BUSINESS ACCOUNTING 2

D1419325

Business Accounting 2

Frank Wood BSc(Econ), FCA

With contributions from J Townsley, BCom, FCA

Fifth Edition

Pitman

PITMAN PUBLISHING

128 Long Acre, London, WC2E 9AN
A Division of Longman Group (UK) Ltd

© Frank Wood 1968
Longman Group UK Ltd 1973, 1979, 1984, 1989

Fifth edition published in Great Britain 1989

British Library Cataloguing in Publication Data

Wood, Frank
  Business accounting 2-5th ed.
  1. Accounting
  I. Title
  657

ISBN 0 273 03120 1   ISE edition

ISBN 0 273 02974 6

Printed and bound in Great Britain

Contents

Preface to the fifth edition

This is the second volume of the textbook. It completes the coverage of the financial accounting part of the following examinations:

Institute of Chartered Accountants in England & Wales: PEI

Association of Accounting Technicians: Final paper

Chartered Association of Certified Accountants: 2.9 Advanced Accounting Practice

Chartered Institute of Management Accountants: Stage 2 Financial Accounting

General Certificate of Education: 'A' Level (most syllabuses)

Institute of Chartered Secretaries & Administrators: Parts 1 & 2

London Chamber of Commerce: Levels: 2 & 3

Royal Society of Arts: Stages 2 & 3

Chapters 19, dealing with the notes accompanying published accounts, and 33 on acquisition and merger accounting, were not the fourth edition.

The chapters now numbered 13, 31, 32, 34 and 36 have been completely rewritten and chapters 16, 20 and 38 have been substantially amended.

This volume examines all the current statements of Standard Accounting Practice in as much detail as needed by most students at this level. Those taking Stage 2 of the professional accountancy examinations will need a much more detailed study of them, as they can represent a complete examination paper.

I wish to acknowledge the permission to use part examination papers granted by the Institute of Chartered Accountants in England and Wales, the Chartered Association of Certified Accountants, the Chartered Institute of Management Accountants, the Association of Accounting Technicians, the Institute of Chartered Secretaries and Administrators, the University of London, the Associated Examining Board, the Joint Matriculation Board and the Welsh Joint Education Committee.

Frank Wood

Matrix of subjects covered

Examining bodies

CHAPTERS	AAT FINAL	ACCA 2.9	CIMA STAGE 2	ICAEW PEI	LCC LEVELS 2 & 3	RSA STAGES 2 & 3	GCE 'A' LEVEL	ICSA PART 2 & 3
1 Bills of exchange	O	X	X	X	X	O	O	O
2 Joint venture accounts	O	X	X	X	X	O	X	O
3 Consignment accounts	X	X	O	X	X	O	O	O
4 Partnership dissolution	X	X	O	X	X	X	X	X
5 Branch accounts	X	X	X	X	X	X	X	X
6 Container accounts	X	X	X	X	O	O	O	O
7 Royalty accounts	X	X	X	X	X	O	O	O
8 Hire purchase and payment by instalments	X	X	X	X	X	O	X	O
9 Limited companies: general background	X	X	X	X	X	X	X	X
10 The issue of shares and debentures	X	X	X	X	X	X	X	X
11 Companies: redemption of shares etc	O	X	X	X	X	O	X	X
12 Limited companies taking over other businesses	X	X	X	X	X	X	X	X
13 Taxation in accounts	X	X	X	X	O	X	X	X
14 Provisions, reserves and liabilities	X	X	X	X	X	X	X	X
15 The increase and reduction of share capital	X	X	X	X	X	O	X	X
16 Statements of standard accounting practice	X	X	X	X	X	X	X	X
17 Company profit & loss accounts	X	X	X	X	X	X	X	X
18 Company balance sheets	X	X	X	X	X	X	X	X
19 Published accounts accompanying notes	X	X	X	X	X	O	X	X
20 SSAP 20: funds flow	X	X	X	X	X	X	X	X
21 Investment accounts	O	X	O	X	X	O	X	O
22 Contract accounts	O	O	O	X	O	O	O	X
23 Value added statements	O	X	X	X	O	O	X	X
24 Consolidated accounts: introduction	X	X	X	X	X	X	X	X
25 Consolidation of balance sheets: basic mechanics I	X	X	X	X	X	X	X	X
26 Consolidation of balance sheets: basic mechanics II	X	X	X	X	X	X	X	X
27 Inter-company dealings: indebtedness and unrealised profit in stocks	X	X	X	X	X	X	X	X
28 Consolidated accounts: Acquisition of shares in subsidiaries at different dates	O	X	X	X	X	X	O	X
29 Inter-company dividends	X	X	X	X	X	X	X	X
30 Consolidated balance sheets: sundry matters	X	X	X	X	X	X	X	X
31 Consolidation of the accounts of vertical group of companies	O	X	X	X	X	O	O	X
32 Consolidated profit and loss accounts	X	X	X	X	X	O	X	X
33 Acquisition & merger accounting	O	X	X	X	X	O	O	X
34 Associated companies	O	X	X	X	O	O	O	X
35 Budgeting	O	X	X	X	X	X	X	X
36 Discounting techniques	O	O	O	X	O	X	X	O
37 Accounting ratios: further	X	X	X	X	X	X	X	X
38 Interpretation of Accounts	X	X	X	X	X	X	X	X
39 Alternatives to historic cost accounting	X	X	X	X	O	O	X	X

1
Bills of exchange

When goods are supplied to someone on credit, or services performed for him, then that person becomes a **debtor**. The creditor firm would normally wait for payment by the debtor. Until payment is made the money owing is of no use to the creditor firm as it is not being used in any way. This can be remedied by factoring the debtors, which involves passing the debts over to a finance firm. They will pay an agreed amount for the legal rights to the debts.

Another possibility is that of obtaining a bank overdraft, with the debtors accepted as part of the security on which the overdraft has been granted.

Yet another way that can give the creditor effective use of the money owing to him is for him to draw a bill of exchange on the debtor. This means that a document is drawn up requiring the debtor to pay the amount owing to the creditor, or to anyone nominated by him at any time, on or by a particular date. He sends this document to the debtor who, if he agrees to it, is said to 'accept' it by writing on the document that he will comply with it and appends his signature. The debtor then returns the bill of exchange to the creditor. This document is then legal proof of the debt. The debtor is not then able to contest the validity of the debt but only for any irregularity in the bill of exchange itself. The creditor can now act in one of three ways:

(a) He can negotiate the bill to another person in payment of a debt. That person may also renegotiate it to someone else. The person who possesses the bill at maturity, i.e. the date for payment of the bill, will present it to the debtor for payment.

(b) He may 'discount' it with a bank. 'Discount' here means that the bank will take the bill of exchange and treat it in the same manner as money deposited in the bank account. The bank will then hold the bill until maturity when it will present it to the debtor for payment. The bank will make a charge to the creditor for this service known as a discounting charge.

(c) The third way open to the creditor is for him to hold the bill until maturity when he will present it to the debtor for payment. In this case, apart from having a document which is legal proof of the debt and could therefore save legal costs if a dispute arose, no benefit has been gained from having a bill of exchange. However, action (a) or (b) could have been taken if the need had arisen.

The creditor who draws up the bill of exchange is known as the **drawer**. The debtor on whom it is drawn is the **drawee**, when accepted he becomes the **acceptor**, while the person to whom the bill is to be paid is the **payee**. In fact it may be recognised that a cheque is a special type of bill of exchange where the drawee is always a bank and in addition is payable on demand. This chapter, however, refers to bills of exchange other than cheques.

To the person who is to receive money on maturity of the bill of exchange the document is known as a 'bill receivable', while to the person who is to pay the sum due on maturity it is known as a 'bill payable'.

Dishonoured bills

When the debtor fails to make payment on maturity the bill is said to be dishonoured. If the holder is someone other than the drawer then he will have recourse against the person who has negotiated the bill to him, that person will then have recourse against the one who negotiated it to him, and so on until final recourse is had against the drawer of the bill for the amount of money due on the bill. The drawer's right of action is then against the acceptor.

On dishonour a bill is often 'noted'. This means that the bill is handed to a lawyer acting in his capacity as a notary public, who then re-presents the bill to the acceptor. The notary public then records the reasons for it not being discharged. The notary public's fee is known as a **noting charge**. With a foreign bill, in addition to the bill being noted, it is necessary to 'protest' the bill in order to preserve the holder's rights against the drawer and previous endorsers. 'Protest' is the term which covers the legal formalities needed.

The action to be taken by the drawer depends entirely upon circumstances. Often the lack of funds on the acceptor's part is purely temporary. In this case the drawer will negotiate with the acceptor and agree to draw another bill, or substitute several bills of smaller amounts with different maturity dates, for the amount owing, frequently with an addition for interest to compensate for the extended period of credit. Negotiation is the keynote; it must not be thought that acceptors are always sued when they fail to make payment. They are customers, and where future dealings with them are expected to be profitable harsh measures are certainly to be avoided. Legal action should be the last action to be considered. Any interest charged to the acceptor would be debited to his account and credited to an Interest Receivable Account.

Discounting charges and noting charges

From the acceptor's point of view the discounting of a bill is a matter wholly for the drawer or holder to decide. He, the acceptor, has been allowed a term of credit and will pay the agreed price on the maturity of the bill. Therefore the discounting charge is not one that he should suffer; this should be borne wholly by the person discounting the bill.

On the other hand, the noting charge has been brought about by the acceptor's default. It is equitable that his account should be charged with the amount of the expense of noting and protesting.

Retired bills

Instead of waiting until maturity, bills may be retired, i.e. not allowed to run until maturity. They may be paid off before maturity, in which case a rebate is often allowed because the full term of credit has not been taken; or else renewed by fresh bills being drawn and the old ones cancelled, the new bills often including interest because the term of credit has been extended.

Exhibit 1.1

Drawer's books

Goods had been sold by D Jarvis to J Burgon on 1 January 19-6 for £400. A bill of exchange is drawn by Jarvis and accepted by Burgon on 1 January 19-6, the date of maturity being 31 March 19-6. The following accounts show the entries necessary:

(a) If the bill is held by the drawer until maturity when the drawee makes payment.

J Burgon

19-6		£	19-6		£
Jan	1 Sales	400	Jan	1 Bill Receivable	400

Bills Receivable

19-6		£	19-6		£
Jan	1 J Burgon	400	Mar 31	Bank	400

Bank

19-6		£
Mar 31	Bills Receivable	400

(b) Where the bill is negotiated to another party by the drawer, in this case to IDT Ltd on 3 January 19-6

J Burgon

19-6		£	19-6		£
Jan	1 Sales	400	Jan	1 Bill Receivable	400

Bills Receivable

19-6		£	19-6		£
Jan	1 J Burgon	400	Jan	3 IDT Ltd	400

(c) If the bill is discounted with the bank, in this case on 2 January 19-6, the discounting charges being £6.

J Burgon

19-6		£	19-6		£
Jan	1 Sales	400	Jan	1 Bill Receivable	400

Bills Receivable

19-6		£	19-6		£
Jan	1 J Burgon	400	Jan	2 Bank	400

Bank

19-6		£	19-6		£
Jan	2 Bills Receivable	400	Jan	2 Discounting Charges	6

19-6		£
Jan 2 Bank		6

Acceptor's books

The instances (*a*), (*b*) and (*c*) in the drawer's books will result in similar entries in the acceptor's books. From the acceptor's point of view two things have happened, first, the acceptance of the bill, and second, its discharge by payment. The fact that (*a*), (*b*) and (*c*) would result in different payees is irrelevant as far as the acceptor is concerned.

D Jarvis

19-6		£	19-6		£
Jan 1 Bills Payable		400	Jan 1 Purchases		400

Bills Payable

19-6		£	19-6		£
Mar 31 Bank		400	Jan 1 D Jarvis		400

Bank

			19-6		£
			Mar 31 Bill Payable		400

Dishonoured bills and accounting entries

These can be illustrated by reference to Exhibit 1.2

Exhibit 1.2

On 1 April 19-7 A Grant sells goods for £600 to K Lee, a bill with a maturity date of 30 June 19-7 being drawn by Grant and accepted by Lee on 2 April 19-7. On 30 June 19-7 the bill is presented to Lee, but he fails to pay it and it is therefore dishonoured. The bill is noted, the cost of £2 being paid by Grant on 7 July 19-7.

The entries needed will depend on whether or not the bill had been discounted by Grant.

(a) Drawer's books

Where the Bill had not been discounted or renegotiated

K Lee

19-7		£	19-7		£
Apl 1 Sales		600	Apl 2 Bill Receivable		600
Jun 30 Bill Receivable – dishonoured		600			
July 7 Bank: Noting Charge (*a*)		2			

Bills Receivable

19-7		£	19-7		£
Apl 2 K Lee		600	Jun 30 K Lee – bill dishonoured		600

Bank

			19-7		£
			July 7 Noting Charges – K Lee (*a*)		2

Note:

(*a*) As the noting charges are directly incurred as the result of Lee's default, then Lee must suffer the cost by his account being debited with that amount.

Where the Bill has been discounted with a bank

The entries can now be seen as they would have appeared if the bill had been discounted on 5 April 19-7, discounting charges being £9.

K Lee

19-7		£	19-7		£
Apl 1	Sales	600	Apl 2 Bill Receivable		600
Jun 30	Bank – bill dishonoured (*c*)	600			
July 7	Bank: Noting Charge	2			

Bills Receivable

19-7		£	19-7		£
Apl 2	K Lee	600	Apl 5 Bank		600

Bank

19-7		£	19-7		£
Apl 5	Bills Receivable	600	Apl 5 Discounting Charges (*b*)		9
			Jun 30 K Lee – bill dishonoured (*c*)		600
			July 7 Noting Charges – K Lee		2

Discounting Charges

19-7		£
Apl 5	Bank (*b*)	9

Notes:

(*b*) The discounting charges are wholly an expense of A Grant. They are therefore charged to an expense account. Contrast this with the treatment of the noting charges.
(*c*) On maturity the bank will present the bill to Lee. On its dishonour the bank will hand the bill back to Grant, and will cancel out the original amount shown as being deposited in the bank account. This amount is then charged to Lee's personal account to show that he is still in debt.

(b) Acceptor's books

The entries in the acceptor's books will not be affected by whether or not the drawer had discounted the bill.

A Grant

19-7		£	19-7		£
Apl 1	Bill Payable	600	Apl 1 Purchases		600
			Jun 30 Bill Payable – dishonoured		600
			July 7 Noting Charge (*d*)		2

Bills Payable

19-7		£	19-7		£
Jun 30	A Grant – bill dishonoured	600	Apl 1 A Grant		600

5

19-7	£
July 7 A Grant (*d*)	2

Note:

(*d*) The noting charges will have to be reimbursed to A Grant. To show this fact A Grant's account is credited while the Noting Charges Account is debited to record the expense.

Bills receivable as contingent liabilities

The fact that bills had been discounted, but had not reached maturity by the Balance Sheet date, could give an entirely false impression of the financial position of the business unless a note to this effect is made on the Balance Sheet. That such a note is necessary can be illustrated by reference to the following balance Sheets.

Balance Sheet as at 31 December 19-7

		(a)		(b)
	£	£	£	£
Fixed Assets		3,500		3,500
Current Assets:				
Stock	1,000		1,000	
Debtors	1,200		1,200	
Bills Receivable	1,800		–	
Bank	500		2,300	
	4,500		4,500	
less Current Liabilities	3,000		3,000	
Working Capital		1,500		1,500
		5,000		5,000
		£		£
Financed by:				
Capital		5,000		5,000

Balance Sheet (*a*) shows the position if £1,800 of bills receivable were still in hand. Balance Sheet (*b*) shows the position if the bills had been discounted, ignoring discounting charges. To an outsider, Balance Sheet (*b*) seems to show a much stronger liquid position with £2,300 in the bank. However, should the bills be dishonoured on maturity the bank balance would slump to £500. The appearance of Balance Sheet (*b*) is therefore deceptive unless a note is added, e.g. *Note:* There is a contingent liability of £1,800 on bills discounted at the Balance Sheet date. This note enables the outsider to view the bank balance in its proper perspective of depending on the non-dishonour of the bills discounted.

Review questions

Note: Questions without the suffix 'A' have answers shown at the back of this book. Questions with the suffix 'A' are set without answers in this book so that teachers/lecturers can set the questions for classwork or homework.

1.1 N Gudgeon sells goods to two companies on July 1 19-7.

To R Johnson Ltd	£2,460
To B Scarlet & Co Ltd.	£1,500

He draws bills of exchange on each of them and they are both accepted.

He discounts both of the bills with the bank on July 4 19-7, and suffers discounting charges of £80 on Johnson's bill and £65 on Scarlet's bill. On September 1 19-7 the bills mature and Johnson Ltd meets its liability. Scarlet's bill is dishonoured and is duly noted on September 4, the noting charge being £6.

Show the above in the necessary accounts:

(*a*) In the books of Gudgeon.

(*b*) In the books of Scarlet Ltd and of Johnson Ltd.

1.2A P Cummings buys goods from T Victor Ltd on January 21 19-7 for £2,900 and from C Bellamy & Co for £4,160. Bills are drawn on him and he accepts them.

T Victor Ltd discount their bill with their bank on January 29, the discounting charge being £110.

C Bellamy & Co simply keep their bill waiting for maturity.

On maturity of the bills on April 21 19-7, Cummings duly meets (pays) Bellamy's bill. He is unable to pay Victor's bill and it is accordingly dishonoured. Victor duly has it noted on April 28 19-7 the noting charge being £10.

Show the entries necessary in:

(*a*) The books of P Cummings

(*b*) The books of T Victor Ltd

(*c*) The books of C Bellamy & Co

1.3 Draw up a Sales Ledger Control Account for the month of August 19-6 from the following:

19-6

		£
Aug 1	Balances (Dr)	12,370
	Balances (Cr)	105
	Totals for the month:	
	Sales Journal	16,904
	Returns Inwards Journal	407
	Cheques Received from customers	15,970
	Bills receivable accepted	1,230
	Cash received from customers	306
	Bad Debts written off	129
	Cash discounts allowed	604
	Bill receivable dishonoured	177
Aug 31	Balances (Cr)	88
	Balances (Dr)	?

1.4 Indicate by Journal entries how the following would appear in the ledger accounts of (*a*) Noone, (*b*) Iddon.

19-8

Jan 1 Iddon sells goods £420 to Noone, and Noone sends to Iddon a three months' acceptance for this amount.

,, 1 Iddon discounts the acceptance with the Slough Discount Co Ltd, receiving its cheque for £412.

Feb 29 One third of Noone's stock, valued at £3,600, is destroyed by fire. Noone claims on the underwriters at Lloyds with whom he is insured.

Apr 1 The underwriters admit the claim for £3,000 only as the total stock was only insured for £9,000.

,, 4 In view of Noone's difficulties Iddon meets the acceptance due today by giving his cheque for £420 to the Slough Discount Co Ltd; he draws on Noone a further bill for one month for £430 (to include £10 interest) which Noone accepts.

,, 9 Noone receives cheque from the underwriters in settlement of the admitted claim.

May 7 Noone's bank honours the acceptance presented by Iddon as due today.

1.5A Balances and transactions affecting a company's control accounts for the month of May 19-2 are listed below.

	£	
Balances at 1 May 19-2:		
Sales ledger	9,123	(debit)
	211	(credit)
Purchases ledger	4,490	(credit)
	88	(debit)
Transactions during May 19-2:		
Purchases on credit	18,135	
Allowances from suppliers	629	
Receipts from customers by cheque	27,370	
Sales on credit	36,755	
Discounts received	1,105	
Payments to creditors by cheque	15,413	
Contra settlements	3,046	
Allowances to customers	1,720	
Bills of exchange receivable	6,506	
Customers' cheques dishonoured	489	
Cash receipts from credit customers	4,201	
Refunds to customers for overpayment of accounts	53	
Discounts allowed	732	
Balances at 31 May 19-2:		
Sales ledger	136	(credit)
Purchases ledger	67	(debit)

Required:

(*a*) Explain the purposes for which Control Accounts are prepared.

(*b*) Post the Sales Ledger and Purchases Ledger control accounts for the month of May 19-2 and derive the respective debit and credit closing balances on 31 May 19-2.

(*Association of Certified Accountants*)

2

Joint venture accounts

Sometimes it is to the mutual advantage of two or more persons or firms to tackle a particular business venture together instead of engaging in it separately. These are known as **joint ventures**. Early versions of Joint Venture Accounts being kept were by the Venetian merchants trading in the Mediterranean in the fifteenth century. One merchant might provide the ship, another the goods and another the capital. Any profits or losses would then be split in an agreed ratio. Present-day versions are to be found where a produce merchant provides the capital, the transport to market and the selling skills, while the farmer actually grows the produce. The profits are then shared between them. Joint ventures may seem to be exactly the same as partnerships. In fact a joint venture is a form of partnership, but it is limited to a particular transaction. There may be several joint ventures as between the same parties, but each one is a separate venture, and the agreements may be different for each one, e.g. in respect of the sharing of profits and losses.

It must not be thought that joint ventures are an outdated concept. In fact they have become far more important in recent years. The opening up of China to Western businesses has been largely in the form of joint ventures for instance. The idea that they have not existed in a way for several centuries is completely a mistaken one.

Some joint ventures may be of such magnitude that a bank account is opened especially for the venture and separate books kept. The calculation of the profits and the eventual withdrawal of their money by the parties involved is quite a straightforward matter. However, it is usually found that each party will record in his own books only those transactions with which he has been concerned. No one party to the venture will therefore have a full record of all the transactions. An example of this is now given:

Exhibit 2.1

Black, of London, Johnson, of Manchester, and Graham of Glasgow, enter into a joint venture. Black and Johnson are both to supply some of the materials, while only Johnson and Graham will sell the finished goods. Profits are to be shared, Black 3: Johnson 2: Graham 1:

Details of the transactions are:

	£
Black supplied materials costing	450
Johnson supplied materials costing	300
Black paid wages	180
Black paid storage expenses	40
Johnson paid for carriage	90
Graham paid selling expenses	120
Johnson received cash from sales	800
Graham received cash from sales	1,100

Each party has entered in his own books the transactions which have been his concern. He will have opened a 'Joint Venture (with the names of the other two parties) Account'. Payments will have been credited to his Cash Book and debited to the Joint Venture Account. Goods supplied will be credited to his Purchases Account and debited to the Joint Venture Account. This Joint Venture Account will appear as follows:

Black's Books (in London)
Joint Venture with Johnson and Graham

	£
Purchases: Materials	450
Cash: Wages	180
Cash: Storage expenses	40

Johnson's Books (in Manchester)
Joint Venture with Black and Graham

	£		£
Purchases: Materials	300	Cash: sales	800
Cash: Carriage	90		

Graham's Books (in Glasgow)
Joint Venture with Black and Johnson

	£		£
Cash: Selling Expenses	120	Cash: Sales	1,100

Now, as things stand, each party knows only the details concerning the transactions he has recorded in his own books. Each one is unaware of (*a*) the amount of his share of the profit, and (*b*) how much he will have to pay to, or receive from, the other parties in final settlement of the joint venture. The only way that this can be settled is for each person to take a copy of his own Joint Venture Account and to send it to the other parties. Each one will then have the account in his own books and one copy of each of the accounts in the other person's books. As this consists of all records of transactions from the start to the completion of the venture, then the profit or loss is now capable of being calculated by each party to the venture. Each person will therefore draw up a Profit and Loss Account for the venture. This will be called a Joint Venture Memorandum Account. It is a memorandum account because the account itself is not going to be incorporated into each person's double entry recording. All that will be required is an entry in each set of books to record their shares of the profits or losses.

Black, Johnson and Graham
Memorandum Joint Venture Account

	£		£
Materials	750	Sales	1,900
Wages	180		
Storage expenses	40		
Carriage	90		
Selling expenses	120		
Net Profit			
Black (one-half) 360			
Johnson (one-third) 240			
Graham (one-sixth) 120			
	720		
	1,900		1,900

Now that each person's share of the profit is known an entry can be made. The share of the net profit on the venture will need to be credited to that person's Profit and Loss Account. The debit is to the source of the profit, the Joint Venture Account. After the entries have been made the balance on the Joint Venture Account can be carried down. If the balance carried down is a credit one then the person has received more from the joint venture than he is entitled to keep, and he will have to pay this amount to the person(s) who has received less than his entitlement, this being shown by a debit balance.

The Joint Venture Accounts now completed can be shown.

Black's Books (in London)
Joint Venture with Johnson and Graham

	£		£
Purchases: Materials	450	Balance c/d	1,030
Cash: Wages	180		
Cash: Storage expenses	40		
Share of profit transferred to Profit and Loss Account	360		
	1,030		1,030
Balance b/d	1,030	Cash received in settlement:	
		From Johnson	170
		From Graham	860
	1,030		1,030

11

Johnson's Books (in Manchester)

Joint Venture with Black and Graham

	£		£
Purchases: Materials	300	Cash: Sales	800
Cash: Carriage	90		
Share of profit transferred			
to Profit and Loss Account	240		
Balance c/d	170		
	800		800
Cash in settlement to Black	170	Balance b/d	170

Graham's Books (in Glasgow)

Joint Venture with Black and Johnson

	£		£
Cash: Selling expenses	120	Cash: Sales	1,100
Share of profit transferred			
to Profit and Loss Account	120		
Balance c/d	860		
	1,100		1,100
Cash in settlement to Black	860	Balance b/d	860

Review questions

2.1 Ollier and Avon enter a joint venture, to share profits or losses equally, resulting from dealings in second-hand cars. Both parties take an active part in the business, each recording his own transactions. They have no joint banking account or separate set of books.

19-3

Jan   1 Ollier buys three cars for £900.

,, 31 Ollier pays for repairs and respraying of vehicles £60.

Mar 1 Avon pays garage rental £20 and advertising expenses £10.

Apr 12 Avon pays for licence and insurance renewal of vehicles, £36.

Aug 10 Avon buys a vehicle in excellent condition for £100.

,, 31 Ollier sells the four vehicles, to various clients, the sales being completed on this date, totalling £1,600.

Show the relative accounts in the books of both partners.

2.2 Plant, Hoe & Reap entered into a joint venture for dealing in carrots. The transactions connected with this venture were:

19-1

Jan   8 Plant rented land cost £156
,,   10 Hoe supplied seeds cost £48
,,   17 Plant employed labour for planting £105
,,   19 Hoe charged motor expenses £17
,,   30 Plant employed labour for fertilising £36
Feb 28 Plant paid the following expenses: Sundries £10, Labour £18, fertiliser a/c £29
Mar 17 Reap employed labour for lifting carrots £73
,,   30 Sale expenses London paid by Reap £39
,,   31 Reap received cash from sale proceeds gross £987

You are required to show the joint venture accounts in the books of Plant, Hoe & Reap. Also show in full the method of arriving at the profit on the venture which is to be apportioned: Plant seven-twelfths; Hoe three-twelfths; Reap two-twelfths.

Any outstanding balances between the parties are settled by cheque on 30 April.

2.3A Wild, Wood and Bine enter into a joint venture for dealing in antique brass figures. The following transactions took place:

19-4

Mar   1 Wild rented a shop, paying 3 months' rent £150
,,   2 Wood bought a motor van for £2,700
,,   4 Wood bought antiques for £650
,,   15 Bine received cash from sale proceeds of antiques £3,790
,,   28 Wild bought antiques for £1,200
Apr 11 Motor van broke down. Bine agreed to use his own van for the job, until cessation of the joint venture, at an agreed charge of £400
,,   13 Motor van bought on March 2 was sold for £2,100. Proceeds were kept by Wild.
,,   15 Sales of antiques, cash being kept by Wood £780.
,,   18 Lighting bills paid for shop by Bine £120.
,,   30 Bine bought antiques for £440.
May   4 General expenses of shop paid for £800, Bine and Wild paying half each
,,   19 Antiques sold by Bine £990, proceeds being kept by him.
,,   31 Joint venture ended. The antiques still in stock were taken over at an agreed valuation of £2,100 by Wood.

You are required to show the joint venture accounts in the books of each of the three parties. Show in full the workings needed to arrive at the profit on the venture. The profit or loss was to be split: Wood one-half; Wild one-third; Bine one-sixth. Any outstanding balances between the parties were settled on 31 May 19-4.

3
Consignment accounts

A consignment of goods is the sending of them by the owner (the consignor) to his agent (the consignee) who agrees to collect, store and sell them on behalf of the owner. When the two parties are both trading in the same country it is not difficult for sales of goods consigned to an agent to be recorded in the owner's books, in the same manner as sales of goods stored in his own premises. When the owner is in this country and the agent is overseas, modern methods of communication enable the consignor to similarly record sales made on his behalf by the agent, which is, perhaps, the reason why consignment accounts are not met as frequently today. However, in the days before telecommunications and air travel it was usually too difficult for sales by the agent to be entered in the consignor's books, using separate accounts for the overseas customers, so the practice grew of allowing the agent to collect the money from the overseas customers supplied by him, deduct his expenses and commission, and remit the balance to the consignor.

Consignor's records

The difficulty of recording individual overseas sales led to an interesting development in profit measurement long before today's advanced techniques. By drawing up consignment accounts it was possible to measure the profit or loss on each consignment thus allowing the consignor to compare the performance of different agents and to separate such profits or losses from those of his main business.

A consignment account is, in effect, a combined Trading and Profit and Loss Account related solely to the consignment. On the debit side is entered the cost of the goods, transport costs, agent's disbursements such as import duties, dock charges, warehouse rent and distribution expenses, and agent's commission, while on the credit side is entered the proceeds of sales. The difference between the two sides represents the profit or loss. If the agent completes the sales before the end of the consignor's financial year, the accounting work is simple. An example to illustrate the entries in the consignor's books can now be seen.

Exhibit 3.1

Robson, of London, whose financial year ends on 31 December, consigned goods to Boateng, his Agent in Ghana, on 16 January 19-8. Robson had purchased the goods for £500 and paid £50 on 28 February for carriage and freight to Ghana. Boateng paid £25 import duty and £30 distribution expenses. He sold the goods for £750, deducted his disbursements and his commission which was at the rate of 6 per cent of the sales, and, on 20 April 19-8, remitted the balance to Robson. Of course, Boateng's transactions were in cedis but all items were converted into £ sterling for inclusion in Robson's books.

While the student at this stage will readily follow the Consignment Account, he must not consider it in isolation. If he does not understand the other parts of the double entry he will share the unnecessary difficulty regularly experienced by students.

The first occurrence to be recorded is the separation of the £500 cost of the goods from Robson's other purchases. The first entry, letter A, in Robson's books for his consignment to Ghana is therefore:

Debit – Consignment to Boateng, Accra, Ghana
Credit – Goods sent on Consignments

Note that Boateng, the agent, has not been debited – the goods are still the property of Robson, and Boateng has so far incurred no financial obligation to him.

Expenses incurred by the consignor for carriage and freight, letter B, are debited to the Consignment Account and credited to the Cash Book bank columns, unless they are not paid separately, in which case the credit will be on the account of the carrier.

Robson makes no further entries until he receives a report from his agent. This is usually called an 'Account Sales' and it is shown in traditional form in Exhibit 3.2. Robson received it on 23 April and made the recording entries necessary to incorporate its contents into his books.

The sales are entered, letter C, by crediting the Consignment Account (instead of the main Trading Account) and by debiting the agent (who stands in place of the separate overseas customers).

Expenses incurred on Robson's behalf and paid by Boateng, letter D, are entered by a debit on the Consignment Account (instead of the main Profit and Loss Account) and a credit on the agent's account.

The commission due to the agent, normally by way of a percentage on sales, letter E, is debited to the Consignment Account and credited to Boateng.

The account of the agent is closed by recording, letter F, his payment of the balance due which is usually by bank transfer or bill of exchange. The bank column of the Cash Book is debited and the agent's account is credited.

Referring to the Consignment Account, it is noted that the credit side exceeds the debit by £100 which is the measure of the profit. To close the Consignment Account, letter G, it is debited with the £100 and 'Profit and Loss on Consignments' is credited.

Consignment to Boateng, Accra, Ghana

	£		£
Jan 16 (A) Goods sent on		Apl 23 (C) Boateng: Sales	750
consignments	500		
Feb 28 (B) Bank: carriage and freight	50		
Apl 23 (D) Boateng:			
Import duty	25		
Distribution	30		
(E) Commission	45		
(G) Profit and loss			
on consignment	100		
	750		750

Goods sent on Consignments

	£
Apl 23 (A) Consignment to Boateng	500

15

	£			£
Apl 23 (C) Consignment: sales	750	Apl 23 Consignment:		
		(D) Import duty	25	
		Distribution	30	
		(E) Commission	45	
		(F) Bank	650	
	750			750

Profit and Loss on Consignments

		£
	Apl 23 (G) Consignment to Boateng	100

Exhibit 3.2

Account Sales
(Converted into £)

Boateng,
Accra,
Ghana.

Consignment of electrical goods ex MV Enterprise sold on behalf of Robson, London, England.

	£	£
Sales per attached schedule (not reproduced)		750
Payments:		
Import duty	25	
Distribution expenses	30	
Commission: 6 per cent of £750	45	
		100
Balance due for which sight draft enclosed		650

Accra, 2 April 19-8 (signed) Boateng.

Consignor's accounting year and incomplete consignments

When the consignor's accounting year comes to a close and there is an incomplete consignment, the agent will be required to submit an interim report or 'Account Sales'. Two related problems arise:

(a) How is the unsold stock to be valued?

(b) What is the profit earned up to date?

It should be appreciated that these two are so connected that the calculation of one of them will affect the answer to the other.

Unsold stock is valued at cost unless net realisable value or replacement price, as appropriate, is lower. Cost includes all expenditure incurred in bringing the goods to a saleable condition and location and so an appropriate part of carriage, freight, insurance and import duty can properly be included in the valuation. On the Consignment Account the stock so valued is credited above, and debited below, the line. The difference between the two sides above the line is the measure of profit earned up to date and the balance below the line is the asset, or part of it, shown in the Balance Sheet as stock on consignments. Care must be taken to distinguish between expenditure which can be regarded as part of the cost of unsold stock and that which refers only to goods which have been sold, e.g. selling expenses and commission.

Before working through another example which will demonstrate the points discussed, there are two terms to be explained which often feature in consignments.

The first is *del credere commission*. This is an Italian term, based on creed or faith, which refers to additional commission paid to an agent who guarantees the debts incurred by customers supplied by him. To the consignor it is a form of credit insurance.

Second is *pro forma*. In the home trade this refers to an invoice sent to a customer who is required to pay for goods before they are delivered to him. It is used when the supplier does not know the creditworthiness of the customer. When used in the context of consignments, the term means either a value to be used for overseas customs purposes or a minimum selling price. In either case the figure is not brought into the accounts although a student might have to calculate the cost of the goods from the *pro forma* figure. For instance, a problem might use the phrase, 'invoiced *pro forma* at £1,000 being cost plus 25 per cent'. The student is properly expected to be able to calculate the cost figure of £800.

Exhibit 3.3

On 19 August 19-8 Campbell, a merchant in Glasgow, sent a consignment of 50 cases of goods to Katta, his agent in Freetown, Sierra Leone. On 26 August Campbell received Katta's acceptance of a six months' bill of exchange for £2,000 drawn by Campbell and immediately discounted it for £1,950. The goods had cost Campbell £40 per case and carriage, freight and insurance paid by him on 30 September amounted to £50. During the voyage two cases on the consignment were completely destroyed by fire and on 31 October Campbell received the appropriate compensation from the insurance company.

Campbell's accounting year ended on 31 December 19-8 and Katta sent him an interim Account Sales made up to that date. It disclosed that 28 cases had been sold for £60 each and landing charges and import duty, £192, and distribution expenses, £20, had been paid. Commission at 5 per cent on sales plus 2½ per cent *del credere* was charged.

On 15 March 19-9, Campbell received the final Account Sales showing that the remainder of the consignment had been sold for £62 per case, distribution charges, £32, had been paid, and commission was deducted. A bill of exchange was enclosed for the balance due to Campbell.

An insurance claim will normally cover the full cost of the goods up to time of loss, but not the expected profit. In our example, the cost per case is £41 made up of original cost £40 and carriage, etc., £1.

In valuing the stock unsold at 31 December, the original cost and carriage etc., have been apportioned over 50 cases, whereas the landing charges, etc., have been related to the 48 cases landed. The distribution expenses are regarded as selling expenses.

Bills Receivable

		£			£
Aug 26		2,000	Aug 26 Bank		1,950
			Discount charges		50
		2,000			2,000

Consignment to Katta, Freetown, Sierra Leone

		Cases	£			Cases		£
Aug 19	Goods sent on			Oct 31	Bank:			
	consignments	50	2,000		insurance claim	2		82
Sep 30	Bank: Carriage			Dec 31	Katta: Sales	28		1,680
	freight and				Stock c/d	20		
	Insurance		50		$20/50 \times 2,050$		820	
Dec 31	Katta:				$20/48 \times 192$		80	
	Landing charges							900
	and duty		192					
	Distribution		20					
	Commission		126					
	P&L on							
	consignments		274					
		50	2,662			50		2,662
Jan 1	Stock b/d	20	900	Mar 15	Katta: Sales	20		1,240
Mar 15	Katta:							
	Distribution		32					
	Commission		93					
	P&L on							
	consignments		215					
		20	1,240			20		1,240

	£			£
Dec 31 Consignment: Sales	1,680	Aug 26 Bill Receivable		2,000
Balance c/d	658	Dec 31 Consignment:		
		Landing charges		
		and duty		192
		Distribution		20
		Commission		126
	2,338			2,338
Mar 15 Consignment: Sales	1,240	Jan 1 Balance b/d		658
		Mar 15 Consignment:		
		Distribution		32
		Commission		93
		Bank		457
	1,240			1,240

Interim Account Sales

Katta, Freetown, Sierra Leone.

Consignment of goods sold on behalf of Campbell, Glasgow.

	£	£	£
Sales 28 cases at £60 each			1,680
Payments: Landing charges and import duty at £4 per case		192	
Distribution expenses		20	
Commission at 5 per cent	84		
at 2½ per cent *del credere*	42		
		126	
			338
			1,342
Acceptance			2,000
Balance in my favour, carried forward			658

Freetown, Sierra Leone, 31 December 19-8   (signed) Katta

	£	£	£
Sales 20 cases at £62			1,240
Payments: Distribution expenses		32	
Commission at 5 per cent	62		
at 2½ per cent *del credere*	31		
		93	
			125
			1,115
Balance in my favour, brought forward			658
Sight draft herewith			457

Freetown, Sierra Leone, 15 March 19-9

Consignee's records

Although the original cost might be known to the agent, it does not concern him and it should not be entered in his accounts. He will, of course, need to keep a stock record of quantities held but this will be quite separate from the double entry accounts, as it is for any trader.

The consignee's transactions usually commence when he takes possession (but not ownership) of the goods. He will probably pay landing charges and customs duties on behalf of the owner, and he will expect to be reimbursed eventually by subtracting such amounts from those received from the sales of goods. The entries are simply: debit the personal account of the consignor; credit the Bank Account. A Balance Sheet of the agent drawn up just after such a payment would include as a current asset the amount due from the consignor but would not include the stock of goods held on his behalf.

As the sales are made the debits will be either on the Cash or Bank Account, if they are cash sales; or on the personal accounts of the customers, if they are credit sales. The credits will be on the personal account of the consignor and not on the Sales Account (if any).

Commission earned by the consignee is debited to the consignor's Personal Account and credited to a commission account for subsequent transfer to the agent's own Profit and Loss Account.

By way of illustration, the accounts of Katta, the consignee in the second example in the previous section, are shown in Exhibit 3.5. Additional information is introduced in order to show a more complete picture. Assume that Katta sold 15 cases on credit and 2 for cash during October, 7 cases on credit in November, and 4 cases on credit in December. The landing charges and import duty were paid on 31 August and the distribution expenses on 29 December. During 19-9, 20 cases were sold on credit in February and the distribution expenses were paid on 10 March.

Exhibit 3.5

(Books of Katta)
Campbell, Glasgow, UK

	£		£
Aug 26 Bill Payable	2,000	Oct 31 Debtors	900
,, 31 Bank: Landing		Bank	120
charges and		Nov 30 Debtors	420
import duty	192	Dec 31 Debtors	240
Dec 29 Bank: Distribution		Balance c/d	658
charges	20		
,, 31 Commission	126		
	2,338		2,338
Jan 1 Balance b/d	658	Feb 28 Debtors	1,240
Feb 28 Commission	93		
Mar 10 Bank: Distribution			
charges	32		
,, 15 Bill payable	457		
	1,240		1,240

Commission

	£
Dec 31 Campbell	126

Review questions

3.1 On 8 February 19-5 PJ, a London trader, consigned 120 cases of goods to MB, an agent in New Zealand.

The cost of the goods was £25 a case. PJ paid carriage to the port £147 and insurance £93.

On 31 March 19-5 PJ received an Account Sales from MB, showing that 100 cases had been sold for £3,500 and MB had paid freight, at the rate of £2 a case, and port charges amounting to £186. MB was entitled to a commission of 5 per cent on sales. A sight draft for the net amount due was enclosed with the Account Sales.

You are required to show the accounts for the above transactions in the ledger of PJ and to show the transfer to Profit and Loss Account at 31 March 19-5.
(*Institute of Chartered Secretaries and Administrators*)

3.2 On 15 November 19-5, Hughes consigned 300 cases of wooden items to Galvez of Madrid. On 31 December 19-5, Galvez forwarded an account sales, with a draft for the balance, showing the following transactions:
1   250 cases sold at £20 each and 50 at £18 each.
2   Port and duty charges £720.
3   Storage and carriage charges £410.
4   Commission on sales 5% + 1% *del credere*.
Required:
(*a*) Prepare the Account Sales, and
(*b*) Show the Consignment Inward Account in the books of Galvez. Ignore interest.

3.3A Stone consigned goods to Rock on 1 January 19-6, their value being £12,000, and it was agreed that Rock should receive a commission of 5 per cent on gross sales. Expenses incurred by Stone for freight and insurance amount to £720. Stone's financial year ended on 31 March 19-6, and an Account Sales made up to that date was received from Rock. This showed that 70 per cent of the goods had been sold for £10,600 but that up to 31 March 19-6, only £8,600 had been received by Rock in respect of these sales. Expenses in connection with the goods consigned were shown as being £350, and it was also shown that £245 had been incurred in connection with the goods sold. With the Account Sales, Rock sent a sight draft for the balance shown to be due, and Stone incurred bank charges of £12 on 10 April 19-6, in cashing same.

Stone received a further Account Sales from Rock made up to 30 June 19-6, and this showed that the remainder of the goods had been sold for £4,800 and that £200 had been incurred by way of selling expenses. It also showed that all cash due had been received with the exception of a debt for £120 which had proved to be bad. A sight draft for the balance due was sent with the Account Sales and the bank charged Stone £9 on 1 July 19-6, for cashing same. You are required to write up the necessary accounts in Stone's books to record these transactions.

(*Institute of Chartered Accountants*)

3.4A Fleet is a London merchant. During the financial year to 31 March 19-8, he sent a consignment of goods to Sing, his agent in Balli. The details of the transaction were as follows:

(*a*) On 1 April 19-7, 1,000 boxes were sent to Sing. These boxes had originally cost Fleet £20 each.

(*b*) Fleet's carriage, freight and insurance costs of the consignment paid on 30 April 19-7 amounted to £2,000.

(*c*) During the voyage to Balli, ten boxes were lost. On 30 September 19-7, Fleet received a cheque for £220 as compensation from his insurance company for the loss of the boxes.

(*d*) On 1 March 19-8, Fleet received £20,000 from Sing.

(*e*) Both Fleet and Sing's accounting year end is 31 March.

(*f*) On 15 April 19-8, Fleet received the following Interim Account Sales from Sing:

Interim Account Sales

The Water Front
Gama
Balli

31 March 19-8

Consignment of goods sold on behalf of Fleet, London: 950 boxes of merchandise.

	£	£	£
Sales:			
950 boxes at £30 each			28,500
Charges:			
Distribution expenses (at £2 per box)		1,900	
Landing charges and import duty (at £1 per box)		990	
Commission (5% × £28,500)		1,425	
			4,315
Net Proceeds per draft enclosed			£24,185

31 March 19-8
Sing (signed)
Balli

Required:
Prepare the following ledger accounts for the year to 31 March 19-8:
   (*a*) in Fleet's books of account:
      (*i*) Goods sent on consignment account;
      (*ii*) Consignment to Sing's account;
      (*iii*) Sing (consignee) account;
   and
   (*b*) in Sing's books of account;
      (*i*) Fleet (London) account;
      (*ii*) Commission account.
(*Association of Accounting Technicians*)

4

Partnership dissolution

Technically a partnership is dissolved whenever a new partner is admitted or a partner leaves the partnership firm; in addition there may be other reasons why the partnership can no longer be carried on, such as a court order insisting that the partnership be dissolved. Someone may cease to be a partner because of death, retirement, bankruptcy, insanity, etc. In their accepted sense, **dissolution accounts** mean that the debts of the partnership are discharged and the assets distributed in accordance with the partnership deed or the provisions of the Partnership Act 1890. This is also the sense in which the term is used in examinations. However, the full dissolution of a partnership very rarely takes place just because of a change in partners. A full dissolution would in fact normally only take place when some disagreement between the partners that could not be settled amicably had occurred, or where the court had ordered it.

Upon a full dissolution of the partnership then, unless the partners otherwise agree, the amounts obtained from the realisation of the assets plus any amounts paid in by partners to clear off debit balances on Capital or Current Accounts shall be disbursed in the following order:

(*a*) In paying the debts and liabilities of the firm to persons who are not partners. It would in fact be an illegal act to pay any monies due to a partner before the creditors were paid, unless it was obvious that the creditors would be paid in full.

(*b*) In paying to each partner the amount due to him in respect of advances as distinguished from capital. If the amount available is sufficient to pay (*a*) but not (*b*), then the amounts payable will be in proportion to the amount owing. For example, if there was only £3,000 left after (*a*) had been paid, and the advances to be repaid were £4,000 from A and £1,000 from B, then A would receive:

$$\frac{£4,000}{£4,000 \times £1,000} \times £3,000 = £2,400, \text{ and B would receive}$$

$$\frac{£1,000}{£4,000 \times £1,000} \times £3,000 = £600.$$

(*c*) To pay to each partner the amount finally due to him according to his Capital and Current Accounts. Any profit on realisation will, subject to any agreement to the contrary, be credited to the partners' Capital Accounts in their profit- and loss-sharing ratios, while any loss will be debited in the same proportions. If a partner's final net balance on his Capital and Current Accounts is a debit balance, then he will be required to pay that amount into the partnership bank account. Should the partner not be able to meet all, or part, of such a deficiency, then the rule in *Garner* v. *Murray* will apply (*see* page 30) unless otherwise agreed. It should be noted that the *Garner* v. *Murray* rule does not apply in Scotland.

When the business is being realised it is not necessary for all of the assets to be sold to outside parties. Very often one or more of the partners may take over some of the assets. The amount at which such assets will pass to him will be agreed to by all the partners. It is not necessary that he actually pays in an amount for them; it would be more normal for them to be charged to his Capital Account and so reduce the amount finally due to him.

The account opened to record the dissolution is the Realisation Account. This is the account in which the profit or loss on realisation is calculated, so that transfers can be made of the profits or losses to increase or reduce the amounts repayable to the partners, or by them, in respect of their Capital Accounts. To do this, the book values of the assets (with the exception of the cash and bank balances as these already represent 'realised' assets) are transferred to the debit of the Realisation Account, while the amounts realised for them are credited to that account. As the Realisation Account is nothing more than a Profit and Loss Account for a special purpose, an excess of credits over debits indicates a profit on realisation, the converse represents a loss. Any costs of realising the assets will also have been debited to the Realisation Account. The profit or loss on realisation will be divided between the partners in the profit- and loss-sharing ratio and will be transferred to their Capital Accounts.

It is a common failing of students to transfer the liabilities to the Realisation Account. However, as realisation for this purpose means 'sold' it will be obvious that liabilities are not realised, they are discharged, and it would therefore be an error of principle to show them in the Realisation Account. As a matter of convenience it is often found that discounts on creditors, being a gain, are shown on the credit side of the Realisation Account. They could instead be divided in the profit- and loss-sharing ratios and credited to the partners' Capital Accounts.

A fully worked example is shown in Exhibit 4.1. While every account is shown here, it would not be normal in examinations to show every account, the accounts normally shown in examinations have an (S) after the title of the account. This is because these accounts alone will demonstrate that the candidate understands the principles concerned. To show all the other accounts would only be time-consuming and would not really demonstrate the possession of any further knowledge. Of course, in real firms every account is shown.

Exhibit 4.1

On 31 December 19-8, P, Q and R decided to dissolve partnership. They had always shared profits in the ratio of P 3:Q 2:R 1.

Their goodwill was sold for £3,000, the machinery for £1,800 and the stock for £1,900. There were three motor-cars, all taken over by the partners at agreed values, P taking one for £800, Q one for £1,000 and R one for £500. The premises were taken over by R at an agreed value of £5,500. The amounts collected from debtors amounted to £2,700 after bad debts and discounts had been deducted. The creditors were discharged for £1,600, the difference being due to discounts received. The costs of dissolution amounted to £1,000.

Their last Balance Sheet is summarised as:

Balance Sheet as at 31 December 19-8

	£	£	£
Fixed Assets			
Premises			5,000
Machinery			3,000
Motor Vehicles			2,500
			10,500
Current Assets			
Stock		1,800	
Debtors	3,000		
less Provisions for bad debts	200	2,800	
Bank		1,400	
		6,000	
less Current Liabilities			
Creditors		1,700	4,300
			14,800
Capitals: P		6,000	
Q		5,000	
R		3,000	14,000
Current Accounts: P		200	
Q		100	
R		500	800
			14,800

The accounts recording the dissolution are now shown. A description of each entry follows the accounts. The letters (A) to (K) against each entry indicates the relevant description.

Premises

	£			£
Balance b/fwd	5,000	Realisation	(B)	5,000

Machinery

	£			£
Balance b/fwd	3,000	Realisation	(B)	3,000

Motor Vehicles

	£			£
Balance b/fwd	2,500	Realisation	(B)	2,500

Stock

		£				£
Balance b/fwd		1,800	Realisation	(B)		1,800

Debtors

		£				£
Balance b/fwd		3,000	Provisions for bad debts	(A)		200
			Realisation	(B)		2,800

Realisation (S)

		£			£
Assets to be realised:			Bank: Assets sold		
Premises	(B)	5,000	Goodwill	(C)	3,000
Machinery	(B)	3,000	Machinery	(C)	1,800
Motor Vehicles	(B)	2,500	Stock	(C)	1,900
Stock	(B)	1,800	Debtors	(C)	2,700
Debtors	(B)	2,800	Taken over by partners:		
Bank: Costs	(G)	1,000	P: Motor-car	(D)	800
Profit on realisation:	(H)		Q: Motor-car	(D)	1,000
	£		R: Motor-car	(D)	500
P	600		R: Premises	(D)	5,500
Q	400		Creditors:		
R	200	1,200	Discounts	(F)	100
		17,300			17,300

Creditors

		£			£
Bank	(E)	1,600	Balance b/fwd		1,700
Realisation (Discounts)	(F)	100			
		1,700			1,700

Bank (S)

		£			£
Balance b/fwd		1,400	Creditors	(E)	1,600
Realisation: Assets sold			Realisation: Costs	(G)	1,000
Goodwill	(C)	3,000	P: Capital	(K)	6,000
Machinery	(C)	1,800	Q: Capital	(K)	4,500
Stock	(C)	1,900			
Debtors	(C)	2,700			
R: Capital	(J)	2,300			
		13,100			13,100

P Capital (S)

		£			£
Realisation: Motor-car	(D)	800	Balance b/fwd		6,000
Bank	(K)	6,000	Current Account transferred	(I)	200
			Realisation: Share of profit	(H)	600
		6,800			6,800

Provision for Bad Debts

		£			£
Debtors	(A)	200	Balance b/fwd		200

P Current Account

		£			£
P: Capital	(I)	200	Balance b/fwd		200

Q Current Account

		£			£
Q: Capital	(I)	100	Balance b/fwd		100

Q Capital (S)

		£			£
Realisation: Motor-car	(D)	1,000	Balance b/fwd		5,000
Bank	(K)	4,500	Current Account transferred	(I)	100
			Realisation: Share of profit.	(H)	400
		5,500			5,500

R Capital (S)

		£			£
Realisation: Motor-car	(D)	500	Balance b/fwd		3,000
Realisation: Premises	(D)	5,500	Current Account transferred	(I)	500
			Realisation: Share of profit	(H)	200
			Bank	(J)	2,300
		6,000			6,000

	£		£
R: Capital (I)	500	Balance b/fwd	500

Description of transactions:

(A) The provision accounts are transferred to the relevant asset accounts, so that the net balance on the asset accounts may be transferred to the Realisation Account. Dr Provision Accounts, Cr Asset Accounts.

(B) The net book values of the assets are transferred to the Realisation Account. Dr Realisation Account, Cr Asset Accounts.

(C) Assets sold. Dr Bank Account, Cr Realisation Account.

(D) Assets taken over by partners. Dr Partners' Capital Accounts, Cr Realisation Account.

(E) Liabilities discharged. Cr Bank Account, Dr Liability Accounts.

(F) Discounts on creditors. Dr Creditors' Account, Cr Realisation Account.

(G) Costs of dissolution. Cr Bank Account, Dr Realisation Account.

(H) Profit or Loss split in profit/loss-sharing ratio (subject to contrary agreement). Profit — Dr Realisation Account, Cr Partners' Capital Accounts. The converse if a loss.

(I) Transfer the balances on the partners' Current Accounts to their Capital Accounts.

(J) Any partner with a Capital Account in deficit, i.e. debits exceed credits, must now pay in the amount needed to cancel his indebtedness to the partnership firm. Dr Bank Account, Cr Capital Account.

(K) The credit balances on the partners' Capital Accounts can now be paid to them. Cr Bank Account, Dr Partners' Capital Account.

The payments made under (K) should complete the elimination of all the balances in the partnership books. It should be checked that the balance in hand at the bank, after all other payments and receipts have been made, should exactly equal the amounts to be repaid to the partners. If it does not, then an error has been made. This fact often bewilders students meeting it for the first time. The fact that it should be true is a further reiteration of the accounting equation. The steps in a partnership dissolution may be shown thus for a firm where A takes three-quarters of the profit and B takes one-quarter.

(*a*)   Capital   + Liabilities   = Assets
    A £3,000 + B £2,000   + Creditors £1,000   = £6,000
(*b*) Liabilities discharged

                   Capital = Assets
    A £3,000 + B £2,000   = (£6,000 − £1,000)   = £5,000
(*c*) Assets sold at a loss of £1,200

                   Capital = Assets
  A (£3,000 − ¾ loss £900) £2,100 + B (£2,000 − ¼ loss £300) £1,700
                     = (£5,000 − £1,200) £3,800 Bank

The final bank balance of £3,800 therefore exactly equals the totals of the balances on the partners' Capital Accounts. The equality of Capital + Liabilities = Assets must always hold true, and after the liabilities have been discharged, then it becomes Capital = Assets. The assets are all converted into a final bank balance, any loss on sale having been deducted not only on the assets side but also from the Capital Accounts. The final asset, i.e. the bank balance, will therefore always equal the final balances on the Capital Accounts.

The rule in *Garner* v. *Murray* (does not apply in Scotland)

It sometimes happens that a partner's Capital Account finishes up with a debit balance. Normally the partner will pay in an amount to clear his indebtedness to the firm. However, sometimes he will be unable to pay all, or part, of such a balance. In the case of *Garner* v. *Murray* in 1904 (a case in England) the court ruled that, subject to any agreement to the contrary, such a deficiency was to be shared by the other partners *not* in their profit- and loss-sharing ratios but in the ratio of their 'last agreed capitals'. By 'their last agreed capitals' is meant the credit balances on their Capital Accounts in the normal Balance Sheet drawn up at the end of their last accounting period. It must be borne in mind that the balances on their Capital Accounts after the assets have been realised may be far different from those on the last Balance Sheet. Where a partnership deed is drawn up it is commonly found that agreement is made to use normal profit- and loss-sharing ratios instead, thus rendering the *Garner* v. *Murray* rule inoperative. The *Garner* v. *Murray* rule does not apply to partnerships in Scotland.

Exhibit 4.2

After completing the realisation of all the assets, in respect of which a loss of £4,200 was incurred, but before making the final payments to the partners, the Balance Sheet appears:

Balance Sheet

	£	£
Cash at bank		6,400
		6,400
Capitals: R	5,800	
S	1,400	
T	400	
	7,600	
less Q (debit balance)	1,200	6,400
		6,400

According to the last Balance Sheet drawn up before the dissolution, the partners' Capital Account credit balances were: Q £600; R £7,000; S £2,000; T £1,000; while the profits and losses were shared Q 3:R 2:S 1:T 1.

Q is unable to meet any part of his deficiency. Each of the other partners therefore suffer the deficiency as follows:

$$\frac{\text{Own capital per Balance Sheet before dissolution}}{\text{Total of all solvent partners' capitals per same Balance Sheet}} \times \text{Deficiency}$$

This can now be calculated.

$$R \quad \frac{£7,000}{£7,000 + £2,000 + £1,000} \times £1,200 = \qquad £840$$

$$S \quad \frac{£2,000}{£7,000 + £2,000 + £1,000} \times £1,200 = \qquad £240$$

$$T \quad \frac{£1,000}{£7,000 + £2,000 + £1,000} \times £1,200 = \qquad £120$$

$$\underline{\qquad} \\ £1,200$$

When these amounts have been charged to the Capital Accounts, then the balances remaining on them will equal the amount of the bank balance. Payments may therefore be made to clear their Capital Accounts.

	Credit Balance B/fwd		Share of deficiency now debited		Final credit balances
	£		£		£
R	5,800	–	840	=	4,960
S	1,400	–	240	=	1,160
T	400	–	120	=	280
Equals the bank balance					6,400

The rule has often been criticised, many parties maintaining that it would be more equitable if the normal profit- and loss-sharing ratios were used. The basic idea behind the rule is that an agreement to share profits and losses refers to those accruing from trading operations, the fact that a partner may not honour his obligations concerning capital is a risk which attaches to capital only. However, in a case such as that shown in Exhibit 4.2 it is possible, if fluctuating Capital Accounts had been used, that both R, S and T could each have started with £1,000 capital each some years ago. R allows a much greater part of his profits to remain in the business than the other partners. It would seem a strange way of rewarding him for the financing benefits which have flowed from R's behaviour to make him suffer a more than proportionate share of Q's deficiency. The rule would act as a deterrent to a partner wishing to leave undrawn profits in the firm. The use of separate agreements to ignore the rule and of Current Accounts which are ignored for this purpose, have been the ways used by the accounting profession to circumvent the *Garner* v. *Murray* decision.

Piecemeal realisation of assets

Frequently the assets may take a long time to realise. The partners will naturally want payments made to them on account as cash is received. They will not want to wait for payments until the dissolution is completed just for the convenience of the accountant. There is, however, a danger that if too much is paid to a partner, and he is unable to repay it, then the person handling the dissolution could be placed in a very invidious position.

Therefore the concept of prudence is brought into play. The view taken is to treat each receipt of sale money as being the last money receivable. Any loss then calculated is shared between the partners in their profit- and loss-sharing ratio. Should any partner's Capital Account then show a debit balance it is assumed that he will be unable to meet such a deficit, and this will be shared (subject to any contrary agreement) between the other partners using the *Garner* v. *Murray* rule. After payment of the liabilities and the costs of dissolution the remainder of the cash is then paid to the partners.

In this manner, even if no further money was received, or should a partner become insolvent, the division of the available cash would be strictly in accordance with the legal requirements. Exhibit 4.3 shows such a series of calculations.

Exhibit 4.3

The following is the summarised Balance Sheet of H, I, J and K as at 31 December 19-5. The partners had shared profits in the ratios H 6:I 4:J 1:K1.

Balance Sheet as at 31 December 19-5

	£
Assets	8,400
	8,400
Capitals:	
H	600
I	3,000
J	2,000
K	1,000
Creditors	1,800
	8,400

On 1 March 19-6 some of the assets were sold for cash £5,000. Out of this the creditors £1,800 and the cost of dissolution £200 are paid, leaving £3,000 distributable to the partners.

On 1 July 19-6 some more assets are sold for £2,100. As all of the liabilities and the costs of dissolution have already been paid, then the whole of the £2,100 is available for distribution between the partners.

On 1 October 19-6 the final sale of the assets realised £1,200.

First Distribution: 1 March 19-6	H £	I £	J £	K £
Capital balances before dissolution	600	3,000	2,000	1,000
Loss if no further assets realised: Assets £8,400 − Sales £5,000 = £3,400 + Costs £200 = £3,600 loss				
Loss shared in profit/loss ratios	1,800	1,200	300	300
	1,200 Dr	1,800 Cr	1,700 Cr	700 Cr
H's deficiency shared in *Garner* v. *Murray* ratios	⅗	600 ⅖	400 ⅙	200
Cash paid to partners (£3,000)		1,200	1,300	500

Second Distribution: 1 July 19-6	H £	I £	J £	K £
Capital balances before dissolution	600	3,000	2,000	1,000
Loss if no further assets realised − Assets £8,400 − Sales (£5,000 + £2,100) = £1,300 + Costs £200 = £1,500 loss				
Loss shared in profit/loss ratios	750	500	125	125
	150 Dr	2,500 Cr	1,875 Cr	875 Cr
H's deficiency shared in *Garner* v. *Murray* ratios		75	50	25
		2,425	1,825	850
less first distribution already paid		1,200	1,300	500
Cash now paid to partners (£2,100)		1,225	525	350

Third and Final Distribution: 1 October 19-6	H £	I £	J £	K £
Capital balances before dissolution	600	3,000	2,000	1,000
Loss finally ascertained − Assets £8,400 − Sales (£5,000 + £2,100 + £1,200) = £100 + Costs £200 = £300 loss				
Loss shared in profit/loss ratios	150	100	25	25
	450 Cr	2,900 Cr	1,975 Cr	975 Cr
(No deficiency now exists on any Capital Account) *less* first and second distributions	−	2,425	1,825	850
Cash now paid to partners (£1,200)	450	475	150	125

In any subsequent distribution following that in which all the partners have shared, i.e. no partner could then have had a deficiency left on his Capital Account, all receipts of cash are divided between the partners in their profit- and loss-sharing ratios.

Following the above method would give the same answer for these subsequent distributions but obviously an immediate division in the profit- and loss-sharing ratios would be quicker. The reader is invited to try it to satisfy himself that it would work out at the same answer.

Review questions

4.1 Moore and Stephens, who share profits and losses equally, decide to dissolve their partnership as at 31 March 19-1.

Their balance sheet on that date was as follows:

		£		£
Capital Account: Moore		2,000	Buildings	800
	Stephens	1,500	Tools and fixtures	850
		———	Debtors	2,800
		3,500	Cash	1,800
Sundry creditors		2,750		
		6,250		6,250

The debtors realised £2,700, the buildings £400 and the tools and fixtures £950. The expenses of dissolution were £100 and discounts totalling £200 were received from creditors.

Prepare the accounts necessary to show the results of the realisation and of the disposal of the cash.

4.2 X, Y and Z have been in partnership for several years, sharing profits and losses in the ratio 3:2:1. Their last balance sheet which was prepared on 31 October 19-1 is as follows:

Balance Sheet of X, Y and Z
as at 31 October 19-1

		£		£	£
Capital X		4,000	*Fixed Assets*		
Y		4,000	at cost	20,000	
Z		2,000	*less* depreciation	6,000	
		10,000			14,000
			Current Assets		
			Stock	5,000	
Current liabilities			Debtors	21,000	
Bank	13,000				
Creditors	17,000				26,000
		30,000			
		£40,000			£40,000

Despite making good profits during recent years they had become increasingly dependent on one credit customer Smithson and in order to retain his custom they had gradually increased his credit limit until he owed the partnership £18,000. It has now been discovered that Smithson is insolvent and that he is unlikely to repay any of the money owed by him to the partnership. Reluctantly X, Y and Z have agreed to dissolve the partnership on the following terms:

(*i*) The stock is to be sold to Nelson Ltd for £4,000.

(*ii*) The fixed assets will be sold for £8,000 except for certain items with a book value of £5,000 which will be taken over by X at an agreed valuation of £7,000.

(*iii*) The debtors, except for Smithson, are expected to pay their accounts in full.

(*iv*) The costs of dissolution will be £800 and discounts received from creditors will be £500.

Z is unable to meet his liability to the partnership out of his personal funds.

Required:

(*a*) The realisation account.

(*b*) The capital accounts to the partners recording the dissolution of the partnership.

(*Associated Examining Board*)

4.3A The following trial balance has been extracted from the books of Gain and Main as at 31 March 19-2; Gain and Main are in partnership sharing profits and losses in the ratio 3 to 2:

	£	£
Capital Accounts:		
Gain		10,000
Main		5,000
Cash at Bank	1,550	
Creditors		500
Current Accounts:		
Gain		1,000
Main	2,000	
Debtors	2,000	
Depreciation: Fixtures and Fittings		1,000
Motor Vehicles		1,300
Fixtures and Fittings	2,000	
Land and Buildings	30,000	
Motor Vehicles	4,500	
Net Profit (for the year to 31 March 19-2)		26,250
Stock, at cost	3,000	
	£45,050	£45,050

In appropriating the net profit for the year, it has been agreed that Main should be entitled to a salary of £9,750. Each partner is also entitled to interest on his opening capital account balance at the rate of 10% per annum.

Gain and Main have decided to convert the partnership into a limited company, Plain Limited, as from 1 April 19-2. The company is to take over all the assets and liabilities of the partnership, except that Gain is to retain for his personal use one of the motor vehicles at an agreed transfer price of £1,000.

The purchase consideration will consist of 40,000 ordinary shares of £1 each in Plain Limited, to be divided between the partners in profit sharing ratio. Any balance on the partners current accounts is to be settled in cash.

You are required to:

Prepare the main ledger accounts of the partnership in order to close off the books as at 31 March 19-2.

(*Association of Accounting Technicians*)

4.4A A, B and C are partners sharing profits and losses in the ratio 2:2:1. The balance sheet of the partnership as at 30 September 19-7 was as follows:

	£		£	£
Freehold premises	18,000	Capital Accounts		
Equipment and machinery	12,000	A	22,000	
Motor cars	3,000	B	18,000	
Inventory	11,000	C	10,000	
Debtors	14,000			50,000
Bank	9,000	Loan Account — A		7,000
		Creditors		10,000
	£67,000			£67,000

The partners agreed to dispose of the business to CNO Limited with effect from 1 October 19-7 under the following conditions and terms:

(*i*) CNO Limited will acquire the goodwill, all fixed assets and the inventory for the purchase consideration of £58,000. This consideration will include a payment of £10,000 in cash and the issue of 12,000 10 per cent Preference Shares of £1 each at par, and the balance by the issue of £1 Ordinary Shares at £1.25 per share.

(*ii*) The partnership business will settle amounts owing to creditors.

(*iii*) CNO Limited will collect the debts on behalf of the vendors.

Purchase consideration payments and allotments of shares were made on 1 October 19-7.

The partnership creditors were paid off by 31 October 19-7 after the taking of cash discounts of £190.

CNO Limited collected and paid over all partnership debts by 30 November 19-7 except for bad debts amounting to £800. Discounts allowed to debtors amounted to £400.

Required:

(*a*) Journal entries (including those relating to cash) necessary to close the books of the partnership, and

(*b*) Set out the basis on which the shares in CNO Limited are allotted to the partners.

Ignore interest.

(*Institute of Chartered Secretaries and Administrators*)

4.5 Amis, Lodge and Pym were in partnership sharing profits and losses in the ratio 5:3:2. The following trial balance has been extracted from their books of account as at 31 March 19-8:

	£	£
Bank interest received		750
Capital accounts (as at 1 April 19-7):		
Amis		80,000
Lodge		15,000
Pym		5,000
Carriage inwards	4,000	
Carriage outwards	12,000	
Cash at bank	4,900	
Current accounts:		
Amis	1,000	
Lodge	500	
Pym	400	
Discounts allowed	10,000	
Discounts received		4,530
Drawings:		
Amis	25,000	
Lodge	22,000	
Pym	15,000	
Motor vehicles:		
at cost	80,000	
accumulated depreciation (at 1 April 19-7)		20,000
Office expenses	30,400	
Plant and machinery:		
at cost	100,000	
accumulated depreciation (at 1 April 19-7)		36,600
Provision for bad and doubtful debts		
(at 1 April 19-7)		420
Purchases	225,000	
Rent, rates, heat and light	8,800	
Sales		404,500
Stock (at 1 April 19-7)	30,000	
Trade creditors		16,500
Trade debtors	14,300	
	£583,300	£583,300

Additional information:

(a) Stock at 31 March 19-8 was valued at £35,000.

(b) Depreciation on the fixed assets is to be charged as follows:

Motor vehicles – 25% on the reduced balance

Plant and machinery – 20% on the original cost.

There were no purchases or sales of fixed assets during the year to 31 March 19-8.

(c) The provision for bad and doubtful debts is to be maintained at a level equivalent to 5% of the total trade debtors as at 31 March 19-8.

(d) An office expense of £405 was owing at 31 March 19-8, and some rent amounting to £1,500 had been paid in advance as at that date. These items had not been included in the list of balances shown in the trial balance.

(*e*) Interest on drawings and on the debit balance on each partner's current account is to be charged as follows:

	£
Amis	1,000
Lodge	900
Pym	720

(*f*)   According to the partnership agreement, Pym is allowed a salary of £13,000 per annum. This amount was owing to Pym for the year to 31 March 19-8, and needs to be accounted for.

(*g*)   The partnership agreement also allows each partner interest on his capital account at a rate of 10% per annum. There were no movements on the respective partners' capital accounts during the year to 31 March 19-8, and the interest had not been credited to them as at that date.

Note: The information given above is sufficient to answer part (*a*) (*i*) and (*ii*) of the question, and notes (*h*) and (*i*) below are pertinent to requirements (*b*) (*i*), (*ii*) and (*iii*) of the question.

(*h*)   On 1 April 19-8, Fowles Limited agreed to purchase the business on the following terms:

(*i*)   Amis to purchase one of the partnership's motor vehicles at an agreed value of £5,000, the remaining vehicles being taken over by the company at an agreed value of £30,000;

(*ii*)   the company agreed to purchase the plant and machinery at a value of £35,000 and the stock at a value of £38,500;

(*iii*)   the partners to settle the trade creditors: the total amount agreed with the creditors being £16,000;

(*iv*)   the trade debtors were not to be taken over by the company, the partners receiving cheques on 1 April 19-8 amounting to £12,985 in total from the trade debtors in settlement of the outstanding debts;

(*v*)   the partners paid the outstanding office expense on 1 April 19-8, and the landlord returned the rent paid in advance by cheque on the same day;

(*vi*)   as consideration for the sale of the partnership, the partners were to be paid £63,500 in cash by Fowles Limited, and to receive 75,000 in £1 ordinary shares in the company, the shares to be apportioned equally amongst the partners.

(*i*)   Assume that all the matters relating to the dissolution of the partnership and its sales to the company took place on 1 April 19-8.

Required:

(*a*) Prepare:

(*i*)   Amis', Lodge's and Pym's trading, profit and loss and profit and loss appropriation account for the year to 31 March 19-8;
and

(*ii*)   Amis', Lodge's and Pym's current accounts (in columnar format) for the year to 31 March 19-8 (the final balance on each account is to be then transferred to each partner's respective capital account);
and

(*b*)   Compile the following accounts:

(*i*)   the partnership realisation account for the period up to and including 1 April 19-8;

(*ii*)   the partners' bank account for the period up to and including 1 April 19-8;
and

(*iii*) the partners' capital accounts (in columnar format) for the period up to and including 1 April 19-8.

Note: Detailed workings should be submitted with your answer.

(*Association of Accounting Technicians*)

4.6A Proudie, Slope and Thorne were in partnership sharing profits and losses in the ratio 3:1:1. The draft balance sheet of the partnership as at 31 May 19-6 is shown below:

	£'000 Cost	£'000 Depreci- ation	£'000 Net Book Value
Fixed Assets			
Land and buildings	200	40	160
Furniture	30	18	12
Motor vehicles	60	40	20
	£290	£98	£192
Current Assets			
Stocks		23	
Trade debtors	42		
less Provision for doubtful debts	1		
		41	
Prepayments		2	
Cash		10	
		76	
less Current Liabilities			
Trade creditors	15		
Accruals	3		
		18	
			58
			£250
Financed by:			
Capital Accounts			
Proudie		100	
Slope		60	
Thorne		40	
			200
Current Accounts			
Proudie		24	
Slope		10	
Thorne		8	
			42
			242
Loan			
Proudie			8
			£250

Additional information:

1 Proudie decided to retire on 31 May 19-6. However, Slope and Thorne agreed to form a new partnership out of the old one, as from 1 June 19-6. They agreed to share profits and losses in the same ratio as in the old partnership.

2 Upon the dissolution of the old partnership, it was agreed that the following adjustments were to be made to the partnership balance sheet as at 31 May 19-6.

(a) Land and buildings were to be revalued at £200,000;

(b) Furniture was to be revalued at £5,000;

(c) Proudie agreed to take over one of the motor vehicles at a value of £4,000, the remaining motor vehicles being revalued at £10,000;

(d) Stocks were to be written down by £5,000;

(e) A bad debt of £2,000 was to be written off, and the provision for doubtful debts was then to be adjusted so that it represented 5% of the then outstanding trade debtors as at 31 May 19-6:

(f) A further accrual of £3,000 for office expenses was to be made;

(g) Professional charges relating to the dissolution were estimated to be £1,000.

3 It has not been the practice of the partners to carry goodwill in the books of the partnership, but on the retirement of a partner it had been agreed that goodwill should be taken into account. Goodwill was to be valued at an amount equal to the average annual profits of the three years expiring on the retirement. For the purpose of including goodwill in the dissolution arrangement when Proudie retired, the net profits for the last three years were as follows:

	£'000
Year to 31 May 19-4	130
Year to 31 May 19-5	150
Year to 31 May 19-6	181

The net profit for the year to 31 May 19-6 had been calculated before any of the items listed in 2 above were taken into account. The net profit was only to be adjusted for items listed in 2(d), 2(e) and 2(f) above.

4 Goodwill is not to be carried in the books of the new partnership.

5 It was agreed that Proudie's old loan of £8,000 should be repaid to him on 31 May 19-6, but any further amount owing to him as a result of the dissolution of the partnership should be left as a long-term loan in the books of the new partnership.

6 The partners' current accounts were to be closed and any balances on them as at 31 May 19-6 were to be transferred to their respective capital accounts.

Required:

(a) Prepare the revaluation account as at 31 May 19-6.

(b) Prepare the partners' capital accounts as at the date of dissolution of the partnership, and bring down any balances on them in the books of the new partnership.

(c) Prepare Slope and Thorne's balance sheet as at 1 June 19-6.

(*Association of Accounting Technicians*)

4.7 Lock, Stock and Barrel have been in partnership as builders and contractors for many years. Owing to adverse trading conditions it has been decided to dissolve the partnership. Profits are shared Lock 40% Stock 30% Barrel 30%. The partnership deed also provides that in the event of a partner being unable to pay off a debit balance the remaining partners will treat this as a trading loss.

The latest partnership balance sheet was as follows:

Fixed tangible assets	Cost £	Depreciation £	£
Freehold yard and buildings	20,000	3,000	17,000
Plant and equipment	150,000	82,000	68,000
Motor vehicles	36,000	23,000	13,000
	206,000	108,000	98,000

Current assets		
Stock of land for building		75,000
Houses in course of construction		115,000
Stocks of materials		23,000
Debtors for completed houses		62,000
		275,000
Current liabilities		
Trade creditors	77,000	
Deposits and progress payments	82,000	
Bank overdraft	132,500	
		291,500

Excess of current liabilities over current assets	(16,500)
	81,500

Partners' capital accounts		
Lock		52,000
Stock		26,000
Barrel		3,500
		81,500

During the six months from the date of the latest balance sheet to the date of dissolution the following transactions have taken place:

	£
Purchase of materials	20,250
Materials used for houses in course of construction	35,750
Payments for wages and subcontractors on building sites	78,000
Payments to trade creditors for materials	45,000
Sales of completed houses	280,000
Cash received from customers for houses	225,000
Payments for various general expenses	12,500
Payments for administration salaries	17,250
Cash withdrawn by partners: Lock	6,000
Stock	5,000
Barrel	4,000

All deposits and progress payments have been used for completed transactions.

Depreciation is normally provided each year at £600 on the freehold yard and buildings, at 10% on cost for plant and equipment and 25% on cost for motor vehicles.

The partners decide to dissolve the partnership on 1 February 19-7 and wish to take out the maximum cash possible, as items are sold. At this date there are no houses in course of construction and one third of the stock of land had been used for building.

It is agreed that Barrel is insolvent and cannot bring any money into the partnership. The partners take over the partnership cars at an agreed figure of £2,000 each. All other vehicles were sold on 28 February 19-7 for £6,200. At the same date stocks of materials were sold for £7,000, and the stock of the land realised £72,500. On 30 April 19-7 the debtors paid in full and all the plant and equipment was sold for £50,000.

The freehold yard and buildings realised £100,000 on 1 June 19-7, on which date all remaining cash was distributed.

There are no costs of realisation or distribution.

Required:

(*a*) Prepare a partnership profit and loss account for the six months to 1 February 19-7, partners' capital accounts for the same period and a balance sheet at 1 February 19-7.

(*b*) Show calculations of the amounts distributable to the partners.

(*c*) Prepare a realisation account and the capital accounts of the partners to the final distribution.

(*Chartered Association of Certified Accountants*)

5
Branch accounts

From an accounting point of view, a firm which has branches is either one which keeps all the financial accounts at the head office, or it is one where each branch maintains its own full accounting system.

Where the head office maintains all the accounts

The purpose behind the accounts is not merely to record transactions so that changes in assets, liabilities or capital can be calculated but also attempts wherever possible to keep a check by remote control as to whether or not the firm is being defrauded of goods or cash. For a firm with branches this is obviously of utmost importance. The managers who run the businesses are thus handling considerable amounts of money and goods, and the actual feeling of not being able to be seen continually by the head office staff may well induce the manager or his staff, into feeling that they could misappropriate large sums of cash or goods without being found out.

The solution of the problem will differ between firms. One firm with several branches which only sold expensive luxury cars could keep control easily, because the number of cars bought and sold would be relatively few, and the location of each car could be traced with very little effort. The opposite of this would be a grocery firm with hundreds of branches selling numerous different lines of goods. To keep a check on each carton of salt or bag of flour is clearly uneconomic even if it could be done, and not many customers would be happy to wait at the cashier's desk while all the reference numbers on the goods sold were recorded.

The accounting solution to this is extremely simple in its basic form. This is to translate all the transactions at the branch into selling prices. Taking a small branch as an example, and given various pieces of information, it is possible to calculate the closing stock, if wastages, breakages and pilfering by customers are ignored.

	£
Stock on hand at 1 January – at selling price	500
January – Goods sent to the Branch by the Head Office – at selling price	4,000
January – Sales by the Branch – obviously at selling price	3,800

The calculation of the closing stock becomes:

	£
Opening Stock 1 January (selling price)	500
add Goods sent to the Branch (selling price)	4,000
Goods which the Branch had available for sale (selling price)	4,500
less Goods Sold (selling price)	3,800
Closing Stock at 31 January should therefore be (selling price)	700

An allowance will be made for wastages, breakages and pilferages, this being based on experience. For instance, it may be normal to allow a figure of 1 per cent of goods sent to the branch to cover those items, therefore an actual stock at selling price of £700 less £40 (1 per cent of £4,000) = £660 would be tolerated. An actual stock of less than £660 would call for investigation. The allowance may well differ as between branches, for instance in Uptown the pilferage rate may be very small whereas in Lowtown there may be a high incidence of pilferages. An oil firm with branches (e.g. petrol stations) situated in many countries will obviously allow more for evaporation of petrol in hot climates than it will in cold climates. Experience and common sense are the only guides.

If a manager, or one of his staff is suspected of fraud, then the policy of the firm will dictate the action to be taken. It may involve the transfer of the manager to another branch to see whether or not the deficiencies cease at the old branch and restart at his new branch. A branch which only transfers managers when they are suspected of fraud will, of course, merely put the man on his guard. Some firms therefore transfer managers fairly frequently, but accounting needs should always be the servant of the firm and not the master.

It may well have occurred to the reader that the manager could say that the stock was a certain figure even though it was not true. For instance, a manager who has stolen £1,000 in goods or cash may try to cover this up by overstating his stock by £1,000. To counteract this many firms will carry out spot inspections of stock. This means that representatives of the firm may call at the branch without notifying the manager in advance and conduct a stocktaking. Then they will compare the actual stock with the stock calculated as follows (all items being shown at selling price):

1 Stock per the branch manager at the date of the last stocktaking by the branch.

2 Add goods received by branch since the date of (1).

3 Less sales since the date of (1).

4 Less allowances for wastages, etc.

5 The stock should be equal to (1 + 2) − (3 + 4).

The knowledge that such spot checks are carried out will act as a deterrent to showing false stock figures.

The head office will normally insist that all branches will bank their full cash takings each day. The money will be paid into a local bank and special paying-in slips will be used so that the amount deposited will be transferred through the banking system into the firm's main bank account at the head office's bank. Each entry will be coded so that the head office will be able to tell quickly if a branch is not banking its takings. Cash payments made by the branch will be kept on a basis similar to the petty cash imprest system, with the head office reimbursing the amount spent at regular intervals.

The double column system

At regular intervals, obviously at least once a year, but usually more frequently, the head office may draft a Trading and Profit and Loss Account for each branch. The Trading Account can be shown with two columns, one in which goods sent to the branch or in stock are shown at cost price, i.e. the normal basis for any business. This column is therefore part of a normal Trading Account for the branch. The other column will show all Trading Account items at selling price. This is the column where deficiencies in trading can be compared with the normal deficiency allowed for wastages, pilferages, etc. It is not a part of the double-entry recording; it is a memorandum column for control purposes only.

Exhibit 5.1

This is drafted up from the following details for a firm which sells goods at a uniform mark-up of 33⅓ per cent profit on cost price:

	£
Stock 1 Jan 19-8 (at cost)	1,200
Goods sent to the Branch during the year (at cost)	6,000
Sales (selling price)	7,428
Stock 31 December 19-8 (at cost)	1,500
Allowances for wastage, etc., 1 per cent of Sales Expenses	1,000

As the actual deficiency of £172 exceeds the amount to be tolerated, i.e. 1 per cent of £7,428 = £74 approximately, this means that an investigation will be made.

This method is suitable where all the sales are for cash, there being no sales on credit.

Branch Trading and Profit and Loss Account for the year ended 31.12.19-8

	At selling price			At selling price	
	£	£		£	£
Stock 1 Jan 19-8	1,600	1,200	Sales	7,428	7,428
Goods from Head			Deficiency		
Office	8,000	6,000	(difference)	172	
	9,600	7,200			
less Stock 31 Dec 19-8	2,000	1,500			
	7,600	5,700			
Gross Profit c/d		1,728			
	7,600	7,428		7,600	7,428
Expenses		1,000	Gross Profit b/d		1,728
Net Profit		728			
		1,728			1,728

The stock and debtors system

Where a branch also sells goods on credit terms then further refinements are necessary to ensure that the control element applies also to debtors. This system can either be operated on the basis that the control element is built in as part of the double entry effected, or else as memoranda columns so far as the stock is concerned. The method using memoranda columns would certainly appear to have all the benefits of simplicity and ease of operation, and is the one to be preferred in practice. The fully integrated method does, however, seem to be preferred by examiners, perhaps this is because this method is indicative of the way that will be illustrated of calculating gross profits using profit margins only.

Using the following basic data, Exhibit 5.2 shows the records where the memoranda method is used, while Exhibit 5.3 shows the records where the fully integrated method is in use.

Data: A branch sells all its goods at a uniform mark-up of 50 per cent profit on cost price. Credit customers are to pay their accounts direct to the head office.

		£
First day of the period –		
Stock (at cost)	A	2,000
Debtors	B	400
During the period –		
Goods sent to the Branch (at cost)	C	7,000
Sales – Cash	D	6,000
Sales – Credit	E	4,800
Cash remitted by Debtors to Head Office	F	4,500
At the close of the last day of the period –		
Stock (at cost)	G	1,800
Debtors	H	700

The letters A to H beside the figures have been inserted in order that the entries in Exhibit 5.3 can be more easily understood. The entries for each of the above items will have the relevant letter shown beside it.

Exhibit 5.2

Memoranda columns in use
Branch Stock

	Selling price memo. only			Seling price memo. only	
	£	£		£	£
Stock b/fwd	3,000	2,000	Sales: Cash	6,000	6,000
Goods Sent	10,500	7,000	Credit	4,800	4,800
Gross Profit to			Stock c/d	2,700	1,800
Profit and Loss		3,600			
	13,500	12,600		13,500	12,600
Stock b/d	2,700	1,800			

Branch Debtors

		£			£
Balances b/fwd		400	Cash		4,500
Branch Sales		4,800	Balances c/d		700
		5,200			5,200
Balances b/d		700			

Goods sent to Branches

	£		£
Transfer to Head Office		Branch Stock	7,000
Trading Account	7,000		

	£
Branch Stock Office – Cash Sales	6,000
Branch Debtors	4,500

The branch Stock Account is thus in effect a Trading Account, and is identical to the type used in the Double Column System. In addition, however, a Branch Debtors Account is in use.

The balance of the Goods Sent to Branches Account is shown as being transferred to the Head Office Trading Account. This figure is deducted from the purchases in the Head Office Trading Account, in order that goods bought for the branch can be disregarded when the gross profit earned by the head office is being calculated.

The fully integrated system introduces the idea that the gross profit earned by a firm can be calculated by reference to profit margins only. A simple example illustrates this point. Assume that a self-employed travelling salesman sells all his goods at cost price plus 25 per cent for profit. At the start of a week he has £4 stock at cost, he buys goods costing £40, he sells goods for £45 (selling price) and he has goods left in stock at the end of the week which had cost him £8. A normal Trading Account based on this data is shown below.

Trading Account for the week ended ...

	£	£
Sales		45
less Cost of Goods Sold:		
Opening Stock	4	
add Purchases	40	
	44	
less Closing Stock	8	36
Gross Profit		9

This could, however, also be shown as:

	£
Profit made when opening stock is sold	1
Profit made when purchases are sold	10
Profit made when all goods are sold	11
But he still has left unsold goods (cost £8) on which the profit still has to be realised	2
Therefore profit realised	9

This could be expressed in account form as:

Salesman's Adjustment Account

	£		£
Gross Profit	9	Unrealised Profit b/fwd	1
Unrealised Profit c/d	2	Goods Bought	10
	11		11

The full integrated system uses a form of adjustment account. Goods sent to the branch are shown at cost price in an account for that purpose, while the Branch Stock Account is shown at selling price. To show one entry at selling price and the other at cost would mean that debit amounts would not equal credit amounts, thus violating double entry principles. To rectify this a Branch Adjustment Account is opened and the profit loading on the goods is recorded to preserve the equality of amounts of debit and credit entries. The Branch Stock Account by being entirely concerned with selling prices acts as a control upon stock deficiencies, while the branch Adjustment Account shows the amount of gross profit earned during the period. In the example seen worked out in Exhibit 5.3 a stock deficiency does not exist. The action required when such a deficiency arises is demonstrated later in this chapter.

Exhibit 5.3

Branch Stock (Selling Price)

		£			£
Balance b/fwd	A	3,000	Sales: Cash	D	6,000
Goods sent to Branch	C	10,500	Credit	E	4,800
			Balance c/d	G	2,700
		13,500			13,500
Balance b/d	G	2,700			

Branch Debtors (Selling Price)

		£			£
Balances b/fwd	B	400	Cash	F	4,500
Branch Stock	E	4,800	Balances c/d	H	700
		5,200			5,200
Balances b/d	H	700			

Goods sent to Branches (Cost Price)

	£			£
Transfer to Head Office Trading Account	7,000	Branch Stock	C	7,000

		£			£
Gross Profit to Profit			Unrealised Profit		
and Loss		3,600	b/fwd	A	1,000
Unrealised Profit c/d	G	900	Branch Stock –		
			goods sent	C	3,500
		4,500			4.500
			Unrealised Profit b/d	G	900

The opening and closing stock are shown in the Branch Stock Account at selling price. However, the Balance Sheet should show the stock at cost price (if for simplicity the fact that the net realisable value etc., may be lower than cost can be ignored). The previous Balance Sheet should therefore have shown stock at cost £2,000. This is achieved by having a compensating £1,000 credit balance brought forward in the Branch Adjustment Account, so that the debit balance of £3,000 in the Branch Stock Account, when it comes to being shown in the Balance Sheet, has the £1,000 credit balance deducted to show a net figure of £2,000. Similarly, at the close of the period the balance sheet will show stock at £1,800 (Branch Stock debit balance £2,700 less Branch Adjustment credit balance £900).

The fully integrated system – further considerations

(a) Returns

Goods may be returned:
(i)   From the branch stock to the head office.
(ii) From the branch debtors to the branch stock.
(iii) From the branch debtors to the head office.

To show the entries needed look at a firm which sells goods at cost plus 25 per cent profit, and according to the categories stated the following goods were returned, all prices shown being selling prices: (i) £45, (ii) £75, (iii) £15. The entries needed are:

Branch Stock (Selling Price)

		£			£
Returns from Debtors	(ii)	75	Returned to Head Office	(i)	45

Branch Adjustment (Profit Loading)

		£
Returns from Branch	(i)	9
Returns from Debtors	(iii)	3

Goods Sent to Branches (Cost Price)

		£
Returns from Branch	(i)	36
Returns from Debtors	(iii)	12

Branch Debtors (Selling Price)

			£
	Returns to Branch	(ii)	75
	Returns to Head Office	(iii)	15

Entries (ii) both being in accounts shown at selling price were two in number, i.e., £75 Dr and £75 Cr Entries (i) and (iii) each needed entries in three accounts, (i) being £45 Cr and £9 Dr and £36 Dr, (iii) being £15 Cr and £12 Dr and £3 Dr.

(b) Different physical and book stock figures

It has been assumed so far that the stock figures according to the accounts have been exactly the same as the actual stocks on hand. This will rarely be true, as there are almost bound to be errors made in selling prices, giving wrong change in cash sales, breakages, wastages, pilferages, or it could perhaps be that goods have been sold at a different profit mark-up from that which is normal in the business.

The stock to be carried forward in the Branch Stock Account is, however, the selling price of the actual stock on hand. The difference between the actual stock and the unadjusted balance on the stock account will normally be a deficiency of stock. The converse would only apply where goods had been sold at higher than normal profit mark-up. A deficiency of stock is entered by crediting the difference to the Branch Stock Account and debiting a similar amount to the Branch Adjustment Account. The converse applies to an excess of stock.

To understand why this should be so, a firm's accounts can be seen where a deficiency of stock exists.

Exhibit 5.4

A firm with one branch has a uniform mark-up of 50 per cent. The following details are known:

	£
Opening Stock – at selling price	1,800
Goods sent to the Branch – at selling price	6,000
Sales by the Branch – at selling price	6,300
Closing Stock – per actual stocktaking – at selling price	1,350

Branch Stock (Selling Price)

	£		£
Balance b/fwd	1,800	Sales	6,300
Goods sent to Branch	6,000	Deficiency (difference between the two sides of the account)	150
		Balance c/d	1,350
	7,800		7,800
Balance b/d	1,350		

	£		£
Branch Stock (deficiency)	150	Unrealised Profit in	
		Opening Stock b/fwd	600
Gross Profit to Profit and		Goods sent to Branch	2,000
Loss	2,000		
Unrealised Profit in Closing			
Stock c/d	450		
	2,600		2,600

		£
	Unrealised Profit in Stock	
	b/d	450

Suppose an ordinary Trading Account had been drafted, it would have appeared:

Trading Account for the period ...

	£	
Sales		6,300
less Cost of Goods Sold:		
Opening Stock	1,200	
add Goods from Head Office	4,000	
	5,200	
less Closing Stock	900	4,300
Gross Profit		2,000

Thus the profit calculated by the normal method and the Branch Adjustment method remains the same. The fact that the Adjustment Account is charged with the full selling price of the stock deficiency is because the gross profit part of the deficiency, £50, had already been taken into account in the £2,000 credited to the Adjustment Account, as it has not been realised it must be cancelled. In addition, the cost of the stock deficiency, £100, is a charge when calculating the gross profit, e.g. goods breakages mean less gross profit.

Missing Figures

It is the common practice of many examiners to omit certain figures when giving details for questions using the Stock and Debtors system. The student is entitled in such a case to assume that where one figure is missing in an account, then that figure may be taken to be the difference between the totals of the two sides.

Where each branch maintains full accounting records

This would very rarely be found in a firm with many branches, it is more common in a firm with just one or two or a few branches, and is particularly relevant where the branch is large enough to warrant a separate accounting staff being employed.

A branch cannot operate on its own without resources, and it is the firm that provides these in the first instance. The firm will want to know how much money it has invested in each branch, and from this arises the concept of Branch and Head Office Current Accounts. The relationship between the branch and the head office is seen as that of a debtor/creditor identity. The current accounts are medias where the branch is shown as a debtor in the head office records, while the head office is shown as a creditor in the branch records. This is purely for expediency, because as the branch and the head office both belong to the same firm it is apparent that a firm cannot owe money to itself.

The current accounts are used for those transactions that are concerned with supplying resources to the branch or in retrieving resources. For such transactions full double entry records are needed both in the branch records and also in the head office records, i.e. each item will be recorded twice in each set of records. Some transactions will, however, concern the branch only, and these will merely need two entries in the branch records and none in the head office records. Exhibit 5.5 shows several transactions and the records needed.

Exhibit 5.5

A firm with its head office in London opened a branch in Manchester. The following transactions took place in the first month:

A Opened a bank account at Manchester by transferring £1,000 from the London bank account.

B Bought premises in Manchester, paying by cheque drawn on the London bank account, £5,000.

C Manchester bought a motor van, paying by cheque £600 from its own bank account.

D Manchester bought fixtures on credit from A B Equipment Ltd, £900.

E London supplied a machine valued at £250 from its own machinery.

F Manchester bought goods from suppliers, paying by cheque on its own account, £270.

G Manchester's cash sales banked immediately in its own bank account, £3,000.

H Goods invoiced at cost to Manchester during the month by London (no cash or cheques being paid specifically for these goods by Manchester), £2,800.

I A cheque is paid to London by Manchester as general return of funds, £1,800.

J Goods returned to London by Manchester – at cost price, £100.

The exact dates have been deliberately omitted. It will be seen later that complications arise because of differences in the time of transactions. Each transaction has been identified by a capital letter. The relevant letter will be shown against each entry in the accounts.

Head Office Records (in London)
Manchester Branch Current Account

		£			£
Bank	A	1,000	Bank	I	1,800
Bank – Premises	B	5,000	Returns from Branch	J	100
Machinery	E	250			
Goods sent to Branch	H	2,800			

Bank

		£			£
Manchester Branch	I	1,800	Manchester Branch	A	1,000
			Manchester Premises	B	5,000

Machinery

		£			£
			Manchester Branch	E	250

Goods sent to Branch

		£				£
Returns from Branch	J	100	Manchester Branch		H	2,800

Branch Records (in Manchester)
Head Office Current Account

		£				£
Returns	J	100	Bank		A	1,000
Bank	I	1,800	Premises		B	5,000
			Machinery		E	250
			Goods from Head Office		H	2,800

Bank

		£				£
Head Office	A	1,000	Motor Van		C	600
Cash Sales	G	3,000	Purchases		F	270
			Head Office		I	1,800

Premises

		£
Head Office	B	5,000

Motor Van

		£
Bank	C	600

Fixtures

		£
A B Equipment Ltd	D	900

A B Equipment Ltd

				£
		Fixtures	D	900

Machinery

		£
Head Office	E	250

Purchases

		£
Bank	F	270

Sales

				£
		Bank	G	3,000

Goods from Head Office

		£				£
Head Office	H	2,800	Head Office – returns		J	100

It can be seen that items, C, D, F and G are entered only in the Manchester records. This is because these items are purely internal transactions and are not concerned with resources flowing between London and Manchester.

Profit or loss and current accounts

The profit earned by the branch (or loss incurred by it) does not belong to the branch. It belongs to the firm and must therefore be shown as such. The head office represents the central authority of the firm and profit of the branch should be credited to the Head Office Current Account, any loss being debited.

The branch will therefore draw up its own Trading and Profit and Loss Account. After agreement with the head office the net profit will then be transferred to the credit of the Head Office Current Account. The head office in its own records will then debit the Branch Current Account and credit its own Profit and Loss Account. Taking the net profit earned in Exhibit 5.5 as £700, the two sets of books would appear thus:

Head Office Records (in London)
London Profit and Loss Account

			£
	Net Profit earned by the Manchester Branch		700

Manchester Branch Current Account

	£		£
Bank	1,000	Bank	1,800
Bank: Premises	5,000	Returns from Branch	100
Machinery	250		
Goods sent to Branch	2,800		
Net profit to main Profit and Loss Account	700	Balance c/d	7,850
	9,750		9,750
Balance b/d	7,850		

Branch Records (in Manchester)
Manchester Profit and Loss Account

	£
Net Profit carried to the Head Office Current Account	700

Head Office Current Account

	£		£
Returns to Head Office	100	Bank	1,000
Bank	1,800	Premises	5,000
		Machinery	250
		Goods from Head Office	2,800
Balance c/d	7,850	Profit and Loss Account	700
	9,750		9,750
		Balance b/d	7,850

The combined balance sheet

After the Trading and Profit and Loss Accounts have been drawn up a Balance Sheet is required for the whole firm. The branch will send its trial balance to the head office which will add the assets in its own trial balance to those in the branch trial balance to give the total for each type of asset to be shown in the Balance Sheet, and a similar procedure will be carried out for the liabilities.

In the trial balances the Head Office Current Accounts will be a debit balance while the Branch Current Accounts will be a credit balance, e.g. the two figures of £7,850 in the London and Manchester books. These therefore cancel out and are not shown in the combined Balance Sheet. This is in order, as the two balances do not in fact represent assets or liabilities, but are merely a measure of the resources at the branch.

Items in transit

It was stated earlier that the timing of transactions raised complications. Obviously a cheque sent by a Manchester branch one day would probably arrive in London the next day, while goods sent from London to Manchester, or returned from Manchester to London, could well take longer than that. Both the head office and the branch will have entered the transactions at the dates of remittance or receipt, and as the remittance from one place will occur on one day and the receipt occur at the other place on another day, then where items are in transit at the end of a financial period each set of records will not contain identical figures. This will mean that the balances on the current accounts will not be equal to one another.

It is, however, necessary to have identical amounts of balances on the current accounts so that they will cancel out when the combined Balance Sheet is prepared. As the two sets of records contain some figures which are different from each other they must somehow be reconciled so that the balances carried down are the same. Which set of figures are to be altered? The answer is one of expediency. It would be normal to find the most experienced accountants at the head office, and therefore the amendments should all be made in the head office books, instead of leaving it to junior accountants at the branches who would be more likely to make mistakes. Also if there are several branches the problems of communicating specific instructions to several accountants some distance away make it easier for all amendments to be made at the head office.

Exhibit 5.6 is for a second month of the business shown in Exhibit 5.5. However, whereas there were no items in transit at the end of the first month, this does not hold true at the conclusion of the second month.

Exhibit 5.6

Head Office Records (showing current accounts only)

	£
Goods sent to Branch	3,700
Cheques received from Branch	2,950
Returns received from Branch	440
Branch Records	
Goods received from Head Office	3,500
Cheques sent to Head Office	3,030
Returns sent to Head Office	500

It may be assumed that the net profit as shown by the Profit and Loss Account of the branch is £800.

Branch Records (in Manchester)

Head Office Current Account

	£		£
Bank	3,030	Balance b/fwd	7,850
Returns to Head Office	500	Goods from Head Office	3,500
Balance c/d	8,620	Net Profit	800
	12,150		12,150
		Balance b/d	8,620

Head Office Records (in London)

Manchester Branch Current Account

	£			£
Balance b/fwd	7,850	Bank	B	2,950
Goods sent to Branch	A 3,700	Returns received	C	440
Net Profit	800			

At this point the following items are observed to be in transit at the end of the period (these should be confirmed to ensure that they are not merely errors in accounting records):

1 Goods sent to the branch amounting to £200 (£3,700 − £3,500).

2 Cheques sent by the branch amounting to £80 (£3,030 − £2,950).

3 Returns from the branch amounting to £60 (£500 − £440).

A needs amending to £3,500. This is done by crediting the account with £200.

B needs amending to £3,030. This is done by crediting the account with £80.

C needs amending to £500. This is done by crediting the account with £60.

As these are items in transit they need to be taken to the period in which they arrive, i.e. the next month. This is effected by carrying them down as balances into the next period. The Branch Current Account will now be completed.

It may appear at first sight to be rather strange that all the items in transit are shown as debit balances. However, it must be appreciated that goods (including returns) and money in transit are assets of the firm at the end of a financial period. That they are in transit is merely stipulating that the assets are neither at the head office nor at the branch but are somewhere else. Assets are always shown as debit balances and there is no reason why it should be different just because they have not reached their destination on a certain date.

	£		£
Balance b/fwd	7,850	Bank	2,950
Goods sent to Branch	3,700	Returns Received	440
Net Profit	800	Goods in Transit c/d	200
		Cheques in Transit c/d	80
		Returns in Transit c/d	60
		Balance c/d	8,620
	12,350		12,350
Balance b/d	8,620		
Goods in Transit b/d	200		
Cheques in Transit b/d	80		
Returns in Transit b/d	60		

All of these four balances are shown in the trial balance. When the combined Balance Sheet is being prepared the balance of the two current accounts, i.e. in this case £8,620, will cancel out as it is a debit balance in one trial balance and a credit balance in the other. The goods in transit £200 and the returns in transit £60, both being goods, are added to the stock in the Balance Sheet. This is because stock is made up of the following items:

At the end of the second month:

	£
Stock at London	
add Stock at Manchester	
add Stocks in Transit (£200+£60)	260
Total Stock	

Similarly, the balance for cheques or remittances in transit is added to the bank balances at London and Manchester.

	£
Bank Balance at London	
add Bank Balance in Manchester	
add Remittances in Transit	80

This is rather like a man who has £14 in one pocket and £3 in another. He takes a £5 note from the pocket containing the larger amount and is transferring it to his other pocket when someone asks him to stay perfectly still and calculate the total cash in his possession. He therefore has:

	£
Pocket 1	9
Pocket 2	3
Cash in Transit	5
	17

Using the figures already given in Exhibit 5.6 but adding some further information, trial balances for London Head Office and the Manchester Branch are now shown in Exhibit 5.7 after the Profit and Loss accounts have been drawn up for the second month.

Exhibit 5.7

Trial Balances as at 29 February 19-8

	London Head Office Dr	London Head Office Cr	Manchester Branch Dr	Manchester Branch Cr
	£	£	£	£
Premises	10,000		5,000	
Machinery	2,000		400	
Fixtures	3,100		1,400	
Motor Vans	1,500		900	
Closing Stock	3,800		700	
Debtors	1,100		800	
Bank	12,200		600	
Head Office Current Account				8,620
Branch Current Account	8,620			
Goods in Transit	200			
Cheques in Transit	80			
Returns in Transit	60			
Creditors		1,300		1,180
Capital Account as at 1 Jan 19-8		37,860		
Net Profit for the two months (Branch £1,500 + Head Office £2,000)		3,500		
	42,660	42,660	9,800	9,800

The combined Balance Sheet can now be drawn up.

Balance Sheet as at 29 February 19-8

	£	£
Fixed Assets		
Premises		15,000
Machinery		2,400
Fixtures		4,500
Motor Vans		2,400
		24,300
Current Assets		
Stocks	4,760	
Debtors	1,900	
Bank	12,880	
	19,540	
less Current Liabilities		
Creditors	2,480	
Working Capital		17,060
		41,360
Capital		
Balance at 1 January 19-8		37,860
add Net Profit:		
London		2,000
Manchester		1,500
		41,360

Notes:

Stocks:		£	Bank:		£
	London	3,800	Bank: London		12,200
	Manchester	700	London		600
	In Transit		In Transit		80
	(£200 + £60)	260			
		4,760			12,880

Foreign branch accounts

The treatment of the accounts of foreign branches is subject to only one exception from that of branches in your own country. This is concerned with the fact that when the trial balance is drawn up by the branch then this will be stated in a foreign currency. To amalgamate these figures with your own country's figures will mean that the foreign branch figures will have to be translated into your currency.

There are rules for general guidance as to how this can be done. SSAP 20: Foreign Currency Translation: gives rules for organisations to follow. These are the ones which will be shown.

The amount of a particular currency which one can obtain for another currency is known as the exchange rate. Taking an imaginary country with a currency called chips, there might be a general agreement that the exchange rate should stay about 5 chips to equal £1. At certain times the exchange rate will exactly equal that figure, but due to all sorts of economic reasons it may well be 5.02 chips to £1 on one day and 4.97 chips to £1 several days later. In addition, some years ago there may have been an act of devaluation by one of the countries involved; the exchange rate could well have then been 3 chips to £1. To understand more about exchange rates and devaluation the reader of this book would be well advised to read a relevant economics textbook.

It is clear, however, that all items in the trial balance should not be converted to your currency on the basis of the exchange rate ruling at the date of the trial balance. The rules in SSAP 20 have been devised in an attempt to bring about conversion into your currency so as not to distort reported trading results.

Now for the rules:

1 (*a*) Fixed assets at the exchange rate ruling when the assets were bought. This method is known as the **temporal method**. If fixed assets have been bought on different dates, then different rates will have to be used for each separate purchase.

(*b*) Depreciation on the fixed assets at the same rate as the fixed assets concerned.

2 Current assets and current liabilities – at the rate ruling at the date of the trial balance. This is known as the **closing method**.

3 Opening stock in the Trading Account – at the rate ruling at the previous Balance Sheet date.

4 Goods sent by the head office to the branch, or returns from the branch – at the actual figures shown in the Goods sent to Branches Account in the head office books.

5 Trading and Profit and Loss Account items, other than depreciation, opening and closing stocks, or goods sent to or returned by the branch – at the average rate for the period covered by the accounts.

6 The Head Office Current Account – at the same figures as shown in the Branch Current Account in the head office books.

When the conversion of the figures into your currency is completed, the totals of the debit and credit sides of your currency trial balance will not normally be equal to one another. This is due to different exchange rates being taken for conversion purposes. A balancing figure will therefore be needed to bring about the equality of the totals. For this purpose a Difference on Exchange Account will be opened and a debit entry made therein if the lesser total is on the debit side of the credit side. When the head office redrafts the Profit and Loss Account any debit balance on the Difference on Exchange Account should be transferred to it as an expense. A credit balance on the Difference on Exchange Account should be transferred to the credit of the Profit and Loss Account as a gain.

In consolidated accounts, special rules are applied for foreign exchange conversion.

Exhibit 5.8

An example of the conversion of a trial balance into UK currency is now shown. The branch is in Flavia, and the unit of currency is the Flavian dollar. The exchange rates needed are:

(a) On 1 January 19-3, 10 dollars = £1
(b) On 1 January 19-5, 11 dollars = £1
(c) On 1 January 19-8, 17 dollars = £1
(d) On 31 December 19-8, 15 dollars = £1
(e) If no further information were given the average rate for 19-8 would have to be taken as (c) + (d) ÷ 2, i.e. 16 dollars = £1. This is not an advisable procedure in practice, the fact that the average has been calculated from only two readings could mean that the average calculated might be far different from a more accurate one calculated from a larger number of readings.

Trial Balance as on 31 December 19-8

	Dr (dol)	Cr (dol)	Exchange rates	Dr £	Cr £
Fixed Assets:					
Bought 1 Jan 19-3	10,000		10=£1	1,000	
Bought 1 Jan 19-5	8,800		11=£1	800	
Stock 1 Jan 19-8	6,800		17=£1	400	
Expense Accounts	8,000		16=£1	500	
Sales		32,000	16=£1		2,000
Goods from Head Office	21,900		£ per account in Head Office books	1,490	
Head Office Current Account		43,000	£ per account in Head Office books		3,380
Debtors	9,000		15=£1	600	
Creditors		4,500	15=£1		300
Bank	15,000		15=£1	1,000	
	79,500	79,500		5,790	5,680
Difference on Exchange Account					110
				5,790	5,790

The stock at 31 December 19-8 is 12,000 dollars. When the Trading Account is drawn up this will be converted at 15 dollars = £1, i.e. £800.

Review questions

5.1 Octopus Ltd, whose head office is at Cardiff, operates a branch at Swansea. All goods are purchased by head office and invoiced to and sold by the branch at cost plus 33⅓ per cent.

Other than a sales ledger kept at Swansea, all transactions are recorded in the books at Cardiff.

The following particulars are given of the transactions at the branch during the year ended 28 February 19-7.

	£
Stock on Hand, 1 March 19-6, at invoice price	4,400
Debtors on 1 March 19-6	3,946
Stock on Hand, 28 February 19-7, at invoice price	3,948
Goods sent from Cardiff during the year at invoice price	24,800
Credit Sales	21,000
Cash Sales	2,400
Returns to Head Office at invoice price	1,000
Invoice value of goods stolen	600
Bad Debts written off	148
Cash from Debtors	22,400
Normal loss at invoice price due to wastage	100
Cash Discount allowed to Debtors	428

You are required to write up the Branch Stock Account and Branch Total Debtors Account for the year ended 28 February 19-7, as they would appear in the head office books.

(Institute of Chartered Accountants)

5.2 RST Limited is a family-controlled company which operates a chain of retail outlets specialising in motor spares and accessories.

Branch stocks are purchased by a centralised purchasing function in order to obtain the best terms from suppliers.

A 10% handling charge is applied by head office to the cost of the purchases, and branches are expected to add 25% to the resulting figure to arrive at normal selling prices, although branch managers are authorised to reduce normal prices in special situations. The effect of such reductions must be notified to head office.

On 1 April 19-6, a new branch was established at Derham. The following details have been recorded for the year ended 31 March 19-7:

	£
Purchase cost to head office of stock transferred to Derham	82,400
Derham branch sales: cash	89,940
credit	1,870
Stocks transferred from Derham to other branches, at normal selling prices	3,300
Authorised reductions from normal selling prices during the year	2,250

All records in respect of branch activities are maintained at head office, and the branch profit margin is dealt with through a branch stock adjustment account.

Required:
  (a) Prepare
     (i)   the branch stock account (maintained at branch selling prices)
    (ii) the branch stock adjustment account
The *book stock* should be taken for this part of the question.

(b) List four of the possible reasons for the stock difference revealed when a physical stocktaking at the Derham branch on 31 March 19-7 showed stock valued at selling prices amounting to £14,850.

(c) State which of the following is the figure to be included in RST Limited's balance sheet at 31 March 19-7, for Derham branch stock:

- (i) £11,138
- (ii) £11,880
- (iii) £10,800
- (iv) None of these.

Justify your choice with appropriate calculations.
(Chartered Institute of Management Accountants)

5.3A Paper Products has a head office in London and a branch in Bristol. The following information has been extracted from the head office books of account as at 31 March 19-6:

Information relating to the branch

Balances	*Opening* £'000	*Closing* £'000
Branch bank account (positive balance)	3	12
Branch debtors	66	81
Branch stock (at transfer price)	75	90

Transactions during the year	£'000
Bad debts written off	15
Branch general expenses	
(paid from bank branch account)	42
Cash received from credit customers and banked	390
Cash sales banked	120
Cash transferred from branch to head office bank account	459
Credit sales	437
Discounts allowed to credit customers	9
Goods returned by credit customers	8
Goods returned from branch	
(at transfer price from head office)	30
Goods sent to branch	
(at transfer price from head office)	600

Information relating to head office

Balances	*Opening* £'000	*Closing* £'000
Stock	180	220

Transactions during the year	£'000
Bad debts written off	24
Cash sales	1,500
Credit sales	2,000
Discounts allowed to credit customers	29
General expenses	410
Goods returned by credit customers	40
Purchases	2,780

Additional information:

1 Most of the accounting records relating to the branch are kept by the head office in its own books of account.

2 All purchases are made by the head office, and goods are invoiced to the branch at selling price, that is, at cost price plus 50%.

Required

(*a*) Write up the following ledger accounts for the year to 31 March 19-6, being careful to bring down any balances as at that date:

- (*i*)   Branch stock account;
- (*ii*) goods sent to branch account;
- (*iii*) branch stock adjustment account;
- (*iv*) branch debtors account; and
- (*v*)   branch bank account;

(*b*) Compile Paper Products trading, and profit and loss account for the year to 31 March 19-6.

(*c*) Examine briefly the merits and demerits of Paper Products' method of branch book-keeping including comments on the significance of the 'balancing figure' in the Branch stock account.

(Association of Accounting Technicians)

5.4 Stone and Millington are in partnership as retailers of books. Stone manages the head office where new books are sold and Millington manages a branch that sells second-hand books. All books are purchased by the head office and second-hand books are invoiced to the branch at cost plus 25%. The partnership agreement allows for interest on capital accounts at 10% per annum and each partner receives a commission of 15% of the net profits of his shop. The remaining profits or losses are shared equally.

The trial balances as at 31 December 19-1 were as follows.

	Head Office		Branch	
	£	£	£	£
Capital accounts		11,000		11,000
Drawings	8,000		8,000	
Fixtures – net book value	10,000		12,000	
Stock at cost 31 December 19-0	4,000			
Stock at invoiced value 31 December 19-0			6,000	
Sales		60,000		40,000
Purchases	50,000			
Goods sent to branch at invoiced value		20,000	18,000	
Branch and head office current account	3,000			1,000
Salaries	3,500		2,500	
Rent	7,500		4,500	
Administration	6,000		–	
Provision for unrealised profit		1,200		
Creditors		800		1,000
Bank	1,000		2,000	
	93,000	93,000	53,000	53,000

The following additional information is available.

(*a*) Stock at 31 December 19-1 (excluding goods in transit) amounted to: head office (cost) £5,000 and branch (invoiced value) £7,000.

(b) The fixtures and fittings for both the head office and the branch are to be depreciated at 20% per annum on the reducing balance method.

(c) On 31 December 19-1 the head office sent to the branch books at invoiced value of £2,000 which were not recorded in the books of the branch until 3 January 19-2.

Any adjustments necessary are to be made in the head office books.

Prepare trading, profit and loss accounts, in columnar format, for the head office, branch and combined head office and branch for the year ended 31 December 19-1 and the appropriation account for that year. Prepare the balance sheet as at 31 December 19-1.

(Joint Matriculation Board)

5.5 Packer and Stringer were in partnership as retail traders sharing profits and losses: Packer three-quarters, Stringer one-quarter. The partners were credited annually with interest at the rate of 6 per cent per annum on their fixed capitals, no interest was charged on their drawings.

Stringer was responsible for the buying department of the business. Packer managed the head office and Paper was employed as the branch manager. Packer and Paper were each entitled to a commission of 10 per cent of the net profits (after charging such commission) of the shop managed by him.

All goods were purchased by head office and goods sent to the branch were invoiced at cost.

The following was the trial balance as on 31 December 19-4.

	Head office books		Branch books	
	Dr	Cr	Dr	Cr
	£	£	£	£
Drawings Accounts and Fixed Capital Accounts:				
Packer	2,500	14,000		
Stringer	1,200	4,000		
Furniture and Fittings, at cost	1,500		1,100	
Furniture and Fittings, provision for depreciation as on 31 December 19-3		500		350
Stock on 31 December 19-3	13,000		4,400	
Purchases	37,000			
Goods sent to Branches		18,000	17,200	
Sales		39,000		26,000
Provision for doubtful debts		600		200
Branch and Head Office Current Accounts	6,800			3,600
Salaries and Wages	4,500		3,200	
Paper, on account of commission			240	
Carriage and Travelling Expenses	2,200		960	
Administrative Expenses	2,400			
Trade and General Expenses	3,200		1,800	
Sundry Debtors	7,000		3,000	
Sundry Creditors		5,800		400
Bank Balances	600			1,350
	81,900	81,900	31,900	31,900

You are given the following additional information:

(a) Stocks on 31 December 19-4, amounted to: head office £14,440, branch £6,570.

(b) Administrative expenses are to be apportioned between head office and the branch in proportion to sales.

(c) Depreciation is to be provided on furniture and fittings at 10 per cent of cost.

(d) The provision for doubtful debts is to be increased by £50 in respect of head office debtors and decreased by £20 in the case of those of the branch.

(e) On 31 December 19-4 cash amounting to £2,400, in transit from the branch to head office, has been recorded in the branch books but not in those of head office, and on that date goods invoiced at £800, in transit from head office to the branch, had been recorded in the head office books but not in the branch books.

Any adjustments necessary are to be made in the head office books.

You are required to:

(a) prepare Trading and Profit and Loss Accounts and the Appropriation Account for the year ended 31 December 19-4, showing the net profit of the head office and branch respectively.

(b) prepare the Balance Sheet as on that date, and

(c) show the closing entries in the Branch Current Accounts giving the make-up of the closing balance.

Income tax is to be ignored.

(Institute of Chartered Accountants)

5.6 L R, a trader, commenced business on 1 January 19-9, with a head office and one branch.

All goods were purchased by the head office and goods sent to the branch were invoiced at a fixed selling price of 25 per cent above cost. All sales, both by the head office and the branch, were made at the fixed selling price.

The following trial balance was extracted from the books at the head office at 31 December 19-9.

Trial Balance

	£	£
Capital		52,000
Drawings	1,740	
Purchases	123,380	
Sales		83,550
Goods sent to branch (at selling price)		56,250
Branch current account	24,550	
Fixed assets	33,000	
Debtors and creditors	7,980	11,060
General expenses	8,470	
Balance at bank	3,740	
	202,860	202,860

No entries had been made in the head office books for cash in transit from the branch to head office at 31 December 19-9, £1,000.

When the balances shown below were extracted from the branch books at 31 December 19-9, no entries had been made in the books of the branch for goods in transit on that date from head office to branch, £920 (selling price).

In addition to the balances which can be deduced from the information given above, the following balances appeared in the branch books on 31 December 19-9.

	£
Fixed assets	6,000
General expenses	6,070
Debtors	7,040
Creditors (excluding head office)	1,630
Sales	51,700
Balance at Bank	1,520

When stock was taken on 31 December 19-9, it was found that there was no shortage at the head office, but at the branch there were shortages amounting to £300, at selling price.

You are required to prepare trading and profit and loss accounts (i) for head office and (ii) for the branch, as they would have appeared if goods sent to the branch had been invoiced at cost, and a balance sheet of the whole business as on 31 December 19-9.

Head Office and branch stocks are to be valued at cost.

Ignore depreciation of fixed assets.

(Institute of Chartered Secretaries and Administrators)

5.7 E G Company Limited, a manufacturing business, exports some of its products through an overseas branch whose currency is 'florins', which carries out the final assembly operations before selling the goods.

The trial balances of the head office and branch at 30 June 19-8 were:

	Head Office		Branch	
	£	£	'Fl.'	'Fl.'
Freehold buildings at cost	14,000		63,000	
Debtors/creditors	8,900	9,500	36,000	1,560
Sales		104,000		432,000
Authorised and issued capital		40,000		
Components sent to branch		35,000		
Head office/branch accounts	60,100			504,260
Branch cost of sales			360,000	
Depreciation provision, machinery		1,500		56,700
Head office cost of sales (including goods to branch)	59,000			
Administration costs	15,200		18,000	
Stock at 30 June 19-8	28,900		11,520	
Profit and loss account		2,000		
Machinery at cost	6,000		126,000	
Remittances		28,000	272,000	
Balance at bank	4,600		79,200	
Selling and distribution costs	23,300		28,800	
	220,000	220,000	994,520	994,520

The following adjustments are to be made:

1 The cost of sales figures include a depreciation charge of 10 per cent per annum on cost for machinery.

2 A provision of £300 for unrealised profit in branch stock is to be made.

3 On 26 June 19-8 the branch remitted 16,000 'Fl.'; these were received by the head office on 4 July and realised £1,990.

4 During May a branch customer in error paid the head office for goods supplied. The amount due was 320 'Fl.' which realised £36. It has been correctly dealt with by head office but not yet entered in the branch books.

5 A provision has to be made for a commission of 5 per cent of the net profit of the branch after charging such commission, which is due to the branch manager.

The rates of exchange were:

At 1 July 19-7	10 'Fl.'=£1
At 30 June 19-8	8 'Fl.'=£1
Average for the year	9 'Fl.'=£1
On purchase of buildings and machinery	7 'Fl.'=£1

You are required to prepare, for internal use:
  (*a*) detailed operating accounts for the year ended 30 June 19-8;
  (*b*) combined head office and branch balance sheet as at 30 June 19-8;
  (*c*) the branch account in the head office books, in both sterling and currency, the opening balance on 1 July 19-7 being £25,136 (189,260 'Fl').
  Taxation is to be ignored.
(Chartered Institute of Management Accountants)

5.8 OTL Ltd commenced business on 1 January 19-0. The head office is in London and there is a branch in Highland. The currency unit of Highland is the crown.
  The following are the trial balances of the head office and the Highland branch as at 31 December 19-0:

	Head office		Highland branch	
	£	£	crowns	crowns
Branch account	65,280			
Balances at bank	10,560		66,000	
Creditors		21,120		92,400
Debtors	18,480		158,400	
Fixed assets (purchased 1 January 19-0)	39,600		145,200	
Head office account				316,800
Profit and loss account (net profit for the year)		52,800		79,200
Issued share capital		86,400		
Stocks	26,400		118,800	
	160,320	160,320	488,400	488,400

The trial balance of the head office was prepared before any entries had been made in respect of any profits or losses of the branch.

Remittance from head office to branch and from branch to head office were recorded in the books at the actual amounts paid and received.

The rates of exchange were:

On 1 January 19-0	5 crowns=£1
Average rate for year 19-0	4.4 crowns=£1
On 31 December 19-0	4 crowns=£1

Required:

(*a*) The trial balance of the Highland branch as at 31 December 19-0, in sterling.

(*b*) The closing entries, as at 31 December 19-0, in the branch account in the books of the head office.

(*c*) A summary of the balance sheet of OTL Ltd as at 31 December 19- 0.

Ignore depreciation of fixed assets.

Ignore taxation.

(Institute of Chartered Secretaries and Administrators)

5.9A Home Ltd is incorporated in the UK and rents mobile homes to holidaymakers in this country and in Carea. The company has a head office in London and a branch in Carea where the local currency is 'mics'. The following balances are extracted from the books of the head office and its 'self-accounting' branch at 31 December 19-4.

	Head office £	Branch Mics
Debit balances		
Fixed assets at cost	450,000	900,000
Debtors and cash	17,600	36,000
Operating costs	103,700	225,000
Branch current account	42,600	–
	613,900	1,161,000
Credit balances		
Share capital	200,000	–
Retained profit, 1 January 19-4	110,800	–
Sales revenue	186,300	480,000
Creditors	9,700	25,000
Head office current account	–	420,000
Accumulated depreciation	107,100	236,000
	613,900	1,161,000

The following information is provided regarding exchange rates, some of which is relevant.

The fixed assets of the branch were acquired when there were 8 mics to the £. Exchange rates ruling during 19-4 were:

	Mics to the £
1 January	6
Average	5
31 December	4

There are no cash or goods in transit between head office and branch at the year end.

Required:

The final accounts of Home Ltd for 19-4. The accounts should be expressed in £'s sterling and, for this purpose, the conversion of mics should be made in accordance with the temporal method of translation as specified in SSAP 20 entitled 'Foreign Currency Translation'.

(Institute of Chartered Secretaries and Administrators)

6
Container accounts

A container is anything in which goods are contained. This may consist of a packet containing cigarettes, a large wooden crate containing tractor parts, or a liquid gas cylinder. Some will be returnable by the purchaser after use, an obvious example being the gas cylinder, while others such as the cigarette packet will be disposed of at will by the customer. The returnable containers will often be subject to a deposit being charged to the customer, a refund being allowed when the container is returned in good condition to the supplier.

In suppliers' books it is therefore convenient to divide containers into those which are (1) not chargeable to the customers, and (2) where a deposit charge is made to the customer.

Containers not charged to customers

Many containers will be treated as manufacturing expenses, e.g. cigarette packets, flour bags or tin cans containing foods. Theoretically they are a distribution expense if the contents and the containers are regarded as being two distinct items, and as such would be chargeable to the Profit and Loss Account, but really the containers for such items are an integral part of the goods sold and are therefore chargeable to the Manufacturing Account. On the other hand, returnable cylinders in which goods are delivered would be chargeable to the Profit and Loss Account.

There will normally be a stock of containers in hand at the end of each accounting period. Exhibit 6.1 shows an account for cartons in which salt is packed for sale.

Exhibit 6.1

	£
Stock of containers 1 January 19-6	100
Containers bought in the year ended 31 December 19-6	2,800
Stock of containers 31 December 19-6	300

Containers

19-6	£	19-6	£
Jan 1 Stock b/d	100	Dec 31 Manufacturing account	2,600
Dec 31 Cash (during the year)	2,800	,, 31 Stock c/d	300
	2,900		2,900
19-7			
Jan 1 Stock b/d	300		

For returnable containers on which deposits are not charged the question of whether or not accurate statistical records would be kept would depend on the nature and value of containers.

Containers on which deposits are charged to customers

There are containers which many purchasers would not return if they were not charged with a deposit refunded only on return. These are obviously containers which require more than a marginal effort to return, or those which could be put to alternative uses. The deposit chargeable must therefore be sufficient to discourage the purchaser from keeping the containers after use, but should not be so great as to deter him from buying the goods in the first place. In some instances a time limit is fixed within which the container is to be returned to obtain a cancellation of the deposit charged. Common sense must however prevail, as it would be unwise to refuse refunds of deposits in circumstances which could bring about a worsening in the firm's relationship with customers it wished to retain.

Accounting must therefore fulfil two needs, (a) it must enable some form of check on the stock of containers, and (b) it must reveal the amount of deposit returnable to customers. This can be satisfied, for (a) a Containers Stock Account can be kept, and for (b) a Containers Suspense Account may be opened.

Volume 1 has already illustrated the need for the depreciation of containers to be provided normally by the Revaluation method. The Container Stock Account will therefore provide for the depreciation element by the process of revaluing the containers at the end of each accounting period. Each container account may also include, in addition to the £ columns, further columns for quantities and for the monetary rates at which the transactions are carried out.

Exhibit 6.2

A new firm, IVY and Co, sells its goods in crates on which a deposit is chargeable to the customer, a credit being allowed on their return within three months.

During the year ended 31 December 19-5:

A 50 crates were bought for £3 each.

B 180 crates were sent to customers, these being charged to their accounts at £4 deposit each. You may well wonder how 180 crates can be sent out when only 50 have been bought by IVY and Co. The fact is that the figure of 180 consists of recounting the same crates, as they are sent out and returned several times each year. However, during the year 180 debits of £4 each have been made in customers' accounts.

C 150 crates were returned by customers, credits being entered in their accounts for £4 each.

D 10 crates were kept by customers beyond the three months' limit, and they therefore forfeited their right to return them to obtain a refund of the deposit.

E 2 crates were damaged and were sold for £1 each.

On 31 December 19-5 the following facts are relevant:

F There were 20 returnable crates with customers.

G There were 18 crates at IVY's warehouse.

The stock of crates at 31 December 19-5 are to be valued at £2 each to provide for depreciation through usage.

The identifying letters A to G are shown against the recorded transactions in the accounts that now follow.

Containers Stock

	Rate	No.	£			Rate	No.	£
			£					£
19-5					**19-5**			
Dec 31 Cash (during the year) A	3	50	150		Dec 31 Containers Suspense: kept by customers D	4	10	40
					,, 31 Cash: damaged crates E	1	2	2
					,, 31 Profit and Loss: Cost of container usage			32
					,, 31 Stock: c/d In Warehouse G	2	18	36
					At Customers F	2	20	40
		50	150				50	150
19-6								
Jan 1 Stock b/d								
In Warehouse G	2	18	36					
At Customers F	2	20	40					

Containers Suspense

	Rate	No.	£			Rate	No.	£
			£					£
19-5					**19-5**			
Dec 31 Sales Ledger: crates credited to customers' accounts on return C	4	150	600		Dec 31 Sales Ledger: crates charged to customers' accounts B	4	180	720
,, 31 Containers Stock: kept by customers D	4	10	40					
,, 31 Deposits on crates returnable c/d F	4	20	80					
		180	720				180	720
					19-6			
					Jan 1 Deposits on crates returnable b/d F	4	20	80

The Balance Sheet will show the balances in the following manner:

IVY & Co
Balance Sheet as at 31 December 19-5

	£
Current Assets	
Crates – at valuation	76
Current Liabilities	
Containers Suspense – deposits returnable	80

Sometimes containers are charged out to customers at an initial price greater than that allowed on their return. The difference therefore represents a hiring charge. If the same data is taken as in Exhibit 6.2 but instead of £4 being allowed on return this had been restricted to £3 instead, then the accounts would have appeared as follows:

Containers Stock

Date	Particulars	Rate	No. £	£	Date	Particulars	Rate	No. £	£
19-5					19-5				
Dec 31	Cash (during the year)	3	50	150	Dec 31	Containers Suspense: kept by customers	3	10	30
Dec 31	Profit and Loss: Profit on container usage			138	,, 31	Cash: damaged crates	1	2	2
					,, 31	Containers Suspense: Hiring charge			180
					,, 31	Stock: c/d In Warehouse	2	18	36
						At Customers F	2	20	40
			50	288				50	288
19-6									
Jan 1	Stock b/d								
	In Warehouse	2	18	36					
	At Customers	2	20	40					

Containers Suspense

Date	Particulars	Rate	No. £	£	Date	Particulars	Rate	No. £	£
19-5					19-5				
Dec 31	Sales Ledger: crates credited to customers' accounts on return		150	450	Dec 31	Sales Ledger: crates charged to customers' accounts	4	180	720
,, 31	Containers Stock: kept by customers	3	10	30					
,, 31	Containers Stock Hiring charge			180					
,, 31	Deposits on crates returnable	3	20	60					
			180	720				180	720
					19-6				
					Jan 1	Deposits on crates returnable b/d	3	20	60

The Balance Sheet would have appeared in the following manner:

IVY & Co
Balance Sheet as at 31 December 19-5

	£
Current Assets	
Crates – at valuation	76
Current Liabilities	
Containers Suspense – deposits returnable	60

Review questions

6.1 S Limited delivers its product to customers in returnable containers. These are invoiced to the customer at £20 each and, if returned in good condition within six months, are credited in full. The containers are purchased for £10 each.

At 30 June 19-6, there were 2,000 containers held in S Limited's warehouse and provision was made in the 19-6 accounts for an estimated liability in respect of 5,500 containers in customers' hands. During 19-7, 1,250 new containers were purchased and 120 were scrapped.

8,750 containers were charged to customers and 9,050 containers were returned within the six-month period.

At 30 June 19-7, the physical stocktaking showed 3,390 containers in the warehouse and information derived from customers indicated that there was a potential liability in respect of 4,950 containers. The stocks of containers are valued at cost price.

Required:
Prepare the containers stock account and the containers suspense account necessary to record these transactions in the books of S Limited:
(Chartered Institute of Management Accountants)

6.2 Lagg Ltd sells its goods in cases. These cases are purchased by the company at £6 per case, but each case is written down to a standard book value (SBV) of £5 per case immediately it is purchased. For stocktaking purposes, all cases are valued at £5 per case irrespective of whether they are still in stock or in the hands of the customers. Cases are charged out to customers at £10 per case, but the customer is credited with £8 per case if the case is returned in good condition within three months of receipt.

The following information relates to the year to 31 March 19-7:

		Cases
1	Stock of cases at 1 April 19-6:	
	In stock	1,000
	In hands of customers 1 January 19-6	3,000

2 During the year, 2,000 cases were purchased.

3 25,000 cases were issued to customers.

4 23,000 cases were returned by customers within the time limit.

5 1,500 cases were not returned within the time limit and were duly paid for by the customers. Cases still in the hands of customers at 31 March 19-7 had all been invoiced since 1 January 19-7.

6 100 cases kept in stock by Lagg had been damaged and were beyond repair.

7 £1,400 had been spent on repairing some slightly damaged cases.

8 50 other damaged cases had been sold for £2 per case.

In order to keep an accurate record of its transactions in cases, Lagg maintains (*inter alia*) the following accounts:
(*a*) a cases stock account in which cases are recorded at their standard book value;
(*b*) a cases suspense account in which cases in the hands of customers are recorded at their return price;
(*c*) a cases sent to customers account in which cases sent to customers are recorded at their issue price;
and
(*d*) a cases profit and loss account.

Required:

Write up the following accounts in the books of Lagg Ltd for the year to 31 March 19-7;
  (*a*) cases stock account;
  (*b*) cases suspense account;
  (*c*) cases sent to customers account;
    and
  (*d*) cases profit and loss account.
(Association of Accounting Technicians)

6.3A KRR Ltd sells goods in containers which are charged to customers at £2.00 each. Customers are credited with £1.25 for each container returned within four months.

On 31 December 19-7, there were 1,580 containers on the company's premises and 5,520 containers, the time limit for the return of which has not expired, were held by customers.

During 19-8:

(i)   KRR Ltd purchased 8,700 containers for £1 each.

(ii) 26,460 containers were charged to customers.

(iii) 23,720 containers were returned by customers and credited to them.

On 31 December 19-8, customers held 6,000 containers, the time limit for the return of which had not expired.

For purposes of the annual accounts of KRR Ltd, all stocks of containers on the company's premises and returnable containers in the possession of customers are valued, at £1 each.

You are required to show the container stock account and the container trading account for the year 19-8. These accounts should be provided with additional memorandum columns in which quantities are to be shown.
(Institute of Chartered Secretaries and Administrators)

6.4A The G Company supplies gas in expensive containers which are returnable after use. These containers cost £20 each and are charged out to customers on sale or return within six months at £26 each. Provided they are returned within the six months period they are credited at £23 each. As each container is returned it is inspected and overhauled at a cost of £2.

At the end of the year the company values all returnable containers in customers' hands and containers held in stock at £16 each.

You are advised that:

	At the beginning of the year	At the end of the year
Containers held by the company	2,760	3,144
Returnable containers held by customers	4,790	2,910

During the year 3,100 new containers were purchased, 20,620 were invoiced to customers and 17,960 were returned. On inspection 260 required additional repairs costing £325 and 56 had to be sold as scrap for £60.

From the information given above prepare:
  (*a*) returnable containers suspense account;
  (*b*) an account showing the profit or loss on dealings in containers.
(Chartered Institute of Management Accountants)

7
Royalty accounts

In some classes of business the owner of some form of privilege or monopoly can allow other firms to utilise this right, the owner being remunerated by reference to the extent which it has been used. The name given to payments for certain of these rights is 'royalty'. Instances of payments of royalties are as follows:

(a) For the extraction of minerals from the ground.

(b) The publisher of a book remunerating the author.

(c) For the use of a patent.

Where the remuneration is simply a case of a fixed amount per unit of use the accounting necessary is quite straightforward. The payer of the royalty will simply charge it as an expense in a Royalty Account.

Complications start to appear when a certain minimum amount is payable per annum even though the actual use of the right may result in a lesser figure for royalties. Such agreements are commonly found in the case of mining and quarrying. These agreements are understandable because of the desire of the owner to be certain of a minimum income. Without a minimum amount the lack of activity on the part of the user would result in a small income for the owner. Carried to extremes no activity would result in no income. On the other hand, the user would probably feel aggrieved if he not only had to pay the minimum amount in a period of low activity but also have to pay the full amount in a period of high activity. The part of the minimum amount not represented by use of the right, in the case of a mine, is known as 'short workings'. It is very often found that royalty agreements provide for such short workings to be carried forward to reduce royalties payable in future years where the activity results in the royalties being in excess of the minimum agreed amount. A limit is usually set upon the number of years for which such short workings can be carried forward for this purpose. Once the final date has been reached, such short workings are then irrecoupable. Exhibit 7.1 illustrates such a case.

Exhibit 7.1

The lessee of a mine is to pay £1 for each ton of ore extracted. The minimum rent is to be £400 per annum. Any payments for short workings are recoupable only in the two years following that in which they occurred. The following table shows the effect of extraction figures contained in column (a). As the minimum rent is £400, then obviously column (b) must never show a figure of less than £400.

Year	(a) Tons extracted	(b) Payable	(c) Short workings carried forward	(d) Short workings recouped	(e) Short workings now irrecoupable
		£	£	£	£
1	420	420			
2	310	400	90		
3	560	470		90	
4	280	400	120		
5	440	400	80	40	
6	450	400		50	30
7	780	780			

Notes:

Column (c) shows the value of the short working at the end of each year which can still be set off against future royalties. £120 is carried forward at the end of year 4, of this £40 is set off against the royalties for year 5, leaving £80 to be carried forward at the end of year 5.

Column (e). The £120 short workings originating in year 4 are partly recouped by £40 in year 5 and £50 in year 6. The remaining £30 can no longer be recouped as the time limit of two years following the year of origin comes into play. The £30 cannot therefore be carried forward to year 7, so that it is in year 6 that it is shown as being irrecoupable.

The short workings carried forward can in fact be likened to the prepayment of an expense. The minimum amount exceeds the actual royalties, therefore the excess is in effect a prepayment of royalties.

All of the accounting calculations have now been made, the only action necessary is that the table is to be translated into double entry terms. This now follows. It is assumed that the financial year is the same as the calendar year and that the landlord is paid on the last day of each year.

Royalties

	£		£
Year 1		Year 1	
Dec 31 Landlord	420	Dec 31 Operating Account (A)	420
Year 2		Year 2	
Dec 31 Landlord	310	Dec 31 Operating	310

Royalties

	£		£
Year 3		Year 3	
Dec 31 Landlord	560	Dec 31 Operating	560
Year 4		Year 4	
Dec 31 Landlord	280	Dec 31 Operating	280
Year 5		Year 5	
Dec 31 Landlord	440	Dec 31 Operating	440
Year 6		Year 6	
Dec 31 Landlord	450	Dec 31 Operating	450
Year 7		Year 7	
Dec 31 Landlord	780	Dec 31 Operating	780

Short Workings

	£		£
Year 2		Year 3	
Dec 31 Landlord	90	Dec 31 Landlord (recouped amount)	90
Year 4		Year 5	
Dec 31 Landlord	120	Dec 31 Landlord (recouped amount)	40
		Year 5	
		Dec 31 Balance c/d	80
	120		120
Year 6		Year 6	
Jan 1 Balance b/d	80	Dec 31 Landlord (recouped amount)	50
		,, 31 Profit and Loss – amount now irrecoupable	30
	80		80

Landlord

	£		£
Year 1		Year 1	
Dec 31 Cash	420	Dec 31 Royalties	420

Landlord

	£		£
Year 2		**Year 2**	
Dec 31 Cash	400	Dec 31 Royalties	310
		,, 31 Short Workings	90
	400		400
Year 3		**Year 3**	
Dec 31 Short Workings –	90	Dec 31 Royalties	
recouped			560
,, 31 Cash	470		
	560		560
Year 4		**Year 4**	
Dec 31 Cash	400	Dec 31 Royalties	280
		,, 31 Short Workings	120
	400		400
Year 5		**Year 5**	
Dec 31 Short Workings –	40	Dec 31 Royalties	440
recouped			
,, 31 Cash	400		
	440		440
Year 6		**Year 6**	
Dec 31 Short Workings –	50	Dec 31 Royalties	
recouped			450
,, 31 Cash	400		
	450		450
Year 7		**Year 7**	
Dec 31 Cash	780	Dec 31 Royalties	780

Operating Account for the year(s) ended 31 December . . . (extracts)

	£
Year 1 Royalties	420
Year 2 ,,	310
Year 3 ,,	560
Year 4 ,,	280
Year 5 ,,	440
Year 6 ,,	450
Year 7 ,,	780

Profit and Loss Account for the year(s) ended 31 December . . . (extracts)

£

Year 6 Irrecoupable Short Workings
    Written off (B)   30

Balance Sheet(s) as at 31 December (extracts)
Current Assets

	£
Year 2 Short Workings Recoupable	90
Year 4 Short Workings Recoupable	120
Year 5 Short Workings Recoupable	80

Notes:

(A) The term Operating Account is used. This could instead be called a Working Account or a similar name could be used; in the case of a manufacturer it would be Manufacturing Account. Where royalties are paid per unit of use they can be seen to be an example of what in costing would be called a direct expense.

(B) The irrecoupable short workings can hardly be charged to an Operating Account, as they are an expense connected with non-operation.

It must not be thought that the method described is the only one by which the double entry can be carried out. Obviously the various methods finish up with the same answers eventually, it is merely the ways by which these answers are worked out that are different.

Sub-leases

Quite often a concern obtains a lease of a mine, quarry, land etc., and is given the right to sub-let part of the asset to someone else, i.e. a sub-lessee. Just as it may have to pay a minimum rent to the owner of the asset, with a right to a carry forward of short workings, then so may the lessee make similar sorts of agreements with the sub-lessees.

The entries in the lessee's books are the reverse of those used for royalties payable. Usually separate accounts for royalties payable and royalties receivable are opened. If the royalties payable and receivable are at the same rate, the royalties receivable will be transferred to the royalties payable account at each year end, so that the *net* royalties will be charged as a expense in the Operating Account. If the royalties charged to the sub-lessee are at a higher rate, the excess must be transferred to the credit of the Profit and Loss Account.

To help avoid confusion, the short workings of the sub-lessee are entered in a 'Short Workings Allowable' account', while the short workings to be recovered from the landlord are entered in a 'Short Workings Recoverable' account.

Revision questions

7.1 Smoker, who had patented a tobacco filter, granted to Piper & Co a licence for seven years to manufacture and sell the filter on the following terms:

(i) Piper & Co to pay a royalty of £1 for every 100 filters sold with a minimum payment of £1,000 per annum. Calculations to be made annually as on 31 December, and payment on 31 January.

(ii) If, for any year, the royalties calculated on filters sold amount to less than £1,000, Piper & Co may set off the deficiency against royalties payable in excess of that sum in the next two years.

The number of filters sold were:

Year to 31 December

19-1	60,000
19-2	80,000
19-3	120,000
19-4	140,000

You are required to show the ledger accounts recording the above transactions in respect of royalties in the books of Piper & Co, which are closed annually on 31 December.

(Institute of Chartered Accountants)

7.2A Some years Dunbar Ltd had been granted a licence to extract a mineral deposit from some land owned by Berwick plc. The terms of the licence were as follows:

1 Dunbar Ltd was to pay Berwick plc a royalty of £2 for each ton of mineral deposit extracted, subject to a minimum payment of £10,000 per annum.

2 If in any year, the total amount of mineral extracted was less than 5,000 tons, Dunbar was to be allowed to recoup any deficiency against royalties payable in excess of that amount during the following two years.

3 Both Dunbar's and Berwick's financial year end is 31 December, and Dunbar agreed to settle the amount due to Berwick on the next 31 January following the financial year end.

During the first five years of the agreement, the following tons of mineral deposit were extracted by Dunbar.

Year to 31 December	*Quantity in tons*
19-1	6,000
19-2	4,000
19-3	3,000
19-4	5,500
19-5	8,000

Required:

Write up the following ledger accounts in the books of Dunbar Ltd for each of the five years to 31 December 19-1, 19-2, 19-3, 19-4 and 19-5 respectively:

    (*a*) royalties;

    (*b*) short-workings:

      and

    (*c*) Berwick plc.

Note: The above accounts must be balanced at the end of each financial year, and any balance on the respective accounts brought down at the beginning of the next financial year.

(Association of Accounting Technicians)

7.3 Shipton, who had patented an automatic door closer, granted Doors Ltd a licence for ten years to manufacture and sell the door closer on the following terms.

(i) Doors Ltd to pay a royalty of £1 for every closer sold with a minimum payment of £500 per annum. Calculations to be made annually as on 31 December and payment to be made on 31 January.

(ii) If, for any year, the royalties calculated on closers sold amount to less than £500, Doors Ltd may set off the deficiency against royalties payable in excess of that sum in the next two years.

With effect from the end of the second year the agreement was varied and a minimum annual payment of £400 was substituted for £500, the other terms of the annual agreement remaining unchanged.

The numbers of the closers sold were:

Year ended 31 December

19-2	200
19-3	400
19-4	600
19-5	500

You are required to show the ledger accounts recording the above transactions in respect of the royalties in the books of Doors Ltd which are closed annually on 31 December.

(Institute of Chartered Accountants)

7.4A Laurie Ltd (sand and gravel merchants) entered into an agreement to purchase from Sands Ltd over a period of five years such quantities of sand as they might require from time to time and which they were to extract from a sand pit belonging to Sands Ltd on the following terms:

1 Laurie Ltd to pay a royalty of 10p per ton for all material extracted with a minimum rent of £2,000 per annum.

2 If, for any of the first three years, the royalties on sand extracted fall short of the minimum rent, the shortfall is to be set off against any royalties payable in excess of the rent for those three years.

3 The following quantities were extracted:

	Tons
First year	4,000
Second year	16,000
Third year	28,000

Prepare the ledger accounts recording these transactions in the books of Laurie Ltd, assuming that the payments due for any year were made during the following year.

Income Tax is to be ignored.

(Chartered Association of Certified Accountants)

8

Hire purchase and payment by instalments

When goods are bought under a hire purchase agreement, the legal title to the goods does not pass to the purchaser until every instalment has been paid and a small amount, usually included in the last payment, is paid which legally exercises an option to buy the goods. Thus to buy on hire purchase is legally to hire the goods until a certain time, when an option can be exercised to take over the legal title to the goods. Normally the hire purchaser is not compelled to complete the transaction. If he so wishes he may return the goods and not pay any further instalments. He will, however, forfeit the right to have any of his previous instalments repaid to him. On default the seller can reclaim the goods, subject to certain provisions of the Hire Purchase Acts.

In contrast to this are credit sales payable by instalments, in which the absolute ownership passes immediately to the purchaser. The seller cannot reclaim the goods, but can sue for the unpaid instalments. There is also a class of sale known as a 'conditional sale agreement', which legally has some of the characteristics of both hire purchase and credit sale transactions.

A book on Hire Purchase Law should be studied for the precise legal position of the three types of sales payable for by instalments. From the accounting point of view the three types have a great deal in common. The total amount payable for the asset is made up of (a) the cash price, this being the amount that would have been payable if payment had been made immediately on acquisition instead of being paid for by instalments, and (b) the interest element. A firm would not normally sell goods for exactly the same price to customer (i) who is being given two years to pay for the goods by regular instalments, than they would to customer (ii) who is to pay immediately for the goods. Therefore customer (i) will have to pay something extra to compensate the selling firm for extra administration expenses, the risk element of default by the purchaser, and the loss of working capital for a period of time. The rate of interest should therefore be fixed so that it is adequate to cover these items.

Exhibit 8.1

A car which had a cash sale price of £500 might have a hire purchase price of £600 calculated as follows:

	£
Cash Price	500
add Hire Purchase Interest – 10 per cent of £500 for two years	100
Hire Purchase Price	600

Payable by 24 monthly instalments of £25 each.

Substitute the words 'credit sale' or 'conditional sale' for the words 'hire purchase' and the facts apply to these other two cases.

Of course, requirements concerning deposits and lengths of repayment allowed change with various governmental attempts to control the economy. If a deposit of £100 had been required, the agreement for the car may have been as follows:

Exhibit 8.2

	£
Cash Price	500
add Hire Purchase Interest – 10 per cent of £400 for two years	80
Hire Purchase Price	580

Deposit of £100 paid, therefore the interest is only calculated on the actual amount owing, i.e. £500 − £100 = £400. Payment is completed by 24 monthly instalments of £20 each.

From this point in the chapter the items dealt with will be goods bought and sold on hire purchase. The accounting treatment of credit sale and conditional sale items can well be exactly the same for hire purchase items. Therefore in each of the examples the substitution of 'credit sale' or 'conditional sale' would convert the method from being one used only for hire purchase.

Hire purchaser's books

Because of the restriction on the resale of goods bought on hire purchase the goods normally bought by a firm are in the nature of fixed assets. There are those who maintain that as the legal title to the goods does not pass until the final payment has been made, then it is wrong to bring the full cash price into the books until this has been done. This would seem to be an extreme view in most cases, and one which should normally be avoided. The vast majority of firms enter into hire purchase agreements with the intention of honouring them. Hire purchase is nothing more than the means of financing the purchase of a fixed asset. To capitalise only the proportion of the cash price actually paid is a case of the concept of prudence being carried to extremes. It is also misleading to anyone who is interested in the analysis of the Balance Sheet, as the fixed assets which have been used to win the profits are not fully represented. This method will not therefore be used in this book.

The main problem is that of splitting the amount actually paid between that which refers to hire purchase interest and that which refers to a reduction in the amount of the cash price still owing. Hire purchase interest is normally the cost of borrowing money which is used to buy a fixed asset. Like the cost of borrowing money generally, such as bank overdraft interest or loan interest, it is revenue expenditure and should therefore be charged to the Profit and Loss Account. The cash price is the actual cost of the asset itself; the fact that the asset is bought on hire purchase has no relevance as far as the asset itself is concerned. The extra money paid for hire purchase is due, not to the asset itself but because the firm did not possess the amount of liquid resources available at the time of purchase to pay for the asset immediately. The cash price is therefore capital expenditure and will have to be shown accordingly in the Balance Sheet. If the hire purchase agreement was begun and terminated in the same accounting period, then the apportioning of the amount actually paid between hire purchase interest and the cash price would be a simple matter. If a car was bought for a total hire purchase price of £96, being cash price £90 and hire purchase interest £6, and this was paid by six monthly instalments of £16 each, then the Cash Book would show credits of £96 in all and the debits would be £90 in the Motor Car Account and £6 in the Hire Purchase Interest Account. Either an intermediate account called a Hire Purchase Account could be used to which the £96 would be debited, and the £90 and the £6 then transferred to the relevant accounts, or else with every credit of £16 in the Cash Book the debits could be made of £1 in the Hire Purchase Interest Account and of £15 in the Motor Car Account. The full cash price of £90 would still show in the Balance Sheet, because the purchase is completed before the year end.

On the other hand where the agreement is not started and completed within the accounting period, then the separation of the interest from the proportion of the cash price paid is not a simple matter. The aim is to show the full cash price of the asset in the Balance Sheet. If not fully paid for, then the amount owing will have to also be shown in the Balance Sheet as being owed. This is similar to any asset bought which has not been paid for at the Balance Sheet date. However, the liability to be shown is not the amount of the hire purchase price that is to be paid, but is instead confined to the part of the cash price which still has to be paid. The hire purchase interest which has to be paid in the future is not a liability of the firm at that point in time. Interest is essentially based on the time factor and is only charged in the Profit and Loss Account when it accrues. Therefore future hire purchase interest will only be chargeable as an expense during the years when it accrues, and is not chargeable in this year's Profit and Loss Account. This is rather like saying that if premises were bought they would be shown as an asset in the Balance Sheet, and that if they were only partly paid for, then the liability would also be shown in the Balance Sheet, but revenue expenditure such as rates will only appear in the accounts, and therefore in the Balance Sheet as a liability as it falls due.

How accurately this can be done depends on whether or not the 'true' running rate of interest is known. In Exhibit 8.3 below the rate of interest is stated to be 10 per cent per annum. This interest is only payable on the amounts actually owing from time to time, i.e. the interest is calculated on the reducing balance owed. On the other hand, if the interest is calculated as a percentage rate of the original amount owing, then this is not a 'true' running rate of interest. An example of this is in Exhibit 8.1 where a car is bought for £500 and the interest chargeable is said to be 10 per cent. The 10 per cent for two years was calculated by reference to the £500, the original amount owing. However, after each instalment has been paid the amount of the £500 still owing will fall. The 'true' running rate of interest refers to the interest rate per annum which would have to be applied to each reducing balance so as to bring the amount owing down to zero after the payment of the last instalment.

The method of calculating the 'true' rate of interest is covered in Chapter 36. That chapter also contains a method, known as the 'Rule of 78', that can be used by firms which want to keep their mathematical computations at a low level. By law the Annual Percentage Rate (APR) has to be shown on all details to customers when goods are sold on hire purchase or similar agreements. This also approximates to the 'true' rate.

In considering financing operations one must consider like with like. It is no use comparing the nominal rate of interest offered by one organization against the 'true' rate offered by another. Comparison can only be achieved by data calculated on the same basis, and therefore the two rates should be expressed as 'true' rates. An example of this is the bank overdraft on which interest is expressed in 'true' interest terms, while a personal bank loan is in 'nominal' rate terms.

The necessary accounts needed can now be considered.

Exhibit 8.3

True rate of interest known. Equal instalments

A machine is bought for £3,618 hire purchase price from Suppliers Ltd on 1 January 19-3, being paid for by three instalments of £1,206 on 31 December 19-3, 19-4 and 19-5. The cash price is £3,000. The true rate of interest is 10 per cent. (For convenience all figures are rounded off, fractions of pounds are not shown.)

Machinery

			£
19-3			
Jan 1 Suppliers Ltd	A		3,000

Suppliers Ltd

			£				£
19-3				19-3			
Dec 31 Bank	B		1,206	Jan 1 Machinery	A		3,000
,, 31 Balance c/d	D		2,094	Dec 31 HP Interest	C		300
			3,300				3,300
19-4				19-4			
Dec 31 Bank	B		1,206	Jan 1 Balance b/d	D		2,094
,, 31 Balance c/d	D		1,097	Dec 31 HP Interest	C		209
			2,303				2,303
19-5				19-5			
Dec 31 Bank	B		1,206	Jan 1 Balance b/d	D		1,097
				Dec 31 HP Interest	C		109
			1,206				1,206

Hire Purchase Interest

			£				£
19-3				19-3			
Dec 31 Suppliers Ltd	C		300	Dec 31 Profit and Loss	E		300
19-4				19-4			
Dec 31 Suppliers Ltd	C		209	Dec 31 Profit and Loss	E		209
19-5				19-5			
Dec 31 Suppliers Ltd	C		109	Dec 31 Profit and Loss	E		109

Provision for Depreciation: Machinery

			£
19-3			
Dec 31 Profit and Loss	F		600
19-4			
Dec 31 Profit and Loss	F		600
19-5			
Dec 31 Profit and Loss	F		600

		£	£
19-3	Machinery (at cost)	3,000	
	less Depreciation	600	2,400
	Owing on Hire Purchase Agreement		2,094
19-4	Machinery (at cost)	3,000	
	less Depreciation to date	1,200	1,800
	Owing on Hire Purchase Agreement		1,097
19-5	Machinery (at cost)	3,000	
	less Depreciation to date	1,800	1,200

Description of entries:

A   When the asset is acquired the cash price is debited to the asset account and the credit is in the supplier's account.

B   The instalments paid are credited to the Bank Account and debited to the supplier's account.

C   The interest is credited to the supplier's account for each period as it accrues, and debited to the expense account, later to be transferred to the Profit and Loss Account for the period E.

D   The balance carried down each year is the amount of the cash price still owing.

F   Depreciation provisions are calculated on the full cash price, as the depreciation of an asset is in no way affected by whether or not it has been fully paid for.

The Balance Sheet consists of balance A the cash price, less balance F the amount of cash price apportioned as depreciation. Balance D the amount of the cash price still owing at each Balance Sheet date is shown as a liability.

True rate of interest known. Unequal instalments

Sometimes the cash price portion is repaid by equal instalments, while the interest portion is paid as it accrues. As the interest falls due, the proportion of the cash price owing on which the interest is based is being reduced each year, thus it will be obvious that the total repayments will be different for each accounting period.

Assuming that the same details applied as above, but that £1,000 was to be paid off the cash price each year, plus the whole of the interest as it accrued, then Suppliers Ltd Account would appear as follows:

Exhibit 8.4

Suppliers Ltd

19-3		£	19-3		£
Dec 31	Bank	1,300	Jan 1 Machinery		3,000
,, 31	Balance c/d	2,000	Dec 31 HP Interest (10 per cent of		
			£3,000)		300
		3,300			3,300
19-4			19-4		
Dec 31	Bank	1,200	Jan 1 Balance b/d		2,000
,, 31	Balance c/d	1,000	Dec 31 HP Interest (10 per cent of		
			£2,000)		200
		2,200			2,200
19-5			19-5		
Dec 31	Bank	1,100	Jan 1 Balance b/d		1,000
			Dec 31 HP Interest (10 per cent of		
			£1,000)		100
		1,100			1,100

All the ways in which the debit and credit entries were made in Exhibit 8.3 will be repeated in this case. The only difference will be that the figures will be governed by the transfers now to be effected from Suppliers Ltd Account.

The seller's books

There are a considerable number of ways of drawing up the final accounts of a business which sells goods on hire purchase and of calculating the amounts to be shown therein. The methods chosen should be suitable for the particular firm and needs obviously vary. There is a vast gulf between the old-established firm which sells quality goods to well-known reputable customers, and the back-street firm which sells cheap, easily breakable goods, to anyone without enquiring very deeply as to the customer's creditworthiness.

It can, however, be stipulated that the interest earned from hire purchase sales is earned because money is owed to the firm for a period of time. The interest that should be credited to the Trading Account is therefore the amount which has accrued during the period covered by the account.

On the other hand the profit made on the goods sold is usually either:

(a) Treated as being profit of the firm entirely in the period in which it was first sold to the purchaser, i.e. when the agreement was entered into and the goods delivered to him.

(b) A proportion of the profits is brought into the Trading Account, this being in the ratio which the cash actually received during the period bears to the total cash receivable.

It is inappropriate in a book at this level to go into intricate details of the methods used in practice by firms. With firms that have many hire purchase transactions the methods of apportioning interest and profit are often ones of expediency, exact accuracy often being too costly to achieve. Therefore in an examination the examiner's instructions should always be carried out, he may be envisaging such a situation. The fact that the examinee may disagree with the method used is irrelevant for this purpose.

Exhibit 8.5 shows the accounts needed by a firm with two departments, one department uses method (*a*), while the other department uses method (*b*).

Exhibit 8.5

A Phelps started business on 1 January 19-5. He sold cash registers of a uniform type which cost him £90 each, for a cash price of £120, and also on hire purchase terms for £140, being payable by a deposit of £20 followed by three instalments of £40 each on the first, second and third anniversaries of the date of the contract. The total price of £140 included compound interest at 10 per cent on the reducing balance owed (calculated after each year's payment) of the normal cash price. It is assumed that the sales were evenly spread over the year.

He also sold calculators of a uniform type on hire purchase only. These required an initial deposit of £6 followed by 12 quarterly instalments of £2 each over a period of three years. The cost of calculators was £18 each.

The following trial balance was extracted as on 31 December 19-5:

	£	£
Capital: Cash Introduced		50,000
Fixed Assets	10,000	
Hire Purchase Sales – Cash Registers (200 at £140 each)		28,000
Cash Sales – Cash Registers (50 at £120 each)		6,000
Cash collected from hire purchasers of calculators (1,000 calculators sold)		9,600
Debtors	24,000	
Purchases – Cash Registers (350 at £90)	31,500	
Purchases – Calculators (1,200 at £18)	21,600	
Bank	8,900	
Creditors		6,400
Salaries and General Expenses	4,000	
	100,000	100,000

It was decided to take credit, in the annual accounts, for the normal gross profit (excluding interest) on cash registers sold to customers and to apportion the interest on a time basis.

In view of the large number of transactions in calculators, and the difficulty of apportioning the interest, it was decided to adopt for this section of the business the alternative method of taking credit for the profit, including interest, on calculators only in proportion to the cash collected.

Stocks were valued at cost, being cash registers (100) £9,000, and calculators (200) £3,600.

The following accounts demonstrate the methods used. The letters A to H refer to the narratives which follow the accounts and are needed to explain those items that are not self-evident.

Cash Registers Trading Account for the year ended
31 December 19-5

			£	£
Cash Sales				6,000
Hire Purchase Sales — at cash prices		A		24,000
Hire Purchase Interest		C		1,000
				31,000
less Cost of Goods Sold:				
Purchases			31,500	
less Closing Stock			9,000	22,500
Gross Profit c/d				8,500

Cash Registers – Interest Suspense

		£			£
Trading Account –			Hire Purchase Sales –		
10% per annum on			Interest included in Hire		
£20,000 for six months	C	1,000	Purchase Price	B	4,000
Interest not yet earned c/d	D	3,000			
		4,000			4,000

Cash Registers – Hire Purchase Sales

		£		£
Interest Suspense –			Debtors	28,000
200 × £20	B	4,000		
Trading Account –				
Cash Price of Sales	A	24,000		
		28,000		28,000

A   As the interest factor of profit is being calculated separately the cash price of goods sold on hire purchase is transferred so that the goods factor of profit can be dealt with.
B   The whole interest factor is transferred to the suspense account.
C   The apportionment of the interest earned in this period is now calculated. For simplicity it has been stated that the sales were spread evenly throughout the year. This means that the average time that money was owing was six months. The interest of 10 per cent per annum is based on the part of the cash price owing. As only the deposits of £20 were paid in this year the balance of £100 of the cash price was therefore owing for each machine, i.e. 200 machines = £20,000. As this money had been owed for six months on average, then the interest is £20,000 for six months at the rate of 10 per cent per annum = £1,000. This now needs transferring to the Trading Account as it constitutes part of this year's profit.

Of course, if the sales have not been spread evenly over the year, then the interest earned would have been different. If most of the sales had taken place at the start of the year the average time that each £100 was owing would be greater than six months, if

91

most of the sales had taken place at the end of the year, then each £100 would have been owing for an average time of less than six months. It all depends on the facts. Calculations must therefore be based on the facts in each firm.

D   When the goods have been sold on hire purchase the total hire purchase price has been debited to each customer's account. However, of the £4,000 total hire purchase interest, £3,000 still has to be earned and is accordingly carried forward to the next accounting period. As the figure of debtors includes this amount, then the debtors need to be shown net in the Balance Sheet after the deduction of the unearned interest.

E   As the interest factor and the profit on goods factor are not being separated for profit calculations, there is no need to show them separately.

F   The provision for unrealised profit is debited to the Trading Account, and will be credited to a Provision for Unrealised Profit Account. At the end of each accounting period the provision will need adjusting, sometimes it will have to be increased, this will be done by debiting the Trading Account and crediting the Provision Account. At other times the provision will need reducing, this will necessitate the debiting of the Provision Account and the crediting of the Trading Account. It will now be seen to work in a similar manner to a Bad Debts Provision Account, the main difference being that provision for unrealised profits affects the Trading Account while provision for bad debts affects the Profit and Loss Account instead. Also, like the bad debts example, the balance of the Provision for Unrealised Profit Account is deducted from the instalments owing in the Balance Sheet.

The provision is calculated thus:

$$\frac{\text{Cash yet to be collected}}{\text{Total Cash collectable from the Sales}} \times \text{Total Gross Profit (incl. interest)}$$

$$= \frac{20,400}{30,000}\text{(G)} \times \text{£12,000(H)} = \text{£8,160}$$

Calculators Trading Account for the year ended 31 December 19-5

		£	£
Sales at Hire Purchase Price	E		30,000
Purchases		21,600	
less Closing Stock		3,600	
Cost of Goods Sold		18,000	
Provision for Unrealised Profit	F	8,160	26,160
Gross Profit c/d			3,840

G   The £20,400 is found by taking the total cash collectable from the sales less the amount already collected: i.e. £30 × 1,000 = £30,000 *less* £9,600 (see trial balance) = Cash yet to be collected £20,400.

H   This figure is found by taking the profit for each calculator (including interest) and multiplying by the number of units sold. Hire purchase price £30 *less* cost £18 = £12 profit (including interest) per unit. 1,000 units sold, therefore £12 × 1,000 = £12,000 total profit.

Profit and Loss Account for the year ended 31 December 19-5

		£
Gross Profit b/d		
On Cash Registers		8,500
On Calculators		3,840
		12,340
less Salaries and General Expenses		4,000
Net Profit		8,340

Balance Sheet as at 31 December 19-5

	£	£	£
Fixed Assets			10,000
Current Assets			
Stocks		12,600	
Hire Purchase Instalments not yet due			
Cash Registers	24,000		
less Provision for Interest not due	3,000	21,000	
Calculators	20,400		
less Provision for Unrealised Profit	8,160	12,240	
Bank		8,900	
		54,740	
less Current Liabilities			
Creditors		6,400	48,340
			58,340
Financed by:			
Capital			
Cash Introduced		50,000	
add Net Profit		8,340	58,340
			58,340

Repossessions

If in the accounts shown, some of the people buying calculators had defaulted on their payments and the goods had been repossessed, then this would need special accounting treatment. The sums paid by the customers would have been forfeited by them. On the other hand, the repossessed items taken back into stock are not new and will therefore have to be revalued accordingly.

The Calculator Trading Account can now be reconstructed if, in addition to the transactions already described, a further 10 calculators on which a total of £8 each had been paid were repossessed (i.e. 1,010 sold originally, 10 of these being repossessed later). On 31 December 19-5 they were not valued at cost, i.e. £18 each, but were valued as being worth £13 each.

	£	£
Sales at Hire Purchase Price		30,000
Instalments Received on Repossessions		80
		30,080
less Cost of Goods Sold:		
Purchases	21,600	
less Stock*	3,550	
	18,050	
Provision for Unrealised Profit	8,160	26,210
Gross Profit		3,870

*The final stock is now made up of:

	£
Unsold Items – 190 × £18	3,420
Items Repossessed – 10 × £13	130
	3,550

The gross profit is now £3,870. This can be explained as follows:

	£	£
Original profit		3,840
Additional transactions –		
Received instalments 10 × £8	80	
Loss of value – cost *less* new value £18 − £13 = £5 × 10	50	
Therefore additional profit		30
Revised Profit		3,870

Company accounts

A change introduced first by the 1981 Companies Act is that an amount owing on a hire-purchase contract cannot now be deducted from the value of the asset in the balance sheet. This still applies with the 1985 Companies Act.

SSAP 21: accounting for leases and hire purchase contracts

In August 1984 SSAP 21 was issued. The background was stated in the following terms:

Leasing and hire purchase contracts are means by which companies finance the right to use of the purchase of fixed assets. In the UK there is normally no provision in a lease contract for legal title to the leased asset to pass to the lessee during the term of a lease. In contrast under a hire purchase contract the hirer may acquire legal title by exercising an option to purchase the asset upon fulfilment of certain conditions (normally the payment of an agreed number of instalments). Current tax legislation provides for capital allowances to be claimed by the lessor under a lease contract and by the hirer under a hire purchase contract.

Lessors fall into three broad categories. They may be companies, including banks and finance houses, which provide finance under lease contracts to enable a single customer to acquire the use of an asset for the greater part of its useful life; they may operate a business which involves the renting out of assets for varying periods of time probably to more than one customer; or they may be manufacturer or dealer lessors who use leasing as a means of marketing their products, which may involve leasing a product to one customer or to several customers. As a lessor and lessee are both parties to the same transaction it is appropriate that the same definitions should be used and the accounting treatment recommended should ideally be complementary. However, this will not mean that the recorded balances in both financial statements will be the same, because the pattern of cash flows and the taxation consequences will be different.

Leases can appropriately be classified into finance leases and operating leases. The distinction between a finance lease and an operating lease will usually be evident from the substance of the contract between the lessor and the lessee. A finance lease usually involves repayment to a lessor by a lessee of the full cost of the asset together with a return on the finance provided by the lessor. As such, a lease of this type is normally non-cancellable or cancellable only under certain conditions, and the lessee enjoys substantially all the risks and rewards associated with the ownership of an asset, other than the legal title.

An operating lease involves the lessee paying a rental for the hire of an asset for a period of time which is normally substantially less than its useful economic life. The lessor retains the risks and rewards of ownership of an asset in an operating lease and normally assumes responsibility for repairs, maintenance and insurance.

Briefly, this standard requires that a finance lease should be accounted for by the lessee as if it were the purchase of the property rights in an asset with simultaneous recognition of the obligation to make future payments, in the same way that a hire purchase is normally accounted for. Under an operating lease, only the rental will be taken into account by the lessee. The standard recognises that the substance of a transaction rather than its legal form should govern the accounting treatment.

Review questions

8.1 An engineering concern purchased machines on the HP system over a period of three years paying £846 down on 1 January 19-3, and further annual payments of £2,000 due on 31 December 19-3, 19-4 and 19-5.

The cash price of the machine was £6,000, the vendor company charging interest at 8 per cent per annum on outstanding balances.

Show the appropriate ledger accounts in the purchaser's books for the three years and how the items would appear in the balance sheet at 31 December 19-3; depreciation at 10 per cent per annum on the written down value is to be charged and interest calculated to the nearest £.

8.2A On 1 January 19-3 J Donkins bought a machine (cash price £2,092) from CD & Co Ltd on the following hire purchase terms. Donkins was to make an immediate payment of £600 and three annual payments of £600 on 31 December in each year. The rate of interest chargeable is 10 per cent per annum.

Donkins depreciates this machinery by 10 per cent on the diminishing balance each year.

(*a*) Make the entries relating to this machine in Donkin's ledger for the year 19-3, 19-4 and 19-5. (All calculations are to be made to the nearest £.)

(*b*) Show how the item machinery would appear in the Balance Sheet as at 31 December 19-3.

8.3 Bulwell Aggregates Ltd wish to expand their transport fleet and have purchased three heavy lorries with a list price of £18,000 each. Robert Bulwell has negotiated hire purchase finance to fund this expansion, and the company has entered into a hire purchase agreement with Granby Garages plc on the 1 January 19-1. The agreement states that Bulwell Aggregates will pay a deposit of £9,000 on 1 January 19-1, and two annual instalments of £24,000 on 31 December 19-1, 19-2, and a final instalment of £20,391 on 31 December 19-3.

Interest is to be calculated at 25% on the balance outstanding on 1 January each year and paid on 31 December each year.

The depreciation policy of Bulwell Aggregates Ltd is to write off the vehicles over a four year period using the straight line method and assuming a scrap value of £1,333 for each vehicle at the end of its useful life.

The cost of the vehicles to Granby Garages is £14,400 each.

Required:

(*a*) Account for the above transactions in the books of Bulwell Aggregates Ltd, showing the entries in the Profit and Loss Account and Balance Sheet for the years 19-1, 19-2, 19-3 and 19-4.

(*b*) Account for the above transactions in the books of Granby Garages plc, showing the entries in the Hire Purchase Trading Account for the years 19-1, 19-2, 19-3. This is the only hire purchase transaction undertaken by this company.

Calculations to the nearest £.

(*Association of Accounting Technicians*)

8.4A J York was acquiring two cars under hire purchase agreements, details of which are as follows:

Registration Number	JY 1	JY 2
Date of purchase	31 May 19-6	31 October 19-6
Cash price	£18,000	£24,000
Deposit	£3,120	£4,800
Interest (deemed to accrue evenly over the period of the agreement)	£1,920	£2,400

Both agreements provided for payment to be made in twenty-four monthly instalments commencing on the last day of the month following purchase.

On 1 September 19-7, vehicle JY 1 became a total loss. In full settlement on 20 September 19-7:

(*a*) an insurance company paid £12,500 under a comprehensive policy, and

(*b*) the hire purchase company accepted £6,000 for the termination of the agreement.

The firm prepared accounts annually to 31 December and provided depreciation on a straight line basis at a rate of 20 per cent per annum for motor vehicles, apportioned as from the date of purchase and up to the date of disposal.

All instalments were paid on due dates.

The balance on the Hire Purchase Company Account in respect of vehicle JY 1 is to be written off.

You are required to record these transactions in the following accounts, carrying down the balances as on 31 December 19-6, and 31 December 19- 7:

(*a*) Motor Vehicles,

(*b*) Depreciation,

(*c*) Hire Purchase Company,

(*d*) Assets Disposal.

8.5 RJ commenced business on 1 January 19-8. He sells refrigerators, all of one standard type, on hire purchase terms. The total amount, including interest, payable for each refrigerator, is £300. Customers are required to pay an initial deposit of £60, followed by eight quarterly instalments of £30 each. The cost of each refrigerator to RJ is £200.

The following trial balance was extracted from RJ's books as on 31 December 19-8.

Trial Balance

	£	£
Capital		100,000
Fixed Assets	10,000	
Drawings	4,000	
Bank overdraft		19,600
Creditors		16,600
Purchases	180,000	
Cash collected from customers		76,500
Bank interest	400	
Wages and salaries	12,800	
General expenses	5,500	
	£212,700	£212,700

850 machines were sold on hire-purchase terms during 19-8.

The annual accounts are prepared on the basis of taking credit for profit (including interest) in proportion to the cash collected from customers.

You are required to prepare the hire purchase trading account, and the profit and loss account for the year 19-8 and balance sheet as on 31 December 19-8.

Ignore depreciation of fixed assets.

Show your calculations.

(*Institute of Chartered Secretaries and Administrators*)

8.6A Object Limited is a retail outlet selling word processing equipment both for cash and on hire purchase terms. The following information has been extracted from the books of account as at 31 August 19-6:

	Dr £	Cr £
Authorised, issued and fully paid share capital (ordinary shares of £1 each)		75,000
Administration and shop expenses	130,000	
Cash at bank and in hand	6,208	
Cash received from hire purchase customers		315,468
Cash sales		71,000
Depreciation of premises and equipment (at 1 September 19-5)		45,000
Hire purchase debtors (at 1 September 19-5)	2,268	
Premises and equipment at cost	100,000	
Profit and loss account (at 1 September 19-5)		8,000
Provision for unrealised profit (at 1 September 19-5)		1,008
Purchases	342,000	
Stock (at 1 September 19-5)	15,000	
Trade creditors		80,000
	£595,476	£595,476

Additional information:

1 The company's policy is to take credit for gross profit (including interest) for hire purchase sales in proportion to the instalments collected. It does this by raising a provision against the profit included in hire purchase debtors not yet due.

2 The cash selling price is fixed at 50% and the hire purchase selling price at 80% respectively above the cost of goods purchased.

3 The hire purchase contract requires an initial deposit of 20% of the hire purchase selling price, the balance to be paid in four equal instalments at quarterly intervals. The first instalment is due three months after the agreement is signed.

4 Hire Purchase sales for the year amounted to £540,000 (including interest).

5 In February 19-6 the company repossessed some goods which had been sold earlier in the year. These goods had been purchased for £3,000, and the unpaid instalments on them amounted to £3,240. They were then taken back into stock at a value of £2,500. Later on in the year they were sold on cash terms for £3,500.

6 Depreciation is charged on premises and equipment at a rate of 15% per annum on cost.

Required:
Prepare Object Limited's trading, and profit and loss account for the year to 31 August 19-6, and a balance sheet as at that date.
Your workings should be submitted.
(*Association of Accounting Technicians*)

8.7A On 1 January 19-6, F Limited commenced business selling goods on hire-purchase. Under the terms of the agreements, an initial deposit of 20 per cent is payable on delivery, followed by four equal quarterly instalments, the first being due three months after the date of sale.

During the year sales were made as follows:

HP

Cost price Sales price

	£	£
10 January	150	225
8 March	350	525
12 May	90	135
6 July	200	300
20 September	70	105
15 October	190	285
21 November	160	240

The goods sold in July were returned in September and eventually sold in November for £187 cash. All other instalments are paid on the due dates.

It may be assumed that:

(a) gross profit and interest are credited to profit and loss account in the proportion that deposits and instalments received bear to hire purchase price, or

(b) the cost is deemed to be paid in full before any credit is taken for gross profit and interest.

You are to prepare for the first year of trading, a hire purchase trading account compiled firstly on assumption (a) and secondly on assumption (b) and give the relevant balance sheet entries under each assumption.

Workings should be clearly shown.

(*Chartered Institute of Management Accountants*)

8.8 The following information relates to vehicles of the Magic Motorcoach Company Ltd, a bus and coach tour operator.

Date Purchased	Motor Coach	Cost (Cash Price)	Date Sold	Sales Proceeds	Hire Purchase Finance
		£		£	£
1.1.19-4	'Polly'	63,200	31.3.19-6	22,000	43,200
30.9.19-4	'Dolly'	70,800	30.6.19-6	33,600	50,400
31.7.19-5	'Molly'	82,600			64,800
31.3.19-6	'Ena'	100,200			75,600
30.6.19-6	'Tina'	116,400			82,800

Additional information:

(a) All coaches are purchased from Mushroom Coach Dealers plc, and the hire purchase finance is arranged through Moneconomic Financing plc at a flat rate of 10% per year payable in 24 equal instalments. The first instalment is due one month after the date of purchase.

(b) Using a rate of 35% depreciation (reducing balance method), it is company policy to charge a full year's depreciation in the year of purchase and none in the year of disposal.

(c) All coaches are given a female name to identify them as individual members of the fleet of coaches. The amount shown as sales proceeds on the disposal of 'Dolly' was in fact a trade-in allowance on the purchase of 'Tina'. Because only 21 of the instalments had been paid, the legal title to 'Dolly' was vested in the finance company, until Magic Motorcoach Company Ltd obtained ownership by paying an agreed settlement figure of £7,450.

(*d*) Because the Magic Motorcoach Company Ltd did not meet its financial obligations, the finance company repossessed 'Tina' after 3 instalments had been paid and obtained £60,000 for it on the open market. The finance company duly presented the Magic Motorcoach Company Ltd with an invoice for the amount due to Moneconomic Financing plc of £22,630 on 31 December 19-6.

(*e*) The year end of the Magic Motorcoach Company Ltd is 31 December.

Required:

Write up the ledger accounts, in the books of Magic Motorcoach Company Ltd, for the following:

    Motor coaches at cost

    Accumulated depreciation

    Fixed assets disposal

    Hire purchase interest

    Hire purchase creditors

      You should show clearly:

    (*i*) the charge or credit to the profit and loss account for each year

    (*ii*) the balances brought down at 31 December 19-4, 19-5 and 19-6.

(*Chartered Association of Certified Accountants*)

8.9A Smith and Jones are partners in Western Co which has a high street shop dealing in domestic electrical goods both for outright sale and under hire purchase agreements. Whilst Smith was working on the partnership records at home there was a fire which destroyed some of the records.

    Smith and Jones have provided you with:

(*a*) a draft profit and loss account for the first year's trading to 31 March 19-5 and a draft balance sheet at that date;

(*b*) a list of debtor balances.

    The first year's accounts had been produced by an accountant who was not a member of the Association.

    The draft accounts for the first year's trading are as follows:

Profit and loss account for the year ended 31 March 19-5

	£	£
Sales		95,000
Purchases	58,379	
less closing stock	10,500	
		47,879
		47,121
Rent and rates	7,500	
Wages	10,250	
Printing, stationery and miscellaneous expenses	746	
Suspense	3,250	
		21,746
		25,375
Share of profit – Smith	12,688	
Jones	12,687	
		25,375

Balance sheet at 31 March 19-5

	£	£
Shop fixtures, fittings and equipment		15,500
Stock	10,500	
Debtors	43,692	
Cash at bank	933	
	55,125	
Creditors	6,250	
		48,875
		64,375
Partners' capital accounts		
Smith – capital introduced	25,000	
profit	12,688	
	37,688	
drawings	3,500	
		34,188
Jones – capital introduced	22,000	
profit	12,687	
	34,687	
drawings	4,500	
		30,187
		64,375

On investigating the first year's draft accounts it is discovered that:

(*a*) All hire purchase sales are for a two year period and 16% of the cash price is added for interest. On signing a hire purchase contract the customer pays 20% of the cash price as deposit and thereafter 24 equal instalments are paid at monthly intervals.

(*b*) Sales in the draft accounts include the full amount of the hire purchase sales including the interest charged for the full two year period. The partners consider that hire purchase interest should be spread over the 24 month period on a 'rule of 78' basis, and they have been told that the factor for a two year contract is 300. Credit should be taken for the cash sales price in the month of sale. The calculations of interest using the 'rule of 78' are shown in the schedule of hire purchase sales (note (*h*)).

(*c*) A sum of £2,300 in outright sales not paid for in the year were not recorded as debtors although the figure is included in sales.

(*d*) A payment of £950 for fittings for the shop was made in the year. This amount is in the cash book but has not been posted to any nominal ledger account.

(*e*) No depreciation has been provided on the shop fixtures, fittings and equipment. 15% on the reducing balance is agreed to be appropriate.

(*f*) Closing stock has been understated by £500.

(*g*) All hire purchase instalments due have been paid.

(*h*) The records for the year to 31 March 19-5 show the hire purchase sales to be:
Hire Purchase Sales

19-4	Total including HP interest £	Interest included £	Amount relating to year to 31 March 19-5 Factor	£
April	1,160	160	209	111
May	2,320	320	195	208
June	1,740	240	180	144
July	6,380	880	164	481
August	5,220	720	147	353
September	2,900	400	129	172
October	6,960	960	110	352
November	8,700	1,200	90	360
December	9,280	1,280	69	294
19-5				
January	7,830	1,080	47	169
February	4,176	576	24	46
March	7,540	1,040	–	–

(*Author's note:* 'Rule 78' calculations of interest are shown in Chapter X, page X.)
An analysis of the debtors list reveals the following information at 31 March 19-6:

Ordinary debtors for sales £2,450

Hire purchase debtors	Balance	No of instalments paid	Interest included Factor	£
19-4/5 Sales	40	23	1	1
	160	22	3	3
	180	21	6	5
	880	20	10	29
	900	19	15	36
	600	18	21	28
	1,680	17	28	90
	2,400	16	36	144
	2,880	15	45	192
	2,700	14	55	198
	1,584	13	66	127
17,124	3,120	12	78	270
19-5/6 Sales	3,640	11	91	340
	4,480	10	105	448
	6,000	9	120	640
	5,120	8	136	580
	4,760	7	153	571
	6,480	6	171	821
	7,600	5	190	1,013
	9,600	4	210	1,344
	12,600	3	231	1,848
	14,080	2	253	2,159
	7,360	1	276	1,178
88,440	6,720	0	300	1,120

Included in the balance for which 15 instalments have been paid is a debtor for £360 who has defaulted, his goods had been repossessed and sold for £25. There are no other bad debts or defaults.

The following information is relevant to the second year's trading:

(*i*)   The margin on sales has remained constant throughout the year at 45% of sales price (before adding hire purchase interest). One month's credit is taken on purchases. Purchases in March 19-6 were £8,000.

(*ii*)   Rent and rates remained at the same level as in 19-4/5, wages amounted to £12,000 in the year.

(*iii*)   Printing, stationery and miscellaneous expenses were £1,550 for the year.

(*iv*)   Amounts paid into the bank in respect of non-hire purchase sales were £15,250.

(*v*)   Smith has withdrawn £80 per week from the business during the year and Jones has withdrawn £100 per week.

(*vi*)   Closing stock of goods for resale had the same value as at 31 March 19-5.

(*vii*)   All sales moneys were banked intact and all expenses and withdrawals were made by cheque payments.

Required:

(*a*) A revised profit and loss account for the year ended 31 March 19-5 and a balance sheet as at that date.

(*b*) A profit and loss account for the year ended 31 March 19-6 and a balance sheet as at that date.

(*Chartered Association of Certified Accountants*)

9

Limited companies: general background

An introduction was made to the accounts of limited companies in Volume 1. It was intended to show some of the basic outlines of the Final Accounts of limited companies to those people who would be finishing their studies of accounting with the completion of Volume 1. This volume now carries the study of limited companies accounting to a more advanced stage.

The Act of Parliament now governing limited companies is the Companies Act 1862. In this volume we are concerned only with basic principles, as the complications are better left until the reader has reached a more advanced stage in his/her studies.

The Companies Act 1985 is the descendant of modern limited liability company legislation which can be traced back to the passing of the Companies Act 1862. This act was a triumph for the development of the limited liability principle which had been severely restricted since the so-called 'Bubble Act' of 1720, this latter act being the remedy for a multitude of spectacular frauds perpetrated behind the cloak of limited liability. Not until 1862 was general prejudice overcome, and the way paved for the general use of the limited liability principle which is now commonplace. Company law therefore consists of the Companies Act 1985, together with a considerable body of case law which has been built up over the years. It must be borne in mind that there are still a number of Chartered Companies in existence which were incorporated by Royal Charter, such as the Hudson's Bay Company, or else which were formed by special Acts of Parliament, such as the Mersey Docks and Harbour Board.

The 1985 Companies Act is a consolidation act which brought together no fewer than five separate companies acts which were in force at the same time, each one adding to and amending the one before it. These were the Companies Acts of 1948, 1967, 1976, 1980 and 1981. Now there is just the one companies act in force and that is the Companies Act 1985.

The 1981 Companies Act had, as its prime purpose, the harmonisation of company law in the European Economic Community (EEC). The Act also brought in a completely new development in the United Kingdom. Before this act companies had to disclose certain information. The way that the accounts were drawn up, so long as the necessary information was shown, was completely at the discretion of the company itself. The 1981 Act however set out detailed rules on the format of the accounts, all of these are now part of the 1985 Companies Act and these will be considered later in this book.

The 1985 Companies Act account requirements do not apply to banks, insurance companies and shipping companies. They therefore may continue to produce accounts as before. Banks and Insurance companies will be the subject of separate future EEC directives.

The Companies Act also covers companies with unlimited liability. These are now very rarely met in practice. Also covered are companies limited by guarantee, which may or may not have a share capital, but the Companies Act 1985 forbids the future formation of such companies, if they have a share capital. Both of these types of limited company are relatively unimportant, and therefore any future reference to a 'limited company' or merely a 'company' will be concerned with limited liability companies of the normal type.

Until the act of 1980 you could not tell from the title of a company whether it was a private company or a public company. With the passing of the act of 1980, however, public companies were required to end their names with the words 'public limited company'. Such a public limited company would have to have a minimum issued share capital of £50,000. Instead of using the words 'public limited company' in full, the abbreviation 'plc', or in capitals PLC, may be used. If the registered office is in Wales the Welsh equivalent is permitted, this is 'cwmni cyfyngedig cyhoeddus'.

A private company, on the other hand, does not have to state that it is a private company. This means that should the words 'public limited company', or the abbreviation, or the Welsh equivalent, not be shown, then the company is a private limited company.

Another change which may be noted is that the minimum number of persons who may form a public company is now two, instead of seven the number which used to prevail before the 1980 Act.

The outstanding feature of a limited company is that, no matter how many individuals have bought shares in it, yet it is treated in its dealings with the outside world as if it were a person in its own right, it is said to be a separate 'legal entity'. Just as the law can create this separate legal person, then so also can it eliminate it, but its existence can only be terminated by using the proper legal procedures. Thus the identity of the shareholders in a large concern may be changing daily as shares are bought and sold by different people. On the other hand, a small private company may have the same shareholders from when it is incorporated (the day it legally came into being), until the date when liquidation is completed (the cessation of a company, often known also as 'winding up' or being 'wound up'). A prime example of its identity as a separate legal entity is that it may sue its own shareholders, or in turn be sued by them.

The legal formalities by which the company comes into existence can be gleaned from any textbook on Company Law. It is not the purpose of this book to discuss Company Law in any great detail, this is far better left to a later stage of one's studies. As companies must, however, comply with the law, the essential Company Law concerning accounting matters will be dealt with in this book as far as is necessary. This is not a book in which company accounts should be discussed in great detail.

What is important is that the basic principles connected with company accounts can be seen in operation. In order that the student may not be unduly confused, points which very rarely occur, or on which the legal arguments are extremely involved and may not yet have been finally settled, will be left out completely or merely mentioned in passing. This means that some generalisations will bear closer scrutiny when accounting studies reach a more advanced stage.

Each company is governed by two documents, known as the Memorandum of Association and the Articles of Association, generally referred to as the 'memorandum' and the 'articles'. The memorandum consists of five clauses for private companies, and six for public companies, which contain the following details:

1 The name of the company.

2 The part of the UK where the registered office will be situated.

3 The objects of the company.

4 A statement (if a limited liability company) that the liability of its members is limited.

5 Details of the share capital which the company is authorised to issue.

6 A public limited company will also have a clause stating that the company is a public limited company.

The memorandum is said to be the document which discloses the conditions which govern the company's relationship with the outside world.

The principle of limited liability underlying clause 4 has been of the utmost importance in industry and commerce. It is inconceivable that large business units, such as Imperial Chemical Industries Ltd or Great Universal Stores Ltd, could have existed except for a very few instances. The investor in a limited company, who therefore buys shares in it, is a shareholder, the most he can lose is the money he has paid for the shares, or where he has only partly paid for them, then he is also liable for the unpaid part in addition. With public companies, where their shares are dealt in on a Stock Exchange, he can easily sell them whenever he so wishes. The sale of a share in a private company is not so easily effected.

Classes of shares

The main classes of shares are **ordinary** shares and **preference** shares. Unless clearly stated in the memorandum or articles of association preference shares are assumed to be of the cumulative variety already described in Volume 1.

There are also a variety of other shares. The rights attaching to these shares are purely dependent on the skill and ingenuity of the draftsman of the memorandum and articles of association. An entirely new type of share may be created provided it does not contravene the law.

The shares which carry the right to the whole of the profits remaining after the preference shares (and any other fixed dividend shares) have been paid a dividend are often known as the equity share capital or as 'equities'.

Until 1981 the only type of share which could be bought back from the shareholders by the company itself were redeemable preference shares. This has now changed completely, and it will be considered in detail in Chapter 11.

Dividends

In Volume 1, Chapter 39, the calculation of dividends from profits available for distribution was shown. Until the 1980 Act there never had been a definition of 'distributable profits'. The 1980 Act stated that companies must not make a distribution except out of profits available for the purpose. As the definition of profits involves an understanding of factors to be examined in later chapters, this will not be considered in detail until Chapter 14.

Table A

Besides the Memorandum of Association every company must also have Articles of Association. Just as the memorandum governs the company's dealings with the outside world, the articles govern the relationships which exist between the members and the company, between one member and the other members, and other necessary regulations. The Companies Act has a model set of articles known as Table A. A company may, if it so wishes, have its articles exactly the same as Table A, commonly known as 'adopting Table A', or else adopt part of it and have some sections altered. The adoption of the major part of Table A is normal for most private companies. In accounting textbooks, unless stated to the contrary, the accounting examples shown are usually on the basis that Table A has been adopted.

Table A lays down regulations concerning the powers of the directors of the company. On the other hand, the company may draft its own regulations for the powers of directors. Any such regulations are of the utmost importance when it is realised that the legal owners of the business, the shareholders, have entrusted the running of the company to the directors. The shareholders' own rights are largely limited to attending Annual General Meetings and having voting rights thereat, although some shares do not carry voting rights. The Companies Acts make the keeping of proper sets of accounting records and the preparation of Final Accounts compulsory for every company. In addition the accounts must be audited, this being quite different from a partnership or a sole trader's business where an audit is not compulsory at all.

Companies having limited liability, whether they are private or public companies, have to send a copy of their Final Accounts, drawn up in a prescribed manner, to the Registrar of Companies. Chapter 17 is concerned with stating the accounting requirements of the Companies Acts.

The shares of most of the public companies are dealt in on one or other of the recognised Stock Exchanges. The shares of private companies cannot be bought and sold on any Stock Exchange, as this would contravene the requirements for the company being recognised as a 'private' company. The sale and purchase of shares on the Stock Exchanges have no effect on the accounting entries made in the company's books. The only entry made in the company's books when a shareholder sells all, or some, of his shares to someone else, is to record the change of identity of the shareholders. The price at which shares were sold on the Stock Exchange does not enter into the company's books. While no accounting entries are necessary, probably apart from a small charge being made to the shareholder to compensate the company for administrative expenses in recording the change of identity caused by the share transfer and the completion of certain legal documents by the company, the price of the shares on the Stock Exchange has repercussions on the financial policy of the company. If some new shares are to be issued, the fact at what price they are to be issued will be largely dependent on the Stock Exchange valuation. If another firm is to be taken over by the company, part of the purchase price being by the means of shares in the company, then the Stock Exchange value will also affect the value placed upon the shares being given. A takeover bid from another firm may well be caused because the Stock Exchange value of the shares has made a takeover seem worthwhile. It must be recognised that the Stock Exchanges are the 'second-hand market' for a company's shares. The company does not actually sell (normally called 'issue') its shares by using the Stock Exchange as a selling place. The company issues new shares directly to the people who make application to it for the shares at the time when the company has shares available for issue. The company does not sell to, or buy from, the Stock Exchanges. This means that the shares of a public company sold and bought on Stock Exchanges are passing from one shareholder to another person who will then become a shareholder. Apart from the effect upon the financial policies of the firm the double entry accounts of the company are not affected.

Later in this book you are shown whereby the shares of a company may be made into 'stock'. Thus 500 Ordinary Shares of £1 each may be made into £500 Stock. The dividends paid on the shares or the stock would be the same, and the voting powers would also be the same. Apart from administrative convenience there is really no difference between shares and stock.

10

The issue of shares and debentures

The issue of shares

In the case of public companies a new issue of shares can be very costly indeed, and the number of shares issued must be sufficient to make the cost worthwhile. However, for simplicity, so that the principles are not obscured by the difficulties of grappling with large amounts, the numbers of shares shown as issued in the illustrations that follow will be quite small.

Shares can be issued being payable for (*a*) immediately on application, or (*b*) by instalments. The first instances will be of shares being paid for immediately. Issues of shares may take place on the following terms connected with the price of the shares:

(*a*) Shares issued at par. This would mean that a share of £1 nominal value would be issued for £1 each.

(*b*) Shares issued at a premium. In this case a share of £1 nominal value would be issued for more than £1 each, say for £3 each.

(*c*) Until the change per the Companies Act 1980, shares could be issued at a discount. This is now expressly forbidden. Shares each of £5 nominal value might have been issued for £3 each.

This will all seem rather strange at first. How can a £1 share, which states that value on the face of it, be issued for £3 each, and who would be foolish enough to buy it? On the other hand, surely there would have been a queue of people waiting to buy a £5 share for £3 each. The reasons for this apparently strange state of affairs stem from the Companies Act requirement that the Share Capital Accounts always show shares at their nominal value, irrespective of how much the shares are worth or how much they are issued for. To illustrate this, the progress of two firms can be looked at, firm A and firm B. Both firms started in business on 1 January 19-1 and issued 1,000 ordinary shares each of £4 nominal value at par. Ignoring any issue expenses, the Balance Sheets on that date would appear:

Firms A Ltd and B Ltd
Balance Sheet as at 1 January 19-1

	£
Bank	4,000
Capital	4,000

Five years later, on 31 December 19-5, the Balance Sheets show that the companies have fared quite differently. It is to be assumed here, for purposes of illustration, that the Balance Sheet values and any other interpretation of values happen to be identical.

£4,000 capital is needed by A Ltd, and this is to be met by issuing more ordinary shares. Suppose that another 1,000 ordinary shares of £4 nominal value each are issued at par. Column (*a*) shows the Balance Sheet before the issue, and column (*b*) shows the Balance Sheet after the issue has taken place.

A Ltd Balance Sheets (Solution 1) as at 31 December 19-5

	(*a*) £	(*b*) £
Fixed Current Assets (other than bank)	9,000	9,000
Bank	1,000	5,000
	10,000	14,000
Financed by:		
Ordinary Share Capital	4,000	8,000
Profit and Loss	6,000	6,000
	10,000	14,000

Now the effect of what has happened can be appreciated. Before the new issue there were 1,000 shares. As there were £10,000 of assets and no liabilities, then each share was worth £10. After the issue there are 2,000 shares and £14,000 of assets, so that now each share is worth £7. This would be extremely disconcerting to the original shareholders who see the value of each of their shares fall immediately by £3. On the other hand, the new shareholder who has just bought shares for £4 each sees them rise immediately to be worth £7 each. Only in one specific case would this be just, and that is where each original shareholder buys an equivalent number of new shares. Otherwise this obviously cannot be the correct solution. What is required is a price which is equitable as far as the interests of the old shareholders are concerned, and yet will attract sufficient applications to provide the capital required. As in this case the Balance Sheet value and the real value are the same, the answer is that each old share was worth £10 and therefore each new share should be issued for £10 each. The Balance Sheets will now appear:

A Ltd Balance Sheets (Solution 2) as at 31 December 19-5

	(*a*) £	(*b*) £
Fixed and Current Assets (other than bank)	9,000	9,000
Bank	1,000	11,000
	10,000	20,000
Financed by:		
Ordinary Share Capital (at nominal value)	4,000	8,000
Share Premium (see note below)		6,000
Profit and Loss	6,000	6,000
	10,000	20,000

Thus in (*a*) above 1,000 shares own between them £10,000 of assets = £10 each, while in (*b*) 2,000 shares are shown as owning £20,000 of assets = £10 each. Both the old and new shareholders are therefore satisfied with the bargain that has been made.

Note: The Share Premium shown on the Capital side of the Balance Sheet is needed, ignoring for a moment the legal requirements to be complied with in company Balance Sheets, simply because the Balance Sheet would not balance without it. If shares are stated at nominal value, but issued at another price, the actual amount received increases the bank balance, but the Share Capital shown is increased by a different figure. The Share Premium therefore represents the excess of the cash received over the nominal value of the shares issued.

The other, B Ltd, has not fared so well. It has, in fact, lost money. The accumulated losses are reflected in a debit balance on the Profit and Loss Appropriation Account as shown in the following Balance Sheet (*c*). It can be seen that there are £3,000 of assets to represent the shareholders' stake in the firm of 1,000 shares, i.e. each share is worth £3 each. If more capital was needed 1,000 more shares could be issued. From the action taken in the previous case it will now be obvious that each new share of £4 nominal value will be issued for its real value of £3 each. The Balance Sheets will appear:

B Ltd Balance Sheets (correct solution) as at 31 December 19-5

	(c)	(d)
	£	£
Fixed and Current Assets (other than bank)	2,000	2,000
Bank	1,000	4,000
Discounts on Shares (see note below)		1,000
Profit and Loss – Debit balance	1,000	1,000
	4,000	8,000
Ordinary Share Capital	4,000	8,000

Once again, as the share capital is shown at nominal value, but the shares issued at a different figure, the difference being Discounts on Shares must be shown in order that the Balance Sheet may balance. It is, of course, not actually an asset, it is merely a balancing figure needed because the entries already made for an increase in the Ordinary Share Capital and the increase in the bank balance have been at different figures. The figure for Discounts on Shares therefore rectifies the double entry 'error'.

Although shares cannot now be issued at a discount, there will very occasionally still be items in company balance sheets for discounts on shares issued before 1980. Although not listed as an item in the balance sheet formats per the 1985 Companies Act, a separate heading will have to be inserted to accommodate the item.

For the purpose of making the foregoing explanations easier it was assumed that Balance Sheet values and other values were the same. This is very rarely true for all the assets, and in fact there is more than one other 'value'. A Balance Sheet is a historical view of the past based on records made according to the firm's interpretation and use of accounting concepts and conventions. When shares are being issued it is not the historical view of the past that is important, but the view of the future. Therefore the actual premiums and discounts on shares being issued is not merely a matter of Balance Sheet values, but on the issuing company's view of the future and its estimate of how the investing public will react to the price at which the shares are being offered.

It is to be noted that there are no restrictions on issuing shares at par or at a premium.

The actual double entry accounts can now be seen.

Shares payable in full on application

The issue of shares in illustrations (i), (ii) and (iii) which follow are based on the Balance Sheets that have just been considered.

(i) Shares issued at par

1,000 ordinary shares with a nominal value of £4 each are to be issued. Applications, together with the necessary money, are received for exactly 1,000 shares. The shares are then allotted to the applicants.

Bank

		£
Ordinary Share Applicants	A	4,000

Ordinary Share Applicants

		£			£
Ordinary Share Capital	B	4,000	Bank	A	4,000

Ordinary Share Capital

		£
Ordinary Share Applicants	B	4,000

It may appear that the Ordinary Share Applicants Account is unnecessary, and that the only entries needed are a debit in the Bank Account and a credit in the Ordinary Share Capital Account. However, applicants do not always become shareholders; this is shown later. The applicant must make an offer for the shares being issued, accompanied by the necessary money, this is the application. After the applications have been vetted the allotments of shares are made by the company. This represents the acceptance of the offer by the company and it is at this point that the applicant becomes a shareholder. Therefore A represents the offer by the applicant, while B is the acceptance by the company. No entry must therefore be made in the Share Capital Account until B happens, for it is not until that point that the share capital is in fact in existence. The Share Applicants Account is therefore an intermediary account pending allotments being made.

(ii) Shares issued at a premium

1,000 Ordinary Shares with a nominal value of £4 each are to be issued for £10 each (see A Ltd previously). Thus a premium of £6 per share has been charged. Applications and the money are received for exactly 1,000 shares.

Bank

		£		
Balance b/fwd		1,000		
Ordinary Share Applicants		10,000		

Ordinary Share Applicants

		£		£
Ordinary Share Capital	A	4,000	Bank	10,000
Share Premium	B	6,000		
		10,000		10,000

Share Premium

		£
Ordinary Share Applicants	B	6,000

Ordinary Share Capital (A Ltd)

		£
Balance b/fwd		4,000
Ordinary Share Applicants	A	4,000

Note: A is shown as £4,000 because the share capital is shown at nominal value and not as total issued value. B The £6,000 share premiums must therefore be credited to a Share Premium Account to preserve double entry balancing.

(iii) Shares issued at a discount (prior to 1980)

1,000 Ordinary Shares with a nominal value of £4 each are to be issued for £3 each (see B Ltd previously). Thus a discount of £1 per share is being allowed. Applications and the money are received for exactly 1,000 shares.

Bank

	£
Balance b/fwd	1,000
Ordinary Share Applicants	3,000

Ordinary Share Applicants

	£		£
Ordinary Share Capital	4,000	Bank	3,000
		Discounts on Shares	1,000
	4,000		4,000

Ordinary Share Capital

	£
Balance b/fwd	4,000
Ordinary Share Capital	4,000

	£
Ordinary Share Applications	1,000

(iv) Oversubscription and undersubscription for shares

When a public company invites investors to apply for its shares it is obviously very rare indeed if in fact that applications for shares equal exactly the number of shares to be issued. Where more shares are applied for than are available for issue, then the issue is said to be 'oversubscribed'. Where fewer shares are applied for than are available for issue, then the issue has been 'undersubscribed'.

With a brand-new company a minimum amount is fixed as being necessary to carry on any further with the running of the company. If the applications are less than the minimum stated, then the application monies must be returned to the senders. This does not apply to an established company. If therefore 1,000 shares of £1 each are available for issue, but only 875 shares are applied for, then only 875 will be issued, assuming that this is above the fixed minimum figure. The accounting entries will be in respect of 875 shares, no entries being needed for the 125 shares not applied for, as this part does not represent a transaction.

The opposite of this is where the shares are oversubscribed. In this case some sort of rationing is applied so that the issue is restricted to the shares available for issue. The process of selecting who will get how many shares depends on the policy of the firm. Some firms favour large shareholders because this leads to lower administrative costs. Why the costs will be lower will be obvious if the cost of calling a meeting of two companies each with 20,000 shares is considered. H Ltd has 20 shareholders with an average holding of 1,000 shares each. J Ltd has 1,000 shareholders with an average holding of 20 shares each. They all have to be notified by post and given various documents including a set of the final accounts. The cost of printing and sending these is less for H Ltd with 20 shareholders than for J Ltd with 1,000 shareholders. This is only one example of the costs involved, but it will also apply with equal force to many items connected with the shares. Conversely, the directors may prefer to have more shareholders with smaller holdings, one reason being that it decreases the amount of voting power in any one individual's hands. The actual process of rationing the shares is then a simple matter once a policy has been agreed. It may consist of scaling down applications, of drawing lots or some other chance selection, but it will eventually bring the number of shares to be issued down to the number of shares available. Excess application monies will then be refunded by the company.

An issue of shares where 1,000 ordinary shares of £1 nominal value each are to be issued at par payable in full, but 1,550 shares are applied for, will appear as follows:

Bank

	£		£
Ordinary Share Applicants	1,550	Ordinary Share Applicants (refunds)	550

Ordinary Share Applicants

	£		£
Bank	550	Bank	1,550
Ordinary Share Capital	1,000		
	1,550		1,550

Ordinary Share Capital

		£
	Ordinary Share Applicants	1,000

Issue of shares payable by instalments

The shares considered so far have all been issued as paid in full on application. Conversely, many issues are made which require payment by instalments. These are probably more common with public companies than with private companies. It should be noted that a public company is now not allowed to allot a share unless there has been paid on it a sum equal to at least one-quarter of its nominal value plus the whole of any premium.

The various stages, after the initial invitation has been made to the public to buy shares by means of advertisements (if it is a public company), etc., are as follows:

A   Applications are received together with the application monies.
B   The applications are vetted and the shares allotted, letters of allotment being sent out.
C   The excess application monies from wholly unsuccessful, or where the application monies received exceed both the application and allotment monies required, and partly unsuccessful applicants, are returned to them. Usually, if a person has been partly unsuccessful, his excess application monies are held by the company and will reduce the amount needed to be paid by him on allotment.
D   Allotment monies are received.
E   The next instalment, known as the first call, is requested.
F   The monies are received from the first call.
G   The next instalment, known as the second call, is requested.
H   The monies are received from the second call.

This carries on until the full number of calls have been made, although there is not usually a large number of calls to be made in an issue.

The reasons for the payments by instalments becomes obvious if it is realised that a company will not necessarily require the immediate use of all the money to be raised by the issue. Suppose a new company is to be formed, it is to buy land, erect a factory, equip it with machinery and then go into production. This might take two years altogether. If the total sum needed was £1,000,000, the allocation of this money could be:

	£
Cost of land, payable within 1 month	300,000
Cost of buildings, payable in 1 year's time	200,000
Cost of machinery, payable in 18 months' time	200,000
Working capital required in 2 years' time	300,000
	1,000,000

The issue may therefore well be on the following terms:

	Per cent
Application money per share, payable immediately	10
Allotment money per share, payable within 1 month	20
First call, money payable in 12 months' time	20
Second call, money payable in 18 months' time	20
Third call, money payable in 24 months' time	30
	100

The entries made in the Share Capital Account should equal the amount of money requested to that point in time. However, instead of one Share Applicants Account, this is usually split into several accounts to represent the different instalments. For this purpose application and allotment are usually joined together in one account, the Application and Allotment Account, as this cuts out the need for transfers where excess application monies are held over and set off against allotment monies needed. When allotment is made, and not until then, an entry of £300,000 (10 per cent + 20 per cent) would be made in the Share Capital Account. On the first call an entry of £200,000 would be made in the Share Capital Account, likewise £200,000 on the second call and £300,000 on the third call. The Share Capital Account will therefore contain not the monies received, but the amount of money requested. Exhibit 10.1 now shows an instance of a share issue.

Exhibit 10.1

A company is issuing 1,000 7 per cent Preference Shares of £1 each, payable 10 per cent on application, 20 per cent on allotment, 40 per cent on the first call and 30 per cent on the second call. Applications are received for 1,550 shares. A refund of the money is made in respect of 50 shares, while for the remaining 1,500 applied for, an allotment is to be made on the basis of 2 shares for every 3 applied for (assume that this will not involve any fractions of shares). The excess application monies are set off against the allotment monies asked for. The remaining requested instalments are all paid in full. The letters by the side of each entry refer to the various stages outlined earlier.

Bank

		£			£
Application and Allotment:			Application and		
Application monies	A	155	Allotment refund	C	5
Allotment monies					
(£1,000 × 20% *less* excess					
application monies £50)	B	150			
First call	F	400			
Second call	H	300			

Application and Allotment

		£			£
Bank – refund of			Bank	A	155
application monies	C	5	Bank	B	150
Preference Share Capital	B	300			
		305			305

First Call

		£			£
Preference Share Capital	E	400	Bank	F	400

Second Call

		£			£
Preference Share Capital	G	300	Bank	H	300

7 per cent Preference Share Capital

		£			£
			Application and Allotment	B	300
			First Call	E	400
Balance c/d		1,000	Second call	G	300
		1,000			1,000
			Balance b/d		1,000

If more than one type of share is being issued at the same time, e.g. preference shares and ordinary shares, then separate Share Capital Accounts and separate Application and Allotment Accounts and Call Accounts should be opened.

Forfeited shares

Sometimes, although it is probably fairly rare in recent times, a shareholder fails to pay the calls requested from him. The Articles of Association of the company will probably provide that the shareholder will have his shares forfeited, provided that certain safeguards for his protection are fully observed. In this case the shares will be cancelled, and the instalments already paid by the shareholder will be lost to him.

After the forfeiture, the company may reissue the shares, unless there is a provision in the Articles of Association to prevent it. There are certain conditions as to the prices at which the shares can be reissued. These are that the amount received on reissue plus the amount received from the original shareholder should at least equal (*a*) the called-up value where the shares are not fully called up, or (*b*) the nominal value where the full amount has been called up. Any premium previously paid is disregarded in determining the minimum reissue price.

Exhibit 10.2

Take the same information as that contained in Exhibit 10.1, but instead of all the calls being paid, Allen, the holder of 100 shares, fails to pay the first and second calls. He had already paid the application and allotment monies on the required dates. The directors conform to the provisions of the Articles of Association and (A) Allen is forced to suffer the forfeiture of his shares. (B) The amount still outstanding from Allen will be written off. (C) The directors then reissue the shares at 75 per cent of nominal value to J Dougan. (D) Dougan pays for the shares.

First Call

		£			£
Preference Share Capital		400	Bank		360
			Forfeited Shares	(B)	40
		400			400

Second Call

		£			£
Preference Share Capital		300	Bank		270
			Forfeited Shares	(B)	30
		300			300

7 per cent Preference Share Capital

		£			£
Forfeited Shares	(A)	100	Application and Allotment		300
Balance c/d		900	First Call		400
			Second Call		300
		1,000			1,000
			Balance b/d		900
Balance c/d		1,000	J Dougan	(C)	100
		1,000			1,000
			Balance b/d		1,000

		£			£
First Call	(B)	40	Preference Share Capital	(A)	100
Second Call	(B)	30			
Balance c/d		30			
		100			100
J Dougan (see following note)		25	Balance c/d		30
Balance c/d		5			
		30			30

Bank

		£
First Call (£900 × 40%)		360
Second Call (£900 × 30%)		270
J Dougan	(D)	75

J Dougan

	£			£
Preference Share Capital	100	Bank	(D)	75
		Forfeited Shares (discount on reissue) see following note		25
	100			100

The transfer of £25 from Forfeited Shares Account to J Dougan's Account is needed because the reissue was entered in Preference Share Capital Account and Dougan's Account at nominal value, i.e. following standard practice of a Share Capital Account being concerned with nominal values, but Dougan was not to pay the full nominal price. Therefore the transfer of £25 is needed to close his account.

The balance of £5 on the Forfeited Shares Account can be seen to be: Cash Received from original shareholder on application and allotment £30 + from Dougan £75 = £105. This is £5 over the nominal value so that the £5 appears as a credit balance. This is usually stated to be either transferred to a Profit on Reissue of Forfeited Shares Account, but it really cannot be thought that this is followed in practice for small amounts. More normally it would be transferred to the credit of a Share Premium Account.

Calls in advance and in arrear and the balance sheet

At the Balance Sheet date some shareholders will not have paid all the calls made, these are collectively known as **calls in arrear**. On the other hand, some shareholders may have paid amounts in respect of calls not made by the Balance Sheet date. These are **calls in advance**.

Calls in arrear, i.e. 'Called up share capital not paid' is to be shown in the balance sheet in one of the positions shown in the format per the 1985 Companies Act, *see*

Chapter 17. There is no specified place for calls in advance, so this will be inserted in the balance sheet as an extra heading.

Rights issues

The costs of making a new issue of shares can be quite high. A way to reduce the costs of raising new long-term capital in the form of issuing shares may be by way of a rights issue. To do this the company circularises the existing shareholders, and informs them of the new issue to be made and the number of shares which each one of them is entitled to buy of the new issue. In most cases the shareholder is allowed to renounce his rights to the new shares in favour of someone else. The issue is usually pitched at a price which will make the rights capable of being sold, i.e. if the existing shareholder does not want the shares he can renounce them to A who will give him £x for the right to apply for the shares in his place, a right that A could not otherwise obtain. If any shareholder does not either buy the shares or transfer his rights, then the directors will usually have the power to dispose of such shares not taken up by issuing them in some other way.

Debentures

A debenture is a bond, acknowledging a loan to a company, usually under the company's seal, which bears a fixed rate of interest. Unlike shares, which normally depend on profits out of which to appropriate dividends, debenture interest is payable whether profits are made or not.

A debenture may be redeemable, i.e. repayable at or by a specified date. Conversely they may be irredeemable, redemption only taking place when the company is eventually liquidated, or in a case such as when the debenture interest is not paid within a given time limit.

People lending money to companies in the form of debentures will obviously be interested in how safe their investment will be. Some debentures are given the legal right that on certain happenings the debenture holders will be able to take control of specific assets, or of the whole of the assets. They can then sell the assets and recoup the amount due under their debentures, or deal with the assets in ways specified in the deed under which the debentures were issued. Such debentures are known as being secured against the assets, the term **mortgage** debenture often being used. Other debentures have no prior right to control the assets under any circumstances. These are known as **simple** or **naked** debentures.

The issue of debentures

The entries for the issue of debentures are similar to those for shares. It would, however, certainly not be the normal modern practice to issue debentures at a premium. If the word 'debentures' appears instead of 'share capital', then the entries in the accounts would be identical.

Shares of no par value

It can be seen that the idea of a fixed par value for a share can be very misleading. For anyone who has not studied accounting, it may well come as a shock to them to find that a share with a par value of £1 might in fact be issued for £5. If the share is dealt in on the Stock Exchange he might find a £1 share selling at £10 or even £20, or equally well may sell for only 10p.

Another disadvantage of a par value is that it can give people entirely the wrong impression of the activities of a business. If a par value is kept to, and the dividend based on that, then with a certain degree of inflation the dividend figure can look excessive. Many trade union leaders would howl with disapproval if a dividend of 100 per cent was declared by a company. But is this so excessive? Exhibit 10.3 gives a rather different picture.

Exhibit 10.3

Allen buys a share 40 years ago for £1. He is satisfied with a return of 5 per cent on his money. With a 5 per cent dividend he could buy a certain amount of goods which will be called x. Forty years later to buy that same amount of goods, x, he would need, say, 20 times as much money. Previously £5 would have bought x, now it would take £100. To keep his dividend at the same level of purchasing power he would need a dividend now of 100 per cent, as compared with the 5 per cent he was receiving 40 years ago.

In the United States of America, Canada and Belgium as well as other countries, no par value is attached to shares being issued. A share is issued at whatever price is suitable at the time, and the money received is credited to a Share Capital Account.

Review questions

10.1 The authorised and issued share capital of Cosy Fires Ltd was £75,000 divided into 75,000 ordinary shares of £1 each, fully paid. On 2 January 19-7, the authorised capital was increased by a further 85,000 ordinary shares of £1 each to £160,000. On the same date 40,000 ordinary shares of £1 each were offered to the public at £1.25 per share payable as to £0.60 on application (including the premium), £0.35 on allotment and £0.30 on 6 April 19-7.

The lists were closed on 10 January 19-7, and by that date applications for 65,000 shares had been received. Applications for 5,000 shares received no allotment and the cash paid in respect of such shares was returned. All shares were then allocated to the remaining applicants pro rata to their original applications, the balance of the monies received on applications being applied to the amounts due on allotment.

The balances due on allotment were received on 31 January 19-7, with the exception of one allottee of 500 shares and these were declared forfeited on 4 April 19-7. These shares were re-issued as fully paid on 2 May 19-7, at £1.10 per share. The call due on 6 April 19-7 was duly paid by the other shareholders.

You are required:

(*a*) To record the above-mentioned transactions in the appropriate ledger accounts, and

(*b*) To show how the balances on such accounts should appear in the company's Balance Sheet as on 31 May 19-7.

(*Chartered Association of Certified Accountants*)

10.2A During the year to 30 September 19-7, Kammer plc made a new offer of shares. The details of the offer were as follows:

1   100,000 ordinary shares of £1 each were issued payable in instalments as follows:

	Per Share
	£
On application at 1 November 19-6	0.65
On allotment (including the share premium of £0.50 per share) on 1 December 19-6	0.55
On first and final call on 1 June 19-7	0.30
	£1.50

121

2   Applications for 200,000 shares were received, and it was decided to deal with them as follows:

(*a*) to return cheques for 75,000 shares;

(*b*) to accept in full applications for 25,000 shares; and

(*c*) to allot the remaining shares on the basis of three shares for every four shares applied for.

3   On the first and final call, one applicant who had been allotted 5,000 shares, failed to pay the due amount, and his shares were duly declared forfeited. They were then re-issued to Amber Ltd on 1 September 19-7 at a price of £0.80 per share fully paid.

Note: Kammer's issued share capital on 1 October 19-6 consisted of 500,000 ordinary shares of £1 each.

Required:

Record the above transactions in the following ledger accounts:

(*a*) ordinary share capital;

(*b*) share premium;

(*c*) application and allotment;

(*d*) first and final call;

(*e*) forfeited shares; and

(*f*) Amber Ltd's account.

(*Association of Accounting Technicians*)

10.3 M Limited has an authorised share capital of £1,500,000 divided into 1,500,000 ordinary shares of £1 each. The issued share capital at 31 March 19-7 was £500,000 which was fully paid, and had been issued at par. On 1 April 19-7, the directors, in accordance with the company's Articles, decided to increase the share capital of the company by offering a further 500,000 ordinary shares of £1 each at a price of £1.60 per share, payable as follows:

on application, including the premium	£0.85 per share
on allotment	£0.25 per share
on first and final call on 3 August 19-7	£0.50 per share

On 13 April 19-7, applications had been received for 750,000 shares and it was decided to allot the shares to applicants for 625,000 shares, on the basis of four shares for every five shares for which applications had been received. The balance of the money received on application was to be applied to the amounts due on allotment. The shares were allotted on 1 May 19-7, the unsuccessful applicants being repaid their cash on this date. The balance of the allotment money was received in full by 15 May 19-7.

With the exception of one member who failed to pay the call on the 5,000 shares allotted to him, the remainder of the call was paid in full within two weeks of the call being made.

The directors resolved to forfeit these shares on 1 September 19-7, after giving the required notice. The forfeited shares were re-issued on 30 September 19-7 to another member at £0.90 per share.

You are required to write up the ledger accounts necessary to record these transactions in the books of M Limited.

(*Chartered Institute of Management Accountants*)

10.4A Applications were invited by the directors of Grobigg Ltd for 150,000 of its £1 ordinary shares at £1.15 per share payable as follows:

	Per share
On application on 1 April 19-8	£0.75
On allotment on 30 April 19-8 (including the premium of £0.15 per share)	£0.20
On first and final call on 31 May 19-8	£0.20

Applications were received for 180,000 shares and it was decided to deal with these as follows:

1   To refuse allotment to applicants for 8,000 shares.
2   To give full allotment to applicants for 22,000 shares.
3   To allot the remainder of the available shares pro rata among the other applicants.
4   To utilise the surplus received on applications in part payment of amounts due on allotment.

An applicant, to whom 400 shares had been allotted, failed to pay the amount due on the first and final call and his shares were declared forfeit on 31 July 19-8. These shares were re-issued on 3 September 19-8 as fully paid at £0.90 per share.

Show how the transactions would be recorded in the company's books.

(Chartered Association of Certified Accountants)

11

Companies purchasing and redeeming own shares and debentures

Purchasing and redeeming own shares

To a student the words 'purchasing' and 'redeeming' may appear to be exactly the same as far as this chapter is concerned. To all intents and purposes it is the same, for it involves an outflow of cash by the company to get back its own shares and then cancel them. However, from a rather more legal and precise point of view, 'redeeming' means the buying back of shares which were originally issued as being 'redeemable' in that the company stated when they were issued that they would be, or could be, redeemed (i.e. bought back by the company). The terms of the 'redemption' (buying back) would be stated at the time when the shares were issued. However, when shares are issued and are not stated to be 'redeemable' then, when they are bought back by the company it is then said to be the 'purchase' of its shares by the company.

Until 1981 a company in the United Kingdom could not in normal circumstances 'purchase' its own shares. In addition 'redemption' was limited to one type of share, these were 'redeemable preference shares'. This had not been the case in the United States and Europe for many years where companies had, with certain restrictions, been allowed to buy back their own shares. The basic reason why this was not allowed in the UK was the fear that the interests of creditors could be adversely affected if the company used its available cash to buy its own shares, thus leaving less to satisfy the claims of the creditors. The possibilities of abuse with preference shares was considered to be less than with ordinary shares, thus the ability to be able to have redeemable preference shares.

Now, under the Companies Act 1985, a company may, if it is authorised to do so by its articles of association:

(a) Issue redeemable shares of any class (preference, ordinary etc). Redeemable shares include those that are to be redeemed on a particular date as well as those that are merely liable to be redeemed at the discretion of the shareholder or of the company. (Section 45.)

There is an important proviso that a company can only issue redeemable shares if it has in issue shares that are *not* redeemable. Without this restriction a company could issue only redeemable shares, then later redeem all of its shares, and thus finish up without any shareholders.

(b) 'Purchase' its own shares (i.e. shares that were not issued as being redeemable shares). Again there is a proviso that the company must, *after* the purchase, have other shares in issue at least some of which are not redeemable. This again is to stop the company redeeming its whole share capital and thus ceasing to have members. The company must have, after the purchase, at least two members.

Advantages of purchase and redemption of shares

Certainly there are quite a few possible advantages of a company being able to buy back its own shares. These are strongest in the case of private companies. For public companies the main advantage is that those with surplus cash resources could find it useful to be able to return some of this surplus cash back to its shareholders by buying back some of its own shares, rather than have pressure put on them to use such cash in uneconomic ways.

For private companies the main possible advantages would appear to be overcoming snags which occur when a shareholder cannot sell his shares on the 'open market', i.e. a stock exchange. This means that:

(*a*) It will help shareholders who have difficulties in selling their shares to another individual to be able to realise their value when needed, for any reason.

(*b*) People will be more willing to buy shares from private companies. The fear of not being able to dispose of them, previously led to finance being relatively difficult for private companies to obtain from people outside the original main proprietors of the company.

(*c*) In many 'family' companies cash is needed to pay for taxes on the death of the shareholder.

(*d*) Shareholders with grievances against the company can be bought out, thus contributing to the more efficient management of the company.

(*e*) Family owned companies will be helped in their desire to keep control of the company when a family shareholder with a large number of shares dies or retires.

(*f*) Similar to public companies, as described above, the company could return unwanted cash resources back to its shareholders.

(*g*) For both private companies, and for public companies whose shares are not listed on a stock exchange, it may help boost share schemes for employees, as the employees would know that they could fairly easily dispose of the shares instead of being stuck with them.

Accounting entries

The accounting entries for either 'purchase' or 'redemption' of shares are exactly the same, except that the word 'Redeemable' will appear as the first word in the title of the accounts for shares that are redeemable. The figures to be entered will naturally be affected by the **terms** under which shares are redeemed or purchased, but the actual type of **location** of the debits and credits to be made will be the same.

The reader will more easily understand the rather complicated entries needed if he understands the reasoning behind the Companies Act. The protection of the creditor was uppermost in the minds of Parliament. The general idea is that 'capital' should not be returned to the shareholders, except under certain circumstances. If 'capital' is returned to the shareholders, thus reducing the cash and bank balances, then the creditors could lose out badly if there was not then sufficient cash/bank balances to be able to pay their claims. Thus the shareholders, seeing that things were not progressing too well in the company, could get their money out possibly at the expense of the creditors.

There are dividends which can quite legitimately be paid to the shareholders out of distributable profits, but the idea is to stop the shareholders withdrawing their 'capital'. Included under the general heading of 'capital' for this purpose are those particular reserves which cannot be used up for the payment of cash dividends. There are special exceptions to this, namely the 'reduction' of capital by public companies (*see* Chapter

13) and the special powers of a private company to purchase or redeem its own shares out of capital (see later this chapter), but apart from these special cases the company law regulations are intended to ensure that 'capital' figures do not fall when shares are redeemed or purchased. This general purpose is behind the accounting entries which are now to be examined.

It is important to note that in *all* cases shares can only be redeemed or purchased when they are fully paid.

The safeguards for the protection of 'capital' contained in the Companies Act, Sections 159 and 160, may be summarised as follows:

(*a*) In respect of the **nominal** value of shares redeemed or purchased there must be either:

(*i*) A new issue of shares to provide the funds for redemption or purchase
or

(*ii*) Sufficient distributable profits must be available (i.e. a large enough credit balance on the Appropriation Account) which could be diverted from being used up as dividends to being treated as used up for the purpose of redeeming or purchasing the shares. Therefore, when shares are redeemed or purchased other than by out of the proceeds of a new issue, then, and only then, the amount of distributable profits treated as being used up by the nominal value or shares redeemed or purchased is debited to the Appropriation Account and credited to a Capital Redemption Reserve. (Before 1981 this was called a Capital Redemption Reserve Fund. The use of the word 'Fund' has now been dropped.) Thus the old Share Capital will equal the total of the new Share Capital *plus* the Capital Redemption Reserve. The Capital Redemption Reserve is a 'non-distributable' reserve. This means that it cannot be transferred back to the credit of the Appropriation Account, and so increase the profits available for distribution as cash dividends. The process of diverting profits from being usable for dividends means that the non-payment of the dividends leaves more cash in the firm against which creditors could claim if necessary.

In all the examples which follow, the shares being redeemed/purchased could either be redeemable shares or those not specifically stated to be redeemable. Obviously, in a real company, the titles of the accounts would state which shares were redeemable.

To get the reader used to journal entries, and then seeing the effect on the face of the balance sheet, journal style entries will be shown first, followed by the balances for the balance sheet.

Exhibit 11.1

£2,000 Preference Shares are redeemed/purchased at par, a new issue of £2,000 Ordinary Shares at par being made for the purpose.

		Dr £	Cr £
(A1)	Bank	2,000	
(A2)	Ordinary Share Applicants		2,000
	Cash received from applicants		
(B1)	Ordinary Share Applicants	2,000	
(B2)	Ordinary Share Capital		2,000
	Ordinary Shares allotted		
(C1)	Preference Share Capital	2,000	
(C2)	Preference Share Purchase*		2,000
	Shares to be redeemed/purchased		
(D1)	Preference Share Purchase*	2,000	
(D2)	Bank		2,000
	Payment made to redeem/purchase shares		

Note: In all the examples which follow, the shares being purchased/redeemed are preference shares. In fact they could be any type of share, ordinary, preference, preferred ordinary, etc. Secondly, the shares to be redeemed/purchased are transferred to a Preference Share Purchase account. In fact if they were being redeemed it would be a Preference Share Redemption Account. It will make it easier to follow if the answers are standardised.

	Balances Before £		Effect Dr £		Cr £	Balances After £
Net Assets (except Bank)	7,500					7,500
Bank	2,500	(A1)	2,000	(D2)	2,000	2,500
	10,000					10,000
Ordinary Share Capital	5,000			(B2)	2,000	7,000
Ordinary Share Applicants	–	(B1)	2,000	(A2)	2,000	–
Preference Share Capital	2,000	(C1)	2,000			–
Preference Share Purchase	–	(D1)	2,000	(C2)	2,000	–
	7,000*					7,000*
Profit & Loss	3,000					3,000
	10,000					10,000

*Notice: total 'capitals' remain the same.

127

Exhibit 11.2

£2,000 Preference Shares redeemed/purchased at par, with no new issue of shares to provide funds for the purpose. Therefore an amount equal to the nominal value of the shares redeemed *must* be transferred from the Profit & Loss Appropriation Account to the credit of a Capital Redemption Reserve. (Until 1981 the title of this account was the Capital Redemption Reserve Fund. The use of the word 'Fund' here has now ceased.)

	Dr £	Cr £
(A1) Preference Share Capital	2,000	
(A2) Preference Share Purchase		2,000
Shares to be redeemed/purchased		
(B1) Preference Share Purchase	2,000	
(B2) Bank		2,000
Cash paid as purchase/redemption		
(C1) Profit & Loss Appropriation	2,000	
(C2) Capital Redemption Reserve		2,000
Transfer per Companies Act 1985, Section 45		

	Balances Before		Effect			Balances After
			Dr		Cr	
	£		£		£	£
Net Assets (except bank)	7,500					7,500
Bank	2,500			(B2)	2,000	500
	10,000					8,000
Ordinary Share Capital	5,000					5,000
Preference Share Capital	2,000	(A1)	2,000			–
Preference Share Purchase	–	(B1)	2,000	(A2)	2,000	–
Capital Redemption Reserve	–			(C2)	2,000	2,000
	7,000*					7,000*
Profit & Loss	3,000	(C1)	2,000			1,000
	10,000					8,000

*Notice: total 'capitals' (share capital + non-distributable reserves) remain the same at £7,000.

Exhibit 11.3

£2,000 Preference Shares redeemed/purchased at par, being £1,200 from issue of Ordinary Shares at par and partly by using Appropriation Account balance.

	Dr £	Cr £
(A1) Bank	1,200	
(A2) Ordinary Share Applicants		1,200
Cash received from applicants		
(B1) Ordinary Share Applicants	1,200	
(B2) Ordinary Share Capital		1,200
Ordinary Shares allotted		
(C1) Profit & Loss Appropriation	800	
(C2) Capital Redemption Reserve		800
Part of redemption/purchase not covered by new issue, to comply with Companies Act 1985		
(D1) Preference Share Capital	2,000	
(D2) Preference Share Purchase		2,000
Shares being redeemed/purchased		
(E1) Preference Share Purchase	2,000	
(E2) Bank		2,000
Payment made for redemption/purchase		

	Balances Before £		Effect Dr £		Cr £	Balances After £
Net Assets (except bank)	7,500					7,500
Bank	2,500	(A1)	1,200	(E2)	2,000	1,700
	10,000					9,200
Ordinary Share Capital	5,000			(B2)	1,200	6,200
Ordinary Share Applicants	–	(B1)	1,200	(A2)	1,200	–
Preference Share Capital	2,000	(D1)	2,000			–
Preference Share Purchase	–	(E1)	2,000	(D2)	2,000	–
Capital Redemption Reserve	–			(C2)	800	800
	7,000*					7,000*
Profit & Loss	3,000	(C1)	800			2,200
	10,000					9,200

*Notice: total 'capitals' remain the same.

(*b*) The next requirement under Section 160, Companies Act 1985, when shares are being redeemed/purchased at a premium, but they were *not* originally issued at a premium, then an amount equal to the premium *must* be transferred from the Appropriation Account to the credit of the Share Purchase/Redemption Account. This again is to divert profits away from being distributable to being part of 'capital'.

Exhibit 11.4

£2,000 Preference Shares which were originally issued at par are redeemed/purchased at a premium of 20 per cent. There is no new issue of shares for the purpose. In this example the Ordinary Shares had been originally issued at a premium, thus the reason for the Share Premium Account being in existence. However it is *not* the Ordinary Shares which are being redeemed and therefore the Share Premium *cannot* be used for the premium on redemption/purchase of the preference shares.

	Dr £	Cr £
(A1) Preference Share Capital	2,000	
(A2) Preference Share Purchase		2,000
Shares being redeemed/purchased		
(B1) Profit & Loss Appropriation	400	
(B2) Preference Share Purchase		400
Premium on purchase/redemption of shares *not* previously issued at premium		
(C1) Profit & Loss Appropriation	2,000	
(C2) Capital Redemption Reserve		2,000
Transfer because shares redeemed/purchased out of distributable profits		
(D1) Preference Share Purchase	2,400	
(D2) Bank		2,400
Payment on purchase/redemption		

	Balances Before £		Dr £		Cr £	Balances After £
Net Assets (except bank)	7,500					7,500
Bank	2,500			(D2)	2,400	100
	10,000					7,600
Ordinary Share Capital	4,500					4,500
Preference Share Capital	2,000	(A1)	2,000			–
Preference Share Purchase	–	(D1)	2,400	(A2)	2,000	–
				(B2)	400	
Capital Redemption Reserve	–			(C2)	2,000	2,000
Share Premium	500					500
	7,000*					7,000*
		(C1)	2,000			
Profit & Loss	3,000	(B1)	400			600
	10,000					7,600

*Notice: Total 'Capitals' remain the same.

130

(*c*) Under Section 160, para 2, Companies Act 1985. When shares are being redeemed or purchased at a premium,

and

they were originally issued at a premium,

and

a new issue of shares is being made for the purpose, then the Share Premium Account *can* have an amount calculated as follows transferred to the credit of the Share Purchase/Redemption Account. This is shown as (E).

Share Premium Account

		£
Balance before new issue	(A)	xxx
Add Premium on new issue	(B)	xxx
Balance after new issue	(C)	xxx
Amount that *may* be transferred	(E)	
is lesser of:		
Premiums that were received when it first issued the shares now being redeemed/purchased (D)		xxx
or		
Balance after new issue (C) above		xxx
Transfer to Share Purchase/Redemption	(E)	xxx
New Balance for Balance Sheet (could be nil)		xxx

Where the amount being deducted (E) is *less* than the premium paid on the *current* redemption or purchase, then an amount equivalent to the difference must be transferred from the debit of the Appropriation Account to the credit of the Share Purchase/Redemption Account. (An instance of this is shown in Exhibit 11.5.) This again diverts profits away from being distributable.

Exhibit 11.5

£2,000 Preference Shares originally issued at premium of 20 per cent now being purchased/redeemed at a premium of 25 per cent. The position can be shown in three different companies if for the purpose of purchase/redemption:

Company 1 issues 2,400 Ordinary £1 shares at par
Company 2 issues 2,000 Ordinary £1 shares at 20 per cent premium
Company 3 issues 1,600 Ordinary £1 shares at 50 per cent premium.

		Company 1 £	Company 2 £	Company 3 £
Balance before new issue	(A)	150*1	400	400
Premium on new issue			400	800 (B)
Balance after new issue	(C)	150	800	1,200
Amount transferable to Share Purchase/ Redemption is therefore lower of (C) or original premium on issue (£400)		150*2	400*2	400*2
New balance for balance sheet		–	400	800

*1 In Company 1 it is assumed that of the original £400 premium the sum of £250 had been used up to issue bonus shares (see Chapter 14 later).

*2 As these figures are less than the premium of £500 *now* being paid, the differences (Company 1 £350: Companies 2 and 3 £100 each) must be transferred from the debit of the Appropriation Account to the credit of the Preference Share/Purchase Redemption Account.

Journal Entries:	Company 1 Dr £	Company 1 Cr £	Company 2 Dr £	Company 2 Cr £	Company 3 Dr £	Company 3 Cr £
(A1) Bank	2,400		2,400		2,400	
(A2) Ordinary Share Applicants		2,400		2,400		2,400
Cash Received from Applicants						
(B1) Ordinary Share Applicants	2,400		2,400		2,400	
(B2) Ordinary Share Capital		2,400		2,000		1,600
(B3) Share Premium		–		400		800
Ordinary Shares Allotted						
(C1) Preference Share Capital	2,000		2,000		2,000	
(C2) Preference Share Purchase		2,000		2,000		2,000
Shares being redeemed/purchased						
(D1) Share Premium Account	150		400		400	
(D2) Preference Share Purchase		150		400		400
Amount of Share Premium Account used for redemption/ purchase						
(E1) Profit & Loss Appropriation	350		100		100	
(E2) Preference Share Purchase		350		100		100
Excess of premium payable over amount of share premium account usable for the purpose						
(F1) Preference Share Purchase	2,500		2,500		2,500	
(F2) Bank		2,500		2,500		2,500
Amount paid on redemption/ purchase						

Exhibit 11.6

The following balance sheet for the three companies of Exhibit 11.5 are given *before* the purchase/redemption. The balance sheets are then shown *after* purchase/redemption.

Balance Sheets (*before* redemption/purchase)

	Company 1 £	Company 2 £	Company 3 £
Net Assets (except bank)	7,500	7,500	7,500
Bank	2,500	2,500	2,500
	10,000	10,000	10,000
Ordinary Share Capital	4,850	4,600	4,600
Preference Share Capital	2,000	2,000	2,000
Share Premium	150	400	400
	7,000	7,000	7,000
Profit & Loss Account	3,000	3,000	3,000
	10,000	10,000	10,000

Balance Sheets (*after* redemption/purchase)

	Company 1 £	Company 2 £	Company 3 £
Net Assets (except bank)	7,500	7,500	7,500
Bank	2,400	2,400	2,400
	9,900	9,900	9,900
Ordinary Share Capital	7,250	6,600	6,200
Share Premium	–	400	800
	7,250	7,000	7,000
Profit & Loss Account	2,650	2,900	2,900
	9,900	9,900	9,900

Private companies: redemption or purchase of shares out of capital

The Companies Act 1981, section 54, introduced a *new* power for a *private* company to redeem/purchase its own shares where *either* it has insufficient distributable profits for the purpose *or* it cannot raise the amount required by a new issue. Previously it would have had to apply to the court for 'capital reduction' as per Chapter 14. The 1981 legislation made it far easier to achieve the same objectives, both in terms of time and expense. This is carried on in the 1985 Act.

A book on Company Law should be read for the detail of the various matters which must be dealt with. A very brief outline may be given as follows:

(*a*) The Company must be authorised to do so by its articles of association.

(*b*) Directors, to certify that, after the 'permissible capital payment', the company will be able to carry on as a going concern during the next twelve months, and be able to pay its debts immediately after the payment and also during the next twelve months.

(*c*) Auditors to make a satisfactory report.

(*d*) Permissible capital payment is the amount by which the price of redemption or purchase exceeds aggregate of (i) company's distributable profits and (ii) proceeds of any new issue. This means that a private company should use its available profits and any share proceeds before making a payment out of capital.

Permissible capital payments

(*a*) Where the 'permissible capital payment' is *less* than the nominal value of shares redeemed/purchased, the amount of the difference *shall* be transferred to the Capital Redemption Reserve from the Appropriation Account (or undistributed profits). Section 171, para (4), Companies Act 1985.

(*b*) Where the 'permissible capital payment' is *greater* than the nominal value of shares redeemed/purchased, *any* non-distributable reserves (e.g. share premium account, capital redemption reserve, revaluation reserve, etc) or fully paid share capital can be reduced by the excess, Section 171, para (5), Companies Act 1985.

This can best be illustrated by taking two companies R & S with similar account balances *before* the purchase/redemption, but redeeming on different terms:

Exhibit 11.7

	Before £		Dr £		Cr £	After £
Company R						
Net Assets (except bank)	2,500					2,500
Bank	7,500			(B2)	4,000	3,500
	10,000					6,000
Ordinary Shares	1,000					1,000
Preference Shares	4,000	(A1)	4,000			–
Non-Distributable Reserves	2,000					2,000
Capital Redemption Reserve				(C2)	3,000	3,000
Preference Share Purchase	–	(B1)	4,000	(A2)	4,000	
	7,000					
Profit & Loss	3,000	(C1)	3,000			
	10,000					6,000

Preference Shares redeemed at par £4,000. No new issue.

Therefore pay	£4,000
less Profit and Loss Account	£3,000
Permissible capital payment	£1,000
Nominal amount shares redeemed/purchased	£4,000
less Permissible capital payment	£1,000
Deficiency to transfer to Capital Redemption Reserve (C1 & C2)	£3,000

(A1) and (A2) represents transfer of shares redeemed/purchased

(B1) and (B2) represents payment to shareholders.

	Before		Dr		Cr	After
Company S	£		£		£	£
Net Assets (except bank)	2,500					2,500
Bank	7,500			(D2)	7,200	300
	10,000					2,800
Ordinary Share Capital	1,000					1,000
Preference Shares	4,000	(A1)	4,000			–
ſ Non-Distributable Reserves	2,000	(C1)	200			1,800
₹ Capital Redemption Reserve	–					–
Preference Share Purchase		(D1)	7,200	(A2)	4,000	
				(B2)	3,000	
				(C2)	200	
	7,000					2,800
Profit & Loss	3,000	(B1)	3,000			–
	10,000					2,800

Preference Shares redeemed/purchased at premium 80%. No new issue.

Therefore pay	£7,200
less Profit and Loss Account	£3,000
Permissible capital payment	£4,200
Permissible capital payment	£4,200
less Nominal amount redeemed/purchased	£4,000
Excess from *any* of non-distributable reserves (or capital) (C1 & C2)	£200

(A1) and (A2) represents shares redeemed/purchased

(B1) and (B2) is transfer to redemption/purchase account of part of source of funds

(D1) and (D2) is payment to shareholders.

Cancellation of shares purchased/redeemed

All shares purchased/redeemed must be cancelled immediately. They cannot be kept in hand by the company and traded in like any other commodity.

Redemption of debentures

Unless they are stated to be irredeemable, debentures are redeemed according to the terms of the issue. The necessary funds to finance the redemption may be from:

(*a*) An issue of shares or debentures for the purpose.

(*b*) The liquid resources of the company.

Resembling the redemption of redeemable preference shares, when the redemption is financed as in (*a*), no transfer of profits from the Profit and Loss Appropriation Account to a Reserve Account is needed. However, when financed as in

(b) it is good accounting practice, although not legally necessary, to divert profits from being used as dividends by transferring an amount equal to the nominal value redeemed from the debit of the Profit and Loss Appropriation Account to the credit of a Reserve Account.

Redemption may be effected:

1 By annual drawings out of profits.

2 By purchase in the open market when the price is favourable, i.e. less than the price which will have to be paid if the company waited until the last date by which redemption has to be carried out.

3 In a lump sum to be provided by the accumulation of a sinking fund.

These can now be examined in more detail.

Regular annual drawings out of profits

(a) When redeemed at a premium

In this case the source of the bank funds with which the premium is paid should be taken to be (a) Share Premium Account, or if this does not exist, or the premium is in excess of the balance on the account, then any part not covered by a Share Premium Account is deemed to come from (b) The Profit and Loss Appropriation Account. Exhibit 11.8 shows the effect on a Balance Sheet where there is no Share Premium Account, while Exhibit 11.9 illustrates the case when a Share Premium Account is in existence.

Exhibit 11.8

Starting with the Before Balance Sheet, £400 of the debentures are redeemed at a premium of 20 per cent.

Balance Sheets

	Before	+ or −	After
	£	£	£
Other Assets	12,900		12,900
Bank	3,400	−480(A)	2,920
	16,300		15,820
Share Capital	10,000		10,000
Debenture Redemption Reserve	−	+400(B)	400
Debentures	2,000	−400(A)	1,600
Profit and Loss	4,300	−400(B)	
		−80(A)	3,820
	16,300		15,820

Exhibit 11.9

Starting with the Before Balance Sheet, £400 of the debentures are redeemed at a premium of 20 per cent.

Balance Sheets

	Before	+ or −	After
	£	£	£
Other Assets	13,500		13,500
Bank	3,400	−480(A)	2,920
	16,900		16,420
Share Capital	10,000		10,000
Share Premium	600	−80(A)	520
Debenture Redemption Reserve	−	+400(B)	400
Debentures	2,000	−400(A)	1,600
Profit and Loss	4,300	−400(B)	3,900
	16,900		16,420

In both Exhibits 11.8 and 11.9 the Debenture Redemption Reserve Account is built up each year by the nominal value of the debentures redeemed each year. When the whole issue of debentures has been redeemed, then the balance on the Debenture Redemption Reserve Account should be transferred to the credit of a General Reserve Account. It is, after all, an accumulation of undistributed profits.

(b) Redeemed – originally issued at a discount

The discount originally given was in fact to attract investors to buy the debentures, and is therefore as much a cost of borrowing as is debenture interest. The discount therefore needs to be written off during the life of the debentures. It might be more rational to write it off to the Profit and Loss Account, but in fact accounting custom, as permitted by law, would first of all write it off against any Share Premium Account or, secondly, against the Profit and Loss Appropriation Account.

The amounts written over the life of the debentures.

(*a*) Equal annual amounts over the life of the debentures.

(*b*) In proportion to the debenture debt outstanding at the start of each year. Exhibit 11.10 shows such a situation.

Exhibit 11.10

£30,000 debentures are issued at a discount of 5 per cent. They are repayable at par over five years at the rate of £6,000 per annum.

Year	Outstanding at start of each year	Proportion written off		Amount
	£			£
1	30,000	$^{30}\!/_{90} \times £1,500$	=	500
2	24,000	$^{24}\!/_{90} \times £1,500$	=	400
3	18,000	$^{18}\!/_{90} \times £1,500$	=	300
4	12,000	$^{12}\!/_{90} \times £1,500$	=	200
5	6,000	$^{6}\!/_{90} \times £1,500$	=	100
	90,000			1,500

Redeemed by purchase in the open market

A sum equal to the cash actually paid on redemption should be transferred from the debit of the Profit and Loss Appropriation Account to the credit of the Debenture Redemption Reserve Account. The sum actually paid will of course have been credited to the Cash Book and debited to the Debentures Account.

Any discount (or profit) on purchase will be transferred to a Reserve Account. Any premium (or loss) on purchase will be deemed to come out of such a Reserve Account, or if no such account exists or it is insufficient, then it will be deemed to come out of the Share Premium Account. Failing the existence of these accounts any loss must come out of the Profit and Loss Appropriation Account. It may seem that purchase would not be opportune if the debentures had to be redeemed at a premium. However, it would still be opportune if the premium paid was not as high as the premium to be paid if the final date for redemption was awaited.

Redemption of debentures by a sinking fund

Where debentures are issued which are redeemable (and most are redeemable) consideration should be given to the availability of cash funds at the time.

This method involves the investment of cash outside the business. The aim is to make the regular investment of money which, together with the accumulated interest or dividends, is sufficient to finance the redemption of the debentures at the requisite time.

Before calculations become too involved a simple proposition can be examined. As each period's interest (or dividend) is received, then that amount is immediately reinvested. Apart from the reinvestment of interest the other money taken for investment is to be an equal amount each period. This being so, if the money is to be invested at 5 per cent per annum, and the debenture is £500 to be redeemed in five years' time, then how much should be taken for investment each year? If £100 was taken each year for five years, then this would amount to more than £500 because of the interest and of the interest on the reinvested interest. Most readers will recognise this as money being invested as compound interest. Therefore something less than £100 per annum is needed. The exact amount can be calculated by the use of the compound interest formula. Chapter 36 illustrates how the amount needed can be calculated. As these calculations are left until later in the book, a summarised set of tables is now shown to help the student at this stage.

Annual Sinking Fund Instalments to Provide £1

Years	3%	3½%	4%	4½%	5%
3	0.323530	0.321933	0.320348	0.318773	0.317208
4	0.239028	0.237251	0.235490	0.233744	0.232012
5	0.188354	0.186481	0.184627	0.182792	0.180975
6	0.154597	0.152668	0.150761	0.148878	0.147017
7	0.130506	0.128544	0.126609	0.124701	0.122819
8	0.112456	0.110476	0.108527	0.106609	0.104721
9	0.098433	0.096446	0.094493	0.092574	0.090690
10	0.087230	0.085241	0.083291	0.081378	0.079504

The table gives the amount required to provide £1 at the end of the relevant number of years. To provide £1,000 multiply by 1,000, to provide for £4,986 multiply by 4,986.

Double entry records for sinking fund

When the annual instalment has been found, the double entry needed each year is:
Annual instalment:
>> Dr Profit and Loss Appropriation
>> Cr Debenture Redemption Reserve

Investment of 1st instalment:
>> Dr Debenture Sinking Fund Investment
>> Cr Bank

Interest/Dividends on Sinking Fund Investment
>> Dr Bank
>> Cr Debenture Redemption Reserve

Investment of 2nd and later instalments (These consist of equal annual instalment plus interest/dividend just received)
>> Dr Debenture Sinking Fund Investment
>> Cr Bank

Exhibit 11.11

Debentures of £10,000 are issued on 1 January 19-1. They are redeemable five years later on 31 December 19-5 on identical terms. The company therefore decides to set aside an equal annual amount, which at an interest rate of 5 per cent will provide £10,000 on 31 December 19-5. According to the table £0.180975 invested annually will provide £1 in five years' time. Therefore £0.180975 × 10,000 will be needed annually = £1,809.75.

Profit and Loss Appropriation for years ended 31 December
(19-1) Debenture Redemption Reserve 1,809.75
(19-2) Debenture Redemption Reserve 1,809.75
(19-3) Debenture Redemption Reserve 1,809.75
(19-4) Debenture Redemption Reserve 1,809.75
(19-5) Debenture Redemption Reserve 1,809.75

Debenture Redemption Reserve

	£		£
		19-1	
		Dec 31 Profit and Loss	1,809.75
		19-2	
		Dec 31 Bank Interest	
19-2		(5% of £1,809.75)	90.49
Dec 31 Balance c/d	3,709.99	Dec 31 Profit and Loss	1,809.75
	3,709.99		3,709.99
		19-3	
		Jan 1 Balance b/d	3,709.99
		Dec 31 Bank: Interest	
19-3		(5% of £3,709.99)	185.49
Dec 31 Balance c/d	5,705.23	Dec 31 Profit and Loss	1,809.75
	5,705.23		5,705.23
		19-4	
		Jan 1 Balance b/d	5,705.23
		Dec 31 Bank Interest	
19-4		(5% of £5,705.23)	285.26
Dec 31 Balance c/d	7,800.24	Dec 31 Profit and Loss	1,809.75
	7,800.24		7,800.24
		19-5	
		Jan 1 Balance b/d	7,800.24
		Dec 31 Bank: Interest	
19-5		(5% of £7,800.24)	390.01
Dec 31 Debentures now redeemed	10,000.00	Dec 31 Profit and Loss	1,809.75
	10,000.00		10,000.00

Debenture Sinking Fund Investment

19-1	£		£
Dec 31 Bank	1,809.75		
19-2			
Dec 31 Bank (see note A)	1,900.24		
19-3			
Dec 31 Bank (see note B)	1,995.24		
19-4		19-5	
Dec 31 Bank (see note C)	2,095.01	Dec 31 Cash: Sale of Investment	7,800.24
	7,800.24		7,800.24

Cash Invested	*A*	*B*	*C*
	£	£	£
The yearly instalment	1,809.75	1,809.75	1,809.75
add interest received reinvested immediately	90.49	185.49	285.26
	1,900.24	1,995.24	2,095.01

Bank (extracts)

19-1		£	19-1		£
Jan 1	Debentures (issued)	10,000.00	Dec 31	Debenture Sinking Fund Investment	1,809.75
19-2			19-2		
Dec 31	Debenture Redemption Reserve (Interest on Investment)	90.49	Dec 31	Debenture Sinking Fund Investment	1,900.24
19-3			19-3		
Dec 31	Debenture Redemption Reserve (Interest on Investment)	185.49	Dec 31	Debenture Sinking Fund Investment	1,995.24
19-4			19-4		
Dec 31	Debenture Redemption Reserve (Interest on Investment)	285.26	Dec 31	Debenture Sinking Fund Investment	2,095.01
19-5			19-5		
Dec 31	Debenture Redemption Reserve (Interest on Investment)	309.01	Jan 1	Debentures (Redemption)	10,000.00

Debentures

19-6		£	19-1		£
Jan 1	Bank (Redemption)	10,000.00	Jan 1	Bank	10,000.00

The instalment for 19-5 is not in fact invested, nor is the interest received on 31 December 19-5 reinvested. The money to redeem the debentures is required on 1 January 19-6, and there is not much point (even if it was possible, which would very rarely hold true) in investing money one day only to withdraw it the day afterwards. The amount required is £10,000 and is available from the following sources:

	£
Dec 31 19-5 Sale of investment	7,800.24
,, 31 19-5 Interest received but not reinvested	390.01
,, 31 19-5 The fifth year's instalment not invested	1,809.75
	10,000.00

Sometimes debentures bought in the open market are not cancelled, but are kept 'alive' and are treated as investments of the sinking fund. The annual appropriation of profits is credited to the Sinking Fund Account, while the amount expended on the purchase of the debentures is debited to the Sinking Fund Investment Account. Interest on such debentures is debited to the Profit and Loss Account and credited to the Sinking Fund Account, thus the interest, as far as the Sinking Fund Account is concerned, is treated in the same fashion as if it was cash actually received by the firm from an outside investment. The sum expended on investments will then be equal to the annual appropriation + the interest on investments actually received + the interest on debentures kept in hand.

Review questions

11.1 Given the same commencing balance sheet, now shown, Exercises 11.1(i) to 11.1(v) inclusive are based on it.

RSV Ltd
Balance Sheet

	£
Net Assets (except bank)	20,000
Bank	13,000
	33,000
Preference Share Capital	5,000
Ordinary Share Capital	15,000
Share Premium	2,000
	22,000
Profit and Loss	11,000
	33,000

Note that each of questions 11.1(i) to (v) are independent of each other. They are not cumulative.

11.1(i) RSV Ltd, per 11.1, redeems £5,000 Preference Shares at par, a new issue of £5,000 Ordinary Shares at par being made for the purpose. Show the balance sheet after completion of these transactions. Workings are to be shown as journal entries.

11.1(ii) RSV Ltd, per 11.1, redeems £5,000 Preference Shares at par, with no new issue of shares to provide funds. Show the balance sheet after completing the transaction. Workings: show journal entries.

11.1(iii) RSV Ltd, per 11.1, redeems £5,000 Preference Shares at par. To help finance this an issue of £1,500 Ordinary Shares at par is effected. Show the balance sheet after these transactions have been completed, also show the necessary journal entries.

11.1(iv) RSV Ltd, per 11.1, redeems £5,000 Preference Shares at a premium of 25 per cent. There is no new issue of shares for the purpose. In this question the Share Premium Account is taken as being from the issue of Ordinary Shares some years ago. Show the balance sheet after these transactions have been completed, and the supporting journal entries.

11.1(v) RSV Ltd, per 11.1, redeems £5,000 Preference Shares at a premium of 40 per cent. There is an issue of £7,000 Ordinary Shares at par for the purpose. The Preference Shares had originally been issued at a premium of 30 per cent. Show the balance sheet after these transactions have been completed, also supporting journal entries.

11.2A Questions 11.2A(i) to 11.2(v) are based on the same commencing balance sheet, as follows:

BAR Ltd
Balance Sheet

	£
Net Assets (except bank)	31,000
Bank	16,000
	47,000
Preference Share Capital	8,000
Ordinary Share Capital	20,000
Share Premium	4,000
	32,000
Profit and Loss	15,000
	47,000

Note that questions 11.2A(i) to (v) are independent of each other. They are not cumulative.

11.2A(i) BAR Ltd, per 11.2A, purchases £10,000 of its own Ordinary Share Capital at par. To help finance this £7,000 Preference Shares are issued at par. Show the necessary journal entries and the balance sheet after the transactions have been completed.

11.2A(ii) BAR Ltd, per 11.2A, purchases £12,000 of its own Ordinary Shares at a premium of 20 per cent. No new issue of shares is made for the purpose. It is assumed that the Share Premium account is in respect of the issue of Preference Shares some years before. Show the balance sheet after the transactions have been completed, also the supporting journal entries.

11.2A(iii) BAR Ltd, per 11.2A, purchases all the Preference Share Capital at par. These shares were not originally Redeemable Preference Shares. There is no new issue of shares to provide funds. Show the requisite journal entries, and the closing balance sheet when the transaction has been completed.

11.2A(iv) BAR Ltd, per 11.2A, purchases £12,000 of its own Ordinary Shares at par, a new issue of £12,000 Preference Shares at par being made for the purpose. Show the journal entries needed and the balance sheet after completing these transactions.

11.2A(v) BAR Ltd, per 11.2A, purchases £6,000 Ordinary Shares at a premium of 50 per cent, they had originally been issued at a premium of 20 per cent. There is an issue of £10,000 Preference Shares at par for the purpose. Show the amended balance sheet, together with journal entries.

11.3 A company's balance sheet appears as follows:

	£
Net Assets (except bank)	12,500
Bank	13,000
	25,500
Preference Share Capital	5,000
Ordinary Share Capital	10,000
Non-Distributable Reserves	6,000
	21,000
Profit and Loss	4,500
	25,500

Required:

(*a*) If £6,000 of the ordinary shares were purchased at par, there being no new issue of shares for the purpose, show the journal entries to record the transactions and the amended balance sheet.

(*b*) If, instead of (i), £6,000 ordinary shares were purchased at a premium of 100 per cent, there being no new issue of shares for the purpose, show the journal entries to record the transactions and the amended balance sheet.

11.4A Debentures of £30,000 are issued on 1 January 19-3. Redemption is to take place, on equal terms, 4 years later. The company decides to put aside an equal amount to be invested at 5 per cent which will provide £30,000 on maturity. Tables show that £0.232012 invested annually will produce £1 in 4 years' time.

You are required to show:

(*a*) Debenture Redemption Reserve account
(*b*) Debenture Sinking Fund Investment account
(*c*) Debentures account
(*d*) Profit and Loss account extracts.

11.5 Some years ago M plc had issued £375,000 of 10% Debentures 19-6/19-0 at par. The terms of the issue allow the company the right to re-purchase these debentures for cancellation at or below par, with an option to redeem, at a premium of 1%, on 30 September 19-6. To exercise this option the company must give three months' notice which it duly did on 30 June 19-6 indicating its intention to redeem all the debentures outstanding at 30 September 19-6.

M plc had established a sinking fund designed to accumulate the sum of £378,750 by 30 September 19-6 and had appropriated profits annually and invested these, together with the interest from such investments and the profits made on any realisations from time to time. A special No 2 bank account was established specifically to deal with the receipts and payments relating to the debentures and the sinking fund.

By 30 June 19-6 annual contributions amounting to £334,485, together with the interest on the sinking fund investments of £39,480, had all been invested except for £2,475 which remained in the No 2 bank account at that date.

The only investments sold, prior to 30 June 19-6, had cost £144,915 and realised £147,243. This was used to repurchase debentures with a par value of £150,000.

Transactions occurring between 1 July and 30 September 19-6 were:
  (i) interest received on the sinking fund investments:

$$7 \text{ July} - £1,756$$
$$13 \text{ September} - £1,455$$

  (ii) proceeds from the sale of investments:

$$2 \text{ August} - £73,215 \text{ (book value was £69,322)}$$
$$25 \text{ September} - £160,238 \text{ (remaining investments)}$$

  (iii) redemption of all the debentures, on 30 September, with the exception of £15,000 held by B Limited. The company had received notice of a garnishee order.*

  (iv) M plc deposited with the W Bank plc the sum of £15,150 on 30 September 19-6.

  You are to ignore debenture interest and income tax.

You are required, from the information given above, to prepare the ledger accounts (including the No 2 bank account) in the books of M plc for the period 30 June to 30 September 19-6, showing the transfer of the final balances to the appropriate accounts.

*Note – Garnishee Order

This order, issued by the court, instructs M plc not to release the money owing to B Limited until directed by the court to do so.
(*Chartered Institute of Management Accountants*)

11.6A The following information relates to the White Rabbit Trading plc:

Summarised balance sheet as at 31 January 19-7

	£000
Fixed assets	2,400
Investments	120
Net current assets	1,880
	4,400
Financed by:	
Capital and reserves	
Ordinary shares of 50p each fully paid	2,000
Redeemable shares of £1 each (19-7/19-1)	500
Share premium	200
Revaluation surplus	400
Profit and loss account	900
	4,000
Long-term liabilities	
8% Debentures (19-7/19-0)	400
	4,400

On 1 February 19-7 the company closed the list of applications for 400,000 ordinary shares at a premium of 50p. The shares were to be paid for as follows: 60p on application, 25p on allotment and 15p on the first and final call, which was to be made on 1 May 19-7. A total of £1,320,000 was received, the shares were allotted and

145

£1,032,000 was returned to unsuccessful applicants. The call money was received by 31 May from all shareholders, with the exception of two shareholders, one of whom had been allotted 500 shares. The other subscriber for 100 shares still owed £25 for allotment in addition to the call money. Eventually both lots of shares were forfeited and reissued to an existing shareholder for a payment of £500 which was duly received.

At a board meeting on 15 February 19-7 the directors decided to make a fresh issue of 500,000 £1 redeemable shares at a premium of 60p, and to redeem all of the existing redeemable shares at a premium of 40p. The shares had originally been issued for £1.20 each. All moneys due on application were duly received by 31 March 19-7, and the redemption took place on 6 April 19-7.

In January 19-5 White Rabbit plc had purchased, for cash, 80,000 25p ordinary shares in March Hares Ltd for £25,000, and this is included in investments on the balance sheet at 31 January 19-7. On 1 April 19-7 the company purchased 400,000 out of a total issue of 500,000 25p ordinary shares in March Hares Ltd, by exchanging 200,000 of its own ordinary shares.

The 8% debentures were redeemed on 15 May 19-7 at a 10% premium, and on the same date £500,000 7% debentures (19-0/19-3) were issued at a discount of 5%.

Required:
Show the full journal entries to record the above events, including cash/bank transactions, in the books of White Rabbit Trading plc.
(*Chartered Association of Certified Accountants*)

12

Limited companies taking over other businesses

Limited companies will often take over other businesses which are in existence as going concerns. The purchase considerations may either be in cash, by giving the company's shares to the owners, by giving the company's debentures, or by any combination of these three factors.

It must not be thought that because the assets bought are shown in the selling firm's books at one value that the purchasing company must record the assets taken over in its own books at the same value. The values shown in the purchasing company's books are those values at which the company is buying the assets, such values being frequently quite different than those shown in the selling firm's books. As an instance of this, the selling firm may have bought premises many years ago for £1,000 but they may now be worth £5,000. The company buying the premises will obviously have to pay £5,000 and it is therefore this value that is recorded in the buying company's books. Alternatively, the value at which it is recorded in the buying company's books may be less than that shown in the selling firm's books. Where the total purchase consideration exceeds the total value of the identifiable assets then such excess is the goodwill, and will need entering in a Goodwill Account in the purchasing company's books. Should the total purchase consideration be less than the values of the identifiable assets, then the difference would be entered in a Capital Reserve Account.

Before the accounting entries necessary to record the purchase of a going business are looked at, it must be pointed out that such recording of the transactions is the simple end of the whole affair. The negotiations that take place before agreement is reached, and the various strategies undertaken by the various parties is a study in itself. The accounting entries are in effect the 'tip of the iceberg', i.e. that part of the whole affair which is seen by the eventual reader of the accounts.

Taking over a sole trader's business

It is easier to start with the takeover of the simplest sort of business unit, that of a sole trader. Some of the Balance Sheets shown will be deliberately simplified so that the principles involved are not hidden behind a mass of complicated calculations.

Exhibit 12.1

Earl Ltd is to buy the business of M Kearney. The purchase consideration is to be £6,000 cash, the company placing the following values on the assets taken over – Machinery £3,000, Stock £1,000. The goodwill must therefore be £2,000, because the total price of £6,000 exceeds the values of Machinery £3,000 and Stock £1,000 by the sum of £2,000. The company's Balance Sheets will be shown before and after the takeover, it being assumed that the transactions are all concluded immediately.

M Kearney
Balance Sheet

	£
Machinery	1,700
Stock	1,300
	3,000
Capital	3,000

Earl Ltd
Balance Sheet(s)

	Before £	+ or − £	After £
Goodwill		+2,000	2,000
Machinery	11,000	+3,000	14,000
Stock	5,000	+1,000	6,000
Bank	9,000	−6,000	3,000
	25,000		25,000
Share Capital	20,000		20,000
Profit and Loss	5,000		5,000
	25,000		25,000

Exhibit 12.2

Suppose the purchase had been made instead by issuing 7,000 shares of £1 each at par to Kearney. The goodwill would then be £7,000 − assets taken over £4,000 = £3,000. The Balance Sheets of Earl Ltd would be:

Earl Ltd
Balance Sheets

	Before £	+ or − £	After £
Goodwill		+3,000	3,000
Machinery	11,000	+3,000	14,000
Stock	5,000	+1,000	6,000
Bank	9,000		9,000
	25,000		32,000
Share Capital	20,000	+7,000	27,000
Profit and Loss	5,000		5,000
	25,000		32,000

Exhibit 12.3

If the purchase had been made by issuing 5,000 shares of £1 each at a premium of 50 per cent, then the total consideration would have been worth £7,500, which, if the assets of £4,000 are deducted leaves goodwill of £3,500. The Balance Sheets would then be:

Earl Ltd
Balance Sheet(s)

	Before £	+ or − £	After £
Goodwill		+3,500	3,500
Machinery	11,000	+3,000	14,000
Stocks	5,000	+1,000	6,000
Bank	9,000		9,000
	25,000		32,500
Share Capital	20,000	+5,000	25,000
Share Premium		+2,500	2,500
Profit and Loss	5,000		5,000
	25,000		32,500

Exhibit 12.4

Now if the purchase had been made by the issue of 1,000 shares of £1 each at a premium of 40 per cent, £3,000 worth of 7 per cent debentures at par and £4,000 in cash, then the total purchase consideration would be shares valued at £1,400, debentures valued at £3,000 and cash £4,000, making in all £8,400. The assets are valued at £4,000, the goodwill must be £4,400. The Balance Sheets would appear:

Earl Ltd
Balance Sheet(s)

	Before £	+ or − £	After £
Goodwill		+4,400	4,400
Machinery	11,000	+3,000	14,000
Stocks	5,000	+1,000	6,000
Bank	9,000	−4,000	5,000
	25,000		29,400
Share Capital	20,000	+1,000	21,000
Share Premium		+ 400	400
Profit and Loss	5,000		5,000
Debentures		+3,000	3,000
	25,000		29,400

In each of Exhibits 12.1 to 12.4 it has been assumed that all transactions were started and completed within a few moments. The fact is that an intermediary account would be created but then closed almost immediately when the purchase consideration was handed over. Taking Exhibit 12.3 as an example, there will be a credit in the Share Capital Account and in the Share Premium Account, and debits in the Goodwill, Machinery and Stock Accounts. Nevertheless, shares cannot be issued to goodwill, machinery or stocks. They have in fact, been issued to M Kearney. This means that there should have been an account for M Kearney, but that the balance on it was cancelled on the passing of the purchase consideration. The actual accounts for Exhibit 12.3 were as follows in the books of Earl Ltd:

Share Premium

			£
		M Kearney	2,500

Share Capital

	£		£
Balance c/d	25,000	Balance b/fwd	20,000
		M Kearney	5,000
	25,000		25,000
		Balance b/d	25,000

Profit and Loss

			£
		Balance b/fwd	5,000

Goodwill

	£
M Kearney	3,500

Machinery

	£		£
Balance b/fwd	11,000		
M Kearney	3,000	Balance c/d	14,000
	14,000		14,000
Balance b/d	14,000		

Stock

	£		£
Balance b/d	5,000		
M Kearney	1,000	Balance c/d	6,000
	6,000		6,000
Balance c/d	6,000		

(In actual fact the £1,000 would probably be entered in the Purchases Account. It does, however, obviously increase the actual amount of stock.)

Bank

	£
Balance b/fwd	9,000

	£	Assets Taken Over	£
Consideration Passing:			
Share Capital	5,000	Goodwill	3,500
Share Premium	2,500	Machinery	3,000
		Stock	1,000
	7,500		7,500

Some accountants would have preferred to use a Business Purchase Account instead of a personal account such as that of M Kearney.

Sometimes the company taking over the business of a sole trader not only pays a certain amount for the assets but also assumes responsibility for paying the creditors in addition. Take the case of a sole trader with assets valued at Premises £5,000 and Stock £4,000. To gain control of these assets the company is to pay the sole trader £11,000 in cash, and in addition the company will pay off creditors £1,000. This means that the goodwill is £3,000, calculated as follows:

	£	£
Paid by the company to gain control of the sole trader's assets:		
Cash to the Sole Trader		11,000
Cash to the Sole Trader's Creditors		1,000
		12,000
The Company receives Assets	£	
Premises	5,000	
Stock	4,000	
		9,000
Excess paid for Goodwill		3,000

Partnership business taken over by a limited company

The entries are the same as for those of taking over a sole trader's business, with the exception that there will be a personal account for each partner. There are, however, difficulties about the distribution of shares as between the partners when the balances on their Capital Accounts are not in the same ratio with one another as their profit-sharing ratios. This is, however, better left to a more advanced stage of studies in accounting.

The partnership will, of course, show a Realisation Account in its own books. The total purchase consideration will be credited to the Realisation Account and debited to the company's personal account. The discharge of the purchase consideration will close the partnership books.

The takeover of a limited company by another limited company

One company may take over another company by one of two methods:

1 By buying all the assets of the other company, the purchase consideration being by cash, shares or debentures. The selling company may afterwards be wound up, the liquidators either distributing the purchasing company's shares and debentures between the shareholders of the selling company, or else the shares and debentures of the buying company may be sold and the cash distributed instead.

2 By giving its own shares and debentures in exchange for the shares and debentures of the selling company's share and debenture holders. Exhibit 12.5 is an illustration of each of these methods.

Exhibit 12.5

The following are the Balance Sheets of three companies as on the same date.

	R Ltd	*S Ltd*	*T Ltd*
	£	£	£
Buildings	13,000	–	1,000
Machinery	4,000	2,000	1,000
Stock	3,000	1,000	2,000
Debtors	2,000	1,000	3,000
Bank	1,000	2,000	3,000
	23,000	6,000	10,000
Share Capital (£1 shares)	18,000	3,000	5,000
Profit and Loss	2,000	1,000	4,000
Current Liabilities	3,000	2,000	1,000
	23,000	6,000	10,000

Balance Sheets

R takes over S by exchanging with the shareholders of S two shares in R at a premium of 10 per cent for every share they hold in S.

R takes over T by buying all the assets of T, the purchase consideration being 12,000 £1 shares in R at a premium of 10 per cent, and R will pay off T's creditors. R values T's assets at Buildings £2,000, Machinery £600, Stock £1,400, Debtors £2,500, and the Bank is £3,000, a total of £9,500.

R's deal with the shareholders of S means that R now has complete control of S Ltd, so that S Ltd becomes what is known as a subsidiary company of R Ltd, and will be shown as an investment in R's Balance Sheet.

On the other hand, the deal with T has resulted in the ownership of the assets resting with R. These must therefore be added to R's assets in its own Balance Sheet. As R has given 12,000 £1 shares at a premium of 10 per cent plus taking over the responsibility for creditors £1,000, the total purchase consideration for the assets taken over is £12,000+£1,200 (10 per cent of £12,000)+£1,000=£14,200. Identifiable assets as already stated are valued at £9,500, therefore the goodwill is £14,200−£9,500=£4,700.

The distinction between the acquisition of the two going concerns can be seen to be a rather fine one. With S the shares are taken over, the possession of these in turn giving rise to the ownership of the assets. In the books of R this is regarded as an investment. With T the actual assets and liabilities are taken over so that the assets now directly belong to R. In the books of R this is therefore regarded as the acquisition of additional assets and liabilities and not as an investment (using the meaning of 'investment' which is used in the Balance Sheets of companies). The Balance Sheet of R Ltd therefore becomes:

	Before £	+ or −	£	After £
Goodwill		+(T)	4,700	4,700
Buildings	13,000	+(T)	2,000	15,000
Machinery	4,000	+(T)	600	4,600
Investment in S at cost		+	6,600	6,600
Stock	3,000	+(T)	1,400	4,400
Debtors	2,000	+(T)	2,500	4,500
Bank	1,000	+(T)	3,000	4,000
	23,000			43,800
Share Capital	18,000	+(S)	6,000	
		+(T)	12,000 =	36,000
Share Premium		+(S)	600	
		+(T)	1,200 =	1,800
Profit and Loss	2,000			2,000
Current Liabilities	3,000	+(T)	1,000	4,000
	23,000			43,800

No entry is necessary in the books of S Ltd, as it is merely the identity of the shareholders that has changed. This would be duly recorded in the register of members, but this is not really an integral part of the double entry accounting system.

If, however, T Ltd is now liquidated, then a Realisation Account must be drawn up and the distribution of the shares (or cash if the shares are sold) to the shareholders of T Ltd must be shown. Such accounts would appear as follows:

Books of T Ltd
Realisation

	£		£
Book Values of Assets Disposed Of:		R Ltd: Total Purchase Consideration	14,200
Buildings	1,000		
Machinery	1,000		
Stock	2,000		
Debtors	3,000		
Bank	3,000		
Profit on Realisation transferred to Sundry Shareholders	4,200		
	14,200		14,200

Share Capital

	£		£
Sundry Shareholders	5,000	Balance b/fwd	5,000

Profit and Loss

	£		£
Sundry Shareholders	4,000	Balance b/fwd	4,000

Creditors

	£		£
R Ltd – taken over	1,000	Balance b/fwd	1,000

R Ltd

	£		£
Realisation:		Creditors	1,000
Total Consideration	14,200	Sundry Shareholders: 12,000 £1 shares received at premium of 10 per cent	13,200
	14,200		14,200

Sundry Shareholders

	£		£
R Ltd; 12,000 £1 shares at premium of 10 per cent	13,200	Share Capital	5,000
		Profit and Loss	4,000
		Profit on Realisation	4,200
	13,200		13,200

It can be seen that the items possessed by the sundry shareholders have been transferred to an account in their name. These are (i) the share capital which obviously belongs to them, (ii) the credit balance on the Profit and Loss Account built up by withholding cash dividends from the shareholders, and (iii) the profit on realisation which they, as owners of the business, are entitled to take. As there were 5,000 shares in T Ltd, and 12,000 shares have been given by R Ltd, then each holder of 5 shares in T Ltd will now be given 12 shares in R Ltd to complete the liquidation of the company.

The exchange of debentures

Sometimes the debentures in the company taking over are to be given in exchange for the debentures of the company being taken over. This may be straightforward on the basis of £100 debentures in company A in exchange for £100 debentures in company B. However, the problem often arises where the exchange is in terms of one of both sets of debentures being at a discount or at a premium. The need for such an exchange may be two-fold:

(a) To persuade the debenture holders in Company B to give up their debentures some form of inducement may be needed, such as letting them have A's debentures at a discount even though they may well be worth the par value.

(b) There may be a difference in the debenture interest rates. For instance, a person with a £100 7 per cent debenture would not normally gladly part with it in exchange for a £100 6 per cent debenture in another company. The first debenture gives him £7 a year interest, the second one only £6 per year. Thus the debenture in the second company may be issued at a discount to redeem the debenture in the first company at a premium. As the amount of interest is only one factor, there are also others such as the certainty of the debenture holder regaining his money if the firm had to close down, the precise terms of the exchange cannot be based merely on arithmetical calculations of interest rates, but it is one of the measures taken when negotiating the exchange of debentures.

Exhibit 12.6

(i) D Ltd is to give the necessary debentures at a discount of 10 per cent necessary to redeem £9,000 debentures in J Ltd at a premium of 5 per cent. The problem here is to find exactly what amount of debentures must be given by D Ltd.

Answer: $\text{Total nominal value of debentures in J Ltd to be redeemed (exchanged)} \times \dfrac{\text{Redeemable value of each £100 debenture of J Ltd}}{\text{Issue value of each £100 debenture of D Ltd}}$

$$=\text{Total nominal value of D Ltd to be issued}$$
$$=£9,000 \times \frac{105}{90} = £10,500$$

Thus, to satisfy the agreement, debentures of D Ltd of a total nominal value of £10,500 are issued at a discount of 10 per cent to the debenture holdings of J Ltd.

(ii) H Ltd is to give the necessary debentures at par to redeem £5,000 debentures in M Ltd at a premium of 4 per cent.

$$£5,000 \times \frac{104}{100} = \text{Debentures of £5,200 nominal value are given by H Ltd at par.}$$

Profit (or loss) prior to incorporation

Quite frequently companies take over businesses from a date which is actually before the company was itself incorporated. It could be that two persons enter into business and start trading with the intention of running the business as a limited company. However, it takes more than a few days to attend to all the necessary formalities before the company can be incorporated. Obviously it depends on the speed with which the formation is pushed through and the solution of any snags which crop up. When the company is in fact incorporated it may enter into a contract whereby it adopts all the transactions retrospectively to the date that the firm, i.e. with two persons it was a partnership, had started trading. This means that the company accepts all the benefits and disadvantages which have flowed from the transactions which have occurred. The example used was that of a brand-new business; it could well have been an old-established business that was taken over from a date previous to incorporation.

Legally a company cannot earn profits before it comes into existence, i.e. is incorporated, and therefore to decide what action will have to be taken such profits will first of all have to be calculated. Any such profits are of a capital nature and must be transferred to a Capital Reserve Account, normally titled Pre-Incorporation Profit Account or Profit Prior to Incorporation Account. That this should be so is apparent if it is realised that though the actual date from which the transactions have been adopted falls before the date of incorporation, yet the price at which the business is being taken over is influenced by the values of the assets, etc., at the date when the company actually takes over, i.e. the date of incorporation. Suppose that Doolin and Kershaw start a business on 1 January 19-5 with £1,000 capital, and very shortly afterwards Davie and Parker become interested as well, and the four of them start to form a company in which they will all become directors, Davie and Parker to start active work when the company is incorporated. The company is incorporated on 1 May 19-5 and the original owners of the business, Doolin and Kershaw, are to be given shares in the new company to compensate them for handing over the business. If they know, not necessarily with precision, that the original £1,000 assets will have grown to net assets of £6,000, then they most certainly would not part with the business to the company for £1,000. Ignoring goodwill they would want £6,000 of shares. Conversely, if the net assets will shrink to £400, then would Davie and Parker be happy to see £1,000 of shares handed over? This means that the price at which the business is taken over is dependent on the expected value at the date of the company incorporation, and not at the value at the date on which the company is supposed to take over. Taking the case of the increase in net assets to £6,000 the £5,000 difference is made up of profits. If these profits could be distributed as dividends, then in effect the capital payment of £6,000 in shares is being part used up for dividend purposes. This is in direct contradiction to the normal accounting practice of retaining capital intact (the accountant's meaning of 'capital' and not the meaning given to 'capital' by the economist). The £5,000 profits must therefore be regarded as not being available for dividends. They are thus a capital reserve.

Although the profit cannot be regarded as free for use as dividends, any such loss can be taken to restrict the dividends which could be paid out of the profits made after incorporation. This is the concept of prudence once again coming into play, and if the price paid on take-over was misjudged and a high figure was paid, only to find out later that a loss had been made, then the restriction of dividends leads to the capital lost being replaced by assets held back within the firm. Alternatively the amount of the pre-incorporation loss could be charged to a Goodwill Account, as this is also another way of stating that a higher price has been paid for the assets of the firm than is represented by the value of the tangible assets taken over.

It is possible for the profits up to the date of incorporation to be calculated quite separately from those after incorporation. However, the cost of stocktaking, etc., may be felt to be not worth while merely to produce accounts when in fact the accounts could be left until the normal financial year end. This is invariably the case in examination questions. Therefore when the accounts for the full financial year are being made up, they will consist of profits before and after incorporation. The accounts must therefore be split to throw up the two sets of profit (or loss), so that distinction can be made between those profits usable, and those not usable, for dividend purposes. There is no hard-and-fast rule as to how this shall be done. Known facts must prevail, and where an arbitrary apportionment must be made it should meet the test of common sense in the particular.case. Exhibit 12.7 shows an attempt to calculate such profits.

Exhibit 12.7

Slack and King, partners in a firm, are to have their business taken over as from 1 January 19-4 by Monk Ltd which is incorporated on 1 April 19-4. It was agreed that all profits made from 1 January 19-4 should belong to the company, and that the vendors be entitled to interest on the purchase price from 1 January to date of payment. The purchase price was paid on 30 April 19-4, including £1,600 interest. A Profit and Loss Account is drawn up for the year ended 31 December 19-4. This is shown as column (X). This is then split into, before incorporation, shown as column (Y), after incorporation, being column (Z). The methods used to apportion the particular items are shown after the Profit and Loss Account, the letters (A) to (I) against the items being the references to the notes. These particular methods must definitely not be used in all cases for similar expenses, they are only an indication of different methods of apportionment. The facts and the peculiarities of each firm must be taken into account, and no method should be slavishly followed. Assume for this example that all calendar months are of equal length.

Monk Ltd
Profit and Loss Account for the year ended 31 December 19-4

		(X) Full year £	£	(Y) Pre-incorporation £	£	(Z) After £	£
Gross Profit	(A)		38,000		8,000		30,000
less:							
Partnership Salaries	(B)	1,000		1,000			
Employees Remuneration	(C)	12,000		3,000		9,000	
General Expenses	(C)	800		200		600	
Commission on Sales	(D)	1,700		200		1,500	
Distribution Expenses	(E)	1,900		400		1,500	
Bad Debts	(F)	100		20		80	
Bank Overdraft Interest	(G)	200				200	
Directors' Remuneration	(H)	5,000				5,000	
Directors' Expenses	(H)	400				400	
Debenture Interest	(H)	500				500	
Depreciation	(C)	1,000		250		750	
Interest paid to Vendors	(I)	1,600		1,200		400	
			26,200		6,270		19,930
Net Profit			11,800				
Transferred to Capital Reserves					1,730		
Carried down to the Appropriation Account							10,070

Notes:

(A) For the three months to 31 March Sales amounted to £40,000, and for the remaining nine months they were £150,000. Gross profit is at a uniform rate of 20 per cent of selling price throughout the year. Therefore the gross profit is apportioned (Y) 20 per cent of £40,000 = £8,000, and (Z) 20 per cent of £150,000 = £30,000.

(B) The Partnership salaries of the vendors, Slack and King, obviously belong to (Y), because that is the period of the partnership.

(C) These expenses, in this particular case, have accrued evenly throughout the year and are therefore split on the time basis of Y three twelfths, Z nine-twelfths.

(D) Commission to the salesmen was paid at the rate of ½ per cent on sales up to 31 March, and 1 per cent thereafter. The commission figure is split:

(Y) ½ per cent of £40,000	=	200
(Z) 1 per cent of £150,000	=	1,500
		1,700

(E) In this particular case (but not always true in every case) the distribution expenses have varied directly with the value of sales. They are therefore split:

(Y) $\dfrac{\text{Y Sales}}{\text{Total Sales}} \times \text{Expenses} = \dfrac{40,000}{190,000} \times £1,900 = \text{⁴⁄₁₉} \times £1,900 = £400$

(Z) $\dfrac{\text{Z Sales}}{\text{Total Sales}} \times \text{Expenses} = \dfrac{150,000}{190,000} \times £1,900 = \text{¹⁵⁄₁₉} \times £1,900 = £1,500$

(F) The bad debts were two in number:

(i) In respect of a sale in January, the debtor dying penniless in March, £20.

(ii) In respect of a sale in June, the debtor being declared bankrupt in December, £80.

(G) The bank account was never overdrawn until June, so that the interest charged must be for period (Z).

(H) Only in companies are such expenses as Directors' Salaries, Directors' Expenses and Debenture Interest to be found. These must naturally be shown in period (Z).

(I) The interest paid to the vendors was due to the fact that the company was receiving all the benefits from 1 January but did not in fact pay any cash for the business until 30 April. This is therefore in effect loan interest which should be spread over the period it was borrowed, i.e. three months to (Y) and 1 month to (Z).

Review questions

12.1 Checkers Ltd was incorporated on 1 April 19-5 and took over the business of Black and White, partners, as from 1 January 19-5. It was agreed that all profits made from 1 January should belong to the company and that the vendors should be entitled to interest on the purchase price from 1 January to date of payment. The purchase price was paid on 31 May 19-5 including £1,650 interest.

The following is the Profit and Loss Account for the year to 31 December 19-5:

	£		£
Salaries of Vendors	1,695	Gross Profit	28,000
Wages and General Expenses	8,640		
Rent and Rates	860		
Distribution Expenses	1,680		
Commission on Sales	700		
Bad Debts	314		
Interest paid to Vendors	1,650		
Directors' Remuneration	4,000		
Directors' Expenses	515		
Depreciation	£		
Motors	1,900		
Machinery	575		
	2,475		
Bank Interest	168		
Net Profit	5,303		
	28,000		28,000

You are given the following information:

1 Sales amounted to £20,000 for the three months to 31 March 19-5 and £50,000 for the

nine months to 31 December 19-5. Gross Profit is at a uniform rate of 40 per cent of selling price throughout the year, and commission at a rate of 1 per cent is paid on all sales.

2 Salaries of £1,695 were paid to the vendors for their assistance in running the business up to 31 March 19-5.

3 The Bad Debts written off are:

(a) A debt of £104 taken over from the vendors.

(b) A debt of £210 in respect of goods sold in August 19-5.

4 On 1 January 19-5 motors were bought for £7,000 and machinery for £5,000. On 1 March 19-5 another motor van was bought for £3,000, and on 1 October 19-5 another machine was added for £3,000. Depreciation has been written off motors at 20 per cent per annum, and machinery 10 per cent per annum.

5 Wages and general expenses and rent and rates accrued at an even rate throughout the year.

6 The bank granted an overdraft in June 19-5.

Assuming all calendar months are of equal length.

(a) Set out the Profit and Loss Account in columnar form, so as to distinguish between the period prior to the company's incorporation and the period after incorporation.

(b) To state how you would deal with the profit prior to incorporation.

(c) To state how you would deal with the results prior to incorporation if they turned out to be a net loss.

12.2 On 31 December 19-6 Breeze Ltd acquired all the assets, except the investments, of Blow Ltd.

The following are the summaries of the Profit and Loss Account of Blow Ltd for the years 19-4, 19-5 and 19-6:

	19-4 £	19-5 £	19-6 £		19-4 £	19-5 £	19-6 £
Motor Expenses	1,860	1,980	2,100	Trading Profits	22,050	25,780	25,590
Depreciation of Plant				Investment Income	290	340	480
Machinery	4,000	3,200	2,560	Rents Received	940	420	–
Bank Overdraft Interest	180	590	740	Profit on Sale of Property		4,800	
Wrapping Expenses	840	960	1,020				
Preliminary Expenses Written off	–	690	–				
Net Profit	16,400	23,920	19,650				
	23,280	31,340	26,070		23,280	31,340	26,070

The purchase price is to be the amount on which an estimated maintainable profit would represent a return of 25 per cent per annum.

The maintainable profit is to be taken as the average of the profits of the three years 19-4, 19-5 and 19-6, after making any necessary adjustments.

You are given the following information:

(a) The cost of the plant and machinery was £20,000. It is agreed that depreciation should have been written off at the rate of 12½ per cent per annum using the straight line method.

(b) A form of new plastic wrapping material introduced on to the market means that wrapping expenses will be halved in future.

(c) By a form of long-term rental of motor vehicles, it is estimated that motor expenses will be cut by one-third in future.

(d) Stock treated as valueless at 31 December 19-3 was sold for £1,900 in 19-5.

(e) The working capital of the new company is such that an overdraft is not contemplated.

(f) Management remuneration has been inadequate and will have to be increased by £1,500 a year in future.

You are required to set out your calculation of the purchase price. All workings must be shown. In fact, your managing director, who is a non-accountant, should be able to decipher how the price was calculated.

12.3 CJK Ltd was incorporated on 15 December 19-9 with an authorised capital of 200,000 ordinary shares of £0.20 each to acquire as at 31 December 19-9 the businesses of C K, a sole trader, and RP Ltd, a company.

From the following information you are required to prepare:

(a) the realisation and capital accounts in the books of CK and RP Ltd showing the winding up of these two concerns;

(b) the journal entries to open the books of CJK Ltd, including cash transactions and the raising of finance;

(c) the balance sheet of CJK Ltd after the transactions have been completed.

The balance sheet of CK as at 31 December 19-9 is as follows:

Balance Sheet

	£
Freehold premises	8,000
Plant	4,000
Stock	2,000
Debtors	5,000
Cash	200
	19,200
Capital	16,000
Creditors	3,200
	19,200

The assets (excluding cash) and the liabilities were taken over at the following values: freehold premises £10,000, plant £3,500, stock £2,000, debtors £5,000 less a bad debts provision of £300, goodwill £7,000, creditors £3,200 less a discount provision of £150. The purchase consideration, based on these values, was settled by the issue of shares at par.

The balance sheet of RP Ltd as at 31 December 19-9 is as follows:

	£
Freehold premises	4,500
Plant	2,000
Stock	1,600
Debtors	3,400
	11,500
Share capital: 10,000 shares at £0.40 each	4,000
Revenue surplus	2,500
Creditors	1,500
Bank overdraft	3,500
	11,500

The assets and liabilities were taken over at book value with the exception of the freehold premises which were revalued at £5,500. The purchase consideration was a cash payment of £1 and three shares in CJK Ltd at par in exchange for every two shares in RP Ltd.

Additional working capital and the funds required to complete the purchase of RP Ltd were provided by the issue for cash of:

(i) 10,000 shares at a premium of £0.30 per share;

(ii) £8,000 7 per cent Debenture Stock at 98.

The expenses of incorporating CJK Ltd were paid, amounting to £1,200.

(*Chartered Institute of Management Accountants*)

12.4A The Balance Sheet of Hubble Ltd as at 31 May 19-0 is shown below.

Hubble Ltd

	£	£
Fixed Assets:		
Freehold Premises at Cost		375,000
Plant and Machinery at Cost		
less Depreciation £48,765		101,235
Motor Vehicles at Cost		
less Depreciation £1,695		6,775
Current Assets:		483,010
Stock in Trade	102,550	
Debtors	96,340	
Cash in Hand	105	
		198,995
		682,005
Authorised Share Capital		
650,000 Ordinary Shares of £1 each		650,000
Issued Share Capital:		
400,000 Ordinary Shares of £1 each Fully Paid		400,000
Profit and Loss Account		180,630
Current Liabilities		580,630
Trade Creditors	63,200	
Bank Overdraft	38,175	
		101,375
		682,005

Hubble Ltd agreed to purchase at this date the Freehold Premises, Plant and Machinery and Stock of A Bubble at agreed valuations of £100,000, £10,000 and £55,000, respectively. The purchase price was to be fully settled by the issue to Bubble of 120,000 Ordinary Shares of £1 each in Hubble Ltd, and a cash payment to Bubble of £25,000. Bubble was to collect his debts and to pay his creditors.

Hubble Ltd sold one of its own premises prior to taking over Bubble for £75,000 (cost £55,000) and revalued the remainder at £400,000 (excluding those acquired from Bubble).

You are required to:

(*a*) Show the journal entries, including cash items, in the books of Hubble Ltd to give effect to the above transactions, and

(*b*) Show the Balance Sheet of Hubble Ltd after completing them.

(*Chartered Association of Certified Accountants*)

12.5A From the following information you are required to:

(*a*) prepare a statement apportioning the unappropriated profit between the pre-incorporation and post-incorporation period, showing the basis of apportionment;

(*b*) show the share capital and profits on the balance sheet of the company as at 31 March 19-0.

VU Limited was incorporated on 1 July 19-9 with an authorised share capital of 60,000 ordinary shares of £1 each, to take over the business of L and Sons as from 1 April 19-9.

The purchase consideration was agreed at £50,000 for the net tangible assets taken over, plus a further £6,000 for goodwill.

Payment was satisfied by the issue of £30,000 8 per cent Debentures and 26,000 ordinary shares both at par, on 1 August 19-9. Interest at 10 per cent per annum on the purchase consideration was paid up to this date.

The company raised a further £20,000 on 1 August 19-9 by the issue of ordinary shares at a premium of £0.25 per share.

The abridged profit and loss account for the year to 31 March 19-0 was as follows:

	£	£
Sales:		
1 April 19-9 to 30 June 19-9	30,000	
1 July 19-9 to 31 March 19-0	95,000	
		125,000
Cost of Sales for the year	80,000	
Depreciation	2,220	
Directors' Fees	500	
Administration Salaries and Expenses	8,840	
Sales Commission	4,375	
Goodwill Written Off	1,000	
Interest on Purchase Consideration, Gross	1,867	
Distribution Costs (60 per cent variable)	6,250	
Preliminary Expenses written off	1,650	
Debentures Interest, Gross	1,600	
Proposed Dividend on Ordinary Shares	7,560	
		115,862
Unappropriated Profit carried forward		9,138

The company sells one product only, of which the unit selling price has remained constant during the year, but due to improved buying the unit cost of sales was reduced by 10 per cent in the post-incorporation period as compared with the pre-incorporation period.

Taxation is to be ignored.

(*Chartered Institute of Management Accountants*)

12.6A Rowlock Ltd was incorporated on 1 October 19-8 to acquire Rowlock's mail order business, with effect from 1 June 19-8.

The purchase consideration was agreed at £35,000 to be satisfied by the issue on 1 December 19-8 to Rowlock or his nominee of:

20,000 Ordinary Shares of £1 each, fully paid, and £15,000 7 per cent Debentures.

The entries relating to the transfer were not made in the books which were carried on without a break until 31 May 19-9.

On 31 May 19-9 the trial balance extracted from the books is:

	£	£
Sales		52,185
Purchases	38,829	
Wrapping	840	
Postage	441	
Warehouse Rent and Rates	921	
Packing Expenses	1,890	
Office Expenses	627	
Stock on 31 May 19-8	5,261	
Director's Salary	1,000	
Debentures Interest (gross)	525	
Fixed Assets	25,000	
Current Assets (other than stock)	9,745	
Current Liabilities		4,162
Formation Expenses	218	
Capital Account – Wysocka, 31 May 19-8		29,450
Drawings Account – Wysocka, 31 May 19-8	500	
	85,797	85,797

You also ascertain the following:

1 Stock on 31 May 19-9 amounted to £4,946.

2 The average monthly sales for June, July and August were one-half of those for the remaining months of the year. The gross profit margin was constant throughout the year.

3 Wrapping, postage and packing expenses varied in direct proportion to sales, whilst office expenses were constant each month.

4 Formation expenses are to be written off.

You are required to prepare the Trading and Profit and Loss Account for the year ended 31 May 19-9 apportioned between the periods before and after incorporation, and Balance Sheet as on that date.

(*Chartered Institute of Management Accountants*)

13
Taxation in accounts

This chapter is concerned with the entries made in the accounts of firms in respect of taxation. It is not concerned with the actual calculations of the taxes. Taxation legislation is now extremely complex and contains many exceptions to the general rules applicable to companies. It is impossible in a book at this level to delve into too many of the complications, and it should therefore be appreciated that, as far as companies are concerned though the facts in this chapter apply to the great majority of limited companies, there are some other complications in a small minority of cases.

Taxation can be split between:

1 Direct taxes, payable to the Inland Revenue, this being the government department responsible for the calculation and collection of the taxes. For a company these taxes are corporation tax and income tax.

SSAP 8 deals with the treatment of taxation in company accounts, this SSAP will be adhered to in this chapter.

2 Value Added Tax, abbreviated as VAT. This has been dealt with in Volume 1.

Limited companies: corporation tax and income tax

The tax which limited companies suffer is known as **corporation tax**. It is legally an appropriation of profits, it is not an expense, and it should therefore be shown in the Profit and Loss Appropriation Account. Two law cases, many years ago, did in fact settle any arguments as to whether it was an expense or appropriation, both cases being decided in favour of the view that it was an appropriation of profits.

When a company makes profits, then such profits are assessable to corporation tax. It does not mean that corporation tax is payable on the net profits as shown in the accounts. What it does mean is that the corporation tax is assessable on the profit calculated after certain adjustments have been made to the net profit shown according to the Profit and Loss Account. There adjustments are not made in the actual accounts, they are made in calculations performed quite separately from the drafting of Finance Accounts. Suppose that K Ltd has the following Profit and Loss Account:

K Ltd Profit and Loss Account for the year ended 31 March 19-8

	£	£
Gross Profit		100,000
less: General Expenses	30,000	
Depreciation of Machinery	20,000	
		50,000
Net Profit		50,000

The depreciation provision for machinery is the accounting figure used for the financial accounts. It is not usually the same figure as that allowed by the Inland Revenue for the depreciation of the machinery. The allowances made for depreciation by the Inland Revenue are known as **capital allowances**. These are calculated by rules which usually vary at one point or another from the methods applied by the company in determining depreciation provisions. A detailed study of a textbook on taxation would be necessary to see exactly how capital allowances are calculated. In some fairly rare cases, hardly ever found in large or medium-sized concerns but probably more common in very small firms, the capital allowances are calculated and the financial provision for depreciation is taken at the same figure. In the case of K Ltd assume that the capital allowances amount to £27,000, and that the rate of corporation tax is 40 per cent on assessable profits. The calculation of the corporation tax liability would be.

	£
Net Profit per the Financial Accounts	50,000
add Depreciation provision not allowed as a deduction for corporation tax purposes	20,000
	70,000
less Capital Allowances	27,000
Adjusted Profits assessable to corporation tax	43,000

As the corporation tax is assumed to be at the rate of 40 per cent of assessable profits, the corporation tax liability will be £43,000 × 40 per cent = £17,200. Sometimes the adjusted profits are greater than the net profits shown in the financial accounts, but may equally well be less. This illustrates the fact that it is relatively rare for the external observer to be able to calculate the corporation tax payable merely by knowing the net profit made by the company. In fact, there are also other items than depreciation provisions that need adjusting to find the correct assessable profits for corporation tax purposes. All that is needed here is the understanding that profit per the Profit and Loss Account is normally different from assessable profit for corporation tax calculations.

The rate of corporation tax is fixed by the Chancellor of the Exchequer in his budget, normally presented to Parliament in April of each year. There have been budgets in other months of the year, but it is normal practice for the March/April budget to fix corporation tax rates. This rate is to be applied to the assessable profits of companies earned during the twelve months to 31 March before the budget. If the Chancellor announced in April 19-8 that the rate was to be 45 per cent, then this refers to each company's adjusted profits for the government financial year 1 April 19-7 to 31 March 19-8. Likewise, if in April 19-4 the corporation tax rate was announced as 40 per cent, this would refer to profits from 1 April 19-3 to 31 March 19-4. A company whose financial year end is not 31 March will therefore span two governmental financial years.

Example

Company T Ltd. Adjusted profits for the year ended 31 December 19-8 £160,000.

Rates of corporation tax:
    For the government financial year ended 31.3.19-8, 45 per cent.
    For the government financial year ended 31.3.19-9, 40 per cent.

	£
3 months' profit 1.1.19-8 to 31.3.19-8	
3/12 months × £160,000 = £40,000 × 45 per cent	18,000
9 months' profit 1.4.19-8 to 31.12.19-8	48,000
9/12 months × £160,000 = £120,000 × 40 per cent	66,000

Corporation tax – when payable

Starting from 1 April 1990 all companies will have a payment date of 9 months after the end of each accounting period. Until then companies trading before 1 April 1965 would normally have had a payment date later than that, but transitional regulations bring both these companies, and the ones formed later, on to the same basis of 9 months' delay following the end of the accounting period. It is not necessary here to study these transitional arrangements, it is better left to your books on taxation. We will assume a payment date 9 months after the accounting period throughout this book. For the rest of this chapter, unless mentioned otherwise, corporation tax will be assumed to be at the rate of 40 per cent for the purposes of illustration. In fact, companies with relatively small profits can pay at a lower rate than companies with greater profits.

Advance corporation tax

Basic features

When a dividend is paid by the company, a sum equal to a fraction of that figure must be paid to the Inland Revenue by the company as Advance Corporation Tax (ACT). The fraction to be found will depend on the standard rate of income tax in operation at the time.
    The fraction will be found thus:

$$\frac{\text{Standard rate of income tax}}{100 - \text{standard rate}}$$

Therefore, given different rates of income tax would give rise to the following rates of ACT:

Standard rate of Income Tax	30%	27%	25%
Workings	$\dfrac{30}{100\text{-}30}$	$\dfrac{27}{100\text{-}27}$	$\dfrac{25}{100\text{-}25}$
Rate of ACT	$= \frac{3}{7}$	$= \frac{27}{73}$	$= \frac{1}{3}$

For the purposes of illustration only, the standard rate of income tax will be taken as 30 per cent, making the ACT fraction $\frac{3}{7}$.

ACT is in fact a prepayment of the main or mainstream corporation tax bill of a company. The ACT is calculated *when* dividends are paid. The mainstream corporation tax can only be ascertained when accounts are submitted to the Inland Revenue after the end of an accounting period. ACT is payable within 3 months of a dividend payment.

Exhibit 13.1

These companies with income chargeable to corporation tax of £100,000 have dividend policies whereby they distribute:
  (a) Nothing
  (b) 50 per cent of available income
  (c) 100 per cent of available income.

	(a)		(b)		(c)	
	Profits	Tax	Profits	Tax	Profits	Tax
	£	£	£	£	£	£
Taxable	100,000		100,000		100,000	
Corporation Tax 40%	40,000	40,000	40,000	40,000	40,000	40,000
	60,000		60,000		60,000	
Dividend – net cash paid to shareholder	Nil		30,000		60,000	
	60,000		30,000		–	
ACT payable on dividend ³⁄₇		–		12,857		25,714
Mainstream Corporation Tax		40,000		27,143		14,286

Restrictions on set-offs of ACT

There is a limit to how much ACT can be set-off against mainstream corporation tax. The limit is calculated as follows:

Take company's profits assessable to Corporation Tax (excluding capital gains) say (A)	£100,000
ACT limit = Income Tax rate (30%) × (A)	£30,000

Any ACT not set-off against mainstream corporation tax for the period can be carried back and set-off against corporation tax for the past six years. Any excess which then still exists can be carried forward against future corporation tax liabilities without any time limit.

Given Corporation Tax as 40%, Income Tax as 30% the following would result in three companies with distributions of (A) £75,000, (B) £50,000, (C) £25,000

	Company A £	Company B £	Company C £
Taxable Profits	100,000	75,000	50,000
Basic Corporation Tax 40%	40,000	30,000	20,000
less ACT on Distribution			
Lower of			
(i) ACT on Distributions			
£75,000 × 3/7	32,142		
£50,000 × 3/7		21,428	
£25,000 × 3/7			10,714
or (ii) ACT limit of			
30% × £100,000	30,000		
30% × £75,000		22,500	
30% × £50,000			15,000
ACT set-off therefore is	30,000	21,428	10,714
Mainstream Corporation Tax	10,000	8,572	9,286

The unrelieved ACT of £2,142 for Company A is available for relief in another accounting period. Companies B and C have got full relief for ACT.

Proposed dividends

(a) The ACT which may be offset against the basic CT liability relates to dividends paid (less received) *during* the accounting period *irrespective* of the period *for which* the dividends are payable.

(b) ACT is due only when a dividend is *paid* not when it is *proposed*. It follows that ACT on a dividend proposed at the end of the accounting period will be offset against the basic CT liability of the next following accounting period (i.e. of the period in which the dividend is paid).

Writing off irrecoverable ACT

Any irrecoverable ACT (i.e. ACT the recoverability of which is not reasonably certain and foreseeable) should be written off in the profit and loss account in which the related dividend is shown.

There are two different views on the presentation in the profit and loss account of irrecoverable ACT written off. One view is that irrecoverable ACT should be treated as part of the tax charge upon the company to be deducted in arriving at profits after tax (known as the net basis); the other that the irrecoverable ACT, being a cost stemming from the payment of a dividend, should be treated as an appropriation like the dividend itself (known as the nil basis). Of the two methods, the first is supported by SSAP 8 as the appropriate accounting treatment because unrelieved ACT constitutes tax upon the company or group, as opposed to tax on the shareholders, and is not an appropriation of profits. It is appreciated, however, that some readers or analysts of accounts may wish for their purposes to regard irrecoverable ACT in some other manner. The amount of irrecoverable ACT should therefore be disclosed separately if material.

Income tax

As already stated, companies do not pay income tax, instead they suffer corporation tax. In the case of sole traders income tax is not directly connected with the business, as the calculation of it depends on whether the sole trader is married or not, the number of dependants that he may have and their ages, the amount and type of other income received by him, etc. It should therefore be charged to the Drawings Account.

The income tax charged upon a partnership is also subject to the personal situation of the partners. The actual apportionment of the tax between the partners must be performed by someone who has access to the personal tax computations, it most certainly is not apportioned in the partners' profit-sharing ratios. When the apportionment has been made each partner should have the relevant amount debited to his Drawings Account.

Sole traders and partnerships are not liable to corporation tax.

Income tax does, however, come into the accounts of limited companies in that the company, when paying charges such as debenture interest or some sorts of royalties, will deduct income tax from the amount to be paid to the debenture holder or royalty owner. This figure of income tax is then payable by the company to the Inland Revenue. This means simply that the company is acting as a tax collector on behalf of the Inland Revenue. Suppose the company has 1,000 different debenture holders, then it is far easier for the Inland Revenue if the company pays only the net amount (i.e. the amount of debenture interest less income tax) due to each debenture holder and then pays the income tax deducted, in one figure, to the Inland Revenue. This saves the Inland Revenue having to trace 1,000 debenture holders and then collect the money from them. It obviously cuts down on the bad debts that the Inland Revenue might suffer, it makes it more difficult to evade the payment of income tax, and all this plus the fact that it makes it cheaper for the Inland Revenue to administer the system.

For the rest of this chapter it will be assumed that the standard rate of income tax is 30 per cent. This rate will obviously differ from time to time. In addition where an individual has a high income he/she will pay rates of income tax which will exceed 30 per cent. However, a company will deduct income tax at the standard rate, even though individual debenture holders may have to pay income tax at higher rates, or indeed pay no income tax at all.

This means that if a company had 8 per cent debentures amounting to £100,000 then, assuming that the debenture interest was payable in one amount, cheques amounting to a total of £5,600 (8 per cent of £100,000 = £8,000 less 30 per cent income tax, £2,400 = £5,600), will be paid to the debenture holders. A cheque for £2,400 will then be paid to the Inland Revenue by the company. Assume that debenture holder AB is liable on his income to income tax at the rate of 30 per cent, and that he receives interest of £70 net (i.e. £100 gross less income tax £30), on his debenture of £1,250 then he has already suffered his rightful income tax by deduction at the source, he will thus not get a further bill from the Inland Revenue for the £30 tax, he has already suffered the full amount due by him, and the company will have paid the £30 income tax as part of the total income tax cheque of £2,400.

On the other hand debenture holder CD may not be liable to income tax because his income is low, or that he has a large number of dependants or other such circumstance for which he obtains liability from having to pay any income tax. If he has a debenture of £1,000 he will receive a cheque for interest amounting to £56 (i.e. £80 gross less income tax £24). As he is not liable to income tax, but as £24 of his money has been included in the total cheque paid by the company to the Inland Revenue of £2,400, then he will be able to claim a refund of £24 from the Inland Revenue. Such a claim is made direct to the Inland Revenue, the company has nothing to do with the refund.

With another debenture holder, EF, this person is liable to a higher rate of income tax, say 40 per cent, on his income. If he has a debenture of £25,000, then the company will pay a cheque to him of £1,400 (£2,000 gross less income tax £600). In fact he is really liable to £800 income tax (£2,000 at 40 per cent) on this income. As £600 income tax has been taken from him and handed over by the company, included in the total cheque of £2,400 income tax paid to the Inland Revenue by the company, then eventually the Inland Revenue will send an extra demand for income tax of £200 (£800 liable less £600 already paid). The company will have nothing to do with this extra demand.

Of course, a company may well have bought debentures or may own royalties, etc., in another company. This may mean that the company not only pays charges, such as debenture interest, but also receives similar items from other companies. The company will receive such items net after income tax has been deducted. When the company both receives and pays such items, it may set off the tax already suffered by it from such interest, etc., received against the tax collected by it from its own charges, just paying the resultant net figure of income tax to the Inland Revenue.

The figures of charges to be shown as being paid or received by the company in the company's own Profit and Loss Account are the gross charges, i.e. the same as they would have been if income tax had never been invented. An exhibit will now be used to illustrate this more clearly.

Exhibit 13.3

RST Ltd has 7 per cent debentures amounting to £10,000 and has bought a £4,000 debenture of 10 per cent in a private company, XYZ Ltd. During the year cheques amounting to £490 (£700 less 30 per cent) have been paid to debenture holders, and a cheque of £280 (£400 less 30 per cent) has been received from XYZ Ltd. Instead of paying over the £210 income tax deducted on payment of debenture interest, RST Ltd waits until the cheque is received from XYZ Ltd, and then pays a cheque for £90 (£210 collected by it less £120 already suffered by deduction by XYZ Ltd) to the Inland Revenue in settlement.

Debenture Interest Payable

	£		£
Cash	490	Profit and Loss	700
Income Tax	210		
	700		700

Debenture Interest Receivable

	£		£
Profit and Loss	400	Cash	280
		Income Tax	120
	400		400

	£		£
Unquoted Investment Income	120	Debenture Interest	210
Cash	90		
	210		210

It may well have been the case that, although the income tax had been deducted at source from both the payment out of the company, and the amount received, no cash has been paid specifically to the Inland Revenue by the company by the balance sheet date. This means that the balance of £90 owing to the Inland Revenue will be carried down as a credit balance and will be shown under Current Liabilities in the balance sheet.

Corporation tax and the imputation system

When a dividend is paid by a company, this is done without any specific deduction of tax of any kind from the dividend payment. However, the dividend has been paid out of the balance of profits remaining after corporation tax has been charged. In addition, although this has not been deducted specifically from the dividend cheques, a sum equal to $\frac{3}{7}$ of the dividend has to be paid as Advance Corporation Tax. The final part of what is called the Imputation System is that the recipient of the dividend is entitled to a tax credit. The tax credit will equal $\frac{3}{7}$ of the actual amount of the dividend received. (On the assumption of 30 per cent income tax rate.)

This works out in this way. An individual, not a company, who has 700 shares of £1 each in a company will receive a dividend cheque for £70 if the company pays a dividend of 10 per cent on its shares. When he declares the income on his tax return he will have to show the figure of the actual income received plus a tax credit equal to $\frac{3}{7}$ of that figure, i.e. in this case £70 + $\frac{3}{7}$ of £70 = £100. Assuming an income tax rate of 30 per cent he would normally have to pay £30 income tax on this income of £100, but he is able to set off the tax credit he is entitled to, making a liability of nil. On the other hand, if his personal reliefs are such that he would not have to pay any income tax at all, then he will be able to get a refund of the £30 tax credit from the Inland Revenue. If his income is so great that he has to pay a higher rate of income tax than 30 per cent, then the Inland Revenue will send him a tax-demand for the extra income tax.

When it comes to companies buying shares in other companies there are a few differences. Some terminology is necessary here. 'Franked Investment Income' consists of the dividend received, plus the tax credit, by a UK resident company from another UK resident company. A 'Franked Payment' is a dividend, plus the relevant advance corporation tax, payable by a UK resident company.

As far as the franked investment income is concerned the double entry is as follows:

Cash received:
  Dr Bank
  Cr Investment Income

Tax credit:
  Dr Tax on profit on ordinary activities
  Cr Investment Income

This means that if company A received a dividend of £560 from company B there will also be a tax credit of £240 (3/7 of £560). The accounts will appear as:

Bank

	£
Investment Income	560

Investment Income

Profit and Loss	800	Bank	560
		Tax on profit on ordinary activities	240
	800		800

The profit and loss account will therefore include £800 investment income, while the £240 tax will be included in the total figure of taxation which will include corporation tax.

As far as the calculation of the payment of ACT by company A is concerned, it will be able to deduct the figure of £240 from its next ACT payment. This is for the *calculation part* only, it does not affect basic double entry.

Although the payments of advance corporation tax are affected as stated, the full payment of corporation tax liability will be affected only as regards the allocation of it between the advance corporation tax part and the mainstream part.

Dividends proposed, and not paid, at the year end are simply shown gross, as are dividends receivable but not yet actually received. No entry is made for tax in these cases.

Deferred taxation

It was pointed out earlier in the chapter that profits *per the accounts* and profits *on which tax is payable* are often quite different from each other. The main reasons for this are:

(*a*) The figure of depreciation shown in the profit and loss account may be far different than the Inland Revenue's figure for 'capital allowances', which is *their* way of calculating allowances for depreciation.

(*b*) Some items of expense charged in the profit and loss account will not be allowed by the Inland Revenue as expenses. Examples are political donations, fines for illegal acts, and expenses of entertaining UK customers.

Timing differences. In the case of capital allowances under (*a*) above, the amount of 'depreciation' charged for an asset over the years will eventually equal the amount allowed by the Inland Revenue as 'capital allowances'. Where the difference lies is in the periods when these items will be taken into account.

For instance, let us take an asset which will be used for three years and then put out of use. It costs £4,800 and will be sold three years later for £2,025. Depreciation rate is to be 33⅓ per cent straight line. Inland Revenue capital allowances are 25 per cent reducing balance.

Years ended 5 April	19-2	19-3	19-4	Total
	£	£	£	£
Depreciation in accounts	925	925	925	2,775
Capital allowances in tax calculations	1,200	900	675	2,775
Timing differences	+275	−25	−250	nil

Let us suppose that profits for each year, after charging depreciation amounted to £1,000. A comparison of profits per accounts and profits for tax purposes becomes as follows:

Years ended 5 April	19-2	19-3	19-4	Total
	£	£	£	£
Profits per accounts after depreciation	1,000	1,000	1,000	3,000
Profits for tax purposes	725	1,025	1,250	3,000
Differences	−275	+25	+250	nil

As you can see, profits have in fact remained the same at £1,000 it is the timing difference of capital allowances which gives different figures for tax purposes. Take the point of view that profits of £1,000 per year give a more sensible picture than the £725; £1,025; £1,250 per the Inland Revenue calculations. The company's way of depreciating is probably more suitable than the Inland Revenue's method which does not vary between different companies.

You may well be asking if it matters at all. Analysts and potential investors and shareholders themselves place a great reliance on 'earnings per share after tax' (EPS). Suppose that the corporation tax was 40 per cent for each of the three years and that there were 10,000 shares. This would give the following figures:

Tax based on 'real profits', i.e. company's calculations

	19-2	19-3	19-4
	£	£	£
Profits per accounts before taxation	1,000	1,000	1,000
less Corporation Tax (40%)	400	400	400
Profit after tax	600	600	600
Earnings per share ÷ 10,000	6.0p	6.0p	6.0p

Tax based on Inland Revenue calculations

	19-2	19-3	19-4
	£	£	£
Profits per accounts before taxation	1,000	1,000	1,000
less Corporation Tax:			
40% × £725	290		
40% × £1,025		410	
40% × £1,250			500
Profits after tax	710	590	500
Earnings per share ÷ 10,000	7.1p	5.9p	5.0p

In truth each of the years have been equally as profitable as one another, as shown by 6.0p earnings per share each year. On the other hand, if no adjustment is made, the accounts when based on actual tax paid would show 7.1p; 5.9p; 5.0p. This would confuse shareholders and would-be shareholders.

So as not to distort the picture given by accounts the concept of 'deferred taxation' was brought in by accountants. This was given approval in SSAP15 (revised) Accounting for Deferred Taxation. The double entry is as follows:

(i) In the years when taxation is *lower* than it would be on comparable accounting profits:

Dr Profit and Loss Appropriation account
Cr Deferred Taxation account

with the amount of taxation understated.

(ii) In the years when taxation is *higher* than it would be on comparable accounting profits:

Dr Deferred Taxation account
Cr Profit and Loss Appropriation Account

with the amount of taxation overstated.

We will now look at Exhibit 13.4 to see how the Profit and Loss Appropriation account and Deferred Taxation account would have been drawn up for the example given above.

To make the exhibit follow the wording for published company accounts, instead of 'Profit per accounts before taxation' we will call it instead 'Profit on ordinary activities before taxation'.

Exhibit 13.4

Profit and Loss Appropriation Account for the years ended 5 April

	19-2		19-3		19-4	
	£	£	£	£	£	£
Profit on ordinary activities before taxation		1,000		1,000		1,000
Tax on profit on ordinary activities:						
Corporation Tax	290		410		500	
Deferred Taxation	110	400	(10)	400	(100)	400
Profit on ordinary activities after taxation		600		600		600

For purposes of shareholders, stock exchange analysts, would-be shareholders, etc. the profit after taxation figures on which Earnings per Share (EPS) would be calculated is the figure of £600 for each of the three years. The distortion has thus been removed.

Assuming that Corporation Tax is payable on 1 January following each accounting year end, the accounts for Corporation Tax and Deferred Tax would be as follows:

Corporation Tax

19-2		£	19-2		£
Apl	5 Balance c/d	290	Apl	5 Profit and Loss Appropriation	290
		290			290
19-3			19-2		
Jan	1 Bank	290	Apl	6 Balance b/d	290
			19-3		
Apl	5 Balance c/d	410	Apl	5 Profit and Loss Appropriation	410
		700			700
19-4			19-3		
Jan	1 Bank	410	Apl	6 Balance b/d	410
			19-4		
Apl	5 Balance c/d	500	Apl	5 Profit and Loss Appropriation	500
		910			910
			19-4		
			Apl	6 Balance b/d	500

Deferred Taxation

19-2		£	19-2		£
Apl	5 Balance c/d	110	Apl	5 Profit and Loss Appropriation	110
		110			110
19-3			19-2		
Apl	5 Profit and Loss Appropriation	10	Apl	6 Balance b/d	110
Apl	5 Balance c/d	100			
		110			110
19-4			19-3		
Apl	5 Profit and Loss Appropriation	100	Apl	6 Balance b/d	100
		100			100

The balance sheets would appear:

	19-2	19-3	19-4
	£	£	£
Creditors: amounts falling due within one year			
Corporation Tax	290	410	500
Provisions for liabilities and charges			
Deferred Taxation*	110	100	–

* Any Advance Corporation Tax (ACT) recoverable would be shown as a deduction from this figure.

Permanent differences. Differences in profits for accounts purposes and those for tax purposes because of non-allowable items such as political donations, entertaining expenses etc, are not adjusted for.

A fully worked example

Exhibit 13.5 shows the accounts in which tax will be involved for the first year of a new company, Harlow Ltd. Exhibit 13.6 follows with the second year of that company. This should make your understanding easier, to consider one year alone very often leaves the student with many unanswered questions in his mind.

To get you used to different tax rates, we have changed corporation tax rates used to 35% and income tax to 25%.

Exhibit 13.5

Harlow Ltd has just finished its first year of trading on 31 December 19-4. Corporation tax throughout was 35% and income tax was 25%. You are given the following information:

(A) Net trading profit for the year was £165,000, before adjustment for debenture interest.

(B) Debenture interest (net) of £12,000 was paid on 31 December 19-4 and (C) the income tax deducted was paid on the same date.

(D) An ordinary interim dividend of 10 per cent on the 210,000 £1 ordinary shares was paid on July 1st 19-4, and (E) the requisite ACT on October 1st 19-4.

(F) A proposed final ordinary dividend of 25 per cent for the year is to be accrued.

(G) Depreciation of £12,000 has been charged before arriving at net trading profit. Capital allowances of £37,000 have been approved by the Inland Revenue. Account for timing differences.

(H) Corporation tax on the first year's trading is expected to be £38,500.

You ar required to:
   (*a*) Show double-entry accounts (other than bank) to record the above
   (*b*) Prepare extracts from the profit and loss account and balance sheet

Exhibit 13.6 will carry on to Harlow Ltd's second year in trading.

Debenture Interest

19-4		£	19-4	£
Dec 31 Bank	(B)	12,000	Dec 31 Profit and Loss	16,000
Dec 31 Income Tax	(C)	4,000		
		16,000		16,000

Income Tax

19-4			£	19-4			£
Dec 31 Bank	(C)	4,000		Dec 31 Debenture Interest	(C)	4,000

Ordinary Dividends

19-4			£	19-4		£
Jul 1 Bank	(D)	21,000		Dec 31 Profit and Loss		73,500
Dec 31 Accrued c/d		52,500				
		73,500				73,500

Deferred Taxation

19-4	£	19-4		£
Dec 31 Balance c/d	8,750	Dec 31 Profit and Loss*	(G)	8,750

* (V) Allowed £37,000 but only charged £12,000
= £25,000 × 35% corporation tax deferred = £8,750

Corporation Tax

19-4	£	19-4		£
Dec 31 Balance c/d	38,500	Dec 31 Profit and Loss	(H)	38,000

Advance Corporation Tax

19-4		£	19-4	£
Oct 1 Bank (⅓ × £21,000)	(E)	7,000	Dec 31 Balance c/d	7,000

Profit and Loss Account (extracts) for the year ended 31 December 19-4

		£	£
Net trading profit	(A)		165,000
less debenture interest	(B)		16,000
Profit on ordinary activities before taxation			149,000
Corporation tax	(H)	38,500	
Deferred taxation	(G)	8,750	47,250
Profit on ordinary activities after taxation			101,750
less dividends on ordinary shares:			
Interim paid 10 per cent	(D)	21,000	
Proposed final dividend 25 per cent		52,500	
			73,500

Balance sheets (extracts) as at 31 December 19-4

Creditors: amounts falling due within one year	£
Proposed ordinary dividend	52,500
Corporation tax	38,500
Deferred tax (8,750 – ACT recoverable 7000)	1,750

Exhibit 13.6

Harlow Ltd, as per Exhibit 13.5 has now finished its second year of trading. From 19-4 there will be four balances (concerned with the exhibit) to be brought forward. These accounts are:

Proposed ordinary dividend	(A)	Cr	£52,500
Corporation tax	(B)	Cr	£38,500
Deferred taxation	(C)	Cr	£8,750
ACT recoverable	(D)	Dr	£7,000

The following information is given to you:

(E) The proposed ordinary dividend £52,500 was paid on 1 March 19-5 (F) the ACT was paid on 1 June 19-5. Corporation tax remains at 35% and income tax at 25%.

(G) Shares had been bought in STU Ltd and franked investment income in the form of a dividend of £1,500 (excluding tax credits) was received on 31 August 19-5.

(H) An interim dividend of 15 per cent on the 210,000 £1 ordinary shares was paid on 1 July 19-5 and (I) the ACT on it paid on 30 September 19-4.

(J) Debentures had been bought in RRR Ltd and interest (net) of £4,500 was received on 30 December 19-5.

(K) Harlow Ltd paid its own debenture interest (net) of £12,000 on 31 December 19-5, and (L) the income tax account (net) was paid on the same date.

(M) The corporation tax due for 19-4 was paid on 30 September 19-5.

(N) A final ordinary dividend for the year of 30 per cent was proposed. This will be paid in March 19-6.

(O) Corporation tax for the year ended 31 December 19-5 is expected to be £41,300.

(P) Depreciation of £28,000 has been charged in the accounts, while capital allowances amounted to £22,000.

(Q) Net trading profit after deducting depreciation, but before adjusting for the above was £178,000.

It would have been quite possible to open a 'Tax on Profit on Ordinary Activities account' and transfer tax items to their prior to closing to the Profit and Loss Account. We will now use this method.

Ordinary Dividends

19-5			£	19-5			£
Mar 1 Bank	(E)		52,500	Jan 1 Balance b/f	(A)		52,500
Jul 1 Bank Interim	(H)		31,500	Dec 31 Profit and Loss			94,500
Dec 31 Accrued c/d	(N)		63,000				
			147,000				147,000

(Franked) Investment Income

19-5		£	19-5			£
Dec 31 Profit and Loss		2,000	Aug 31 Bank	(G)		1,500
			Aug 31 Tax on profit on ordinary activities			500
		2,000				2,000

Debenture Interest Payable

19-5		£	19-5	£
Dec 31 Bank	(K)	12,000	Dec 31 Profit and Loss	16,000
Dec 31 Income tax		4,000		
		16,000		16,000

Debenture Interest Receivable

19-5	£	19-5		£
Dec 31 Profit and Loss	6,000	Dec 30 Bank	(J)	4,500
		Dec 30 Income Tax		1,500
	6,000			6,000

Income Tax

19-5		£	19-5	£
Dec 30 Debenture Interest			Dec 31 Debenture Interest	
Receivable		1,500	payable	4,000
Dec 31 Bank	(L)	2,500		
		4,000		4,000

Deferred Taxation

19-5		£	19-5		£
Dec 31 Tax on profit on			Jan 1 Balance b/f	(C)	8,750
ordinary activities					
(6000 × 35%)	(P)	2,100			
Dec 31 Balance c/d		6,650			
		8,750			8,750

Advance Corporation Tax

19-5		£	19-5	£
Jan 1 Balance b/f	(D)	7,000	Sep 30 Corporation tax – set-off*	7,000
Jan 1 Bank ⅓ × 52,500	(F)	17,500	Dec 31 Balance c/d	27,500
Sep 30 Bank ⅓ × 31,500 – 500 (FII)	(I)	10,000		
		34,500		34,500

* *Note*: only the ACT paid in 19-4 can be set-off against the tax for 19-4

Corporation Tax

19-5		£	19-5			£
Sep 30 ACT (recovered)		7,000	Jan 1 Balance b/f	(B)	38,500
Sep 30 Bank	(M)	31,500	Dec 31 Tax on profit on		
			ordinary activities	(O)	41,300
Dec 31 Accrued c/d		41,300			
		79,800			79,800

Tax on Profit on Ordinary Activities

19-5		£	19-5			£
Aug 31 Franked Investment			Dec 31 Deferred Taxation	(P)	2,100
Income		500			
Dec 31 Corporation Tax	(O)	41,300	Dec 31 Profit and Loss		39,700
		41,800			41,800

Profit and Loss Account (extracts) for the year ended 31 December 19-5

		£	£
Net trading profit	(Q)		178,000
add debenture interest received		6,000	
franked investment income		2,000	8,000
			186,000
less debenture interest payable			16,000
Profit on ordinary activities before taxation			170,000
Tax on profit on ordinary activities			39,700
Profit on ordinary activities after taxation			130,300
less dividends on ordinary shares			
Interim paid 15 per cent		31,500	
Proposed final dividend		63,000	94,500

Balance Sheet (extracts) as at 31 December 19-5

Creditors: amounts falling due within one year	£
Proposed Ordinary Dividend	63,000
Corporation Tax	41,300
Deferred Tax (6,650 – ACT recoverable 27,500)	(20,850)

Review questions

Note: At the time of writing no suitable questions from professional examinations were available. Up to this time the complications relating to companies formed before 1965, and which are not relevant after 1990, have figured in most specialised tax questions.

For those taking examinations with little tax content, questions 13.5 and 13.6A will be sufficient for your purposes.

13.1 Long Acre Ltd has just finished its first year of trading to 31 December 19-3. Corporation tax throughout was 35% and income tax 25%. You are given the following information:

     (i)   Net trading profit, after adjustment for (ii) but before other adjustments, was £220,000.

     (ii)   Depreciation of £50,000 was charged in the accounts. Capital allowances amounted to £90,000.

     (iii) An interim dividend of 5 per cent on 400,000 £1 ordinary shares was paid on 1 July 19-3.

     (iv) ACT on (iii) was paid on 30 September 19-3.

     (v)   Debenture interest of £9,600 (net) was paid on 31 December 19-3.

     (vi) Income tax deducted from debenture interest was paid on 31 Jan 19-4.

     (vii) A final dividend of 7½ per cent was proposed for the year.

     (viii) Corporation tax for the year was estimated to be £90,000.

You are required to:

    (*a*) Draw up the double-entry accounts recording the above (except bank).

    (*b*) Show the relevant extracts from the profit and loss account and the balance sheet.

Note that question 13.2A is concerned with the second year of trading for Long Acre Ltd.

13.2A Long Acre Ltd has just finished its second year of trading to 31 December 19-4. Balances per 13.1 need to be brought forward into this question. Tax rates are the same as for 19-3.

The following information is available:

     (i)   The proposed final dividend for 19-3, 13.1, was paid on 31 January 19-4.

     (ii)   ACT on (i) was paid on 31 March 19-4.

     (iii) Shares in Covent Ltd were bought on 1 January 19-4. A dividend of £2,400 (excluding tax credits) was received on 30 September 19-4. This is franked investment income.

     (iv) Debentures in Covent Ltd, were bought 1 July 19-4. Debenture interest of £7,200 (net) was paid to us on 31 December 19-4.

     (v)   Debenture interest of £9,600 (net) was paid by us on 31 December 19-4.

     (vi) Income tax owing to the Inland Revenue for 19-4 was not paid by us until 19-5. The 19-3 income tax had been paid on 30 January 19-4.

     (vii) An interim dividend of 7½ per cent on 400,000 £1 ordinary shares was paid by us on 10 July 19-4.

     (viii) ACT on (vii) was paid by us on 10 October 19-4.

     (ix) A final dividend of 17½ per cent was proposed for the year.

     (x)   Depreciation of £70,000 was charged in the accounts. Capital allowances amounted to £96,000.

     (xi) Net trading profit (before taking into account (iii), (iv), and (v) was £360,000).

     (xii) The Corporation Tax due for 19-3 was paid on 1 October 19-4. Corporation Tax for the year to 31 December 19-4 is expected to be £95,000.

You are required to:

    (*a*) Draw up the double-entry accounts recording the above (except bank).

    (*b*) Show the relevant extracts from the profit and loss account for the year and balance sheet at the year end.

Question 13.3 is a typical professional examination question. It is not easy. Remember to bring forward the balances from the previous year which will often have to be deduced. The letters (A) to (N) against the information will make it easier for you to check the answer against that given at the back of the book.

13.3 Corporation tax for financial years 19-1, 19-2, and 19-3 was 35% and Income Tax for each year was 25%.

(A) Barnet Ltd's draft profit and loss account for the year ended 31 December 19-2 shows net trading profit of £560,000. This figure is before taking into account (B) and (C1) and (C2).

(B) Debenture interest paid on 30 November 19-2 (gross) was £80,000. Ignore accruals.

(C1) Fixed rate interest received is £24,000 net, excluding tax credits. Date received 31 October 19-2. Ignore accruals.

(C2) A dividend of £900 was received from CD Ltd on 1 September. This is franked investment income.

(D) Depreciation, already charged before calculating net trading profit, was £50,000. This compares with £90,000 capital allowances given by the Inland Revenue. There is to be full provision for all timing differences for 19-2.

(E) The income tax bill (net) in respect of (B) and (C1) was paid on 15 December 19-2.

(F) Preference dividend paid on 30 June 19-2 £18,000.

(G) Ordinary interim dividend paid 15 July 19-2 £75,000.

(H) Proposed final ordinary dividend for 19-2 (paid in 19-3) was £120,000.

(I) Proposed final ordinary dividend for 19-1 (paid 31 March 19-2) was £90,000.

(J) There was a credit balance on deferred taxation account on 31 December 19- 1 of £67,000.

(K) Mainstream tax for 19-1 had been provided for at £115,000 but was finally agreed at £112,000 (paid on 30 September 19-2).

(L) Corporation tax for 19-2 is estimated to be £154,000.

(M) ⅓ ACT is paid in each case two months after dividends paid.

(N) ACT paid in 19-1 but which had not been set-off against Corporation Tax in 19-1 amounted to £49,000.

You are required to enter up the following accounts for the year ended 31 December 19-2 for Barnet Ltd: Deferred Tax; Income Tax; Interest Receivable; Debenture Interest; Franked Investment Income; Advance Corporation Tax; Corporation Tax; Tax on Profit on Ordinary Activities; Preference Dividends; Ordinary Dividends; Profit and Loss Accounts Extracts. Also Balance Sheet extracts as at 31 Dec 19-2.

13.4A KK Ltd has a trading profit, before dealing with any of the undermentioned items, for the year ended 31 December 19-9 of £200,000. You are to complete the Profit and Loss and Appropriation Account for the year and balance sheet extracts as at the end of the year.

(*a*) The standard rate of income tax is taken as being 30 per cent.

(*b*) KK Ltd has bought £80,000 of 10 per cent debentures in another company. KK Ltd receives its interest, less income tax, for the year on 15 December 19-9.

(*c*) KK has issued £150,000 of 8 per cent debentures, and pays interest, less income tax for the year on 20 December 19-9.

(*d*) No cheque has been paid to the Inland Revenue for income tax.

(*e*) KK Ltd has a liability for Corporation Tax, based on the year's profits for 19-9, of £97,000.

(*f*) KK Ltd owns 60,000 ordinary shares of £1 each in GHH Ltd, and receives a cheque for the dividend of 20 per cent in November 19-9. GHH Ltd is neither a subsidiary company nor a related company.

(*g*) KK Ltd proposed a dividend of 15 per cent on the 100,000 ordinary shares of £1 each, payable out of the profits for 19-9.

(*h*) Transfer £20,000 to General Reserve.

(*i*) Unappropriated profits brought forward from last year amounted to £19,830.

13.5 BG Ltd has a trading profit for the year ended 31 December 19-7, before dealing with the following items, of £50,000. You are to complete the Profit and Loss Account and Appropriation Account and show the balance sheet extracts.

(*a*) The standard rate of income tax is taken as being 30 per cent.

(*b*) BG Ltd had £40,000 of 9 per cent debentures. It sent them cheques for debenture interest for the year less income tax on 31 December 19-7.

(*c*) BG Ltd had bought £10,000 of 11 per cent debentures in another company. It received a year's interest, less income tax, on 30 December 19-7.

(*d*) No cheque has been paid to the Inland Revenue for income tax.

(*e*) BG Ltd had bought 15,000 ordinary shares of £1 each in MM Ltd. MM Ltd paid a dividend to BG Ltd of 20 per cent on 30 November 19-7. MM Ltd is a 'related company'.

(*f*) BG Ltd had a liability for Corporation Tax, based on the profits for 19-7, of £24,000.

(*g*) BG proposed a dividend of 30 per cent on its 70,000 ordinary shares of £1 each, out of the profits for 19-7.

(*h*) Transfer £5,000 to General Reserve.

(*i*) Unappropriated profits brought forward from last year amounted to £9,870.

14
Provisions, reserves and liabilities

A **provision** is an amount written off or retained by way of providing for depreciation, renewals or diminution in value of assets; or retained by way of providing for any known liability of which the amount cannot be determined with 'substantial' accuracy. This therefore covers such items as Provisions for Depreciation. A **liability** is an amount owing which can be determined with substantial accuracy.

Sometimes, therefore, the difference between a provision and a liability hinges around what is meant by 'substantial' accuracy. Rent owing at the end of a financial year would normally be known with precision, this would obviously be a liability. Legal charges for a court case which has been heard, but for which the lawyers have not yet submitted their bill, would be a provision. The need for the distinction between liabilities and provision will not become obvious until Chapter 18, where the requirements of the Companies Acts regarding disclosures in the Final Accounts are examined.

A 'Revenue Reserve' is where an amount has been voluntarily transferred from the Profit and Loss Appropriation Account by debiting it, thus reducing the amount of profits left available for cash dividend purposes, and crediting a named Reserve Account. The reserve may be for some particular purpose, such as a Foreign Exchange Reserve Account created just in case the firm should ever meet a situation where it would suffer loss because of devaluation of a foreign currency, or it could be a General Reserve Account.

Such transfers are, in fact, an indication to the shareholders that it would be unwise at that particular time to pay out all the available profits as dividends. The resources represented by part of the profits should more wisely and profitably be kept in the firm, at least for the time being. Revenue Reserves can be called upon in future years to help swell the profits shown in the Profit and Loss Appropriation Account as being available for dividend purposes. This is effected quite simply by debiting the particular Reserve Account and crediting the Profit and Loss Appropriation Account.

A General Reserve may be needed because of the effect of inflation. If the year 19-3 a firm needs a working capital of £4,000, the volume of trade remains the same for the next three years but the price level increases by 25 per cent, then the working capital requirements will now be £5,000. If all the profits are distributed the firm will still only have £4,000 working capital which cannot possibly finance the same volume of trade as it did in 19-3. Transferring annual amounts of profits to a General Reserve instead of paying them out as dividends is one way to help overcome this problem. On the other hand it may just be the convention of conservatism asserting itself, with a philosophy of 'it's better to be safe than sorry', in this case to restrict dividends because the funds they would withdraw from the business may be needed in a moment of crisis. This is sometimes overdone, with the result that the firm has excessive amounts of liquid funds being inefficiently used, whereas if they were paid out to the shareholders, who after all are the owners, then the shareholders could put the funds to better use themselves.

This then leaves the question of the balance on the Profit and Loss Appropriation Account, if it is a credit balance. Is it a Revenue Reserve? There is no straightforward answer to this, the fact that it has not been utilised for dividend purposes could mean that it has been deliberately held back and as such could be classified as a Revenue Reserve. On the other hand, there may be a balance on the account just because it is inconvenient to pay dividends in fractions of percentages.

Capital reserves

A Capital Reserve is normally quite different from a Revenue Reserve. It is a reserve which is not available for transfer to the Profit and Loss Appropriation Account to swell the profits shown as available for cash dividend purposes. Most Capital Reserves can never be utilised for cash dividend purposes; notice the use of the word 'cash', as it will be seen later that Bonus Shares may be issued as a 'non-cash' dividend.

The ways that Capital Reserves are created must therefore be looked at.

Capital reserves created in accordance with the Companies Acts

The Companies Act states that the following are Capital Reserves and can never be utilised for the declaration of dividends payable in cash.

(*a*) Capital Redemption Reserve. *See* Chapter 11.

(*b*) Share Premium Account. *See* Chapter 10.

(*c*) Revaluation Reserve. Where an asset has been revalued then an increase is shown by a debit in the requisite asset account and a credit in the Revaluation Account. The recording of a reduction in value is shown by a credit in the asset account and a debit in the Revaluation Account.

Created by case law

The Companies Act 1985 defines distributable profits, described later in this chapter, but generally it can be said that if a company keeps to 'generally accepted accounting principles' then this will be said to be realised profits. As accounting develops and changes there will obviously be changes made in the 'generally accepted accounting principles'.

There will however, be law cases which will establish whether or not a profit has been realised and is therefore available for cash dividend purposes, i.e. the item could be transferred to a Capital Reserve account instead of a Revenue Reserve account and vice versa. Many of the law cases arising before 1985, deciding which profits had to go to Capital Reserve and which to Revenue Reserve will still apply. These are all items which will be studied by students moving to more advanced studies at a later stage. The new definition will however give rise to further law cases.

Capital reserves put to use

These can only be used in accordance with the Companies Acts. The following description of the actions which can be taken assumes that in fact the articles of association are the same as Table A for this purpose, and that therefore there are no provisions in the articles to prohibit such actions.

Capital Redemption Reserve (for creation, *see* Chapter 11)

(i) To be applied in paying up unissued shares of the company as fully-paid shares. These are commonly called 'bonus shares', and are dealt with in Chapter 15.

(ii) Can be reduced only in the manner as to reduction of share capital (*see* Chapter 15).

(iii) Can be reduced, in the case of a private company, where the permissible capital payment is greater than the nominal value of shares redeemed/purchased, (*see* Chapter 11).

Share Premium Account (for creation, *see* Chapter 10)

(i) The same provision referring to bonus shares as exists with the Capital Redemption Reserve.

(ii) Writing off preliminary expenses.

(iii) Writing off expenses and commission paid on the issue of shares or debentures.

(iv) In writing off discounts on shares or debentures issued (for creation of these accounts, *see* Chapter 10).

(v) Providing any premium payable on redemption or purchases of shares or debentures.

Revaluation reserve

Where the directors are of the opinion that any amount standing to the credit of the revaluation reserve is no longer necessary then the reserve must be reduced accordingly. An instance of this would be where an increase in the value of an asset had been credited to the revaluation account, and there had subsequently been a fall in the value of that asset.

The revaluation reserve may also be reduced where the permissible capital payment exceeds the nominal value of the shares redeemed/purchased.

Profits prior to incorporation (for creation, *see* Chapter 12)

These can be used for the issuing of bonus shares, in paying up partly paid shares, or alternatively they may be used to write down goodwill or some such similar fixed asset.

Created by case law

These can be used in the issue of bonus shares or in the paying up of partly paid shares.

Distributable profit

The Companies Act 1985, sections 263 to 281, and paragraph 91 of Schedule 4 covers the position regarding distributable profit. The first statutory definition was in the Companies Act of 1980, so previous to that it had been based on case law.

The basic rule for all companies (with the exception of investment companies) is that:

Accumulated realised profits less accumulated realised losses = distributable profits.

'Realised profits' (or realised losses) are the ones calculated by reference to the generally accepted accounting principles applying at the time *when* the accounts were prepared. This basically means that SSAPs will apply unless they come into conflict with the Companies Act itself.

Normally the revenue reserves, including any credit balance on the Profit and Loss Account, would equal distributable profit. The Companies Act 1985 does provide for three possible adjustments, outlined below.

Development costs

Under Section 269 any development costs which have been capitalised have to be deducted from distributable profits, *unless* there are special circumstances justifying the capitalisation. Normally this means that SSAP 13 will apply.

Depreciation on revalued assets

There is a conflict here between SSAP 12 and section 275 of the Companies Act 1985. SSAP 12 requires depreciation on revalued assets to be based on the revalued amounts. However, section 275 allows the extra depreciation because of the revaluation to be *added back* when calculating distributable profit.

Distributions in kind

Where a company makes a non-cash distribution, for example by giving an investment, and that item (i.e. in this case the investment) has been revalued, it could generally be said that part of the distribution was unrealised profit locked into the investment. However, section 275 allows this because the 'unrealised' profit is 'realised' by the distribution (from the company's viewpoint, anyway).

Distributions and auditors' reports

Section 271 prohibits any particular distribution if the auditor's report is qualified, with one exception. That is that if the amount involved is *not* material and the auditor agrees to this fact, then distribution of an item can take place.

If a distribution is unlawfully made, any member knowing it to be so could be made to repay it. If the company could not recover such distributions then legal proceedings could be taken against the directors.

Review questions

14.1 An extract from the draft accounts of Either Ltd at 30 November 19-5, shows the following figures before allowing for any dividend which might be proposed:

	£000s
Ordinary shares of £1 each	400
6% preference shares of £1 each	150
Capital redemption reserve	300
Revaluation reserve	125
General reserve	80
Profit and loss account	13
	1,068
Operating profit before taxation for the year	302
Taxation	145
	£157

Additional information includes:

(*a*) The revaluation reserve consists of an increase in the value of freehold property following a valuation in 19-3. The property concerned was one of three freehold properties owned by the company and was subsequently sold at the revalued amount.

(*b*) It has been found that a number of stock items have been included at cost price, but were being sold after the balance sheet date at prices well below cost. To allow for this, stock at 30 November 19-5 would need to be reduced by £35,000.

(*c*) Provision for directors' remuneration should be made in the sum of £43,000.

(*d*) Included on the balance sheet is £250,000 of research and development expenditure carried forward.

(*e*) No dividends have yet been paid on either ordinary or preference shares for the year to 30 November 19-5, but the directors wish to pay the maximum permissible dividends for the year.

(*f*) Since the draft accounts were produced it has been reported that a major customer of Either Ltd has gone into liquidation and is unlikely to be able to pay more than 50p in the £ to its creditors. At 30 November 19-5 this customer owed £60,000 and this has since risen to £180,000.

(*g*) It has been decided that the depreciation rates for plant and machinery are too low but the effect of the new rates has not been taken into account in constructing the draft accounts. The following information is available:

	£
Plant and machinery	
Purchases at the commencement of the business on	
1 December 19-1 cost	100,000
Later purchases were 1 June 19-3	25,000
29 February 19-4	28,000
31 May 19-4	45,000
1 December 19-4	50,000

In the draft accounts depreciation has been charged at the rate of 25% using the reducing balance method and charging a full year's depreciation in the year of purchase. It has been decided to change to the straight line method using the same percentage but charging only an appropriate portion of the depreciation in the year of purchase. There have been no sales of plant and machinery during the period.

Required:

(*a*) Calculate the maximum amount which the directors of Either Ltd may propose as a dividend to be paid to the ordinary shareholders whilst observing the requirements of the Companies Act. Show all workings and state any assumptions made.

(*b*) Outline and discuss any differences which might have been made to your answer to (*a*) if the company were a public limited company.

For the purposes of this question you may take it that corporation tax is levied at the rate of 50%.

(*Chartered Association of Certified Accountants*)

15

The increase and reduction of the share capital of limited companies

Alteration of capital

A limited company may, if so authorised by its articles, and the correct legal formalities are observed, alter its share capital in any of the following ways.

1 Increasing its share capital by new shares, e.g. increase Authorised Share Capital from £5,000 to £15,000.

2 Consolidate and divide all or any of its share capital into shares of a larger amount than its existing shares, for instance to make 5,000 Ordinary Shares of £1 each into 1,000 Ordinary Shares of £5 each.

3 Convert all or any of its paid-up shares into stock, and reconvert that stock into shares of any denomination, e.g. 10,000 Ordinary Shares of £1 each made into £10,000 Ordinary Stock.

4 Subdivide all, or any, of its shares into shares of smaller denominations, e.g. 1,000 Ordinary Shares of £6 each made into 2,000 Ordinary Shares of £3 each, or 3,000 Ordinary Shares of £2 each, etc.

5 Cancel shares which have not been taken up. This is 'diminution' of capital, not to be confused with reduction of capital described later in the chapter. Thus a firm with an Authorised Capital of £10,000 and an Issued Capital of £8,000 can alter its capital to be Authorised Capital £8,000 and Issued Capital £8,000.

Bonus shares

These are shares issued to existing shareholders free of charge. An alternative name is 'scrip issue'.

If the articles give the power, and the requisite legal formalities are observed, the following may be applied in the issuing of bonus shares:

1 The balance of the Profit and Loss Appropriation Account.

2 Any other revenue reserve.

3 Any capital reserve, e.g. Share Premium.

This thus comprises all of the reserves.

The reason why this should ever be needed can be illustrated by taking a somewhat exaggerated example, shown in Exhibit 15.1.

Exhibit 15.1

A company, Better Price Ltd, started business fifty years ago with 1,000 Ordinary Shares of £1 each and £1,000 in the bank. The company has constantly had to retain a proportion of its profits to finance its operations, thus diverting them from being used for cash dividend purposes. Such a policy has conserved working capital.

The firm's Balance Sheet as at 31 December 19-7 is shown as:

Better Price Ltd
Balance Sheet as at 31 December 19-7
(before bonus shares are issued)

	£
Fixed Assets	5,000
Current Assets less Current Liabilities	5,000
	10,000
Share Capital	1,000
Reserves (including Profit and Loss Appropriation balance)	9,000
	10,000

If in fact an annual profit of £1,500 was now being made, this being 15 per cent on capital employed, and £1,000 could be paid annually as cash dividends, then the dividend declared each year would be 100 per cent, i.e. a dividend of £1,000 on shares of £1,000 nominal value. It is obvious that the dividends and the share capital have got out of step with one another. Employees and trade unions may well become quite belligerent, as owing to the lack of accounting knowledge, or even misuse of it, it might be believed that the firm was making unduly excessive profits. Customers, especially if they are the general public, may also be deluded into thinking that they were being charged excessive prices, or, even though this could be demonstrated not to be true because of the prices charged by competitors, they may well still have the feeling that they were somehow being duped.

In point of fact, an efficient firm in this particular industry or trade may well be only reasonably rewarded for the risks it has taken by making a profit of 15 per cent on capital employed. The figure of 100 per cent for the dividend is due to the very misleading convention in accounting in the UK of calculating dividends in relationship to the nominal amount of the share capital.

If it is considered, in fact, that £7,000 of the reserves could not be used for dividend purposes, due to the fact that the net assets should remain at £8,000, made up of Fixed Assets £5,000 and working capital £3,000, then besides the £1,000 Share Capital which cannot be returned to the shareholders there are also £7,000 reserves which cannot be rationally returned to them. Instead of this £7,000 being called reserves, it might as well be called capital, as it is needed by the business on a permanent basis.

To remedy this position, as well as some other needs less obvious, bonus shares were envisaged. The reserves are made non-returnable to the shareholders by being converted into share capital. Each holder of one Ordinary Share of £1 each will receive seven bonus shares (in the shape of seven ordinary shares) of £1 each. The Balance Sheet, if the bonus shares had been issued immediately, would then appear:

Better Price Ltd
Balance Sheet as at 31 December 19-7
(after bonus shares are issued)

	£
Fixed Assets	5,000
Current Assets *less* Current Liabilities	5,000
	10,000
Share Capital (£1,000+£7,000)	8,000
Reserves (£9,000−£7,000)	2,000
	10,000

When the dividends of £1,000 per annum are declared in the future, they will amount to $\dfrac{£1,000}{£8,000} \times \dfrac{100}{1} = 12.5$ per cent. This will cause less disturbance in the minds of employees, trade unions, and customers.

Of course the issue of bonus shares may be seen by any of the interested parties to be some form of diabolical liberty. To give seven shares of £1 each free for one previously owned may be seen as a travesty of social justice. In point of fact the shareholders have not gained at all. Before the bonus issue there were 1,000 shares that owned between them £10,000 of net assets. Therefore, assuming just for this purpose that the book 'value' is the same as any other 'value', each share was worth £10. After the bonus issue each previous holder now has eight shares for every one share he held before. If he had owned one share only, he now owns eight shares. He is therefore the owner of $\dfrac{8}{8,000}$ part of the firm, i.e. a one-thousandth part. The 'value' of the net assets are £10,000, so that he owns £10 of them, so his shares are worth £10. This is exactly the same 'value' as that applying before the bonus issue was made.

It would be useful in addition, to refer to other matters for comparison. Anyone who had owned a £1 share fifty years ago, then worth £1, would now have (if he was still living after such a long time) eight shares worth £8. A new house of a certain type fifty years ago might have cost £x, it may now cost £$8x$, the cost of a bottle of beer may now be y times greater than it was fifty years ago, a packet of cigarettes may be z times more and so on. Of course, the firm has brought a lot of trouble on itself by waiting so many years to capitalise reserves. It should have been done by several stages over the years.

This is all a very simplified, and in many ways an exaggerated version. There is, however, no doubt that misunderstanding of accounting and financial matters have caused a great deal of unnecessary friction in the past and will probably still do so in the future. Yet another very common misunderstanding is that the assumption the reader was asked to accept, namely that the Balance Sheet values equalled 'real values', is often one taken by the reader of a Balance Sheet. Thus a profit of £10,000 when the net assets book values are £20,000 may appear to be excessive, yet in fact a more realistic value of the assets may be saleable value, in which case the value may be £100,000.

The accounting entries necessary are to debit the Reserve Accounts utilised, and to credit a Bonus Account. The shares are then issued and the entry required to record this is to credit the share capital Account and to debit the Bonus Account. The Journal entries would be:

The Journal

	Dr	Cr
	£	£
Reserve Account(s) (show each account separately)	7,000	
Bonus Account		7,000
Transfer of an amount equal to the bonus payable in fully-paid shares		
Bonus Account	7,000	
Share Capital Account		7,000
Allotment and issue of 7,000 shares of £1 each, in satisfaction of the bonus declared		

Rights issue

A company can also increase its share capital by making a Rights Issue. This is the issue of shares to existing shareholders at a price lower than the ruling market price of the shares.

The price at which the shares of a very profitable company are quoted in the Stock Exchange is usually higher than the nominal value of the shares. For instance, the market price of the shares of a company might be quoted at £2.50 while the nominal value per share is only £1.00. If the company has 8,000 shares of £1 each and declares a rights issue of one for every eight held at a price of £1.50 per share, it is obvious that it will be cheaper for the existing shareholders to buy the rights issue at this price instead of buying the same shares in the open market for £2.50 per share. Assume that all the rights issue were taken up, then the number of shares taken up will be 1,000 (i.e. 8,000 ÷ 8). And the amount paid for them will be £1,500. The Journal entries will be:

The Journal

	Dr	Cr
	£	£
Cash	1,500	
Share Capital		1,000
Share Premium		500
Being the rights issue of 1 for every 8 shares		
held at a price of £1.50 nominal value being £1.00.		

It is to be noted that because the nominal value of each share is £1.00 while £1.50 was paid, the extra 50p constitutes a share premium to the company.

Reduction of capital

Where capital is not represented by assets

Any scheme for the reduction of capital needs to go through the legal formalities via the shareholders and other interested parties, and must receive the consent of the court. It is assumed that all of this has been carried out correctly.

Capital reduction means in fact that the share capital, all of it if there is only one class such as ordinary shares, or all or part of it if there is more than one class of shares, has been subjected to a lessening of its nominal value, or of the called-up part of the nominal value.

Thus:

(*a*) A £4 share might be made into a £3 share.

(*b*) A £5 share might be made into a £1 share.

(*c*) A £3 share, £2 called up, might be made into a £1 share fully paid up.

(*d*) A £5 share, £3 called-up, might be made into a £3 share £1 called up.

Any other variations.

Why should such a step be necessary? The reasons are rather like the issue of bonus shares in reverse. In this case the share capital has got out of step with the assets, in that the share capital is not fully represented by assets. Thus Robert Ltd may have a Balance Sheet as follows:

Robert Ltd
Balance Sheet as at 31 December 19-7

	£
Net Assets	30,000
Ordinary Share Capital	
10,000 Ordinary Shares of £5 each fully paid	50,000
less Debit Balance — Profit and Loss Account	20,000
	30,000

The net assets are shown at £30,000, it being felt in this particular firm that the book value represented a true and fair view of their 'actual value'. The company will almost certainly be precluded from paying dividends until the debit balance on the Profit and Loss Appropriation Account has been eradicated and a credit balance brought into existence. Some firms, in certain circumstances, may still pay a dividend even though there is a debit balance, but it is to be assumed that Robert Ltd is not one of them. If profits remaining after taxation are now running at the rate of £3,000 per annum, it will be more than seven years before a dividend can be paid. As the normal basic reason for buying shares is to provide income, although there may well enter another reason such as capital appreciation, the denial of income to the shareholders for this period of time is serious indeed.

A solution would be to cancel, i.e. reduce, the capital which was no longer represented by assets. In this case there is £20,000 of the share capital which can lay no claim to any assets. The share capital should therefore be reduced by £20,000. This is done by making the shares into £3 shares fully paid instead of £5 shares. The Balance Sheet would become:

Robert Ltd
Balance Sheet as at 31 December 19-7

	£
Net Assets	30,000
	30,000
Ordinary Share Capital	30,000
	30,000

Now that there is no debit balance on the Profit and Loss Appropriation Account the £3,000 available profit next year can be distributed as dividends.

Of course, the firm of Robert Ltd is very much a simplified version. Very often both preference and ordinary shareholders are involved and sometimes debenture holders as well. Even creditors occasionally sacrifice part of the amount owing to them, the idea being that the increase in working capital so generated will help the firm to achieve prosperity, in which case the creditors hope to enjoy the profitable contact that they used to have with the firm. The whole of these capital reduction schemes are matters of negotiation between the various interested parties. For instance, preference shareholders may be quite content for the nominal value of their shares to be reduced if the rate of interest they receive is increased. As with any negotiation the various parties will put forward their points of view and discussions will take place, until eventually a compromise solution is arrived at. When the court's sanction has been obtained, the accounting entries are:

(a) For amounts written off assets.
    Debit Capital Reduction Account.
    Credit Various Asset Accounts.
(b) For reduction in liabilities (e.g. creditors).
    Debit liability accounts.
    Credit Capital Reduction Account.
(c) The reduction in the share capital.
    Debit Share Capital Accounts (each type).
    Credit Capital Reduction Account.
(d) If a credit balance now exists on the Capital Reduction Account.
    Debit Capital Reduction Account (to close).
    Credit Capital Reserve.

It is very unlikely that there would ever be a debit balance on the Capital Reduction Account, as the court would very rarely agree to any such scheme which would bring about that result.

Capital Reduction schemes for private companies will be used less frequently with the advent of powers to companies to purchase their own shares. The new powers given will normally be more suitable for private companies.

Where some of the assets are no longer needed

Where some of the firm's assets are no longer needed, probably due to a contraction in the firm's activities, a company may find itself with a surplus of liquid assets. Subject to the legal formalities being observed, in this case the reduction of capital is effected by returning cash to the shareholders, i.e.:

(*a*) Debit Share Capital Account (with amount returnable).

Credit Sundry Shareholders

(*b*) Debit Sundry Shareholders.

Credit Bank (amount actually paid).

Such a scheme could be objected to by the creditors if it affected their interests.

Review questions

15.1 The Merton Manufacturing Co Ltd has been in business for many years making fitted furniture and chairs. During 19-4 and 19-5 substantial losses have been sustained on the manufacture of chairs and the directors have decided to concentrate on the fitted furniture side of the business which is expected to produce a profit of at least £22,500 per annum before interest charges and taxation. A capital reduction scheme has been proposed under which:

(i) a new ordinary share of 50p nominal value will be created;

(ii) the £1 ordinary shares will be written off and the shareholders will be offered one new ordinary share for every six old shares held;

(iii) the £1, 6% redeemable preference shares will be cancelled and the holders will be offered for every three existing preference shares, one new ordinary share and £1 of a new 8% debenture;

(iv) the existing 11½% debenture will be exchanged for a new debenture yielding 8% and in addition existing debenture holders will be offered one new ordinary share for every £4 of the old debenture held;

(v) existing reserves will be written off;

(vi) goodwill is to be written off;

(vii) any remaining balance of write off which is necessary is to be achieved by writing down plant and equipment; and

(viii) existing ordinary shareholders will be invited to subscribe for two fully paid new ordinary shares at par for every three old shares held.

The balance sheet of the Merton Manufacturing Co Ltd immediately prior to the capital reduction is as follows:

	£	£
Fixed intangible assets		
Goodwill at cost less amounts written off		50,000
Fixed tangible assets		
Freehold land and buildings at cost		95,000
Plant and equipment at cost	275,000	
less Depreciation to date	89,500	
		185,500
		330,500
Current assets		
Stocks	25,000	
Debtors	50,000	
	75,000	
Current liabilities	£	
Creditors	63,500	
Bank overdraft	15,850	
	79,350	
Excess of current liabilities		(4,350)
		326,150
Long-term loan		
11½% debenture, secured on the freehold		
land and buildings		100,000
		226,150
		£
Share capital and reserves		
£1 ordinary shares fully paid		90,000
6% £1 redeemable preference shares fully paid		150,000
Share premium account		25,000
Profit and loss account		(38,850)
		226,150

On a liquidation freehold land and buildings are expected to produce £120,000, plant and equipment £40,000, stocks £15,000 and debtors £45,000. Goodwill has no value.

There are no termination costs associated with ceasing the manufacture of chairs.

Required:

(a) Assuming that the necessary approval is obtained and that the new share issue is successful, produce a balance sheet of the company showing the position immediately after the scheme has been put into effect.

(b) Show the effect of the scheme on the expected earnings of the old shareholders.

(c) Indicate the points which a preference shareholder should take into account before voting on the scheme.

Corporation tax may be taken at 33⅓%. The tax credit on dividends may be taken at 25%.

(Chartered Association of Certified Accountants)

15.2 Deflation Ltd, which had experienced trading difficulties, decided to reorganise its finances.

On 31 December 19-5 a final trial balance extracted from the books showed the following position:

	£	£
Share Capital, authorised and issued:		
150,000 6 per cent Cumulative Preference Shares of £1 each		150,000
200,000 Ordinary Shares of £1 each		200,000
Share Premium Account		40,000
Profit and Loss Account	114,375	
Preliminary Expenses	7,250	
Goodwill (at cost)	55,000	
Trade Creditors		43,500
Debtors	31,200	
Bank Overdraft		51,000
Leasehold Property (at cost)	80,000	
,, ,, (provision for depreciation)		30,000
Plant and Machinery (at cost)	210,000	
,, ,, (provision for depreciation)		62,500
Stock in Hand	79,175	
	577,000	577,000

Approval of the Court was obtained for the following scheme for reduction of capital:

1 The preference shares to be reduced to £0.75 per share.
2 The ordinary shares to be reduced to £0.125 per share.
3 One £0.125 ordinary share to be issued for each £1 of gross preference dividend arrears; the preference dividend had not been paid for three years.
4 The balance on share premium account to be utilised.
5 Plant and machinery to be written down to £75,000.
6 The profit and loss account balance, and all intangible assets, to be written off.

At the same time as the resolution to reduce capital was passed, another resolution was approved restoring the total authorised capital to £350,000, consisting of 150,000 6 per cent cumulative preference shares of £0.75 each and the balance in ordinary shares of £0.125 each. As soon as the above resolutions had been passed 500,000 ordinary shares were issued at par, for cash, payable in full upon application.
You are required:

(*a*) to show the journal entries necessary to record the above transactions in the company's books, and

(*b*) to prepare a Balance Sheet of the company, after completion of the scheme.
(*Institute of Chartered Accountants*)

15.3 On 31 March 19-6 the following was the Balance Sheet of Finer Textiles

Balance Sheet

	£	£
Fixed Assets		
Goodwill and Trade Marks as valued	225,000	
Plant and Machinery (at cost *less* depreciation)	214,800	
Furniture and Fittings (at cost *less* depreciation)	12,600	
		452,400
Current Assets:		
Stock-in-Trade	170,850	
Sundry Debtors	65,100	
Cash in Hand	150	
		236,100
		688,500
Authorised Capital:		
150,000 7 per cent Preference Shares of £1 each	150,000	
2,100,000 Ordinary Shares of £0.5 each	1,050,000	
		1,200,000
Issued and Fully Paid Capital		
150,000 7 per cent Preference Shares of £1 each	150,000	
1,200,000 Ordinary Shares of £0.5 each	600,000	
		750,000
Capital Reserve		48,000
		798,000
Deduct Profit and Loss Account (debit balance)		183,900
		614,100
Current Liabilities		
Sundry Creditors		31,800
Bank Overdraft		42,600
		688,500

The following scheme of capital reduction was sanctioned by the Court and agreed by the shareholders:

(i) Preference shares were to be reduced to £0.75 each.
(ii) Ordinary shares were to be reduced to £0.2 each.
(iii) The capital reserve was to be eliminated.
(iv) The reduced shares of both classes were to be consolidated into new ordinary shares of £1 each.
(v) An issue of £150,000 8 per cent Debentures at par was to be made to provide fresh working capital.
(vi) The sum written off the issued capital of the company and the capital reserve to be used to write off the debit balance of the Profit and Loss Account and to reduce fixed assets by the following amounts:

Goodwill and trade marks	£210,000
Plant and machinery	£ 45,000
Furniture and fittings	£ 6,600

(vii) The bank overdraft was to be paid off out of the proceeds of the debentures which were duly issued and paid in full.

A further resolution was passed to restore the authorised capital of the company to 1,200,000 ordinary shares of £1 each.

Prepare journal entries (cash transactions to be journalised) to give effect to the above scheme and draw up the Balance Sheet of the company after completion of the scheme.

15.4 The Balance Sheet of Planners Ltd on 31 March 19-6 was as follows:

Balance Sheet

	£	£
Goodwill		20,000
Fixed Assets		100,000
		120,000
Current Assets:		
Stock	22,000	
Work in Progress	5,500	
Debtors	34,000	
Bank	17,500	
		79,000
Capital Expenses:		
Formation Expenses		1,000
		200,000
Issued Share Capital:		
120,000 Ordinary Shares of £1 each		120,000
50,000 6 per cent Cumulative Preference Shares of £1 each		50,000
		170,000
less Profit and Loss Account Debit Balance		40,000
		130,000
6 per cent Debentures		50,000
Current Liabilities:		
Creditors		20,000
		200,000

The dividend on the preference shares is £9,000 in arrears. A scheme of reconstruction was accepted by all parties and was completed on 1 April 19-6.

A new company was formed, Budgets Ltd, with an authorized share capital of £200,000, consisting of 200,000 ordinary shares of £1 each. This company took over all the assets of Planners Ltd. The purchase consideration was satisfied partly in cash and partly by the issue, at par, of shares and debentures by the new company in accordance with the following arrangements:

1 The creditors of the old company received, in settlement of each £10 due to them, £7 in cash and three fully paid ordinary shares in the new company,

2 The holders of preference shares in the old company received seven fully paid ordinary shares in the new company to every eight preference shares in the old company and three fully paid ordinary shares in the new company for every £5 of arrears of dividend.

3 The ordinary shareholders in the old company received one fully paid share in the new company for every five ordinary shares in the old company.

4 The holders of 6 per cent debentures in the old company received £40 cash and £60 6 per cent debentures issued at par for every £100 debenture held in the old company.

5 The balance of the authorised capital of the new company was issued at par for cash and was fully paid on 1 April 19-6.

6 Goodwill was eliminated, the stock was valued at £20,000 and the other current assets were brought into the new company's books at the amounts at which they appeared in the old company's balance sheet. The balance of the purchase consideration represented the agreed value of the fixed assets.

You are required to show:
   (*a*) The closing entries in the Realisation Account and the Sundry Shareholders Account in the books of Planners Ltd.
   (*b*) To show your calculation of:
(i) The Purchase Consideration for the Assets, and (ii) the agreed value of the fixed assets.
   (*c*) The summarised balance sheet of Budgets Ltd as on 1 April 19-6.
15.5 The summarised Balance Sheet of Owens Ltd at 31 December 19-9 was as follows:

	£
Freehold Premises	60,000
Plant	210,000
Stock	64,000
Debtors	70,000
Development Expenditure	75,000
Cash at Bank	6,000
Profit and Loss Account	85,000
	570,000
Issued Capital:	
150,000 6 per cent Preference Shares of £1 each	150,000
300,000 Ordinary Shares of £1 each	300,000
Creditors	120,000
	570,000

A capital reduction scheme has been sanctioned under which the 150,000 preference shares are to be reduced to £0.75 each, fully paid, and the 300,000 ordinary shares are to be reduced to £0.10 each, fully paid.

Development expenditure and the debit balance on Profit and Loss Account are to be written off, the balance remaining being used to reduce the book value of the plant.

Prepare the journal entries recording the reduction scheme and the balance sheet as it would appear immediately after the reduction. Narrations are not required in connection with journal entries.

16

Statements of standard accounting practice and allied statements

Introduction

The external users of accounts need to be able to be sure that reliance can be placed by them on the methods used by a business in calculating its profits and balance sheet values. In the late 1960s there was a general outcry that the standards used by different businesses were showing vastly different profits on similar data. In the UK a controversy had arisen following the takeover of AEI Ltd by GEC Ltd. In fighting the takeover bid made by GEC, the AEI directors had produced a forecast, in the 10th month of their financial year, that the profit before tax for the year would be £10 million. After the takeover the accounts of AEI for that same year showed a loss of £4½ million. The difference was attributed to being £5 million as 'matters substantially of fact' and £9½ million to 'adjustments which remain matters substantially of judgement'.

There was a general outcry in the financial pages of the national press against the failure of the accounting profession to lay down consistent principles for businesses to follow.

In December 1969 the Institute of Chartered Accountants in England and Wales issued a 'Statement of Intent in Accounting Standards in the 1970s. The council of the institute then laid down a five point plan to advance accounting standards. Since then the other main accountancy bodies have joined with the institute in helping to produce standards.

Prior to the issuing of any standard a great deal of preparatory work is done which culminates in the publication of an Exposure Draft (ED). Copies of the exposure draft are then sent to those with a special interest in the topic. The accountancy journals also give full details of the exposure drafts. After full and proper consultation, when it is seen to be desirable, an accounting standard on the topic may then be issued.

There is, however, no general law compelling people to observe the standards. The only method of ensuring compliance with the standards is through the professional bodies using their own disciplinary procedures on their members.

This book deals with the main outlines of all SSAPs issued to the date that the book was written. It does not deal with all the many detailed points contained in the SSAPs and EDs. It would be a far larger book if this was attempted. Students at the later stages of their professional examinations will need to get full copies of all SSAPs and study them thoroughly.

This chapter now deals with all the existing SSAPs which are not specifically dealt with elsewhere.

International accounting standards

The International Accounting Standards Committee (IASC) was established in 1973. Representatives from each of the founder members, which includes the UK, sit on the committee as well as co-opted members from other countries.

The need for an IASC has been said to be mainly:

(*a*) The considerable growth in international investment. This means that it is desirable to have similar methods the world over so that investment decisions are more compatible.

(*b*) The growth in multinational firms. These firms have to produce accounts covering a large number of countries. Standardisation between countries makes the accounting work that much easier and reduces costs.

(*c*) As quite a few countries now have their own standard setting bodies it is desirable that their efforts should be harmonised.

(*d*) For poor countries which cannot afford to have standard setting bodies, the IASC can help them by letting them use the international standards instead of setting their own standards.

In the United Kingdom the SSAPs have precedence over International Accounting Standards. In fact most of the provisions of International Accounting Standards are incorporated in existing SSAPs.

SSAP 1: accounting for associated companies (revised 1982)

This standard is dealt with as a separate topic in Chapter 34 of this book.

SSAP 2: disclosure of accounting policies (issued 1971)

This SSAP does not set out to give a basic theoretical framework of accounting. It accepts the view that there may well be more than one accounting method which could be adopted in many cases, as the circumstances of different organisations will vary. Such varying practices may well be suitable in particular cases, but the users of accounting statements should be made aware of which practice has been used in each case.

The standard also requires disclosure when the generally accepted accounting concepts are not complied with. The ones specifically mentioned as being generally applied are accruals, consistency, going-concern and prudence. In fact the SSAP does not mention other concepts and conventions generally recognised in the academic world, described in Volume 1, although it accepts that there are other concepts than the four mentioned.

Accounting bases are the methods which could be used in applying the concepts. It should be recognised that these are subject to limitations imposed by adherence to legislation and SSAPs. At the same time management must exercise its own judgement in choosing the bases to apply in their particular circumstances.

Accounting policies are the accounting bases judged by management to be the most appropriate. There should be a note attached to the accounts explaining the policies chosen. Five examples are given to illustrate where judgements may easily vary. These are:

1 Methods of depreciating fixed assets.
2 The valuation of stocks and of work-in-progress.
3 Capitalisation of development expenditure.
4 The recognition of profit on long-term contracts.
5 Hire purchase or instalment transactions.

SSAP 3: earnings per share (revised 1974)

Students taking examinations where this is dealt with in detail (e.g. ACCA paper 2.8) should read the actual standard itself. However the main outline can be given here, but remember that it omits a considerable amount.

Earnings per share (EPs) is a widely used stock market measure. The SSAP tries to bring about a more consistent method to aid comparability and reduce misunderstandings.

EPS is the profit in pence per share calculated as follows:

	£	£
Profit on ordinary activities after taxation		xxxx
less minority interest	xxx	
less preference dividends	xxx	xxxx
Profit available to equity shareholders		xxxx

$$\text{EPS} = \frac{\text{Profit available to equity shareholders}}{\text{Number of equity shares}} = \text{EPS in pence}$$

Problems arise with the following items, which the SSAP gives detailed instructions as to the methods to be chosen.

1 *Taxation charges*. In particular Advance Corporation Tax (ACT) complications and unrelieved overseas tax can make comparability difficult. The 'net' method calculates EPS bringing tax charges in full. The 'nil' distribution method calculates tax charges as though there was no irrecoverable ACT or unrelieved overseas tax. If there is a material difference between the EPS using both the 'nil' and 'net' methods of charging for taxation, then both 'nil' and 'net' EPS figures should be given.

2 *Changes in capital structure*. Share issues during a period complicate the calculations of EPS. Shares can be issued:

(*a*) At full market prices

(*b*) Bonus issues

(*c*) Share exchange (e.g. on takeovers)

(*d*) Rights issues.

Adjustments not given here, need to be made in each case.

3 *Future dilutions*. Items such as:

(*a*) Where a company has issued shares on which dividends can only be calculated on future earnings.

(*b*) Convertible debentures which can be converted into ordinary shares in the future.

(*c*) Where the company has issued options to buy ordinary shares in the future.

In each case adjustments, not given here, need to be made.

SSAP 4: accounting for government grants (issued 1974)

Many different types of grants are, or have been obtainable from government departments. Where these relate to revenue expenditure, e.g. subsidies on wages, they should be credited to revenue in the period when the revenue is incurred.

Where there are grants relating to capital expenditure, then SSAP 4 states that they should be credited to revenue *over the expected useful life of the asset*. This may be achieved by:

(*a*) Crediting the fixed asset account by the amount of the grant, depreciation then being on the net figure. This method will accordingly spread the benefit of the grant over the life of the asset, as each year's depreciation figure will be correspondingly reduced.

(*b*) Treating the amount of the grant as a deferred credit, a portion of which is credited to the profit and loss account annually, over the life of the asset, thus reducing the cost of depreciation. If this method is chosen, the amount of the deferred credit should, if material, be shown separately. It should not be shown as part of shareholders' funds.

It will be appreciated that the net effect of both methods (*a*) and (*b*) will be the same as far as the profit and loss accounts are concerned.

SSAP 5: accounting for value added tax (issued 1974)

All that needs to be noted here is that Volume 1 of this book fully complies with SSAP 5. There is no need here to go into further detail.

SSAP 6: extraordinary items and prior year adjustments (revised 1978)

Normal trading profit or loss has always had to be taken into the profit and loss account. However, previous to SSAP 6, there had always been the possibility that 'extraordinary' items affecting profit and loss could avoid the profit and loss account and be carried direct to reserves. In this way they would not be exposed to the view of the readers of the accounts. SSAP 6 seeks to remedy this deficiency. All extraordinary items, with certain specified exceptions, now have to go through the Profit and Loss Account.

In addition prior year adjustments, before this SSAP, were often dealt with by adjusting the Reserves. These now have to pass through the Profit and Loss Account and their nature and size disclosed.

Extraordinary items, for the purposes of this statement, are those items which derive from events or transactions outside the ordinary activities of the business and which are both material and expected not to recur frequently or regularly. They do not include items which, though exceptional on account of size and incidence (and which may therefore require separate disclosure), derive from the ordinary activities of the business. Neither do they include prior year items merely because they relate to a prior year.

Extraordinary items derive from events outside the ordinary activities of the business; they do not include items of abnormal size and incidence which derive from the ordinary activities of the business. The classification of items as extraordinary will depend on the particular circumstances – what is extraordinary in one business will not necessarily be extraordinary in another. Subject to this, examples of extraordinary items could be the profits or losses arising from the following:

(*a*) the discontinuance of a significant part of a business;

(*b*) the sale of an investment not acquired with the intention of resale;

(*c*) writing off intangibles; including goodwill, because of unusual events or developments during the period; and

(*d*) the expropriation of assets.

Prior year adjustments, that is prior year items which should be adjusted against the opening balance of retained profits or reserves, are rare and limited to items arising from changes in accounting policies and from the correction of fundamental errors. They are discussed in the paragraphs that follow. The majority of prior year items however should be dealt with in the profit and loss account of the year in which they are recognised and shown separately if material. They arise mainly from the corrections and adjustments which are the natural result of estimates inherent in accounting and more particularly in the periodic preparation of financial statements. Estimating future events and their effects requires the exercise of judgement and will require reappraisal as new events occur, as more experience is acquired or as additional information is obtained. Since a change in estimate arises from new information or developments it should not be given retrospective effect by a restatement of prior years. Sometimes a change in estimate may have the appearance of a change in accounting policy and care is necessary in order to avoid confusing the two. For example, the future benefits of a cost may have become doubtful and a change may be made from amortising the cost over the period of those benefits to writing it off when incurred. Such a change should be treated as a change in estimate and not as a change in accounting policy. Prior year items are not extraordinary merely because they relate to a prior year; their nature will determine their classification.

SSAP 7: accounting for changes in the purchasing power of money (issued 1974)

This was the original standard on inflation accounting, later replaced by SSAP 16.

SSAP 8: treatment of tax under the imputation system (revised 1977)

This can be understood by reference to Chapter 13 of this book which adheres throughout to this SSAP.

SSAP 9: stocks and work in progress (revised 1980)

Due to the many varying kinds of businesses and conditions in companies this SSAP cannot be too rigid. There simply cannot be one system of valuation for stocks and work in progress. All that the standard can do is to narrow down the different methods that could be used.

Basically the valuation should:
1 be valued at the lower of cost or net realisable value.
2 not recognise profit in advance, but should account immediately for anticipated losses.

Net realisable value consists of the expected selling price less any expenses necessary to sell the product. This may be below cost because of obsolescence, deterioration and similar factors.

SSAP 9 also defines 'cost' and certainly in the case of a manufacturing business it will also include overhead expenses, so that prime cost could not be used. The definition is:

Cost is defined in relation to the different categories of stocks and work in progress as being that expenditure which has been incurred in the normal course of business in bringing the product or service to its present location and condition. This expenditure should include, in addition to cost of purchase (as defined later) such costs of conversion (as defined later) as are appropriate to that location and condition.

Cost of purchase comprises purchase price including import duties, transport and handling costs and any other directly attributable costs, less trade discounts, rebates and subsidies.

Cost of conversion comprises:

(a) costs which are specifically attributable to units of production, i.e. direct labour, direct expenses and sub-contracted work;

(b) production overheads (as defined later);

(c) other overheads, if any, attributable in the particular circumstances of the business to bringing the product or service to its present location and condition.

Production overheads: based on the normal level of activity, taking one year with another: all of them should be included including fixed production overheads. Obviously neither selling nor general administration costs should be included in cost.

Notice that abnormal costs should not be included, as they should not have the effect of increasing stock valuation.

The LIFO and base stock methods should not be used, as they do not provide an up-to-date valuation. Although the LIFO is not accepted by the SSAP, yet the Companies Act 1985 accepts the LIFO method.

Long-term contract work

It is not proposed to discuss it here. The contents of Chapter 22 of this book conforms to SSAP 9.

SSAP 10: statement of sources and application of funds (revised 1978)

This is contained in Chapter 21 of this book.

SSAP 11: this was a standard on deferred tax now replaced by SSAP 15.

SSAP 12: accounting for depreciation (revised 1987)

This SSAP applies to all fixed assets, except for:

1 Investment properties, dealt with in SSAP 19.
2 Goodwill, dealt with in SSAP 22.
3 Development cost, dealt with in SSAP 13.
4 Investments.

First of all some terms are defined:

Depreciation: 'is the measure of wearing out, consumption or other reduction in the useful economic life of a fixed asset whether arriving from use, effluxion of time or obsolescence through technological or market changes.'

Useful economic life: 'of an asset is the period over which the present owner will derive economic benefits from its use.'

Residual value: 'is the realisable value of the asset at the end of its economic life, based on prices prevailing at the date of acquisition or revaluation, where this has taken place. Realisation costs should be deducted in arriving at residual values.'

Recoverable amount: 'is the greater of the net realisable value of an asset (at the date of the balance sheet) and where appropriate, the amount recoverable from its further use.'

The standard lays down that all assets with a finite life (i.e. a life that does not go on forever) should be depreciated by allocating cost less residual value (or revalued amount less residual value) over their useful economic lives.

The standard recognises that there are various methods of providing for depreciation, such as straight line, reducing balance, depletion unit etc. It does not however, try to insist on which method should be used. The system chosen should be the one most appropriate to the type of asset and kind of business.

Whatever method is used it should be used consistently. A change in method should only be made when it becomes more suitable. Where a change is made the effect, if material, should be shown as a note attached to the accounts.

The depreciation should be calculated in the value as shown on the balance sheet and not on any other figure. It *must* be charged against the profit and loss account, and *not* against reserves.

Asset lives should be estimated in a realistic way and not artificially shortened. The lives should be reviewed regularly, at least every five years. Where revisions bring about material changes for accumulated depreciation it should be treated as an exceptional item under SSAP 6.

Asset revaluation

Any permanent reduction should be written off immediately, the remainder being written off over the asset's remaining life. Such adjustments are via the profit and loss account.

Any increased value does not mean that depreciation should not be charged. The new value is the one at which future depreciation should be based. Depreciation charged before revaluation should not be credited back to profit and loss.

Land and buildings

Freehold land. As this normally lasts forever there is no need to depreciate, except in cases of reduction of value by such factors as land erosion, extraction of minerals, dumping of toxic waste, etc.

Buildings. These should be depreciated, except that if the amount is not material and life is expected to be very long then there will be no need to charge depreciation. If estimated residual value equals or is more than net value depreciation can be ignored.

Notes to accounts

The following should be disclosed:
1 Method of depreciation used.
2 Economic life or depreciation rate in use.
3 Total depreciation for period.
4 Depreciable assets – gross amount and accumulated depreciation.

SSAP 13: accounting for research and development (issued 1977)

SSAP 13 is concerned with this topic. It divides research and development expenditure under three headings:

(*a*) Pure (or basic) research: original investigation undertaken in order to gain new scientific or technical knowledge and understanding. Basic research is not primarily directed towards any specific practical aim or application;

(*b*) Applied research: original investigation undertaken in order to gain new scientific or technical knowledge and directed towards a specific practical aim or objective;

(*c*) Development: the use of scientific or technical knowledge in order to produce new or substantially improved materials, devices, products, processes, systems or services prior to the commencement of commercial production.

Expenditure incurred on pure and applied research can be regarded as part of a continuing operation required to maintain a company's business and its competitive position. In general, one particular period rather than another will not be expected to benefit and therefore it is appropriate that these costs should be written off as they are incurred.

The development of new and improved products is, however, distinguishable from pure and applied research. Expenditure on such development is normally undertaken with a reasonable expectation of specific commercial success and of future benefits arising from the work, either from increased revenue and related profits or from reduced costs. On these grounds it may be argued that such expenditure should be deferred to be matched against the future revenue.

It will only be practicable to evaluate the potential future benefits of development expenditure if:

(*a*) there is a clearly defined project: and

(*b*) the related expenditure is separately identifiable.

(1)

The outcome of such a project would then need to be examined for:

(*a*) its technical feasibility; and

(*b*) its ultimate commercial viability considered in the light of factors such as:

    (*i*) likely market conditions (including competing products);

    (*ii*) public opinion;

    (*iii*) consumer and environmental legislation.

(2)

Furthermore a project will only be of value:

(*a*) if further development costs to be incurred on the same project together with related production, selling and administration costs will be more than covered by related future revenues; and

(*b*) adequate resources exist, or are reasonably expected to be available, to enable the project to be completed and to provide any consequential increases in working capital.

(3)

The elements of uncertainty inherent in the considerations set out in paragraphs marked as (1) and (2) are considerable. There will be a need for different persons having differing levels of judgement to be involved in assessing the technical, commercial and financial viability of the project. Combinations of the possible different assessments which they might validly make can produce widely differing assessments of the existence and amounts of future benefits.

If these uncertainties are viewed in the context of the concept of prudence, the future benefits of most development projects would be too uncertain to justify carrying the expenditure forward. Nevertheless, in certain industries it is considered that there are numbers of major development projects that satisfy the stringent criteria set out in paragraphs (1) (2) and (3). Accordingly, where expenditure on development projects is judged on a prudent view of available evidence to satisfy these criteria, it may be carried forward and amortised over the period expected to benefit.

At each accounting date the unamortised balance of development expenditure should be examined project by project to ensure that it still fulfils the criteria in paragraphs (1) (2) and (3). Where any doubt exists as to the continuation of those circumstances the balance should be written off.

Fixed assets may be acquired or constructed in order to provide facilities for research and/or development activities. The use of such fixed assets will usually extend over a number of accounting periods and accordingly they should be capitalised and written off over their usual life.

Since the appearance of SSAP 13 in December 1977 the treatment of Research and Development Costs has been brought into law. The Companies Act 1985 specifically states that costs of research cannot be treated as assets. As far as development costs are concerened, the 1985 Act states:

If any amount is included in a company's balance sheet in respect of development costs the following information shall be given in a note to the accounts –

(*a*) the period over which the amount of those costs originally capitalised is being or is to be written off; and

(*b*) the reasons for capitalising the development costs in question.

SSAP 14: group accounts (issued 1978)

This standard is observed in the chapters in this book relating to groups of companies.

Holding companies should produce consolidated accounts, with the exception that a holding company which is itself a wholly-owned subsidiary of another company need not produce them.

Subsidiaries may be excluded from consolidated accounts for the following reasons (subject usually to the Government's Department of Trade permission):

1 Figures are too insignificant to be useful to the group's shareholders.
2 It would be harmful or misleading (see notes below) to the group's business.
3 The business of the subsidiary and holding company cannot reasonably be compared.

Misleading, for (2) above, might mean that:

1 The holding company does not control the subsidiary even though it owns more than 50 per cent of the equity shares, e.g. has less than 50 per cent of voting rights or does not control composition of the board.
2 Restrictions, e.g. by overseas governments on companies abroad, mean that control cannot properly be exercised for the foreseeable future.
3 Control is to be temporary.

Uniform accounting methods are to be followed throughout the group except in exceptional cases. Any material effects caused by different methods should be disclosed. Accounting year ends in the group to be the same as far as is possible.

SSAP 15: accounting for deferred taxation (revised 1985)

The description of the methods of accounting for deferred taxation is given in Chapter 13. It follows SSAP 15 exactly and there is no need to repeat it here.

SSAP 16: current cost accounting (issued 1980 : suspended 1985)

The outlines of this out-dated SSAP are given in Chapter 39 of this book.

SSAP 17: accounting for post-balance sheet events (issued 1980)

Quite often there will be events occurring after a balance sheet date which will provide evidence of the value of assets, or of the amounts of liabilities, as at the balance sheet date. Obviously any event up to the balance sheet date will have affected the balance sheet. Then, once the board of directors have formally approved the accounts it becomes impossible to alter the accounts. However, there is the period between these dates during which events may throw some light upon the valuation of assets or amounts of liabilities. SSAP 17 directs its attention to such events during this period.

SSAP 17 brings in two new terms – 'adjusting events' and 'non-adjusting events'.

Adjusting events

These are events which provide additional evidence relating to conditions existing at the balance sheet date. They require changes in amounts to be included in financial statements. Examples of adjusting events are now given:

(*a*) **Fixed assets.** The subsequent determination of the purchase price or of the proceeds of sale of assets purchased or sold before the year end.

(*b*) **Property.** A valuation which provides evidence of a permanent diminution in value.

(*c*) **Investments.** The receipt of a copy of the financial statements or other information in respect of an unlisted company which provides evidence of a permanent diminution in the value of a long-term investment.

(*d*) **Stocks and work in progress.**

    (*i*) The receipt of proceeds of sales after the balance sheet date or other evidence concerning the net realisable value of stocks.

    (*ii*) The receipt of evidence that the previous estimate of accrued profit on a long-term contract was materially inaccurate.

    (*e*) **Debtors.** The renegotiation of amounts owing by debtors, or the insolvency of a debtor.

    (*f*) **Dividends receivable.** The declaration of dividends by subsidiaries and associated companies relating to periods prior to the balance sheet date of the holding company.

    (*g*) **Taxation.** The receipt of information regarding rates of taxation.

    (*h*) **Claims.** Amounts received or receivable in respect of insurance claims which were in the course of renegotiation at the balance sheet date.

    (*i*) **Discoveries.** The discovery of errors or frauds which show that the financial statements were incorrect.

Non-adjusting events

These are events which arise after the balance sheet date and concern conditions which did not exist at that time. Consequently they do not result in changes in amounts in financial statements. They may, however, be of such materiality that their disclosure is required by way of notes to ensure that financial statements are not misleading. Examples of non-adjusting events which may require disclosure are now given:

    (*a*) **Mergers** and acquisitions.

    (*b*) **Reconstructions** and proposed reconstructions.

    (*c*) **Issues** of shares and debentures.

    (*d*) **Purchases and sales of fixed assets** and investments.

    (*e*) **Loss of fixed assets** or stocks as a result of a catastrophe such as fire or flood.

    (*f*) **Opening new trading activities** or extending existing trading activities.

    (*g*) **Closing a significant part of the trading activities** if this was not anticipated at the year end.

    (*h*) **Decline in the value** of property and investments held as fixed assets, if it can be demonstrated that the decline occurred after the year end.

    (*i*) **Changes in rates of foreign exchange.**

    (*j*) **Government action**, such as nationalisation.

    (*k*) **Strikes** and other labour disputes.

    (*l*) **Augmentation of pension benefits.**

SSAP 18: accounting for contingencies (issued 1980)

The definition given in SSAP 18 is 'Contingency is a condition which exists at the balance sheet date, where the outcome will be confirmed only on the occurrence or non-occurrence of one or more uncertain future events. A contingent gain or loss is a gain or loss dependent on a contingency'.

    The over-riding concern is the concept of prudence. Quite simply, if one is in doubt then contingent losses must be taken into account but contingent gains are left out. If there is a material contingent loss then it should be accrued if it can be estimated with reasonable accuracy. Otherwise it should be disclosed by way of notes to the accounts.

SSAP 19: accounting for investment properties (issued 1980)

Under the accounting requirements of SSAP 12 'accounting for depreciation', fixed assets are generally subject to annual depreciation charges to reflect on a systematic basis the wearing out, consumption or other loss of value whether arising from use, effluxion of time or obsolescence through technology and market changes. Under those requirements it is also accepted that an increase in the value of such a fixed asset does not generally remove the necessity to charge depreciation to reflect on a systematic basis the consumption of the asset.

A different treatment is, however, required where a significant proportion of the fixed assets of an enterprise is held not for consumption in the business operations but as investments, the disposal of which would not materially affect any manufacturing or trading operations of the enterprise. In such a case the current value of these investments, and changes in that current value, are of prime importance rather than a calculation of systematic annual depreciation. Consequently, for the proper appreciation of the financial position, a different accounting treatment is considered appropriate for fixed assets held as investments (called in this standard 'investment properties').

Investment properties may be held by a company which holds investments as part of its business such as an investment trust or a property investment company.

Investment properties may also be held by a company whose main business is not the holding of investments.

Where an investment property is held on a lease with a relatively short unexpired term, it is necessary to recognise the annual depreciation in the financial statements to avoid the situation whereby a short lease is amortised against the investment revaluation reserve whilst the rentals are taken to the profit and loss account.

This statement requires investment properties to be included in the balance sheet at open market value. The statement does not require the valuation to be made by qualified or independent valuers; but calls for disclosure of the names or qualifications of the valuers, the bases used by them and whether the person making the valuation is an employee or officer of the company. However, where investment properties represent a substantial proportion of the total assets of a major enterprise (e.g. a listed company) the valuation thereof would normally be carried out:

(a) annually by persons holding a recognised professional qualification and having recent post-qualification experience in the location and category of the properties concerned; and

(b) at least every five years by an external valuer.

SSAP 20: foreign currency translation (issued 1983)

The roles of SSAP 20 are already shown in Chapter 5 of this book. There is only need here for a few extra comments.

Hyper-inflation

If there is hyper-inflation the methods described in Chapter 5 may not give a fair view of the results. In these cases it may first of all be necessary to produce accounts adjusted for inflation.

Hedging against exchange losses

Losses incurred may be set off against profits made in the computation of exchange dealings.

Disclosure

The method to translate currencies should be disclosed. Net profits/net losses on translation must be disclosed, irrespective as to whether they are shown in the profit and loss account or as a movement of reserves.

SSAP 21: accounting for leases and hire purchase (isssued 1984)

Details of SSAP 21 are given in Chapter 8.

SSAP 22: accounting for goodwill (issued 1984)

Although this is contained in Volume 1, it is repeated here for the benefit of those not having that volume in their possession. In addition, a note follows which is applicable for those who will be studying Chapters 24 to 34 on consolidated (group) accounts.

This standard was issued in January 1985. A brief summary of it is as follows:

1 Purchased goodwill should normally be eliminated as an asset from the books on acquisition. This should normally be achieved by writing it off against the reserves of the company.

2 In some companies, where special needs are appropriate, the purchased goodwill can be 'amortised' (i.e. depreciated) year by year over its useful economic life.

3 Goodwill which has not been bought, but which has been created within the company (inherent goodwill) should never be brought into the books at all.

4 Where there is 'negative goodwill' (i.e. purchase price for assets is less than value of assets), then this should be added to the reserves in the balance sheet of the company.

In the chapters dealing with group accounts, a figure for goodwill will often be calculated. It must be borne in mind that this is subject to the contents of SSAP 22 just as much as for a company simply buying the business of a sole trader or partnership.

SSAP 23: accounting for acquisitions and mergers (issued 1985)

This standard is dealt with in Chapter 33.

SSAP 24: accounting for pension costs (issued 1988)

The details will have to be studied if you proceed to a higher level in accounting. Basically the objective is that the employer should recognise the expected cost of providing pensions on a 'systematic and rational basis' over the period which he derives benefit from the employees' services.

Statements of recommended practice (SORPs)

In 1986 the Accounting Standards Committee (ASC) issued the first statement of Recommended Practice (SORP). It is important to note that they are different from SSAPs. With SSAPs their provisions must be carried out, unless there is sufficient and adequate evidence to prove otherwise, and in addition any non-compliance must be clearly stated.

The SORP simply sets out what is considered to be the best practice on a particular topic, in respect of which it is not considered suitable to issue a SSAP at that time. Companies are simply encouraged to use the SORP. No action will be taken by the accounting bodies if a SORP is not followed.

A sub-category of SORPs was introduced, called 'franked SORPs'. Generally these will refer to topics which are of limited application, for a specific industry. Franked SORPs will normally be drafted by a working party whose work will be overseen by the ASC. When the ASC agrees with the final draft of the SORP it will then be 'franked'.

Normally all SORPs will be preceded by Statements of Intent (SOI). Thus, as an Exposure Draft (ED) will precede an SSAP so will a SOI precede a SORP.

It is not the intention that this book should cover the SOIs which have been issued. Any student who needs such knowledge later in his studies will have to go to more specialised books.

Review questions

16.1 In preparing its accounts for the year to 31 May 19-7, Whiting plc had been faced with a number of accounting problems, the details of which were as follows:

(*i*) The company had closed down its entire American operations which represented a significant part of Whiting plc's business.

(*ii*) The corporation tax for the year to 31 May 19-6 had been over-provided by £5,000.

(*iii*) Land and buildings had been revalued at an amount well in excess of the historic cost (note: the current value is to be adjusted in the accounts).

(*iv*) A trade debtor had gone into liquidation owing Whiting plc an amount equivalent to 20% of Whiting's turnover for the year. It is highly unlikely that any of this debt will ever be repaid.

(*v*) During the year, the company changed its method of valuing stock. If the same method had been adopted in the previous year, the profits for that year would have been considerably less than had previously been reported.

Required:

    (*a*) Being careful to give your reasons, explain how each of the above matters should be treated in the accounts of Whiting plc for the year to 31 May 19-7 if the company follows the requirements of SSAP 6 (extraordinary items and prior year adjustments);

and

    (*b*) outline the provisions of SSAP 22 (accounting for goodwill) for the treatment of both non-purchased and purchased goodwill in the balance sheets of companies and groups of companies.

(*Association of Accounting Technicians*)

16.2 The directors are preparing the published accounts of Dorman plc for the year to 31 October 19-5. The following information is provided for certain of the items which are to be included in the final accounts.

(*i*) Stocks of raw material, monolite

	£
Cost	26,500
Replacement cost	48,100

(*ii*) Stocks of finished goods:

	Paramite	Paraton
	£	£
Direct costs	72,600	10,200
Proportion of fixed factory overhead	15,300	4,600
Proportion of selling expenses	6,870	1,800
Net realisable value	123,500	9,520

(*iii*) **Plant and machinery.** An item of plant was shown in the 19-4 accounts at a net book value of £90,000 (£160,000 cost less accumulated depreciation £70,000). The plant was purchased on 1 November 19-2 and has been depreciated at 25% reducing balance. The directors now consider the straight line basis to be more appropriate: they have estimated that at 1 November 19-4 the plant had a remaining useful life of six years and will possess zero residual value at the end of that period.

(*iv*) **Freehold property.** The company purchased a freehold property for £250,000 11 years ago, and it is estimated that the land element was worth £50,000 at that date.

The company has never charged depreciation on the property but the directors now feel that it should have done so; the building is expected to have a total useful life of forty years.

(*v*) **Research expenditure:** incurred in an attempt to discover a substitute for raw materials currently purchased from a politically sensitive area of the world amounted to £17,500 during the year.

(*vi*) **Development expenditure:** on Tercil, which is nearly ready for production, amounted to £30,000. Demand for Tercil is expected significantly to exceed supply for at least the next four years.

(*vii*) **Accident.** On 1 December 19-5 there was a fire in the warehouse which damaged stocks, other than the items referred to in (*i*) and (*ii*) above. The book value of these stocks was £92,000. The company has discovered that it was under-insured and only expects to recover £71,000 from the insurers.

(*viii*) **Investments.** Dorman purchased 30,000 ordinary shares in Lilleshall Ltd on 1 November 19-4 for £96,000, and immediately succeeded in appointing two of its directors to Lilleshall's board. The issued share capital of Lilleshall consists of 100,000 ordinary shares of £1 each. The profits of Lilleshall for the year to 31 October 19-5 amounted to £40,000. (Ignore taxation.)

Required:

Explain how each of the above items should be dealt with in the published accounts of Dorman plc.

(*Institute of Chartered Secretaries and Administrators*)

16.3A In preparing the published accounts of a company, briefly state the significant accounting/disclosure requirements you would have in mind in ensuring that the accounts comply with best accounting practice as embodied in the statements of standard accounting practice:

(*a*) Value added tax.

(*b*) Earnings per share.

(*c*) The disclosure requirements of each major class of depreciable assets.

(*d*) Research expenditure.

(*e*) Capital-based grants relating to fixed assets.

(*f*) Goodwill on consolidation.

(*g*) The disclosure requirements relating to generally accepted fundamental accounting concepts.

(*h*) The accounts of a subsidiary company having similar activities to that of the holding company.

(*Association of Accounting Technicians*)

16.4A Oldfield Enterprises Limited was formed on 1 January 19-5 to manufacture and sell a new type of lawn mower. The book-keeping staff of the company have produced monthly figures for the first ten months to 31 October 19-5 and from these figures together with estimates for the remaining two months, Barry Lamb, the managing director has drawn up a forecast profit and loss account for the year to 31 December 19-5 and a balance sheet as at that date.

These statements together with the notes are submitted to the board for comment. During the board meeting discussion centres on the treatment given to the various assets. The various opinions are summarised by Barry Lamb who brings them, with the draft accounts, to you as the company's financial adviser.

Oldfield Enterprises Ltd
Draft profit and loss account for the year to 31 December 19-5

	£000s	£000s
Sales		3,000
Cost of sales		1,750
Gross profit		1,250
Administration overheads	350	
Selling and distribution overheads	530	
		880
Net profit before taxation		370

Draft balance sheet at 31 December 19-5

Fixed assets – tangible	Cost	Depreciation and Amortisation	Net
	£000s	£000s	£000s
Leasehold land and buildings	375	125	250
Freehold land and buildings	350	–	350
Plant and machinery	1,312	197	1,115
	2,037	322	1,715

Fixed assets – intangible			
Research and development			375
Currrent assets			
Stock		375	
Debtors		780	
		1,155	
Current liabilities			
Creditors	250		
Bank overdraft	125	375	
			780
			2,870
Share capital			2,500
Net profit for year			370
			2,870

Notes

(a) Administration overheads include £50,000 written off research and development.

(b) The lease is for 15 years and cost £75,000, buildings have been put up on the leasehold land at a cost of £300,000. Plant and machinery has been depreciated at 15%. Both depreciation and amortisation are included in cost of sales.

Opinions put forward

Leasehold land and buildings.

The works director thinks that although the lease provides for a rent review after three years the buildings have a 50-year life. The buildings should therefore be depreciated over 50 years and the cost of the lease should be amortised over the period of the lease.

The managing director thinks that because of the rent review clause the whole of the cost should be depreciated over three years.

The sales director thinks it is a good idea to charge as much as the profits will allow in order to reduce the tax bill.

Freehold land and buildings.

The works director thinks that as the value of the property is going up with inflation no depreciation is necessary.

The sales director's opinion is the same as for leasehold property.

The managing director states that he has heard that if a property is always kept in good repair no depreciation is necessary. This should apply in the case of his company.

Plant and machinery.

The managing director agrees with the 15% for depreciation and proposes to use the reducing balance method.

The works director wants to charge 25% straight line.

Research and development.

The total spent in the year will be £425,000. Of this £250,000 is for research into the cutting characteristics of different types of grass, £100,000 is for the development of an improved drive system for lawn mowers and £75,000 is for market research to determine the ideal lawn mower characteristics for the average garden.

The managing director thinks that a small amount should be charged as an expense each year.

The works director wants to write off all the market research and 'all this nonsense of the cutting characteristics of grass'.

The sales director thinks that, as the company has only just started, all research and development expenditure relates to future sales so all this year's expenditure should be carried forward.

Stock.

Both the managing director and the works director are of the opinion that stock should be shown at prime cost.

The sales director's view is that stocks should be shown at sales price as the stock is virtually all sold within a very short period.

Required:

(*a*) You are asked to comment on each opinion stating what factors should be taken into account to determine suitable depreciation and write off amounts.

(*b*) Indicate what amounts should, in your opinion, be charged to profit and loss and show the adjusted profit produced by your recommendations, stating clearly any assumptions you may make.

(*Chartered Association of Certified Accountants*)

16.5 The accountant of Hook, Line and Sinker, a partnership of seven people has asked your advice in dealing with the following items in the partnership accounts for the year to 31 May 19-7.

(*a*)   (*i*) Included in invoices prepared and dated in June 19-7 were £60,000 of goods despatched during the second half of May 19-7.

(*ii*) Stocks of components at 31 May 19-7 include parts no longer used in production. These components originally cost £50,000 but have been written down for purposes of the accounts to £25,000. Scrap value of these items is estimated to be £1,000. Another user has expressed interest in buying these parts for £40,000.

(b) After May 19-7 a customer who accounts for 50% of Hook, Line and Sinker sales suffered a serious fire which has disrupted his organisation. Payments for supplies are becoming slow and Hook, Line and Sinker sales for the current year are likely to be substantially lower than previously. This customer owed £80,000 to Hook, Line and Sinker at 31 May 19-7.

(c) During the year to 31 May Hook, Line and Sinker commenced a new advertising campaign using television and expensive magazine advertising for the first time. Sales during the year were not much higher than previous years as the partners consider that the effects of advertising will be seen in future years.

Expenditure on advertising during the year is made up of:

	£
Television	50,000
Advertisements in magazines	60,000
Advertisements in local papers	25,000

All the expenditure has been treated as expense in the accounts but the partners wish to carry forward three-quarters of the television and magazine costs as it is expected that this cost will benefit future years' profits and because this year's profits will compare unfavourably with previous years if all the expenditure is charged in the accounts.

(d) Three projects for the construction of sinkers have the following cost and revenue characteristics:

	Project A	Project B	Project C
Degree of completion	75%	50%	15%
	£	£	£
Direct costs to date	30,000	25,000	6,000
Sales price of complete project	55,000	50,000	57,500
Overheads allocated to date	4,000	2,000	500
Costs to complete – Direct	10,000	25,000	40,000
– Overheads	2,000	2,000	3,000

No profits or losses have been included in the accounts.

(e) After considerable discussion with management, the sales of a newly developed special purpose hook have been given the following probabilities:

First year of production

Sales	Probability
£	
15,000	0.2
30,000	0.5
40,000	0.3

Second year of production

Increase over first year	Probability
£	
10,000	0.1
20,000	0.5
30,000	0.4

Second year sales may be assumed independent of first year levels.

Cost-volume-profit analysis shows that the break-even point is £50,000.

Production of the special purpose hook started prior to the end of the accounting year and stocks of the finished product are included at cost amounting to £20,000. It has been decided that if there is less than 0.7 probability of break even being reached in the second year then stocks should be written down by 25%.

(f) During the year it was discovered that some stock sheets had been omitted from the calculations at the previous year end. The effect is that opening stock for the current year, shown as £35,000 should be £42,000. No adjustment has yet been made.
Required:
Discuss the treatment of each item with reference to relevant Statements of Standard Accounting Practice, and accounting concepts and conventions. Recommend appropriate treatment for each item showing the profit effect of each recommendation made.
(Chartered Association of Certified Accountants)
16.6 The chief accountant of Uncertain Ltd is not sure of the appropriate accounting treatment for a number of events occurring during the year 19-5/6.

(a) A significant number of employees have been made redundant, giving rise to redundancy payments of £100,000 which have been included in manufacturing cost of sales.

(b) One of Uncertain Ltd's three factories has been closed down. Closure costs amounted to £575,000. This amount has been deducted from reserves in the balance sheet.

(c) The directors have changed the basis of charging depreciation on delivery vehicles. The difference between the old and new methods amounts to £258,800. This has been charged as a prior year adjustment.

(d) During October 19-6 a fire occurred in one of the remaining factories belonging to Uncertain Ltd and caused an estimated £350,000 of additional expenses. This amount has been included in manufacturing cost of sales.

(e) It was discovered on 31 October 19-6 that a customer was unable to pay his debt to the company of £125,000. The £125,000 was made up of sales in the period July to September 19-6. No adjustment has been made in the draft accounts for this item.

Uncertain Ltd
Draft profit and loss account for the year ended 30 September 19-6

	£	£
Sales		5,450,490
Manufacturing cost of sales		3,284,500
Gross profit		2,165,990
Administration expenses	785,420	
Selling expenses	629,800	
		1,415,220
		750,770
Corporation tax (50%)		375,385
		375,385
Proposed dividend on ordinary shares		125,000
		250,385
Prior year adjustment	258,800	
Corporation tax	129,400	
		129,400
		120,985

Required:

(a) Write a report to the chief accountant of Uncertain Ltd with suggestions for appropriate treatment for each of the items (a) to (e), with explanations for your proposals.

(b) Amend the draft profit and loss account to take account of your proposals.

(Chartered Association of Certified Accountants)

17

The final accounts of limited companies: profit and loss accounts

When a company draws up its own Final Accounts, purely for internal use by the directors and the management, then it can draft them in any way which is considered most suitable. Drawing up a Trading and Profit and Loss Account and Balance Sheet for the firm's own use is not necessarily the same as drawing up such accounts for examination purposes. If a firm wishes to charge something in the Trading Account which perhaps in theory ought to be shown in the Profit and Loss Account, then there is nothing to prevent the firm from so doing. The examinee, on the other hand, must base his answers on accounting theory and not on the practice of his own firm.

When it comes to publication, i.e. sent to the shareholder or to the Registrar of Companies, then the Companies Act 1985, Schedule 4, lays down the information which *must* be shown and also *how* it should be shown. Prior to 1981, provided the necessary information was shown it was completely up to the company exactly *how* it was shown. The provisions of the 1981 Act brought the United Kingdom into line with the Fourth Directive of the EEC, and therefore the freedom previously available to companies on *how* to show the information has been taken away from them. There are however some advantages to be gained from such standardisation.

The current 1985 Act however does give companies the choice of two alternative formats (layouts) for balance sheets, and four alternative formats for profit and loss accounts. As the reader of this chapter will most probably be studying this for the first time, it would be inappropriate to give all the details of all the formats. Only the far more advanced student would need such details. In this book therefore the reader will be shown an internal profit and loss account which can easily be adapted to cover publication requirements under the 1985 Act, also a balance sheet.

All companies, even the very smallest, have to produce accounts for shareholders giving the *full* details required by the 1985 Act. 'Small' and 'medium' companies, as later defined, can however file 'modified' accounts with the Registrar of Companies. These will be examined later.

The format that will be used for the published profit and loss account in this book, out of the four formats which could be used, is Format 1. The reasons for this choice are that it is in a vertical style, which is much more modern and also more likely to gain extra marks from examiners, and in addition is much more like common UK practice before 1981. An example of Format 2, also in vertical style, is shown as Exhibit 17.5. Formats 3 and 4 are in horizontal style and are not shown in this book.

The Companies Act 1985, Schedule 4, shows Format 1 as in Exhibit 17.1.

Exhibit 17.1

Profit and loss account formats
Format 1

1 Turnover
2 Cost of sales
3 Gross profit or loss
4 Distribution costs
5 Administrative expenses
6 Other operating income
7 Income from shares in group companies
8 Income from shares in related companies
9 Income from other fixed asset investments
10 Other interest receivable and similar income
11 Amounts written off investments
12 Interest payable and similar charges
13 Tax on profit or loss on ordinary activities
14 Profit or loss on ordinary activities after taxation
15 Extraordinary income
16 Extraordinary charges
17 Extraordinary profit or loss
18 Tax on extraordinary profit or loss
19 Other taxes not shown under the above items
20 Profit or loss for the financial year

Obviously this is simply a list, and it does not show where sub-totals should be placed. The important point is that the items 1 to 20 have to be displayed in that order. Obviously if some items do not exist for the company in a given year then those headings will be omitted from the published profit and loss account. Thus if the company has no sorts of investments then items 7, 8, 9, 10 and 11 will not exist, so, that item 6 will be followed by item 12 in that company's published profit and loss account. The actual numbers on the left-hand side of items do not have to be shown in the published accounts.

Exhibit 17.2 shows a Trading and Profit and Loss Account drawn up for internal use by the company. This could be drawn up in any way as far as the law is concerned because the law does not cover accounts prepared solely for the company's internal use. If the internal accounts were drawn up in a completely different fashion to those needed for publication, then there would be quite a lot of work to do to reassemble the figures, into a profit and loss account for publication. In Exhibit 17.2 the internal accounts have been drawn up in a style which makes it much easier to get the figures for the published profit and loss account. As examination questions may ask for both (i) internal and (ii) published accounts, it makes it simpler for the students if the internal *and* published accounts follow a similar order of display.

Exhibit 17.2 (accounts for internal use)

Block plc

Trading & Profit & Loss Account for the year ended 31 March 19-8

	£	£	
Turnover			765,000
less Cost of Sales:			
Stock 1 April 19-7		105,000	
Add Purchases		460,000	
		565,000	
less Stock 31 March 19-8		126,000	439,000
Gross Profit			326,000
Distribution Costs:			
Salaries & Wages	50,000		
Motor Vehicles Costs: Distribution	21,000		
General Distribution Expenses	15,000		
Depreciation: Motors	4,000		
Machinery	3,000	93,000	
Administrative Expenses:			
Salaries & Wages	44,000		
Directors' Remuneration	20,000		
Motor Vehicle Costs: Administrative	8,000		
General Administrative Expenses	31,000		
Auditors' Remuneration	2,000		
Depreciation: Motors	3,000		
Machinery	2,000	110,000	203,000
			123,000
Other Operating Income: Rents Receivable			7,000
			130,000
Income from shares in related companies		2,500	
Income from shares from non-related companies		1,500	
Other Interest Receivable		1,000	5,000
			135,000
Interest Payable:			
Loans Repayable within five years		500	
Loans Repayable in ten years' time		1,500	2,000
Profit on ordinary activities before taxation			133,000
Tax on Profit on ordinary activities			48,000
Profit on ordinary activities after taxation			85,000
Retained profits brought forward from last year			55,000
			140,000
Transfer to General Reserve		15,000	
Proposed ordinary dividend		60,000	75,000
Retained profits carried forward to next year			65,000

Exhibit 17.3 (Accounts for publication)

Block plc

Profit and Loss Account for the year ended 31 March 19-8

		£	£
1	Turnover		765,000
2	Cost of Sales		439,000
3	Gross Profit		326,000
4	Distribution Costs	93,000	
5	Administrative Expenses	110.000	203,000
			123,000
6	Other Operating Income		7,000
			130,000
8	Income from Shares in Related Companies	2,500	
9	Income from Other Fixed Asset Investments	1,500	
10	Other Interest Receivable	1,000	5,000
			135,000
12	Interest Payable:		2,000
	Profit on Ordinary Activities before Taxation		133,000
13	Tax on Profit on Ordinary Activities		48,000
14	Profit for the year on Ordinary Activities after Taxation		85,000
	Retained Profits from last year		55,000
			140,000
	Transfer to General Reserve	15,000	
	Proposed Ordinary Dividend	60,000	75,000
	Retained Profits Carried to Next Year		65,000

Exhibit 17.2 is redrafted into a form suitable for publication and shown as Exhibit 17.3. The following notes are applicable.

The figures in the left-hand side of Exhibit 17.3 do *not* have to be published. They are shown for the benefit of the reader of this book.

It would be legally possible for the internal accounts, as shown in Exhibit 17.2 to be published just as they are, because all the items are shown in the correct order. This would not have been possible if the internal accounts were drafted in a completely different order. However, the Companies Act does not force companies to publish full accounts, as a company's competitors may thereby be given information which would lead to them being placed in a better competitive position against the company. The law therefore states the minimum information which must be disclosed, a company can show more than the minimum should it so wish.

Format Item 1. Turnover is defined as the amounts derived from the provision of goods and services falling within the company's ordinary activities, net after deduction of V.A.T. and trade discounts.

Format: Items 2, 4 and 5. The figures for Cost of Sales, Distribution costs and Administrative expenses must include any depreciation charges connected with these functions. In the case of Block plc, because of the type of business, there are depreciation charges as part of Distribution costs and Administration expenses but not for Cost of Sales.

Format Item 6. This is operating income which does not fall under Item 1. Such items as rents receivable, royalties receivable might be found under this heading. It all depends on what the 'ordinary activities' of the company are, as Item 6 is for operating 'outside' the ordinary activities.

Format Item 7. When the reader reaches Chapter 24 of this book he will be introduced to holding companies and subsidiaries. Such companies are under 'common' control, i.e. the holding company owns sufficient shares to 'control' the activities of the subsidiary. The holding company and all its subsidiaries are a 'group'. Any dividends received by a company from its investments in shares in any member of the 'group' have to be shown separately.

Format Item 8. The term 'related company' was a new term introduced by the 1981 Companies Act. A 'related company' is defined as a non-group company in which an investor company holds a long-term 'qualifying capital interest' (i.e. an interest in voting equity shares) for the purpose of securing a contribution to the investor's own activities by the exercise of control or influence. Where the equity stake exceeds 20 per cent, there is a presumption of such influence unless the contrary is shown.

Format Item 12. This includes bank interest on loans and overdrafts, debenture interest etc.

In the published Profit and Loss Account for Block plc there are no items per the format numbered 7, 11, 15, 16, 17, 18, and 19. After item 20, Profit for the year, there are several more lines, those of retained profits brought forward and carried forward, transfer to reserves and proposed dividends. Although the format omits them, they are in fact required according to the detailed rules accompanying the Format. This also applies to the line 'Profit on Ordinary Activities before Taxation.

It would have been possible to amalgamate items, for instance 4 and 5 could have been shown as one item as 'Net Operating Expenses £203,000'. In this case included in the notes appended to the accounts would be an item showing how the figure of £203,000 was made up.

In the notes attached to the profit and loss account, Section 53 Companies Act 1985, requires that the following be shown separately:

(*a*) Interest on bank loans, overdrafts and other loans

(i) repayable within 5 years from the end of the accounting period

(ii) finally repayable after 5 years from the end of the accounting period.

(*b*) Amounts set aside for redemption of share capital and for redemption of loans.

(*c*) Rents from land, if material.

(*d*) Costs of hire of plant and machinery.

(*e*) Auditors' remuneration, including expenses.

Section 55 requires a note, where a company carries on business of two or more classes differing substantially from each other, of the amount of turnover for each class of business and the division of the profit and loss before taxation between each class. Information also has to be given of the turnover between geographical markets.

Section 56, requires notes concerning numbers of employees, wages and salaries, social security costs and pension costs.

Exhibit 17.4 gives a Profit and Loss Account for a company which has amounts for each of items 1 to 20 inclusive. In addition the extra lines are shown, although they were omitted from the Format 1 in the Companies Act. The monetary figures are given so that the reader can see where sub-totals can be shown.

Exhibit 17.4

Profit and Loss Account: Format 1

		£	£000's £
1	Turnover		800
2	Cost of sales		500
3	Gross profit or loss		300
4	Distribution costs	60	
5	Administrative expenses	40	100
			200
6	Other operating income		30
			230
7	Income from shares in group companies	20	
8	Income from shares in related companies	10	
9	Income from other fixed asset investments	5	
10	Other interest receivable and similar income	15	
			50
			280
11	Amounts written off investments	4	
12	Interest payable and similar charges	16	
			20
	Profit or loss on ordinary activities before taxation		260
13	Tax on profit or loss on ordinary activities		95
14	Profit or loss on ordinary activities after taxation		165
15	Extraordinary income	16	
16	Extraordinary charges	4	
17	Extraordinary profit or loss	12	
18	Tax on extraordinary profit or loss	5	
			7
			172
19	Other taxes not shown under the above items		8
20	Profit or loss for the financial year		164
	Retained Profits from last year		60
			224
	Transfers to Reserves	40	
	Dividends Paid and Proposed	100	140
	Retained Profits Carried to Next Year		84

Allocation of expenses

It will be obvious under which heading most expenses will be shown whether they are

(i) Cost of Sales, or

(ii) Distribution Costs, or

(iii) Administrative Expenses.

However, some items are not so easy to allocate with certainty as the Companies Acts do not define these terms. Some companies may choose one heading for a particular item, while another company will choose to include that item under another heading. These items can now be examined.

(a) **Discounts Received**. These are for prompt payment of amounts owing by us. Where they are for payments to suppliers of goods they could be regarded as either being a reduction in the cost of goods, or alternatively as being a financial recompense, i.e. the reward for paying money on time. If regarded in the first way it would be deducted from Cost of Sales, whereas the alternative approach would be to deduct it from Administrative Expenses.

However, these discounts are also deducted when paying bills in respect of Distribution Costs or Administrative Expenses, and it would also be necessary to deduct from these headings if the Cost of Sales deduction approach is used. As this raises complications in the original recording of discounts received, it would be more suitable in this book if all cash discounts received are deducted in arriving at the figure of Administrative Expenses.

(b) **Discounts Allowed**. To be consistent in dealing with discounts, this should be included in Administrative Expenses.

(c) **Bad Debts**. These could either be regarded as an expense connected with sales, after all they are sales which are not paid for. The other point of view is that for a debt to become bad, at least part of the blame must be because the proper administrative procedures in checking on customers' creditworthiness has not been thorough enough. In this book all bad debts will be taken as being part of Administrative Expenses.

Exhibit 17.5

The previous exhibit, 17.4, is now shown as it might appear in Format 2.

Profit and Loss Account: Format 2

		£	£	£000's £
1	Turnover			800
2	Change in stocks of finished goods and in Work in Progress			45
3	Own work capitalised			25
4	Other operating income			30
				900
5	(a) Raw materials and consumables	290		
	(b) Other external charges	190	480	
6	Staff costs:			
	(a) Wages and salaries	110		
	(b) Other pension costs	12	122	
7	(a) Depreciation and other amounts written off tangible and intangible fixed assets	50		
	(b) Exceptional amounts written off current assets	10	60	
8	Other operating charges		8	670
				230
9	Income from shares in group companies		20	
10	Income from shares in related companies		10	
11	Income from other fixed asset investments		5	
12	Other interest receivable and similar income		15	50
				280
13	Amounts written off investments		4	
14	Interest payable and similar charges		16	20
	Profit or loss on ordinary activities before taxation			260
15	Tax on profit or loss on ordinary activities			95
16	Profit or loss on ordinary activities after taxation			165
17	Extraordinary income		16	
18	Extraordinary charges		4	
19	Extraordinary profit or loss		12	
20	Tax on extraordinary profit or loss		5	7
				172
21	Other taxes not shown under the above items			8
22	Profit or loss for the financial year			164
	Retained Profits from last year			60
				224
	Transfers to Reserves		40	
	Dividends Paid and Proposed		100	140
	Retained Profits Carried to Next Year			84

Note: Obviously the author has had to invent figures for items 2, 3, 5, 6, 7 and 8, as it would be impossible to deduce them from the figures shown in Exhibit 17.4.

Review questions

17.1 From the following selected balance of Rogers plc as at 31 December 19- 2 draw up (i) A Trading and Profit and Loss Account for internal use, and (ii) a Profit and Loss Account for publication.

	£
Profit and Loss Account as at 31 December 19-1	15,300
Stock 1 January 19-2	57,500
Purchases	164,000
Sales	288,000
Returns Inwards	11,500
Returns Outwards	2,000
Carriage Inwards	1,300
Wages & Salaries (see note (*b*))	8,400
Rent & Rates (see note (*c*))	6,250
General Distribution Expenses	4,860
General Administrative Expenses	3,320
Discounts Allowed	3,940
Bad Debts	570
Debenture Interest	2,400
Motor Expenses (see note (*d*))	7,200
Interest Received on Bank Deposit	770
Income from shares in related companies (gross)	660
Motor Vehicles at cost: Administrative	14,000
Distribution	26,000
Equipment at cost: Administrative	5,500
Distribution	3,500
Royalties Receivable	1,800

Notes: (*a*) Stock at 31 December 19-2 £64,000.

(*b*) Wages and Salaries are to be apportioned: Distribution Costs ⅓rd, Administrative Expenses ⅔rds.

(*c*) Rent and Rates are to be apportioned: Distribution Costs 60%, Administrative Expenses 40%.

(*d*) Apportion Motor Expenses equally between Distribution Costs and Administrative Expenses.

(*e*) Depreciate Motor Vehicles 25% and Equipment 20% on cost.

(*f*) Accrue auditors' remuneration of £500.

(*g*) Accrue Corporation Tax for the year on ordinary activity profits £30,700.

(*h*) A sum of £8,000 is to be transferred to General Reserve.

(*i*) An ordinary dividend of £30,000 is to be proposed.

17.2 You are given the following selected balances of Federal plc as at 31 December 19-4. From them draw up (i) a Trading and Profit and Loss Account for the year ended 31 December 19-4 for internal use and (ii) A Profit and Loss Account for publication.

	£
Stock 1 January 19-4	64,500
Sales	849,000
Purchases	510,600
Carriage Inwards	4,900
Returns Inwards	5,800
Returns Outwards	3,300
Discounts Allowed	5,780
Discounts Received	6,800
Wages (putting goods into saleable condition)	11,350
Salaries and Wages: Sales and Distribution staff	29,110
Salaries and Wages: Administrative Staff	20,920
Motor Expenses (see note (c))	15,600
Rent & Rates (see note (d))	25,000
Investments in related companies (market value £66,000)	80,000
Income from shares in related companies	3,500
General Distribution Expenses	8,220
General Administrative Expenses	2,190
Bad Debts	840
Interest from Government Securities	1,600
Haulage Costs: Distribution	2,070
Debenture Interest Payable	3,800
Profit and Loss Account: 31 December 19-3	37,470
Motor Vehicles at cost: Distribution and Sales	75,000
Administrative	35,000
Plant & Machinery at cost: Distribution and Sales	80,000
Administrative	50,000
Production	15,000
Directors' Remuneration	5,000

Notes:

(*a*) The production department puts goods bought into a saleable condition.

(*b*) Stock at 31 December 19-4 £82,800

(*c*) Apportion Motor Expenses: Distribution ⅔rds, Administrative ⅓rd.

(*d*) Apportion Rent and Rates: Distribution 80%, Administrative 20%.

(*e*) Write £14,000 off the value of Investments in related companies.

(*f*) Depreciation Motor Vehicles 20% on cost, Plant and Machinery 10% on cost.

(*g*) Accrue auditors' remuneration £2,000.

(*h*) Accrue Corporation Tax on ordinary activity profits £74,000.

(*i*) A sum of £20,000 is to be transferred to Debenture Redemption Reserve.

(*j*) An ordinary dividend of £50,000 is to be proposed.

17.3 The following information has been extracted from the books of account of Rufford plc for the year to 31 March 19-6:

	Dr £000	Cr £000
ACT (paid on 14 October 19-5)	3	
Administration expenses	97	
Deferred taxation		24
Depreciation on office machinery (for the year to 31 March 19-6)	8	
Depreciation on delivery vans (for the year to 31 March 19-6)	19	
Distribution costs	33	
Dividends received (from a UK listed company on 31 July 19-5)		14
Factory closure expenses (net of tax)	12	
Interest payable on bank overdraft (repayable within five years)	6	
Interim dividend (paid on 30 September 19-5)	21	
Interest receivable		25
Purchases	401	
Retained profit at 31 March 19-5		160
Sales (net of VAT)		642
Stock at 1 April 19-5	60	

Additional information:

1 Administrative expenses include the following items:

	£ 000
Auditors' remuneration	20
Directors' emoluments	45
Travelling expenses	1
Research expenditure	11
Hire of plant and machinery	12

2 It is assumed that the following tax rates are applicable for the year to 31 March 19-6:

	%
Corporation tax	50
Income tax	30

3 There was an overprovision for corporation tax of £3,000 relating to the year to 31 March 19-5.

4 Corporation tax payable for the year to 31 March 19-6 (based on the profits for that year) is estimated to be £38,000. The company, in addition, intends to transfer a further £9,000 to its deferred taxation account.

5 A final dividend of £42,000 for the year to 31 March 19-6 is expected to be paid on 2 June 19-6.

6 Stock at 31 March 19-6 was valued at £71,000.

7 As a result of a change in accounting policy, a prior year charge of £15,000 (net of tax) is to be made.

8 The company's share capital consists of 420,000 ordinary shares of £1 each. There are no preference shares, and no change had been made to the company's issued share capital for some years.

Required:

(*a*) In so far as the information permits, prepare the company's published profit and loss account for the year to 31 March 19-6 in the vertical format in accordance with the Companies Act and with related statements of standard accounting practice.

(NB A statement of the company's accounting policies is not required.)

(*b*) Prepare balance sheet extracts in order to illustrate the balances still remaining in the following accounts at 31 March 19-6:

    (i)   corporation tax;

    (ii) advanced corporation tax;

    (iii) proposed dividend; and

    (iv) deferred taxation.

(NB a detailed balance sheet is not required.)

(Association of Accounting Technicians)

17.4A The following balance has been extracted from the books of Falconer plc as on 31 August 19-4. From them draw up (i) A Trading and Profit and Loss Account, for internal use, for the year ended 31 August 19-4, also (ii) A Profit and Loss Account for publication for the year.

	£
Purchases	540,500
Sales	815,920
Returns Inwards	15,380
Returns Outwards	24,620
Carriage Inwards	5,100
Wages – Productive	6,370
Discounts Allowed	5,890
Discounts Received	7,940
Stock 31 August 19-3	128,750
Wages & Salaries: Sales and Distribution	19,480
Wages & Salaries: Administrative	24,800
Motor Expenses: Sales and Distribution	8,970
Motor Expenses: Administrative	16,220
General Distribution Expenses	4,780
General Administrative Expenses	5,110
Rent and Rates (see note (*c*))	9,600
Directors' Remuneration	12,400
Profit and Loss Account: 31 August 19-3	18,270
Advertising Costs	8,380
Bad Debts	1,020
Hire of Plant and Machinery (see note (*b*))	8,920
Motor Vehicles at cost: Sales & Distribution	28,000
Administrative	36,000
Plant and Machinery: Distribution	17,500
Debenture Interest Payable	4,800
Income from Shares in group companies	12,800
Income from Shares in related companies	10,500
Preference Dividend Paid	15,000
Profit on disposal of investments	6,600
Tax on profit on disposal of investments	1,920

Notes:

(*a*) Stock at 31 August 19-4 £144,510.

(*b*) The hire of plant and machinery is to be apportioned: Productive £5,200, Administrative £3,720.

(*c*) Rent and Rates to be apportioned: Distribution ⅔rds, Administrative ⅓rd.

(*d*) Motors are to be depreciated at 25% on cost, Plant and Machinery to be depreciated at 20% on cost.

(*e*) Auditors' remuneration of £1,700 to be accrued.

(*f*) Corporation tax on profit from ordinary activities for the year is estimated at £59,300.

(*g*) Transfer £25,000 to General Reserve.

(*h*) Ordinary dividend of £60,000 is proposed.

17.5A From the following balance of Danielle plc you are to draw up (i) a Trading and Profit and Loss Account for the year ended 31 December 19-6, for internal use, and (ii) a Profit and Loss Account for publication:

	£
Plant and Machinery, at cost (see note (*c*))	275,000
Bank Interest Receivable	1,850
Discounts Allowed	5,040
Discounts Received	3,890
Hire of Motor Vehicles: Sales and Distribution	9,470
Hire of Motor Vehicles: Administrative	5,710
Licence Fees Receivable	5,100
General Distribution Expenses	11,300
General Administrative Expenses	15,800
Wages and Salaries: Sales and Distribution	134,690
Administrative	89,720
Directors' Remuneration	42,000
Motor Expenses (see note (*e*))	18,600
Stock 31 December 19-5	220,500
Sales	880,000
Purchases	405,600
Returns Outwards	15,800
Returns Inwards	19,550
Profit and Loss Account as at 31 December 19-5	29,370

Notes:

(*a*) Stock at 31 December 19-6 £210,840.

(*b*) Accrue Auditors' Remuneration £3,000.

(*c*) Of the Plant and Machinery, £150,000 is Distributive in nature, whilst £125,000 is for Administration.

(*d*) Depreciate Plant and Machinery 20% on cost.

(*e*) Of the Motor Expenses ⅔rds is for Sales and Distribution and ⅓rd for Administration.

(*f*) Corporation Tax on Ordinary Profits is estimated at £28,350.

(*g*) Proposed ordinary dividend is £50,000.

(*h*) A sum of £15,000 is to be transferred to General Reserve.

18

The final accounts of limited companies: balance sheets

The Companies Act 1985 sets out two formats for the balance sheet, one vertical and one horizontal. The method chosen for this book is that of Format 1 because this most resembles previous UK practice. As it is the vertical style format it will also be looked upon with favour by examiners.

Format 1 is shown as Exhibit 18.1. Monetary figures have been included to illustrate it more clearly.

Exhibit 18.1

Balance Sheet – Format 1

				£000's	
			£	£	£
A	CALLED UP SHARE CAPITAL NOT PAID*				10
B	FIXED ASSETS				
I	Intangible assets				
	1	Development costs	20		
	2	Concessions, patents, licences, trade marks and similar rights and assets	30		
	3	Goodwill	80		
	4	Payments on account	5	135	
II	Tangible assets				
	1	Land and buildings	300		
	2	Plant and machinery	500		
	3	Fixtures, fittings, tools and equipment	60		
	4	Payments on account and assets in course of construction	20	880	
III	Investments				
	1	Shares in group companies	15		
	2	Loans to group companies	10		
	3	Shares in related companies	20		
	4	Loans to related companies	5		
	5	Other investments other than loans	30		
	6	Other loans	16		
	7	Own shares	4	100	1,115
C	CURRENT ASSETS				
I	Stock				
	1	Raw materials and consumables	60		
	2	Work in progress	15		
	3	Finished goods and goods for resale	120		
	4	Payments on account	5	200	
II	Debtors				
	1	Trade debtors	200		
	2	Amounts owed by group companies	20		
	3	Amounts owed by related companies	10		
	4	Other debtors	4		
	5	Called up share capital not paid*	–		
	6	Prepayments and accrued income**	–	234	

III		Investments			
	1	Shares in group companies	40		
	2	Own shares	5		
	3	Other investments	30		
			—	75	
IV		Cash at Bank and in Hand		26	
				535	
D		PREPAYMENTS AND ACCRUED INCOME**		15	
				550	
E		CREDITORS: AMOUNTS FALLING DUE WITHIN ONE YEAR			
	1	Debenture loans	5		
	2	Bank loans and overdrafts	10		
	3	Payments received on account	20		
	4	Trade creditors	50		
	5	Bills of exchange payable	2		
	6	Amounts owed to group companies	15		
	7	Amounts owed to related companies	6		
	8	Other creditors including taxation and social security	54		
	9	Accruals and deferred income***	–	162	
F		NET CURRENT ASSETS (LIABILITIES)			388
G		TOTAL ASSETS LESS CURRENT LIABILITIES			1,513
H		CREDITORS: AMOUNTS FALLING DUE AFTER MORE THAN ONE YEAR			
	1	Debenture loans	20		
	2	Bank loans and overdrafts	15		
	3	Payments received on account	5		
	4	Trade creditors	25		
	5	Bills of exchange payable	4		
	6	Amounts owed to group companies	10		
	7	Amounts owed to related companies	5		
	8	Other creditors including taxation and social security	32		
	9	Accruals and deferred income***	–	116	
I		PROVISIONS FOR LIABILITIES AND CHARGES			
	1	Pensions and similar obligations	20		
	2	Taxation, including deferred taxation	40		
	3	Other provisions	4	64	
J		ACCRUALS AND DEFERRED INCOME***		20	200
					1,313
K		CAPITAL AND RESERVES			
I		Called up share capital			1,000
II		Share premium account			100
III		Revaluation reserve			20
IV		Other reserves:			
	1	Capital redemption reserve	40		
	2	Reserve for own shares	10		
	3	Reserves provided for by the articles of association	20		
	4	Other reserves	13		83
V		PROFIT AND LOSS ACCOUNT			110
					1,313

(*); (**); (***) These items may be shown in either of the two positions indicated.

It should be noted that various items can be shown in alternative places, i.e.
Called up share capital not paid, either in position A or position CII 5.
Prepayments and accrued income, either CII 6 or as D.
Accruals and deferred income, either E9 or H9, or in total as J.

Items preceded by letters or Roman numerals must be disclosed on the face of the balance sheet, e.g. B Fixed Assets, (K) II Share Premium Account, whereas those shown with Arabic numerals (you may call them ordinary numbers, 1, 2, 3, 4, etc) may be combined where they are not material or the combination facilitates assessment of the company's affairs. Where they are combined the details of each item should be shown in the notes accompanying the accounts. The actual letters, roman numerals or arabic numbers do *not* have to be shown on the face of the published balance sheets.

The following also apply to the balance sheet in Format 1.

BI Intangible assets. These are assets not having a 'physical' existence as compared with tangible assets which do have a physical existence. For instance you can see and touch the tangible assets of land and buildings, plant and machinery etc, whereas Goodwill does not exist in a physical sense.

For each of the items under Fixed Assets, whether they are Intangible Assets, Tangible Assets or Investments, the notes accompanying the accounts must give full details of (i) cost, at beginning and end of financial year, (ii) effect on that item of acquisitions, disposals, revaluations etc. during the year, and (iii) full details of depreciation, i.e. accumulated depreciation at start of year, depreciation for year, effect of disposals on depreciation in the year and any other adjustments.

All fixed assets, including property and goodwill must be depreciated over the period of the useful economic life of each asset. Prior to this many companies had not depreciated property because of rising money values of the asset. Costs of research must not be treated as an asset, and development costs may be capitalised only in special cases. Any hire-purchase owing must not be deducted from the assets concerned. Only goodwill which has been purchased can be shown as an asset, internally generated goodwill must not be capitalised. (This does not refer to goodwill in consolidated accounts, see Chapter 28.)

Where an asset is revalued, normally this will be fixed assets being shown at market value instead of cost, any difference on revaluation must be debited or credited to a revaluation reserve, see KIII in the Format.

Investments shown as CIII will be in respect of those not held for the long term.

Two items which could previously be shown as assets, (i) preliminary expenses, these are the legal expenses etc in forming the company, and (ii) expenses of and commission on any issue of share or debentures, must not now be shown as assets. They can be written off against any Share Premium Account balance, alternatively they should be written off to profit and loss account.

Full details of each class of share capital, and of authorised capital, will be shown in notes accompanying the balance sheet.

Choice of formats

The Act leaves the choice of a particular format for the Balance Sheet and the Profit and Loss Account to the directors. Once adopted the choice must be adhered to in subsequent years except in the case that there are special reasons for the change. If a change is made then full reasons for the change must be stated in the notes attached to the accounts.

Fundamental accounting principles

The Companies Act 1985 sets out the accounting principles (or 'valuation rules' as they are called in the Fourth Directive of the EEC) to be followed when preparing company financial statements.

The following principles are stated in the Act, the reader can be referred to Chapter 10 of Business Accounting 1 for a fuller discussion of some of them.

(*a*) A company is presumed to be a going concern.

(*b*) Accounting policies must be applied consistently from year to year.

(*c*) The prudence concept must be followed.

(*d*) The accruals concept must be observed.

(*e*) Each component item of assets and liabilities must be valued separately. As an instance of this, if a company has five different types of stock, each type must be valued separately at the lower of cost and net realisable value, rather than be valued on an aggregate basis.

(*f*) Amounts in respect of items representing assets or income may *not* be set off against items representing liabilities or expenditure. Thus an amount owing on a hire purchase contract cannot now be deducted from the value of the asset in the balance sheet, although this was often done before 1981.

True and fair view

If complying with the requirements of the 1985 Act would cause the accounts not to be 'true and fair' then the directors must set aside such requirements. This should not be done lightly, and it would not be common to find such instances.

Reporting requirements for small and medium companies

Small and medium-sized companies do not have to file a full set of final accounts with the registrar of companies. They could, if they wished, send a full set of final accounts, but what they *have* to file is a minimum of 'modified accounts'. They would still have to send a full set to their own shareholders, the 'modified accounts' refer only to those filed with the Registrar.

The definition of 'small' and 'medium' companies is if, for the financial year in question and the previous year, the company comes within the limits of at least 'two' of the following three criteria:

Criteria	Size	
	Small	Medium
Balance Sheet Total (i.e. total assets)	£700,000	£2,800,000
Turnover	£1,400,000	£5,750,000
Average number of employees	50	250

Modified accounts of small companies

(*a*) Neither a profit and loss account nor a directors' report has to be filed with the Registrar.

(*b*) A modified balance sheet showing only those items to which a letter or Roman numeral are attached (*see* Format 1, Exhibit 18.1) has to be shown. For example the total for CI Stocks has to be shown, but not the figures for each of the individual items comprising this total.

Modified accounts of medium companies

(a) The Profit and Loss Account per Format 1 does not have to show item 1 Turnover or item 2 Cost of Sales. It will therefore begin with the figure of Gross Profit or Loss.

(b) The analyses of turnover and profit normally required as notes to the accounts need not be given.

(c) The balance sheet, however, must be given in full.

Notes to the accounts: review questions on published company accounts including notes required by law are shown at the end of Chapter 19.

Review questions

18.1 The following balances remained in the books of Owen Ltd on 31 Dec 19-1, *after* the Profit and Loss Account and Appropriation Account had been drawn up. You are to draft the balance sheet as at 31 Dec 19-1 in accordance with the Companies Act.

	Dr £	Cr £
Ordinary Share Capital: £1 shares		50,000
Preference Share Capital: 50p shares		25,000
Calls Account (Ordinary Shares)	150	
Development Costs	3,070	
Goodwill	21,000	
Land and Buildings – at cost	48,000	
Plant and Machinery – at cost	12,500	
Provision for Depreciation: Buildings		16,000
Provision for Depreciation: Plant and Machinery		5,400
Shares in Related Companies	35,750	
Stock: Raw Materials	3,470	
Stock: Finished Goods	18,590	
Debtors: Trade	17,400	
Amounts Owed by Related Companies	3,000	
Prepayments	1,250	
Debentures (*see* note 1)		10,000
Bank Overdraft (repayable within 6 months)		4,370
Creditors: Trade (payable within 1 year)		12,410
Bills Payable (*see* note 2)		3,600
Share Premium		20,000
Capital Redemption Reserve		5,000
General Reserve		4,000
Profit and Loss Account		8,400
	164,180	164,180

Notes:

1 Of the debentures £6,000 is repayable in 3 months' time, while the other £4,000 is repayable in 5 years' time.

2 Of the Bills Payable, £1,600 is in respect of a bill to be paid in 4 months' time and £2,000 for a bill payable in 18 months' time.

3 The depreciation charged for the year was: Building £4,000, Plant and Machinery £1,800.

18.2 After the profit and loss, appropriation account has been prepared for the year ended 30 September 19-4, the following balances remain in the books of Belle Works plc. You are to draw up a balance sheet in accordance with the Companies Act.

	£	£
Ordinary Share Capital		70,000
Share Premium		5,000
Revaluation Reserve		10,500
General Reserve		6,000
Foreign Exchange Reserve		3,500
Profit and Loss		6,297
Patents Trade Marks and Licences	1,500	
Goodwill	17,500	
Land and Buildings	90,000	
Provision for Depreciation: Land and Buildings		17,500
Plant and Machinery	38,600	
Provision for Depreciation: Plant and Machinery		19,200
Stock of Raw Materials: 30 September 19-4	14,320	
Work in Progress: 30 September 19-4	5,640	
Finished Goods: 30 September 19-4	13,290	
Debtors: Trade	11,260	
Debtors: Other	1,050	
Prepayments and Accrued Income	505	
Debentures (redeemable in 6 months' time)		6,000
Debentures (redeemable in 4½ years' time)		12,000
Bank Overdraft (repayable in 3 months)		3,893
Trade Creditors (payable in next 12 months)		11,340
Trade Creditors (payable after 12 months)		1,260
Bills of Exchange (payable within 12 months)		4,000
Corporation Tax (payable in 9 months' time)		14,370
National Insurance (payable in next month)		305
Pensions Contribution Owing		1,860
Deferred Taxation		640
	193,665	193,665

18.3 The following trial balance has been extracted from the books of Baganza plc as at 30 September 19-7:

	£'000	£'000
Advance corporation tax (paid on interim dividend)	87	
Administrative expenses	400	
Called up share capital		
(1,200,000, ordinary shares of £1 each)		1,200
Cash at bank and in hand	60	
Corporation tax		
(overpayment for the year to 30 September 19-6)		20
Deferred taxation (at 1 October 19-6)		460
Distribution costs	600	
Dividends received (on 31 March 19-7)		249
Extraordinary item (net of tax)		1,500
Freehold property:		
at cost	2,700	
accumulated depreciation (at 1 October 19-6)		260
Interim dividend (paid on June 19-7)	36	
Investments in United Kingdom companies	2,000	
Plant and machinery:		
at cost	5,200	
accumulated depreciation (at 1 October 19-6)		3,600
Profit and loss account (at 1 October 19-6)		2,109
Purchases	16,000	
Research expenditure	75	
Stock (at 1 October 19-6)	2,300	
Tax on extraordinary item		360
Trade creditors		2,900
Trade debtors	2,700	
Turnover		19,500
	£32,158	£32,158

Additional information:

1 The stock at 30 September 19-7 was valued at £3,600,000.

2 Depreciation for the year to 30 September 19-7 is to be charged on the historic cost of the fixed assets as follows:

Freehold property: 5%

Plant and machinery: 15%

3 The basic rate of income tax is assumed to be 27%.

4 The directors propose a final dividend of 60p per share.

5 The company was incorporated in 1970.

6 Corporation tax based on the profits for the year at a rate of 35% is estimated to be £850,000.

7 A transfer of £40,000 is to be made to the Deferred Taxation Account.

Required:

In so far as the information permits, prepare Baganza plc's profit and loss account for the year to 30 September 19-7, and a balance sheet as at that date in accordance with the Companies Act 1985 and appropriate statements of standard accounting practice.

However, formal notes to the accounts are not required, although detailed workings should be submitted with your answer, which should include your calculation of earnings per share.

(*Association of Accounting Technicians*)

18.4 The trial balance of Payne Peerbrook plc as on 31 December 19-6 is as follows:

	Dr £	Cr £
Preference Share Capital: £1 shares		50,000
Ordinary Share Capital: 50p shares		60,000
General Reserve		45,000
Exchange Reserve		13,600
Profit and Loss Account as on 31 December 19-5		19,343
Stock 31 December 19-5	107,143	
Sales		449,110
Returns Inwards	11,380	
Purchases	218,940	
Carriage Inwards	2,475	
Wages (putting goods into a saleable condition)	3,096	
Wages: Warehouse Staff	39,722	
Wages and Salaries: Sales Staff	28,161	
Wages and Salaries: Administrative Staff	34,778	
Motor Expenses (*see* note ii)	16,400	
General Distribution Expenses	8,061	
General Administrative Expenses	7,914	
Debenture Interest	10,000	
Royalties Receivable		4,179
Directors' Remuneration	18,450	
Bad Debts	3,050	
Discounts Allowed	5,164	
Discounts Received		4,092
Plant and Machinery at cost (*see* note iii)	175,000	
Provision for Depreciation: Plant and Machinery		58,400
Motor Vehicles at cost (*see* note ii)	32,000	
Provision for Depreciation: Motors		14,500
Goodwill	29,500	
Development Costs	16,320	
Trade Debtors	78,105	
Trade Creditors		37,106
Bank Overdraft (repayable any time)		4,279
Bills of Exchange payable (all due within 1 year)		6,050
Debentures (redeemable in 5 years' time)		80,000
	845,659	845,659

Notes:

(*i*) Stock of Finished Goods on 31 December 19-6 £144,081.

(*ii*) Motor Expenses and Depreciation on Motors to be apportioned: Distribution ¾ths, Administrative ¼th.

(*iii*) Plant and Machinery depreciation to be apportioned. Cost of Sales ⅕th; Distribution ⅗ths: Administrative ⅕th.

(*iv*) Depreciate the following fixed assets on cost: Motor Vehicles 25%, Plant and Machinery 20%.

(*v*) Accrue Corporation Tax on profits of the year £14,150. This is payable 1 October 19-7.

(*vi*) A preference dividend of £5,000 is to be paid and an ordinary dividend of £10,000 is to be proposed.

You are to draw up:

(*a*) A Trading and Profit and Loss Account for the year ended 31 December 19-6 for internal use, and

(*b*) A Profit and Loss Account for publication, also a Balance Sheet as at 31 December 19-6.

19

Published accounts of limited companies: accompanying notes

The Companies Act 1985 requires that the following additional notes are given to accompany the published balance sheet.

1 Particulars of turnover

An analysis of turnover into:

(a) each class of business;

(b) geographical markets;

and, in addition, the amount of profit or loss before taxation, in the opinion of the directors, attributable to each class of business.

Such disclosure does not have to be made if it would be prejudicial to the business of the company. The fact of non-disclosure would have to be stated.

An example of such a note might be as follows:

Analysis of turnover

	Turnover	Profit
Motors	26,550,000	2,310,000
Aircraft	58,915,000	4,116,000
	£85,465,000	£6,426,000

The geographical division of turnover is:

United Kingdom	32,150,000
The Americas	43,025,000
Rest of the World	10,290,000
	£85,465,000

2 Particulars of staff

(a) Average number employed by the company (or by group in consolidated accounts), divided between categories of workers, e.g. between manufacturing and administration.

(b) (i) Wages and salaries paid to staff.

(ii) Social security costs of staff.

(iii) Other pension costs for employees.

Where format two of the profit and loss account per the Companies Act is used, (i), (ii) and (iii) are already shown in the body of the profit and loss account and need not be repeated.

(c) Number of employees (excluding those working wholly or mainly overseas) earning over £30,000, analysed under successive multiples of £5,000. Exclude pension contributions.

Here is an example of a note concerning higher-paid employees. The number of employees earning over £30,000 was 28, analysed as follows:

Gross salaries	Number of employees
£30,000–35,000	16
£35,001–40,000	8
£40,001–45,000	4
	28

3 Directors' emoluments

(*a*) Aggregate amounts of:

   (i)   emoluments, including pension contributions and benefits in kind. Distinction to be made between those emoluments as fees and those for executive duties;

   (ii) pensions for past directors;

   (iii) compensation for loss of office.

(*b*) The chairman's emoluments and those of the highest paid director, if paid more than the chairman. In both cases pension contributions are to be excluded.

(*c*) Number of directors whose emoluments, excluding pension contributions, fall within each bracket of £5,000.

   (*d*) Total amounts waived by directors and numbers concerned.

The disclosures under (*b*) and (*c*) above are not needed for a company being neither a holding nor subsidiary company where its directors' emoluments under (*a*) do not exceed £60,000. The disclosures under (*b*) and (*c*) are also not necessary for directors working wholly or mainly overseas.

   An illustration is now given:

Name	Fee (as directors)	Remuneration (as executives)	Pension contributions
A (Chairman)	£5,000	£85,000	£20,000
B	£2,500	£95,000	£30,000
C	£2,500	£55,000	£15,000
D	£1,500	£54,000	£12,500
E	£1,500	£30,000	£10,000

Note to accounts:

Directors' remuneration: the amounts paid to directors were as follows:

Fees as directors	£ 13,000
Other Emoluments, including pension contributions	£406,500

Emoluments of the Chairman – excluding pension contributions – amounted to £90,000, and those of the highest paid director to £97,500. Other directors' emoluments were in the following ranges:

£30,001 to £35,000	1
£55,001 to £60,000	2

4 Various charges to be shown as notes

(*a*) auditors' remuneration, including expenses;

(*b*) hire of plant and machinery;

(*c*) interest payable on (i) bank loans, overdrafts and other loans repayable by instalments or otherwise within five years; (ii) loans of any other kind;

(*d*) Depreciation:
  (i)   amounts of provisions for both tangible and intangible assets,
  (ii) effect on depreciation of change of depreciation method,
  (iii) effect on depreciation of revaluation of assets.

5 Income from listed investments

6 Rents receivable from land, after deducting outgoings

7 Taxation (see also SSAP 8 Corporation tax)

(*a*) Tax change split between:
  (i)   UK corporation tax, and basis of computation;
  (ii) UK income tax, and basis of computation;
  (iii) irrecoverable VAT;
  (iv) tax attributable to franked investment income.

(*b*) If relevant, split between tax on ordinary and tax on extraordinary activities.

(*c*) Show, as component part, charge for deferred tax.

(*d*) Any other special circumstances affecting tax liability.

8 Extraordinary and exceptional items and prior year adjustments

(*See* SSAP 6.)

9 Redemption of shares and loans

Show amounts set aside for these purposes.

10 Earnings per share (listed companies only)

(*See* SSAP 3.)

11 Statement showing movements on reserves

The directors' report

As well as a balance sheet and profit and loss account, the shareholders must also receive a directors' report. The contents of the report are given in the Companies Act, but no formal layout is given. Such a report is additional to the notes, which have to be attached to the accounts; the directors' report does not replace such notes.

(*a*) A fair review of the development of the business of the company (and its subsidiaries) during the financial year and of the position at the end of the year. The dividends proposed and transfers to reserves should be given.

(*b*) Principal activities of the company and any changes therein.

(*c*) Post balance sheet events, i.e. details of important events affecting company (and its subsidiaries) since the end of the year.

(*d*) Likely future developments in the business.

(*e*) An indication of research and development carried on.

(*f*) Significant changes in fixed assets. In the case of land, the difference between book and market values, if significant.

(*g*) Political and charitable contributions; if, taken together, these exceed £200 there must be shown:
  (i)   separate totals for each classification;
  (ii) where political contributions exceeding £200 have been made, the names of recipients and amounts;

(*h*) Details of own shares purchased.

(*i*) Employees:

    (i) statement concerning health, safety and welfare at work of company's employees;

    (ii) for companies with average workforce exceeding 250, details of employment of disabled people.

(*j*) Indication of activities in research and development;

(*k*) Directors:

    (i) names of all persons who had been directors during any part of the financial year;

    (ii) their interests in contracts;

    (iii) for each director, the name, also:

- the number of shares held at the start of the year;
- the number of shares held at the end of the year;
- for each director elected in the year there shall also be shown shares held when elected;
- all the above to show nil amounts where appropriate.

Note: under the Companies Act 1985 the directors' report is subject to external audit. If the external auditors' judgement is that the directors' report is inconsistent with the audited company accounts, then this must be stated in the auditors' report.

Illustrative company accounts: specimen question 1

F Clarke Ltd are specialist wholesalers. This is their trial balance at 31 December 19-4.

	Dr £	Cr £
Ordinary share capital: £1 shares		1,000,000
Share premium		120,000
General reserve		48,000
Profit and Loss account as at 31.12.19-3		139,750
Stock: 31.12.19-3	336,720	
Sales		4,715,370
Purchases	2,475,910	
Returns outwards		121,220
Returns inwards	136,200	
Carriage inwards	6,340	
Carriage outwards	43,790	
Warehouse wages (average no. of workers 59)	410,240	
Salesmens' salaries (average no. of workers 21)	305,110	
Administrative wages and salaries	277,190	
Plant and machinery	610,000	
Motor vehicle hire	84,770	
Provision for depreciation: plant and machinery		216,290
General distribution expenses	27,130	
General administrative expenses	47,990	
Directors' remuneration	195,140	
Rents receivable		37,150
Trade debtors	1,623,570	
Cash at bank and in hand	179,250	
Trade creditors (payable before 31.3.19-5)		304,570
Bills of exchange payable (payable 28.2.19-5)		57,000
	6,759,350	6,759,350

Notes:

(a) Stock at 31.12.19-4: £412,780, consists of goods for resale.

(b) Plant and machinery is apportioned: distributive 60%; administrative 40%.

(c) Accrue auditors' remuneration: £71,000.

(d) Depreciate plant and machinery: 20% on cost.

(e) Of the motor hire, £55,000 is for distributive purposes.

(f) Corporation tax on profits, at a rate of 35%, is estimated at £238,500, and is payable on 1.10.19-5.

(g) There is a proposed ordinary dividend of 37½% for the year.

(h) All of the sales are of one type of goods. Net sales of £3,620,000 have been made in the UK with the remainder in Europe, and are shown net of VAT.

(i) Pension contributions for staff amounted to £42,550 and social security contributions to £80,120. These figures are included in wages and salaries in the trial balance. No employee earned over £30,000.

(j) Plant of £75,000 had been bought during the year.

(k) Directors' remuneration has been as follows:

	£
Chairman	46,640
Managing Director	51,500
Finance Director	46,000
Marketing Director	43,000
	187,140

In addition each of them drew £2,000 as directors' fees. Pensions are the personal responsibility of directors.

Required:

Subject to the limits of the information given you, draw up profit and loss account for the year ended 31 December 19-4, and a balance sheet as at that date. They should be in published form and accompanied by the necessary notes prescribed by statute.

Specimen answer 1

F Clarke Ltd: Workings

Turnover: Sales	4,715,370	Cost of sales:	
less Returns in	136,200	Opening stock	336,720
	4,579,170	*add* Purchases	2,475,910
		less Returns out	121,220
			2,354,690
		add Carriage in	6,340	2,361,030
			2,697,750
		less Closing stock	412,780
			2,284,970

Distribution costs		Administrative expenses	
Warehouse wages	410,240	Wages and salaries	277,190
Salesmens' salaries	305,110	Motor hire	29,770
Carriage out	43,790	General expenses	47,990
General expenses	27,130	Directors' remuneration	150,140
Motor hire	55,000	Auditors' remuneration	71,000
Depreciation: plant	73,200	Depreciation: plant	48,800
			624,890
Marketing Director's			
remuneration	45,000		
	959,470		

Profit and loss account for the year ended 31 December 19-4

	£	£
Turnover		4,579,170
Cost of sales		2,284,970
Gross Profit		2,294,200
Distribution costs	959,470	
Administrative expenses	624,890	1,584,360
		709,840
Other operating income		37,150
Profit on ordinary activities before taxation		746,990
Tax on profit on ordinary activities		238,500
Profit on ordinary activities after taxation		508,490
Retained profits from last year		139,750
		648,240
Proposed ordinary dividend		375,000
Retained profits carried forward to next year		273,240

(b) F Clarke Ltd
Balance sheet as at 31 December 19-4

Fixed assets	£	£	£
Tangible assets			
Plant and machinery			271,710
Current assets			
Stock			
Finished goods and goods for resale		412,780	
Debtors			
Trade debtors		1,623,570	
Cash at bank and in hand		179,250	
		2,215,600	
Creditors: amounts falling due within one year			
Trade creditors	304,570		
Bills of exchange payable	57,000		
Other creditors including taxation and social security	684,500	1,046,070	
Net current assets			1,169,530
Total assets less current liabilities			1,441,240
Capital and reserves			
Called-up share capital			1,000,000
Share premium account			120,000
Other reserves:			
General reserve			48,000
Profit and loss account			273,240
			1,441,240

Notes to the accounts

1 Turnover

This is the value, net of VAT, of goods of a single class of business.
Turnover may be analysed as follows:

	£
United Kingdom	3,620,000
Europe	899,170
	4,519,170

2 Employees

Average number of workers was:

Warehousing	59
Sales	21
	80

Remuneration of employees was

Wages and salaries	764,760
Social security costs	80,120
Pension contributions	42,550
	687,430

3 Directors' remuneration

The amounts paid to directors were as follows:

Fees as directors	8,000
Other emoluments	187,140

Emoluments of the Chairman amounted to £46,640, and those of the highest paid director £51,500. Other directors' emoluments were in the following ranges:

£40,001–45,000	1
£45,001–50,000	1

4 Operating profit is shown after charging

	£
Auditors' remuneration	71,000
Hire of motors	84,770

5 Fixed assets

Plant and machinery

Cost at 1.1.19-4	535,000	
Additions	75,000	610,000
Depreciation to 31.12.19-3	216,290	
Charge for the year	122,000	338,290
		271,710

6 Other creditors including taxation

Proposed dividend	375,000	
Auditors' remuneration	71,000	
Corporation tax	238,500	684,500

Illustrative company accounts: specimen question 2

The trial balance of Quartz plc on 31 December 19-3 was as follows

	Dr £000	Cr £000
Preference share capital: £1 shares		200
Ordinary share capital: £1 shares		1,000
Exchange reserve		75
General reserve		150
Profit and loss account 31.12.19-2		215
Sales		4,575
Purchases	2,196	
Carriage inwards	38	
Stock 31.12.19-2	902	
Wages (adding value to goods)	35	
Wages: warehousing	380	
Wages and salaries: administrative	220	
Wages and salaries: sales	197	
Motor expenses	164	
Bad debts	31	
Debenture interest	40	
Bank overdraft interest	19	
General distribution expenses	81	
General administrative expenses	73	
Directors' remuneration	210	
Investments: related companies	340	
Income from shares in related companies		36
Discounts allowed and received	55	39
Profit on property sale		100
Buildings: at cost	1,200	
Plant and machinery: at cost	330	
Motor vehicles: at cost	480	
Provisions for depreciation:		
Land and buildings		375
Plant and machinery		195
Motors		160
Goodwill	40	
Patents, licences and trade marks	38	
Trade debtors and creditors	864	392
Bank overdraft (repayable any time)		21
Debentures 10%		400
	7,933	7,933

Notes

(*a*) Stock at 31.12.19-3: £1,103,000 at cost.

(*b*) Motor expenses and depreciation on motors to be apportioned: distribution 75%; administrative 25%.

(*c*) Depreciation on buildings and plant and machinery to be apportioned: distribution 50%; administrative 50%.

(*d*) Depreciate on cost: motor vehicles 25% plant and machinery 20%.

(e) Accrue corporation tax on profits of the year £236,000. This is payable 1 October 19-4.

(f) A preference dividend of 10% is to be paid and an ordinary dividend of 50% is to be proposed.

(g) During the year new vehicles were purchased at a cost of £60,000.

(h) During June 19-3 one of the buildings, which had originally cost £130,000, and which had a written-down value at the date of the sale of £80,000, was sold for £180,000. The profit of £100,000 is regarded as extraordinary. The capital gains tax liability will be £30,000. Depreciation on buildings to be charged against the year's profits £60,000. The buildings are revalued by B & Co., Chartered Surveyors at £1,500,000 at 31.12.19-3 (and this figure is to be included in the accounts).

(i) Directors' remuneration was as follows:

	£
Marketing	42,000
Chairman	37,000
Managing	61,000
Finance	50,000
	190,000

In addition each director drew £5,000 fees.

(j) Of the goodwill, 50% is to be written off during this year, and 50% in the following year.

(k) The debentures are to be redeemed in five equal annual instalments, starting in the following year 19-4.

(l) The investments are in listed companies with a market value at 31 December 19-3 of £438,000.

(m) Auditors' remuneration, including expenses, was £7,000.

You are required to prepare a balance sheet as at 31 December 19-3. It should:
(a) conform to the requirements of the Companies Act, 1985;
(b) conform to the relevant Statements of Standard Accounting Practice;
(c) be shown in vertical form;
(d) give the notes necessary to the accounts.

Quartz plc: workings				Dist.	Admin.
Cost of sales:		Wages		577	220
Opening stock	902	Motor expenses		123	41
add Purchases	2,196	General		81	73
add Carriage in	38	Depreciation: plant		33	33
			motors	90	30
	3,136		buildings	30	30
less Closing stock	1,103	Directors		47	163
		Discounts (net) 55–39			16
	2,033	Debenture Interest			40
Wages (added value)	35	Bank Interest			19
		Bad Debts			31
	2,068			981	696

(a) Quartz plc
Profit and loss account for the year ended 31 December 19-4

	£000	£000
Turnover		4,575
Cost of sales		2,068
Gross profit		2,507
Distribution costs	981	
Administrative expenses	696	1,677
		830
Income from shares in related companies		36
Profit on ordinary activities before taxation		866
Tax on profit on ordinary activities		236
Profit for the year on ordinary activities after taxation		630
Extraordinary profit on sale of buildings	100	
Tax on extraordinary profit	30	70
Profit for the financial year		700
Retained profits from last year		215
		915
Goodwill written off	20	
Dividends paid and proposed	520	540
Retained profits carried to next year		375

(b) Quartz plc
Balance sheet as at 31 December 19-3

	£000	£000	£000
Fixed assets			
Intangible assets			
Patents, licences and trade marks		38	
Goodwill		20	
		58	
Tangible assets			
Buildings	1,500		
Plant and machinery	69		
Vehicles	200	1,769	
Investments			
Shares in related companies		340	2,167
Current assets			
Stock	1,103		
Trade debtors	864	1,967	
Creditors: amounts falling due within one year			
Debenture loans	80		
Bank overdraft	21		
Trade creditors	392		
Other creditors	786		
	1,279		
Creditors: amounts falling due after more than one year			
Debenture loans	320	1,599	368
			2,535
Capital and reserves			
Called-up share capital			1,200
Revaluation reserve			735
Other reserves			225
Profit and loss account			375
			2,535

Notes to the accounts
1 Share capital called up is:

200,000 10% preference shares of £1 each	200,000
1,000,000 ordinary shares of £1 each	1,000,000
	£1,200,000

2 Accounting policies

Goodwill has been written off 20,000 against this year. The directors intend to write off the remaining £20,000 against next year's profits.

3 Tangible assets

	Buildings £000	Plant £000	Vehicles £000
Cost at 1.1.19-4	1,330	330	480
Disposals (at cost)	(130)	–	–
Adjustment for revaluation	735		
	1,935	330	480
Depreciation at 1.1.19-4	425	195	160
Provided in year	60	66	120
Disposals	(50)		
	435	261	280
Net book values	1,500	69	200

The extraordinary profit of £100,000 in the profit and loss account was in respect of buildings with a written down value of £80,000 which were sold for £180,000.

4 Investments

The market value of investments at 31 December 19-3 was £438,000.

5 Ten per cent debenture loans

These are redeemable in five equal annual instalments, starting next year. Interest of £40,000 is charged in this year's accounts.

6 Other creditors including taxation:

Preference dividend proposed	20,000
Ordinary dividend proposed 50%	500,000
Corporation tax based on year's profits	236,000
Capital gains tax on extraordinary profit on buildings	30,000
	786,000

7 Other reserves

Exchange reserve	75,000
General reserve	150,000
	225,000

8 Directors' remuneration

The amounts paid to directors were as follows:

Fees as directors	20,000	
Other emoluments	190,000	210,000

Emoluments of the chairman amounted to £42,000 and those of the highest paid director £66,000. Other directors' emoluments were in the following ranges:

£45,001 to £50,000	1
£50,001 to £55,000	1

9 Operating profit is shown after charging:

	£
Auditors' remuneration	7,000
Bank overdraft interest	19,000

Review questions

19.1 The following trial balance of X Limited, a non-listed company, has been extracted from the books after the preparation of the profit and loss and appropriation accounts for the year ended 31 March 19-7.

	£000	£000
Ordinary share capital – authorised, allotted and called-up fully paid shares of £1 each		1,000
12% debentures (repayable in 9 years)		500
Deferred taxation		128
Provisions for depreciation:		
plant and machinery at 31 March 19-7		650
freehold properties at 31 March 19-7		52
vehicles at 31 March 19-7		135
Investments (listed), at cost	200	
Trade debtors and prepayments	825	
Corporation tax		360
Advance corporation tax recoverable	120	
Proposed final dividend		280
Tangible fixed assets:		
freehold properties at 31 March 19-7	1,092	
plant and machinery at 31 March 19-7	1,500	
vehicles at 31 March 19-7	420	
Profit and loss account – balance at 31 March 19-7		386
Share premium account		150
Trade creditors and accruals		878
Research and development costs	35	
Stocks:		
raw materials	200	
work-in-progress	50	
finished goods	250	
Bank balance	439	
Revaluation reserve on freehold properties		612
	5,131	5,131

You are also provided with the following information:

1 Investments

The listed investments consist of shares in W plc quoted on the stock exchange at £180,000 on 31 March 19-7. This is not considered to be a permanent fall in the value of this asset.

2 Trade debtors and prepayments

The company received notice, during April 19-7, that one of its major customers, Z Limited, had gone into liquidation. The amount included in trade debtors and prepayments is £225,000 and it is estimated that a dividend of 24p in the £ will be paid to unsecured creditors.

3 Taxation

(a) Corporation tax

The figure in the trial balance is made up as follows:

	£000
based on profits for the year	174
tax on extraordinary item (see note 4)	96
advance corporation tax on proposed dividend	120
	390
less advance corporation tax paid during the year	30
	360

(b) Deferred taxation

A transfer of £50,000 was made from the profit and loss account during the year ended 31 March 19-7.

4 Tangible fixed assets

(a) In arriving at the profit for the year, depreciation of £242,000 was charged, made up of freehold properties £12,000; plant and machinery £150,000 and vehicles £80,000.

(b) During the year to 31 March 19-7, new vehicles were purchased at a cost of £200,000.

(c) During March 19-7, the directors sold one of the freehold properties which had originally cost £320,000 and which had a written-down value at the date of the sale of £280,000. A profit of £320,000 on the sale, which was regarded as extraordinary, has already been dealt with in arriving at the profit for the year. The estimated corporation tax liability in respect of the capital gain will be £96,000, as shown in *note* 3. After this sale, the directors decided to have the remaining freehold properties revalued, for the first time, by Messrs V & Co, Chartered Surveyors and to include the revalued figure of £1,040,000 in the 19-7 accounts.

5 Research and development costs

The company carries out research and development and accounts for it in accordance with the relevant Accounting Standard. The amount shown in the trial balance relates to development expenditure on a new product scheduled to be launched in April 19-7. Management is confident that this new product will earn substantial profits for the company in the coming years.

6 Stocks

The replacement cost of the finished goods, if valued at 31 March 19-7, would amount to £342,000.

You are required to prepare a balance sheet at 31 March 19-7 to conform to the requirements of the Companies Act and relevant Statements of Standard Accounting Practice, in so far as the information given allows. The vertical format must be used.

The notes necessary to accompany this statement should also be prepared.

Workings should be shown, but comparative figures are not required.

(Chartered Institute of Management Accountants)

19.2 The following information has been extracted from the books of account of Billinge public limited company as at 30 June 19-6:

	Dr £'000	Cr £'000
Administration expenses	242	
Cash at bank and in hand	107	
Cash received on sale of fittings		3
Corporation tax (over-provision for the previous year)		10
Deferred taxation		60
Depreciation on fixtures, fittings, tools and equipment (at 1 July 19- 5)		132
Distribution costs	55	
Factory closure costs	30	
Fixtures, fittings, tools and equipment at cost	340	
Profit and loss account (at 1 July 19-5)		40
Purchase of equipment	60	
Purchases of goods for resale	855	
Sales (net of VAT)		1,500
Share capital (450,000 authorised, issued and fully paid ordinary shares of £1 each)		450
Stock (at 1 July 19-5)	70	
Trade creditors		64
Trade debtors	500	
	£2,259	£2,259

Additional information:

1 The company was incorporated in 1970.

2 The stock at 30 June 19-6 (valued at the lower of cost or net realisable value) was estimated to be worth £100,000.

3 Fixtures, fittings, tools and equipment all relate to administrative expenses. Depreciation is charged on them at a rate of 20% per annum on cost. A full year's depreciation is charged in the year of acquisition, but no depreciation is charged in the year of disposal.

4 During the year to 30 June 19-6, the company purchased £60,000 of equipment. It also sold some fittings (which had originally cost £20,000) for £3,000 and for which depreciation of £15,000 had been set aside.

5 The corporation tax based on the profits for the year at a rate of 35% is estimated to be £85,000. A transfer of £40,000 is to be made to the deferred taxation account. Tax relief of £15,000 is available against the factory closure costs.

6 The company proposes to pay a dividend of 20p per ordinary share.

7 The standard rate of income tax is 30%.

Required:

In so far as the information permits, prepare Billinge public limited company's profit and loss account for the year to 30 June 19-6, and a balance sheet as at that date in accordance with the Companies Act and appropriate statements of standard accounting practice.

(Association of Accounting Technicians)

19.3A Cosnett Ltd is a company principally involved in the manufacture of aluminium accessories for camping enthusiasts.

The following trial balance was extracted from the books at 30 September 19-5.

	£	£
Issued ordinary share capital (£1 shares)		600,000
Retained profit at 1 October 19-4		625,700
Debentures redeemable 2,010		150,000
Bank loan		25,000
Plant and machinery at cost	1,475,800	
Accumulated depreciation to 30 September 19-5		291,500
Investments in UK companies at cost	20,000	
Turnover		3,065,800
Dividends from investments (amount received)		2,800
Loss arising on factory closure	86,100	
Cost of sales	2,083,500	
Political and charitable contributions	750	
Distribution costs	82,190	
Salaries of office staff	42,100	
Directors' emoluments	63,000	
Rent and rates of offices	82,180	
Hire of plant and machinery	6,700	
Travel and entertainment expenses	4,350	
General expenses	221,400	
Trade debtors	396,100	
Trade creditors and accruals		245,820
Stocks	421,440	
Bank	17,950	
Interim dividend paid	21,000	
Interest charged	19,360	
Provision for deferred taxation		45,100
Advance corporation tax	7,800	
	5,051,720	5,051,720

You are provided with the following additional information:

(*a*) The company's shares are owned, equally, by three brothers: John, Peter and Henry Phillips; they are also the directors.

(*b*) The bank loan is repayable by five equal annual instalments of £5,000 commencing 31 December 19-5.

(*c*) The investments were acquired with cash, surplus to existing operating requirements, which will be needed to pay for additional plant the directors plan to acquire early in 19-6.

(*d*) On 1 January 19-5 the company closed a factory which had previously contributed approximately 20% of the company's total production requirements.

(*e*) Trade debtors include £80,000 due from a customer who went into liquidation on 1 September 19-5; the directors estimate that a dividend of 20p in the £ will eventually be received.

(*f*) Trade creditors and accruals include:

(i) £50,000 due to a supplier of plant, of which £20,000 is payable on 1 January 19-6 and the remainder at the end of the year.

(ii) Accruals totalling £3,260.

(g) The mainstream corporation tax liability for the year is estimated at £120,000.

(h) The directors propose to pay a final dividend of 10.5p per share and to transfer £26,500 to the deferred tax account.

Note: An advance corporation tax rate of ³⁄₇ may be assumed.

Required:

The profit and loss account of Cosnett Ltd for the year to 30 September 19-5 and balance sheet at that date together with relevant notes attached thereto. The accounts should comply with the minimum requirements of the Companies Act and Statements of Standard Accounting Practice so far as the information permits.

(Institute of Chartered Secretaries and Administrators)

19.4A The following trial balance has been extracted from the books of Arran plc as at 31 March 19-7:

	£'000	£'000
Administrative expenses	95	
Advance corporation tax paid	6	
Called up share capital (all ordinary shares of £1 each)		210
Cash at bank and in hand	30	
Debtors	230	
Deferred taxation (at 1 April 19-6)		60
Distribution costs	500	
Fixed asset investments	280	
Franked investment income		7
Interim dividend paid	21	
Overprovision of last year's corporation tax		5
Land and buildings at cost	200	
Land and buildings: accumulated depreciation at 1 April 19-6		30
Plant and machinery at cost	400	
Plant and machinery: accumulated depreciation at 1 April 19-6		170
Profit and loss account (at 1 April 19-6)		235
Profit on extraordinary item (before taxation)		50
Purchases	1,210	
Sales		2,215
Stocks at 1 April 19-6	140	
Trade creditors		130
	£3,112	£3,112

Additional information:

1 Stocks at 31 March 19-7 were valued at £150,000.

2 Depreciation for the year to 31 March 19-7 is to be charged against administrative expenses as follows:

	£'000
Land and buildings	5
Plant and machinery	40

3 Assume that the basic rate of income tax is 30%.

4 Corporation tax of £165,000 is to be charged against profits on ordinary activities for the year to 31 March 19-7.

5 £4,000 is to be transferred to the Deferred Taxation Account.

6 Corporation tax of £15,000 is payable on the extraordinary profit.

7 The company proposes to pay a final ordinary dividend of 30p per share.

Required

In so far as the information permits, prepare the company's profit and loss account for the year to 31 March 19-7 and a balance sheet as at that date in accordance with the Companies Act 1985 and related statements of standard accounting practice. (*Note:* Profit and loss account and balance sheet notes are not required, but you should show the basis and computation of earnings per share at the foot of the profit and loss account, and your workings should be submitted.)

(Association of Accounting Technicians)

19.5A The following trial balance has been extracted from the books of account of Greet plc as at 31 March 19-8:

	Dr £'000	Cr £'000
Administrative expenses	210	
Called up share capital (ordinary shares of £1 fully paid)		600
Debtors	470	
Cash at bank and in hand	40	
Corporation tax (overprovision in 19-7)		25
Deferred taxation (at 1 April 19-7)		180
Distribution costs	420	
Extraordinary item		60
Fixed asset investments	560	
Franked investment income (amount received)		73
Plant and machinery:		
At cost	750	
Accumulated depreciation (at 31 March 19-8)		220
Profit and loss (at 1 April 19-7)		182
Purchases	960	
Stock (at 1 April 19-7)	140	
Trade creditors		260
Turnover		1,950
	£3,550	£3,550

Additional information:

1 Stock at 31 March 19-8 was valued at £150,000.

2 The following items (inter alia) *are already included* in the balances listed in the above trial balance:

	Distribution costs £'000	Administrative expenses £'000
Depreciation (for the year to 31 March 19-8)	27	5
Hire of plant and machinery	20	15
Auditors' remuneration	–	30
Directors' emoluments	–	45

3 The following rates of taxation are to be assumed:

	%
Corporation tax	35
Income tax	27

4 The corporation tax charge based on the profits for the year is estimated to be £52,000.

5 A transfer of £16,000 is to be made to the credit of the deferred taxation account.

6 The extraordinary item relates to the profit made on the disposal of a factory in Belgium following the closure of the company's entire operations in that country. The corporation tax payable on the extraordinary item is estimated to be £20,000.

7 The company's authorised share capital consists of 1,000,000 ordinary shares of £1 each.

8 A final ordinary dividend of 50p per share is proposed.

9 There were no purchases or disposals of fixed assets during the year.

10 The market value of the fixed assets investments as at 31 March 19-8 was £580,000. There were no purchases or sales of such investments during the year.

Required:

In so far as the information permits, prepare the company's published profit and loss account for the year to 31 March 19-8 and a balance sheet as at that date in accordance with the Companies Act and with related statements of standard accounting practice.

Relevant notes to the profit and loss account and balance sheet and detailed workings should be submitted with your answer, but a statement of the company's accounting policies is not required.

(Association of Accounting Technicians)

19.6 The accountant of Scampion plc a retailing company listed on the London Stock Exchange has produced the following draft financial statements for the company for the year to 31 May 19-7.

Profit and Loss account year to 31 May 19-7

	£000	£000
Sales		3,489
Income from investments		15
		3,504
Purchases of goods and services	1,929	
Value added tax paid on sales	257	
Wages and salaries including pension scheme	330	
Depreciation	51	
Interest on loans	18	
General administration		
expenses – Shops	595	
– Head office	25	
		3,205
Net profit for year		299
Corporation tax at 40%		120
Profit after tax for year		179

Balance Sheet at 31 May 19-7

	£000	£000
Fixed assets		
Land and buildings		1,178
Fixtures, fittings, equipment and motor vehicles		194
Investments		167
		1,539
Current assets		
Stock	230	
Debtors	67	
Cash at bank and in hand	84	
	381	
Current liabilities		
Creditors	487	
		(106)
		1,433
Ordinary share capital (£1 shares)		660
Reserves		703
Loans		70
		1,433

You discover the following further information:

(i) Fixed assets details are as follows:

	Cost	Depreciation	Net
	£000	£000	£000
Freehold land and buildings	1,212	34	1,178
Fixtures, fittings and equipment	181	56	125
Motor vehicles	137	68	69

Purchases of fixed assets during the year were freehold land and buildings £50,000, fixtures, fittings and equipment £40,000, motor vehicles £20,000. The only fixed asset disposal during the year is referred to in Note (x). Depreciation charged during the year was £5,000 for freehold buildings, £18,000 for fixtures, fittings and equipment, and £28,000 for motor vehicles. Straight-line depreciation method is used assuming the following lives: Freehold buildings 40 years, fixtures, fittings and equipment 10 years and motor vehicles 5 years.

(ii) A dividend of 10 pence per share is proposed.

(iii) A valuation by Bloggs & Co Surveyors shows the freehold land and buildings to have a market value of £1,350,000.

(iv) Loans are:

£20,000 bank loan with a variable rate of interest repayable by 30 September 19-7;

£50,000 12% debenture repayable 2001;

£100,000 11% debenture repaid during the year.

There were no other loans during the year.

(v) The income from investments is derived from fixed asset investments (shares in related companies) £5,000 and current asset investment (government securities) £10,000.

(vi) At the balance sheet date the shares in related companies (cost £64,000) are valued by the directors at £60,000. The market value of the government securities is £115,000 (cost £103,000).

(vii) After the balance sheet date but before the financial statements are finalised there is a very substantial fall in share and security prices. The market value of the government securities had fallen to £50,000 by the time the directors signed the accounts. No adjustment has been made for this item in the accounts.

(viii) Within two weeks of the balance sheet date a notice of liquidation was received by Scampion plc concerning one of the company's debtors. £45,000 is included in the balance sheet for this debtor and enquiries reveal that nothing is likely to be paid to any unsecured creditor. No adjustment has been made for this item in the accounts.

(ix) The corporation tax charge is based on the accounts for the year and there are no other amounts of tax owing by the company.

(x) Reserves at 31 May 19-6 were:

	£
Revaluation reserve	150,000
Share premium account	225,000
Profit and loss account	149,000

The revaluation reserve represents the after tax surplus on a property which was valued in last year's balance sheet at £400,000 and sold during the current year at book value.

Required:

A profit and loss account for the year to 31 May 19-7 and a balance sheet at that date for Scampion plc complying with the Companies Act in so far as the information given will allow.

Ignore advance corporation tax and related tax credit on investment income.

(Chartered Association of Certified Accountants)

20

SSAP 10: Statement of source and application of funds

In Volume 1 the reader was introduced to Flow of Funds Statements. The present chapter deals specifically with SSAP 10, which requires that all audited financial accounts of enterprises with a turnover of more than £25,000 per annum should be accompanied by a funds statement. For the purpose of SSAP 10 'funds' are working capital, consequently cash flow statements are excluded.

The following *minimum* information (if appropriate and material) has to be shown:

(*a*) net profit or loss, with adjustments for items not using or providing funds,

(*b*) dividends paid,

(*c*) acquisitions and disposals of fixed and other non-current assets,

(*d*) funds raised for long-term capital, e.g. shares, loan capital,

(*e*) redemptions and purchases of long-term capital,

(*f*) changes in working capital, analysed between component parts, and movements in net liquid funds.

The basic layout, without figures, is now shown in Exhibit 20.1.

Exhibit 20.1

Statement of Source and Application of Funds
Year ended ...

	£	£
Source of funds		
Profit before tax		X
Adjustments for items not involving the movement of funds: Depreciation		X
Total generated from operations		X
Funds from other sources		
Issue of shares for cash	X	
Issue of loan capital	X	X
		X
Application of funds		
Dividends paid	X	
Tax paid	X	
Purchase of fixed assets	X	X
Increase/decrease in working capital		X
Increase/Decrease in stocks	X	
Increase/Decrease in debtors	X	
Decrease/Increase in creditors	X	
Movement in net liquid funds:		
Increase/Decrease in Cash Balances	X	
Short-term investments	X	X	X

The basic layout cannot be adhered to for all possible items. For instance, if there had been no purchase of fixed assets, but instead there had been a sale of fixed assets, then 'Sale of fixed assets' would appear under 'Funds from other sources'.

Two examples will now be worked through, Exhibit 20.2 and 20.3. Some points must be stressed:

(i) It is taxation **paid**, not taxation charged, that is needed.

(ii) It is dividends **paid**, not dividends proposed, that is needed.

(iii) Do *not* include any profit on sales of fixed assets, such profit is already automatically included in any figure of sales of fixed assets.

(iv) Look for other adjustments to the starting figure of profit before tax which do not involve movement by funds, e.g. provisions for bad debts.

Exhibit 20.2

PQ Ltd
Balance Sheets as at 31 December

	19-6				19-7	
	£	£	£	£	£	£
Fixed Assets at cost		3,200			4,000	
less Depreciation		1,200	2,000		1,600	2,400
Current Assets						
Stock		4,218			5,654	
Debtors		1,560			1,842	
Bank		840			695	
		6,618			8,191	
less Current Liabilities						
Creditors	922			988		
Taxation	306			410		
Proposed Dividend	500	1,728	4,890	750	2,148	6,043
			6,890			8,443
Finance by:						
Issued Share Capital			5,000			6,000
Profit and Loss Account			1,890			2,443
			6,890			8,443

PQ Ltd
Profit and Loss Account for the year ended 31 December 19-7

	£
Profit on ordinary activities before taxation (after charging depreciation £400)	1,713
Tax on profit on ordinary activities	410
	1,303
Undistributed profits from last year	1,890
	3,193
Proposed Dividend	750
Undistributed Profits carried on to next year	2,443

PQ Ltd
Statement of Source and Application of Funds
Year ended 31 December 19-7

		£	£
Source of funds			
Profit before tax			1,713
Add depreciation			400
Total generated from operations			2,113
Funds from other sources			
Issue of shares for cash			1,000
Application of funds			3,113
Dividends paid	(B)	500	
Tax paid	(C)	306	
Purchase of fixed assets		800	1,606
Increase in working capital		(A)	1,507
Increase in stocks		1,436	
Increase in debtors		282	
Increase in creditors	(D)	(66)	
		1,652	
Decrease in Cash balances		145 (A)	1,507

Notes

(A) Obviously if the statement has been drawn up correctly, then it should balance, in this case at £1,507 for each of these two figures.

(B) Dividend **paid**. The year's proposed dividend is £750 and the item shown as owing in the balance sheet is also £750. Therefore the dividend **paid** is that shown as owing at 31.12.19-6 £500.

(C) Tax shown as owing at 31.12.19-6 £306 has obviously been paid in the year, leaving only this year's taxation shown as owing.

(D) An increase in creditors would help reduce working capital, therefore shown in brackets, i.e. it is deducted from the other figures.

A more complicated example will now be shown in Exhibit 20.3.

Exhibit 20.3

ST Ltd

Balance Sheets as at 31 December		19-7				19-8	
	£	£	£	£	£	£	£
Fixed Assets at cost		5,600				8,300	
less Depreciation		2,300	3,300			3,150	5,150
Current Assets							
Stock		7,204				5,516	
Debtors	3,120			3,994			
less Provision for Bad Debts	210	2,910		180	3,814		
Cash		60				90	
		10,174				9,420	
less Current Liabilities							
Creditors	1,520			1,416			
Taxation	580			735			
Proposed Dividend	800			1,200			
Bank Overdraft	105	3,005	7,169	629	3,980	5,440	
			10,469				10,590
Financed by:							
Issued Share Capital			4,000				5,000
Share Premium Account			—				1,000
Profit and Loss Account			3,469				4,090
Loan Capital			3,000				500
			10,469				10,590

ST Ltd

Profit and Loss Account for the year ended 31 December 19-8

	£
Profit on ordinary activities before taxation*	2,556
Tax on profit on ordinary activities	735
	1,821
Undistributed profits from last year	3,469
	5,290
Proposed dividend	1,200
Undistributed Profits carried to next year	4,090

*Includes profit on fixed assets sold of £85. The items sold had cost £1,120, had been depreciated £740, and were sold for £465.

The change in provision for bad debts had also been taken into account before arriving at profit of £2,556.

1,000 Ordinary Shares of £1 had been issued at a price of £2 per share. In the Balance Sheet the Issued Share Capital increases by £1,000 and the Share Premium Account increases by £1,000. In the Fund Statement the overall impact of issuing the shares of £2,000 will be shown.

In getting the figures together for the Statement of Source and Application of Funds, some figures need to be deduced so that the profit figure can be adjusted. These are (a) cost of fixed assets bought and (b) depreciation charged. To find these it is necessary to reconstruct (a) the fixed asset account and (b) the depreciation account. The figures needed will be those necessary to balance the accounts. (In a real company these figures would be readily available, but examiners are fond of making students deduce the figures instead.)

Workings   *Fixed Assets Account*

19-8		£	19-8		
					£
Jan 1 Balance b/fwd		5,600	Dec 31 Assets Disposal		1,120
Dec 31 Bank (missing figure)		3,820	,, 31 Balance c/fwd		8,300
		9,420			9,420

Provision for Depreciation Account

19-8	£	19-8	£
Dec 31 Assets Disposal	740	Jan 1 Balance b/fwd	2,300
,, 31 Balance c/fwd	3,150	Dec 31 Profit & Loss (missing figure)	1,590
	3,890		3,890

Now that the cost of fixed assets, and of the depreciation has been calculated, the preparation of the statement can be done.

ST Ltd
Statement of Source and Application of Funds
Year ended 31 December 19-8

	£	£
Source of funds		
Profit before tax		2,556
add Depreciation		1,590
		4,146
less Reduction in provisions for Bad Debts	30	
,, Profit on Fixed Assets	85	115
Total generated from operations		4,031
Funds from other sources		
Issue of shares for cash (at a premium of £1,000)	2,000	
Sale of fixed assets	465	2,465
		6,496
Application of funds		
Dividends paid	800	
Tax paid	580	
Purchase of fixed assets	3,820	
Repayment of loan capital	2,500	7,700
Decrease in working capital		(1,204)
Decrease in stocks	(1,688)	
Increase in debtors	874	
Decrease in creditors	104	
	(710)	
Decrease in net liquid funds*	(494)	(1,204)

*Increase in overdraft 629−105 = 524 less increase in cash 30 = 494 net.

Review questions

20.1 Draw up a flow of funds statement, in accordance with SSAP 10, for the year 19-5 from the following information:

JJ Ltd
Balance Sheets at 31 December

	19-4			19-5		
	£	£	£	£	£	£
Fixed Assets at cost		8,650			11,170	
less Depreciation		2,890	5,760		3,905	7,265
Current Assets						
Stock		3,720			3,604	
Debtors		4,896			5,001	
Bank		544			–	
		9,160			8,605	
Less Current Liabilities						
Creditors	2,072			1,854		
Bank Overdraft	–			116		
Taxation	856			620		
Proposed Dividend	500	3,428	5,732	600	3,190	5,415
			11,492			12,680
Financed by:						
Issued Share Capital			10,000			10,000
Profit and Loss Account			1,492			2,680
			11,492			12,680

Profit and Loss Account for the year ended 31 December 19-5

	£
Profit on ordinary activities before taxation (after charging depreciation £1,015)	2,408
Tax on profit on ordinary activities	620
	1,788
Undistributed profits from last year	1,492
	3,280
Proposed dividend	600
Undistributed Profits carried to next year	2,680

20.2A Draw up a flow of funds statement, in accordance with SSAP 10, for the year 19-8 from the following:

TX Ltd
Balance Sheets as at 31 December

	19-7			19-8		
	£	£	£	£	£	£
Fixed Assets at cost		6,723			7,418	
less Depreciation		2,946	3,777		3,572	3,846
Current Assets						
Stock		6,012			8,219	
Debtors	4,192			4,381		
less Provision for Bad Debts	200	3,992		240	4,141	
Cash		100			35	
		10,104			12,395	
less Current Liabilities						
Creditors	2,189			2,924		
Taxation	622			504		
Proposed Dividend	1,200			750		
Bank Overdraft	416	4,427	5,677	294	4,472	7,923
			9,454			11,769
Debentures			3,000			2,000
			6,454			9,769
Issued Share Capital			6,000			7,500
Profit and Loss Account			454			2,269
			6,454			9,769

Profit and Loss Account for the year ended 31 December 19-8

	£
Profit on ordinary activities before taxation*	3,069
Tax on profit on ordinary activities	504
	2,565
Undistributed profits from last year	454
	3,019
Proposed dividend	750
Undistributed Profits carried to next year	2,269

*Includes loss on fixed assets sold of £114. The items sold had cost £2,070, had been depreciated £1,290 and were sold for £666.

20.3 Albert Dejonge, a sole proprietor, received the following summarised balance sheets from his accountant for the years ended 31 December 19-4 and 31 December 19-5:

Balance Sheet as at 31 December

19-4 £		19-5 £
50,000	Capital	63,000
15,000	Net profit	25,000
65,000		88,000
9,000	*less* Drawings	12,000
56,000		76,000
20,000	Long-term loan finance	25,000
7,500	Trade creditors	9,000
1,500	Expenses owing	1,000
£85,000		£111,000
	Assets	
24,000	Premises	31,000
19,000	Motor vehicles (Net book value)	21,000
17,000	Stock	35,300
16,000	Trade debtors	19,000
1,000	Expenses in advance	600
7,500	Balance at bank	3,000
500	Cash	1,100
£85,000		£111,000

Notes:

1 There had been no purchases or sales of premises but the premises had been revalued at £31,000. Dejonge does not provide for depreciation on his premises.

2 An additional motor vehicle was purchased on 1 January 19-5 at cost £6,000. There were no other sales or purchases of vehicles.

3 During the latter part of 19-5, Dejonge had noted that his bank balance was falling and on 1 December 19-5 he arranged a bank overdraft facility with a limit of £10,000.

4 At the end of December 19-5, after stocktaking, £6,000 of stock had been destroyed by fire, and only £3,000 of the cost is to be recovered from the insurance company. No entries had been made in the accounts, and the closing stock figure had not been adjusted for the loss of the stock.

Dejonge told his accountant that he was very worried about his falling bank balance and he could not understand why this had happened when his profit for 19-5 was much better than 19-4.

Required:

A source and application of funds statement showing the change in working capital over the year.

(Associated Examining Board GCE 'A' level)

20.4A Trimble and Partners have the following balance sheets at 31 December 19-6 and 19-7:

	19-6		19-7	
	£	£	£	£
Fixed assets		42,000		56,000
Current assets: Stock	14,000		28,600	
Debtors	29,400		28,800	
Bank	4,200		7,000	
	47,600		64,400	
Current liabilities: Creditors	36,400		43,400	
		11,200		21,000
		53,200		77,000
Capital Accounts: Trimble		21,300		36,600
Crisp		16,100		23,500
Poole		15,800		16,900
		53,200		77,000

Notes: (i) The movements on the capital accounts during 19-7 were:

(£)	Trimble	Crisp	Poole
Opening balances	21,300	16,100	15,800
Capital introduced	10,000	4,000	–
Shares of Net Profit	15,500	11,300	9,900
Interest on Capital	1,280	1,000	950
	48,080	32,400	26,650
less Drawings	11,480	8,900	9,750
	36,600	23,500	16,900

(ii) Changes in fixed assets were as follows in 19-7:

	Cost	Depreciation	Net Book Value
	£	£	£
Opening balances	84,000	42,000	42,000
Additions	23,800		
Provision for year		2,800	
Disposals*	(16,800)	(9,800)	
Closing balances	91,000	35,000	56,000

*There was a 'loss on disposals' charged in the profit and loss account, amounting to £1,400.

Required:

Prepare a statement of source and application of funds for the year ended 31 Dec 19-7.

(University of London: GCE 'A' level)

20.5 The summarised balance sheets of Whitehead Ltd at 31 May 19-6 and 19-7 are as follows:

	19-6		19-7	
	£	£	£	£
Fixed Assets				
Freehold land and property at valuation		180,000		300,000
Plant and machinery at cost	70,000		100,000	
less aggregate depreciation	20,000		35,000	
		50,000		65,000
Fixtures and fittings at cost	25,000		20,000	
less aggregate depreciation	10,000		12,000	
		15,000		8,000
		245,000		373,000
Investments at cost		20,000		28,000
Current Assets				
Stocks	20,000		24,000	
Debtors	32,000		18,000	
Balance at bank	14,000		34,000	
		66,000		76,000
		331,000		477,000
Issued Capital				
£1 Ordinary Shares fully paid	200,000		200,000	
Reserves				
Share premium	50,000		50,000	
Retained earnings	35,000		55,000	
Land revaluation	–		120,000	
		285,000		425,000
Current Liabilities				
Creditors	26,000		22,000	
Proposed dividends	20,000		30,000	
		46,000		52,000
		331,000		477,000

Additional information:

1 There was a revaluation of the freehold land and property during the year ended 31 May 19-7. There were no purchases or sales of property and it is company policy not to provide for depreciation of freehold property.

2 There have been no disposals of plant and machinery nor purchases of fixtures and fittings during the year ended 31 May 19-7. Fixtures and fittings have been depreciated by £5,000 in the year ended 31 May 19-7.

3 An interim dividend of £10,000 for the year ended 31 May 19-7 was paid during the year.

Required:

A sources and application of funds statement for the year ended 31 May 19-7 showing the change in working capital over that year.

(Associated Examining Board GCE 'A' level)

20.6A The following summarised balance sheets had been prepared for Morisco Plc as at 30 June 19-6 and 30 June 19-7

19-6 £000		Balance Sheet as at 30 June		*19-7* £000
		Authorised Capital		
100		200,000 50p ordinary shares		100
100		100 000 £1 10% preference shares		100
200				200
		Issued Capital		
75		50p ordinary shares fully paid		100
100		£1 preference shares fully paid		100
65		Share premium		65
80		Retained earnings		115
320				380
		Loan Capital		
40		11% Debentures 1990-91		40
360				420

£000	£000	Fixed Assets	£000	£000
	150	Freehold land and building at cost		150
95		Plant and machinery at cost	120	
35		*less* aggregate depreciation	50	
	60			70
	210			220
		Current Assets		
56		Stock	160	
60		Trade debtors	55	
98		Balance at bank	55	
23		Cash	15	
237			285	
		Less Current Liabilities	£ 000's	
75		Trade creditors	70	
12	150	Proposed dividends	15	85	200
	360			420

Profit and loss appropriation account for
the year ended 30 June 19-7

	19-7
	£000
Net profit	95
less dividends	35
Retained earnings	60

Additional information:

1 There were no sales or purchases of freehold land and buildings.

2 Plant and machinery which cost £20,000 was sold for £5,000 in May 19-7. The aggregate depreciation as at 1 July 19-6 was £10,000. No depreciation was provided in the year of sale.

New plant and machinery had been purchased on 1 June 19-7 for £45,000.

There were no other sales or purchases of plant and machinery.

3 To celebrate the company's Silver Jubilee a bonus issue of ordinary shares had been made on 1 July 19-6. The issue was on a 1 for 3 basis and financed wholly from retained earnings.

Required

(*a*) A sources and applications of funds statement for Morisco Plc for the year ended 30 June 19-7.

Show the change in working capital over the year.

(*b*) Comment on the change in the working capital.

(Associated Examining Board: GCE 'A' level)

20.7A The accountant of a private company has been able to get the use of a computer to produce the spreadsheets shown below but as yet the computer lacks a program to print out final accounts. The accountant nevertheless expects to use the spreadsheet data to reconstruct a summary profit and loss account and source and application of funds statements for the year to 30 April 19-6.

Movements of Assets during the year 19-5/-6 (£'000s)

	Balance Sheet value last year	Depreciation or Amortisation for year	Additions during year	Sales during year	Other changes	Balance Sheet value this year
Goodwill	–	–	40	–	–	40
Property	760	(36)	–	–	–	724
Plant and vehicles	540	(84)	420	(60)	–	816
Stocks	230	–	–	–	24	254
Debtors	254	–	–	–	76	330
Bank and cash	50	–	–	–	14	64
	1,834	(120)	460	(60)	114	2,228

Movement of Liabilities during the year 19-5/-6 (£'000s)

	Balance Sheet value last year	New Capital issued	Payments during year	Transfers to reserves and for provisions	Other changes	Balance Sheet value this year
Ordinary Shares (£1 each)	1,060	440	–	–	–	1,500
Deferred taxation	36	–	–	176	–	212
General reserve	152	–	–	32	–	184
Creditors	136	–	–	–	24	160
Provision for Corporation tax	340	–	(340)	52	–	52
Provision for net dividend	110*	–	(110)	120	–	120
	1,834	440	(450)	380	24	2,228

Notes:
(i) Proceeds of £40,000 were received from the sale of plant and vehicles.
(ii) During the year the company redeemed 10,000 of its £1 ordinary shares for £125,000 wholly out of distributable profits and this transaction has not been included in the spreadsheets.

Required:

(a) Reconstruct the profit and loss account for the year to 30 April 19- 6.

(b) Prepare a source and application of funds statement for the year to 30 April 19-6 in good style.

(Institute of Chartered Secretaries and Administrators)

20.8 The following information has been extracted from the financial records of Forest plc for each of the four years 31 October 19-4 to 31 October 19-7 inclusive:

Year to 31 October	19-4	19-5	19-6	19-7
	£'000	£'000	£'000	£'000
Turnover	800	600	900	1,200
Cost of sales	(480)	(360)	(630)	(840)
Gross profit	320	240	270	360
Profit/(loss) before taxation	30	(85)	(95)	(20)
Taxation	(5)	–	–	–
Profit after taxation	25	(85)	(95)	(20)
Extraordinary items	(10)	150	(30)	(40)
Dividends	(50)	(50)	–	–
Retained profits/(losses)				
for the year	(35)	15	(125)	(60)
Assets employed:				
Tangible fixed assets	900	810	700	500
Net current assets	125	230	465	605
Total assets less				
current liabilities	1,025	1,040	1,165	1,105
Creditors: amounts falling due				
after more than one year	–	–	(250)	(250)
	£1,025	£1,040	£915	£855
Capital and reserves:				
Called up share capital	800	800	800	800
Profit and loss account	225	240	115	55
	£1,025	£1,040	£915	£855

Additional information:

	19-4	19-5	19-6	19-7
	£'000	£'000	£'000	£'000
Goods purchased during the year	700	550	420	890
Purchase of fixed assets				
during the year	85	95	90	–
Depreciation charge for the year	185	185	200	200
Taxation paid during the year	30	5	–	–

Balances at 31 October	19-4	19-5	19-6	19-7
	£'000	£'000	£'000	£'000
Stocks	270	460	250	300
Trade debtors	80	60	375	600
Cash at bank and in hand	(40)	(90)	(20)	10
Trade creditors	(130)	(150)	(140)	(305)
Debenture loans	–	–	(250)	(250)

Notes:
1 Assume a nil rate of inflation.
2 Assume that all purchases and sales of goods are made on credit terms.

Required:

Prepare and present in columnar form, Forest plc's statement of source and application of funds for *each* of the three years to 31 October 19-5, 19-6 and 19-7 respectively.

(Association of Accounting Technicians)

20.9A The following information relates to X plc. The company's accounting year ends on 30 September.

Balance sheets of X plc at the end of	19-6		19-7	
	£000	£000	£000	£000
Tangible fixed assets (*note 1*)		945		1,662
Current assets				
Stocks	1,225		1,488	
Debtors	700		787	
Short-term investments	175		262	
Cash at bank	184		186	
	2,284		2,723	
less:				
Creditors:				
amounts falling due within one year:				
Bank overdraft	52		105	
Trade creditors	525		735	
Expense creditors	9		10	
Taxation	140		228	
Proposed dividends	140		175	
	866		1,253	
Net current assets		1,418		1,470
Total assets *less* current liabilities		2,363		3,132
Creditors:				
amounts falling due after more than one year:				
Long-term loan		525		700
		1,838		2,432
Capital and reserves:				
Called-up ordinary share capital		1,225		1,400
Share premium account		–		87
General reserve		525		787
Profit and loss account		88		158
		1,838		2,432

Summary profit and loss account for the year ended 30 September 19-7

	£000	£000
Profit on ordinary activities before taxation		735
Corporation tax		228
Profit on ordinary activities after taxation		507
less:		
Proposed dividend	175	
Transfer to General reserve	262	
		437
		70
Retained profit brought forward		88
Retained profit carried forward		158

Note 1 – Schedule of tangible fixed assets:

	Freehold premises 19-6	Plant and machinery	Freehold premises 19-7	Plant and machinery
	£000	£000	£000	£000
At cost	560	455	560	718
Additions during the year	–	263	280	700
	560	718	840	1,418
less Depreciation	35	298	53	543
Net book value	525	420	787	875

You are required to

(*a*) prepare a sources and application of funds statement for X plc, for the year ended 30 September 19-7, conforming to the requirements of Statement of Standard Accounting Practice No 10, in so far as this is possible from the information given;

(*b*) write a short commentary on the statement prepared in (*a*) above.

(Chartered Institute of Management Accountants)

20.10 You are presented with the following forecasted information relating to Blackley Limited for the three months to 31 March 19-7:

Forecasted profit and loss accounts (abridged) for the three months to 31 March 19-7

	Jan 19-7 £'000	Feb 19-7 £'000	March 19-7 £'000
Sales	250	300	350
Cost of goods sold	(200)	(240)	(280)
Gross profit	50	60	70
Depreciation	(3)	(20)	(4)
Administration, selling and distribution expenses	(37)	(40)	(42)
Forecasted net profit	£10	–	£24

Forecasted balances at	31 Dec 19-6 £'000	31 Jan 19-7 £'000	28 Feb 19-7 £'000	31 March 19-7 £'000
Debit balances				
Tangible fixed assets at cost	360	240	480	480
Investments at cost	15	5	5	10
Stocks at cost	40	30	40	55
Trade debtors	50	65	75	80
Cash at bank and in hand	80			
Credit balances				
Debentures (10%)	–	–	–	50
Trade creditors	80	120	140	150
Taxation	8	–	–	–
Proposed dividend	15	–	–	–

Additional information:

1 Sales of tangible fixed assets in January 19-7 were expected to realise £12,000 in cash.

2 Administration, selling and distribution expenses were expected to be settled in cash during the month in which they were incurred.

Required:

(a) Calculate Blackley Limited's forecasted net cash position at 31 January, 28 February and 31 March 19-7 respectively; and

(b) prepare a forecasted statement of source and application of funds for the three months to 31 March 19-7.

(*Association of Accounting Technicians*)

21
Investment accounts

It is possible to envisage a situation where the only external investment made by a firm is in the form of money in an account with a **savings bank**, which had, say, an interest rate of 5 per cent per annum. Interest is calculated to 31 December each year and a cheque for the interest is sent to the account holder to arrive on 31 December. Such a type of account adhering to these dates would be very rare in practice. However, with such an account the accounting entries needed by the investing firm would be very simple indeed. If £400 was invested by a firm in such an account on 1 January 19-4 and eventually withdrawn on 31 December 19-7, then assuming that the firm's financial year was equated with the calendar year, the Cash Book for each year would be debited with £20 while each year's Investment Income Account would be credited with £20. The balance of the Investment Income Account, £20, would be transferred to the credit side of the Profit and Loss Account for each of the years ended 31 December 19-4, 19-5, 19-6 and 19-7. On the withdrawal of the £400 the Cash Book would be debited with £400 and the credit entry would be made in the Investment Account, thereby cancelling the original debit entry made when the cash was invested.

Most investments, however, are not of this sort, and have complicating factors. Investments can be divided into two main classes, **government stocks** and **investments in limited companies**, the latter may take the form of shares, stock or debentures. In this chapter government stocks will be dealt with first. Taxation will be ignored until it is mentioned specifically.

Government stocks

With government stock the price is always quoted for that of £100 nominal value. Prices on the Stock Exchange will vary in accordance with supply and demand. Thus, Treasury 3 per cent Stock may be shown as 45. This means that on the Stock Exchange the price for £100 nominal value of the stock was £45. The purchaser of the stock will receive interest at the rate of £3 each year as interest payable is always based on the nominal value and not the Stock Exchange value.

Interest is payable at regular intervals depending on the stock concerned. Taking a government stock which carried interest at 5 per cent per annum, interest may be payable quarterly on 31 March, 30 June, 30 September and 31 December. Imagine that a person was willing to sell stock of £1,200 nominal value at 80, i.e. for £960 on 1 Jan (£80 for £100 nominal value, therefore £80×12 = £960 for £1,200 nominal value). The purchaser is to receive the whole of the next interest on 31 March, this being £1,200 at 5 per cent per annum for three months = £15. The seller has received interest up to 31 December, the day before he sold the stock. Ownership of stock and ownership of interest have therefore both been on the same time scale. If market conditions do not change, consider the case of a person who is to sell the stock on 1 February, and the purchaser was still to receive all of the £15 interest on 31 March. The seller will not want to sell at the same price, for as January's interest is not to be received by him, the ownership of the stock and the right to receive interest have moved on to a different time scale. The seller is not now merely selling stock, he is also selling the right to one month's interest in addition. He would therefore now want £980+ one month's interest £5 = £965. When the purchaser pays £965 he will want to record the purchase in his own books. He will accordingly split this price as to £960 paid for the stock, a capital item, and the cost of income £5. When the full quarter's interest £15 is received, the £5 cost will be deducted in the income calculation leaving net income for the period as £10. This accords with the evidence, as two months' ownership for February and March is worth £1,200×5 per cent per annum × two months = £10. The seller would also apportion the selling price £1,205 as to £1,200 for the stock and £5 for the interest, The £5 interest would then be shown as investment income in his books. This is in fact, saying that where the interest is bought and sold as part of a total price, then interest received is not equal to interest accrued. The apportionment of cost and selling price is the way by which investment income can be equated with the duration of the ownership of the investment, i.e. fifteen months' ownership should show fifteen months' investment income.

Where the price of the stock does not include the right to the next instalment of interest it is stated to be *ex div* or e.d.; this stands for **excluding dividend**. Where it does include the right to receive the next instalment of interest, irrespective of how long the stock has been owned it is known as *cum div*, meaning **including dividend**. All prices are *cum div* unless stated specifically to be *ex div*.

Because of the necessity to keep income separate from the capital cost of the investment, each Investment Account has a column for income and a column for capital. In addition a column is used to show the nominal value of the stock, this being used for convenience and does not form part of the double-entry system. Brokerage charges and stamp duties are part of the capital cost of the investment and are included in the cheque paid to the firm's stockbrokers. Brokerage charges on sale are deducted from the cheque remitted by the stockbrokers for the sale proceeds, so that as the sale price is brought in net they have been effectively charged.

Exhibit 21.1

Brent Ltd bought £10,000 3 per cent Government Stock at 40 *ex div* on 1 January 19-6, the cheque for the stock £4,000 plus brokerage charges £100 being £4,100. The interest is received on 31 March, 30 June, 30 September and 31 December 19-6. During 19-7 interest is received on 31 March, and all the stock is sold for 43 *cum div* on 31 May, the cheque being £4,190, made up of £4,300 total proceeds *less* £110 brokerage charges. The financial year end of Brent Ltd is 31 December.

The following shows the entries in the Investment Account for the years ended 31 December 19-6 and 19-7.

	Nominal	Income	Capital			Nominal	Income	Capital
	£	£	£			£	£	£
19-6				19-6				
Jan 1 Cash	10,000		4,100	Mar 31 Cash			75	
Dec 31 Investment				Jun 30 ,,			75	
Income to				Sep 30 ,,			75	
Profit and Loss		300		Dec 31 ,,			75	
				,, 31 Balance c/d		10,000		4,100
	10,000	300	4,100			10,000	300	4,100
19-7				19-7				
Jan 1 Balance b/d	10,000		4,100	Mar 31 Cash			75	
Dec 31 Investment				May 31 ,, (A)		10,000	50	4,410
Income to				Sale Proceeds				
Profit and Loss		125						
,, 31 Profit on sale to								
Profit and Loss			40					
	10,000	125	4,140			10,000	125	4,140

(A) As the stock is sold *cum div*, Brent Ltd is therefore including in the selling price the value of two months' interest for April and May = $\frac{2}{12} \times 3$ per cent $\times$ £10,000 = £50. The £4,190 sale price is accordingly apportioned £50 as to income and £4,140 as to capital.

To illustrate matters further, Exhibit 21.2 shows an investment where there are both extra purchases and sales of part of the investment.

Exhibit 21.2

On 1 January 19-4 Green Ltd bought £4,000 6 per cent Government Stock at £90, the cheque of £3,680 paid being £3,600 for the stock and £80 for the brokerage charges. Interest is receivable each year on 31 March, 30 June, 30 September, and 31 December.

Investment – 6 per cent Government Stock

Debit side

Date	Particulars		Nominal £	Income £	Capital £
19-4					
Jan 1	Cash		4,000		3,680
Dec 31	Investment Income to Profit and Loss			240	
			4,000	240	3,680
19-5					
Jan 1	Balance b/d		4,000		3,680
Jun 1	Adjustment for sale at *ex div* price	(B)		10	
Dec 31	Investment Income to Profit and Loss	(C)		115	
			4,000	125	3,680
19-6					
Jan 1	Balance b/d		1,000		920
Feb 1	Cash		5,000		4,345
Jun 1	Adjustment of purchase at *ex div* price	(E)	1,000	25	910
" 1		(F)			5
Dec 31	Investment Income to Profit and Loss			370	
			7,000	395	6,180
19-7					
Jan 1	Balance b/d		7,000		6,180

Credit side

Date	Particulars		Nominal £	Income £	Capital £
19-4					
Mar 31	Cash			60	
Jun 30	"			60	
Sep 30	"			60	
Dec 31	"			60	
31	Balance c/d		4,000		3,680
			4,000	240	3,680
19-5					
Feb 1	Cash Sale proceeds	(A)	1,000	5	945
Mar 31	Cash (£3,000 × 6% × 3 months)			45	
Jun 1	Cash Sale proceeds	(B)	2,000		1,710
1	Adjustment for sale at *ex div* price				10
30	Cash (£3,000 × 6% × 3 months)			45	
Sep 30	Cash (£1,000 × 6% × 3 months)			15	
Dec 31	Cash (£1,000 × 6% × 3 months)			15	
31	Profit and Loss – on Sale of Investments	(D)			95
31	Balance c/d		1,000		920
			4,000	125	3,680
19-6					
Mar 31	Cash (£6,000 × 6% × 3 months)			90	
Jun 1	Adjustment of purchase at *ex div* price			5	
30	Cash (£7,000 × 6% × 3 months)			90	
Sep 30	Cash (£7,000 × 6% × 3 months)			105	
Dec 31	Cash (£7,000 × 6% × 3 months)	(E)		105	
31	Balance c/d		7,000		6,180
			7,000	395	6,180

On 1 February 19-5 £1,000 nominal value of the stock is sold *cum div*, the net proceeds being £950.

1 June 19-5, £2,000 nominal value sold *ex div*, net proceeds after brokerage being £1,710.

1 February 19-6, £5,000 nominal value bought *cum div*, the cost including brokerage being £4,370.

1 June 19-6, £1,000 nominal value bought *ex div*, cost including brokerage being £910.

On page 286 is the Investment Account in Green's books for the financial years ended 31 December 19-4, 19-5 and 19-6. Taxation is ignored.

Notes:

(*a*) The sale proceeds £950 represent the sale of the right to one month's interest, £1,000×6 per cent per annum for one month = £5, plus the right to the actual stock itself. This must therefore be the balance of the net sale proceeds, £950−£5 = £945.

(*b*) The sale at an *ex div* price means that Green Ltd will receive interest for June on this £2,000 of stock even though the stock itself had passed out of Green Ltd's ownership. The actual net sale price is therefore £1,720, which is made up of £1,710 actually received plus £10 for the right to one month's interest retained. This is adjusted by debiting the Income column with £10 to cancel the income which was not equated with ownership, and crediting the Capital column with £10 representing the actual reduction in the sale price caused by selling at an *ex div* price. (*c*) will illustrate the validity of debiting the income column, as without this entry the amount of investment income transferred to the Profit and Loss Account would not agree with the facts relating to the duration of the investment and the rate of interest.

(*c*) The correctness of this can be proved if the interest actually accrued during ownership is calculated:

		£
6 per cent per annum on £4,000 for one month	=	20
6 per cent per annum on £3,000 for four months	=	60
6 per cent per annum on £1,000 for seven months	=	35
		115

(*d*)

	£	£
Cost of £1,000 nominal value of stock £3,680×¼=	920	
Sold on 1 February 19-5 for	945	25 profit
Cost of £2,000 nominal value of stock £3,680×½=	1,840	
Sold on 1 June 19-5 for (adjusted net sale price)	1,720	120 loss
		95 net loss

(*e*) The stock bought on 1 June 19-6 for £910 *ex div* meant that June's ownership would not bring in any interest on this stock. The price paid for the stock would have been reduced by the amount of June's interest, i.e. £1,000 at 6 per cent per annum for one month = £5. The true price paid therefore was £915. This is represented by a debit of £5 in the Capital column, while a credit of £5 in the Income column is made to show that ownership of fixed interest stock does in fact bring in a return of interest in accordance with the length of ownership.

(*f*) This can be proved to be correct.

		£
£1,000 at 6 per cent per annum for one month	=	5
£6,000 at 6 per cent per annum for four months	=	120
£7,000 at 6 per cent per annum for seven months	=	245
		370

Investment in limited companies

In the cases where stocks, shares and debentures carry a fixed rate of interest the treatment is the same as with Government Stocks. However, where the investment is not of the fixed interest type, e.g. ordinary shares, the next dividend receivable is not known on purchase or sale. On the declaration of the next dividend an adjustment can be made, so that the account will contain the same balances as it would have done if the next dividend had been known, and the necessary apportionments taken place at sale or purchase rather than wait until the dividend had been declared. In theory these adjustments should always be made, but in practice they are usually ignored where the purchase and sale of investments do not constitute the main business of the firm.

Review questions

21.1 The following transactions of Trust Ltd took place during the year ended 30 June 19-7:

19-6

1 July	Purchased £12,000 4 per cent Consolidated Loan (interest payable 1 February and 1 August) at 60½ *cum div*.
12 July	Purchased 2,000 ordinary shares of £0.5 each in Abee Ltd for £4,000.
1 August	Received half-year's interest on 4 per cent Consolidated Loan.
15 August	Abee Ltd made a bonus issue of three ordinary shares for every two held. Trust Ltd sold 2,500 of the bonus shares for £1 each.
1 October	Purchased 5,000 ordinary shares of £1 each in Ceedee Ltd at £0.775 each.

19-7

2 January	Sold £3,000 4 per cent Consolidated Loan at 61 *ex div*.
1 February	Received half-year's interest on 4 per cent Consolidated Loan.
1 March	Received dividend of 18 per cent on shares in Abee Ltd.
1 April	Ceedee Ltd made a 'rights' issue of one share for every two held at £0.5 per share. 'Rights' sold on market for £0.25 per share.
1 June	Received dividend of 12½ per cent on shares in Ceedee Ltd.

Required:

Write up the relevant investment accounts as they would appear in the books of Trust Ltd for the year ended 30 June 19-7, bringing down the balances as on that date.

Ignore brokerage and stamp duty.

(*Institute of Chartered Accountants*)

21.2 On 31 March 19-5 the investments held by Jowetts of Mayfair Ltd included 6,000 Ordinary shares of £1 each fully paid in Composite Interest Ltd, such shares appearing in the books at £7,200. It is not the practice of Jowetts of Mayfair Ltd to make apportionments of dividends received or receivable.

Jowetts of Mayfair Ltd sold 1,000 shares on 31 May 19-5 for £1,965. On 20 September 19-5 Composite Interest Ltd:

(a) Issued by way of a bonus issue three fully paid shares for every five held on 31 August 19-5.

(b) It gave the right to shareholders to apply for one share for every two actually held on 31 August 19-5, the price to be £1.05 per share payable in full on application.

The shares issued under (a) and (b) were not to participate in the dividend for the year ended 31 August 19-5.

The bonus shares were received. For the rights issue 1,800 shares were taken up and paid for on 30 September 19-5. The rights on the remaining shares were sold for £0.3 per share, the money for this being received on 15 November 19-5.

On 17 December 19-5 Composite Interest Ltd declared and paid a final dividend of 20 per cent for the year ended 31 August 19-5, and on 15 March 19-6 an interim dividend of 5 per cent for the year ended 31 August 19-6.

Show the investment account for the year ended 31 March 19-6 as it would appear in the books of Jowetts of Mayfair Ltd.

Expenses of sale are to be ignored.

21.3A Stag Ltd is an investment company making up its accounts to 31 December in each year.

The following transactions have been extracted from the company's records for 19-9.

19-9

1 January	Purchased 1,000 ordinary shares of £0.25 each in Bull Ltd at £1.75 per share.
12 February	Purchased £2,000 ordinary stock in Bear Ltd for £1,500.
1 March	Received dividend of 20 per cent on shares in Bull Ltd.
24 April	Bull Ltd made a bonus issue of one share for every four held.
2 May	Received dividend of 2½ per cent on ordinary stock in Bear Ltd.
10 May	Bull Ltd announced a rights issue of two ordinary shares for every five held on that date, at £1.25 per share. Rights sold on market for £0.5 per share.
1 August	Applied for £5,000 7¼ per cent Loan stock in Bear Ltd issued at £98 per cent, and payable half on application and the balance in two equal instalments on 1 October and 1 December. The application was successful.
16 September	Received dividend of 30 per cent on shares in Bull Ltd.
1 October	Paid instalment on loan stock in Bear Ltd.
20 November	Received dividend of 3 per cent on ordinary stock in Bear Ltd.
1 December	Paid final instalment on loan stock in Bear Ltd.

Required:

Write up the accounts for the investments in Bull Ltd and Bear Ltd as they would appear in the books of Stag Ltd for the year ended 31 December 19-9, bringing down the balances as on that date.

Ignore stamp duty, brokerage and taxation.

(Institute of Chartered Accountants)

21.4A HM Ltd bought £10,000 nominal of Peatshire 6 per cent Loan Stock at 92 *cum div* on 30 April 19-8. Interest on the stock is paid half-yearly on 30 June and 31 December. £4,000 of the stock was sold at 94 *ex div* on 30 November 19-8.

HM Ltd prepares final accounts annually to 31 March.

Prepare the investment account in the company's ledger from the date of the purchase to 1 April 19-9.

Ignore brokerage, stamp duty and taxation and make apportionments in months.

21.5A On 1 April 19-7, FRY Ltd purchased 10,000 ordinary shares of £1 each, fully paid, in TLS Ltd at a cost of £20,500.

On 1 September 19-7, TLS Ltd declared and paid a dividend of 15 per cent on its ordinary shares for the year ended 30 June 19-7.

On 1 November 19-7, TLS Ltd gave its eight members the right to subscribe for one ordinary share for every eight held on 1 November 19-7, at a price of £1.5 per share, payable in full on application.

On 15 November 19-7, FRY Ltd purchased for £0.4 per share the rights of another shareholder in TLS Ltd to subscribe for 750 shares under the rights issue.

On 30 November 19-7, FRY Ltd applied and paid for all the shares in TLS Ltd to which it was then entitled.

On 8 September 19-8, TLS Ltd declared and paid a dividend for the year ended 30 June 19-8, of 15 per cent on all ordinary shares, including those issued in 19-7.

On 1 October 19-8, FRY Ltd sold 4,500 ordinary shares in TLS Ltd for £9,875.

The accounting year of FRY Ltd ends on 31 December.

FRY Ltd does not make apportionments of dividends received or receivable. When part of a holding of shares is sold, it is the practice of this company to calculate the cost of the shares sold as an appropriate part of the average cost of all the shares held at the date of the sale.

You are required to show the investment account in the books of FRY Ltd for the two years ended 31 December 19-7, and 31 December 19-8, bringing down the balance at the end of each year.

Ignore taxation.

(*Institute of Chartered Secretaries and Administrators*)

22
Contract accounts

The span of production differs between businesses, and some fit into the normal pattern of annual accounts easier than others do. A farmer's accounts are usually admirably suited to the yearly pattern, as the goods they produce are in accordance with the seasons, and therefore repeat themselves annually. With a firm whose production span is a day or two the annual accounts are also quite suitable.

On the other hand, there are businesses whose work does not conform to a financial year's calculation of profits. Assume that a firm of contractors has only one contract being handled, and that is the total construction of a very large oil refinery complex. This might take five years to complete. Not until it is completed can the actual profit or loss on the contract be correctly calculated. However, if the company was formed especially with this contract in mind, the shareholders would not want to wait for five years before the profit could be calculated and dividends paid. Therefore an attempt is made to calculate profits yearly. Obviously, most firms will have more than one contract under way at a time, and also it would be rare for a contract to take such a long time to complete.

For each contract an account is opened. It is, in fact, a form of Trading Account for each contract. Therefore if the firm has a contract to build a new technical college it may be numbered Contract 71. Thus a Contract 71 Account would be opened. All expenditure traceable to the contract will be charged to the Contract Account. This is far easier than ascertaining direct expenses in a factory, as any expenditure on the site will be treated as direct, e.g. wages for the manual workers on the site, telephone rental for telephones on the site, hire of machinery for the contract, wages for the timekeepers, clerks, etc., on the site.

The contractor is paid by agreement on the strength of architects' certificates in the case of buildings, or engineers' certificates for an engineering contract. The architect, or engineer, will visit the site at regular intervals and will issue a certificate stating his estimate of the value of the work done, in terms of the total contract price (the sale price of the whole contract). Thus he may issue a certificate for £10,000. Normally the terms governing the contract will contain a clause concerning retention money. This is the amount, usually stated as a percentage, which will be retained, i.e. held back, in case the contract is not completed by a stated date, or against claims for faulty workmanship, etc. A 10 per cent retention in the case already mentioned would lead to £9,000 being payable by the person for whom the contract was being performed.

The administration overhead expenses not traceable directly to the sites are sometimes split on an arbitrary basis and charged to each contract. Of course, if there was only one contract, then all the overhead expenses would quite rightly be chargeable against it. On the other hand if there are twenty contracts being carried on, any apportionment must be arbitrary. No one can really apportion on a 'scientific' basis the administration overhead expenses of the managing director's salary, the cost of advertising to give the firm the right 'image', the costs of running accounting machinery for the records of the whole firm, and these are only a few of such expenses. In a fashion similar to the departmental accounts principle in Chapter 34 of Volume 1, it sometimes gives misleading results, and it is therefore far better left for the administrative overhead expenses which are obviously not chargeable to a contract to be omitted from the Contract Accounts. The surplus left on each Contract Account is thus the 'contribution' of each contract to administrative overhead expenses and to profit.

Exhibit 22.1

Contract 44 is for a school being built for the Blankshire County Council. By the end of the year the following items have been charged to the Contract Account:

	Contract 44
Wages – Labour on Site	£5,000
Wages – Foreman and Clerks on the Site	600
Materials	4,000
Sub-contractors on the Site	900
Other Site Expenses	300
Hire of Special Machinery	400
Plant Bought for the Contract	2,000

The entries concerning expenditure traceable direct to the contract are relatively simple. These are charged to the Contract Account. These can be seen in the Contract Account shown on the next page.

Architects' certificates have been received during the year amounting to £14,000, it being assumed for this example that the certificate related to all work done up to the year end. A retention of 10 per cent is to be made, and the Blankshire County Council has paid £12,600. The £14,000 has been credited to a holding account called an Architects' Certificates Account, and debited to the Blankshire County Council Account. The total of the Architects' Certificates Account now needs transferring to the Contract 44 Account. It is, after all, the 'sale' price of the work done so far, and the Contract Account is a type of Trading Account. The £12,600 received has been debited to the Cash Book and credited to Blankshire County Council Account, which now shows a balance of £1,400, this being equal to the retention money.

The cost of the stock of the materials on the site unused is not included in the value of the architects' certificates and is therefore carried forward to the next year at cost price. The value of the plant at the end of the year is also carried forward. In this case the value of the cost of the plant not yet used is £1,400. This means that £2,000 has been debited for the plant and £1,400 credited, thus effectively charging £600 for depreciation. Assume that the stock of unused materials cost £800.

The Contract 44 Account will now appear:

Contract 44

	£		£
Wages – Labour on Site	5,000	Architects' Certificates	14,000
Wages – Foreman and Clerks on the Site	600	Stock of Unused Materials c/d	800
		Value of Plant c/d	1,400
Materials	4,000		
Sub-contractors on the Site	900		
Other Site Expenses	300		
Hire of Special Machinery	400		
Plant Bought for the Contract	2,000		

The difference between totals of the two sides (Credit side £16,200, Debit side £13,200) can be seen to be £3,000. It would be a brave person indeed who would assert that the profit made to date was £3,000. The contract is only part completed, and costly snags may crop up which would dissipate any potential profit earned, or snags may have developed already, such as subsidence, which has remained unnoticed as yet. The concept of prudence now takes over. The normal custom is, barring any evidence to the contrary, for the apparent profit (in this case £3,000) to have the following formula applied to it:

$$\text{Apparent profit} \times \tfrac{2}{3} \times \frac{\text{Cash received}}{\text{Work certified}} = \text{Amount which can be utilised for dividends, etc.}$$

In this case this turns out as $£3,000 \times \tfrac{2}{3} \times \dfrac{12,600}{14,000} = £1,800.$

There are variations on the formula under differing circumstances, but it is the formula which is usually propounded as being the most suitable.

Why two-thirds? Why not three-quarters? This is a fair question, and all that can be said is that the rule-of-thumb method devised years ago happened to be two-thirds. This was acceptable to accountants and business people. Just as technology has changed so also the two-thirds rule needs re-examination in a rapidly changing world. Modern techniques of building and engineering have undoubtedly minimised errors and snags compared with the past, therefore a much higher figure than two- thirds may now be quite justifiable.

The Contract 44 Account can now be completed:

Profit and Loss Account

	£
Profits from contracts:	
Contract 43	
Contract 44	1,800
Contract 45	

	£
Plant (Contract 44 part)	1,400
Stock (Contract 44 part)	800

	£
Profit reserve on Contract 44	1,200

Contract 44

	£		£
Wages – Labour on Site	£5,000	Architects' Certificates	14,000
Wages – Foreman and Clerks on		Stock of Unused Materials c/d	800
the Site	600	Value of Plant c/d	1,400
Materials	4,000		
Sub-contractors on the Site	900		
Other Site Expenses	300		
Hire of Special Machinery	400		
Plant Bought for the Contract	2,000		
Profit to the Profit and Loss			
Account	1,800		
Reserve (the part of the apparent			
profit not yet recognised as			
earned) c/d	1,200		
	16,200		16,200
Stock of Unused Materials b/d	800	Reserve b/d	1,200
Value of Plant b/d	1,400		

In the case shown there has been an apparent profit of £3,000, but the action would have been different if instead of revealing such a profit, the Contract Account had in fact shown a loss of £3,000. In such a case it would not be two-thirds of the loss to be taken into account but the whole of it. Thus £3,000 loss would have been transferred to the Profit and Loss Account. This is in accordance with the concept of prudence which states that profits may be underestimated but never losses.

It is in fact not always the case that an engineer or architect will certify the work done up to the financial year end. He may call several days earlier than the year end. The cost of work done, but not certified at the year end, will therefore need carrying down as a balance to the next period when certification will take place.

SSAP 9 includes the valuation of long-term contract work in progress. The contents of this chapter do in fact conform to the statements made in SSAP 9.

Before SSAP 9 many contractors had only taken profit into account when the contract was completed. The advent of SSAP 9 has brought in anticipation of profit before completion of contract, although prudence is still very much a guiding concept.

Review questions

22.1 The final accounts of Diggers Ltd are made up to 31 December in each year. Work on a certain contract was commenced on 1 April 19-5 and was completed on 31 October 19-6. The total contract price was £174,000, but a penalty of £700 was suffered for failure to complete by 30 September 19-6.

The following is a summary of receipts and payments relating to the contract:

	During 19-5	During 19-6
Payments:		
Materials	25,490	33,226
Wages	28,384	45,432
Direct Expenses	2,126	2,902
Purchases of Plant on 1 April 19-5	16,250	–
Receipts		
Contract Price (*less* penalty)	52,200	121,100
Sale, on 31 October 19-6, of all plant purchased on 1 April 19-5	–	4,100

The amount received from the customer in 19-5 represented the contract price of all work certified in that year less 10 per cent retention money.

When the annual accounts for 19-5 were prepared it was estimated that the contract would be completed on 30 September 19-6, and that the market value of the plant would be £4,250 on that date. It was estimated that further expenditure on the contract during 19-6 would be £81,400.

For the purposes of the annual accounts, depreciation of plant is calculated, in the case of uncompleted contracts, by reference to the expected market value of the plant on the date when the contract is expected to be completed, and is allocated between accounting periods by the straight-line method.

Credit is taken, in the annual accounts, for such a part of the estimated total profit, on each uncompleted contract, as corresponds to the proportion between the contract price of the work certified and the total contract price.

Required:

Prepare a summary of the account for this contract, showing the amounts transferred to profit and loss account at 31 December 19-5 and 31 December 19-6.

22.2 Stannard and Sykes Ltd are contractors for the construction of a pier for the Seafront Development Corporation. The value of the contract is £300,000, and payment is by engineer's certificate subject to a retention of 10 per cent of the amount certified, this to be held by the Seafront Development Corporation for six months after the completion of the contract.

The following information is extracted from the records of Stannard and Sykes Ltd.

	£
Wages on site	41,260
Materials delivered to site by supplier	58,966
Materials delivered to site from store	10,180
Hire of Plant	21,030
Expenses charged to Contract	3,065
Overheads charged to Contract	8,330
Materials on site at 30 November 19-8	11,660
Work certified	150,000
Payment received	135,000
Work in progress at cost (not the subject of a certificate to date)	12,613
Wages accrued 30 November 19-8	2,826

Required:

Prepare the Pier Contract Account to 30 November 19-8, and suggest a method by which profit could be prudently estimated.

(*Chartered Association of Certified Accountants*)

22.3A Cantilever Ltd was awarded a contract to build an office block in London and work commenced at the site on 1 May 19-5.

During the period to 28 February 19-6, the expenditure on the contract was as follows:

	£
Materials issued from stores	9,411
Materials purchased	28,070
Direct expenses	6,149
Wages	18,493
Charge made by the company for administration expenses	2,146
Plant and machinery purchased on 1 May 19-5, for use at site	12,180

On 28 February 19-6, the stock of materials at the site amounted to £2,164 and there were amounts outstanding for wages £366 and direct expenses £49.

Cantilever Ltd has received on account the sum of £64,170 which represents the amount of Certificate No. 1 issued by the architects in respect of work completed to 28 February 19-6, after deducting 10 per cent retention money.

The following relevant information is also available:

(*a*) the plant and machinery has an effective life of five years, with no residual value, and

(*b*) the company only takes credit for two-thirds of the profit on work certified.

Required:

(*a*) to prepare a contract account for the period to 28 February 19-6, and

(*b*) to show your calculation of the profit to be taken to the credit of the company's Profit and Loss Account in respect of the work covered by Certificate No 1.

(*Institute of Chartered Accountants*)

22.4A You are required to prepare the contract account for the year ended 31 December 19-0, and show the calculation of the sum to be credited to the profit and loss account for that year.

On 1 April 19-0 MN Ltd commenced work on a contract which was to be completed by 30 June 19-1 at an agreed price of £520,000.

MN Ltd's financial year ended on 31 December 19-0, and on that day expenditure on the contract totalled £263,000 made up as under:

	£
Plant	30,000
Materials	124,000
Wages	95,000
Sundry expenses	5,000
Head office charges	9,000
	263,000

Cash totalling £195,000 had been received by 31 December 19-0 representing 75 per cent of the work certified as completed on that date, but in addition, work costing £30,000 had been completed but not certified.

A sum of £9,000 had been obtained on the sale of materials which had cost £8,000 but which had been found unsuitable. On 31 December 19-0 stocks of unused materials on site had cost £10,000 and the plant was valued at £20,000.

To complete the contract by 30 June 19-1 it was estimated that:

(*a*) the following additional expenditures would be incurred:

	£
Wages	64,000
Materials	74,400
Sundry expenses	9,000

(*b*) further plant costing £25,000 would be required;

(*c*) the residual value of all plant used on the contract at 30 June 19-1 would be £15,000;

(*d*) head office charges to the contract would be at the same annual rate plus 10 per cent.

It was estimated that the contract would be completed on time but that a contingency provision of £15,000 should be made. From this estimate and the expenditure already incurred, it was decided to estimate the total profit that would be made on the contract and to take to the credit of the profit and loss account for the year ended 31 December 19-0, that proportion of the total profit relating to the work actually certified to that date.

(*Chartered Institute of Management Accountants*)

23
Value added statements

A great deal of discussion has taken place in recent years about the desirability of not simply interpreting results in terms of profits only. One way of doing this is in terms of the value added by the business itself to the resources acquired by it in transforming them into the final product. The production of such 'value added statements' was recommended in the *Corporate Report 1975*.

Such value added can be taken to represent in monetary terms, the net output of an enterprise. This is the difference between the total value of its output and the value of the inputs of materials and services obtained from other enterprises. The value added is seen to be due to the combined efforts of capital, management and employees, and the statement shows how the value added has been distributed to each of these factors.

As an example the Profit and Loss Account of Growth Ltd shown below is then restated in value added terms:

Growth Ltd
Profit and Loss Account for the year ended 31 December 19-1

	£	£
Turnover		765,000
Cost of Sales*		439,000
Gross Profit		326,000
Distribution Costs*	93,000	
Administrative Expenses*	108,000	201,000
		125,000
Interest Payable		2,000
Profit on Ordinary Activities before Taxation		123,000
Tax on Profit on Ordinary Activities		44,000
Profit for the year on Ordinary Activities after Taxation		79,000
Undistributed Profits from last year		55,000
		134,000
Transfer to General Reserve	15,000	
Proposed Ordinary Dividend	60,000	75,000
Undistributed Profits Carried to Next Year		59,000

Note: Costs* include:	£
Wages, pensions and other employee benefits	220,000
Depreciation	74,000
All other costs were bought in from outside	346,000
(£439,000+£93,000+£108,000)	£640,000

Growth Ltd

Statement of Value Added for the year ended 31 December 19-1

	£	£
Turnover		765,000
Bought in materials and services		346,000
Value Added		419,000
Applied the following way:		
To pay employees wages, pensions and other benefits		220,000
To pay providers of capital		
Interest on loans	2,000	
Dividends to Shareholders	60,000	62,000
To pay government		
Corporation Tax Payable		44,000
To provide for maintenance and expansion of assets:		
Depreciation	74,000	
Retained Profits	19,000	93,000
		419,000

The reader can see that the retained profits £19,000 is made up of the increase in undistributed profits (£59,000 – £55,000) £4,000 + transfer to general reserve £15,000 = £19,000.

The value added statement can be seen to be a means of reporting the income for all the groups which contribute to an organisation's performance. It is therefore relevant to the information needed by all of these groups, something which is not well served by an ordinary profit and loss account.

Review questions

23.1 Manvers Ltd includes with its financial statements each year a statement of value added. The draft value added statement for the year ended 31 May 19-6 is as follows:

	£	£
Revenue from sales		204,052
Bought in materials and services		146,928
Value added by the company		57,124

Applied to:

The benefit of employees

	£	£
Salaries	16,468	
Deductions for income tax and national insurance	3,352	
	13,116	
Pension schemes	2,810	
Employees' profit sharing schemes	525	
Welfare and staff amenities	806	
		17,257

Central and Local Government

	£	£
Value added tax	30,608	
Corporation tax	985	
Local rates	325	
Tax etc. deducted from salaries and loan interest	3,832	
		35,750

The providers of capital

	£	£
Interest on loan capital	1,600	
Income tax deducted	480	
	1,120	
Interest on bank overdrafts	250	
Dividends to shareholders of the company	500	
		1,870

The replacement of assets and the expansion of the business

	£	£
Depreciation	1,835	
Retained profits	412	
		2,247
		57,124

Discussion among the board of directors on the draft figures has revealed a wide variation of opinion on the usefulness of the value added statement to the readers of the accounts.

Some board members say that the added value statement is confusing as it is only a redrafting of the results which are shown in the profit and loss account which gives all the information necessary. Another view is that the statement of changes in financial position is far more important and this should be given in place of the value added statement.

Required:

(a) A report to the directors showing the advantages of the value added statement comparing it with the profit and loss account and the source and application of funds statement. Your report should deal specifically with the points raised in discussion by the directors.

(b) Construct a profit and loss account from the information given.

(c) Calculate the operating profit for use in a statement of changes in financial position.

(*Chartered Association of Certified Accountants*)

24

Consolidated accounts: introduction

The owners of a company are its shareholders. The purchase of ordinary shares normally gives a person three main rights, these being proportionate to the number of shares held by him. These are:

(*a*) Voting rights.

(*b*) A right to an interest in the net assets of the company. (Net assets means assets less liabilities.)

(*c*) A right to an interest in the profits earned by the company.

Because of the voting rights the ordinary shareholder is normally entitled to vote at shareholders' meetings. Preference shareholders on the other hand do not normally have full voting rights, their votes usually being restricted to where their dividends are in arrears or where their special rights are being varied. The reader should also realise that debenture shareholders carry no right to vote at general meetings.

At shareholders' meetings the ordinary shareholder, by virtue of his voting rights, is able to show his approval or disapproval (in accordance with the number of shares owned by him) of the election of directors. The directors appoint the officers of the company and manage its affairs. Therefore any group of shareholders acting together, who between them own more than 50 per cent of the voting shares of the company, can control the election of directors and, as a consequence, they can control the policies of the company through the directors. This would also hold true if any one shareholder owned more than 50 per cent of the voting shares.

One company may hold shares in another company; therefore if one company wishes to obtain control of another company it can do so by obtaining more than 50 per cent of the voting shares in that company.

Holding companies and subsidiary companies

A company, S Ltd, has an issued share capital of 1,000 ordinary shares of £1 each. On 1 January 19-6 H Ltd buys 501 of these shares from Jones, a shareholder, for £600. H Ltd will now have control of S Ltd because it has more than 50 per cent of the voting shares. H Ltd is called the 'holding' company and S Ltd is said to be its 'subsidiary' company.

Now just because the identity of S Ltd's shareholders has changed it does not mean that the balance sheet of S Ltd will be drafted in a different fashion. Looking only at the balance sheet of S Ltd no one would be able to deduce that H Ltd owned more than 50 per cent of the shares, or even that H Ltd owned any shares at all in S Ltd. After obtaining control of S Ltd both H Ltd and S Ltd will continue to maintain their own sets of accounting records and to draft their own balance sheets. In fact if the balance sheets of H Ltd and S Ltd are looked at, both before and after the purchase of the shares, then any differences can be noted.

Exhibit 24.1

(*a*) Before H Ltd acquired control of S Ltd.

H Ltd Balance Sheet as at 31 December 19-5

	£	£
Fixed Assets		2,000
Current Assets:		
Stock-in-Trade	2,900	
Debtors	800	
Bank	1,300	
		5,000
		7,000
Share Capital		5,000
Profit and Loss Account		2,000
		7,000

S Ltd Balance Sheet as at 31 December 19-5

	£	£
Fixed Assets		400
Current Assets:		
Stock-in-Trade	400	
Debtors	200	
Bank	100	
		700
		1,100
Share Capital		1,000
Profit and Loss Account		100
		1,100

(b) After H Ltd acquired control of S Ltd the balance sheets would appear as follows before any further trading took place:

H Ltd Balance Sheet as at 1 January 19-6

	£	£
Fixed Assets		2,000
Investment in Subsidiary Company		600
Current Assets:		
Stock-in-Trade	2,900	
Debtors	800	
Bank	700	
		4,400
		7,000
Share Capital		5,000
Profit and Loss Account		2,000
		7,000

S Ltd Balance Sheet as at 1 January 19-6

	£	£
Fixed Assets		400
Current Assets:		
Stock-in-Trade	400	
Debtors	200	
Bank	100	
		700
		1,100
Share Capital		1,000
Profit and Loss Account		100
		1,100

The only differences can be seen to be those in the balance sheets of H Ltd. The bank balance has been reduced by £600, this being the cost of shares in S Ltd, and the cost of the shares now appears as 'Investment in Subsidiary Company £600'. The balance sheets of S Ltd are completely unchanged.

From the Profit and Loss Account point of view, the appropriation section of S Ltd would also be completely unchanged after H Ltd takes control. H Ltd would however see a change in its Profit and Loss Account when a dividend is received from S Ltd, in this case the dividends received would be shown as Investment Income on the credit side of the Profit and Loss Account. Remember that dividends payable are charged to the Appropriation section of the paying company's Profit and Loss Account, while dividends received are in the main part of the receiving company's Profit and Loss Account.

The need for consolidated accounts

Imagine a shareholder of H Ltd receiving H Ltd's Balance Sheet and Profit and Loss Account annually. After H Ltd's acquisition of the shares in S Ltd then £600 would appear as an asset in H Ltd's Balance Sheet. As the shares of S Ltd are now not so readily marketable, remembering that over 50 per cent are owned by H Ltd, it would be normal to find the investment remaining at cost, i.e. £600. The Profit and Loss Account would show dividends received from S Ltd. The cost of the investment in S Ltd and the dividends received from S Ltd would be the only items referring to the subsidiary in the records of H Ltd.

Anyone investing in H Ltd is, because of its majority shareholding in S Ltd, therefore also investing in S Ltd as well. Therefore just as the other assets and liabilities change over the years in H Ltd and the shareholders are very much concerned with the changes, so also does the shareholder of H Ltd want to know about the changes in the assets and liabilities of S Ltd. He is not, however, a shareholder of S Ltd, and therefore is not automatically entitled to a set of final accounts of S Ltd annually. Correspondingly, if the situation was to stay put at that point, the shareholder of H Ltd would not get a proper accounting view of his investment. This is accentuated if in fact the holding company was one with 20 subsidiaries, owning a different percentage of the shares in each one, and with all kinds of interindebtedness and inter-company sales – all of which need special treatment as seen later in this book.

The only way that a shareholder in H Ltd can see clearly, in accounting terms, how his investment is progressing is for him to receive a consolidated set of the accounts of both companies showing the overall effect of his investment.

Different methods of acquiring control of one company by another

So far the acquisition of control in S Ltd was by H Ltd buying more than 50 per cent of the shares in S Ltd from Jones, i.e. buying shares on the open market. This is by no means the only way of acquiring control, so by way of illustration some of the other methods are now described.

(a) S Ltd may issue new shares to H Ltd amounting to over 50 per cent of the voting shares. H Ltd pays for the shares in cash.

(b) H Ltd could purchase over 50 per cent of the voting shares of S Ltd on the open market by exchanging for them newly issued shares of H Ltd.

Or, acting through another company:

(c) H Ltd acquires more than 50 per cent of the voting shares in S1 Ltd for cash, and then S1 Ltd proceeds to acquire all of the voting shares of S2 Ltd. S2 Ltd would then be a sub-subsidiary of H Ltd.

These are only some of the more common ways by which one company becomes a subsidiary of another company.

The nature of a group

Wherever two or more companies are in the relationship of holding and subsidiary companies then a 'group' is said to exist. When such a group exists then besides the Final Accounts of the Holding company itself, then to comply with legal requirements, there must be a set of Final Accounts prepared in respect of the group as a whole. These group accounts are usually known as 'consolidated accounts', because the accounts of all the companies have had to be consolidated together to form one Balance Sheet and one Profit and Loss Account.

Sometimes holding companies carry on trading as well as investing in their subsidiaries. There are however other holding companies that do not trade at all, the whole of their activities being concerned with investing in other companies.

Teaching method

The method used in this book for teaching consolidated accounts is that of showing the reader the adjustments needed on the face of the consolidated balance sheet, together with any workings necessary shown in a normal arithmetical fashion. The reasons why this method of illustrating consolidated accounts has been chosen are as follows:

(*a*) The author believes that it is his job to try to help the reader understand the subject, and not just to be able to perform the necessary manipulations. He believes that, given understanding of what is happening, then the accounting entries necessary follow easily enough. Showing the adjustments on the face of the balance sheet gives a 'birds-eye view' so that it is easier to see what is happening, rather than trace one's way laboriously through a complex set of double-entry adjustments made in ledger accounts.

(*b*) The second main reason is that this would be a much lengthier and more costly book if all of the double-entry accounts were shown. It is better for a first look at consolidated accounts to be an introduction to the subject only, rather than be at one and the same time both an introduction and a very detailed survey of the subject. If the reader can understand the consolidated accounts shown in this book then he/she will have a firm foundation which will enable him/her to tackle the more difficult and complicated aspects of the subject.

Group accounts (SSAP 14)

This SSAP deals with group accounts, or consolidated accounts as they are known in this book. The requirements of the SSAP are fully observed in what is written in the chapters which follow.

25

Consolidation of balance sheets: basic mechanics I

This chapter is concerned with the basic mechanics of consolidating balance sheets. The figures used will be quite small ones, as there is no virtue in obscuring the principles involved by bringing in large amounts. For the sake of brevity some abbreviations will be used. As the consolidation of the accounts of either two or three companies, but no more, will be attempted, then the abbreviations will be 'H' for the holding company, 'S1' the first subsidiary company, and 'S2' the second subsidiary company. Where there is only one subsidiary company it will be shown as 'S'. Unless stated to the contrary, all the shares will be ordinary shares of £1 each.

It will make the problems of the reader far easier if relatively simple balance sheets can be used to demonstrate the principles of consolidated accounts. To this end the balance sheets which follow in the next few chapters will usually have only two sorts of assets, those of stock and cash at bank. This will save a great deal of time and effort. If every time a consolidated balance sheet was to be drawn up the reader had to deal with assets of Land, Buildings, Patents, Motor Vehicles, Plant and Machinery, Stock, Debtors and Bank balances, then this would be an unproductive use of time.

Rule 1

The first rule is that in consolidation like things cancel out each other. In fact 'Cancellation Accounts' are in fact what consolidation accounts are all about. It also helps the reader to see the issue more clearly if the consolidated balance sheet is constructed immediately after H has bought the shares in S. In fact this would not be done in practice, but it is useful to use the method from a teaching point of view.

Exhibit 25.1

100 per cent of the shares of S bought at balance sheet value.

H has just bought all the shares of S. Before consolidation the balance sheets of H and S appear as follows:

H Balance Sheet

	£
Investment in subsidiary S (A)	6
Bank	4
	10
Share Capital	10
	10

	£
Stock	5
Bank	1
	6
Share Capital (B)	6
	6

Now the consolidated balance sheet can be drawn up. The rule about like things cancelling out each other can now be applied. As can be seen, item (A) in H's balance sheet and item (B) in S's balance sheet are concerned with exactly the same thing, namely the 6 ordinary shares of S; and for the same amount, for the shares are shown in both balance sheets at £6. These are cancelled when the consolidated balance sheet is drafted.

H & S Consolidated Balance Sheet

	£
Stock	5
Bank (£4+£1)	5
	10
Share Capital	10
	10

Exhibit 25.2

100 per cent of the shares of S bought for more than balance sheet value.

H Balance Sheet

		£
Investment in subsidiary S: 6 shares	(C)	9
Bank		1
		10
Share Capital		10
		10

		£
Stock		5
Bank		1
		6
Share Capital	(D)	6
		6

Now (C) and (D) refer to like things, but the amounts are unequal. What has happened is that H has given £3 more than the book value for the shares of S. In accounting, where the purchase money for something exceeds the stated value then the difference is known as Goodwill. This is still adhered to in the consolidation of balance sheets. The consolidated balance sheet is therefore:

H and S Consolidated Balance Sheet

	£
Goodwill (C) £9−(D) £6	3
Stock	5
Bank (£1+£1)	2
	10
Share Capital	10
	10

Exhibit 25.3

100 per cent of the shares of S bought for less than balance sheet value.

H Balance Sheet

		£
Investment in subsidiary S: 6 shares	(E)	4
Stock		5
Bank		1
		10
Share Capital		10
		10

S Balance Sheet

	£
Stock	5
Bank	1
	6
Share Capital (F)	6
	6

H has bought all of the shares of S, but has given only £4 for £6 worth of shares at balance sheet values. The £2 difference is the opposite of Goodwill. Contrary to what many people would think, this is not 'Badwill' as such a word is not an accounting term. The uninitiated might look upon the £2 as being 'profit' but your knowledge of company accounts should tell you that this difference could never be distributed as cash dividends. It is therefore a 'Capital Reserve' and will be shown accordingly in the consolidated balance sheet. The consolidated balance sheet therefore appears as:

H and S Consolidated Balance Sheet

	£
Stock (£5+£5)	10
Bank (£1+£1)	2
	12
Share Capital	10
Capital Reserve (F) £6 − (E) £4	2
	12

Cost of control

In fact the expression **cost of control** could be used instead of goodwill. This expression probably captures the essence of the purchase of the shares rather than calling it goodwill. It is precisely for the sake of gaining control of the assets of the company that the shares are bought. However the expression goodwill is more widely used and is correspondingly the one that will be used through the remainder of this book. (You can now attempt Review Questions 25.1, 25.2 and 25.3.)

Important note: Remember that SSAP 22 (accounting for goodwill) applies to all the goodwill figures you will be calculating in the next few chapters. It will be up to the company exactly how it will apply SSAP 22.

Rule 2

This states that, although the whole of the shares of the subsidiary have not been bought, nonetheless the whole of the assets of the subsidiary company (subject to certain inter-company transactions described later) will be shown in the consolidated balance sheet.

This rule comes about because of the choice made originally between two possible methods that could have been chosen. Suppose that H bought 75 per cent of the shares of S then the balance sheets could be displayed in one of two ways, e.g.

H and S Consolidated Balance Sheet

	£
Goodwill	*xxxx*
Assets of H: 100 per cent	*xxxx*
Assets of S: 75 per cent	*xxxx*
	xxxx
Share Capital of H	*xxxx*
	xxxx

H and S Consolidated Balance Sheet

	£
Goodwill	*xxxx*
Assets of H: 100 per cent	*xxxx*
Assets of S: 100 per cent	*xxxx*
	xxxx
Share Capital of H	*xxxx*
Claims of outsiders which equal 25 per cent of the assets of S	*xxxx*
	xxxx

It can be seen that both balance sheets show the amount of assets which H owns by virtue of its proportionate shareholding. On the other hand the second balance sheet gives a fuller picture, as it shows that H has control of all of the assets of S, although in fact it does not own all of them. The claims of outsiders comes to 25 per cent of S and obviously they cannot control the assets of S, whereas H, with 75 per cent, can control the whole of the assets even though they are not fully owned by it. The second balance sheet method gives rather more meaningful information and is the method that is usually used for consolidated accounts.

Assume that S has 6 shares of £1 each and that it has one asset, namely stock £6. H buys 4 shares for £1 each, £4. If the whole of the assets of S £6 are to be shown on the assets side of the consolidated balance sheet, and the cancellation of only £4 is to take place on the other side, then the consolidated balance sheet would not balance. Exhibit 25.4 shows this in detail before any attempt is made to get the consolidated balance sheet to balance.

Exhibit 25.4

H Balance Sheet

	£
Investment in subsidiary: 4 shares (bought today)	4
Stock	5
Bank	1
	10
Share Capital	10
	10

S Balance Sheet

	£
Stock	6
Share Capital	6

Now as the two extra shares have not been bought by H then they cannot be brought into any calculation of goodwill or capital reserve. H has in fact bought four shares with a balance sheet value of £1 each, £4, for precisely £4. There is therefore no element of goodwill or capital reserve. But on the other hand the consolidated balance sheet per Rule 2 must show the whole of the assets of S. This gives a consolidated balance sheet as follows:

H and S Consolidated Balance Sheet

	£
Stock (£5+£6)	11
Bank	1
Share Capital	10

Quite obviously the balance sheet totals differ by £2. What is this £2? On reflection it can be seen to be the £2 shares not bought by H. These shares belong to outsiders, they are not owned by the group. These outsiders also hold less than 50 per cent of the voting shares of S, in fact if they owned more then S would not be a subsidiary company. The title given to the outside shareholders is the apt one therefore of **Minority Interest**. As the whole of the assets of S are shown in the consolidated balance sheet then part of these assets are owned by the minority interest. This claim against the assets is therefore shown on the capital side of the consolidated balance sheet. The consolidated balance sheet becomes:

		£
Stock (£5+£6)		11
Bank		1
		12
Share Capital		10
Minority Interest		2
		12

This therefore is the convention of showing the whole of the assets of the subsidiary (less certain inter-company transactions) in the consolidated balance sheet, with the claim of the minority interest shown on the other side of the balance sheet.

Exhibit 25.5

Where less than 100 per cent of the subsidiary's shares are bought at more than book value.

H Balance Sheet

		£
Investment in subsidiary: 6 shares	(G)	8
Stock		11
Bank		1
		20
Share Capital		20
		20

S Balance Sheet

		£
Stock		7
Bank		3
		10
Share Capital	(I)	10
		10

H has bought 6 shares only, but has paid £8 for them. As the book value of the shares is £6, the £2 excess must therefore be Goodwill. The cancellation is therefore £6 from (G) and £6 from (I), leaving £2 of (G) to be shown as Goodwill in the consolidated balance sheet. The remaining £4 of (I) is in respect of shares held by the minority interest.

	£
Goodwill	2
Stock (£11+£7)	18
Bank (£1+£3)	4
	24
Share Capital	20
Minority Interest	4
	24

Exhibit 25.6

Where less than 100 per cent of the shares in the subsidiary are bought at less than book value.

H Balance Sheet

		£
Investment in subsidiary: 7 shares	(J)	5
Stock		13
Bank		2
		20
Share Capital		20
		20

S Balance Sheet

		£
Stock		9
Bank		1
		10
Share Capital	(K)	10
		10

Seven shares of S have now been bought for £5. This means that £5 of (J) and £5 of (K) cancel out with £2 shown as Capital Reserve. The remaining £3 of (K) is in respect of the shares held by the minority interest and will be shown as such in the consolidated balance sheet.

	£
Stock (£13+£9)	22
Bank (£2+£1)	3
	25
Shares	20
Capital Reserve	2
Minority Interest	3
	25

You can now attempt Review Questions 25.6 and 25.7.

Taking over subsidiaries with reserves

So far, for reasons of simplification, the examples given have been of subsidiaries having share capital but no reserves. When reserves exist, as they do in the vast majority of firms, it must be remembered that they belong to the ordinary shareholders. This means that if H buys all the 10 shares of S for £15, and S at that point of time has a credit balance of £3 on its Profit and Loss Account and a General Reserve of £2, then what H acquires for its £15 is the full entitlement/rights of the 10 shares measured by/shown as:

	£
10 Shares	10
Profit and Loss	3
General Reserve	2
	15

This means that the £15 paid and the £15 entitlements as shown will cancel out each other and will not be shown in the consolidated balance sheet. This is shown by the balance sheets shown in Exhibit 25.7

Exhibit 25.7

Where 100 per cent of the shares are bought at book value when the subsidiary has reserves.

H Balance Sheet

		£
Investment in subsidiary : 10 shares	(L)	15
Stock		11
Bank		2
		28
Share Capital		20
Profit and Loss		5
General Reserve		3
		28

		£
Stock		9
Bank		6
		15
Share Capital	(M1)	10
Profit and Loss	(M2)	3
General Reserve	(M3)	2
		15

H and S Consolidated Balance Sheet

	£
Stock (£11+£9)	20
Bank (£2+£6)	8
	28
Share Capital	20
Profit and Loss	5
General Reserve	3
	28

The cost of the shares (L) £15 is cancelled out exactly against (M1) £10+(M2)£3+(M3)£2=£15. These are therefore the only items cancelled out and the remainder of the two balance sheets of H and S are then combined to be the consolidated balance sheet.

Exhibit 25.8

Where 100 per cent of the shares are bought at more than book value when the subsidiary has reserves.

H Balance Sheet

		£
Investment in subsidiary: 10 shares	(N)	23
Stock		7
Bank		5
		35
Share Capital		20
Profit and Loss		9
General Reserve		6
		35

		£
Stock		15
Bank		2
		17
Share Capital	(O1)	10
Profit and Loss	(O2)	4
General Reserve	(O3)	3
		17

H paid £23 (N) for the entitlements (O1)£10+(O2)£4+(O3)£3=£17, so that a figure of £6 will be shown in the consolidated balance sheet for Goodwill.

H and S Consolidated Balance Sheet

	£
Goodwill	6
Stock (£7+£15)	22
Bank (£5+£2)	7
	35
Share Capital	20
Profit and Loss	9
General Reserve	6
	35

Exhibit 25.9

Where 100 per cent of the shares in the subsidiary are bought at below book value when the subsidiary has reserves.

H Balance Sheet

		£
Investment in subsidiary: 10 shares	(P)	17
Stock		10
Bank		8
		35
Share Capital		20
Profit and Loss		6
General Reserve		9
		35

		£
Stock		16
Bank		5
		21
Share Capital	(Q1)	10
Profit and Loss	(Q2)	8
General Reserve	(Q3)	3
		21

H has paid £17 (P) for the benefits of (Q1)£10+(Q2)£8+(Q3)£3=£21. This means that there will be a Capital Reserve of £21−£17=£4 in the consolidated balance sheet, while (P), (Q1), (Q2) and (Q3) having been cancelled out will not appear.

H and S Consolidated Balance Sheet

	£
Stock (£10+£16)	26
Bank (£8+£5)	13
	39
Share Capital	20
Profit and Loss	6
General Reserve	9
Capital Reserve	4
	39

Exhibit 25.10

Where less than 100 per cent of the shares are bought in a subsidiary which has reserves, and the shares are bought at the balance sheet value.

H Balance Sheet

		£
Investment in subsidiary: 8 shares	(R)	24
Stock		15
Bank		6
		45
Share Capital		20
Profit and Loss		17
General Reserve		8
		45

		£
Stock		21
Bank		9
		30

		£
Share Capital	(T1)	10
Profit and Loss	(T2)	5
General Reserve	(T3)	15
		30

The items (R) and the parts of (T1), (T2) and (T3) which are like things need to be cancelled out. The cancellation takes place from the share capital and reserves of S as follows:

	Total at acquisition date	Bought by H 80 per cent	Held by Minority Interest
	£	£	£
Share Capital	10	8	2
Profit and Loss	5	4	1
General Reserve	15	12	3
	30	24	6

The amount paid by H was £24, and as H acquired a total of £24 value of shares and reserves the cancellation takes place without there being any figure of Goodwill or Capital Reserve. The consolidated balance sheet therefore appears:

H and S Consolidated Balance Sheet

	£
Stock (£15+£21)	36
Bank (£6+£9)	15
	51

	£
Share Capital	20
Profit and Loss	17
General Reserve	8
Minority Interest	6
	51

Partial control at a price not equal to balance sheet value

In Exhibit 25.10 the amount paid for the 80 per cent of the shares of S was equal to the balance sheet value of the shares in that it amounted to £24. Very rarely will it be so, as the price is normally different from balance sheet value. If an amount paid is greater than the balance sheet value then the excess will be shown as Goodwill in the consolidated balance sheet, while if a smaller amount than balance sheet value is paid then the difference is a Capital Reserve and will be shown as such in the consolidated balance sheet. Using the balance sheet figure of S in Exhibit 25.10 then if H had paid £30 for 80 per cent of the shares of S then the consolidated balance sheet would show a Goodwill figure of £6, while if instead £21 only had been paid then the consolidated balance sheet would show £3 for Capital Reserve.

When the acquisition of two subsidiaries brings out in the calculations a figure of Goodwill in respect of the acquisition of one subsidiary, and a figure for Capital Reserve in respect of the acquisition of the other subsidiary, then the net figure only will be shown in the consolidated balance sheet. For instance if H had acquired two subsidiaries S1 and S2 where the calculations showed a figure of £10 for Goodwill on the acquisition of S1 and a figure of £4 for Capital Reserve on the acquisition of S2, then the consolidated balance sheet would show a figure for Goodwill of £6. Given figures instead of £11 Goodwill for S1 and £18 Capital Reserve for S2 then the consolidated balance sheet would show a Capital Reserve of £7.

The final Exhibit in this chapter is a composite one, bringing in most of the points already shown.

Exhibit 25.11

Where two subsidiaries have been acquired, both with reserves, full control being acquired of one subsidiary and a partial control of the other subsidiary.

H Balance Sheet

		£
Investment in subsidiaries:		
S1 10 shares	(U)	37
S2 7 shares	(V)	39
Stock		22
Bank		2
		100
Share Capital		40
Profit and Loss		50
General Reserve		10
		100

		£
Stock		19
Bank		11
		30
Share Capital	(W1)	10
Profit and Loss	(W2)	12
General Reserve	(W3)	8
		30

S2 Balance Sheet

		£
Stock		42
Bank		18
		60
Share Capital	(X1)	10
Profit and Loss	(X2)	30
General Reserve	(X3)	20
		60

With the acquisition of S1 H has paid £37 for (W1)£10+(W2)£12+(W3)£8=£30, giving a figure of £7 for Goodwill. With the acquisition of S2 H has given £39 for 7/10ths of the following: (X1)£10+(X2)£30+(X3)£20=£60×7/10ths=£42, giving a figure of £3 for Capital Reserve. As the net figure only is to be shown in the consolidated balance sheet then it will be Goodwill £7 – Capital Reserve £3 = Goodwill (net) £4.

		£
Goodwill		4
Stock (£22+£19+£42)		83
Bank (£2+£11+£18)		31
		118
Share Capital		40
Profit and Loss		50
General Reserve		10
Minority Interest:		
3/10ths of (X1)	3	
3/10ths of (X2)	9	
3/10ths of (X3)	6	
		18
		118

Now work through Review Questions 25.10 and 25.11.

Review questions

25.1 The following balance sheets were drawn up immediately H Ltd had acquired control of S Ltd. You are to draw up a consolidated balance sheet.

H Balance Sheet

	£
Investment in S: 100 shares	110
Stock	60
Bank	30
	200
Share Capital	200
	200

S Balance Sheet

	£
Stock	80
Bank	20
	100
Share Capital	100
	100

25.2 You are to draw up a consolidated balance sheet from the following balance sheets of H Ltd and S Ltd which were drawn up immediately H Ltd had acquired the shares in S Ltd.

H Balance Sheet

	£
Investment in S Ltd:	
3,000 shares	2,700
Fixed Assets	2,000
Stock	800
Debtors	400
Bank	100
	6,000
Share Capital	6,000
	6,000

S Balance Sheet

	£
Fixed Assets	1,800
Stock	700
Debtors	300
Bank	200
	3,000
Share Capital	3,000
	3,000

25.3 Draw up a consolidated balance sheet from the following balance sheets which were drawn up as soon as H Ltd had acquired control of S Ltd.

H Balance Sheet

	£
Investment in S Ltd: 60,000 shares	60,000
Fixed Assets	28,000
Stock	6,000
Debtors	5,000
Bank	1,000
	100,000
Share Capital	100,000
	100,000

S Balance Sheet

	£
Fixed Assets	34,000
Stock	21,000
Debtors	3,000
Bank	2,000
	60,000
Share Capital	60,000
	60,000

25.4A H Ltd acquires all the shares in S Ltd and then the following balance sheets are drawn up. You are to draw up a consolidated balance sheet.

H Balance Sheet

	£
Investment in S Ltd	29,000
Fixed Assets	5,000
Stock	4,000
Debtors	3,000
Bank	1,000
	42,000
Share Capital	42,000
	42,000

S Balance Sheet

	£
Fixed Assets	12,000
Stock	6,000
Debtors	4,000
Bank	2,000
	24,000
Share Capital	24,000
	24,000

25.5A Draw up a consolidated balance sheet from the balance sheets of H Ltd and S Ltd that were drafted immediately the shares in S Ltd were acquired by H Ltd.

H Balance Sheet

	£
Investment in S Ltd: 63,000 shares	50,000
Fixed Assets	18,000
Stock	5,000
Debtors	4,000
Bank	3,000
	80,000
Share Capital	80,000
	80,000

S Balance Sheet

	£
Fixed Assets	48,000
Stock	6,000
Debtors	5,000
Bank	4,000
	63,000
Share Capital	63,000
	63,000

25.6 H Ltd acquires 60 per cent of the shares in S Ltd. Balance Sheets are then drafted immediately. You are to draw up the consolidated balance sheet.

H Balance Sheet

	£
Investment in S Ltd: 1,200 shares	1,500
Fixed Assets	900
Stock	800
Debtors	600
Bank	200
	4,000
Share Capital	4,000
	4,000

	£
Fixed Assets	1,100
Stock	500
Debtors	300
Bank	100
	2,000
Share Capital	2,000
	2,000

25.7 H Ltd acquires 95 per cent of the shares of S Ltd. The following balance sheets are then drafted. You are to draw up the consolidated balance sheet.

H Balance Sheet

	£
Investment in S: 2,850 shares	2,475
Fixed Assets	2,700
Stock	1,300
Debtors	1,400
Bank	125
	8,000
Share Capital	8,000
	8,000

S Balance Sheet

	£
Fixed Assets	625
Stock	1,700
Debtors	600
Bank	75
	3,000
Share Capital	3,000
	3,000

25.8A H Ltd buys 66⅔ per cent of the shares in S Ltd. You are to draw up the consolidated balance sheet from the following balance sheets constructed immediately control had been achieved.

H Balance Sheet

	£
Investment in S: 600 shares	540
Fixed Assets	1,160
Stock	300
Debtors	200
Bank	100
	2,300
Share Capital	2,300
	2,300

S Balance Sheet

	£
Fixed Assets	400
Stock	200
Debtors	240
Bank	60
	900
Share Capital	900
	900

25.9A After H Ltd acquired 75 per cent of the shares of S Ltd the following balance sheets are drawn up.

H Balance Sheet

	£
Investments in S Ltd: 1,200 shares	1,550
Fixed Assets	2,450
Stock	1,000
Debtors	800
Bank	200
	6,000
Share Capital	6,000
	6,000

S Balance Sheet

	£
Fixed Assets	800
Stock	400
Debtors	250
Bank	150
	1,600
Share Capital	1,600
	1,600

25.10 Immediately after H Ltd had acquired control of S1 Ltd and S2 Ltd the following balance sheets were drawn up. You are to draw up a consolidated balance sheet.

H Balance Sheet

	£
Investments in subsidiaries:	
S1 Ltd (3,000 shares)	3,800
S2 Ltd (3,200 shares)	4,700
Fixed Assets	5,500
Current Assets	2,500
	16,500
Share Capital	10,000
Profit and Loss Account	6,500
	16,500

S1 Balance Sheet

	£
Fixed Assets	2,200
Current Assets	1,300
	3,500
Share Capital	3,000
Profit and Loss Account	400
General Reserve	100
	3,500

	£
Fixed Assets	4,900
Current Assets	2,100
	7,000
Share Capital	4,000
Profit and Loss Account	1,000
General Reserve	2,000
	7,000

25.11 Immediately after H Ltd had acquired control of S1 Ltd and S2 Ltd the following balance sheets were drawn up. You are to draw up a consolidated balance sheet.

H Balance Sheet

	£
Investment in subsidiaries:	
S1 Ltd (1,800 shares)	4,200
S2 Ltd (2,000 shares)	2,950
Fixed Assets	4,150
Current Assets	2,100
	13,400
Share Capital	10,000
Profit and Loss Account	2,000
General Reserve	1,400
	13,400

S1 Balance Sheet

	£
Fixed Assets	3,500
Current Assets	2,500
	6,000
Share Capital	3,000
Profit and Loss Account	1,200
General Reserve	1,800
	6,000

S2 Balance Sheet

	£
Fixed Assets	1,800
Current Assets	1,400
	3,200
Share Capital	2,000
Profit and Loss Account	500
General Reserve	700
	3,200

25.12A Immediately after H Ltd had achieved control of S1 Ltd and S2 Ltd the following balance sheets are drawn up. You are to draw up the consolidated balance sheet.

H Balance Sheet

	£
Investments in subsidiaries:	
S1 Ltd 4,000 shares	6,150
S2 Ltd 6,000 shares	8,950
Fixed Assets	3,150
Current Assets	2,050
	20,300
Share Capital	15,000
Profit and Loss Account	2,000
General Reserve	3,300
	20,300

S1 Balance Sheet

	£
Fixed Assets	5,300
Current Assets	1,200
	6,500
Share Capital	4,000
Profit and Loss Account	1,100
General Reserve	1,400
	6,500

	£
Fixed Assets	6,000
Current Assets	3,450
	9,450
Share Capital	7,000
Profit and Loss Account	1,400
General Reserve	1,050
	9,450

25.13A The following balance sheets of H Ltd, S1 Ltd and S2 Ltd were drawn up as soon as H Ltd had acquired the shares in both subsidiaries. You are to draw up a consolidated balance sheet.

H Balance Sheet

	£
Investments in subsidiaries:	
S1 Ltd 3,500 shares	6,070
S2 Ltd 2,000 shares	5,100
Fixed Assets	2,030
Current Assets	1,400
	14,600
Share Capital	11,000
Profit and Loss Account	1,000
General Reserve	2,600
	14,600

S1 Balance Sheet

	£
Fixed Assets	4,800
Current Assets	2,400
	7,200
Share Capital	5,000
Profit and Loss Account	900
General Reserve	1,300
	7,200

	£
Fixed Assets	2,800
Current Assets	900
	3,700
Share Capital	2,000
Profit and Loss Account	1,400
General Reserve	300
	3,700

26

Consolidation of balance sheets: basic mechanics II

In the last chapter the consolidation of balance sheets was looked at as if the consolidated balance sheets were drawn up immediately the shares in the subsidiary had been acquired. However, this is very rarely the case in practice, and therefore the consolidation of balance sheets must be looked at as at the time it actually takes place, i.e. at the end of the accounting period some time after acquisition has taken place. Correspondingly, the balance on the profit and loss account of the subsidiary, and possibly the balances on the other reserve accounts, will have altered when compared with the figures at the date of acquisition.

In Chapter 25 the Goodwill, or Capital Reserve, was calculated at the date of acquisition, and this calculation will stay unchanged as the years go by. It is important to understand this. Say, for instance, that the calculation was made of Goodwill on 31 December 19-3 and that the figure was £5,000. Even if the calculation was made one year later, on 31 December 19-4, then the calculation must refer to the reserves, etc., as on 31 December 19-3 as this is when they were acquired, and so the figure of Goodwill will still be £5,000. This would be true even if 5 years went by before anyone performed the calculation. In practice therefore, once the figure of Goodwill has been calculated then there is absolutely no need to re-calculate it every year. However, in examinations the Goodwill figure will still have to be calculated by the student even though the consolidated balance sheet that he is drawing up is 5, 10 or 20 years after the company became a subsidiary. This has to be done because the previous working papers are not available to an examinee.

It would be outside the law and good accounting practice for any company to return its capital to the shareholders, unless of course special permission was granted by the court[1]. Similarly, if a holding company was to pay its money in acquiring a company as a subsidiary, and then distribute as dividends the assets that it had bought then this is really the same as returning its capital to its shareholders. This can best be illustrated by a simple example.

H pays £15 to acquire 100 per cent of the shares of S, and the share capital of S consists of £10 of shares and £5 profit and loss account. Thus to acquire a capital asset, i.e. ownership of S, the holding company has parted with £15. If the balance of the profit and loss account of S was merely added to the profit and loss balance of H in the consolidated balance sheet then the £5 balance of S could be regarded as being distributable as cash dividends to the shareholders of H. As this £5 of reserves has been bought as a capital asset then such a dividend would be the return of capital to the shareholders of S, and to prevent this the balance of the profit and loss account of S on

[1]Since the 1981 Companies Act powers have been given to companies to purchase own shares.

acquisition is capitalised, i.e. it is brought into the computation as to whether there is goodwill or capital reserve and not shown in the consolidated balance sheet as a profit and loss account balance. On the other hand the whole of any profit made by S since acquisition will clearly belong to H's shareholders as H owns 100 per cent of the shares of S.

Exhibit 26.1

Where the holding company holds 100 per cent of the subsidiary company's shares.

H acquires the shares on 31 December 19-4. The balance sheets one year later are as follows:

H Balance Sheet as at 31 December 19-5

		£
Investment in subsidiary: 10 shares bought 31/12/19-4	(A)	18
Stock		11
Bank		3
		32
Share Capital		20
Profit and Loss		12
		32

S Balance Sheet as at 31 December 19-5

			£
Stock			14
Bank			2
			16
Share Capital	(B)		10
As at 31/12/19-4	(C)	5	
Profit for 19-5	(D)	1	
			6
			16

The shares were acquired on 31 December 19-4, therefore the calculation of the Goodwill or Capital Reserve is as the position of those firms were at that point in time. Thus for (A) £18 the firm of H obtained the following at 31 December 19-4, Shares (B) £10 and Profit and Loss (C) £5 = £15. Goodwill therefore amounted to £3. The profit of S made during 19-5 is since acquisition and does not therefore come into the Goodwill calculation. The figure of (D) £1 is a reserve which belongs wholly to H, as H in fact owns all of the shares of S. This (D) £1 is added to the reserves shown in the consolidated balance sheet.

H Consolidated Balance Sheet as at 31 December 19-5

	£
Goodwill	3
Stock (£11+£14)	25
Bank (£3+£2)	5
	33

	£
Share Capital	20
Profit and Loss (H £12+S£1)	13
	33

Exhibit 26.2

Where the holding company holds 100 per cent of the shares of the subsidiary and there is a post acquisition loss.

H Balance Sheet as at 31 December 19-5

		£
Investment in subsidiary:		
10 shares bought 31/12/19-4	(E)	19
Stock		10
Bank		4
		33

	£	£
Share Capital		20
Profit and Loss:		
As at 31/12/19-4	7	
add Profit 19-5	6	
		13
		33

S Balance Sheet as at 31 December 19-5

		£
Stock		9
Bank		2
		11

		£	£
Share Capital	(F)		10
Profit and Loss			
As at 31/12/19-4	(G)	4	
less Profit 19-5	(I)	3	
			1
			11

In calculating Goodwill, against the amount paid (E) £19 are cancelled the items (F) £10 and (G) £4, thus the Goodwill is £5. The loss (I) has been incurred since acquisition. A profit since acquisition, as in Exhibit 26.2, adds to the reserves in the consolidated balance sheet, therefore a loss must be deducted.

H Consolidated Balance Sheet as at 31 December 19-5

	£
Goodwill	5
Stock (£10+£9)	19
Bank (£4+£2)	6
	30
Share Capital	20
Profit and Loss (£13−(I)£3)	10
	30

Exhibit 26.3

Where the holding company acquires less than 100 per cent of the shares of the subsidiary and there is a post acquisition profit.

H Balance Sheet as at 31 December 19-5

		£
Investment in subsidiary: 8 shares bought 31/12/19-4	(J)	28
Stock		7
Bank		3
		38
Share Capital		20
Profit and Loss	£	
As at 31/12/19-4	10	
add Profit 19-5	8	
		18
		38

S Balance Sheet as at 31 December 19-5

			£
Stock			28
Bank			2
			30
Share Capital	(K)		10
Profit and Loss		£	
As at 31/12/19-4	(L)	15	
add Profit 19-5	(M)	5	
	(N)		20
			30

H has given (J) £28 to take over 80 per cent of (K)+(L) i.e. 80 per cent of (£10+£15) = £20. Therefore Goodwill is £8. The profit for 19-5 (M) £5 is also owned 80 per cent by H = £4, and as this has been earned since the shares in S were bought the whole of this belongs to the shareholders of H and is also distributable to them, therefore it can be shown with other Profit and Loss Account balances in the consolidated balance sheet.

The Minority Interest is 20 per cent of (K) £10+(N) £20=£6. It must be pointed out that, although the holding company splits up the profit and loss account balances into pre-acquisition and post-acquisition, there is no point in the Minority Interest doing likewise. It would however amount to exactly the same answer if they did, because 20 per cent of (K) £10+(L)£15+(M)£5 still comes to £6, i.e. exactly the same as 20 per cent of (N) £20+(K)£10 = £6.

H Consolidated Balance Sheet as at 31 December 19-5

	£
Goodwill	8
Stock (£7+£28)	35
Bank (£3+£2)	5
	48
Share Capital	20
Profit and Loss (H£18+£4)	22
Minority Interest: (Shares £2+Profit and Loss £4)	6
	48

If there had been a post-acquisition loss then this would have been deducted from H's balance of Profit and Loss Account £18 when the consolidated balance sheet was drawn up.

Review questions

26.1 H Ltd buys 100 per cent of the shares of S Ltd on 31 December 19-5. The balance sheets of the two companies on 31 December 19-6 are as shown, you are to draw up a consolidated balance sheet as at 31 December 19-6.

H Balance Sheet as at 31 December 19-6

	£	£
Investment in subsidiary:		
4,000 shares bought 31/12/19-5		5,750
Fixed Assets		5,850
Current Assets		2,400
		14,000
Share Capital		10,000
Profit and Loss Account:		
As at 31/12/19-5	1,500	
add Profit for 19-6	2,500	
		4,000
		14,000

S Balance Sheet as at 31 December 19-6

	£	£
Fixed Assets		5,100
Current Assets		1,500
		6,600
Share Capital		4,000
Profit and Loss Account:		
As at 31/12/19-5	800	
add Profit for 19-6	1,800	
		2,600
		6,600

26.2 H Ltd buys 70 per cent of the shares of S Ltd on 31 December 19- 8. The balance sheets of the two companies on 31 December 19-9 are as follows. You are to draw up a consolidated balance sheet as at 31 December 19-9.

H Balance Sheet as at 31 December 19-9

	£	£
Investment in S Ltd:		
7,000 shares bought 31/12/19-8		7,800
Fixed Assets		39,000
Current Assets		22,200
		69,000
Share Capital		50,000
Profit and Loss Account:		
As at 31/12/19-8	4,800	
add Profit for 19-9	9,200	
		14,000
General Reserve		5,000
		69,000

S Balance Sheet as at 31 December 19-9

	£	£
Fixed Assets		8,400
Current Assets		4,900
		13,300
Share Capital		10,000
Profit and Loss Account:		
As at 31/12/19-8	1,700	
less Loss for 19-9	400	
		1,300
General Reserve (unchanged since 19-5)		2,000
		13,300

26.3A H Ltd bought 55 per cent of the shares in S Ltd on 31 December 19-6. From the following balance sheets you are to draw up the consolidated balance sheet as at 31 December 19-7.

H Balance Sheet as at 31 December 19-7

	£	£
Investment in S Ltd: 2,750 shares		4,850
Fixed Assets		13,150
Current Assets		13,500
		31,500
Share Capital		30,000
Profit and Loss Account:		
As at 31/12/19-6	900	
add Profit for 19-7	600	
		1,500
		31,500

S Balance Sheet as at 31 December 19-7

	£	£
Fixed Assets		4,600
Current Assets		3,100
		7,700
Share Capital		5,000
Profit and Loss Account:		
As at 31/12/19-6	700	
add Profit for 19-7	500	
		1,200
General Reserve (unchanged since 19-3)		1,500
		7,700

26.4 H buys shares in S1 and S2 on 31 December 19-4. You are to draft the consolidated balance sheet as at 31 December 19-5 from the following:

H Balance Sheet as at 31 December 19-5

	£	£
Investment:		
S1: 6,000 shares		8,150
S2: 8,000 shares		11,400
Fixed Assets		21,000
Current Assets		12,000
		52,550
Share Capital		40,000
Profit and Loss Account:		
As at 31/12/19-4	2,350	
add Profit for 19-5	5,200	
		7,550
General Reserve		5,000
		52,550

S1 Balance Sheet as at 31 December 19-5

	£	£
Fixed Assets		9,900
Current Assets		4,900
		14,800
Share Capital		10,000
Profit and Loss Account:		
As at 31/12/19-4	1,100	
add Profit for 19-5	1,700	
		2,800
General Reserve (same as 31/12/19-4)		2,000
		14,800

S2 Balance Sheet as at 31 December 19-5

	£	£
Fixed Assets		6,000
Current Assets		4,000
		10,000
Share Capital		8,000
Profit and Loss Account:		
As at 31/12/19-4	500	
less Loss for 19-5	300	
		200
General Reserve (same as 31/12/19-4)		1,800
		10,000

26.5A H Ltd bought 40,000 shares in S1 Ltd and 27,000 shares in S2 Ltd on 31 December 19-2. The following balance sheets were drafted as at 31 December 19-3. You are to draw up a consolidated balance sheet as at 31 December 19-3.

H Balance Sheet as at 31 December 19-3

	£	£
Investments in subsidiaries:		
S1 Ltd 40,000 shares		49,000
S2 Ltd 27,000 shares		30,500
Fixed Assets		90,000
Current Assets		80,500
		250,000
Share Capital		200,000
Profit and Loss Account:		
As at 31/12/19-2	11,000	
add Profit for 19-3	16,000	
		27,000
General Reserve		23,000
		250,000

S1 Balance Sheet as at 31 December 19-3

	£	£
Fixed Assets		38,200
Current Assets		19,200
		57,400
Share Capital		50,000
Profit and Loss Account:		
As at 31/12/19-2	3,000	
less Loss for 19-3	1,600	
		1,400
General Reserve (as at 31/12/19-2)		6,000
		57,400

S2 Balance Sheet as at 31 December 19-3

	£	£
Fixed Assets		31,400
Current Assets		14,600
		46,000
Share Capital		36,000
Profit and Loss Account:		
As at 31/12/19-2	4,800	
add Profit for 19-3	3,400	
		8,200
General Reserve (as at 31/12/19-2)		1,800
		46,000

27

Inter-company dealings: indebtedness and unrealised profit in stocks

When a subsidiary company owes money to the holding company, then the amount owing will be shown as a debtor in the holding company's balance sheet and as a creditor in the subsidiary company's balance sheet. Such debts in fact have to be shown separately from other debts so as to comply with the Companies Acts. Such a debt between these two companies is however the same debt, and following the rule that like things cancel out, then the consolidated balance sheet will show neither debtor nor creditor for this amount as cancellation will have taken place. The same treatment would apply to debts owed by the holding company to the subsidiary, or to debts owed by one subsidiary company to another subsidiary company. The treatment is exactly the same whether the subsidiary is 100 per cent owned or not.

Exhibit 27.1

Where the subsidiary company owes money to the holding company.

H Balance Sheet

		£	£
Investment in subsidiary: 10 shares			10
Stock			13
Debtors:			
Owing from subsidiary	(A)	4	
Other debtors		7	
			11
Bank			1
			35
Share Capital			20
Profit and Loss			6
Creditors			9
			35

	£	£
Stock		6
Debtors		13
Bank		3
		22
Share Capital		10
Creditors:		
Owing to holding company (B)	4	
Other creditors	8	
		12
		22

H & S Consolidated Balance Sheet

	£
Stock (£13+£6)	19
Debtors (£7+£13)	20
Bank (£1+£3)	4
	43
Share Capital	20
Profit and Loss	6
Creditors (£9+£8)	17
	43

Unrealised profit in stock-in-trade

It is possible that companies in a group may not have traded with each other. In that case the stocks-in-trade at the balance sheet date will not include goods bought from another member of the group. Again it is also possible that the companies may have traded with each other, but at the balance sheet date all of the goods traded with each other may have been sold to firms outside the group, and the result is that none of the companies in the group will have any of such goods included in their stock-in-trade.

However, it is also possible that the companies have traded with each other, and that one or more of the companies has goods in its stock-in-trade at the balance sheet date which have been bought from another group member. If the goods have been traded between members of the group at cost price, then the consolidated balance sheet would not be altered just because of a change in the location of stocks-in-trade. This means that it would not offend accounting practice by adding together all of the stock figures and showing them in the consolidated balance sheet, as the total will be the total of the cost of the unsold goods within the group.

Conversely, goods are usually sold between members of the group at prices above the original cost price paid by the first member of the group to acquire them. If all such goods are sold by group members to firms outside by the balance sheet date then no adjustments are needed in the consolidated balance sheet, because the goods will not then be included in the stocks-in-trade. It would however be more usual to find that some of the goods had not been sold by one of the companies at the balance sheet date, so that company would include these goods in its stock-in-trade in its own balance sheet. Suppose that the holding company H owns all the shares in S, the subsidiary, and that H had sold goods which had cost it £12 to S for £20. Assume in addition that S had sold none of these goods by the balance sheet date. In the balance sheet of S the goods will be included in stock-in-trade at £20, while the profits made by H will include the £8 profit recorded in buying the goods for £12 and selling them for £20. Although this is true from each company's point of view, it most certainly is not true from the group viewpoint. The goods have not passed to anyone outside the group, and therefore the profit of £8 has not been realised by the group.

Going back to the basic accounting concepts, the realisation concept states that profit should not be recognised until the goods have been passed to the customer. As the consolidated accounts are concerned with an overall picture of the group, and the profits have not been realised by the group, then such profits should be eliminated. Accordingly the figure of £8 should be deducted from the profit and loss account of H on consolidation, and the same amount should be deducted from the stock-in-trade of S on consolidation. This cancels an unrealised inter-group profit.

If H had sold goods which had cost it £12 to S, a 100 per cent owned subsidiary, for £20, and S had sold ¾ of the goods for £22 by the balance sheet date then the picture would be different. H will have shown a profit in its profit and loss account for these sales of £8. In addition S will have shown a profit in its profit and loss account for the sales made of £7, i.e. £22−¾ of £20. The two profit and loss accounts show total profits of £8+£7 = £15. So far however, looking at the group as a whole, these goods have cost the group £12. Three-quarters of these have been sold to firms outside the group, so that cost of goods sold outside the group is ¾×£12 = £9, and as these were sold by S the profit realised by the group is £22−£9 = £13. This is £2 less than that shown by adding up the separate figures for each company in the group. Thus the group figures would be over-stated by £2 if the separate figures were merely added together without any adjustment. In addition the stock-in-trade would be overvalued by £2 if the two separate figures were added together because the remaining stock-in-trade of S includes one-quarter of the goods bought from H, i.e. ¼×£20 = £5, but the original cost of the group was ¼×£12 = £3. The adjustment needed is that in the consolidation process £2 will be deducted from the profit and loss balance of H and £2 will be deducted from the stock-in-trade of S, thus removing any unrealised inter-group profits.

This could be expressed in tabular form as:

(a)	Cost of goods to H	£12
(b)	Sold to S for	£20
(c)	Sold by S, ¾ for	£22
(d)	Stock of S at balance sheet date at cost to S ¼ of (b)	£5
(e)	Stock of S at balance sheet date at cost to H ¼ of (a)	£3
(f)	Excess of S balance sheet value of stock over cost to group (d)−(e)	£2

(g) Profit shown in H profit and loss account (b)−(a) = £8
(i) Profit shown in S profit and loss account (c) £22 − ¾ of (b) £15 = £7
(j) Profit shown in the profit and loss accounts of H and S = (g) + (i) = £15
(k) Actual profit made by the group dealing with outsiders (c) £22 less (¾ of (a) £12) £9 = £13

(*l*) Profit recorded by individual companies exceeds profit made by the group's dealing with outsiders (*j*) − (*k*) = £2

The action needed for the consolidated balance sheet is therefore to deduct (*f*) £2 from the stock figures of H and S, and to deduct (*l*) £2 from the profit and loss account figures of H and S.

Exhibit 27.2

Where the stock-in-trade of one company includes goods bought from another company in the group.

H Balance Sheet as at 31 December 19-3

	£	£
Investment in subsidiary:		
10 shares bought 31/12/19-2		16
Stock-in-Trade		24
Bank		6
		46
Share Capital		20
Profit and Loss Account:		
As at 31/12/19-2	8	
Profit for 19-3 (C)	18	
		26
		46

S Balance Sheet as at 31 December 19-3

	£	£
Stock-in-Trade (D)		22
Bank		3
		25
Share Capital		10
Profit and Loss Account:		
As at 31/12/19-2	6	
Profit for 19-3	9	
		15
		25

During the year H sold goods which had cost it £16 to S for £28, i.e. recording a profit for H of £12. Of these goods two-thirds had been sold by S at the balance sheet date, leaving one-third in stock-in-trade. This means that the stock-in-trade of S (D) includes £4 unrealised profit ($\frac{1}{3} \times £12$). The figure of H's profit for the year (C) £18 also includes £4 unrealised profit. When consolidating the two balance sheets £4 therefore needs deducting from each of those figures.

In Exhibit 27.2 the subsidiary has been wholly owned by the holding company. The final figures would have been exactly the same if it had been the subsidiary which had sold the goods to the holding company instead of vice-versa.

H Consolidated Balance Sheet as at 31 December 19-3

	£
Stock-in-Trade (S £22 − £4 + H £24)	42
Bank (H £6 + S £3)	9
	51
Share Capital	20
Profit and Loss Accounts (S £9 + H £8 + £18 − £4)	31
	51

Partially-owned subsidiaries and unrealised profits

So far the examples looked at have been those where wholly owned subsidiaries have been concerned. The situation can be different when the subsidiary is only partly owned.

In Exhibit 27.2 the unrealised profit in stock-in-trade was £4, and in that case the subsidiary was 100 per cent controlled. Suppose that in fact the ownership of shares was 75 per cent then there would be more than one possibility:

(a) (i) That £4 is deducted from the stock-in-trade figure in the consolidated balance sheet, and correspondingly £4 is deducted from the profit and loss account of H when it is consolidated, there being no adjustment for minority interest,

or

(ii) That £4 is deducted from the stock-in-trade figure in the consolidated balance sheet. To correspond with this a proportion is deducted from the minority interest, in this case £4×25 per cent = £1, whilst the remaining holding company proportion of 75 per cent, £3, is deducted from H profit and loss account when consolidated.

(b) That the profit to be cancelled out be restricted to the proportion of control of the subsidiary. In this particular case the part of the profit to be cancelled out is restricted to 75 per cent, i.e. £3. This has to be deducted both from the stock-in-trade of S on consolidation and from the profit and loss account of H.

None of these methods is incorrect, and they are all in use. With (b) the view is taken that only part of the sale, in this case 75 per cent, is connected with the group, the other part of the sale of 25 per cent being to the minority interest and therefore this 25 per cent of profits can be said to be realised.

Obviously there are advocates for each of these methods. A student at his first acquaintance with consolidated accounts is more likely to want to master the basic mechanics, leaving the study of the suitability of certain methods until later in his course. The simplest to operate is certainly method (a) (i) and in point of fact it accords with the author's opinion of the best method. In using any of these methods the student should always indicate in his answer that he/she realises that more than one method could have been used. An asterisk against this part of the answer with a brief note shown below the balance sheet is sufficient, but it is dangerous to omit such a note, as the specimen answer from which the examiner is marking may have used one of the other methods, and it would be quite easy for him to mark the answer as wrong if a note was not appended.

Exhibit 27.3

Where the stock-in-trade of one company includes goods bought from another company in the group, and the holding company does not have 100 per cent of the shares in the subsidiary.

H Balance Sheet as at 31 December 19-6

	£	£
Investment in subsidiary:		
8 shares bought 31/12/19-5		16
Stock-in-Trade		25
Bank		1
		42
Share Capital		20
Profit and Loss Account:		
As at 31/12/19-5	3	
Profit for 19-6	19	
		22
		42

S Balance Sheet as at 31 December 19-6

	£	£
Stock-in-Trade		27
Bank		3
		30
Share Capital		10
Profit and Loss Account:		
As at 31/12/19-5	5	
Profit for 19-6	15	
		20
		30

Included in the stock-in-trade of S at 31 December 19-6 are goods bought by H for £10 and sold to S for £15. S had not sold any of these goods before 31 December 19-6.

		Methods	
	(ai)	*(aii)*	*(b)*
Goodwill	4	4	4
Stock-in-Trade:			
(ai) (25+27−5)	47		
(aii) (25+27−5)		47	
(b) (25+27−4)			48
Bank	4	4	4
	55	55	56
Share Capital	20	20	20
Profit and Loss Account:			
(ai) (S 80%×15+H3+19−5)	29		
(aii) (S 80%×15+H3+19−4)		30	
(b) (S 80%×15+H3+19−4)			30
Minority Interest:			
(ai) (Shares 2+P/Loss 20%×20)	6		
(aii) (Shares 2+P/Loss 20%×20=4−1)		5	
(b) (Shares 2+P/Loss 20%×20=4)			6
	55	55	56

Review questions

27.1 You are to draw up a consolidated balance sheet from the following details as at 31 December 19-9.

H Balance Sheet as at 31 December 19-9

	£	£
Investment in subsidiary:		
1,000 shares bought 31/12/19-8		2,800
Fixed Assets		1,100
Stock		1,200
Debtors		2,100
Bank		200
		7,400
Share Capital		2,000
Profit and Loss Account:		
As at 31/12/19-8	1,500	
Profit for 19-9	2,200	
		3,700
General Reserve		800
Creditors		900
		7,400

S Balance Sheet as at 31 December 19-9

	£	£
Fixed Assets		1,200
Stock		900
Debtors		1,400
Bank		300
		3,800
Share Capital		1,000
Profit and Loss Account:		
As at 31/12/19-8	950	
Profit for 19-9	1,150	
		2,100
Creditors		700
		3,800

During the year H had sold goods which had cost £150 to S for £240. None of these goods had been sold by the balance sheet date.

At the balance sheet date H owes S £220.

27.2 Draw up a consolidated balance sheet as at 31 December 19-4 from the following:

H Balance Sheet as at 31 December 19-4

	£	£
Investment in subsidiary:		
6,000 shares bought 31/12/19-3		9,700
Fixed Assets		9,000
Stock		3,100
Debtors		4,900
Bank		1,100
		27,800
Share Capital		20,000
Profit and Loss Account:		
As at 31/12/19-4	6,500	
Loss for 19-5	2,500	
		4,000
Creditors		3,800
		27,800

	£	£
Fixed Assets		5,200
Stock		7,200
Debtors		3,800
Bank		1,400
		17,600
Share Capital		10,000
Profit and Loss Account:		
As at 31/12/19-4	3,500	
Profit for 19-5	2,000	
		5,500
Creditors		2,100
		17,600

At the balance sheet date S owes H £600.

During the year H sold goods which had cost £300 to S for £500. Threequarters of these goods had been sold by S by the balance sheet date.

27.3 Draw up a consolidated balance sheet from the following details as at 31 December 19-8.

H Balance Sheet as at 31 December 19-8

	£	£
Investment in subsidiaries:		
S1 30,000 shares bought 31/12/19-7		39,000
S2 25,000 shares bought 31/12/19-7		29,000
Fixed Assets		22,000
Stock		26,000
Debtors		13,000
Bank		5,000
		134,000
Share Capital		100,000
Profit and Loss Account:		
As at 31/12/19-7	14,000	
add Profit for 19-8	9,000	
		23,000
General Reserve		2,000
Creditors		9,000
		134,000

S1 Balance Sheet as at 31 December 19-8

	£	£
Fixed Assets		22,000
Stock		11,000
Debtors		8,000
Bank		3,000
		44,000
Share Capital		30,000
Profit and Loss Account:		
As at 31/12/19-7	8,000	
less Loss for 19-8	5,000	
		3,000
General Reserve (as at 31/12/19-7)		4,000
Creditors		7,000
		44,000

S2 Balance Sheet as at 31 December 19-8

	£	£
Fixed Assets		21,000
Stock		9,000
Debtors		7,000
Bank		1,000
		38,000
Share Capital		30,000
Profit and Loss Account:		
As at 31/12/19-7	1,200	
add Profit for 19-8	1,800	
		3,000
Creditors		5,000
		38,000

At the balance sheet date S2 owed S1 £500 and H owed S2 £900.

During the year H had sold goods costing £2,000 to S1 for £2,800. Of these goods one-half had been sold by the year end. He had also sold goods costing £500 to S2 for £740, of which none had been sold by the year end.

27.4A You are presented with the following information from the Seneley group of companies for the year to 30 September 19-6:

	Seneley plc £'000	Lowe Ltd £'000	Wright Ltd £'000
Tangible fixed assets	225	300	220
Investments			
Shares in group companies:			
Lowe Ltd	450	–	–
Wright Ltd	130	–	–
	580	–	–
Current assets			
Stocks	225	150	45
Trade debtors	240	180	50
Cash at bank and in hand	50	10	5
	515	340	100
Creditors: amounts falling due within one year			
Trade creditors	(320)	(90)	(70)
Net current assets	195	250	30
	1,000	550	250
Capital and reserves			
Called-up share capital	800	400	200
Profit and loss account	200	150	50
	1,000	550	250

Additional information:

(*a*) The authorised, issued and fully paid share capital of all three companies consists of £1 ordinary shares.

(*b*) Seneley purchased 320,000 shares in Lowe Ltd on 1 October 19-3, when Lowe's profit and loss account balance stood at £90,000.

(*c*) Seneley purchased 140,000 shares in Wright Ltd on 1 October 19-5, when Wright's profit and loss account balance stood at £60,000.

(*d*) During the year to 30 September 19-6, Lowe had sold goods to Wright for £15,000. These goods had cost Lowe £7,000, and Wright still had half of these goods in stock as at 30 September 19-6. Minority interests are not charged with their share of any unrealised stock profits.

(*e*) Included in the respective trade creditor and trade debtor balances as at 30 September 19-6 were the following inter-company debts:
- Seneley owed Wright £5,000;
- Lowe owed Seneley £20,000; and
- Wright owed Lowe £25,000.

(*f*) Seneley writes off any goodwill arising on consolidation to reserves.

Required

Prepare the Seneley group's consolidated balance sheet as at 30 September 19-6. Your workings should be submitted.

(*Association of Accounting Technicians*)

27.5A You are to draw up a consolidated balance sheet as at 31 December 19-3 from the following:

H Balance Sheet as at 31 December 19-3

	£	£
Investment in subsidiaries:		
S1 75,000 shares bought 31/12/19-2		116,000
S2 45,000 shares bought 31/12/19-2		69,000
Fixed Assets		110,000
Stock		13,000
Debtors		31,000
Bank		6,000
		345,000
Share Capital		300,000
Profit and Loss Account:		
As at 31/12/19-2	22,000	
less Loss for 19-3	7,000	
		15,000
General Reserve (as at 31/12/19-2)		7,000
Creditors		23,000
		345,000

S1 Balance Sheet as at 31 December 19-3

	£	£
Fixed Assets		63,000
Stock		31,000
Debtors		17,000
Bank		3,000
		114,000
Share Capital		75,000
Profit and Loss Account:		
As at 31/12/19-2	11,000	
add Profit for 19-3	12,000	
		23,000
Creditors		16,000
		114,000

	£	£
Fixed Assets		66,800
Stock		22,000
Debtors		15,000
Bank		4,000
		107,800
Share Capital		80,000
Profit and Loss Account:		
As at 31/12/19-2	12,800	
less Loss for 19-3	2,400	
		10,400
General Reserve (as at 31/12/19-2)		6,400
Creditors		11,000
		107,800

At the balance sheet date S1 owed H £2,000 and S2 £500, and H owed S2 £1,800.

H had sold goods which had cost £2,000 to S2 for £3,200, and of these goods one-half had been sold by S2 by the year end.

28

Consolidated accounts: acquisition of shares in subsidiaries at different dates

Up to this point the shares bought in subsidiary companies have all been bought at one point in time for each company. However, it is a simple fact that shares are often bought in blocks at different points in time, and that the first purchase of shares in a company may not give the buyer a controlling interest.

For instance, a company S has an issued share capital of 100 ordinary shares of £1 each, and the only reserve of S is the balance of the profit and loss account which was £50 on 31 December 19-4, and two years later on 31 December 19-6 it was £80. H buys 20 shares on 31 December 19-4 for £36 and a further 40 shares on 31 December 19-6 for £79. There are two possibilities open when calculating pre-acquisition profits, and therefore Goodwill or capital Reserve. These are:

(a) To calculate these on the basis of shares bought as at date of each purchase, i.e. as at 31 December 19-4 and 31 December 19-6.

(b) To calculate them on the basis of the shares held when control was achieved, i.e. as at 31 December 19-6.

This would give different answers which are now shown.

	£	£
Method (a)		
Shares bought 31/12/19-4	20	
Proportion of Profit and Loss Account as at 31/12/19-4: 20 per cent × £50	10	
		30
Shares bought 31/12/19-6	40	
Proportion of Profit and Loss Account as at 31/12/19-6: 40 per cent × £80	32	
		72
		102

	£	£
Paid 31/12/19-4	36	
Paid 31/12/19-6	79	
		115

Goodwill therefore £115 − £102 =	£13	

Method (b)

Shares bought	60	
Profit and Loss Account of subsidiary of which control achieved 31/12/19-6:		
60 per cent × £80	48	
		108

Paid 31/12/19-4	36	
Paid 31/12/19-6	79	
		115

Goodwill therefore £115 − £108 = £7.

There does not seem to be any doubt that method (a) would be preferable for examination purposes. In fact both methods are used in practice. It would seem that method (b) would be preferred in practice where the shares bought prior to control constituted a relatively small part of the issued share capital, especially if in the earlier stages eventual control was not visualised. On the other hand where the purchases are all part of an overall plan to gain control of the company then method (a) is preferred.

In addition it has been conveniently assumed so far that all shares have been bought exactly on the last day of an accounting period. This will just not be so, most shares being bought part way through an accounting period. Unless specially audited accounts are drawn up as at the date of acquisition there is no up-to-date figure of Profit and Loss Account as at the date of acquisition. As this is needed for the calculation of Goodwill or Capital Reserve the figure has to be obtained somehow. Naturally enough specially audited accounts would be the ideal for the purpose of the calculation, but if they are not available a second-best solution is necessary. In this instance the Profit and Loss balance according to the last balance sheet before the acquisition of the shares is taken, and an addition made (or deduction – if a loss) corresponding to the proportion of the year's profits that had been earned before acquisition took place. This is then taken as the figure of pre-acquisition profits for Goodwill and Capital Reserve calculations.

Exhibit 28.1

Calculation of pre-acquisition profits, and goodwill, where the shares are bought part way through an accounting period.

H bought 20 of the 30 issued ordinary shares of S for £49 on 30 September 19-5. The accounts for S are drawn up annually to 31 December. The balance sheet of S as at 31 December 19-4 showed a balance on the Profit and Loss Account of £24. The profit of S for the year ended 31 December 19-5 disclosed a profit of £12.

	£	£
Shares bought		20
Profit and Loss Account:		
Balance at 31/12/19-4	24	
add Proportion of 19-5 profits before acquisition 9/12×£12	9	
	33	
Proportion of pre-acquisition profits		
20 shares owned out of 30, ⅔ × £33		22
		42

Paid for shares £49

Therefore Goodwill is £49 − £42 = £7

Review questions

28.1 On 31 December 19-4 S Ltd had Share Capital £40,000 and Reserves of £24,000. Two years later the Share Capital has not altered but the Reserves have risen to £30,000. The following shares were bought by H Ltd 10,000 on 31 December 19-4 for £23,500, and on 31 December 19-6 14,000 for £31,000. Assuming that this completed an overall plan to gain control of the company you are to calculate the figure of Goodwill/Capital Reserve for the consolidated balance sheet as at 31 December 19-6.

28.2A On 31 December 19-6, S Ltd had share Capital of £400,000 and Reserves of £260,000. Three years later the Share Capital is unchanged but the Reserves have risen to £320,000. The following shares were bought by H Ltd 100,000 on 31 December 19-6 for £210,000 and 200,000 on 31 December 19-9 for £550,000. This completed the plan to take control of the company. Calculate the figure of Goodwill/Capital Reserve for the consolidated balance sheet as at 31 December 19-9.

28.3 H Ltd bought 50,000 of the 80,000 issued ordinary £1 shares of S Ltd for £158,000 on 31 August 19-8. S Ltd accounts are drawn up annually to 31 December. The balance sheet of S Ltd on 31 December 19-7 showed a balance on the Profit and Loss Account of £36,000. The profit of S Ltd for the year ended 31 December 19-8 showed a profit of £42,000. Calculate the figure for the Goodwill/Capital Reserve to be shown in the consolidated balance sheet as at 31 December 19-8.

28.4A On 1 January 19-1 S Ltd had a Share Capital of £300,000, a Profit and Loss Account balance of £28,000 and a General Reserve of £20,000. During the year ended 31 December 19-1 S Ltd made a profit of £36,000, none of which was distributed. H Ltd bought 225,000 shares on 1 June 19-1 for £333,000. Calculate the figure of Goodwill/Capital Reserve to be shown in the consolidated balance sheet as at 31 December 19-1.

29

Inter-company dividends

Not from pre-acquisition profits

These dividends are paid by one company to another. They will therefore be shown in the receiving company's own Profit and Loss Account as Investment Income, with a subsequent increase in its final Profit and Loss Appropriation Account balance and an equivalent increase in the bank balance. From the paying company's own accounts point of view, it has shown the dividend as a charge against its own Profit and Loss Appropriation Account, thus reducing the final balance on that account, and when paid there will be a reduction of the bank balance. If the dividend has been proposed, but not paid, at the accounting year end then it will be normal for the proposed dividend to be shown as a current liability in the subsidiary company's balance sheet, and as a current asset on the holding company's balance sheet as dividend owing from the subsidiary.

From the consolidated balance sheet point of view (making an assumption about pre-acquisition profit shown in detail later) no action is needed. It is a past event which is automatically cancelled when drafting the consolidated balance sheet as they are like things.

If paid from pre-acquisition profits

In Chapter 26 the company law principle that dividends should not be paid out of capital was reiterated. To prevent this happening the pre-acquisition profits were capitalized and brought into the Goodwill or Capital Reserve calculation. A company cannot circumvent the principle by buying the shares of a company, part of the purchase price being for the reserves of the subsidiary, and then utilising those reserves by paying itself dividends, and consequently adding those dividends to its own profits and then declaring an increased dividend itself. The next two exhibits are drawn up to illustrate this.

Exhibit 29.1

Dividends paid from post-acquisition profits.

H buys 100 per cent of the shares of S on 31 December 19-4. In 19-5 S pays a dividend of 50 per cent = £5 which H receives. To simplify matters the dividend is declared for 19-5 and paid in 19-5.

	£	£
Investment in subsidiary:		
10 shares bought 31/12/19-4		23
Stock		11
Bank		1
		35
Share Capital		20
Profit and Loss Account:		
As at 31/12/19-4	7	
add Profit for 19-5 (including dividend of £5 from S)	8	
		15
		35

S Balance Sheet as at 31 December 19-5

	£	£	£
Stock			19
Bank			7
			26
Share Capital			10
Profit and Loss Account:			
As at 31/12/19-4		12	
Profit for 19-5	9		
less Dividend paid to H	5	4	16
			26

The dividend is £5 out of profits made since the acquisition of £9. The dividend can be treated as being from post-acquisition profits, and can therefore be shown in the Profit and Loss Account of H as Investment Income and so swell the profits of H available for dividend purposes.

	£
Goodwill (£23−£10−£12)	1
Stock (H £11+ S £19)	30
Bank (H £1+ S £7)	8
	39
Share Capital	20
Profit and Loss Account;	
(H £7+ £8 + S £4)	19
	39

Exhibit 29.2

Dividends paid from pre-acquisition profits.

H Balance Sheet as at 31 December 19-4

	£
Investment in subsidiary:	
10 shares bought 31/12/19-4	23
Stock	7
Bank	1
	31
Share Capital	20
Profit and Loss Account	11
	31

	£
Stock	14
Bank	3
	17
Share Capital	10
Profit and Loss Account	7
	17

H Consolidated Balance Sheet as at 31 December 19-4
(immediately after acquisition)

	£
Goodwill (H £23− S £10− S £7)	6
Stock	21
Bank (H £1+ S £3)	4
	31
Share Capital	20
Profit and Loss Account	11
	31

The consolidated balance sheet already shown was drafted immediately after acquisition. The following balance sheets show the position one year later. It is helpful to remember that the calculation of goodwill does not alter.

H Balance Sheet as at 31 December 19-5

	£	£
Investment in subsidiary:		
£23 originally calculated less dividend from pre-acquisition profits £7)		16
Stock		18
Bank		5
		39
Share Capital		20
Profit and Loss Account:		
As at 31/12/19-4	11	
add Profit for 19-5 (does not include the dividend from S)	8	
		19
		39

S Balance Sheet as at 31 December 19-5

	£	£
Stock		8
Bank		2
		10
		10
Share Capital		10
Profit and Loss Account:		
As at 31/12/19-4	7	
add Profit for 19-5*	0	
less Dividend paid	7	–
		10

*For simplicity the profit of S for 19-5 is taken as being exactly nil.

H Consolidated Balance Sheet as at 31 December 19-5

	£
Goodwill	6
Stock	26
Bank	7
	39
Share Capital	20
Profit and Loss (P £19)	19
	39

It will be noticed that when a dividend is paid out of pre-acquisition profits it is in fact a return of capital to the holding company. Accordingly the dividend is deducted from the original cost of the investment; it is a return of the purchase money rather than be treated as Investment Income of the holding company. A common practice of many examiners, or 'trick' if you prefer to call it that, would have been to treat the receipt as investment income instead of as a refund of capital. Thus the balance sheet of H as at 31 December 19-5 in this exhibit would have read 'Profit and Loss Account £26' instead of 'Profit and Loss Account £19', and the Investment would be shown at £23 instead of £16. This means that the examiner really wants the examinee to adjust what is in fact an incorrect balance sheet, so that the only way is to adjust the holding company's balance sheet before proceeding with the consolidation of the balance sheets of H and S.

Proposed dividend at date of acquisition of shares

Quite frequently there will be a proposed dividend as at the date of the acquisition of the shares, and the holding company will receive the dividend even though the dividend was proposed to be paid from profits earned before acquisition took place. The action taken is similar to that in Exhibit 29.2, in that it will be deducted from the price paid for the shares in order that the net effective price is calculated.

Exhibit 29.3

Shares acquired in a subsidiary at a date when a proposed dividend is outstanding.

H Balance Sheet as at 31 December 19-3

	£	£
Investment in subsidiary:		
10 shares bought 31/12/19-2	22	
less Dividend from pre-acquisition profits	6	
		16
Stock		11
Bank		2
		29
Share Capital		20
Profit and Loss Account:		
As at 31/12/19-2	4	
Profit for 19-3	5	
		9
		29

S Balance Sheet as at 31 December 19-3

	£	£
Stock		19
Bank		4
		23
Share Capital		10
Profit and Loss Account:		
As at 31/12/19-4 (after deducting the proposed dividend £6)	5	
add Profit for 19-3	8	
		13
		23

	£	£
Goodwill (see workings below)		1
Stock		30
Bank		6
		37
Share Capital		20
Profit and Loss Account:		
(H £9 + S £8)		17
		37

Calculation of Goodwill

	£	£
Paid		22
less Shares taken over	10	
less Profit and Loss balance at 31/12/19-2	5	
less Dividend paid from pre-acquisition profits	6	
		21
Goodwill		1

Proposed dividends

When a dividend is proposed by a company it will be shown as a current liability in its balance sheet. This is just as true for a subsidiary company as it would be for a company which is not controlled by another company. It is common practice for the holding company to show a proposed dividend from a subsidiary for an accounting period as being receivable in the same accounting period. Thus the subsidiary will show the proposed dividend as a current liability and the holding company will show it as a current asset. However, as this is merely another form of inter-indebtedness the amounts owing must be cancelled out when drawing up the consolidated balance sheet. Where the subsidiary is owned 100 per cent by the holding company then the two items will cancel out fully.

When the subsidiary is only part-owned there is the question of the minority interest. The cancellation of the part of the proposed dividend payable to the holding company is effected, and the remainder of the proposed dividend of the subsidiary will be that part owing to the minority interest. This can be dealt with in two ways, both acceptable in accounting:

(*a*) The part of the proposed dividend due to the minority interest is added back to the minority interest figure in the consolidated balance sheet.

(*b*) To show the part of the proposed dividend due to the minority interest as a current liability in the consolidated balance sheet.

It must be borne in mind that nothing that has been said refers in any way to the proposed dividends of the holding company. These will simply be shown as a current liability in the consolidated balance sheet.

Method (*b*) would seem to be the better method. For instance, when considering the working capital or liquidity of the group it is essential that all current liabilities due to external parties should be brought into calculation. If the proposed dividend soon to be paid to persons outside the group was excluded, this could render the calculations completely invalid.

Exhibit 29.4

Where a subsidiary has proposed a dividend, and there is a minority interest share in the subsidiary.

This will be shown using method (*b*) just described.

H Balance Sheet as at 31 December 19-3

	£
Investment in subsidiary:	
6 shares bought 31/12/19-1	17
Stock	19
Proposed dividend receivable from S	3
Bank	1
	40
Share Capital	20
Profit and Loss Account	11
Proposed dividend (of the holding company)	9
	40

S Balance Sheet as at 31 December 19-3

	£
Stock	23
Bank	7
	30
Share Capital	10
Profit and Loss Account	15
Proposed Dividend	5
	30

Note: At the date of acquisition of the shares on 31 December 19-1 the profit and loss account balance of S was £10, and there were no proposed dividends at that date.

	£	£
Goodwill (see workings)		5
Stock		42
Bank		8
		55
Share Capital		20
Profit and Loss Account (see workings below)		14
Minority Interest:		
Shares	4	
Profit and Loss 2/5ths	6	
Current Liabilities:		10
Proposed dividends of Holding Company	9	
Owing to Minority Interest	2	
		11
		55

Workings:	£	£	£
Profit and Loss Account:			
H's Profit and Loss balance			11
S's Profit and Loss balance		15	
less Owned by Minority Interest: 2/5ths × £15	6		
less Pre-acquisition profits at 31/12/19-1 bought by holding company: 3/5ths × £10	6		
		12	
			3
			14

Goodwill:			
Paid			17
less Shares bought		6	
less Pre-acquisition profits 3/5ths × £10		6	
			12
			5

If method (*a*) had been used then the consolidated balance sheet would be as shown except for Minority Interest and Current Liabilities. These would have appeared:

	£	£
Minority Interest:		
Shares	4	
Profit and Loss	8	
Current Liabilities:		12
Proposed Dividend		9

Review questions

29.1 The following balance sheets were drawn up as at 31 December 19-7. The person drafting the balance sheet of H Ltd was not too sure of an item and has shown it as a suspense item.

H Balance Sheet as at 31 December 19-7

	£	£
Investment in subsidiary:		
20,000 shares bought 31/12/19-6		29,000
Fixed Assets		40,000
Current Assets		5,000
		74,000
Share Capital		50,000
Profit and Loss Account:		
As at 31/12/19-6	8,000	
add Profit for 19-7	11,000	
		19,000
Suspense*		5,000
		74,000

*The suspense item consists of the dividend received from S in January 19- 7.

S Balance Sheet as at 31 December 19-7

	£	£
Fixed Assets		17,000
Current Assets		10,000
		27,000
Share Capital		20,000
Profit and Loss Account:		
As at 31/12/19-6*	3,000	
add Profit for 19-7	4,000	
		7,000
		27,000

*The balance of £3,000 is after deducting the proposed dividend for 19-6 of £5,000.

Draw up the consolidated balance sheet as at 31 December 19-7.

29.2A The following balance sheets of H Ltd and S Ltd were drawn up as at 31 December 19-4. Draw up the consolidated balance sheet as at that date.

H Balance Sheet as at 31 December 19-4

	£	£
Investment in subsidiary:		
100,000 shares bought 31/12/19-3		194,000
Fixed Assets		250,000
Current Assets		59,000
		503,000
Share Capital		400,000
Profit and Loss Account:		
As at 31/12/19-3	39,000	
add Profit for 19-4*	64,000	
		103,000
		503,000

*The profit figure for 19-4 includes the dividend of £20,000 received from S Ltd for the year 19-3.

S Balance Sheet as at 31 December 19-4

	£	£
Fixed Assets		84,000
Current Assets		49,000
		133,000
Share Capital		100,000
Profit and Loss Account:		
As at 31/12/19-3*	11,000	
add Profit for 19-4	22,000	
		33,000
		133,000

*The balance of £11,000 is after deducting the proposed dividend for 19-3 £20,000.

29.3 Draw up a consolidated balance sheet as at 31 December 19-9 from the following information.

H Balance Sheet as at 31 December 19-9

	£	£
Investment in subsidiary:		
30,000 shares bought 31/12/19-8		47,000
Fixed Assets		44,000
Current Assets		12,000
		103,000
Share Capital		80,000
Profit and Loss Account:		
As at 31/12/19-8	14,000	
add Profit for 19-9	9,000	
		23,000
		103,000

S Balance Sheet as at 31 December 19-9

	£	£
Fixed Assets		36,000
Current Assets		21,000
		57,000
Share Capital		40,000
Profit and Loss Account:		
As at 31/12/19-8	4,000	
add Profit for 19-9	7,000	
		11,000
Proposed Dividend for 19-9		6,000
		57,000

The proposed dividend of S has not yet been brought into the accounts of H Ltd.

29.4A The balance sheets of H Ltd and S Ltd are as follows:

H Balance Sheet as at 31 December 19-4

	£	£
Investment in subsidiary:		
120,000 shares bought 31/12/19-3		230,000
Fixed Assets		300,000
Current Assets		75,000
		605,000
Share Capital		500,000
Profit and Loss Account:		
As at 31/12/19-3	64,000	
add Profit for 19-4	41,000	
		105,000
		605,000

S Balance Sheet as at 31 December 19-4

	£	£
Fixed Assets		203,000
Current Assets		101,000
		304,000
Share Capital		200,000
Profit and Loss Account:		
As at 31/12/19-3	51,000	
add Profit for 19-4	13,000	
		64,000
Proposed Dividend for 19-4		40,000
		304,000

The proposed dividend of S has not yet been brought into the accounts of H Ltd.
Draw up the consolidated balance sheet as at 31 December 19-4.

29.5 The following are the summarised balance sheets of H Ltd and S Ltd at 31 December 19-6.

	H Limited		S Limited	
	£	£	£	£
Tangible fixed assets (see note (a))		320,000		360,000
Loan to S Ltd		50,000		
Investment in S Ltd		250,000		
Current assets:				
Stocks	110,000		50,000	
Debtors	100,000		40,000	
Bank	30,000		10,000	
	240,000		100,000	
Creditors: amounts falling due within one year:				
Trade creditors	190,000		22,000	
Proposed preference dividend	–		8,000	
		(190,000)		(30,000)
Total assets *less* current liabilities		£670,000		£430,000
Capital and reserves:				
Ordinary shares of £1 each, fully paid		500,000		200,000
8% preference shares of £1 each, fully paid		–		100,000
Reserves		170,000		80,000
Loan from H Ltd		–		50,000
		£670,000		£430,000

Notes:
(a) Tangible fixed assets:

H Limited	Cost	Cumulative depreciation	W D V
	£	£	£
Buildings	120,000	10,000	110,000
Plant and machinery	200,000	40,000	160,000
Motor vehicles	80,000	30,000	50,000
	400,000	80,000	320,000

Tangible fixed assets:

S Limited	Cost	Cumulative depreciation	WDV
	£	£	£
Buildings	300,000	100,000	200,000
Plant and machinery	120,000	30,000	90,000
Motor vehicles	130,000	60,000	70,000
	550,000	190,000	360,000

There were no additions or disposals of fixed assets by the group during the year.

(b) H Limited acquired its holding on 1 January 19-6, when the balance on S Limited's reserves stood at £50,000. The investment consists of 150,000 ordinary shares of £1 each, fully paid, purchased for £250,000.

(c) H Limited credited to its profit and loss account a dividend of £7,500 from S Limited in March 19-6, in respect of the shares acquired on 1 January 19-6. S Limited does not intend to pay an ordinary dividend for the year ended 31 December 19-6.

Required:
Prepare a consolidated balance sheet for H Limited and its subsidiary S Limited at 31 December 19-6.
Note: Ignore taxation.
(Chartered Institute of Management Accountants)
29.6 X plc acquired 80% of the ordinary share capital of Y plc on 1 January 19-6 for £300,000.

The following lists of balances of the two companies at 31 December 19-6 were:

	X plc £000	Y plc £000
Called-up share capital:		
400,000 ordinary shares of £1 each, fully paid	400	
300,000 ordinary shares of £0.50 each, fully paid		150
Reserves as at 1 January 19-6	220	90
Retained profits for 19-6	20	18
Trade creditors	130	80
Taxation	30	14
Proposed final dividend	20	10
Depreciation provisions:		
Freehold property	12	6
Plant and machinery	40	12
Current account		14
	872	394
Tangible fixed assets:		
Freehold property, at cost	120	160
Plant and machinery, at cost	183	62
Investment in Y plc	300	
Stocks	80	70
Debtors	160	90
Bank	10	12
Current account	19	
	872	394

Notes:

(*a*) A remittance of £2,000 from Y plc to X plc in December 19-6, was not received by X plc until January 19-7.

(*b*) Goods, with an invoice value of £3,000, were despatched by X plc in December 19-6 but not received by Y plc until January 19-7. The profit element included in this amount was £400.

(*c*) Included in the stock of Y plc at 31 December 19-6, were goods purchased from X plc for £10,000. The profit element included in this amount was £2,000.

(*d*) It is group policy to exclude all profit on any inter-company transactions.

(*e*) No interim dividend was paid in 19-6 by either company.

(*f*) Ignore the ACT on the proposed final dividend.

(*g*) Goodwill is to be written off against reserves.

Required:

Prepare a consolidated balance sheet for X plc and its subsidiary Y plc as at 31 December 19-6.

(*Chartered Institute of Management Accountants*)

29.7A H plc acquired 80% of the ordinary share capital of S plc for £150,000 and 50% of the issued 10% cumulative preference shares for £10,000, both purchases being effected on 1 May 19-7. There have been no changes in the issued share capital of S plc since that date. The following balances are taken from the books of the two companies at 30 April 19-8:

	H plc £000	S plc £000
Ordinary share capital (£1 shares)	300	100
10% cumulative preference shares (50p shares)	–	20
Share premium account	20	10
General reserve	68	15
Profit and loss account	50	35
Trade creditors	35	22
Taxation	50	30
Proposed dividends	15	10
Depreciation		
Freehold property	40	15
Plant and machinery	100	48
	678	305
Freehold property at cost	86	55
Plant and machinery at cost	272	168
Investment in S plc	160	–
Stocks	111	65
Debtors	30	15
Cash	19	2
	678	305

The following additional information is available:

(*a*) Stocks of H plc include goods purchased from S plc for £20,000. S plc charged out these stocks at cost plus 25%.

(*b*) Proposed dividend of S plc includes a full year's preference dividend. No interim dividends were paid during the year by either company.

(*c*) Creditors of H plc include £6,000 payable to S plc in respect of stock purchases. Debtors of S plc include £10,000 due from H plc. The holding company sent a cheque for £4,000 to its subsidiary on 29 April 19-8 which was not received by S plc until May 19-8.

(*d*) At 1 May 19-7 the balances on the reserves of S plc were as follows:

	£000
Share premium	10
General reserve	20
Profit and loss account	30

(*e*) Goodwill is to be written off against reserves.

Required:

(*a*) Prepare a consolidated balance sheet for H plc and its subsidiary S plc at 30 April 19-8. Ignore the ACT on the proposed final dividend

Notes to the accounts are not required. Workings must be shown.

(*b*) explain what is meant by the term 'cost of control' and justify your treatment of this item in the above accounts.

(*Chartered Institute of Management Accountants*)

30

Consolidated balance sheets: sundry matters

Preference shares

It should be remembered that preference shares do not carry voting powers under normal conditions, nor do they possess a right to the reserves of the company. Contrast this with ordinary shares which, when bought, will give the holding company voting rights and also a proportionate part of the reserves of the company.

This means that the calculation of Goodwill or Capital Reserve on the purchase of preference shares is very simple indeed. If 9 Preference Shares of £1 each are bought for £12 then Goodwill will be £3, while if 20 Preference Shares of £1 each are bought for £16 then the Capital Reserve will be £4. The amount of Goodwill or Capital Reserve on the purchase of preference shares is not shown separately from that calculated on the purchase of ordinary shares, instead the figures will be amalgamated to throw up one figure only on the consolidated balance sheet.

Preference Shares owned by the minority interest are simply shown as part of the minority interest figure in the consolidated balance sheet, each share being shown at nominal value.

Sale of fixed assets between members of the group

There is obviously nothing illegal in one company in the group selling items in the nature of fixed assets to another company in the group. If the sale is at the cost price originally paid for it by the first company, then no adjustment will be needed in the consolidated balance sheet. Rather more often the sale will be at a price different from the original cost price. The inter-company unrealised profit must be eliminated in a similar fashion to that taken for the unrealised profit in trading stock as described in Chapter 27.

If the fixed asset is shown at its cost to the group in the consolidated balance sheet rather than at the cost to the particular company, then obviously the depreciation figures on that fixed asset should be adjusted to that based on the group cost rather than of the cost of the particular company.

Exhibit 30.1

H Balance Sheet as at 31 December 19-6

	£	£
Investment in S:		
50 shares bought 31/12/19-5		95
Fixed Assets	78	
less Depreciation	23	
		55
Current Assets		20
		170
Share Capital		100
Profit and Loss Account:		
As at 31/12/19-6	30	
For the year 19-6	40	
		70
		170

S Balance Sheet as at 31 December 19-6

	£	£
Fixed Assets	80	
less Depreciation	20	
		60
Current Assets		35
		95
Share Capital		50
Profit and Loss Account:		
As at 31/12/19-5	20	
For the year 19-6	25	
		45
		95

During the year H Ltd had sold a fixed asset which had cost it £20 to S Ltd for £28. Of the figure of £20 depreciation in the balance sheet of S, £7 refers to this asset and £13 to the other assets. The rate of depreciation is 25 per cent. The £8 profit is included in the figure of £40 profit for 19-6 in the balance sheet of H.

This means that the figure of £8 needs cancelling from the asset costs in the consolidated balance sheet and from the Profit and Loss Account balance. In addition the figure of depreciation needs adjusting downward, from the £7 as shown on the balance sheet of S, to the figure of £5, i.e. 25 per cent depreciation based on the cost of the asset to the group. This in turn means that the figure of profit for S £25 needs increasing by £2, as, instead of the expense of £7 depreciation there will now be a reduced expense of £5. The consolidated balance sheet becomes:

	£	£
Goodwill		25
Fixed Assets	150	
less Depreciation	41	
		109
Current Assets		55
		189
Share Capital		100
Profit and Loss Account:		
(H £70 − £8 + S £25 + £2)		89
		189

Revaluation of fixed assets

The consolidated balance sheet should give a picture that is not clouded by the method of drafting consolidated accounts. The consolidation process is looked at from the point of view that the holding company acquires shares in a company, and thereby achieves control of that company, and, in addition, it is recognised that the reserves are also taken over. It has been seen previously that the economic view is that of taking over the assets of another company, after all one does not buy such shares so that one possesses the share certificates, rather it is for the assets which are taken over and used. The consolidated balance sheet should therefore give the same picture as that which would have been recorded if, instead of buying shares, the assets themselves had been bought directly.

If, therefore, the fixed assets as shown in the balance sheet of the subsidiary were really valued at more than that figure when acquisition took place, then it would be better if the value of the fixed assets in the consolidated balance sheet was to be shown at that figure.

Such a revaluation can either be recorded in the separate accounts of the subsidiary companies themselves, or alternatively it can be brought into the workings when the consolidated balance sheet is drawn up.

It can be seen that, failing attention to the above, some rather strange results can occur. For instance, if H buys all the 10 shares of S for £18 when the reserves are £5, then the Goodwill calculation normally is:

	£	£
Cost		18
less share	10	
less reserves	5	
		15
Goodwill		£3

However, H might have bought the shares of S because it thought that, instead of the value of £15 assets as shown on the balance sheet of S (represented on the other side of the balance sheet by Shares £10 and Reserves £5), the assets were really worth £17.

In the eyes of H Ltd therefore it is giving £18 for physical assets worth £17 and the Goodwill figure is correspondingly £18−£17= £1. Assuming that the difference is in the recorded value of fixed assets, then the consolidated balance sheet will be showing a wrong picture if it shows Goodwill £3 and Assets £15. The revaluation upwards of the fixed assets by £2, and the consequent reduction of the Goodwill figure by £2 will redress the view.

Where there are depreciation charges on the revalued assets then this also will need adjusting.

Exhibit 30.2

H Balance Sheet as at 31 December 19-6

	£	£
Investment in subsidiary:		
30 shares bought 31/12/19-5		56
Fixed Assets	80	
less Depreciation for the year	16	
		64
Current Assets		26
		146
Share Capital		100
Profit and Loss Account:		
As at 31/12/19-5	20	
add Profit 19-6	26	
		46
		146

S Balance Sheet as at 31 December 19-6

	£	£
Fixed Assets	50	
less Depreciation for the year	10	
		40
Current Assets		14
		54
Share Capital		30
Profit and Loss Account:		
As at 31/12/19-5	3	
add Profit 19-6	21	
		24
		54

At the point in time when H bought the shares in S, the assets in S were shown at a value of £33 in the balance sheet of S. In fact however H valued the fixed assets as being worth £20 higher than that shown. The consolidated balance sheet will therefore show them at this higher figure. In turn the depreciation, which is at the rate of 20 per cent, will be £4 higher. The consolidated balance sheet therefore appears:

H and S Consolidated Balance Sheet as at 31 December 19-6

	£	£
Goodwill		3
Fixed Assets		
(£80+£70)	150	
less Depreciation (£16+£14)	30	
		120
Current Assets		40
		163
Share Capital		100
Profit and Loss Account:		
(H £46+ S £21 — increased depreciation £4)		63
		163

Review questions

30.1 From the following balance sheets and further information you are to draw up a consolidated balance sheet as at 31 December 19-8.

H Balance Sheet as at 31 December 19-8

	£	£
Investment in S:		
200,000 shares bought 31/12/19-7		340,000
Fixed Assets	300,000	
less Depreciation	100,000	
		200,000
Current Assets		103,000
		643,000
Share Capital		500,000
Profit and Loss Account:		
As at 31/12/19-7	77,000	
add Profit for 19-8	66,000	
		143,000
		643,000

	£	£
Fixed Assets	210,000	
less Depreciation	40,000	
		170,000
Current Assets		102,000
		272,000
		200,000
Share Capital		
Profit and Loss Account:		
As at 31/12/19-7	40,000	
add Profit for 19-8	32,000	
		72,000
		272,000

During the year H Ltd had sold a fixed asset, which had cost it £40,000 to S for £50,000. S has written off 20 per cent, i.e. £10,000 as depreciation for 19-8.

30.2A From the following balance sheets and supplementary information you are to draw up a consolidated balance sheet as at 31 December 19-5.

H Consolidated Balance Sheet as at 31 December 19-5

	£	£
Investment in S:		
10,000 shares bought 31/12/19-4		23,000
Fixed Assets	84,000	
less Depreciation	14,000	
		70,000
Current Assets		20,000
		113,000
		75,000
Share Capital		
Profit and Loss Account:		
As at 31/12/19-4	15,000	
add Profit for 19-5	23,000	
		38,000
		113,000

	£	£
Fixed Assets	26,000	
less Depreciation	10,000	
		16,000
Current Assets		12,000
		28,000
Share Capital		10,000
Profit and Loss Account:		
As at 31/12/19-4	6,000	
add Profit for 19-5	7,000	
		13,000
General Reserve		
(as at 31/12/19-4)		5,000
		28,000

During the year H sold a fixed asset to S. It had cost H £3,000 and it was sold to S for £5,000. S had written off £500 as depreciation during 19-5.

30.3

H Balance Sheet as at 31 December 19-7

	£	£
Investment in S:		
60,000 shares bought on 31/12/19-6		121,000
Fixed Assets	90,000	
less Depreciation for year	24,000	
		66,000
Current Assets		40,000
		227,000
Share Capital		150,000
Profit and Loss Account:		
As at 31/12/19-6	44,000	
add Profit for 19-7	33,000	
		77,000
		227,000

	£	£
Fixed Assets	70,000	
less Depreciation for year	7,000	
		63,000
Current Assets		28,000
		91,000
Share Capital		60,000
Profit and Loss Account:		
As at 31/12/19-6	17,000	
add Profit for 19-7	14,000	
		31,000
		91,000

When H Ltd bought the shares of S Ltd it valued the fixed assets at £95,000 instead of the figure of £70,000 as shown in the balance sheet of S.

Draw up a consolidated balance sheet as at 31 December 19-7.

30.4A

H Balance Sheet as at 31 December 19-5

	£	£
Investment in S:		
30,000 shares bought 31/12/19-4		53,400
Fixed Assets	60,000	
less Depreciation for year	6,000	
		54,000
Current Assets		10,600
		118,000
Share Capital		80,000
Profit and Loss Account:		
As at 31/12/19-7	27,000	
add Profit for 19-5	11,000	
		38,000
		118,000

	£	£
Fixed Assets	40,000	
less Depreciation for year	4,000	
		36,000
Current Assets		11,000
		47,000
Share Capital		30,000
Profit and Loss Account:		
As at 31/12/19-4	8,000	
add Profit for 19-5	9,000	
		17,000
		47,000

When H Ltd took control of S Ltd it valued the fixed assets at 31/12/19-4 at £50,000 instead of £40,000 as shown.

Draw up the consolidated balance sheet as at 31 December 19-5.

31

Consolidation of the accounts of a vertical group of companies

Subsidiaries and sub-subsidiaries

So far we have considered the case of holding companies having a direct interest in their subsidiary companies. In each case the holding company itself has bought the shares in its subsidiary companies. In each case over 50 per cent of the voting shares have been bought. In a straightforward case, where the holding company, H1 has bought shares in subsidiary companies S1 and S2 it could be represented by a diagram (Exhibit 31.1).

Exhibit 31.1

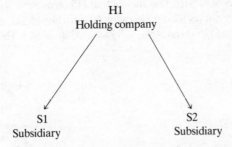

Suppose instead that H2 bought 100 per cent of the shares in S3, and that S3 then itself bought 100 per cent of the shares in S4. Because H2 controls S3 completely, and S3 controls S4 completely, therefore H2 controls both S3 and S4. This is shown as Exhibit 31.2.

If H3 owned S5 100 per cent, but S5 only owned 80 per cent of S6, then we can say that H3 owns 100% of 80% of S6 (*see* Exhibit 31.3). Similarly if in another case H4 owned 75% of S7, and S7 owns 80 per cent of S8, then H4 owns 75% $\times$ 80% = 60% (*see* Exhibit 31.4).

A subsidiary owned through the investment of another subsidiary is known as a **sub-subsidiary**.

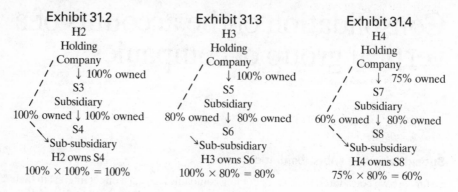

Exhibit 31.2	Exhibit 31.3	Exhibit 31.4
H2	H3	H4
Holding	Holding	Holding
Company	Company	Company
↓ 100% owned	↓ 100% owned	↓ 75% owned
S3	S5	S7
Subsidiary	Subsidiary	Subsidiary
100% owned ↓ 100% owned	80% owned ↓ 80% owned	60% owned ↓ 80% owned
S4	S6	S8
Sub-subsidiary	Sub-subsidiary	Sub-subsidiary
H2 owns S4	H3 owns S6	H4 owns S8
100% × 100% = 100%	100% × 80% = 80%	75% × 80% = 60%

In Exhibits 31.2, 31.3 and 31.4 the eventual ownership by H of each sub-subsidiary exceeds 50 per cent.

There will be cases where the ownership of the sub-subsidiary by the holding company is less than 50 per cent. Exhibit 31.5 shows where H5 owns 80 per cent of S9, and S9 owns 60 per cent of S10. This means that H5 owns 80% × 60% = 48% of S10. Exhibit 31.6 similarly shows where H6 owns 60 per cent of S11 and S11 owns 55 per cent of S12. Therefore H6 owns 60% × 55% = 33% of S13. Exhibits 31.5 and 31.6 illustrate the ownership.

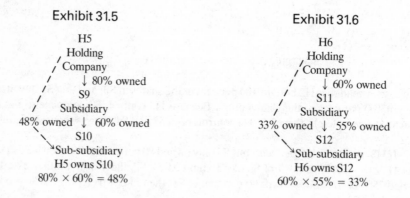

Exhibit 31.5	Exhibit 31.6
H5	H6
Holding	Holding
Company	Company
↓ 80% owned	↓ 60% owned
S9	S11
Subsidiary	Subsidiary
48% owned ↓ 60% owned	33% owned ↓ 55% owned
S10	S12
Sub-subsidiary	Sub-subsidiary
H5 owns S10	H6 owns S12
80% × 60% = 48%	60% × 55% = 33%

It might look as though S10 is not a sub-subsidiary of H5, because H5 owns less than 50 per cent of S10. However, H5 controls S9 as its ownership is over 50 per cent, and in turn S9 controls S10 as it owns more than 50 per cent. Effectively, therefore, H5 controls S10, and as such S10 is its sub-subsidiary.

Necessity for consolidated accounts and the Companies Act

Section 229 of the Companies Act 1985 exempts a wholly-owned, subsidiary from preparing consolidated accounts. For instance, in Exhibit 31.2 the subsidiary S3 would not have to prepare consolidated accounts, neither would S5 in Exhibit 31.3. This is due to the fact that there are no minority interest shareholders of S3 or of S5 to want to know the separate affairs of those subsidiaries.

However in each of cases S7, S9 and S11 in Exhibit 31.4, 31.5 and 31.6, there are minority shareholders. In practice, therefore, those subsidiary companies would have to prepare consolidated accounts, e.g. in Exhibit 31.4 consolidating S7 and S8.

Methods of consolidating accounts

There are in fact two methods of consolidating the accounts.

(a) The first one follows the reasoning already given in this chapter, i.e. computing the holding company's interest in the subsidiaries and the sub-subsidiaries and taking that percentage of the capital and reserves of these companies into the consolidation process. For instance in Exhibit 31.5 the capital and reserves would give 100% of H5 + 80% of S9 + 48% of S10.

(b) The second method first consolidates the balance sheets of the subsidiary and sub-subsidiary, and when that is done it is then consolidated with the balance sheet of the holding company. This recognises the fact that subsidiaries with minority interests have to produce consolidated accounts.

For an examination method (a) is to be preferred. It is a quicker method, and usually you will be short of time in an examination. Also an examination question will almost certainly ask for consolidation for all the companies and therefore there will be no need to do the intermediate consolidation. This book will therefore use method (a) only.

Consolidation technique

We are concerned here with method (a), just described. This is often called the 'direct' method. It follows mainly the same techniques as described in earlier chapters, but two points need stressing:

(a) **Cost of control account**, and the entry for the cost of investment.

(i) For subsidiaries, debit total cost of investment to cost of control account

(ii) For subsidiaries, debit cost of control account only with the proportion concerned with the holding company's share in the subsidiary which controls the sub-subsidiary. Debit minority interest account with the balance.

Given H investing £20,000 to buy 80% of shares of S1, then S1 investing £10,000 to buy 60% of shares of S2, the entries in the Cost of Control account (or its workings) would be:

Cost of Control

Cost of shares in S1	20,000
Cost of shares in S2 (80%)	8,000

The remaining proportion of investment by S1 is then debited to a Minority Interest account (or its workings)

Minority Interest

	£
Cost of shares in S2 (20%)	2,000

(b) Apportionment of share capital and reserves to cost of control account and to minority interest account.

(i) Cost of control. Take only the group's ultimate share of sub-subsidiary's share capital and reserves.

(ii) Minority interest. Include the balance of sub-subsidiary's share capital and reserves.

In the illustration given in (a (ii)) where H bought 80% of S1, and S1 bought 60% of S2, the ultimate share of the group is 80% × 60% = 48%. Therefore in the consolidated accounts 48% should come into group calculations and 52% shown in minority interest workings. Double entry: Cr Cost of Control account: Dr (appropriate) Reserve account.

A worked example (without proposed dividends)

Exhibit 31.7

H Ltd owns 80 per cent of the ordinary share capital of S1 Ltd. In turn S1 Ltd owns 75 per cent of the ordinary share capital of S2 Ltd. Both investments had been acquired on 31 December 19-4, one year previous to the following balance sheets:

Balance sheets December 19-5

	H Ltd		S1 Ltd		S2 Ltd	
	£000	£000	£000	£000	£000	£000
Fixed assets		40		4		27
Investments:						
Shares in S1		41				
Shares in S2				25		
Net current assets		19		6		28
		100		35		55
Share Capital		40		10		20
Profit and Loss						
As at 31.12.19-4	24		5		15	
add Profit 19-5	36	60	10	15	20	35
General reserve at 31.12.19-4				10		
		100		35		55

Ownership of H can be seen to be 80% of S1 and 80% × 75% = 60 per cent of S2. Any goodwill on acquisition to be written off to profit and loss.

We now will prepare a consolidated balance sheet on 31 December 19-5, one year after both acquisitions. In previous chapters the illustrations have been given on the face of the balance sheets. In this more complicated example we will use double entry accounts for the main items.

H Ltd and its subsidiaries

Consolidated Balance Sheet as at 31 December 19-5

	£000
Fixed Assets	71
Net Current Assets	53
	124
Share Capital	40
Profit and Loss (*see* account below)	60
	100
Minority interest (*see* account below)	24
	124

In the accounts which follow (ai), (aii), (bi) and (bii) refer to consolidation techniques already described.

Cost of Control

	£000		£000
Cost of Shares in S1 (ai)	41	Share capital S1 80% × 10	8
Cost of Shares in S2 80% (aii)	20	Share capital S2 60% × 20 (bi)	12
		Pre-acquisition Reserves:	
		Profit and Loss S1 80% × 5	4
		Profit and Loss S2 60% × 12	9
		General Reserve S1 80% × 10	8
		Profit and Loss: Goodwill written off	20
	61		61

Minority Interest

	£000		£000
Cost of shares in S2 20% (aii)	5	Share Capital S1 20%	2
Balance to consolidated balance sheet	24	Share Capital S2 40% (bii)	8
		Profit and Loss S1 20%	3
		Profit and Loss S2 40% (bii)	14
		General Reserve S1 20% × 10	2
	29		29

Profit and Loss

	£000		£000
Minority interest S1	3	H	60
Minority interest S2	14	S1	15
Cost of Control S1: Pre-acquisition	4	S2	35
Cost of Control S2: Pre-acquisition	9		
Cost of Control: Goodwill written off	20		
Balance to consolidated balance sheet	60		
	110		110

General Reserve

	£000		£000
Cost of Control 80% × 10	8	S1 balance b/f	10
Minority interest 20% × 10	2		
	10		10

A worked example (with proposed dividends)

Take the same companies as in Exhibit 31.7, but in this case the companies have proposed dividends at 31 December 19-5 of H Ltd £16,000, S1 Ltd £5,000, S2 Ltd £20,000. The balance sheets would have appeared:

Balance Sheets 31 December 19-5

	H Ltd		S1 Ltd		S2 Ltd	
	£000	£000	£000	£000	£000	£000
Fixed assets		40		4		27
Investments						
Shares in S1		41				
Shares in S2				25		
Net current assets (as before)		19		6		28
Dividends to be received	(80% of S1)	4	(75% of S2) 15			
		104		50		55
Share Capital		40		10		20
Profit and Loss	24		5		15	
As at 31.12.19-4 retained profits for 19-5						
(*see* below)	24	48	20	25	–	15
General reserve				10		
Proposed Dividends		16		5		20
		104		50		55

Note			
Retained Profit	H	S1	S2
Net profits 19-5	36	10	20
less proposed dividends	16	5	20
	20	5	–
add dividends receivable			
H 80% of S1 × 5	4		
S1 75% of S2 × 20		15	–
	24	20	–

Now a consolidated balance sheet can be drawn up.

H Ltd and its subsidiaries
Consolidated Balance Sheet as at 31 December 19-5

	£000
Fixed Assets	71
Net Current Assets	53
	124
Share Capital	40
Profit and Loss (*see* account below)	44
	84
Minority interest (*see* account below)	24
Proposed dividend	16
	124

The cost of control figures and goodwill in this Exhibit are the same as for Exhibit 31.7 as circumstances at dates of acquisition had not changed.

Profit and Loss

	£000			£000
Minority interest:		Balances	H	48
S1 20% × 25	5		S1	25
S2 40% × 15	6		S2	15
Cost of control (as before) S1	4			
Cost of control (as before) S2	9			
Cost of control: goodwill written off	20			
Balance to consolidated balance sheet	44			
	88			88

Minority Interest

	£000		£000
Cost of shares in S2 (20%)	5	Profit and Loss S1	5
Balance to consolidated		Profit and Loss S2	6
balance sheet	24	General Reserve 20%	2
		Share Capital S1 20%	2
		Share Capital S2 40%	8
		Proposed dividends S1	1
		Proposed dividends S2 (see note (a))	5
	29		29

Proposed Dividends

			£000
Minority interest S1	1	H	16
Minority interest S2 (20%)	5	S1	5
Consolidated balance sheet (H)	16	S2	20
Cancel against dividends receivable	19		
	41		41

Dividends Receivable

	£000		£000
H	4	Cancel against proposed	
S1	15	dividends (note (b))	19
	19		19

Notes:

(a) Credit is given to minority for 25% of S2 dividend, not 40%. This is because 25% is the amount actually received by them, while 75% is received by S1, and the minority interest in this dividend is automatically calculated when we calculate the S1 minority interest in profit and loss balance £25,000 at 20%. As the £25,000 figure already includes the dividend from S2 it should not be double-counted.

(b) The balances on dividends proposed and receivable cancel out, so nothing appears in the consolidated balance sheet.

(c) It would have been possible to show the proposed dividends applicable to minority shareholders, S1 £1,000 and S2 £5,000 as a current liability in the consolidated balance sheet, rather than show it as part of minority interest. This would seen to be the better method. For instance, when considering the working capital or liquidity of the group it is essential that all current liabilities due to external parties should be brought into calculation. If the proposed dividend soon to be paid to persons outside the group was excluded, this could render the calculations completely invalid.

Review questions

31.1 From the following balance sheets you are to draft a consolidated balance sheet for the group of H, S1 and S2.

H Balance Sheet as at 31 December 19-7

	£	£
Investment in S1:		
9,000 shares bought 31/12/19-6		23,000
Fixed Assets		99,000
Current Assets		25,000
		147,000
Share Capital		100,000
Profit and Loss Account:		
As at 31/12/19-6	15,000	
add Profit for 19-7	22,000	
		37,000
General Reserve		10,000
		147,000

S1 Balance Sheet as at 31 December 19-7

	£	£
Investment in S2:		
3,500 shares bought 31/12/19-6		6,000
Fixed Assets		22,000
Current Assets		5,000
		33,000
Share Capital		10,000
Profit and Loss Account		
As at 31/12/19-6	7,000	
add Profit for 19-7	16,000	
		23,000
		33,000

S2 Balance Sheet as at 31 December 19-7

	£
Fixed Assets	6,000
Current Assets	3,000
	9,000
Share Capital	5,000
Profit and Loss Account	
As at 31/12/19-6	1,000
add Profit for 19-7	3,000
	4,000
	9,000

31.2A From the following balance sheets prepare a consolidated balance sheet for the group of H, S1 and S2.

H Balance Sheet as at 31 December 19-9

	£	£
Investment in S1:		
16,000 shares bought 31/12/19-8		39,000
Fixed Assets		200,000
Current Assets		40,000
		279,000
Share Capital		200,000
Profit and Loss Account		
As at 31/12/19-8	43,000	
add Profit for 19-9	36,000	
		79,000
		279,000

S1 Balance Sheet as at 31 December 19-9

	£	£
Investment in S2:		
7,000 shares bought 31/12/19-8		13,000
Fixed Assets		16,000
Current Assets		4,000
		33,000
Share Capital		20,000
Profit and Loss Account		
As at 31/12/19-8	6,000	
add Profit for 19-7	4,000	
		10,000
General reserve (as at 31/12/19-8)		3,000
		33,000

	£	£
Fixed Assets		10,500
Current Assets		5,500
		16,000
Share Capital		10,000
Profit and Loss Account		
As at 31/12/19-8	1,000	
add Profit for 19-9	5,000	
		6,000
		16,000

31.3 On 1 April 19-1 Machinery Limited bought 80% of the ordinary share capital of Components Limited and on 1 April 19-3 Machinery Limited was itself taken over by Sales Limited who purchased 75% of the ordinary shares in Machinery Limited.

The balance sheets of the three companies at 31 October 19-5 prepared for internal use showed the following position:

	Sales Ltd		Machinery Ltd		Components Ltd	
	£	£	£	£	£	£
Fixed assets						
Freehold land at cost		89,000		30,000		65,000
Buildings at cost	100,000		120,000		40,000	
less						
Accumulated depreciation	36,000		40,000		16,400	
		64,000		80,000		23,600
Plant and equipment at cost	102,900		170,000		92,000	
less						
Accumulated depreciation	69,900		86,000		48,200	
		33,000		84,000		43,800
		186,000		194,000		132,400

Investments	Sales Ltd		Machinery Ltd		Components Ltd	
	£	£	£	£	£	£
Shares in Machinery at cost		135,000				
Shares in Components at cost				96,000		
Current assets						
Stocks	108,500		75,500		68,400	
Debtors	196,700		124,800		83,500	
Cash at bank	25,200		–		25,400	
		330,400		200,300		177,300
		651,400		490,300		309,700
Current liabilities						
Creditors	160,000		152,700		59,200	
Bank overdraft	–		37,400		–	
Corporation tax	57,400		47,200		24,500	
Proposed dividends	80,000		48,000		12,000	
		297,400		285,300		95,700
		£354,000		£205,000		£214,000
Ordinary shares		200,000		120,000		100,000
10% Preference shares		–		–		40,000
Revenue reserves		154,000		85,000		74,000
		354,000		205,000		214,000

Additional information

(*a*) All ordinary shares are £1 each, fully paid.

(*b*) Preference shares in Components Ltd are 50p each fully paid.

(*c*) Proposed dividends in Components Ltd are:

on Ordinary shares	£10,000
on Preference shares	£2,000

(*d*) Proposed dividends receivable by Sales Ltd and Machinery Ltd are included in debtors.

(*e*) All creditors are payable within one year.

(*f*) Items purchased by Machinery Ltd from Components Ltd and remaining in stock at 31 October 19-5 amounted to £25,000. The profit element is 20% of selling price for Components Ltd.

(*g*) Depreciation policy of the group is to provide for:

(i) buildings – at the rate of 2% on cost each year;

(ii) plant and equipment – at the rate of 10% on cost each year including full provision in the year of acquisition.

These policies are applied by all members of the group.

Included in the plant and equipment of Components Ltd is a machine purchased from the manufacturers, Machinery Ltd on 1 January 19-4 for £10,000. Machinery Ltd recorded a profit of £2,000 on the sale of the machine.

(h) Intra group balances are included in debtors and creditors respectively and are as follows:

				£
Sales Ltd	Creditors	–	Machinery Ltd	45,600
		–	Components Ltd	28,900
Machinery Ltd	Debtors	–	Sales Ltd	56,900
Components Ltd	Debtors	–	Sales Ltd	28,900

(i) A cheque drawn by Sales Ltd for £11,300 on 28 October 19-5 was received by Machinery Ltd on 3 November 19-5.

(j) At 1 April 19-1, reserves in Machinery Ltd were £28,000 and in Components Ltd £20,000. At 1 April 19-3 the figures were £40,000 and £60,000 respectively.

Required:

Prepare a group balance sheet at 31 October 19-5 for Sales Limited and its subsidiaries complying, so far as the information will allow, with the accounting requirements of the Companies Act.

(*Chartered Association of Certified Accountants*)

31.4A Bryon Ltd has held 1,500,000 shares in Carlyle Ltd for many years. At the date of acquisition, the reserves of Carlyle Ltd amounted to £800,000. On 31 March 19-6 Carlyle Ltd bought 400,000 shares in Doyle Ltd for £600,000 and a further 400,000 shares were purchased on 30 June 19-6 for £650,000.

At 30 September 19-6 the balance sheets of the three companies were:

	Bryon Ltd		Carlyle Ltd		Doyle Ltd	
	£	£	£	£	£	£
Freehold land and buildings – cost		950,000		1,375,000		300,000
Plant and equipment						
Cost	500,000		10,000,000		750,000	
Depreciation	280,000		7,500,000		500,000	
		220,000		2,500,000		250,000
		1,170,000		3,875,000		550,000
Investments						
1,500,000 shares in Carlyle Ltd		1,600,000				
800,000 shares in Doyle Ltd				1,250,000		
Stocks	50,000		2,050,000		850,500	
Debtors	325,000		2,675,000		1,700,000	
Cash at bank	25,500		–		16,500	
		400,500		4,725,000		2,567,000
		3,170,500		9,850,000		3,117,000
Creditors under 1 year	91,500		2,385,750		1,395,800	
Proposed dividend	200,000					
Bank overdraft	–		1,450,850		–	
		291,500		3,836,600		1,395,800
		2,879,000		6,013,400		1,721,200
10% Debenture		–		2,000,000		–
		2,879,000		4,013,400		1,721,200
		£		£		£
Ordinary shares of						
£1 each		2,000,000				1,200,000
50p each				1,000,000		
8% Redeemable preference shares of £1 each				2,000,000		
Reserves		879,000		1,013,400		521,200
		2,879,000		4,013,400		1,721,200

Proposed dividends have not yet been provided for on the shares in Carlyle Ltd and Doyle Ltd although Bryon Ltd has included dividends of 5p per share as receivable from Carlyle Ltd in debtors. Dividends on the preference shares were paid for one half year on 1 April 19-6, the next payment date was 1 October 19-6. Dividends on the ordinary shares in Doyle Ltd are proposed at the rate of 10p per share and on Carlyle's shares as anticipated by Bryon.

Profits for the year in Doyle Ltd were £310,000, before making any adjustments for consolidation, accruing evenly through the year.

The directors of Bryon Ltd consider that the assets and liabilities of Carlyle Ltd are shown at fair values but fair values for Doyle Ltd for the purposes of consolidation are:

		£
Freehold land and building		500,000
Plant and equipment – Valuation	968,400	
– Depreciation	639,600	
		328,800

Other assets and liabilities are considered to be at fair values in the balance sheet.

Additional depreciation due to the revaluation of the plant and equipment in Doyle Ltd amounts to £40,000 for the year to 30 September 19-6.

Included in stocks in Carlyle Ltd are items purchased from Doyle Ltd during the last three months of the year, on which Doyle Ltd recorded a profit of £80,000.

On 30 September 19-6 Carlyle Ltd drew a cheque for £100,000 and sent it to Doyle Ltd to clear the current account. As this cheque was not received by Doyle Ltd until 3 October, no account was taken of it in the Doyle Ltd balance sheet.

Required:

Prepare a balance sheet as at 30 September 19-6 for Bryon Ltd and its subsidiaries, conforming with the Companies Act so far as the information given will permit.

Ignore taxation.

(*Chartered Association of Certified Accountants*)

32

Consolidated profit and loss accounts

The consolidated profit and loss account is drawn up to show the profit (or loss) of the whole of the companies in the group, treating the group as a single entity. If all of the subsidiaries are owned 100 per cent, and there are no inter-company dividends or unrealised profits in stock, then it is simply a case of adding together all of the separate profit and loss accounts to form the consolidated profit and loss account. However, such a situation would very rarely be found.

Exhibit 32.1 shows the framework for a consolidated profit and loss account giving details of adjustments needed. Notes (a) to (h) follow the account.

Exhibit 32.1

Specimen Profit and Loss Account for the year ended …

		£000	£000	
Turnover	(a)		200	Holding company
Cost of sales	(b)		120	plus
Gross profit			80	subsidiaries less
Distribution costs		10		cancellation of
Administrative expenses		20	30	inter-company items
Profit on ordinary activities before taxation			50	
Tax on profit on ordinary activities	(c)		14	
Profit on ordinary activities after taxation			36	
Minority interest	(d)		4	
			32	
Extraordinary Profit	(e)	3		
Tax on Extraordinary Profit		1	2	
Profit for the Financial Year			34	
Retained profits from last year	(f)		7	
			41	
Proposed dividend	(g)	15		Holding company
Transfer to reserves	(h)	8	23	only
Retained profits carried to next year			18	

Notes:

(*a*) Turnover. Sales within the group to be deducted.

(*b*) Cost of Sales (i) Deduct purchases within the group. This is the same figure as for (*a*), as the price at which sales are made by one group company is the same figure at which the other group company has bought them. (ii) Adjust for unrealised profit in stock, by reducing closing stock. As cost of sales = opening stock + purchases − closing stock, any reduction in closing stock will increase 'cost of sales'. The balance sheet stock figure will be reduced by unrealised profits.

(*c*) Tax on profit on ordinary activities. This is the sum of tax for all companies within the group.

(*d*) Minority interest

(i) If ordinary shares only issued by subsidiary. Take requisite percentage of subsidiary's profits after taxation.

(ii) If preference shares also issued by subsidiary found by:

Minority interest percentage of preference share capital × total preference dividend for the year

plus

Minority interest percentage of ordinary share capital × balance of profits (i.e. after preference dividend) for the year.

(e.g.) Total Preference Shares £1,000: Minority interest £400.

Total Ordinary Shares £2,000: Minority interest £500.

Total preference dividend for year £150.

Profit of subsidiary after tax but before dividend: £950.

Minority interest is:		
Share of preference dividend: 40% × £150	=	£ 60
Share of balance of profits: 25% × (£950−£150)	=	£200
		£260

(*e*) Extraordinary profits (or losses)

These consist of the holding company plus group's shares in subsidiaries.

(*f*) This is holding company's retained profits

plus

Group's share of post-acquisition profit of subsidiaries.

(*g*) In respect of holding company only.

(*h*) Those of the holding company plus the group's share of the subsidiary's transfers to reserves.

We can now look at two examples:

(*a*) Exhibit 32.2. Consolidation of accounts where subsidiary owned 100 per cent.

(*b*) Exhibit 32.3. Consolidation where there is a minority interest in subsidiary company.

Exhibit 32.2

H Ltd owns 100 per cent of shares in S Ltd. Profit and Loss accounts of these companies for the year to 31 December 19-4 are as follows:

Profit and Loss accounts	H Ltd		S Ltd	
	£000	*£000*	*£000*	*£000*
Turnover		400		280
Cost of sales		270		190
Gross profit		130		90
Distribution costs	20		10	
Administrative expenses	30	50	15	25
Profit on ordinary activities before taxation		80		65
Tax on profit on ordinary activities		17		11
Profit on ordinary activities after taxation		63		54
Retained profits from last year		11		7
		74		61
Proposed dividend	40		30	
Transfer to reserves	5	45	2	32
Retained profits carried to next year		29		29

Notes:

(*a*) H Ltd had sold goods costing £10,000 to S Ltd for £15,000.

(*b*) At the balance sheet date 40 per cent of the goods in (*a*) had not been sold by S Ltd.

(*c*) There are no extraordinary profits or losses.

(*d*) Of the £7,000 retained profits from last year for S Ltd, £3,000 is in respect of post-acquisition profits.

The consolidated profit and loss of the group can now be drawn up.

H Ltd and subsidiary S Ltd
Consolidated Profit and Loss account for the year ended 31 December 19-4

	£000	£000
Turnover (*see* W1)		665
Cost of sales (*see* W2)		447
Gross profit		218
Distribution costs	30	
Administrative expenses	45	75
Profit on ordinary activities before taxation		143
Tax on profit on ordinary activities		28
Profit on ordinary activities after taxation		115
Retained profits from last year (*see* W3)		14
		129
Proposed dividend (W4)	40	
Transfer to reserves (W5)	7	47
Retained profits carried to next year		82

Workings: Letters (*a*) to (*h*) refer to the descriptions given.

(W1) H 400 + S 280 − 15 inter-company sales = 665 (*a*)

(W2) H 270 + S 190 − 15 inter-company purchases + unrealised profit in stock (40% × 5) 2 = 447 (*bi* and ii)

(W3) H 11 + S 3 = 14. Only post-acquisition profits of S included (*f*).

(W4) Only dividend of H included as S dividend will be received by H and will cancel out (*g*).

(W5) H 5 + S (100%) 2 = 7 (*h*).

Exhibit 32.3

H Ltd owns 80 per cent of shares in S Ltd. Profit and loss accounts of the companies for the year to 31 December 19-2 are as follows:

Profit and Loss accounts	H Ltd		S Ltd	
	£000	*£000*	*£000*	*£000*
Turnover		640		330
Cost of sales		410		200
Gross profit		230		130
Distribution costs	35		20	
Administrative expenses	70	105	55	75
Profit on ordinary activities before taxation		125		55
Tax on profit on ordinary activities		29		10
Profit on ordinary activities after taxation		96		45
Extraordinary profit	4		12	
Tax on extraordinary profit	1	3	2	10
Profit for the financial year		99		55
Retained profits from last year		29		25
		128		80
Proposed dividend	60		35	
Transfers to reserves	22	82	10	45
Retained profits carried to next year		46		35

Notes:

(*a*) S Ltd had sold goods costing £20,000 to H Ltd for £30,000.

(*b*) At the balance sheet date 30 per cent of the goods in (*a*) had not been sold by H Ltd.

(*c*) Of the £25,000 retained profits of S Ltd, £15,000 is in respect of post-acquisition profits.

H Ltd and subsidiary S Ltd

Consolidated Profit and Loss accounts for the year ending 31 December 19- 2

	£000	£000
Turnover (*see* W1)		940
Cost of sales (*see* W2)		583
Gross profit		357
Distribution costs	55	
Administrative expenses	125	180
Profit on ordinary activities before taxation		177
Tax on profit on ordinary activities		39
Profit on ordinary activities after taxation		138
Minority interest (*see* W3)		9
		129
Extraordinary profits (net of tax) (W4)		11
Profit for the financial year		140
Retained profits from last year (*see* W5)		41
		181
Proposed dividend (*see* W6)	60	
Transfer to reserves (*see* W7)	30	90
Retained profits carried to next year		91

Workings: Letters (*a*) to (*h*) refer to the descriptions given.

(W1)   H 640 + S 330 − intercompany sales 30 = 940 (*a*).

(W2)   H 410 + S 200 − intercompany purchases 30 + unrealised profit in stock (30% × 10) 3 = 583 (*b*i and ii). The method used here for the unrealised profit is the total one.

(W3)   20 per cent × 45 (profit after taxation of (*b*) = 9 (*di*).

(W4)   H 3 + S (80% × 10) 8 = 11 (*e*).

(W5)   H 29 + S (80% × 15) 12 = 41 (*f*).

(W6)   Only the dividend of H shown. See (*g*).

(W7)   H 22 + S (80% × 10) 8 = 30 (*h*).

Review questions

32.1 The following information relates to the Brodick group of companies for the year to 30 April 19-7:

	Brodick plc £000	Lamlash Ltd £000	Corrie Ltd £000
Turnover	1,100	500	130
Cost of sales	(630)	(300)	(70)
Gross profit	470	200	60
Administrative expenses	(105)	(150)	(20)
Dividend from Lamlash Ltd	24	–	–
Dividend from Corrie Ltd	6	–	–
Profit before tax	395	50	40
Taxation	(65)	(10)	(20)
Profit after tax	330	40	20
Interim dividend	(50)	(10)	–
Proposed dividend	(150)	(20)	(10)
Retained profit for the year	130	10	10
Retained profits brought forward	460	106	30
Retained profits carried forward	£590	£116	£40

Additional information:

(*a*) The issued share capital of the group was as follows:
Brodick plc: 5,000,000 ordinary shares of £1 each;
Lamlash Ltd: 1,000,000 ordinary shares of £1 each;
and
Corrie Ltd: 400,000 ordinary shares of £1 each.

(*b*) Brodick plc purchased 80% of the issued share capital of Lamlash Ltd in 19-0. At that time, the retained profits of Lamlash amounted to £56,000.

(*c*) Brodick plc purchased 60% of the issued share capital of Corrie Ltd in 19-4. At that time, the retained profits of Corrie amounted to £20,000.

(*d*) Brodick plc recognises dividends proposed by other group companies in its profit and loss account.

Required

In so far as the information permits, prepare the Brodick group of companies' consolidated profit and loss account for the year to 30 April 19-7 in accordance with the Companies Act 1985 and related statements of standard accounting practice. (Note: Notes to the profit and loss account are not required, but you should append a statement showing the make up of the 'retained profits carried forward', and your workings should be submitted.)

(*Association of Accounting Technicians*)

32.2A You are presented with the following summarised information for Norbreck plc and its subsidiary, Bispham Ltd:

Profit and loss accounts for the year to 30 September 19-7

	Norbreck plc	Bispham Ltd
	£000	£000
Turnover	1,700	450
Cost of sales	(920)	(75)
Gross profit	780	375
Administration expenses	(300)	(175)
Income from shares in group company	120	–
Profit on ordinary activities before taxation	600	200
Tax on profit on ordinary activities	(30)	(20)
Profit on ordinary activities after taxation	570	180
Dividends paid	(90)	(50)
proposed	(270)	(100)
Retained profit for the year	210	30
Retained profit brought forward	220	70
Retained profit carried forward	£430	£100

Balance sheets at 30 September 19-7	Norbreck plc £000	Bispham Ltd £000
Fixed tangible assets	1,280	440
Investments: Shares in group company	400	–
Current assets:		
Stocks	300	250
Debtors (including for Norbreck plc, the dividend proposed by the subsidiary)	280	150
Cash at bank and in hand	40	10
	620	410
Creditors (amounts falling due within one year):		
Trade creditors	(80)	(160)
Other creditors, taxation and social security	(160)	(70)
Proposed dividend	(270)	(100)
	(510)	(330)
Net current assets	110	80
Total assets less current liabilities	1,790	520
Provisions for liabilities and charges		
Taxation, including deferred taxation	(460)	(20)
	£1,330	£500

	Norbreck plc £000	Bispham Ltd £000
Capital and reserves:		
Called up share capital (ordinary shares of £1 each)	900	400
Profit and loss account	430	100
	£1,330	£500

Additional information:

(*a*) Norbreck plc acquired 80% of the shares in Bispham Ltd on 1 October 19-4. Bispham's profit and loss account balance as at that date was £40,000.

(*b*) Goodwill arising on acquisition is to be written off against the group's retained profits.

(*c*) Norbreck takes credit within its own books of account for any dividends receivable from Bispham.

(*d*) Ignore advance corporation tax.

Required:

Prepare Bispham plc's consolidated profit and loss account for the year to 30 September 19-7 and a consolidated balance sheet as at that date.

Note: Formal notes to the account are not required, although detailed workings should be submitted with your answer. You should also append to the consolidated profit and loss account your calculation of earnings per share and a statement showing the make up of 'retained profits carried forward'.

(*Association of Accounting Technicians*)

32.3A The following figures for the year to 30 April 19-6 have been extracted from the books and records of three companies which form a group:

	Old plc	Field Ltd	Lodge Ltd
	£	£	£
Revenue reserves at 1 May 19-5	30,000	40,000	50,000
Stocks at 1 May 19-5	90,000	150,000	80,000
Sales	1,250,000	875,000	650,000
Purchases	780,000	555,000	475,000
Distribution expenses	125,000	85,000	60,000
Administration expenses	28,000	40,000	72,000
Interim dividends:			
Paid 31 July 19-5, ordinary	45,000	35,000	15,000
Paid 31 October 19-5, preference		4,000	
Share capital – fully paid ordinary shares of £1 each	450,000	350,000	200,000
8% preference shares of £1 each		100,000	
Stocks at 30 April 19-6	110,000	135,000	85,000

Profits are deemed to accrue evenly throughout the year.

Other information:

(*a*) Corporation tax of the following amounts is to be provided on the profits of the year:

Old plc	£125,000
Field Ltd	75,000
Lodge Ltd	20,000

(*b*) Final dividends proposed are:

Old plc	15p per share
Field Ltd	12.5p per share on the ordinary shares and a half years dividend on the preference shares
Lodge Ltd	7.5p per share

(*c*) Field Ltd sells goods for resale to both Old plc and Lodge Ltd. At 30 April 19-6, stocks of goods purchased from Field Ltd are:

in Old plc	£40,000
in Lodge Ltd	28,000

The net profit percentage for Field Ltd on sales of these goods is 25%.

Old plc has £36,000 of these goods in stock at 1 May 19-5.

Total sales in the year by Field Ltd to Old plc were £150,000 and to Lodge Ltd £120,000.

(*d*) Old plc acquired the whole of the ordinary shares in Field Ltd many years ago. 50,000 of the preference shares were acquired on 1 August 19-5. Old plc acquired 120,000 shares in Lodge Ltd on 1 August 19-5.

Required:

A consolidated profit and loss account for Old plc and its subsidiaries for the year ended 30 April 19-6, together with any relevant notes.

(*Chartered Association of Certified Accountants*)

32.4A The following are the trial balances of ATH Ltd, GLE Ltd, and FRN Ltd as on 31 December 19-8.

	ATH Ltd £	GLE Ltd £	FRN Ltd £
Ordinary Share Capital (shares of £1 each, fully paid)	100,000	30,000	20,000
7 per cent Cumulative Preference Share			
Capital (shares of £1 each, fully paid)	–	–	5,000
Profit and Loss Account – balance at 31/12/19-7	15,600	6,000	1,900
Current Liabilities	20,750	15,900	18,350
Sales	194,000	116,000	84,000
Dividend received from GLE Ltd	1,200		
	331,550	167,900	129,250
Fixed Assets	45,000	29,000	25,000
Current Assets	46,000	27,500	22,500
24,000 Ordinary Shares in GLE Ltd at cost	33,700	–	–
20,000 Ordinary Shares in FRN Ltd at cost	21,250	–	–
Cost of Goods Sold	153,000	87,000	63,000
General Expenses	32,600	22,900	18,750
Dividend for 19-8, paid on 31/12/19-8	–	1,500	–
	331,550	167,900	129,250

ATH Ltd acquired the shares in FRN Ltd on 31 December 19-6, when the credit balance on the profit and loss account of FRN Ltd was £700, and acquired the shares in GLE Ltd on 31 December 19-7. No dividend was paid by either ATH Ltd or GLE Ltd for the year 19-7.

No dividend has been paid by FRN Ltd for the years 19-6, 19-7 and 19-8 and none is proposed. The directors of ATH Ltd propose to pay a dividend of £7,000 for 19-8.

The sales of GLE Ltd for 19-8 (£116,000) include £1,000 for goods sold to FRN Ltd and this amount has been debited to purchases account in the books of FRN Ltd. All these goods were sold by FRN Ltd during 19-8.

Required:

A consolidated trading and profit and loss account for the year 19-8 and a consolidated balance sheet as on 31 December 19-8 (not necessarily in a form for publication).

Ignore depreciation of fixed assets and taxation.

(*Institute of Chartered Secretaries and Administrators*)

33

Consolidated accounts: SSAP 23 Acquisition Accounting and Merger Accounting

Methods of combination of companies

When two limited companies are going to combine together in some way, then it is obvious that the shares must come under common ownership. There are two main methods of achieving this, with different possible methods of accounting for the combination.

1 **Acquisition accounting:** when needed.

A common method of combination is for one company, A, to purchase the shares in the other company, B. Often this is managed by making a cash payment to shareholders in B. They have then severed their links with the company. Company A shareholders now control both companies.

Issuing debentures (loan stock) by company A to company B's old shareholders, the new debenture holders, would not have effective voting power in the new group.

For both of these types of combination **acquisition accounting** should be used.

2 **Merger accounting:** when needed.

Alternative to 1 above is where company A does not pay cash or issue debentures to the old shareholders of company B. Instead it issues new equity (ordinary voting) shares to the old shareholders of B. This means that the shareholders of A and B have 'merged' into one, and between them have a joint interest in the new group. It is often called a **pooling** of interest.

A variance on this is the **new entity** method of combination. Here a new company C is formed to take over A and B, giving the old shareholders of A and B new shares in C. Once again the shareholders have 'merged' into one.

For both of these types of combination merger accounting may (not must) be used. If desired, acquisition accounting could be used instead.

Acquisition accounting method

In books of holding company:

(*a*) Shares purchased in a subsidiary company to be shown at cost less dividends received out of pre-acquisition profits.

(*b*) Dividends out of pre-acquisition profits cannot be regarded as available for distribution as dividends by the holding company.

In consolidated final accounts:

(*c*) Assets of the subsidiary to be shown in balance sheet at their fair value at the date of acquisition.

(*d*) The difference between the purchase consideration and the net assets (at fair value) at date of acquisition is treated as goodwill (or capital reserve if a negative figure).

(e) Post-acquisition profits only of the subsidiary to be included in consolidated reserves of the group.

The idea underlying these rules is to stop capital receipts, i.e. dividends from pre-acquisition profits, being paid out as dividends.

The consolidation of balance sheets using the acquisition method is now shown in Exhibit 33.1.

Exhibit 33.1

A Ltd has just made an offer of £270,000 for the whole of the share capital of B Ltd, and this has been accepted. Payment to be by cash. The 'fair value' placed on the tangible fixed assets of B Ltd, for the purposes of the merger is £148,000. Following are the two companies balance sheets, immediately before the merger on 31 December 19-3.

	A Ltd		B Ltd	
	£000			£000
Tangible fixed assets		400		120
Current Assets	450		200	
less current liabilities	130	320	90	110
		720		230
Ordinary shares £1		500		150
Revenue reserves		220		80
		720		230

The balance sheets of A Ltd, and of the group, immediately following the merger, are as follows:

Balance Sheet at 31 December 19-3

		A Ltd			The Group	
		£000	£000		£000	£000
Fixed assets						
Intangible (goodwill)		–		(W2)	12	
Tangible		400		(W3)	548	
Investments		270	670		–	560
Current assets	(W1)	180		(W4)	380	
less Current liabilities		130	50		220	160
			720			720
Share capital			500			500
Reserves			220			220
			720			720

Workings: £000

(W1)	Original current assets 450 − cash paid 270	=	180
(W2)	Paid for shares		270
	less net assets at take-over date	230	
	add increase in value of fixed to a		
	'fair value' 148 − 120 =	28	258
	Goodwill (intangible fixed asset)		12

(W3)   Fixed assets A Ltd 400 + B Ltd 148 = 548

(W4)   A Ltd (after payment) 180 + B Ltd 200 = 380

Merger accounting method

(*a*) Shares issued by the holding company are merely the means of achieving the merger in a technical sense. Consequently no share premium arises. They are shown in the holding company's balance sheet (A Ltd) at nominal value, as addition to share capital.

(*b*) As share premium is not recognised in (*a*) the cost of the investment in the holding company's balance sheet (A Ltd) is the nominal value of shares issued. If the nominal value of the shares is not the same as the stock exchange or similar market valuation, then obviously the 'true' value of the subsidiary is not shown in the 'cost' of the investment.

(*c*) Any dividends received by the holding company (A Ltd) from the subsidiary (B Ltd) can be distributed in full by the holding company. This means that the whole of the subsidiary reserves can be included in the consolidated balance sheet reserves.

(*d*) The assets of the subsidiary are not revalued at 'fair value' at the date of merger. It would not make sense to revalue B Ltd assets and to leave A Ltd assets value at the old values.

Sometimes, however, under the 'new entity' method of merger described on page 410 both companies revalue their assets.

(*e*) Where the total nominal value of the shares issued by the holding company A Ltd, is more than the total nominal value of the shares of B Ltd, the difference is deducted from group reserves. If the total is less, then the shortfall becomes a non-distributable group reserve.

Exhibit 33.2

Taking the same firms of A Ltd and B Ltd as in Exhibit 33.1, but instead of a cash offer of £270,000 – the offer is 200,000 ordinary shares of £1 each at a stock exchange value of £270,000.

The balance sheets of A Ltd and the group immediately after the merger are now shown:

	A Ltd		Group	
	£000	£000	£000	£000
Fixed assets				
Tangible	400			520
Investments	200	600		–
	───			
Current assets	450		650	
less Current liabilities	130	320	220	430
	───	───	───	───
		920		950
		───		───

Workings:

(W1)	Reserve A Ltd	220		
	B Ltd	80		300
		───		

less excess of nominal value shares issued by A Ltd over those exchanged of B Ltd, i.e. 200 − 150	50
	───
	250
	───

Final points per SSAP 23

As per SSAP 23 it is not necessary in the **merger method** to adjust values of the subsidiaries' assets and liabilities to **fair values**. However, adjustments should be made to achieve uniformity of accounting policies between the groups.

Remember that, in a merger, there is no such thing as **pre-acquisition profits**. Profits do not have such a restriction with regards to their distribution.

Review questions

33.1 Large plc, a manufacturer and wholesaler, purchased 600,000 of the 800,000 issued ordinary shares of a smaller company, Small Ltd, on 1 January 19-5 when the retained earnings account of Small Ltd had a credit balance of £72,000.

The latest accounts of the two companies are:

Summary Profit and Loss Accounts for the year to 30 September 19-6 (£'000s)

		Large plc		Small Ltd
Credit sales		10,830		2,000
Cost of sales and production services		3,570		1,100
Gross profit		7,260		900
Administrative and marketing expenses (including depreciation, audit fee and directors' remuneration)		2,592		180
Operating profit		4,668		720
Dividend received from Small Ltd		180		–
Net profit before tax		4,848		720
Taxation	2,304		200	
Net dividend	2,400		240	
		4,704		440
Profit retained		144		280
Brought forward from last year		1,200		192
Carried forward to next year		1,344		472

Summary Balance Sheets at 30 September 19-6 (£'000s)

	Large plc	Small Ltd
Intangible assets:		
Research and development:		
– pure research	20	–
– applied research	30	–
– development	180	–
Goodwill – purchased (at cost less amounts written off)	48	–
– unpurchased	50	–
Fixed assets at cost less depreciation	3,920	728
Investment in Small Ltd	525	–
Current account with Large plc	–	75
Stock	594	231
Debtors	2,250	370
Bank	99	24
	7,716	1,428
less Current account with Small Ltd	75	–
Creditors for goods and services	297	156
	7,344	1,272
Share capital	6,000	800
Retained earnings	1,344	472
	7,344	1,272

Notes:

The intangible asset section of the balance sheet of Large plc has not yet been amended prior to consolidation to take account of the provisions of the Companies Act or the recommendations contained in Statements of Standard Accounting Practice regarding intangible assets.

The stock of Large plc contained goods valued at £108,000 purchased from Small Ltd at production cost plus 50%.

Required:

(*a*) Prepare the consolidated profit and loss account of Large plc and its subsidiary Small Ltd for the year to 30 September 19-6 using the acquisition (purchase) method of consolidation.

(*b*) Prepare the consolidated balance sheet of Large plc and its subsidiary Small Ltd at 30 September 19-6 using the acquisition (purchase) method of consolidation.

(*c*) What would the reserves of the group be if a merger (pooling of interest) method of consolidation were used instead of the acquisition (purchase) method? Briefly explain why there is a difference between the values of the reserves arising from the two methods of consolidation.

(*Institute of Chartered Secretaries and Administrators*)

33.2A Huge plc acquired a holding of 600,000 of the 800,000 ordinary £1 shares of Large plc on 1 October 19-5 when the revenue reserves of Large stood at £320,000.

On 1 October 19-6, the Directors of Medium plc agreed to appoint the Commercial Manager of Huge as one of its directors to enable Huge to participate in its commercial, financial and dividend policy decisions. In exchange, Huge agreed to provide finance to Medium for working capital. On the same day, Huge acquired its holding of 100,000 of the 400,000 ordinary £1 shares of Medium when the revenue reserves of Medium were £150,000. Three months later, the directors of Small plc, who supplied materials to Large, heard of the arrangement between Huge and Medium and suggested that they would be pleased to enter into a similar relationship. The Board of Huge were interested in the proposal and showed their good faith by acquiring a 10% holding in Small which at that time had a debit balance of £2,000 on its profit and loss account.

Balance sheets of the four companies on 30 September 19-7

	Huge £'000s	Large £'000s	Medium £'000s	Small £'000s
Property, plant and machinery	2,004	780	553	85
Investment in Large	650			
Investment in Medium	180			
Investment in Small	12			
Current a/c Medium	40			
Current a/c Small			10	
Stocks	489	303	72	28
Debtors	488	235	96	22
Bank/Cash	45	62	19	5
	3,908	1,390	740	140
less Liabilities due in one year:				
Creditors	318	170	90	10
	3,590	1,220	650	130
Ordinary share capital	2,400	800	400	80
Revenue reserves	1,190	420	210	40
Current a/c Huge			40	
Current a/c Large				10
	3,590	1,220	650	130

Required:

(*a*) Identify which of the four companies should be included in a group consolidation, explaining how and why the treatment of one company in the consolidation may be different from another. Mention any appropriate accounting standards of legislation applicable.

(*b*) Prepare the consolidated balance sheet of the group at 30 September 19-7 using the acquisition (purchase) method of accounting.

(*Institute of Chartered Secretaries and Administrators*)

34

SSAP 1 Accounting for the Results of Associated Companies

The concept of an **associated company** was first put forward in 1971, with the issue of SSAP 1 Accounting for Associated Companies. The SSAP was subject to relatively minor revisions in 1982. The idea behind the SSAP was to ensure that if one company has invested in another company, and can *significantly* influence the affairs of that company, then ordinary investment accounting is not suitable. Rather than simply show dividends received as a measure of income, it would be much more realistic that the investing company's full share of the profit of that company should be incorporated in the investing company's consolidated profit and loss account.

It would be quite rare for the investing company not to have subsidiaries, so we will consider the position of bringing the accounting for associated companies into the consolidated profit and loss account.

Definition

An associated company is defined as a company, not being a subsidiary of the investing group or company, in which:

(*a*) the interest of the investing group or company is effectively that of a partner in a joint venture or a consortium and the investing group or company is in a position to exercise a significant influence over the company in which the investment is made; or

(*b*) the interest of the investing group or company is for the long term and is substantial and, having regard to the disposition of the other shareholdings, the investing group or company is in a position to exercise a significant influence over the company in which the investment is made.

Significant influence over a company is taken to mean participation in the financial and operating policy decisions of that company, including dividend policy, but not necessarily control of those policies.

In respect of (*b*) above, an interest of 20 per cent or more can be deemed to permit significant influence, subject to evidence indicating otherwise. If the interest is less than 20 per cent then normally it will not be an associated company, unless it can be shown to be otherwise.

Effect upon consolidated profit and loss account

Take out: (A) Dividends received or receivable from the associate
Include instead: Group's share of the associates
                    (B) Pre-tax profit
                    (C) Taxation charge
                    (D) Extraordinary items (profit or loss)
                    (E) Group's share of post-acquisition retained profits brought forward.

Effect upon consolidated balance sheet

Rather than   :   the cost of the investment

Show instead   :   the cost of the investment

plus

the group's share of associate's post-acquisition retained profit.

This method of accounting for associates is known as **equity accounting**.

Exhibit 34.1 shows how the associated company's results are incorporated into a consolidated set of accounts.

Exhibit 34.1

A Ltd is a holding company with subsidiaries. It also has 25 per cent of the equity share capital of B Ltd. This was bought for £100,000 three years ago when B Ltd had reserves (retained profits) £20,000.

Profit and Loss Accounts for the year ending 31 December 19-3

	A Ltd & Subsidiaries (consolidated)		B Ltd Associate Comp.	
	£000	£000	£000	£000
Turnover		540		200
Cost of Sales		370		130
Gross Profit		170		70
Distribution Costs	20		3	
Administrative Expenses	40	60	7	10
		110		60
Dividends receivable from B Ltd	(A)	10		
Profit on Ordinary Activities before Taxation		120	(B)	60
Tax on Profit on Ordinary Activities		28	(C)	16
Profit on Ordinary Activities after Taxation		92		44
Extraordinary Profits (net of Tax)		10	(D)	8
Profit for the financial year		102		52
Retained profits from last year		33		32
		135		84
Proposed dividends		60		40
Retained profits carried to next year		75		44

Balance Sheet as at 31 December 19-3 (abbreviated)

	£000	£000
Fixed assets	145	130
Investment in B Ltd at cost	100	–
Net current assets	180	114
	425	244
Share capital (ordinary shares)	350	200
Reserves	75	44
	425	244

Now we can move to the consolidation of B Ltd with A Ltd. As you have already been told the items needing adjusting are:

Take out : (A) Dividends receivable
Include : (B) Group share of pre-tax profit
        (C) Group share of taxation
        (D) Group share of extraordinary items
        (E) Group's share post-acquisition retained profit brought forward

The answer is:

A Ltd Group
Consolidated Profit and Loss Account for the year ending 31 December 19-3

		£000		£000
Turnover				540
Cost of Sales				370
				170
Distribution Costs		20		
Administrative Expenses		40		60
				110
Share of profit of associated company (*see* W1)			(B)	15
Profit on Ordinary Activities before Taxation				125
Tax on Profit on Ordinary Activities (*see* W2)			(C)	32
Profit on Ordinary Activities after Taxation				93
Extraordinary profits (*see* W3)			(D)	12
Profit for the financial year				105
Retained profits from last year (*see* W4)			(E)	36
				141
Proposed dividend				60
Retained profits carried to next year				81

	£000
Fixed assets	145
Investment in B Ltd (*see* W5)	106
Net current assets	180
	431
Share capital	350
Reserves (*see* W6)	81
	431

Workings

(W1) 25% of Profit before taxation of B Ltd × £60 = £15

(W2) A £28 + 25% of B £16 = £32

(W3) A £10 + 25% of B £8 = £12

(W4) A £33 + 25% of B's post-acquisition profits (£32 − £20) £12 = £36

(W5) Cost of 25% share in B =   100

      add retained profits B c/fwd   44

      less pre-acquisition profits   20

      Post-acquisition profits   24

      25% share   6

                                                                106

(W6) Reserves A   75

      add 25% of post-acquisition

        profit of B (*see* W5)   6   81

Investing companies without subsidiaries

All that is needed here is a supplementary statement as shown in Exhibit 34.2.

Exhibit 34.2

Example of a profit and loss account of a company without subsidiaries.

Profit and Loss account of an investing company

	£000	£000
Turnover		2,000
Cost of Sales		1,400
Gross Profit		600
Distribution Costs	175	
Administrative Expenses	125	300
Profit on Ordinary Activities before Taxation		300
Tax on Profit on Ordinary Activities		85
Profit on Ordinary Activities after Taxation		215
Dividends – proposed		80
Amount set aside to reserves		135

Supplementary statement incorporating results of associated companies:

	£000
Share of profits less losses of associated companies	50
less Tax	15
Share of profits after tax of associated companies	35
Profit on ordinary share activities after taxation (as above)	215
Profit attributable to members of the investing company	250
Dividends – proposed	80
Net profit retained (£35,000 by associated companies)	170

Note: The earnings per share figure would be based on £250,000.

Related companies

The Companies Act 1985 refers to 'related companies' rather than 'associated companies'. They are basically the same, the minor differences are not needed by you in this stage of your studies.

35

Budgeting and budgetary control

Part one: an introduction

It can be stated that management control is needed to try to ensure that the organisation achieves its objectives. Once the objectives have been agreed, plans should be drawn up so that the progress of the firm can be directed towards the ends specified in the objectives. Now it must not be thought that plans can be expressed only in accounting terms, for example quality of the product might be best shown in engineering terms, or social objectives shown in a plan concerned with employee welfare. But some of the objectives, such as the attainment of a desired profit, or of the attainment of a desired growth in assets can be expressed in accounting terms. When a plan is expressed quantitatively it is known as a **budget** and the process of converting plans into budgets is known as **budgeting**. In this book we are concerned primarily with budgets shown in monetary terms, i.e. financial budgets.

The budgeting process may be quite formal in a large organisation with committees set up to perform the task. On the other hand in a very small firm the owner may jot down his budget on a piece of scrap paper or even on the back of a used envelope. Some even manage without writing anything down at all, they have done the budgets in their heads and can easily remember them. This book is concerned with budgeting in a formal manner.

Budgets and people

Probably in no other part of accounting is there a greater need for understanding other people than in the processes of budgeting. Budgets are prepared to try to guide the firm towards its objectives. There is no doubt that some budgets that are drawn up are even more harmful to a firm than if none were drawn up at all.

Budgets are drawn up for control purposes, that is an attempt to control the direction that the firm is taking. Many people, however, look upon them, not as a guide, but as a straitjacket. We can look at a few undesirable actions that can result from people regarding budgets as a straitjacket rather than as a guide.

(*a*) The sales manager refuses to let a salesman go to Sweden in response to an urgent and unexpected request from a Swedish firm. The reason – the overseas sales expenses budget has already been spent. The result – the most profitable order that the firm would have received for many years is taken up instead by another firm.

(*b*) The works manager turns down requests for overtime work, because the budgeted overtime has already been exceeded. The result – the job is not completed on time, and the firm has to pay a large sum under a penalty clause in the contract for the job which stated that if the job was not finished by a certain date then a penalty of £20,000 would become payable.

(*c*) Towards the end of the accounting year a manager realises that he has not spent all of his budget for a particular item. He then launches on a spending spree, completely unnecessary items being bought, on the basis that 'If I don't spend this amount this year they will cut down next year when I will really need the money.' The result: a lot of unusable and unnecessary equipment.

(*d*) The education budget has been spent, therefore the education manager will not let anyone go on courses for the rest of the year. The result: the firm starts to fall behind in an industry which is highly technical, the staff concerned become fed up, and the better ones start to look for jobs in other firms which are more responsive to the need to allow personnel to keep in touch with changing technology.

Studies have shown that the more that managers are brought into the budgeting process, then the more successful budgetary control is likely to be. A manager on whom a budget is imposed, rather than a manager who had an active part in the drafting of his budget, is more likely to pay less attention to the budget and use it unwisely in the control process.

Having sounded the warning that needs to be borne in mind constantly when budgeting, we can now look at the positive end of budgeting – to see the advantages of a good budgetary control system.

Budgets and profit planning

The methodology of budgetary control is probably accountancy's major contribution to management. Before we get down to the mechanics of constructing budgets we should first of all look at the main outlines of drafting budgets.

When the budgets are being drawn up the two main objectives must be uppermost in the mind of top management, that is that the budgets are for:

(*a*) Planning. This means a properly co-ordinated and comprehensive plan for the whole business. Each part must interlock with the other parts.

(*b*) Control. Just because a plan is set down on paper does not mean that the plan will carry itself out. Control is exercised via the budgets, thus the name budgetary control. To do this means that the responsibility of managers and budgets must be so linked that the responsible manager is given a guide to help him to produce certain desired results, and the actual achieved results can be compared against the expected, i.e. actual compared with budget.

Preparation of estimates

The first thing to establish is what the limiting factors are in a firm. It may well be the fact that sales cannot be pushed above a certain amount, otherwise it might be the fact that the firm could sell as much as it can produce, but the productive capacity of the firm sets a limit. Whatever the limiting factor is, there is no doubt that this aspect of the firm will need more attention than probably any other. There would not, for instance, be much point in budgeting for the sale of 1,000 units a year if production could not manufacture more than 700, or to manufacture 2,000 a year if only 1,300 of them could be sold.

There is no doubt that usually the most difficult estimate to make is that of sales revenue. This can be done by using one of two methods:

(*a*) Make a statistical forecast on the basis of the economic situation conditions applying reference to the goods sold by the company, and what is known about the actions of competitors.

(*b*) The opposite is to make an internal forecast. This is usually done by asking each salesman, or group of salesmen, to estimate the sales in their own areas, and then total the estimates. Sometimes the salesmen are not asked at all.

Now we should remember that much of the subject matter that you have read about, or are currently reading in Economics, is very relevant here. A knowledge of elasticity of demand, whether the product is a complementary product, e.g. the price of egg-cups is linked to the demand for eggs, whether it is a substitute, e.g. that a rise in the price of butter may induce housewives to turn to other commodities instead, is very relevant in this area. Factors such as whether the firm has a monopoly, whether the firm has many small customers, a few large customers, or even one large customer, are of crucial importance. Estimating sales revenue is very much a matter of taking all the economic factors into account allied to other factors.

The sales budget is, however, more than just a sales forecast. Budgets should show the actions that management is taking to influence future events. If an increase in sales is desired the sales budget may show extra sales, which may well be an indication of the action that management is going to take by means of extra television advertising, making a better product, or to give retailers better profit margins and push up sales in that way.

The production budget

The production budget stems from the sales budget, but the first question that has to be settled is that of the level of the stock of finished goods which will be held by the firm.

If sales are even over the year, then production can also be in keeping with the sales figure, and the stock figure can remain constant. Suppose that the firm sells 50 units every month, then the firm can produce 50 units per month. In almost every firm, a stock level will have to be maintained, the amount of stock will be dependent on factors such as amount of storage space, the estimated amount needed to cater for breakdowns in production or for delays in receiving raw materials etc. Nonetheless, if the stock level was to be a minimum of 70 units it would still mean that production was at the rate of 50 units per month.

On the other hand sales may not be constant. Sales may average 50 units per month, but the figures may well be as follows:

January	20 units	February	30 units	March	60 units
April	80 units	May	70 units	June	40 units

This would mean that if production levels were kept at 50 units per month the stock levels would usually have to be more than 100 units, whilst if the stock levels were to be kept at 100 units minimum the production figures each month would equal the sales figures. We can now compare the two levels of production.

Even production flow

The problem here is to find the stock level that the firm would need on 1st January if (i) sales are as shown, (ii) the stock must not fall below 100 units, (iii) production is to be 50 units per month. It can be found by trial and error. For instance, if you decided to see what would happen if the firm started off with 100 units in stock at 1st January you would find that, after adding production and deducting sales each month, the stock level would fall to 90 units in May. As 100 units of stock is the minimum needed you would need to start off on 1st January with 110 units. The method is that if you start off your calculation with an estimated figure of stock, which must at least be the minimum figure required, then if you find that the lowest figure of stock shown during the period is 10 units less than the minimum stock required, go back and add 10 units to the stock to be held on 1st January. If the lowest figure is 30 units less than required add 30 units to the 1st January stock, and so on. We can now look at the figures in Exhibit 35.1.

Exhibit 35.1

Units	January	February	March	April	May	June
Opening Stock	110	140	160	150	120	100
add Units Produced	50	50	50	50	50	50
	160	190	210	200	170	150
less Sales	20	30	60	80	70	40
Closing Stock	140	160	150	120	100	110

Before we look at the implications of maintaining an even production flow we can look at another example. Try to work it out for yourself before looking at the answer in Exhibit 35.2. The Sales are expected to be January 70, February 40, March 50, April 120, May 140 and June 70. The stock level must not fall below 120 units and an even production flow of 80 units is required. What stock level would there have to be on 1st January?

Exhibit 35.2

Units	January	February	March	April	May	June
Opening Stock	140	150	190	220	180	120
add Units Produced	80	80	80	80	80	80
	220	230	270	300	260	200
less Sales	70	40	50	120	140	70
Closing Stock	150	190	220	180	120	130

It is more important in many firms to ensure a smooth production flow than to bother unduly about stock levels, assuming that the minimum stock level is always attained. If the work is skilled then that type of labour force may take several years to become trained, and skilled labour in many industries does not take kindly to being sacked and re-employed as the demand for the goods fluctuates. This is not always true with skilled labour, for instance in the building industry such craftsmen as bricklayers may go to a builder until he has completed a contract such as building a college, a hospital, or a housing estate, and then leave and go to another employer on the completion of the job.

On the other hand, a skilled engineer concerned with the manufacturer of say, diesel engines, would not expect to be fired and re-employed continuously. The bricklayer has a skill that is easily transferable to many other building employers in an area, whereas the diesel engineer may have only one firm within fifty miles of his home where he can perform his skills properly. A man employed as a labourer might work on a building site in one part of a year and then transfer as a labourer to an engineering factory as a labourer in another part of the year. Whether a firm could carry on production with widely uneven production levels depends so much on the type of firm and the type of labour involved. A firm would only sack skilled labour which it needed again shortly if it could persuade the men or women to come back when required. If the people who had been sacked were likely to find other employment, and not return to the firm when required, then this would mean that the firm would probably keep them on its payroll and production would continue and stocks of finished goods would begin to pile up. Many firms do in fact realise their social obligations by only laying off workers when no other alternative is at all reasonable. In many organisations there are probably more workers from time to time than the firm actually needs – this is known as 'organisational slack', so that there is a leeway between the increasing of production and having to take on extra workers.

Uneven production levels

Some firms by their very nature will have uneven production levels, and this will be accepted by their labour force. An ice-cream firm would find sales at the highest levels in summer, tailing off in winter. It is not really possible to build up stocks of ice-cream very much in the winter for summer sales! Even if it could be done technically, the costs of refrigerating large quantities of ice-cream for several months could hardly be economic. The large labour force used in the summer months will probably include quite a few students occupying their vacation periods profitably, and not able anyway to work at the job all the year round even if they wanted to. Such a kind of firm will normally have a far greater relationship between current stock levels and current sales than a firm which has even production levels.

The calculation of the quantity to be produced is then:

Opening Stock+Units Produced−Sales=Closing Stock

This means that if the opening stock will be 80 units, the sales are expected to be 100 units and the desired closing is 50 units it becomes:

	Units
Opening Stock	80
add Production	?
less Sales	100
Closing Stock	50

Production will, therefore, be the missing figure, i.e. 70 units (80+Production 70 = 150 for sale less actually sold 100 = closing stock 50).

Exhibit 35.3 shows the units to be produced if the following information is known – Stock required 1st January 40, at end of each month, January 60, February 110, March 170, April 100, May 60, June 20. Sales are expected to be January 100, February 150, March 110, April 190, May 70, June 50.

Exhibit 35.3

Units	January	February	March	April	May	June
Opening Stock	40	60	110	170	100	60
Production required (?)	120	200	170	120	30	10
	160	260	280	290	130	70
less Sales	100	150	110	190	70	50
Closing Stock	60	110	170	100	60	20

Linked with the production budget will be a materials purchase budget. It may well be that an order will have to be placed in January, received in March and issued to production in April. The purchase of materials will have to be planned as scientifically as possible.

You are now in a position to be able to tackle questions 35.1 to 35.6 inclusive.

Part two: cash budgets

It is no use budgeting for production and for sales if during the budget period the firm runs out of cash funds. When talking about cash in budgets we are also usually including bank funds, and therefore in this book we will not be differentiating between cash and cheque payments or between cash and cheques received. Cash is, therefore, also budgeted for, so that any shortage of cash can be known in advance and action taken to obtain permission for a loan or a bank overdraft to be available then, rather than wait until the shortage or deficiency occurs. Bank managers, or anyone concerned with the lending of money, certainly resent most strongly one of their customers needing a bank overdraft without prior warning, when in fact the customer could have known if he had drawn up a cash budget in advance which revealed the need for cash funds on a particular date.

The finance needed may not just be by way of borrowing from a bank or finance house, it may well be a long-term need that can only be satisfied by an issue of shares or debentures. Such issues need planning well in advance, and a cash budget can reveal (a) that they will be needed (b) how much is needed and (c) when it will be needed.

We can now look at a very simple case. Without being concerned in this first exhibit with exactly what the receipts and payments are for, just to keep matters simple at this stage, we can see the dangers that are inherent in not budgeting for cash.

Exhibit 39.4

Mr Muddlem had a meeting with his accountant on 1 July 19-3. He was feeling very pleased with himself. He had managed to get some very good orders from customers, mainly because he was now allowing them extra time in which to pay their accounts. Sprite the accountant, said, 'Can you afford to do all that you are hoping to do?'

Muddlem laughed, 'Why, I'll be making so much money I won't know how to spend it.'

'But have you got the cash to finance everything?' asked Sprite.

'If I'm making a good profit then of course I'll have the cash,' said Muddlem. 'I know the bank manager says that any bank overdraft could not be more than £1,000, but I doubt if I need it.'

'Don't let us rely on guesses,' says Sprite. 'Let's work it out.'

After an hour's work the following facts emerge.

(a) Present cash balance (including bank balance) £800.

(b) Receipts from debtors will be: July £2,000, August £2,600, September £5,000, October £7,000, November £8,000, December £15,000.

(c) Payments will be: July £2,500, August £2,700, September £6,900, October £7,800, November £9,900, December £10,300.

This is then summarised:

	July £	August £	Sept £	Oct £	Nov £	Dec £
Balance at start of the month:	+800	+300	+200			
Deficit at the start of the month:				−1,700	−2,500	−4,400
Receipts	2,000	2,600	5,000	7,000	8,000	15,000
	2,800	2,900	5,200	5,300	5,500	10,600
Payments	2,500	2,700	6,900	7,800	9,900	10,300
Balance at end of the month:	+300	+200				+300
Deficit at the end of the month:			−1,700	−2,500	−4,400	

'I'm in an awkward position now,' says Muddlem. 'I just cannot borrow £4,400 nor can I cut down on my sales, and anyway I don't really want to as these new sales are very profitable indeed, If only I'd known this, I could have borrowed the money from my brother only last week but he's invested it elsewhere now.'

'Come and see me tomorrow,' say Sprite. 'There may well be something we can do.'

Fortunately for Muddlem his luck was in. He arrived to see his accountant the following morning waving a cheque. 'My wife won £5,000 on a jackpot bingo last night,' he said.

'Thank goodness for that, at least in future you'll learn to budget ahead for cash requirements. You can't be lucky all the time,' says Sprite.

Timing of cash receipts and payments

In drawing up a cash budget it must be borne in mind that all the payments for units produced would very rarely be at the same time as production itself. For instance the raw materials might be bought in March, incorporated in the goods being produced in April, and paid for in May. On the other hand the raw materials may have been in hand for some time, so that the goods are bought in January, paid for in February, and used in production the following August. Contrary to this, the direct labour part of the product is usually paid for almost at the same time as the unit being produced. Even here a unit may be produced in one week and the wages paid one week later, so that a unit might be produced on say 27 June and the wages for the direct labour involved paid for on 3 July.

Similarly the date of sales and the date of receipt of cash will not usually be at the same time, except in many retail stores. The goods might be sold in May and the money received in August, or even paid for in advance so that the goods might be paid for in February but the goods not shipped to the buyer until May. This is especially true, at least for part of the goods when a cash deposit is left for specially made goods which will take some time to manufacture. A simple example of this would be a made-to-measure suit on which a deposit would be paid at the time of order, the final payment being made when the completed suit is collected by the buyer.

Exhibit 35.5

A cash budget for the six months ended 30 June, 19-3 is to be drafted from the following information.

(a) Opening cash balance at 1 January, 19-3 £3,200.

(b) Sales; at £12 per unit; cash received three months after sale.

Units: 19-2   19-3

Oct	Nov	Dec	Jan	Feb	Mar	April	May	June	July	Aug	Sept
80	90	70	100	60	120	150	140	130	110	100	160

(c) Production: in units.

19-2   19-3

Oct	Nov	Dec	Jan	Feb	Mar	April	May	June	July	Aug	Sept
70	80	90	100	110	130	140	150	120	160	170	180

(d) Raw Materials used in production costs £4 per unit of production. They are paid for two months before being used in production.

(e) Direct Labour. £3 per unit paid for in the same month as the unit produced.

(f) Other variable expenses, £2 per unit, ¾ of the cost being paid for in the same month as production, the other ¼ paid in the month after production.

(g) Fixed Expenses of £100 per month are paid monthly.

(h) A motor van is to be bought and paid for in April for £800. Schedules of payments and receipts are as follows:

Payments: (The month shown in brackets is the month in which the units are produced)

January	£	*February*	£
Raw Materials: 130 (March)×£4	520	140 (April)×£4	560
Direct Labour: 100 (January)×£3	300	110 (February)×3	330
Variable: 100 (January)×¾×£2	150	110 (February)×¾×£2	165
90 (December)×¼×£2	45	100 (January)×¼×£2	50
Fixed:	100		100
	£1,115		£1,205

March	£	*April*	£
Raw Materials: 150 (May)×£4	600	120 (June)×£4	480
Direct Labour: 130 (March)×£3	390	140 (April)×£3	420
Variable: 130 (March)×¾×£2	195	140 (April)×¾×£2	210
110 (February)×¼×£2	55	130 (March)×¼×£2	65
Fixed:	100		100
Motor Van			800
	£1,340		£2,075

May	£	*June*	£
Raw Materials: 160 (July)×£4	640	170 (August)×£4	680
Direct Labour: 150 (May)×£3	450	120 (June)×£3	360
Variable: 150 (May)×¾×£2	225	120 (June)×¾×£2	180
140 (April)×¼×£2	70	150 (May)×¼×£2	75
Fixed:	100		100
	£1,485		£1,395

Receipts: (The month shown in brackets is the month in which the sale was made)

				£
January	80	(October)	×£12	960
February	90	(November)	×£12	1,080
March	70	(December)	×£12	840
April	100	(January)	×£12	1,200
May	60	(February)	×£12	720
June	120	(March)	×£12	1,440

Cash Budget

	Jan £	Feb £	Mar £	April £	May £	June £
Balance from previous month	3,200	3,045	2,920	2,420	1,545	780
add Receipts (per schedule)	960	1,080	840	1,200	720	1,440
	4,160	4,125	3,760	3,620	2,265	2,220
less Payments (per schedule)	1,115	1,205	1,340	2,075	1,485	1,395
Balance carried to next month	3,045	2,920	2,420	1,545	780	825

You should now be able to tackle all of questions 35.7 to 35.11 inclusive.

Part three: co-ordination of budgets

The various budgets have to be linked together and a **Master Budget**, which is really a budgeted set of Final Accounts drawn up. We have in fact looked at the Sales, Production and Cash Budgets. There are, however, many more budgets for parts of the organisation, for instance there may be:

(i) a selling budget.
(ii) an administration expense budget,
(iii) a manufacturing overhead budget,
(iv) a direct labour budget,
(v) a purchases budget,

and so on. In this book we do not wish to get entangled in too many details, but in a real firm with a proper set of budgeting techniques there will be a great deal of detailed backing for the figures that are incorporated in the more important budgets.

Now it may be that when all the budgets have been co-ordinated, or slotted together, the Master Budget shows a smaller profit than the directors are prepared to accept. This will mean recasting budgets to see whether a greater profit can be earned, and if at all possible the budgets will be altered. Eventually there will be a Master Budget that the directors can agree to. This then gives the target for the results that the firm hopes to achieve in financial terms. Remember that there are other targets such as employee welfare, quality product etc. that cannot be so expressed.

The rest of this chapter is concerned with the drawing up of budgets for an imaginary firm, Walsh Ltd, culminating in the drawing up of the Master Budget.

To start with we can look at the last Balance Sheet of Walsh Ltd as at 31 December, 19-4. This will give us our opening figures of stocks of raw materials, stock of finished goods, cash (including bank) balance, creditors, debtors etc.

Walsh Ltd
Balance Sheet as at 31 December 19-4

Fixed Assets	Cost	Depreciation to date	Net
	£	£	£
Machinery	4,000	1,600	2,400
Motor Vehicles	2,000	800	1,200
	6,000	2,400	3,600

Current Assets

Stocks: Finished Goods (75 units)		900	
Raw Materials		500	
Debtors (19×4 October £540 + November £360 + December £450)		1,350	
Cash and Bank Balances		650	
		3,400	

Less Current Liabilities

Creditors for Raw Materials (November £120 + December £180)	300		
Creditors for Fixed Expenses (December)	100	400	
Working Capital			3,000
			6,600

Financed by:

Share Capital: 4,000 shares £1 each	4,000
Profit and Loss Account	2,600
	6,600

The plans for the six months ended 30 June, 19-5 are as follows:

(i) Production will be 60 units per month for the first four months, followed by 70 units per month for May and June.

(ii) Production costs will be (per unit):

	£
Direct Materials	5
Direct Labour	4
Variable Overhead	3
	£12

(iii) Fixed overhead is £100 per month, payable always one month in arrears.

(iv) Sales, at a price of £18 per unit, are expected to be:

	January	February	March	April	May	June
No. of units	40	50	60	90	90	70

(v) Purchases of direct materials (raw materials) will be:

	January	February	March	April	May	June
	£	£	£	£	£	£
	150	200	250	300	400	320

(vi) The creditors for raw materials bought are paid two months after purchase.

(vii) Debtors are expected to pay their accounts three months after they have bought the goods.

(viii) Direct Labour and variable overheads are paid in the same month as the units are produced.

(ix) A machine costing £2,000 will be bought and paid for in March.

(x) 3,000 shares of £1 each are to be issued at par in May.

(xi) Depreciation for the six months: Machinery £450, Motor Vehicles £200.

We must first of all draw up the various budgets and then incorporate them into the Master Budget. Some of the more detailed budgets which can be dispensed with in this illustration will be omitted.

Materials Budget

	January	February	March	April	May	June
Opening Stock £	500	350	250	200	200	250
add Purchases £	150	200	250	300	400	320
	650	550	500	500	600	570
less Used in Production:						
Jan–April 60×£5	300	300	300	300		
May and June 70×£5					350	350
Closing Stock £	350	250	200	200	250	220

Production Budget (in units)

	January	February	March	April	May	June
Opening Stock (units)	75	95	105	105	75	55
add Produced	60	60	60	60	70	70
	135	155	165	165	145	125
less Sales	40	50	60	90	90	70
Closing Stock	95	105	105	75	55	55

Production Cost Budget (in £'s)

	January	February	March	April	May	June	Total
Materials Cost £	300	300	300	300	350	350	1,900
Labour Cost £	240	240	240	240	280	280	1,520
Variable Overhead £	180	180	180	180	210	210	1,140
	720	720	720	720	840	840	4,560

Creditors Budget

	January	February	March	April	May	June
Opening Balance £	300	330	350	450	550	700
add Purchases £	150	200	250	300	400	320
	450	530	600	750	950	1,020
less Payments £	120	180	150	200	250	300
Closing Balance £	330	350	450	550	700	720

Debtors Budget

	January	February	March	April	May	June
Opening Balances	1,350	1,530	2,070	2,700	3,600	4,320
add Sales £	720	900	1,080	1,620	1,620	1,260
	2,070	2,430	3,150	4,320	5,220	5,580
less Received £	540	360	450	720	900	1,080
Closing Balances £	1,530	2,070	2,700	3,600	4,320	4,500

Cash Budget

	January	February	March	April	May	June
Opening Balance £	+650	+550	+210			+1,050
Opening Overdraft £				−2,010	−2,010	
Received (see schedule) £	540	360	450	720	3,900	1,080
	1,190	910	660	1,290	1,890	2,130
Payments (see schedule) £	640	700	2,670	720	840	890
Closing Balance £	+550	+210			+1,050	+1,240
Closing Overdraft £			−2,010	−2,010		

Cash Payments Schedule

	January	February	March	April	May	June
Creditors for goods bought two months previously £	120	180	150	200	250	300
Fixed Overhead £	100	100	100	100	100	100
Direct Labour £	240	240	240	240	280	280
Variable Overhead £	180	180	180	180	210	210
Machinery £			2,000			
£	640	700	2,670	720	840	890

Cash Receipts Schedule

	January	February	March	April	May	June
Debtors for goods sold three months previously £	540	360	450	720	900	1,080
Shares Issued £					3,000	
					3,900	

Master Budget
Forecast Operating Statement for the Six months ended 30 June 19-5

			£
Sales			7,200
less Cost of Goods Sold:			
Opening Stock of Finished Goods		900	
add Cost of Goods Completed		4,560	
		5,460	
less Closing Stock of Finished Goods		660	4,800
Gross Profit			2,400
less			
Fixed Overhead		600	
Depreciation: Machinery	450		
Motors	200	650	1,250
Net Profit			1,150

Forecast Balance Sheet as at 30 June 19-5

Fixed Assets
Tangible Assets

	Cost £	Depreciation to date £	Net £
Machinery	6,000	2,050	3,950
Motor Vehicles	2,000	1,000	1,000
	8,000	3,050	4,950

Current Assets

Stocks: Finished Goods		660
Raw Materials		220
Debtors		4,500
Cash and Bank Balances		1,240
		6,620

Creditors: amounts falling due within 1 year

Creditors for Goods	720		
Creditors for Overheads	100	820	

Net Current Assets	5,800
Total Assets less Current Liabilities	10,750

Capital and Reserves

Called-up Share Capital	7,000
Profit and Loss Account (2,600+1,150)	3,750
	10,750

Capital budgeting

The plan for the acquisition of fixed assets such as machinery, buildings etc. is usually known as a **Capital Budget**. Management will evaluate the various possibilities open to it, and will compare the alternatives. This is a very important part of budgeting. So far in this book it has been assumed that the capital budgeting has already been done.

Questions 35.12 to 35.17 could now be attempted by you.

Part four: further thoughts on budgets

The process of budgeting with the necessary participation throughout management, finally producing a profit plan, is now a regular feature in all but the smallest firms. Very often budgeting is the one time when the various parts of management can really get together and work as a team rather than just as separate parts of an organisation. When budgeting is conducted under favourable conditions, there is no doubt that a firm which budgets will tend to perform rather better than a similar firm that does not budget. Budgeting means that managers can no longer give general answers affecting the running of the firm, they have to put figures to their ideas, and they know that in the end their estimated figures are going to be compared with what the actual figures turn out to be.

It has often been said that the act of budgeting is possibly of more benefit than the budgets which are produced. However, the following benefits can be claimed for good budgeting:

(*a*) The strategic planning carried on by the board of directors or owners can be more easily linked to the decisions by managers as to how the resources of the business will be used to try to achieve the objectives of the business. The strategic planning has to be converted into action, and budgeting provides the ideal place where such planning can be changed into financial terms.

(*b*) Standards of performance can be agreed to for the various parts of the business. If sales and production targets are set as part of a co-ordinated plan, then the sales department cannot really complain that production is insufficient if they had agreed previously to a production level and this is being achieved, nor can production complain if its production exceeds the amount budgeted for and it remains unsold.

(*c*) The expression of plans in comparable financial terms. Some managers think mainly in terms of say units of production, or of tons of inputs or outputs, or of lorry mileage, etc. The effect that each of them has upon financial results must be brought home to them. For instance a transport manager might be unconcerned about the number of miles that his haulage fleet of lorries covers until the cost of doing such a large mileage is brought home to him, often during budgeting, and it may then be and only then that he starts to search for possible economies. It is possible in many cases to use mathematics to find the best ways of loading vehicles, or of the routes taken by vehicles so that fewer miles are covered and yet the same delivery service is maintained. This is just one instance of many when the expression of the plans of a section of a business in financial terms sparks off a search for economies, when otherwise such a search may never be started at all.

(*d*) Managers can see how their work slots into the activities of the firm. It can help to get rid of the feeling of 'I'm only a number not a person', because he can identify his position within the firm and can see that his job really is essential to the proper functioning of the firm.

(*e*) The budgets for a firm cannot be set in isolation. This means that the situation of the business, the nature of its products and its work force etc., must be seen against the economic background of the country. For instance it is no use budgeting for extra labour when labour is in extremely short supply, without realising the implications, possibly that of paying higher than normal wage rates. Increasing the sales target during a 'credit squeeze' needs a full investigation of the effect of the shortage of money upon the demand for the firm's goods and so on.

The charges made against budgeting are mainly that budgets bring about inflexibility, and that managers will not depart from budget even though the departure would bring about a more desirable result. Too many budgets are set at one level of sales or production when in fact flexible budgets (discussed later in this chapter) ought to be used. It is very often the case that budgeting is forced upon managers against their will, instead the firm should really set out first of all to do a 'selling job' to convince managers that budgets are not the monsters so often thought. A trial run for part of a business is far superior than starting off by having a fully detailed budget set up right away for the whole of the business. Learning to use budgets is rather like learning to swim. Let a child get used to the water first and remove its fear of the water, then it will learn to swim fairly easily. For most children (but not all), if the first visit to the baths meant being pushed into the deep end immediately, then reaction against swimming would probably set in. Let a manager become used to the idea of budgeting, without the fear of being dealt with severely during a trial period, and most managers will then become used to the idea and participate properly.

Flexible budgets

So far in this book budgets have been drawn up on the basis of one set of expectations, based on just one level of sales and production. Later, when the actual results are compared with the budgeted results expected in a fixed budget, they will have deviated for two reasons:

1 Whilst the actual and budgeted volumes of production and sales may be the same there may be a difference on actual and budgeted costs.

2 The volumes of actual and budgeted units of sales and production may vary, so that the costs will be different because of different volumes.

The variations, or variances as they are more commonly known, are usually under the control of different managers in the organisation. Variances coming under (1) will probably be under the control of the individual department. On the other hand variances under (2) are caused because of variations in plans brought about by top management because of changing sales, or at least the expectation of changing sales.

Budgets are used for control purposes, therefore a manager does not take kindly to being held responsible for a variance in his spending if the variance is caused by a type (2) occurrence if he is working on a fixed budget. The answer to this is to construct budgets at several levels of volume, and to show what costs etc. they should incur at differenct levels. For instance, if a budget had been fixed at a volume of 500 units and the actual volume is 550, then the manager would undoubtedly feel aggrieved if his costs for producing 550 units are compared with the costs he should have incurred for 500 units. Budgets which do allow for changing levels are called **Flexible Budgets**.

To draft a full set of flexible budgets is outside the scope of this book, but an instance of one department's flexible budget for manufactured overhead can be shown in Exhibit 39.5.

Exhibit 39.5

Data Ltd

Budget of Manufacturing Overhead, Department S

(This would in fact be in greater detail)

Units	400	450	500	550	600
	£	£	£	£	£
Variable overhead	510	550	600	680	770
Fixed overhead	400	400	400	400	400
Total overhead (A)	£910	£950	£1,000	£1,080	£1,170
Direct Labour hours (B)	200	225	250	275	300
Overhead rates (A) divided by (B)	£4.55	£4.22	£4.0	£3.92	£3.9

Notice that the variable costs in this case do not vary in direct proportion to production. In this case once 500 units production have been exceeded they start to climb rapidly. The flexible budget makes far greater sense than a fixed budget. For instance if a fixed budget had been agreed at 400 units, with variable overhead £510, then if production rose to 600 units the manager would think the whole system unfair if he was expected to incur only £510 variable overhead (the figure for 400 units). On the contrary, if the comparison was on a flexible budget then costs at 600 units production would instead be compared with £770 (the figure at 600 units).

Review questions

35.1 What would the production levels have to be for each month if the following data was available:

Units 19-5	Jan	Feb	March	April	May	June
(i) Stocks levels wanted at the end of each month	690	780	1,100	1,400	1,160	940
(ii) Expected sales each month	800	920	1,090	1,320	1,480	1,020

(iii) The stock level at 1 January, 19-5 will be 740 units.

35.2 For the year ended 31 December, 19-9 the sales of units are expected to be:

January	110	July	70
February	180	August	30
March	170	September	170
April	150	October	110
May	120	November	150
June	100	December	190

The opening stock at 1 January 19-9 will be 140 units. The closing stock desired at 31 December, 19-9 is 150 units.

Required:

(*a*) What will production be per month if an even production flow is required and stock levels during the year could be allowed to fall to zero?

(*b*) Given the same information plus the constraint that stock levels must never fall below 80 units, and that extra production will be undertaken in January 19-9 to ensure this, what will be the January production figure?

35.3A (*a*) For each of the following, state three reasons why a firm may wish to keep:

(i) a minimum stock level of finished goods, and

(ii) an even level of production in the face of fluctuating demand.

(*b*) The sales forecast for Douglas & Co for July – December 19-7 is:

	J	A	S	O	N	D
Units	280	200	260	360	400	420

Produce a production budget showing monthly opening and closing stock figures if the firm wishes to maintain an even level of producing 300 units each month, and a minimum stock level of 150 units.

What must the opening stock be at 1 July to achieve this?

(*c*) Under what circumstances, in budgetary control, may a firm's productive capacity prove to be its limiting or key factor?

(*Associated Examining Board: GCE 'A' level*)

35.4 B Ukridge comes to see you in April 19-3. He is full of enthusiasm for a new product that he is about to launch on to the market. Unfortunately his financial recklessness in the past has led him into being bankrupted twice, and he has only just got discharged by the court from his second bankruptcy.

'Look here laddie,' he says, 'with my new idea I'll be a wealthy man before Christmas.'

'Calm down,' you say, 'and tell me all about it.'

Ukridge's plans as far as cash is concerned for the next six months are:

(*a*) Present cash balance (including bank) £5.

(*b*) Timely legacy under a will – being received on 1 May, 19-3, £5,000. This will be paid into the business bank account by Ukridge.

(*c*) Receipts from debtors will be: May £400, June £4,000, July £8,000, August £12,000, September £9,000, October £5,000.

(*d*) Payments will be: May £100, June £5,000, July £11,000, August £20,000, September £12,000, October £7,000.

You are required:

(*a*) To draw up a cash budget, showing the balances each month, for the six months to 31 October, 19-3.

(*b*) The only person Ukridge could borrow money from would charge interest at the rate of 100 per cent per annum. This is not excessive considering Ukridge's past record. Advise Ukridge.

35.5 Draw up a cash budget for N Morris showing the balance at the end of each month, from the following information for the six months ended 31 December 19-2:

(*a*) Opening Cash (including bank) balance £1,200

(*b*) Production in units:

19-2									19-3	
April	*May*	*June*	*July*	*Aug*	*Sept*	*Oct*	*Nov*	*Dec*	*Jan*	*Feb*
240	270	300	320	350	370	380	340	310	260	250

(*c*) Raw Materials used in production cost £5 per unit. Of this 80 per cent is paid in the month of production and 20 per cent in the month after production.

(*d*) Direct Labour costs of £8 per unit are payable in the month of production.

(*e*) Variable expenses are £2 per unit, payable one-half in the same month as production and one-half in the month following production.

(*f*) Sales at £20 per unit:

19-2								19-3	
Mar	*April*	*May*	*June*	*July*	*Aug*	*Sept*	*Oct*	*Nov*	*Dec*
260	200	320	290	400	300	350	400	390	400

Debtors to pay their accounts three months after that in which sales are made.

(*g*) Fixed expenses of £400 per month payable each month.

(*h*) Machinery costing £2,000 to be paid for in October 19-2.

(*i*) Will receive a legacy £2,500 in December 19-2.

(*j*) Drawings to be £300 per month.

35.6 Richard Toms has agreed to purchase the business of Norman Soul with effect from 1 August 19-7. Soul's budgeted working capital at 1 August 19-7 is as follows:

	£	£	£
Current Assets			
Stock at cost	13,000		
Debtors	25,000		
		38,000	
Current Liabilities			
Creditors	10,000		
Bank overdraft	20,000		
		30,000	
			8,000

In addition to paying Soul for the acquisition of the business, Toms intends to improve the liquidity position of the business by introducing £10,000 capital on 1 August 19-7. He has also negotiated a bank overdraft limit of £15,000. It is probable that 10% of Soul's debtors will in fact be bad debts and that the remaining debtors will settle their accounts during August subject to a cash discount of 10%. The opening creditors are to be paid during August. The sales for the first four months of Tom's ownership of the business are expected to be as follows: August £24,000; September £30,000; October £30,000 and November £36,000. All sales will be on credit and debtors will receive a two month credit period. Gross profit will be at a standard rate of 25% of selling price. In addition, in order to further improve the bank position and to reduce his opening stock, Toms intends to sell on 1 August 19-7 at cost price £8,000 of stock for cash. In order to operate within the overdraft limit Toms intends to control stock levels and to organise his purchases to achieve a monthly rate of stock turnover of 3. He will receive one month's credit from his suppliers.

General cash expenses are expected to be £700 per month.

Required:

(a) A stock budget for the four months ending 30 November 19-7 showing clearly the stock held at the end of each month.

(b) A cash budget for the four months ending 30 November 19-7 showing clearly the bank balance at the end of each month.

(*Associated Examining Board: GCE 'A' level*)

35.7A Ian Spiro, formerly a taxi-driver, decided to establish a car-hire business after inheriting £50,000.

His business year would be divided into budget periods each being four weeks.

He commenced business on a Monday the first day of period 1, by paying into a business bank account £34,000 as his initial capital.

All receipts and payments would be passed through his bank account.

The following additional forecast information is available on the first four budget periods of his proposed business venture.

1 At the beginning of period 1 he would purchase 6 saloon cars of a standard type; list price £6,000 each, on which he had negotiated a trade discount of 11%.

2 He estimates that four of the cars will be on the road each Monday to Friday inclusive, and at week-ends all six cars will be on the road. Hire charges as follows:

> Weekday rate   £10 per day per car
> Weekend rate   £18 per day per car

He estimates that this business trading pattern will commence on the Monday of the second week of period 1, and then continue thereafter.

All hire transactions are to be settled for cash.

Note: a week-end consists of Saturday and Sunday. All remaining days are week-days.

3 An account was established with a local garage for fuel, and it was agreed to settle the account two periods in arrear.

The forecast gallon usage is as follows:

Period 1	*Period 2*	*Period 3*	*Period 4*
200	200	400	500

The fuel costs £1.80 per gallon.

4 Servicing costs for the vehicles would amount to £300 per period, paid during the period following the service. Servicing would commence in period 1.

5 Each of his vehicles would be depreciated at 25% per annum on a reducing balance basis.

6 Fixed costs of £200 per period would be paid each period.

7 He had agreed with a local firm to provide 2 cars on a regular basis, Monday to Friday inclusive, as chauffeur driven cars. The agreed rate was £60 a day (per car) payment being made in the following period.

This contract would not commence until the first day of period 2, a Monday.

8 Drawings: Periods 1 & 2 £400 a period.
         Periods 3 & 4 £800 a period.

9 Wages and Salaries:

(*a*) Initially he would employ 3 staff, each on £320 a budget period. Employment would commence at the beginning of period 1.

(*b*) On commencement of the contract the two additional staff employed as chauffeurs would each receive £360 a budget period. Payments are to be made at the end of the relevant period.

10 In anticipation of more business being developed he planned to buy a further three cars for cash in period 4. The cars would cost £6,500 each and it was agreed he would be allowed a trade discount of 10%.

Required:

(*a*) A detailed cash budget for the first four budget periods.

(*b*) An explanation as to why it is important that a business should prepare a cash budget.

(*c*) Identify how a sole proprietor may finance a forecast cash deficit distinguishing between internal and external financial sources.

(*Associated Examining Board: GCE 'A' level*)

35.8A A company's estimated pattern of costs and revenues for the first four months of 19-7 is as follows:

Cost and Revenues: January–April 19-7
(£'000)

Month	Sales	Materials	Wages	Overheads
January	410.4	81.6	16.2	273.6
February	423.6	84.8	16.8	282.4
March	460.8	93.6	18.3	306.7
April	456.3	91.2	18.6	304.5

1 One quarter of the materials are paid for in the month of production and the remainder two months later: deliveries received in November 19-6 were £78,400, and in December 19-6 £74,800.

2 Customers are expected to pay one-third of their debts a month after the sale and the remainder after two months: sales expected for November 19-6 are £398,400, and for December 19-6, £402,600.

3 Old factory equipment is to be sold in February 19-7 for £9,600. Receipt of the money is expected in April 19-7. New equipment will be installed at a cost of £38,000. One half of the amount is payable in March 19-7 and the remainder in August 19-7.

4 Two-thirds of the wages are payable in the month they fall due, and one-third a month later: wages for December 19-6 are estimated at £15,900.

5 £50,000 of total monthly overheads are payable in the month they occur, and the remainder one month later: total overheads for December 19-6 are expected to be £265,200.

6 The opening bank balance at 1 January 19-7 is expected to be an overdraft of £10,600.

Required:

(*a*) Using the information above, prepare the firm's cash budget for the period January–April, 19-7.

(*b*) Provide a statement to show those items in part (*a*) which would appear in a budgeted balance sheet as at 30 April 19-7.

(*University of London: GCE 'A' level*)

35.9 D Smith is to open a retail shop on 1 January, 19-4. He will put in £25,000 cash as capital. His plans are as follows:

(i) On 1 January 19-4 to buy and pay for Premises £20,000, Shop Fixtures £3,000, Motor Van £1,000.

(ii) To employ two assistants, each to get a salary of £130 per month, to be paid at the end of each month. (PAYE tax, National Insurance contributions etc, are to be ignored.)

(iii) To buy the following goods (shown in units):

	Jan	Feb	March	April	May	June
Units	200	220	280	350	400	330

(iv) To sell the following number of units:

	Jan	Feb	March	April	May	June
Units	120	180	240	300	390	420

(v) Units will be sold for £10 each. One-third of the sales are for cash, the other two thirds being on credit. These latter customers are expected to pay their accounts in the second month following that in which they received the goods.

(vi) The units will cost £6 each for January to April inclusive, and £7 each thereafter. Creditors will be paid in the month following purchase. (Value stock-in-trade on FIFO basis.)

(vii) The other expenses of the shop will be £150 per month payable in the month following that in which they were incurred.

(viii) Part of the premises will be sub-let as an office at a rent of £600 per annum. This is paid in equal instalments in March, June, September and December.

(ix) Smith's cash drawings will amount to £250 per month.

(x) Depreciation is to be provided on Shop Fixtures at 10 per cent per annum and on the Motor Van at 20 per cent per annum.

You are required to:

(*a*) Draw up a Cash Budget for the six months ended 30 June, 19-4, showing the balance of cash at the end of each month.

(*b*) Draw up a forecast Trading and Profit and Loss Account for the six months ended 30 June 19-4 and a Balance Sheet as at that date.

35.10A The summarised balance sheet of Newland Traders at 30 May 19-7 was as follows:

	£'000	£'000
Fixed assets at cost		610
less depreciation		264
		346
Current assets		
Stocks	210	
Debtors	315	
Cash at bank and in hand	48	
	573	
less Current liabilities		
Creditors	128	445
		791
Capital and reserves		
Issued capital		600
General reserve		150
Profit and loss account		41
		791

Selling and materials prices at 30 May 19-7 provide for a gross profit at the rate of 25% of sales.

The creditors at 30 May 19-7 represent the purchases for May 19-7, and the debtors the sales for April of £150,000 and May of £165,000.

Estimates of sales and expenditure for the six months to 30 November 19-7 are as follows.

(i) Sales for the period at current prices will be £800,000. Sales for the months of September and October will each be twice those of the sales in each of the other months.

(ii) Stock at the end of each month will be the same as at 30 May 19-7 except that at 30 November 19-7 it will be increased to 20% above that level.

(iii) Creditors will be paid one month after the goods are supplied and debtors will pay two months after the goods are supplied.

(iv) Wages and expenses will be £20,000 a month and will be paid in the month in which they are incurred.

(v) Depreciation will be at the rate of £5,000 a month.

(vi) There will be capital expenditure of £80,000 on 1 September 19-7. Depreciation, in addition to that given in (v) above, will be at the rate of 10% per annum on cost.

(vii) There will be no changes in issued capital, general reserve or prices of sales or purchases.

Required:

(a) Sales and purchases budgets and budgeted trading and profit and loss accounts for the six months ended 30 November 19-7.

(b) A budgeted balance sheet as at 30 November 19-7.

(*c*) A cash flow budget for the six months ended 30 November 19-7 indicating whether or not it will be necessary to make arrangements for extra finance and, if so, your recommendation as to what form it should take.

Show all your calculations.

(*Welsh Joint Education Committee: GCE 'A' level*)

35.11 The balance sheet of Gregg Ltd at 30 June, 19-6 was expected to be as follows:

Balance Sheet 30 June, 19-6

Fixed Assets	Cost	Depreciation to date	Net
Land and Buildings	40,000	–	40,000
Plant and Machinery	10,000	6,000	4,000
Motor Vehicles	6,000	2,800	3,200
Office Fixtures	500	220	280
	56,500	9,020	47,480

Current Assets		
Stock-in-Trade: Finished Goods	1,800	
Raw Materials	300	
Debtors (19-6 May £990 + June £900)	1,890	
Cash and Bank Balances	7,100	11,090
		£58,570

Financed by:	
Share Capital	50,000
Profit and Loss Account	7,820
	57,820

Current Liabilities		
Creditors for Raw Materials		
(April £240+May £140+June £160)	540	
Creditors for variable overhead	210	750
		£58,570

The plans for the six months to 31 December 19-6 can be summarised as:
(i) Production costs per unit will be:

	£
Direct Materials	2
Direct Labour	5
Variable overhead	3
	£10

(ii) Sales will be at a price of £18 per unit for the three months to 30 September and at £18.5 subsequently. The number of units sold would be:

	July	Aug	Sept	Oct	Nov	Dec
Units	60	80	100	100	90	70

All sales will be on credit, and debtors will pay their accounts two months after they have bought the goods.

(iii) Production will be even at 90 units per month.

(iv) Purchases of direct materials – all on credit – will be:

July	Aug	Sept	Oct	Nov	Dec
£	£	£	£	£	£
220	200	160	140	140	180

Creditors for direct materials will be paid three months after purchase.

(v) Direct labour is paid in the same month as production occurs.

(vi) Variable overhead is paid in the month following that in which the units are produced.

(vii) Fixed overhead of £90 per month is paid each month and is never in arrears.

(viii) A machine costing £500 will be bought and paid for in July. A motor vehicle costing £2,000 will be bought and paid for in September.

(ix) A debenture of £5,000 will be issued and the cash received in November. Interest will not start to run until 19-7.

(x) Provide for depreciation for the six months: Motor Vehicles £600, Office Fixtures £30, Machinery £700.

You are required to draw up as a minimum:

(a) Cash Budget, showing figures each month.

(b) Debtors' Budget, showing figures each month.

(c) Creditors' Budget, showing figures each month.

(d) Raw Materials Budget, showing figures each month.

(e) Forecast Operating statement for the six months.

(f) Forecast Balance Sheet as at 31 December, 19-6.

In addition you may draw up any further budgets you may wish to show the workings behind the above budgets.

35.12A Len Auck and Brian Land trade as partners in Auckland Manufacturing Company making components for mini-computers. To cope with increasing demand the partners intend to extend their manufacturing capacity but are concerned about the effect of the expansion on their cash resources during the build up period from January to April 19-6.

The following information is available.

(*a*) The balance sheet of Auckland Manufacturing Company at 31 December 19-5 is expected to be:

	£	£
Fixed assets		
Plant and machinery at cost		65,000
less depreciation		28,000
		37,000
Current assets		
Stocks – raw materials	10,500	
– finished goods	18,500	
Debtors	36,000	
Cash at bank	4,550	
	69,550	
Current liabilities		
Creditors	27,550	
		42,000
		£79,000
Partners' capital accounts –		
Len Auck		40,000
Brian Land		39,000
		£79,000

(*b*) Creditors at 31 December 19-5 are made up of:

	£
Creditors for materials supplied in November and December at	
£13,000 per month	26,000
Creditors for overheads	1,550
	£27,550

(*c*) New plant costing £25,000 will be delivered and paid for in January 19-6.

(*d*) Raw material stocks are to be increased to £12,000 by the end of January 19-6, thereafter raw material stocks will be maintained at that level. Payment for raw materials is made two months after the month of delivery. Finished goods stocks will be maintained at £18,500 throughout the period. There is no work in progress.

(*e*) Sales for the four months are expected to be:

	£
January	18,000
February	22,000
March	22,000
April	24,000

Sales for several months prior to 31 December had been running at the rate of £18,000 per month. It is anticipated that all sales will continue to be paid for two months following the month of delivery.

(*f*) The cost structure of the product is expected to be:

	%
Raw materials	50
Direct wages	20
Overheads, including depreciation	17½
Profit	12½
Selling price	100

(*g*) Indirect wages and salaries included in overheads amount to £900 for the month of January and £1,000 per month thereafter.

(*h*) Depreciation of plant and machinery (including the new plant) is to be provided at £700 per month and is included in the total overheads.

(*i*) Wages and salaries are to be paid in the month to which they relate, all other expenses are to be paid for in the month following the month to which they relate.

(*j*) The partners share profits equally and drawings are £400 per month each.

(*k*) During the period to April an overdraft facility is being requested.

Required:

(*a*) A forecast profit and loss account for the four months January to April 19-6 and a balance sheet as at 30 April 19-6.

(*b*) A month by month cash forecast for the four months showing the maximum amount of finance required during the period.

(*c*) A calculation of the month in which the overdraft facility would be repaid on the assumption that the level of activity in April is maintained.

For the purposes of this question taxation and bank interest may be ignored.

(*Chartered Association of Certified Accountants*)

36
Discounting techniques

Most financial transactions involve interest calculations since interest is the charge for using money over time. If a business wishes to borrow money it will have to pay interest on the amount it borrows. The rate of interest will depend on the going market rates and the lender's assessment of the risk associated with lending to a particular type of customer. The higher the risk the higher the rate of interest.

Simple interest

Simple interest applies where the period involved is not greater than a year. The amount of interest due is calculated from the formula:

Amount of interest (A)
= Principal amount loaned (P) × Rate of Interest (r) × Unit of time (t)

Example: Interest has to be calculated on a loan from a Bank of £198,000 at a rate of 12% per annum for 59 days.

Rates of interest for loans will usually be expressed on an annual basis. The unit of time will therefore be the proportion of a year (365 days) for which the loan was obtained.

Thus $\quad A = P r t$

$$A = £198,000 \times 0.12 \times \frac{59}{365}$$

$$A = £3,840.66$$

Note in the formulae it is convenient to express r as a decimal rather than as a percentage i.e. 0.12 rather than 12%.

Another illustration where simple interest is common is where a business discounts a bill of exchange with a bank. The bill of exchange represents a promise to pay (by a third party usually a customer of the business) a specified sum of money at a fixed future date.

Example: A business holds a bill of exchange which promises to pay £20,000 in 90 days' time. The business wants the cash now not in 90 days and the bank quotes a discount rate of interest of 15% on this type of transaction.

$$A = P r t$$

$$A = £20,000 \times 0.15 \times \frac{90}{365}$$

$$A \times £739.73$$

The bank will thus pay to the business the Principal sum of £20,000 less the

Amount of interest £739.73 which amounts to an immediate cash advance of £19,260.27.

Note that the interest rate which the business has really paid on this transaction is more than 15%. The business has in effect borrowed £19,260.27 for 90 days and paid interest of £739.73. This is equivalent to interest of 15.6% on the amount borrowed of £19,260.27. You can check this by using the interest formula:

$$A = Prt$$

$$r = \frac{A}{Pt}$$

$$r = \frac{739.73}{9260.27 \times \dfrac{90}{365}} = 15.58\%$$

This represents the true rate of interest on the transaction as compared to the nominal rate of 15% used to work out the amount advanced on the bill of exchange. This real rate is officially called the annual percentage rate of charge (APR).

In many borrowing situations it is important to note the difference between the nominal rate quoted by a lender and the real rate of interest being paid. Where a loan has to be repaid by instalments the real rate can be considerably higher than the nominal rate.

Example: John wants to borrow £1,000 for one year. The finance company quote interest of 10% but require £500 to be repaid after six months and the balance at the end of the year.

The interest to be paid is 10% of £1,000 =	£100
The amount borrowed will be 1,000 × ½ year =	500
500 × ½ year =	250
	750
The equivalent amount borrowed for one year is	750

$$r = \frac{A}{Pt} = \frac{100}{750 \times 1}$$

$$r = 13.33\%$$

The real rate of interest is thus 13.33% not 10%, i.e. APR = 13.33%.

Compound interest

Where a period of time greater than one year is involved the process of interest calculation becomes compound. This simply means that interest will become payable on the interest of the earlier period as well as the principal sum. If £100 is deposited in a bank for two years at 10% interest per annum, the interest earned is not twice the simple interest for one year which would be £20 (2×£10). At the end of year one amount of simple interest of £10 would be added to the Principal and the total of £110 then reinvested for the second year at 10% which would earn £11 interest. The total interest earned over two years is thus £21.

If you compare the effect of compounding interest over a period of time with simple interest, for example where the interest earned is withdrawn at the end of each year, the difference is quite dramatic.

Example

Mr A invests £1,000 at 10% and allows the interest to be reinvested each year.

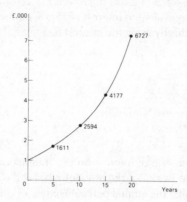

The graph shows the £1,000 increasing over 20 years to a sum of £6,727. Compound Interest is calculated from the formula

Amount (A) = Principal (P) × (1 + rate of interest for the period (r)) to the power of the number of periods (n)

$$A = P(1 + r)^n$$

Example

What will £1,000 invested at 10% per annum compound accumulate to in 10 years?

$$A = P(1 + r)^n$$
$$= 1,000(1 + 0.10)^{10}$$
$$= 2,593.74$$

The computations involved are not much problem if you have a calculator. It is also common to use tables which have been calculated for commonly used rates of interest. The tables are based on £1 invested at the rate of interest as shown in Exhibit 36.1.

Exhibit 36.1

Example of a compound interest table

£1 at compound interest at the end of the period
Rate of interest per period

Period of compounding	1%	2%	5%	10%
1	1.010	1.020	1.050	1.100
2	1.020	1.040	1.103	1.210
3	1.030	1.061	1.158	1.331
4	1.041	1.082	1.216	1.464
5	1.051	1.104	1.276	1.611
10	1.105	1.219	1.629	2.594
50	1.645	2.692	11.462	117.391

Example: You want to know what £500 will accumulate to over three years at 5% per annum interest.

The table shows that £1 invested for 3 periods at 5% will amount to £1.158. Thus £500 will amount to £1.158×500 = £579.

If the compounding process is to take place more often than annually – the rate of interest must be changed to the rate for the compounding period rather than for a year.

Example: What will £500 accumulate to over three years at 5% per annum interest compounded on a quarterly basis?

The periods are now three months and therefore in total there are 12 periods in all. The rate of interest per period will be $0.05 \div 4 = 0.0125$, i.e. $\frac{3}{12} \times$ annual rate,

$$A = P \quad (1+r)^n \quad = 500\,(1.0125)^{12}$$
$$A \qquad\qquad = 580.38$$

Notice that compounding quarterly as compared to annually, as in the previous example, makes a small difference of £1.38 to the accumulated amount. Because for most purposes the difference between annual and more frequent compounding is not material this text will normally use annual compounding.

It is sometimes useful to calculate the rate of return which the increase in an investment represents over a period of time.

Example: Jones bought a house for £10,000 on 1 January 19-1 and sold it for £12,100 on 31 December 19-2. What rate of return does this represent?

Using the tables requires the figures to be expressed in terms of £1. In this case 10,000:12,100 is equivalent to 1:1.210 for a two year period.

Looking across the table on the row for 2 periods compounding it can be seen that the return is equivalent to 10%.

Or using the formula

$$A = \quad P\,(1+r)^n$$

$$r = \sqrt[n]{\frac{A}{P}} - 1 = \sqrt[2]{\frac{12,100}{10,000}} - 1$$

$$= 0.1 \text{ or } 10\%.$$

Present value

In the previous section we calculated that if £1,000 were invested at compound interest of 10% for 10 years it would accumulate to £2,594.

If we posed this question the other way round and asked what would be the value today of £2,594 if received 10 years into the future assuming interest at 10% the answer is a present value of £1,000.

Present value is simply the reciprocal of compound interest and is a useful approach to solving a number of investment problems.

The formula for compound interest is:

$$A = P\,(1+r)^n$$

For the present value calculation we know the Amount (A) and wish to calculate the Principal (P). Divide both sides by $(1+r)^n$ gives

$$P = \frac{A}{(1+r)^n}$$

Example: You are promised a cash gift of £10,000 in two years time. The current rates of interest which you could obtain for this sum is 15%. What is its present value?

$$P = \frac{A}{(1+r)^n} = \frac{10,000}{(1.15)^2}$$

Present Value P = £7,561.4

As with compound interest the use of tables of present values is quite common. For example the values are shown here for the present value of £1 at a rate of interest of 10%. A full table is included in the appendix.

Periods	10%
1	0.909
2	0.826
3	0.751
4	0.683
5	0.621

Example

If you are offered £1,000 at the end of each of the next five years in settlement of a debt of £4,000 should you accept? Assume interest at 10%.

			£
Year	1	£1,000 × 0.909 =	909
	2	£1,000 × 0.826 =	826
	3	£1,000 × 0.751 =	751
	4	£1,000 × 0.683 =	683
	5	£1,000 × 0.621 =	621
		Present Value	3,790

The present value of the five payments is £3,790 which is worth a little less than the debt of £4,000.

Sometimes in investment situations we happen to know in advance the Principal sum and the Amount and want to work out the rate of interest which completes the equation. This rate of interest is called the internal rate of return, or where a business needs to quote the real rate of interest to a customer it is called the annual percentage rate of change (APR).

Example

A friend offers to sell you a lease on some property which will entitle you to equal rent payments at the end of each of the next three years of £1,000.

He wants £2,550 for the lease and you want to calculate what interest rate is included in the deal.

This can be done by trial and error using the present value tables in the appendix. Firstly select a rate of interest as a guess – say 5%.

Year	£	Factor at 5%		£
1	1,000 ×	0.952	=	952
2	1,000 ×	0.907	=	907
3	1,000 ×	0.864	=	864
				2,723

At five per cent interest the present value exceeds the amount asked for the lease of £2,500. A higher rate of interest will be required to reduce the amount closer to target. Try 8% and 9%:

Year	£		Factor at 8%		£		9%		£
1	1,000	×	0.926	=	926	×	0.917	=	917
2	1,000	×	0.857	=	857	×	0.842	=	842
3	1,000	×	0.794	=	794	×	0.772	=	772
					2,577				2,531

The rate of interest which will produce a present value of £2,550 lies between 8% and 9%. If we want to be more exact we can interpolate on an approximate basis as follows:

$$8\% \text{ gives} \qquad 2,577$$
$$\left. \begin{array}{c} - \quad 2,550 \end{array} \right\} \quad 19$$
$$9\% \qquad 2,531 \quad 33$$
$$\overline{46}$$

2,550 is thus $^{19}\!/_{46}$ of 1% below 9%

i.e. $9 - 0.41 = 8.59\%$, i.e. APR $= 8.59\%$

Annuities

An annuity is a series, or one of a series, of equal payments at fixed intervals. For example, rent payable every month, quarter or year, is one form of annuity. The term annuity originated in the field of insurance where in exchange for a lump sum payment or a series of premiums a regular payment would be made to the annuitant during his life. Regular payments such as rents or purchase by instalments occur frequently in business and it is, therefore, useful to know something about the calculation of annuities.

In practice there are a number of different kinds of annuity varying mainly in the details of when the regular payments are made, for example at the beginning or end of the period. In this chapter attention is centred entirely on the Ordinary Annuity in which the equal periodic payments occur at the end of the period. In practice, with a little thought it will be possible to handle most situations with a knowledge of how to calculate an Ordinary Annuity.

Formula for the amount of an ordinary annuity

The amount of an annuity of £1 per period for three periods at 5 per cent interest might be determined as follows:

The first rent payment of £1 accumulates at 5 per cent
interest for two periods and grows to: $\qquad$ £1 $(1 + 0.05)^2 = $ £1.1025
The second rent payment of £1 accumulates at 5 per cent
interest for one period and grows to: $\qquad$ £1.05
The third rent is due at the end of the annuity period $\qquad$ £1.00

These added up to $\qquad$ £3.1525

To develop the formula for the annuity we need to examine the relationship between compound interest, and an annuity of the amount of interest. If £1 is invested for two periods at 5 per cent interest we have shown above that it will accumulate to £1.1025. Deducting the original investment from this amount we are left with the compound interest on £1 for two periods as £0.1025. This amount is simply the amount of an annuity of 5 per cent of £1 for two periods at 5 per cent.

Substituting generalized letters into the formula. This can be set down as:

$$0.05 \times \text{Annuity} = 1\,(1 + 0.05)^2 - 1$$

or

$$\text{Annuity} = 1\,\frac{(1 + 0.05)^2 - 1}{0.05} = \frac{(1.05)^2 - 1}{0.05}$$

$$\text{Annuity} = R\,\frac{(1 + r)^n - 1}{r}$$

Where R = the annuity per period.

As in previous examples tables are available calculated on the basis of £1 to assist calculations: see the Appendix.

Example: A company plans to invest £1,000 at the end of the year for each of the next five years at an interest rate of 5 per cent per annum. How much will have accumulated at the end of the fifth year?

$$£1,000\frac{(1 + 0.05)^5 - 1}{0.05} = £5,525.631$$

or using tables

$$£1,000 \times 5.526 = £5,526$$

It will frequently be useful to know the amount required by way of periodic rents to accumulate to a known future sum, for example when establishing a sinking fund.

It has already been established that where the amount of an annuity = A

$$A = R\,\frac{(1 + r)^n - 1}{r}$$

$$R = \frac{Ar}{(1 + r)^n - 1}$$

Example: A company wishes to set aside equal annual amounts at the end of each year of the next four years, to accumulate to a fund of £5,000 for the replacement of assets. The amounts set aside will be invested at 6 per cent per annum interest. What amounts should be set aside?

$$R = \frac{Ar}{(1 + r)^n - 1} = \frac{5,000(0.06)}{(1.06)^4 - 1} = £1,142.9578$$

This figure can be proved correct by the table below worked (as would be normal) to the nearest £1.

	Deposit £	Interest £	Increase in fund £	Balance of fund £
End of year 1	1,143	–	1,143	1,143
End of year 2	1,143	69	1,212	2,355
End of year 3	1,143	141	1,284	3,639
End of year 4	1,143	218	1,361	5,000

Example: What amount invested annually at 5 per cent per annum will provide £1 in five years time?

$$R = \frac{Ar}{(1 = r)^n - 1} = \frac{1\,(0.05)}{(1.05)^5 - 1} = £0.180975$$

The present value of annuities

It will often be necessary to calculate the present value of an annuity to evaluate a business problem. The present value of an annuity is the amount which if it were invested now at compound interest would be just sufficient to allow for the withdrawal of equal amounts (rents) at the end of a fixed number of periods. For example, we may wish to know whether to pay £135 cash now for a television or five instalments of £30 over the next two-and-a-half years instead. By converting the five instalments to a present cash value we can make direct comparison with the £135 cash price. If the present value of the annuity is more than £135 we should choose to pay cash. If, however, it comes to less than £135 the instalment method is cheaper. The result obtained will depend on the rate of interest used in the calculation.

The present value of an annuity will be equal to the sum of the present values of every individual rent payment. This can be illustrated in the above example, assuming an 8 per cent rate of interest. The calculation shows it better at this rate of interest to pay by instalment.

Period	£	Present Value Multiplier from Tables		£
1	30 ×	0.962	=	28.86
2	30 ×	0.925	=	27.75
3	30 ×	0.889	=	26.67
4	30 ×	0.855	=	25.65
5	30 ×	0.822	=	24.66
				133.59

Note: when taken a half-yearly period the annual rate of interest is halved. The multiplier is therefore from the 4 per cent column of the Present Value tables.

The formula for finding the present value of an ordinary annuity is developed as follows:

Compound discount (equivalent to compound interest) is the amount by which the total investment at compound interest will exceed the original capital. On the basis of £1:

$$\text{Discount} = 1 - \frac{1}{(1 = r)^n}$$

By the same process of argument that was used when developing the formula for an ordinary annuity, it can be shown that the compound discount on £1 at 5 per cent is equal to 5 per cent of the present value of an annuity of £1. Thus

$$r \times \text{Present Value} = 1 - \frac{1}{(1 + r)^n}$$

$$\text{Present Value} = \left[\frac{1 - \dfrac{1}{(1 + r)^n}}{r} \right]$$

Tables are given in the Appendix to show the present values of an annuity of £1.

Example (details per previous example). The present value of five half-yearly payments of £30 at 8 per cent per annum would be:

$$R = \left[\frac{1 - \dfrac{1}{(1 + r)^n}}{r} \right] = 30 \left[\frac{1 - \dfrac{1}{(1 + 0.04)^5}}{0.04} \right] = £133.57$$

or using the tables $30 \times 4.452 = £133.56$.

Finally, to prove that the present value of an annuity is the amount which if it were invested now at compound interest would be just sufficient to allow for the withdrawal of equal amounts at the end of a fixed number of periods, we can show that the present value of £133.57 just calculated would fulfil this condition for withdrawals of £30 over five half-yearly periods with interest at 8 per cent per annum.

		£
Start		133.57
Period 1	Interest	5.34 (133.57 at 8 per cent for 6 months)
	Payment	(30.00)
Balance		108.91
Period 2	Interest	4.35
	Payment	(30.00)
Balance		83.26
Period 3	Interest	3.33
	Payment	(30.00)
Balance		56.59
Period 4	Interest	2.26
	Payment	(30.00)
Balance		28.85
Period 5	Interest	1.15
	Payment	(30.00)
Balance		00.00

Capital budgeting

When a business is planning investment in fixed assets or things which involve a long-term commitment of the organisation's resources then the budgeting process should include interest as an important cost element in the decision about whether to invest or not. This process is what is termed Capital Budgeting.

The process of evaluating investments taking into account interest requires that cash budgets are dealt with rather than the figures used in profit calculations. In profit calculation for example depreciation of fixed assets is included in the expenses. However since depreciation does not involve cash – it is not relevant for capital budgeting. Interest is only relevant to cash flows and it is these that Capital Budgeting concentrates on. The two aspects of cash flows on an investment are the cash outflows on the acquisition and setting up of the project and the cash inflows which are expected to be generated. It is the balance between outflow and inflow which determines whether the investment is worthwhile.

Investment outlays

The cash outlay involved in an investment will include a variety of different items. If for example the investment is in plant and machinery the outlay will include not only the invoice cost of the equipment bought – but also the cost of installation, commissioning which means the costs of a period of adjustment until it operates at full efficiency, and possibly training of new personnel. In addition the introduction of new plant and machinery might involve extra funds for working capital tied up in the operation.

Example

Progress Ltd is planning to introduce new machines. The outlays anticipated on the acquisition are as follows:

	Cash Flow – Outlay
	£
Invoice Cost of Machines	50,000
Carriage Inward	2,000
Installation – cost of wages of own employees	1,000
	53,000
Cost of materials and wages in commissioning machines	5,000
Training Cost – Wages of operatives	2,000
	60,000
Additional Working Capital	14,000
Cash Outlay	74,000

If the outlays in the Example for Progress Ltd had been on machinery designed to replace existing equipment – perhaps justified by claims of greater efficiency for the new machines – then the decision would be taken based on the incremental outlays compared to the incremental inflows – i.e. the net additional cash required to be invested on the new scheme compared to the additional cash earned or saved.

Thus in the example the additional outlay compared with existing machines would not include working capital (assuming outputs are the same) since this is already required in the existing set-up. Also the buying of new equipment – implies that the old can be sold – thus the cash from sale should be deducted from the outlay

		£
i.e.	Cost of Machines and installations etc.	60,000
	less Sale of old machines	10,000
	Net Cash Outlay	50,000

The net outlay of £50,000 will then be compared with the cash saved by using the new process.

This incremental approach is important for assessing improvements and where the equipment is for example part of a large factory where it will be impossible to identify all the cash flow implications of one small part of the total unit.

The Cash outflows on an investment in a large project may be spread over a number of periods. The development can be spread over several years from its first inception. It may therefore be necessary to discount back the outlays to a present value at the start of the project.

Example: The cash outlays on a new factory development were estimated as follows:

	£
Year 1 Development and Buildings	100,000
2 Installation of Equipment	50,000
3 Commissioning	30,000
	180,000

The Present Value of these outflows if interest is assumed to be 10% would be:

Period	£		£
1	100,000 × 0.909	=	90,900
2	50,000 × 0.826	=	41,300
3	30,000 × 0.751	=	22,530
			£154,730

The Present Value of outlays at the start of the project – often called period 0 – is £154,730. This figure would be compared with the Present Value of Inflows.

An important aspect of investment cash flows is that they will give rise to tax implications. The purchase of Plant and Machinery for example will give rise to allowances which can be deducted from taxable income. Thus for a company which buys a new machine for £100,000 and pays Corporation Tax at 35% on its profits the cash flows will be firstly an outlay on purchase of £100,000, secondly its tax bill when due for payment (usually in the next year) will be reduced by the tax on the writing down allowance (the tax equivalent of depreciation). If the writing down allowance is 25% p.a. the tax saved in the first year will be 35% of (25% × 100,000) = £8,750. In the year after the tax saved will be 35% of (25% × 75,000) = £6,562 since the writing down allowance is based on the reducing balance method. The cash flow involved will thus be spread:

Year	0	1	2	3	4	5	etc.
Outlay on machine	£100,000						
Tax saving (£)		8,750	6,562	4,922	3,691	2,769	etc.

The tax saving will continue over the life of the asset.

The actual calculation of tax payments can be complex and requires a detailed knowledge of the tax laws, which are beyond the scope of this book. However in principle all that needs to be taken into account are the cash outflows or inflows for tax which will arise from the investment decision. These may have to be calculated by a person competent in tax.

Cash inflows

The other aspect of the Capital Budgeting process is to estimate the cash which will be generated by the new investment.

If the investment is in something new – then the estimates will be cash budgets of the sales and expenses expected to be generated by the new investment. The approach will be exactly the same as for the operating cash budgets prepared for management in planning its cash requirements – except that the requirement here is usually for the annual figures over the anticipated life of the investment, rather than on a month by month basis.

If the investment is in improvement or replacement of an existing process then the cash inflow will be the savings expected as compared to the existing situation.

As with the cash outflows the net inflows expected from an investment will be subject to tax. The tax consequences of the new business must be worked out and the cash payments for tax included in the calculation of net cash inflows,

Example: The expected results from buying a new machine for £6,000 have been estimated to produce sales of £6,000 per annum for four years and the production costs would be £2,500 for materials, labour and other cash outlays. Working Capital required will be £2,000 which will be recoverable at the end of the fourth year. Depreciation per annum would be £1,500 and the company pays Corporation tax nine months after its accounting year end at 35%. Writing down allowance is 25% p.a.

The profit expected each year is thus:

		£
Sales		6,000
Material, Labour and		
other costs	2,500	
Depreciation	1,500	4,000
		2,000
Corporation Tax		700
Net Profit		1,300

Exhibit 36.2

But for Capital Budgeting the cash flow analysis would be:

Investment outlay	Year 1	2	3	4	5
Cost of Machine	(6,000)				
Working Capital	(2,000)			2,000	
Taxation Allowance on Capital Expenditure		525	394	295	886
	(8,000)	525	394	2,295	886

Cash flows					
Sales	6,000	6,000	6,000	6,000	
Costs of Material and labour etc.	(2,500)	(2,500)	(2,500)	(2,500)	
Tax (35% × 3,500)		(1,225)	(1,225)	(1,225)	(1,225)
	3,500	2,275	2,275	2,275	(1,225)

It is assumed that the machine is scrapped without value in the last year and the remaining balance of allowances are written off. Overall the tax allowances add up to £2,100 which is 35% of £6,000.

Capital expenditure evaluation

There are several ways of working out whether or not a capital expenditure is worthwhile. The simplest systems do not include interest in the evaluation and are therefore deficient in this important respect. They are however frequently used and may be a worthwhile addition to the more complete evaluations which include interest.

Payback

This measures the time taken to recover the cash outlay on the project. If we use the data on cash flows from Exhibit 36.2 the cash figures are as follows:

Year	Investment outlay £	Cash flow £	Net cash flow £	Cumulative cash flow £
1	(8,000)	3,500	(4,500)	(4,500)
2	525	2,275	2,800	(1,700)
3	394	2,275	2,669	969
4	2,295	2,275	4,570	5,539
5	886	(1,225)	(1,339)	5,200

The net cash flow is negative in the first two years but becomes positive in the third year. To work out the time when the cash outlay is recovered assuming the cash flows evenly during the year we calculate $\dfrac{1,700}{2,669} \times 365 \text{ days} = 232 \text{ days}$.

Thus the payback on this project occurs after 2 years 232 days or approximately 2.64 years.

Firms using payback as a method of evaluation would normally have a period fixed as a cut-off point. For example if the cut-off time were 3 years then all projects which had a payback of more than 3 years would be rejected.

The advantage of the payback method is that it emphasises the early return of cash which may be of utmost importance to a firm with liquidity problems. The disadvantage it has is that it ignores the results after payback has been achieved. For example if we had a project which showed a cumulative cash flow of : year 1 £(4,500) and year 2 £400 and no further cash flows then the payback would still be 1.92 years and no regard is given to subsequent years. It would therefore be given a better evaluation than the previous example where cash flows continue into the future. While in this case the difference between the two would be clear – in a more complicated case it may not be easy to discriminate between alternatives.

Accounting rate of return

This is defined as:

$$\frac{\text{Average annual net profit after tax}}{\text{Average investment}}$$

If again we use the information from Exhibit 36.2 we know that the expected profit after tax in each of the four years is expected to be £1,300. The investment in machinery is £6,000 at the start and nil at the end assuming it is being depreciated straight line. The average investment would normally be calculated at ½ the opening value + closing value i.e. ½ (6,000 + 0) = £3,000. The working capital remains constant at £2,000 – the calculation for working capital is the same ½ (2,000 + 2,000) = £2,000. Thus the total average investment would be £3,000 + £2,000 = £5,000. The tax relief on the capital expenditure is included with the corporation tax assessed on profits.

The return is therefore $\dfrac{1,300}{5,000}$ = 26.0%.

This accounting rate of return relates to the results shown in the annual accounts. However as an average it should not be forgotten that there will be significant differences between the start and end of the project's life. In the example given the figures each year would be:

	Year 1		Year 2		Year 3		Year 4	
Net Profit	1,300		1,300		1,300		1,300	
	———	= 17.9%	———	= 22.7%	———	= 30.6	———	= 47.3%
Net Book Value of	7,250		5,720		4,250		2,750	
Machine + Working								
Capital at mid-year								

With a depreciating asset the rate of return appears to increase as the net book value declines, even though profits are constant.

Present value and internal rate of return

So far the methods employed to evaluate capital expenditure have ignored interest which means that only in certain circumstances would these methods approximate to the correct evaluation employing compound interest. Taking the facts again from the previous example in Exhibit 36.2 we can calculate the return assuming a required rate of interest of 15%.

	Investment outlay	Cash flow	Net cash flow
1	(8,000)	3,500	(4,500)
2	525	2,275	2,800
3	394	2,275	2,669
4	2,295	2,275	4,570
5	886	(1,225)	(339)

	Investment outlay		Cash flow		Net cash flow	
1	(8,000)× 0·870 =	(6,960)	3,500 × 0·870 = 3,045	(4,500)× 0·870 =	(3,915)
2	525 × 0·756 =	397	2,275 × 0·756 = 1,720	2,800 × 0·756 =	2,117
3	394 × 0·658 =	259	2,275 × 0·658 = 1,497	2,669 × 0·658 =	1,756
4	2,295 × 0·572 =	1,313	2,275 × 0·572 = 1,301	4,570 × 0·572 =	2,614
5	886 × 0·497 =	440	(1,225)× 0·497 = (609)	(339)× 0·497 =	(169)
		(4,551)	6,954		2,403

The Net Present Value of this project using an interest rate of 15% is £2,403, which indicates that the discounted value of the inflows exceeds the discounted value of the investment outlay by this net amount. The project is therefore worthwhile provided the funds of the business do not cost more than 15%.

The Internal Rate of Return is the rate of interest which will when applied to the cash flows equate Investment Outlay and Cash Inflow or in other words discount the Net Cash Flow to zero.

As was previously illustrated this is done by trial and error. Using the rates from the tables at 50% and 60% we get

Year	Net cash flow	r = 50%		r = 40%	
		factor		factor	
1	(4,500)	0.667	(3,001)	0.714	(3,213)
2	2,800	0.444	1,243	0.510	1,428
3	2,669	0.296	790	0.364	972
4	4,570	0.198	905	0.260	1,188
5	(339)	0.132	(45)	0.186	(63)
Net Present Value			(108)		312

Interpolating between the two one can estimate that the rate producing a Net Present Value of zero will fall $^{108}/_{420} \times 10\%$ below 50%, i.e. at approximately 47% which is the Internal Rate of Return on the Project. The actual return in this project is therefore well above the cost of capital to the company – assuming that this is 15%.

Present value v. IRR

In the majority of cases both the Present Value method and the Internal Rate of Return method will give the same result. In certain circumstances there can be conflict and it is necessary therefore to know which method is yielding the right result.

The circumstances in which the conflict arises is where projects are mutually exclusive – that is where only one can be chosen – and where there are differences in the timing of cash flows or in the size of cash flows on the projects.

Example: The Cash Investment in each of two projects is £10,000. Project A has a cash inflow in year 2 of £13,000 while Project B has a cash inflow in year 5 of £17,620.

Assuming that the rate of interest used by the company is 10% then the Present Value of the projects is

	Cash Outlay	Cash Inflow		Present Value	PV	Net Present
	Year 0	Year 2	Year 5	Factor at 10%	of Inflow	Value
Project A	10,000	13,000		0.826	10,739	738
Project B	10,000		17,620	0.621	10,942	942

Exhibit 36.3

i.e. Project B would be selected.

The Internal Rate of Return on these cash flows is:

Project A approximately 14% ($13,000 \times 0.769 = 9,997$)

and Project B approximately 12% ($17,620 \times 0.567 = 9,991$)

i.e. Project A would be selected.

The conflict in the two measures arises because of the difference in the timing of cash flows between the two alternative investments. Project A produces its cash inflow in year 2 whereas Project B is delayed until year 5. To determine which method is the best selector – the opportunity value of the cash funds generated has to be considered, i.e. what rate of return can be earned on the funds elsewhere. If Project A's inflow can be reinvested at 14% then it is the best choice. However if only 10% can be generated then B is better.

This problem could be looked at rather like a bank deposit problem. Up until the end of year 2 both A & B are overdrawn by £10,000. At the end of year 2 project A receives £13,000 and thus goes into credit for year 3, 4 and 5, if interest is less than 14%, whereas project B stays overdrawn until the end of year 5. Numerically the accounts would be as follows if 10% and 14% interest were charged and earned in the account.

| | Project A | | Project B | |
	using 10%	using 14%	using 10%	using 14%
Year 0	(10,000)	(10,000)	(10,000)	(10,000)
Year 1 interest	(1,000)	(1,400)	(1,000)	(1,400)
	(11,000)	(11,400)	(11,000)	(11,400)
Year 2 interest	(1,100)	(1,596)	(1,100)	(1,596)
cash	13,000	13,000	(12,100)	(12,990)
	900	Say 0		
Year 3 interest	90		(1,210)	(1,819)
	990		(13,310)	(14,815)
Year 4 interest	99		(1,331)	(2,074)
	1,089		(14,641)	(16,889)
Year 5 interest	109		(1,464)	(2,365)
cash	–		17,620	17,620
	1,198	0	1,515	(1,634)

As we showed using the present value approach project B has accumulated a bigger value at the end of the project using 10%. Notice that these end values in year 5 can be discounted back to the Net Present Value at the start, i.e. $1,198 \times 0.621 = 774$ and $1,515 \times 0.621 = 941$ (small differences are due to rounding errors). Using 14% interest Project A just breaks even while Project B loses – remaining in overdraft!

Thus the assumption about what the funds generated will earn elsewhere can be crucial in this type of choice where it is a question of deciding between alternatives which are mutually exclusive. As a rule of thumb many firms choose the Net Present Value since the assumption about the rate of interest earned is likely to be realistic – but this is by no means always so.

The problem just considered also raises the difficulty in general of comparing projects which have different life cycles. For example one project may involve buying equipment which requires replacement every two years while another requires replacement every five years. In comparing the alternatives it may be helpful to work out the annualised cost of each based on a period of time which is the lowest common multiple of the two or more choices. For example a 10 year cycle would be taken for projects with 2 and 5 year lives.

The way to calculate the annualised figure of cash flow is to firstly calculate the net present value of the alternatives. If for example using data in Exhibit 36.3 the NPV of a project with a two year life were £738 and assuming that a 10% rate of interest were appropriate then the annualised figure is the amount of the annuity for two years with a present value of £738. Referring to the tables we can see that the present value of £1 per period for two years at 10% is £1.736. If x is the annualised amount then

$$1.736\,x = 738$$
$$\text{therefore } x = 425$$

Diagrammatically what we have done is convert cash flows as follows:

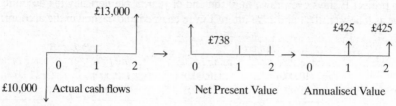

Exhibit 36.4

Using the data from Exhibit 36.3 for Machine B which has a five year life the accumulated net cash flow figure would be calculated using the NPV of £942 and the figure from the tables for the present value of an annuity for five years at 10% which equals 3.791 then

$$3.791\,x = 942$$
$$x = 248$$

We can then compare annualised net cash flow for machine B of £248 with that for machine A of £425. Selecting the alternative with the highest net cash flow on an annualised basis would give project A.

This technique can be used to compare projects on the basis of costs rather than net cash flows – when the alternative with the lowest annualised cost would be selected.

Leasing

Leasing is an important method for many organisations to acquire assets. Things as diverse as motor vehicles, televisions, computers, machinery and buildings are commonly leased rather than bought. In a lease the lessor owns the object and leases it to the user, the lessee. The agreement which is legally binding and non-cancellable usually covers the major part of the economic life of the asset. The lessee in exchange for the use of the asset agrees to pay a rental, keep the item in good condition, insure it and properly service it. The rental payments and other costs are fully chargeable against the taxable profits of the lessee. The lessor as owner of the assets can claim all Capital Allowances for tax purposes against his taxable profits.

Leasing is possible because of the different costs of capital and tax situations between lessors and lessees. For example a company wishing to obtain a computer costing £100,000 may find it attractive to lease because the financial institution funding the operating can borrow at much lower rates than the company and its marginal tax rates against which the capital allowances on the computer can be set are significantly higher for the financial institution than the company.

The problem facing an organisation therefore is to compare the relative attractiveness of obtaining the use of an asset by buying it outright funding from normal sources of capital or whether to lease it.

The interest rate implied in a lease

In the type of decision which has to be made the purchase price of an asset is known, as are the rental terms. From this an interest rate which is the APR can be derived:

A computer costing £100,000 has an expected life of 5 years with no scrap value. It can be leased for £27,740 per annum. The interest rate is that at which:

The Cost of the Item = Present Value of the annual rental payments

$100,000 = 27,740 \times x$ (where x is the factor for the present value of an annuity of £1 for 5 years)

$$\text{therefore} \quad x = \frac{100,000}{27,740} = 3.605$$

By looking across the tables for the present value of an annuity on the five year period it will be seen that 3.605 corresponds to a rate of interest of 12%, i.e. APR = 12%.

If scrap values are involved the calculation would have to be made as in the trial and error method of calculating internal rate of return.

This calculation has ignored the impact of taxation which may be crucial in the ultimate choice between leasing or buying. In the example we have just examined the rental payments would be deducted from taxable income and the net of tax cost would therefore be reduced by the tax borne by the company on its profits. If the tax rate were 42% of profits then the net of tax cost of the lease could be 58% of £27,740 = £16,089 and the corresponding interest rate would be 58% $\times$ 12% = 6.96%. (This ignores possible time lags in obtaining tax relief.)

This net of tax rate of interest can be compared with the organisation's net of tax cost of capital.

Using annualised cost

In the previous section the method of converting cash flows into annualised amounts is one method of comparing the buying decision with the alternative of leasing. The cost of buying the computer we know is £100,000. Capital Allowances for tax purposes of 100% of costs would be obtained in year 1 at the tax rate of 42%. There is a nil residual value at the end of 5 years. The Company's net of tax cost of capital is 10%.

Cash flows

Year		
0	(100,000)	
1	42,000	(assuming tax bill reduced by 42% $\times$ 100,000)
2	–	
3	–	
4	–	
5	–	

$$\text{NPV} = (100,000) - (42,000 \times 0.909) = (61,822)$$

The annualised figure is thus:

$$61,822 = 3.791 \times x$$
$$x = 16,307$$

The annualised cost of buying the asset is £16,307 and should be compared with the net of tax cost of leasing which amounted to £16,089. Since these figures are so close – the organisation would consider all the other factors surrounding the decision before making its choice.

It would also have been possible to compare the NPV of the lease payments with the NPV for buying.

For leasing the NPV net of tax =

Rental $\times$ Present Value of an annuity of £1 for 5 years at 10% =

$$16,089 \times 3.791 = £60,993.$$

The NPV of leasing is an outlay of £60,993 compared to buying of £61,822. Notice that the organisation's costs of capital of 10% has been used to discount the rental payments to a NPV rather than the interest rate implied in the lease of 6.96%. It is normal to use the average cost of capital rather than the marginal rate implicit in the particular transaction.

Notice that the benefits of the investment in the equipment have not been considered. We have simply compared alternative costs of buying or leasing the same equipment. The overall investment decision could be taken by comparing these costs with the benefits accruing from the investment.

The financial implications of leasing

Signing a lease creates a legal obligation to continue paying the rental. The amount of the obligation to the lessor and the benefits obtainable by the organisation under the lease do not normally appear on the face of the organisation's Balance Sheet in conventional accounting. In considering the organisation's financial structure however – a lease represents the equivalent of a loan (as a clear alternative to a direct loan to acquire an asset).

The equivalent loan would be the NPV of the outstanding lease payments discounted by the rate of interest for borrowing. For example the NPV of a five year lease with rental of £27,740 and a rate of interest of 14% (before tax) would be £27,740 × 3.605 = £100,000.

Accounting for leases

In accounting for finance leases the problem is to divide the rental payments into an interest component and a capital repayment element. The rental payments are as was previously mentioned intended to pay for the use of the asset and for the finance required to fund the transaction. To calculate the interest element each period it is necessary to work out the real rate of interest implied in the lease, from knowledge of the rental payments, the period of the lease and the cash value of the assets involved at the start of the period.

If we take a problem with the facts as follows:

1 A rental of £670 per quarter payable in advance.

2 20 quarterly payments starting from 1 January 19-2.

3 The leased asset could be purchased for cash of £10,000 at the start of the lease.

In order to calculate the implied rate of interest it must be remembered that an ordinary annuity calculation relates to payments at the end of the period. In this case we have one payment of £670 at the start and an annuity of £670 for 19 periods. The interest rate at which the present value of these lease payments equals the cash value of £10,000 is the interest rate implied in the lease.

$$\text{Present Value of annuity} = R \left[\frac{1 - \dfrac{1}{(1+i)^{11}}}{i} \right]$$

$$\text{therefore } 10{,}000 = 670 + 670 \left[\frac{1 - \dfrac{1}{(1+i)^{19}}}{i} \right]$$

$$\text{therefore } 9{,}330 = 670 \left[\frac{1 - \dfrac{1}{(1+i)^{19}}}{i} \right]$$

$$i = 0.0332 \text{ or } 3.32\%$$

Note that the initial payment of £670 reduce the cash value of the machine to £9,330 and the calculation then as for an ordinary annuity for 19 periods.

To find the rate of interest using the table for the Present Value of an Annuity requires the initial payment to be dealt with as before. We need to find the interest rate where $9{,}330 = 670 \times$ factor for 19 periods

or

$$\text{factor for 19 periods} = \frac{9{,}330}{670} = 13.925$$

By interpolation $\qquad$ 3% $\qquad$ 14.324

$\qquad\qquad\qquad\qquad\qquad\qquad$ 0.399 $\qquad$ 13.925

$\qquad\qquad\qquad\qquad$ 4% $\qquad$ 13.134

$\qquad\qquad\qquad\qquad\qquad\qquad$ 1.190

$$\frac{0.399}{1.190} = 0.335$$

i.e. 3.3%

Applying the rate of interest of 3.32% (which may in practice be rounded to 3.3%) to the lease data shows the following:

Exhibit 36.5

Calculation of the periodic finance charge in the lease

Period	Capital sum at start of period £	Rental paid £	Capital sum during period £	Finance charge (3.32% per quarter) £	Capital sum at end of period £
1/19-2	100,000	670	9,330	310	9,640
2/19-2	9,640	670	8,970	298	9,268
3/19-2	9,268	670	8,598	285	8,883
4/19-2	8,883	670	8,213	273	8,486
1/19-3	8,486	670	7,816	259	8,075
2/19-3	8,075	670	7,405	246	7,651
3/19-3	7,651	670	6.981	232	7,213
4/19-3	7,213	670	6,543	217	6,760
1/19-4	6,760	670	6,090	202	6,292
2/19-4	6,292	670	5,622	187	5,809
3/19-4	5,809	670	5,139	171	5,310
4/19-4	5,310	670	4,640	154	4,794
1/19-5	4,794	670	4,124	137	4,261
2/19-5	4,261	670	3,591	119	3,710
3/19-5	3,710	670	3,040	101	3,141
4/19-5	3,141	670	2,471	82	2,553
1/19-6	2,553	670	1,883	63	1,946
2/19-6	1,946	670	1,276	42	1,318
3/19-6	1,318	670	648	22	670
4/19-6	670	670	–	–	–
		£13,400		£3,400	

Finance charges for each year of the contract are therefore:

	£
19-2 (310 + 298 + 285 +273)	1,166
19-3	954
19-4	714
19-5	439
19-6	127

The total picture for the five years is as follows:

	Total rental	less	Finance charge	=	Capital repayment
	£		£		£
19-2	2,680		1,166		1,514
19-3	2,680		954		1,726
19-4	2,680		714		1,966
19-5	2,680		439		2,241
19-6	2,680		127		2,553

In the Balance Sheet of the Company the liability under finance leases would be:

	Obligations under finance leases at start of year	less	Capital repayment	=	Obligations under finance leases at end of year
	£		£		£
19-2	10,000		1,514		8,486
19-3	8,486		1,726		6,760
19-4	6,760		1,966		4,794
19-5	4,794		2,241		2,553
19-6	2,553		2,553		–

A small company may consider that the calculations involved in the actuarial method described are too complicated and a simple rule-of-thumb method may be used instead, known as the Rule of 78.

The term arises because it was originally applied over 1 year and 78 is the sum of the number of months from 1 to 12 inclusive. The first month would receive a proportion in reverse order to its position, i.e. $\frac{12}{78}$ the second month would receive $\frac{11}{78}$ and so on till the twelfth month which would receive $\frac{1}{78}$ of the total.

Under this system it is clear that the early periods will receive a heavier allocation than later periods which is what happens when interest is allocated according to the actuarial method. The relationship between the two will however only be approximate since there is no direct relationship. The finance charge to which the proportion is applied is simply the difference between the total payments under the leasing agreement and the cash value of the asset at the start.

If we refer back to the illustration of the actuarial method in Exhibit 36.5 the allocation of the finance charge of £3,400 to the periods concerned using the rule of 78 would be as follows:

	Rental payment number	For Rule of 78	Allocation × £3,400 £	Annual Allocation £
1/19-2	1	19	340	
2/19-2	2	18	322	
3/19-2	3	17	304	
4/19-2	4	16	286	1,252
1/19-3	5	15	268	
2/19-3	6	14	251	
3/19-3	7	13	233	
4/19-3	8	12	215	967
1/19-4	9	11	197	
2/19-4	10	10	179	
3/19-4	11	9	161	
4/19-4	12	8	143	680
1/19-5	13	7	125	
2/19-5	14	6	107	
3/19-5	15	5	89	
4/19-5	16	4	72	393
1/19-6	17	3	54	
2/19-6	18	2	36	
3/19-6	19	1	18	
4/19-6	–	–	–	108
	190	190	3,400	3,400

Period 1/19-2 receives $^{19}/_{190} \times £3,400 = £340$ of the total finance charge and so on. Note that because the payments are at the start of the period there is no allocation to period 4/19-6.

Comparison of the two methods of allocation is as follows:

	Actuarial method £	Rule of 78 £
19-2	1,166	1,252
19-3	954	967
19-4	714	680
19-5	439	393
19-6	127	108
	3,400	3,400

Uncertainty

In the previous sections the budgets of capital expenditures were based on an assumption of average certainty. In reality however different types of project have widely different levels of uncertainty attached to their outcomes. The outcome of replacement of machinery on an existing product line is likely to be much easier to estimate than the result of investment in a totally new product line of an innovatory kind. Methods need to be developed to deal with uncertainty in this type of situation. Some of the most common methods of allowing for uncertainty are described below.

Scaling down benefits and scaling up uncertain costs

Perhaps the commonest method of allowing for uncertainty is to adopt a very conservative approach to the estimated data used in capital budgets. This may simply mean reducing estimates of revenues by a fixed percentage and increasing estimates of costs likewise. Perhaps a more useful approach is to obtain from the estimates a range of likely outcomes which might range over.

'Best	'Most	'Worst
Likely	Likely	Likely
Outcome',	Outcome',	Outcome'.

Continual vigilance is necessary in preparing estimates for capital budgets since people become highly committed to projects and tend to produce figures to prove their case, rather than objective estimates.

Adjusting the cut-off rate

Another common method of allowing for uncertainty is to increase the rate of return required from a project. Most businesses find that the actual rate of return earned by the business as a whole falls short of the returns promised by individual projects. It is always hard after the event to effectively trace what happens – although post-auditing of capital budgets is very desirable in principle. In practice therefore businesses tend to fix cut off rates some way higher than this estimated cost of capital to allow for shortfalls from the budget. Different cut-off rates are also often applied to projects in different classes of uncertainty. Replacement of existing plant will require a lower cut-off than investment in a new and untried development.

Estimates using subjective probabilities

Some organisations have used estimating techniques which require the estimators to consider the range of likely outcomes and relate to them a subjective assessment of the probability of occurrence. For example instead of a single estimate of sales the likely range is associated with its probability.

1	2	3 = 1 × 2
Sale Estimates	Probability of Outcome	Expected Sales
£		
1,000	0.1	100
2,000	0.3	600
3,000	0.4	1,200
4,000	0.2	800
	1.0	2,700

The probability of the outcome in the second column is assigned by the estimator to the range of sales estimates in column one. The probabilities add to one as they cover the full range of likely outcomes. The expected sales from this estimate amount to £2,700.

This type of approach is only likely to prove better than other methods if there is reasonable basis for assigning the probability of outcome – based on analysis of previous experience for example.

Sensitivity analysis

When the data to be analysed has been assembled – particularly if it is to be analysed on a computer – it may be helpful to run the calculation through a number of times – each time varying an item of input to the budget. For example on the first run using the best estimate figures – the present value may be positive. On the second run the sales estimates may be reduced by 10% and the new result compared with the first run. If the second outcome shows a negative present value it is clear that the result is sensitive to the estimates of sales. In this way all the items crucial to the success of the project can be identified and special additional scrutiny given to their validity.

Review questions

36.1 (*a*) What interest will be paid on a loan of £5,300 for 62 days at 17%?

(*b*) A bank offers to discount a bill of exchange for £9,000 with an outstanding period of 70 days at 19% interest. What will the bank pay for the bill of exchange?

36.2A What is the real rate of interest involved in discounting the bill of exchange in 36.1?

36.3 Smith borrows £1,000 on 1 January 19-1 from a moneylender at an interest charge of £200. The repayment terms are £250 at the end of March, June, September and December 19-1. What real rate of interest is he paying?

36.4 How much interest is earned if £4,000 is held for 10 years at 10% p.a. interest compound?

36.5A How much interest would have been earned if the compounding had been applied half-yearly?

36.6A Jones bought some shares on 1 January 19-1 for £8,000 and sold them 4 years later on 31 December 19-4 for £9,728. What compound rate of interest does this increase represent?

36.7 A property developer offers to buy your rights under a lease to rents amounting to £5,000 p.a. for the next seven years. He offers you an immediate cash sum of £20,000. You can invest the money at 12% p.a. interest. Should the offer be accepted?

36.8A Using the information in question 36.7 what interest rate would exactly equate the developers' offer to the rental income?

36.9 A company obtains a loan of £100,000 for five years. One of the conditions of the loan is that the company will each year pay an equal amount into a sinking fund to accumulate over the five years to amount of the loan repayable. The sinking fund will earn interest at 10% p.a. How much must be paid into the sinking fund each year?

36.10A Using the data in 36.9 how much would the amount paid into the sinking fund be if the interest rate was charged to 15% p.a.?

36.11 The Raynor Company's project engineers have made the following estimates of costs on a new project:

19-1

1 January	Rent paid for one year to 31 December 19-1 on premises for the plant	£5,000
31 January	Machinery purchased	£50,000
31 March	Installation costs paid for machinery	£10,000
31 December	Cost of Wages and material in commissioning plant	£15,000

19-2

1 January	Rent paid for year to 31 December 19-2	£5,000
31 March	Further commissioning costs	£8,000
30 June	Training costs for labour	£2,000
30 September	Working Capital provided for inventories and debtors (extra to that required in existing plant)	£10,000
31 December	Cash received from scrap value of old plant replaced by the project	£8,000

Ignoring taxation prepare a statement of the cash outlay on the project in 19-1 and 19-2. The plant is estimated to be in full use on 1 October 19-2.

36.12 Using the data in question 36.11 and assuming that the company is taxed at a rate of 50%, nine months after the end of its financial year on the 31 December, show the impact of tax on the cash flows. For tax purposes the company can obtain 25% p.a. writing down allowance on the cost of machinery in its assessment based on 19-1. The scrap value cash in 19-2 will be fully taxable in that year.

36.13 Using the net of tax cash flows produced in question 36.12 for the years 19-1 to 19-4 only and assuming an interest rate of 15%, what is the present value of the cash flows at the start of the project?

36.14A The annual profit expected from a new project is calculated as follows:

		£
Sales		50,000
Materials, Labour and Overheads	20,000	
Depreciation	5,000	
		25,000
Net Profit before tax		25,000
Corporation Tax at 50%		12,500
Net Profit after tax		12,500

The investment in machinery will take place on 1 July 19-1 amounting to £25,000 it will last five years with no residual value. Working Capital will also be required from 1 July 19-1 amounting to £10,000 and will be recovered at the end of the project. Writing down allowances of 25% p.a. of the cost of machinery can be claimed in the first year. Tax at the rate of 50% of profits is payable 9 months after the accounting year end which is 30 June. Profits on the project will start immediately the machinery is installed.

Prepare a budget of the cash flows arising from the project.

36.15A What is the Present Value of the Net Cash flows in question 36.14A if the interest rate is 10% p.a.

36.16A The installed and commissioned cost of a new machine is estimated to be £100,000. Corporation Tax payable will be reduced by tax on 25% p.a. writing down allowance of the cost of machinery in the year following its purchase. The new machinery is estimated to have a five year life with nil residual value and will be depreciated straight line. The new machine replaces an old piece of equipment which would be depreciated over the next five years at £3,000 per year, if not replaced, and would then have a nil book value. The new equipment is estimated to save material costs each year of £30,000. The old equipment could be sold (in the first year) for £6,000, but tax at 50% would be payable next year. All profits are taxed at 50% payable a year after the accounting date.

Prepare the cash flow statement necessary to evaluate the project.

How will the reported profits change in the financial accounts?

36.17 A project to install new equipment has the following estimated cash flows:

Year	Investment Outlay	Cash Inflow	Net Cash Flow
1	20,000	(11,000)	9,000
2	–	(6,000)	(6,000)
3	–	(3,000)	(3,000)
4	(2,000)	–	(2,000)
	18,000	(20,000)	(2,000)

(figures in brackets represent cash inflows)

What is the payback period for the project?

36.18 Using the data in 36.17 calculate the Net Present Value of the project with a discount rate of 10%.

36.19 Using the data in 36.17 calculate the Internal Rate of Return generated by the project.

36.20A Project Delta involves the outlay of £400,000 at the start of the project with net cash inflow of £200,000 at the end of year 1 and £100,000 at the end of year 2 and £300,000 at the end of year 3.

Calculate – payback period, internal rate of return and net present value with interest at 15%.

36.21A The Rathbone Company buys a machine for £100,000 which will be depreciated straight line over five years to a residual value of £5,000. The Profits estimated on the project will be as follows (for each of the five years)

		£
Sales		60,000
Operating Costs	30,000	
Depreciation	19,000	
		49,000
Net Profit		11,000

Ignoring taxation – what is the accounting rate of return?

36.22A Using the data in 36.21A calculate the internal rate of return. Assume cash arises in the same year as sales – and no working capital is required.

36.23 A company is considering a project which has two possible alternative solutions A or B. The estimated data is shown below – calculate Internal Rate of Return and NPV using 12% interest. Which should be selective?

	Net Cash Outlay Year 0 £	Net Cash Benefit Year 4 £
Project		
A	16,000	(28,984)
B	44,000	(74,324)

36.24A A company is considering two mutually exclusive projects X and Y. Calculate the internal rate of return and NPV at a 10% discount rate. Which alternative should be chosen?

	Net Cash Outlay Year 0 £	Net Cash Benefits Year 2 £	Year 6 £
Project			
X	30,000	(39,012)	–
Y	30,000	–	(59,172)

36.25 A machine is estimated to generate the following cash flows:

Year	Net Cash Flows
0	8,000
1	(4,000)
2	(2,000)
3	(6,000)

(Cash inflow shown in brackets)

1 Calculate the NPV using 12% interest.

2 What is the annualised amount of the net benefits from this project?

36.26 An alternative to the machine in question 36.25 is equipment with an expected life of 6 years. The NPV of the unequal net cash flows from this equpment amounts to £2,624 using 12% interest rate. What is the annualised equivalent of the £2,624 NPV? Would you choose the machine from 36.25 or this equipment – based on annualised benefits?

36.27A The Repair Co is considering alternative investments in machines. Machine X costing £2,000 will last for 3 years only and cost £1,000 p.a. to operate. Machine Y costs £5,000 but will last for 6 years. It will cost £100 p.a. for the first three years and £600 p.a. for the last three years of its life to operate. Calculate the annualised cost of Machine X and Y over a six year period, assuming that the replacement cost for Machine X at the end of year 3 is £1,800 and interest rate of 10%. Which machine would you choose based on this data?

36.28 Some Plant can be leased for five years at a rent of £13,190 per annum. The cash price is £50,000. What is the implied interest rate?

36.29 A company which could buy an asset for £80,000 with a four year life and nil residual value is offered a lease with rental of £26,338 p.a. for four years. The tax rate is 40% – assuming tax relief is obtained in the same year as payments – what is the implicit interest in the lease?

36.30 A company enters into a lease which requires rental payments of £5,000 per annum over 10 years. The rate of interest payable on borrowing for this type of funding is 14%. What is the capital value of the lease?

36.31 Roadwheelers Ltd were considering buying an additional lorry but the company had not yet decided which particular lorry to purchase. The lorries had broadly similar technical specifications and each was expected to have a working life of 5 years.

The following information was available on the lorries being considered:

1

Lorries

	BN Roadhog	FX Sprinter	VR Rocket
Purchase price	£40,000	£45,000	£50,000
Estimated scrap value after 5 years	£ 8,000	£ 9,000	£14,000
Fixed costs other than depreciation	£	£	£
Year 1	2,000	1,800	1,500
Year 2	2,000	1,800	1,500
Year 3	2,200	1,800	1,400
Year 4	2,400	2,000	1,400
Year 5	2,400	2,200	1,400
Variable costs per road mile	6p	8p	7p

2 The company charges 25p per mile for all journeys irrespective of the length of journey and the expected annual mileages over the 5 year period are:

	Miles
Year 1	50,000
Year 2	60,000
Year 3	80,000
Year 4	80,000
Year 5	80,000

3 The company's cost of capital is 10% per annum.

4 It should be assumed that all operating costs are paid and revenues received at the end of year.

5 Present value of £1 at interest rate of 10% per annum:

Year 1	£0.909
Year 2	£0.826
Year 3	£0.751
Year 4	£0.683
Year 5	£0.621

Required
(*a*) (i) Appropriate computations using the net present value method for each of the lorries under consideration.

A report to the directors of Roadwheelers Ltd advising them as to which specific lorry should be purchased.

(*b*) A brief outline of the problems encountered in evaluating capital projects.

(Associated Examining Board GCE A level)

36.32A Hirwaun Pig Iron Co. operate a single blast furnace producing pig iron. The present blast furnace is obsolete and the company is considering its replacement.

The alternatives the company is considering are:

(i) Blast furnace type; Exco. Cost £2 million.

This furnace is of a standard size capable of a monthly output of 10,000 tons. The company expects to sell 80% of its output annually at £150 per ton on a fixed price contract.

The remaining output will be sold on the open market at the following expected prices:

	19-8	19-9	19-0	19-1
Price per ton	£150	£140	£140	£160

(ii) Blast furnace type; Ohio. Cost £3.5 million.

This large furnace is capable of a monthly output of 20,000 tons. A single buyer has agreed to buy all the monthly output at a fixed price which is applicable from 1 January each year.

The prices fixed for the next four years are as follows:

	Payments per ton of output			
	19-8	19-9	19-0	19-1
Price per ton	£130	£130	£140	£170

Additional information:

1 Blast furnaces operate continuously and the operating labour is regarded as a fixed cost. During the next four years the operating labour costs will be as follows:

Exco	£1.2 million per annum
Ohio	£2.5 million per annum

2 Other forecast operating payments (excluding labour) per ton

	19-8	19-9	19-0	19-1
Exco	£130	£130	£135	£135
Ohio	£120	£120	£125	£125

3 It can be assumed that both blast furnaces will have a life of 10 years.

4 The company's cost of capital is 12% per annum.

5 It should be assumed that all costs are paid and revenues received at the end of each year.

6 The following is an extract from the present value table for £1:

	11%	12%	13%	14%
Year 1	£0.901	£0.893	£0.885	£0.877
Year 2	£0.812	£0.797	£0.783	£0.770
Year 3	£0.731	£0.712	£0.693	£0.675
Year 4	£0.659	£0.636	£0.613	£0.592

Required

(a) The forecast budgets for each of the years 19-8–19-1 and for each of the blast furnaces being considered. Show the expected yearly net cash flows.

(b) Appropriate computations using the net present value method for each of the blast furnaces. Exco and Ohio for the first four years.

(c) A report providing a recommendation to the management of Hirwaun Pig Iron Co as to which blast furnace should be purchased. Your report should include a critical evaluation of the method used to assess the capital project.

(Associated Examining Board GCE A level)

36.33 Moray Ferries Ltd own a single ship which provides a short sea ferry service for passengers, private vehicles and commercial traffic. The present ship is nearing the end of its useful life and the company is considering the purchase of a new ship.

The forecast operating budgets using the present ship are as follows:

	19-6 £M	19-7 £M	19-8 £M	19-9 £M	19-0 £M
Estimated Revenue Receipts					
Private traffic	2	3	4.5	6	7
Commercial traffic	3	4	4.5	5	6
	5	7	9.0	11	13
Estimated Operating Payments	4	5	6.5	7.5	9
	1	2	2.5	3.5	4

The ships being considered as a replacement are as described below.

1 Ship A. Cost £10M

This ship is of similar capacity to the one being replaced, but being a more modern ship it is expected that extra business would be attracted from competitors. It is anticipated therefore that estimated revenue receipts would be 10% higher in each year of the present forecast.

There would be no change in operating payments.

2 Ship B. Cost £14M

This modern ship has a carrying capacity 30% greater than the present ship. It is expected that private traffic receipts would increase by £½M a year in each year of the forecast. Commercial traffic receipts are expected to increase by 15% in each of the first two years and by 30% in each of the remaining years.

Operating payments would increase by 20% in each year of the forecast.

Additional information:

3 The company's cost of capital is 15% per annum.
4 It is company policy to assume that ships have a life of 20 years.
5 It should be assumed that all costs are paid and revenues received at the end of each year.
6 The following is an extract from the present value table for £1:

	12%	14%	15%	16%
Year 1	£0.893	£0.877	£0.870	£0.862
Year 2	£0.797	£0.769	£0.756	£0.743
Year 3	£0.712	£0.675	£0.658	£0.641
Year 4	£0.636	£0.592	£0.572	£0.552
Year 5	£0.567	£0.519	£0.497	£0.476

7 All calculations should be made correct to 3 places of decimals.

Required

(*a*) Revised operating budgets for 19-6–19-0 for each of the alternatives being considered.

(*b*) Appropriate computations using the net present value method for each of the ships, A and B.

(*c*) A report providing a recommendation to the management of Moray Ferries Ltd as to which course of action should be followed. Your report should include any reservations that you may have.

(Associated Examining Board GCE A level)

36.34A The Rovers Football Club are languishing in the middle of the First Division of the Football League. The Club have suffered a loss of £200,000 in their last financial year and whilst receipts from spectators have declined over the last five years, recently receipts have stabilised at approximately £1,000,0000 per season. The Club is considering the purchase of the services of one of two new football players, Jimmy Jam or Johnny Star.

Jimmy Jam is 21 years old and considered to be a future international footballer. He is prepared to sign a five year contract with Rovers for a salary of £50,000 per annum. His present club would require a transfer fee of £200,000 for the transfer of his existing contract. With J Jam in the team the Rovers Club would expect receipts to increase by 20%.

Johnny Star is 32 years old and a leading international footballer who is prepared to sign for Rovers on a two year contract before retiring completely from football. He would expect a salary of £200,000 per annum and his present club would require a transfer fee of £100,000 for the transfer of his existing contract. Rovers believe that as a result of signing Star receipts would increase by 40%.

The rate of interest applicable to the transaction is 12% and the following is an extract from the present value table for £1:

	12%
Year 1	0.893
Year 2	0.797
Year 3	0.712
Year 4	0.636
Year 5	0.507

It should be assumed that all costs are paid and revenues received at the end of each year.

Required

A report, incorporating an evaluation of the financial result of engaging each player by the net present value method, providing the Rovers Football Club with information to assist it in deciding which alternative to adopt. Indicate any other factors that may be taken into consideration.

(Associated Examining Board GCE A level)

37

Accounting ratios: a further view

In Volume 1 accounting ratios and the interpretation of final accounts were introduced. The present chapter takes the reader one stage further. On occasion the reader will be required to look again at factors already dealt with in Volume 1, but it may be in greater depth or with a different slant.

Accounting information summarises the economic performance and situation of a business. In order to make use of this information the user needs to analyse and interpret its meaning. When confronted with information it is useful to have a framework of analysis available to make an attempt to distil what is important from the mass of less important data.

A mechanic confronted with a car that is refusing to start has a set of routine checks which will by elimination help to identify the problem. Someone without the appropriate knowledge can feel helpless faced with the complex array of electrical and mechanical parts under the bonnet of a car.

A business is in many ways more complex than a motor car. In a car cause and effect can be traced through a mechanical sequence. A thorough check will show the fault and a repair can be made. If a business's sales decline however, the cause may be clearly identifiable on the other hand the problem may be due to a variety of causes, some of which are human problems and may not be so easily diagnosed. A business consists of people interacting amongst themselves as well as with the mechanical means of production at their disposal. The human behaviour element may not always lend itself to logical and systematic analysis.

Having said this however the first stage in analysis is the development of a systematic review of the accounting data. In this respect accounting ratios are relationships which bring together the results of activity which experience shows identify the key areas for success of the business.

The choice of ratios will be determined by the needs of the user of the information. In this chapter the ratios which are illustrated are divided into main groups which may be identified with the requirements of particular users. However this division whilst it is useful as an aid to our memory and in developing a logical approach should not be taken as a set of rigid rules. A supplier of goods on credit to a firm, will mainly be interested in his customers immediate ability to repay him, which will be measured by liquidity ratios, but he will also be interested in the overall future and prospects of the customer measured by the Profitability and other ratios.

The main parties interested in accounts include shareholders and potential shareholders, creditors, lenders, the Government for taxation and statistical purposes, potential take-over bidders, employees particularly through their trade unions, as well as management. The interests of the various parties have been summarised in Exhibit 37.1 which divides the types of ratio into five main categories. In this book it is not possible to show all possibly useful ratios since these can run to many hundreds, rather generally useful common ratios are illustrated. In practice it is sensible to calculate as many ratios as appear useful for the required objective.

Exhibit 37.1

Examples of parties with an immediate interest	Type of ratio
Potential suppliers of goods on credit; lenders, e.g. bank managers and debenture holders; management.	*Liquidity (credit risk)*: Ratios indicating how well equipped the business is to pay its way.
Shareholders (actual and potential); potential take-over bidders; lenders; management; competitive firms; tax authorities; employees.	*Profitability*: How successfully is the business trading.
Shareholders (actual and potential); potential take-over bidders; management; competitive firms; employees.	*Use of assets*: How effectively are the assets of the firm utilised.
Shareholders (actual and potential); potential take-over bidders; management; lenders and creditors in assessing risk.	*Capital structure*: How does the capital structure of the firm affect the cost of capital and the return to shareholders.
Shareholders (actual and potential); potential take-over bidders; management.	*Investment*: Show how the market prices for a share reflect a company's performance.

Exhibit 37.2 shows a set of accounts prepared for The Rational Company Ltd. The various types of ratio mentioned in Exhibit 37.1 will be illustrated using the data for The Rational Company Ltd.

Exhibit 37.2

The Rational Co Ltd
Profit and Loss Account for the year ended 31 December 19-1

	£	£
Turnover		900,000
Cost of Sales		780,000
Gross Profit		120,000
Distribution Costs	27,000	
Administrative Expenses	30,000	57,000
		63,000
Other Operating Income (Royalties)		4,700
		67,700
Interest Payable		15,700
Profit on Ordinary Activities before Taxation		52,000
Tax on Profit on Ordinary Activities		22,000
Profit for the year on Ordinary Activities after Taxation		30,000
Undistributed Profits from last year		107,400
		137,400
Preference Dividend paid	2,400	
Proposed Ordinary Dividend	15,000	17,400
Undistributed Profits Carried to Next Year		120,000

Rational Co Ltd
Abridged Balance Sheet as at 31 December 19-1

	Cost £	Depreciation £	Net £
Fixed Assets			
Land and Buildings	500,000	140,000	360,000
Plant	40,000	10,000	30,000
	540,000	150,000	390,000
Current Assets			
Stock		90,000	
Debtors		105,000	
Bank		15,000	
		210,000	
less Current Liabilities			
Trade Creditors	21,000		
Bank Overdraft	32,000		
Current Taxation	22,000		
Proposed Ordinary Dividend	15,000	90,000	
Working Capital			120,000
			510,000
Debentures 7%			210,000
			300,000
Capital and Reserves			
Called-up Share Capital			
Ordinary Shares		150,000	
8% Preference Shares		30,000	180,000
Profit and Loss Account			120,000
			300,000

NB The Market Price of an ordinary share at 31 December 19-1 was £3.

Liquidity ratios

The analysis of credit risk was the historic starting point for formal ratio analysis. With widely scattered markets a firm is frequently asked to trade with companies it has little or no knowledge of. The risks of supplying goods on credit to a strange company are fairly obvious and in practice can be very hazardous. Many small businesses have themselves been forced to wind up because a large customer has failed to pay its debt. It is hardly surprising that firms specialising in giving advice on credit risks should have come into existence. These firms started the consistent use of ratios to analyse company balance sheets. Usually they are operating as outsiders and therefore have to rely on published information, in contrast to the management of a business who can obtain much more detailed information about that business. The following ratios are useful in the measurement of liquidity:

The current ratio

The Current Ratio measures Current Assets: Current Liabilities. In general terms we are comparing assets which will become liquid in approximately twelve months with liabilities which will be due for payment in the same period.

In interpreting the ratio a creditor will want to see a sufficiently large amount of current assets to cover liabilities and the eventuality of losses. It is hard, however, to say exactly what is satisfactory since factors of type of industry and overall size and reputation of the firm will play a part. A commonly used rule of thumb would be 2:1, in other words £2 of Current Assets for £1 of Current Liability, but many very good firms show a lower ratio, whilst some bad ones, by over valuing assets, show a much higher ratio. Referring to Exhibit 37.2 the Current Ratio is 210,000:90,000=2.3:1. This may also be conveniently expressed by $\frac{210,000}{90,000} = 2.3$ times.

The acid test ratio

In order to refine the analysis of the Current Ratio another ratio is used which takes only those current assets which are cash or will convert very quickly into cash. This will normally mean Cash and Debtors or Current Assets less Stock in Trade. The Acid Test Ratio may, therefore, be stated as:

Current Assets less Stock in Trade : Current Liabilities.
The ratio calculated from Exhibit 37.2 is:
$$\frac{120,000}{90,000} = 1.3 \text{ times.}$$

This shows that provided Creditors and Debtors are paid at approximately the same time, the company has sufficient liquid resources to meet its current liabilities. If a large proportion of the Current Assets had been in the form of Stock in Trade the liquid position might have been dangerously low.

The ratios shown under Credit Risk have been concerned with liquidity. A useful supplement to this type of analysis is provided by Fund or Cash Flow Statements which have been dealt with in another chapter. From the point of view of management, the forecast cash flow statement is the most useful statement for control of credit. For those outside the firm, however, this information is not usually available and they must rely on the ratios.

Profitability ratios

Profitability is the end product of the policies and decisions taken by a firm, and is its single most important measure of success.

Gross profit/sales

From Exhibit 37.2 the ratio for the Rational Company Ltd is $\frac{120,000}{900,000} = 0.133$ or as a percentage on sales = 13.3 per cent.

It is impossible to state a rule of thumb for this figure which will vary considerably from firm to firm and industry to industry.

Net profit (after tax)/sales

The same comments apply to Net Profit/Sales as to Gross Profit/Sales. The difference between the two ratios will be explained by measuring the ratios of sales to the Expenses in the Profit and Loss Account. The ratio from Exhibit 37.2 is $\frac{30,000}{900,000} = 0 = 03.3$ per cent. This percentage of 3.3 indicates by how much the profit margin can decline before the firm makes losses.

Return on capital employed

Great care must be exercised in measuring ratios of profit to Capital Employed. There are no standard definitions and thus for comparability it is necessary to ensure that the same method is used over time for the same firm or between different firms. Another problem is inherent in comparing profit which arises over a period of time, with Capital Employed which is taken from the Balance Sheet and is thus measured at one point of time. For a proper evaluation the Capital Employed needs to be an average figure for the accounting period in which the profit was calculated. As an external analyst the only data available is at the beginning and end of the accounting period. Since the year end is by no means likely to be representative of the average for a period any calculated figure must be taken with caution. If for example an analyst knows that a major investment in fixed assets took place mid-way through the year he would tend to average the opening and closing figures. If little change has taken place then the year end figure may be used.

Net profit (after tax)/total assets

In this calculation of Return on Capital Employed the Total Assets are defined as all Fixed and other Non-Current Assets plus Working Capital. Working Capital is simply the figure reached by deducting Current Liabilities from Current Assets (assuming that Current Assets exceed Current Liabilities). Using the data from Exhibit 37.2 the working capital is Current Assets £210,000 less Current Liabilities £90,000 = £120,000. The Total Assets are therefore Fixed Assets £390,000 + Working Capital £120,000 = £510,000 and the return is

$$\frac{\text{Net Profit (after tax)}}{\text{Total Assets}} = \frac{30,000}{510,000} = 5.88\%$$

One of the problems with using this approach to Return on Capital is that Net Profit after tax will already have had interest on debentures, loans and overdrafts charged against it and thus if this interest is significant the return on assets will be understated.

Similarly if the Assets of the business include items of an intangible nature such as Goodwill it is often felt that the return on assets is better related to tangible assets alone, since the accounting valuation of intangibles varies so much.

To answer these problems the following ratio is often used:

Net Operating Profit/Operating Assets

The aim here is to take the operating profit which is the outcome of operations before interest charges are made or any investment income is included. This profit will then be taken over Operating Assets which are the tangible assets used in the generation of the Operating Income. Operating Assets will not include intangibles nor investments in shares or other securities outside the firm, whether shown under a separate heading or as Current Assets.

As with the previous calculation of Total Assets it is appropriate to take Working Capital as part of Operating Assets but in this definition it is frequently appropriate to exclude Bank Overdraft from Current Liabilities. Although from a legal point of view and from the Banks intention it is a Current Liability, since repayment can be demanded at short notice, in practice for a well run business the bank is usually happy to maintain an overdraft over extended periods of time. Unlike most of the other Current Liabilities interest is chargeable on overdrafts.

Thus this definition of Return on Capital Employed is Net Operating Profit: Tangible Operating Fixed Assets + (Working Capital + Overdraft). Referring to Exhibit 37.2 this is equal to £390,000 + £120,000 + £32,000 = £542,000. Which is equivalent to:

Share Capital £180,000 + Reserves £120,000 + Debentures £210,000 + Bank overdraft £32,000 = £542,000.

The Net Operating Profit which in Exhibit 37.2 = £67,700 is the profit obtained from the Capital Employed before paying interest or dividends to any of these sources of capital. This return on Capital Employed in the Rational Company Ltd is therefore $\frac{67,700}{542,000} = 12.49$ per cent.

Net profit (after taxes)/owners equity

In this case the net profit after tax (less Preference Dividends) is compared with the Ordinary Shareholders stake in the business, i.e. ordinary share capital plus reserves. From Exhibit 37.2 the ratio is $\frac{£27,600}{£270,000} = 10.2$ per cent.

In contrast to the previous ratio this one is not an overall measure of profitability but is specially concerned with the return an ordinary shareholder might expect.

Use of assets ratios

Although the way assets are utilised will affect profitability, these particular ratios deserve to be evaluated separately as they are of great importance. In effect they show how effectively management has been using the assets at their disposal.

A straightforward ratio between Assets and Sales can be used by the external analyst. For the Rational Co. Ltd we should show:

Land and Buildings	: Sales	360,000:900,000 = 1: 2.5
Plant	: Sales	30,000:900,000 = 1: 30.0
Total Fixed Assets	: Sales	390,000 = 1: 2.3
Stock in Trade	: Sales	90,000:900,000 = 1: 10.0
Debtors	: Sales	105,000:900,000 = 1: 8.6
Cash at Bank	: Sales	15,000:900,000 = 1: 60.0
Total Current Assets	: Sales	210,000:900,000 = 1: 4.3

It is often convenient to express these ratios in terms of 'per £1,000 of sales' to avoid too much 'rounding off'. For example Land and Buildings per £1,000 of sales would be £400, i.e. (360,000 ÷ 900).

A number of these activity ratios are sufficiently important to merit special mention and in some cases detailed development.

Sales/fixed assets

The ratio of Sales to Fixed Assets measures the utilisation a firm is obtaining from its investment in fixed plant. If the ratio is low it indicates that management may not be utilising its plant very effectively. In the illustration from Exhibit 37.2 the ratio is = 2.3 times, or £433.3 per £1,000 of sales.

Stock turnover

This important ratio is measured in the first instance by dividing Sales by Stock in Trade. Since Sales are at Selling Prices, the Stock should also be measured at selling price. Usually an easier way is to divide Sales at Cost Price (which is the Cost of Goods Sold total) by Stock in Trade at cost value. The stock figure used should be an average figure for the year. While the true average will be known to management it will often not be available to outsiders. In this situation a very rough approximation is used by taking the average of the opening and closing stocks, if in the example in Exhibit 37.2, the stock at 1 January had been £50,000 and the stock at 31st December is £90,000 the average would be taken as

$$\frac{50,000 + 90,000}{2} = £70,000.$$

The Stock turnover therefore is

$$\frac{\text{Cost of Goods Sold}}{\text{Stock in Trade}} = \frac{780,000}{70,000} = 11.1 \text{ times.}$$

If the cost of Goods Sold is not known, it may be necessary to use the Sales figure instead. Although this is not a satisfactory basis, it may be better than nothing if like is compared with like. Notice that in this example Stock turnover = 12.86 times if the Sales figure is used (900,000 ÷ 70,000)

Collection period for debtors

The resources tied up in debtors is an important ratio subject. We have already calculated the relationships of debtors to sales which in the example is 1:8.6. This means that for every £8.6 sold there is £1 of debtors outstanding.

This relationship is often translated into the length of time a debtor takes to pay. If we assume that the sales for Rational Ltd are made over the whole of one year, i.e. 365 days this means that on average a debt is outstanding for $365 \times \frac{1}{8.6} = 42.4$ days. Notice that it is assumed sales take place evenly over the year, and we have ignored holidays. However it is useful to know that our customers take about 6 weeks to pay!

In recent years the interest in productivity measurement has focused interest on many ratios which combine information which is not essentially part of the accounts with accounting data. Published Accounts for example are now required to show as supplementary information the average number of people employed by a limited company. This information may be related to Sales to give an index of Sales per employee. For example if the average number employed by the Rational Company were 215 then sales per employee would be $\frac{900,000}{215} = £4,186$. This example is given as an illustration of the development of this type of measurement which may be a useful guide to assessment of a company's performance.

Capital structure ratios

The Capital Structure of a business is important because it has a significant influence on the risk to lenders, and on the return to shareholders.

In the first instance it is worthwhile to express the Balance Sheet in percentage terms. For the Rational Company using the main sub-totals it would be as follows:

Balance Sheet at 31 December 19-1

		% of balance sheet totals
Fixed Assets		130
Current Assets	70	
less Current Liabilities	30	40
		170
less Debentures		(70)
		100
Ordinary Shares		50
Preference Shares		10
Profit and Loss Account		40
		100

Net worth/total assets

From this it can be seen immediately that Ordinary Shares and Preference Shares with the Reserves, which total is often called Net Worth is providing 50 per cent of the financing of Fixed and Current Assets. Thus the ratio Net Worth: Fixed Assets + Current Assets is an important measure of the shareholder stake in a business. (300,000: 390,000 + 210,000 = 1:2).

Fixed assets/net worth

From the Balance Sheet it is also easy to see that a high proportion of the assets (65%) are Fixed Assets. A comparison of the Fixed Assets with Net Worth shows whether the longer term investment usually involved in Fixed Assets is provided by Shareholders. In our example the ratio is £390,000 : £300,000 (or 65% :50%) = 1:0.77. This ratio shows that shareholders are not providing all the investment required to finance the fixed assets quite apart from current assets. The remainder of the funding of assets is provided by borrowing. The important thing here is to ensure that the borrowing is sufficiently long term to match the investment in fixed assets. If the company has to repay borrowing whilst all its resources are locked into assets which cannot easily be converted into cash it can only make repayment by fresh borrowing or new capital issues which may cause problems.

Fixed assets/net worth and long-term loan

Provided the Mortgage Debenture has a reasonably long life the Rational Company provides reasonable cover of its Fixed Assets since Fixed Assets: Net Worth + Long-term Loan are in the ratio 1:1.31 (390:510).

Coverage of fixed charges

This relationship is obtained by dividing net profit by any fixed interest charges or rentals. Since these charges are allowable expenses for tax purposes, the profit before tax will be used. From Exhibit 37.2 the interest charges are £15,700 with no rental expense. The available profit befor tax is £52,000 + £15,700 = £67,700. The Fixed Charges are, therefore, covered

$$\frac{\text{Profit before tax} + \text{Fixed Charges}}{\text{Fixed Charges}} = \frac{67{,}000}{15{,}700} = 4.3 \text{ times.}$$

This is low enough to indicate a company which is high geared.

By 'high geared' is meant a company which has a high proportion of borrowing to net worth. A company with no gearing has all its funds provided by the ordinary shareholder. Gearing has also been measured indirectly in the ratio of Net Worth: Total Assets. The lower the proportion of funds provided from Net Worth, the higher the borrowing and hence gearing.

The coverage of fixed charges gives a very important measure of the extent to which the profit may decline before the company is not able to earn enough to cover the interest etc. it is legally obliged to pay. If charges are not paid legal steps will be taken against the company which usually end in its being taken over or wound up.

Borrowing/net worth

This ratio is the most direct measure of gearing since it indicates the proportions in which all funds are provided for the business. Borrowing is taken as all the long term and current liabilities of the business and Net Worth as Share Capital and Reserves. In this definition Preference Shares are included in net worth. Although the return to Preference Shareholders is a fixed rate interest there is no legal obligation for the company to pay it, hence the inclusion with Net Worth. If you are however looking at the effect of gearing on the return to ordinary shareholders it may then be appropriate to treat Preference Share Dividends as a fixed charge.

The Ratio for Rational Co Ltd is thus £210,000+ £90,000 : 300,000 = 1:1.

Investment ratios

These ratios are important for the investor and financial manager who is interested in the market prices of the shares of a company on the Stock Exchange.

Dividend yield

This measures the real rate of return on an investment in shares, as distinct from the declared dividend rate which is based on the nominal value of a share. The Yield is calculated as follows, illustrated from Exhibit 37.2:

$$\frac{\text{The Dividend per Share}}{\text{Market Price per Share}} = \frac{£1 \times 10 \text{ per cent}}{£3} = 3.3 \text{ per cent.}$$

Dividend cover for ordinary shares

This indicates the amount of profit for an ordinary dividend and indicates the amount of profit retained in the business. The cover is:

$$\frac{\text{Net Profit for the year after Tax } - \text{ Preference Dividend}}{\text{Dividend on Ordinary Shares}}$$

$$= \frac{£30,000 - 2,400}{15,000} = 1.8 \text{ times.}$$

Earnings per ordinary share

As is implied by the name this ratio is

$$\frac{\text{Net Profit for the year after tax } - \text{ Preference Dividend}}{\text{Number of Ordinary Shares}}$$

$$= \frac{£30,000 - 2,400}{150,000} = £0.18 \text{ per share.}$$

The calculation of this important ratio is now covered by the Statement of Standard Accounting Practice 3.

SSAP 3 Earnings per share applies to all UK companies quoted on the stock exchanges. It is impossible to summarise the SSAP in a few words. Students at later stages of professional examinations should obtain the SSAP and read its detailed instructions.

The price earnings ratio

Finally the Price Earnings Ratio relates the earnings per share to the price the shares sell at in the market. From Exhibit 37.2 the ratio is:

$$\frac{\text{Market Price}}{\text{Earnings per Share}} = \frac{£3}{£0.18} = 16.7$$

This relationship is an important indicator to investor and financial manager of the market's evaluation of a share, and is very important when a new issue of shares is due since it shows the earnings the market expects in relation to the current share prices.

Summary of ratios

Type of ratio	Method of calculation

● Liquidity

Current Ratio

$$\frac{\text{Current Assets}}{\text{Current Liabilities}}$$

Acid Test Ratio

$$\frac{\text{Current Assets less Stock in Trade}}{\text{Current Liabilities}}$$

● Profitability

Gross Profit/Sales

$$\frac{\text{Gross Profit}}{\text{Sales}}$$

Net Profit after Tax/Sales

$$\frac{\text{Net Profit after Tax}}{\text{Sales}}$$

● Return on capital employed

Net Profit After Tax/Total Assets

$$\frac{\text{Net Profit After Tax}}{\text{Fixed and Other Assets + Working Capital}}$$

Net Operating Profit/Operating Assets

$$\frac{\text{Net Operating Income}}{\text{Tangible Operating Fixed Assets + Working Capital and Overdraft}}$$

Net Profit (after tax)/Owners Equity

$$\frac{\text{Net Profit after tax less Preference Dividend}}{\text{Ordinary Share Capital + Reserves}}$$

● Use of assets

Asset/Sales

$$\frac{\text{Individual Asset Totals}}{\text{Sales}}$$

Sales/Fixed Assets

$$\frac{\text{Sales}}{\text{Fixed Assets}}$$

Stock Turnover

$$\frac{\text{Cost of Goods Sold}}{\text{Average Stock in trade}}$$

Collection Period for Debtors

$$365 \times \frac{\text{Debtors}}{\text{Sales}}$$

● Capital structure

Net Worth/Total Assets

$$\frac{\text{Ordinary Share Capital + Preference S C + Reserves}}{\text{Fixed Assets + Other Assets + Current Assets}}$$

Fixed Assets/Net Worth

$$\frac{\text{Fixed Assets}}{\text{Net Worth}}$$

Fixed Assets/Net Worth and Long-term Loan

$$\frac{\text{Fixed Assets}}{\text{Net Worth + Long-term Loan}}$$

Coverage of Fixed Charges	$$\dfrac{\textit{Net Profit before tax and Fixed Charges}}{\text{Fixed Charges}}$$
Borrowing/Net Worth	$$\dfrac{\textit{Long Term + Current Liabilities}}{\text{Net Worth}}$$

● *Investment*

Dividend Yield	$$\dfrac{\textit{Dividend per Share}}{\text{Market Price per Share}}$$
Dividend Cover for Ordinary Shares	$$\dfrac{\textit{Net Profit after tax} - \textit{Pref Div}}{\text{Ordinary Share Dividend}}$$
Earnings per Ordinary share	$$\dfrac{\textit{Net Profit after tax} - \textit{Pref Div}}{\text{Number of Ordinary Shares}}$$
Price Earnings Ratio	$$\dfrac{\textit{Market Price per Share}}{\text{Earnings per Share}}$$

Review questions

37.1A Describe the five main groups of ratios and indicate who may be interested in each type.

37.2A Explain what you think the following ratios indicate about a firm:

(*a*) Acid test ratio.

(*b*) Net Operating Profit/Capital Employed.

(*c*) Collection Period for Debtors.

(*d*) Net Worth/Total Assets.

(*e*) Dividend Cover for Ordinary Shares.

37.3A Stock Turnover is sometimes calculated by dividing sales by the average of the opening and closing stock in trade figures. What is wrong with this method of computation?

37.4 For each of the following items select the lettered item(s) which indicate(s) its effect(s) on the company accounts. More than one item may be affected.

1 Declaration and payment of a dividend on Preference Share Capital.

2 Declaration of a proposed dividend on ordinary shares due for payment in one month

3 Purchase of stock in trade for cash.

4 Payment of creditors.

5 Bad Debt written off against an existing provision for Bad and Doubtful Debts.

Effect

A Reduces working capital.

B Increases working capital.

C Reduces current ratio.

D Increases current ratio.

E Reduces acid test ratio.

F Increases acid test ratio.

37.5A Describe four ratios which might help you to assess the profitability of a company and explain their significance.

37.6 A limited company with 100,000 £1 Ordinary Shares as its Capital earns a profit after tax of £15,000. It pays a dividend of 10 per cent. The Market price of the shares is £1.50. What is the:

(a) Yield on Ordinary Shares?
(b) Earnings per share?
(c) Price/Earnings ratio?

37.7A What ratios might be of particular interest to a potential holder of debentures in a limited company?

37.8 The following is a Trading and Profit and Loss Account of a small limited company engaged in manufacturing for the year ending 31 December 19-2.

		£'000
Sales (Credit)		150
Opening Stock	20	
Purchases (credit)	120	
	140	
less Closing Stock	40	
	100	
Direct Manufacturing Expenses	20	
Overhead Expenditure	10	130
Net Profit		20

Balance Sheet at 31 December 19-2

	Cost	Aggreg dep	£'000
Fixed Assets:			
Freehold Property	100	—	100
Plant and Machinery	40	20	20
	140	20	120
Current Assets:			
Stocks at cost		40	
Debtors		50	
Quoted Investments at cost		60	
Bank		20	
		170	
Less Current Liabilities:			
Corporation Tax	10		
Bills Payable	20		
Tax Creditors	60	90	80
			200
5 per cent Debentures			60
			140
Authorised and Issued Share Capital			100
Reserves			40
			140

Required:

Select five major ratios and apply them to the above accounts and comment upon their relevance.

37.9A

Ironsides Limited

Balance Sheet as at 31 December 19-8

	£	£	£
Fixed Assets at cost			7,200,000
Depreciation			2,000,000
			5,200,000
Current Assets			
Stock		1,200,000	
Debtors		800,000	
Investments		600,000	
Cash		200,000	
		2,800,000	
less Current Liabilities			
Creditors	280,000		
Taxation	520,000	800,000	
Working Capital			2,000,000
			7,200,000
6% Debenture		800,000	
5% Mortgage		2,000,000	
Bank Loan 8%		400,000	3,200,000
Capital and Reserves			4,000,000
Share Capital: Ordinary £1 shares			
Authorised		2,500,000	
Issued			2,400,000
General Reserve			1,600,000
			4,000,000

Condensed Profit and Loss Account for year ended 31 December, 19-9.

		£
Sales		12,000,000
Cost of Production		10,320,000
		1,680,000
Gross Profit		
Other Expenses:		
Administration	120,000	
Selling	68,000	
Rent	112,000	
Depreciation	400,000	700,000
		980,000
less Interest		
Bank	32,000	
Mortgage	100,000	
Debenture	48,000	180,000
		800,000
		360,000
less Corporation Tax 45%		
		440,000
less Dividend		400,000
To General Reserve		£40,000

You are required to calculate for Ironsides Ltd ten significant ratios and comment on the meaning.

37.10 The annual accounts of the Wholesale Textile Company Limited have been summarised for 19-1 and 19-2 as follows:

	Year 19-1		Year 19-2	
	£	£	£	£
Sales				
Cash	60,000		64,000	
Credit	540,000	600,000	684,000	748,000
Cost of sales		472,000		596,000
Gross margin		128,000		152,000
• *Expenses*				
Warehousing		26,000		28,000
Transport		12,000		20,000
Administration		38,000		38,000
Selling		22,000		28,000
Debenture interest		–		4,000
		98,000		118,000
Net profit		30,000		34,000

	On 31 Dec.19-1		On 31 Dec. 19-2	
	£	£	£	£
Fixed assets				
(*less* depreciation)		60,000		80,000
Current assets				
Stock	120,000		188,000	
Debtors	100,000		164,000	
Cash	20,000	240,000	14,000	366,000
less Current liabilities				
Trade creditors		100,000		152,000
Net current assets		140,000		214,000
		200,000		294,000
Share Capital		150,000		150,000
Reserves and undistributed profit		50,000		84,000
Debenture loan		–		60,000
		200,000		294,000

You are informed that:

1 All sales were from stocks in the company's warehouse.

2 The range of merchandise was not changed and buying prices remained steady throughout the two years.

3 Budgeted total sales for 19-2 were £780,000.

4 The debenture loan was received on 1 January, 19-2, and additional fixed assets were purchased on that date.

You are required to state the internal accounting ratios that you would use in this type of business to assist the management of the company in measuring the efficiency of its operation, including its use of capital.

Your answer should name the ratios and give the figures (calculated to one decimal place) for 19-1 and 19-2, together with possible reasons for changes in the ratios for the two years. Ratios relating to capital employed should be based on the capital at the year end. Ignore taxation.

38

Interpretation of final accounts

The Interpretation of Final Accounts through the use of ratios can conveniently be divided into two parts. Firstly there is analysis by those outside the firm who are seeking to understand more from the published accounting data. On the other side there is management wishing to interpret a much fuller range of internal information in a meaningful way. In both situations current information will be assessed in relation to past trends of the same business and with comparative information for similar firms.

Comparisons over time

One of the most helpful ways in which accounting ratios can be used is to compare them with previous periods' ratios for the same organisation. Taking as an example Net Profit after Tax/Sales the results for the Rational Co Ltd are as follows:

	19-6	19-5	19-4	19-3	19-2	19-1
Net Profit after Tax/Sales	3.3	3.8	3.1	3.4	3.4	3.5

This year's result (19-6) acquires much more significance when compared to the previous five years. The appreciation of the trends is usually assisted by graphing the results as in Exhibit 38.1.

Exhibit 38.1

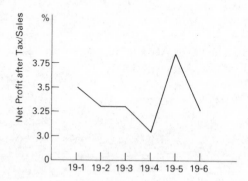

This graph very clearly illustrates how the net profit margin has fluctuated. In this type of case the ratio which is a comparative number is not expected to 'grow' in the way that an expanding firm expects its Sales to grow. Thus for ratios an ordinary graph would normally be appropriate.

However when the ratio points have been plotted it can be helpful to insert a line of best fit to these points. Thus on the graph we drew of Net Profit After Tax/Sales a line of best fit gives a useful idea of the past trends of the ratio as in Exhibit 38.2.

Exhibit 38.2

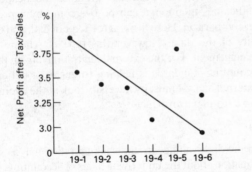

This can be drawn either by eye or better by using a statistical technique such as least squares.

It is very tempting to extend these trend lines into the future as a form of forecast. Past trends should not be used mechanically to predict the future. Only if you are sure that all conditions influencing a ratio are likely to remain constant next year should you extend the trend. Notice that in the graph we have just plotted the linear trend is relatively little influenced by the upturn in the current year. This improvement may in fact represent the start of an upward movement if we had sufficient information to explain it. Thus great care must be taken with predictions.

As with the interpretation of all ratios the best approach is to structure the analysis in an orderly fashion. The pyramid type of structuring explained later in the chapter is a useful model since it links together a set of ratios, in a way that helps to develop understanding – one ratio being explained by other more detailed ratios.

It is also often helpful to combine with the comparison of ratios over time, some information about the trends in the real accounting data. In the example we have just examined of the Net Profit after Tax/Sales ratio it is likely to be helpful for someone interpreting the accounts to have alongside his graphical analysis of the ratio other graphs showing the sales in £ and Net Profit after Tax in £. The ratio analysis must always be kept in the perspective of the real accounting results. The graphs of key figures from the Profit and Loss Account for example can usefully be developed on logarithmic scales to emphasise trends.

Comparisons with other firms

Comparisons over time are useful since they give a perspective on trends developing within a firm. However since firms operate in a competitive environment it is always necessary to have some basis of comparison with other organisations particularly those in the same type of business.

While in principle inter-firm comparisons are very worthwhile there are considerable practical differences. Firstly in many cases organisations are not directly comparable with others in size or in the exact nature of business carried on. A large multinational company can be involved in a wide range of industries and countries of operation, as a whole therefore it is probably unique. Size can in itself have an important bearing on ratios. For example the Capital Structure Ratios of a large public company are not comparable with one which is small and privately owned. Secondly inter-company comparisons are frequently made misleading by differences in accounting methods and factors such as the age structure and location of assets.

Most of the difficulties mentioned can be overcome by a properly structured scheme of inter-firm comparison. Here firms agree to pool data and employ experts to ensure comparability of the data. However this type of scheme is only available internally for the management. For the external analyst relying on published data the development of accounting standards is helping to ensure a better basic source of information. The external analyst must by necessity look at the overall ratios for more general guidelines to a firm's performance.

External analysis

The outsider is at some disadvantage in undertaking ratio analysis since he will have relatively little information about the underlying bases of accounting. He will, however, be able to obtain information which is now published, showing ratios by industry. These are calculated from the published accounts of public companies, and more limited information on accounts of private companies. This information would tend to be in a form similar to that shown in Exhibit 38.3, which is an abbreviated form of a broad schedule of ratios.

Using some information from Exhibit 37.2 in Chapter 37, let us set up the information we have available to assess the Rational Co Ltd which is a Building and Civil Engineering Firm.

Exhibit 38.3

Illustration of Published Ratios by Industry
Quoted Companies Year 19-0 and 19-1

Industry Classification	Year	Financial Performance				Credit Control	
		P/CE %	NP/S %	S/FA times	S/ST times	CA/CL times	LA/CL times
Building and Civil Engineering	19-0	14.5	3.9	7.7	10.1	1.32	0.96
	19-1	14.8	4.6	7.0	7.3	1.36	0.93
Specialist Construction Contractors	19-0	14.5	5.3	6.0	9.8	1.55	1.15
	19-1	17.8	6.0	6.3	12.1	1.66	1.08

Notes:

P	=	Net Operating Profit	ST	=	Stock in Trade
NP	=	Net Profit After Tax	CA	=	Current Assets
CE	=	Capital Employed	CL	=	Current Liabilities
S	=	Sales	LA	=	Liquid Assets or Current Assets
FA	=	Fixed Assets			Less Stock

The ratios shown are the median figures for the companies in the sample. In practice it would be common to show the two quartile figures as well.

Ratio	Rational Co Ltd		Industry Median for Building and Civil Engineering	
	19-0	19-1	19-0	19-1
Operating Profit/Capital Employed	13.2	11.7	14.5	14.8
Net Profit after Tax/Sales	3.8	3.3	3.9	4.6
Sales/Fixed Assets	3.1	2.3	7.7	7.0
Sales/Stock	13.5	12.9	10.1	7.3
Current Assets/Current Liabilities	2.2	2.3	1.32	1.36
Liquid Assets/Current Liabilities	1.1	1.3	0.96	0.93

Whilst it must be appreciated that we are working with only a few ratios and that ideally we would look at least at five years' information we might draw some tentative conclusions:

Operating Profit/Capital Employed is lower than the median figure for the industry. Looking further we see that Sales/Fixed Assets Ratio is considerably below average. The two ratios are closely linked since Sales is an important contributor to Profit and Fixed Assets are part of Capital Employed. Net Profit after tax to Sales is also below average but the company is utilising its stock above the average level. Both the liquidity ratios are above average, which may mean from the company's point of view that too much resources are tied up in non-productive cash or debtor balances, which would also contribute to a low return on capital employed.

In practice we could also look at the quartile figures in addition to the median. Our conclusions from the analysis can only be tentative but there is an impression which develops even from the limited information we have looked at that all is not right with the Rational Co Ltd. Profitability is below average and the explanation seems to lie in a low net profit margin, and low utlisation of fixed assets plus too many liquid assets. The trend of profitability figures cannot be assessed from two years, and it would have been useful to see information covering as many years back such as will give a reasonable guide. In preparing the graphs of trends over time for the ratios it is often very useful to show the Industry Data on the same graph as that from the firm. Using the example previously illustrated the graph for the Rational Co Ltd Profit after Tax/Sales would be improved by adding the Industry Median figures as in Exhibit 38.4.

Exhibit 38.4

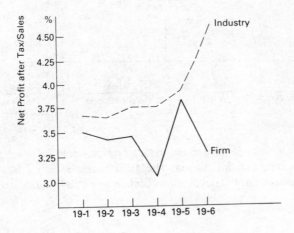

Internal analysis

From a management point of view very useful information can be drawn from a detailed ratio analysis between companies using a full range of information not normally published. The Centre for Inter-firm Comparisons is a specialist organisation undertaking this work, maintaining secrecy as to the identity of participating firms, but ensuring that all firms taking part prepare their information on a comparable basis. Several Trade Associations and Professional Bodies run similar schemes for their members. The Centre for Inter-firm Comparison have developed what is known as the 'pyramid' approach to ratios. This simply means that a key ratio at the top of the pyramid is explained by more detailed ratios which branch out below.

One example is shown in Exhibit 38.5 developed from the key ratio Operating Profit/Operating Assets. Note that Operating Profit is the same as

$$\frac{\text{Sales}}{\text{Operating Assets}} \times \frac{\text{Operating Profit}}{\text{Sales}} \text{ (cancelling out Sales in the multiplication).}$$

Exhibit 38.5

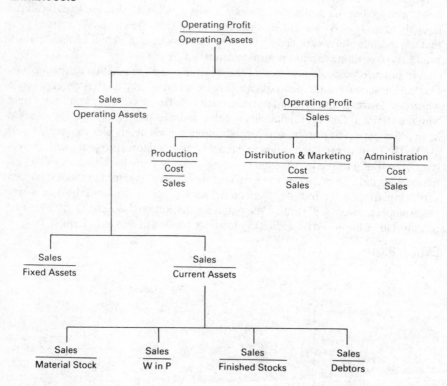

In a working scheme very many detailed ratios would be developed from the framework illustrated in this chapter. The main benefit usually arises by the more general comparison, but the detail allows backup research if things are going wrong.

The ratios are as follows:

Ratio	Last Year	This Year
Return on assets		
1 Operating profit/Operating assets (%)	8.2	11.1
Profit margin on sales and turnover of assets		
2 Operating profit/sales (%)	6.7	5.8
3 Sales/Operating assets (times per year)	2.5	1.7
Departmental costs (as a percentage of sales)		
4 Production	71.0	70.9
5 Distribution and marketing	16.3	18.2
6 Administration	6.0	5.1
Asset utilisation (£'s per £1,000 of sales)		
3a Operating assets	703	653
10 Current assets	593	480
11 Fixed assets	102	101
Current asset utilisation (£'s per £1,000 of sales)		
12 Material stocks	142	141
13 Work in progress	156	152
14 Finished stocks	152	94
15 Debtors	143	103

The results of our firm can now be appraised alongside the other companies in the sample. Our firm is identified by 'C'.

The interfirm comparison

Ratio	A	B	C	D	E
Return on assets					
1 Operating profit/Operating assets (%)	17.2	14.5	11.1	8.6	3.9
Profit margin on sales and turnover of assets					
2 Operating profit/sales (%)	14.0	14.3	5.8	7.9	2.0
3 Sales/Operating assets (times per year)	1.3	1.1	1.7	1.0	2.4
Departmental costs (as a percentage of sales)					
4 Production	74.0	70.5	70.9	71.7	77.0
5 Distribution and marketing	8.5	12.2	18.2	14.2	16.0
6 Administration	3.5	3.0	5.1	6.2	5.0
Asset utilisation (£'s per £1,000 of sales)					
3a Operating assets	842	908	653	1,030	500
10 Current assets	616	609	480	800	370
11 Fixed assets	250	320	101	241	160
Current asset utilisation (£'s per £1,000 of sales)					
12 Material stocks	131	120	141	172	84
13 Work in progress	148	120	132	175	140
14 Finished stocks	203	164	94	259	68
15 Debtors	134	205	123	194	78

Interpreting the Inter-firm Comparison we are able to see that our firm is below two other firms in return on operating assets. This can be traced to Operating Profit/Sales. Note that total departmental costs + operating profit as per cent sales = 100 per cent. The main factor in the profit being below firms A and B is high distribution and marketing costs. Action can be taken on these costs if appropriate.

Since firm C will have details of the general size and description of all the firms in the sample (although the names of firms are confidential) and knows that the Centre for Inter-firm Comparison makes sure that the figures used are comparable, very valuable information can be drawn for management.

When several periods' data is available this type of information is much more readily appreciated in graphical form.

Further thoughts on gearing

In the previous chapter, ratios to measure gearing were discussed. The most important aspect of gearing is its relation to risk.

The break-even chart shows clearly how risk emanates from variations in sales in relation to costs. Risk is usually defined in terms of the variability in profits and of course ultimately in the likelihood of failure, implied in bankruptcy or liquidations. A business with a high proportion of fixed cost will show a much higher rate of increase in profit as sales rise above break-even compared to one with a high proportion of variable cost. Correspondingly the high fixed cost company will show a much more dramatic decline into loss as sales reduce.

Exhibit 38.6

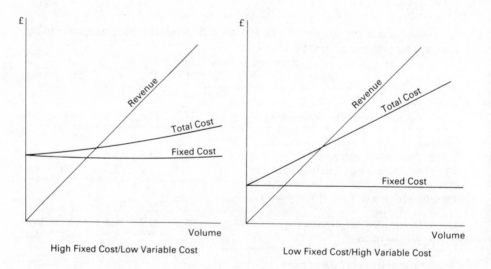

High Fixed Cost/Low Variable Cost   Low Fixed Cost/High Variable Cost

In numerical terms this can be illustrated as follows:

Fixed Costs are £200 and Variable Costs are 60% of Sales. The break-even point is therefore at Sales of £500. The break even is worked out from the fact that we know Fixed Cost is £200 and that the contribution is: Sales – 60% Sales = 40% Sales. Thus every £1 sold will make a contribution of 40p. The point of break even is where contribution equals fixed costs, i.e. $\frac{200}{0.4} = £500$ sales.

	£	£	£	£	£	£
Sales	400	500	600	700	800	900
Variable Cost	240	300	360	420	480	540
Contribution	160	200	240	280	320	360
Fixed Cost	200	200	200	200	200	200
Profit/Loss Before Interest and Tax	−40	0	40	80	120	160

Exhibit 38.7

The impact of changes in sales level can be seen to have a more than proportional impact on profit:

Sales Increase from £600 to £700 = + 16.7%
Profit Increase   £40 to £80 = + 100.0%
Sales Increase from £600 to £800 = + 33.3%
Profit Increase   £40 to £120 = + 200.0%

The effect of the level of fixed cost on the returns of a business is the cause of what has been called gearing. A highly geared company is one with a high proportion of fixed cost.

A business often has to think carefully about investing in new plant because of its impact on gearing. Using the data in Exhibit 38.7 as a starting point we can see the effect on its profitability if the business invests in some new plant the impact will be to increase fixed cost from £200 to £300 and reduce variable cost to 50% of sales. The Break Even Point will move this up to sales of £600.

	£	£	£	£	£	£
Sales	400	500	600	700	800	900
Variable Cost	200	250	300	350	400	450
Contribution	200	250	300	350	400	450
Fixed Cost	300	300	300	300	300	300
Profit/Loss before Interest or Tax	−100	−50	0	50	100	150

The impact of the new investment has been to increase the Break Even Sales from £500 to £600 in exchange for which the rate of profitability has increased. This can best be seen on the graph, Exhibit 38.6, where a higher geared situation shows the widest angle between the Revenue and Total Cost Line.

In numerical terms increasing sales from £700 to £800, i.e. 14.3% increases profits from £50 to £100, i.e. 100%.

The analysis we have examined which relates to the change in gearing from operating factors does not in itself indicate whether the investment is a good one or not. It does however show that new investment can have a significant impact on the operational risk of the business. The decision will have to be taken as to whether the increased profitability justifies the increase in break even position. If sales are hard to come by, this may not be justified.

Financial gearing

The impact of a firm borrowing money and paying interest on it, rather than funding itself entirely from its equity capital is very similar in effect to operational gearing. The interest on borrowing is the same in its impact as a fixed cost.

To illustrate this the data from Exhibit 38.7 will be taken.

	£	£	£	£	£	£
Sales	400	500	600	700	800	900
Profit/Loss before Interest and Tax	−40	0	40	80	120	160

If the business is funded entirely from Ordinary Share Capital amounting to £1,000, then if we ignore tax the rates of return would be

	£	£	£	£	£	£
Sales	400	500	600	700	800	900
$\text{Return} = \dfrac{\text{Profit/Loss}}{\text{Share Capital of £1,000}}$	−4%	0	4%	8%	12%	16%

If instead of funding entirely from ordinary shares. If the business raised its £1,000 funds – £600 from Ordinary Shares and £400 from a 10% Loan then the returns amend would be as follows:

	£	£	£	£	£	£
Sales	400	500	600	700	800	900
Profit/Loss before Interest and Tax	−40	0	40	80	120	160
Interest	−40	−40	−40	−40	−40	−40
Net Profit before tax	−80	−40	0	40	80	120
$\text{Return} = \dfrac{\text{Profit/Loss}}{\text{Share Capital of £600}}$	−13.3%	−6.7%	0	6.7%	13.3%	20%

The impact of borrowing money on the return to the Ordinary Shareholders is to increase the return to him beyond the point where operating profits exceed a return of 10% on the capital, i.e. Sales of £750. After this point the returns to the ordinary shareholder accelerate. Notice however the significant increase in Break Even Point from £500 to £600 and that sales must in fact exceed £750 before the shareholder is better off.

Quite apart from the increased risk from gearing the introduction of borrowing brings a legal risk that the lender may – if for example interest is not paid on time – take a legal charge over the company's assets.

The net cost of borrowing is reduced if tax is taken into account, since the interest charge is deductible from profit subject to tax. If we assumed a 50% tax rate the figures would be as follows:

100% Share Capital

	£	£	£	£	£	£
Sales	400	500	600	700	800	900
Net of Tax Profit/Loss	−20	0	20	40	60	80
Return	−2%	0	2%	4%	6%	8%

60% Share Capital

Net of Tax Profit	−40%	−20	0	20	40	60
Return	−6.7%	−3.3%	0	3.3%	6.7%	10%

Problems with return on capital employed

Considerable difficulty is caused by the wide use of Return on Capital Employed (ROCE) as a measure of the performance of a business. Perhaps the main issue is the valuation of the fixed assets which are subject to depreciation. The problem can be illustrated from the following facts: A business acquires an asset costing £9,000 which will have a life of three years with a nil residual value. Profits generated before depreciation will be £5,000 per annum and the profit after depreciation (straight line) will be £5,000 − £3,000 = £2,000 per annum.

Period	0	1	2	3
Cost value of asset	9,000	9,000	9,000	9,000
less aggregate depreciation	0	3,000	6,000	9,000
	9,000	6,000	3,000	0

In year one if the average value of assets is used the return will be 26.7%

$$(2,000 \ / \ \frac{9,000 + 6,000}{2} \ )$$

and in year 3 it will have increased to 133.3%

$$(2,000 \ / \ \frac{3,000 + 0}{2} \ ).$$

If the profits happened to be earned by using the fully depreciated assets in year 4 – the return would be infinite – in relation to a zero capital value.

The fact which emerges from this example is that if performance is to be judged by ROCE there is an incentive for the manager not to invest in new fixed assets which will increase the capital base. With depreciating assets the performance will appear to improve automatically.

Although much has been written about this problem of measurement, this is no practical alternative that has been adopted. The interpreter of the accounts must be vigilant.

The limitations of ratio analysis

The advantages of ratio analyses which have been brought out in this text are that they provide a consistent and disciplined approach to the analysis of accounts. In addition they are a convenient method of comparing the performance of a particular firm with others and of seeing trends over time. Nonetheless there are dangers in accepting answers which appear to be put forward by ratios in too rigid a manner. The following points are relevant:

1 Accounting Statements present a limited picture only of the business. The information included in accounts does not cover all aspects of the business.

2 The problem associated with differing bases of accounting are nowhere more important than in ratio analysis. In particular differences in valuing fixed assets, depreciation methods and in valuation of stock-in-trade can be mentioned. As you will appreciate from your study of accounting there is usually a variety of accounting methods which may be appropriate to a particular firm.

3 The accounts of large organisations frequently aggregate operations in different industries and an external analyst will not be able to split up the results of one sector from another.

4 Comparison of a firm which finances its fixed plant through rental, thus not showing it as an asset, with a firm which purchases its own assets will be difficult.

5 External analysis of balances can be misleading because the picture at that particular moment of time may not be representative of the year as a whole. For example firms frequently take stock when their stock levels are lowest. Average figures should be used but are not available externally.

6 Interpretation of a change in a ratio needs careful examination of changes in both numerator and denominator. Without a very full and detailed investigation some wrong conclusions can be drawn.

7 There is room for considerable difference between individual companies. It is wrong to lay down too rigid guidelines since what may be good for one successful firm may be wrong for another.

8 In general it is incorrect to compare small firms with very large firms. Many of the general industrial analyses of ratios are overall averages, and are, therefore, not strictly comparable to any particular firm.

The lesson is that while ratios are useful in indicating areas for investigation they cannot be relied upon to answer all the questions raised. Many of the limitations may, however, be reduced if a properly supervised scheme of inter-firm comparison is introduced.

Interpretation of accounts for employees

The interpretation which has been reviewed so far in this chapter has been for people with a good knowledge of the basis of accounting. Many firms have realised in recent years that it can be of great interest to their employees, if they attempt to make important features of the accounts generally available. Experience has tended to show that the average employee is very easily put off if too much detail is presented to him. Most firms attempt therefore to give a much more limited amount of information and to present it as imaginatively as possible in a special employee report. It is always far better to get over a limited amount of important information than to include so much detail that the message is obscured. Those who are interested can look for more detail in the main published accounts.

Firms have developed many different approaches in preparing their reports to employees. Many succeed by capturing interest through good graphics and design. Care must be taken however not to make these reports appear too trivial or condescending. There is a very wide range of approach between different firms many of which include cartoons and 'comic-strip' types of presentation to capture interest. Space is not available here to do justice to this type of presentation. Try to find examples of company reports in libraries.

Review questions

38.1A During 19-3 the comparative financial data from three companies in the same industrial sector was as follows:

	ZA Ltd	XB Ltd	CL Ltd
	£	£	£
Fixed Assets (net)	52,000	76,000	54,000
Current Assets:			
Stock,	48,000	40,000	64,000
Debtors	30,000	56,000	80,000
Cash	42,000	24,000	16,000
	172,000	196,000	214,000
less Current Liabilities			
Creditors	(24,400)	(44,600)	(64,000)
Proposed Dividends	(7,600)	(11,400)	(30,000)
	140,000	140,000	120,000
Issued Capital:			
6 per cent £1 Preference	10,000	40,000	–
£1 Ordinary Shares	70,000	60,000	120,000
Revenue Reserves	60,000	40,000	–
	140,000	140,000	120,000
Average Stock	50,000	72,000	60,000
Sales	250,000	240,000	800,000
Gross Profit	50,000	60,000	80,000
Net Profit	30,000	30,000	30,000

You are required:

(*a*) to write a report analysing and comparing the performance of the three companies;

(*b*) to advise a client with £5,000 to invest in shares of one of the three companies which company and which type of share to select.

38.2 Three companies have the capital structures shown below.

Company	A	B	C
	£'000s	£'000s	£'000s
Ordinary shares	600	400	50
12% Debentures	–	200	550
	600	600	600

The return on capital employed was 20 per cent for each firm in 19-4, and in 19-5 was 10 per cent. Corporation tax in both years was assumed to be 55 per cent, and debenture interest is an allowable expense against corporation tax.

(*a*) Calculate the percentage return on the shareholders' capital for each company for 19-4 and 19-5. Assume that all profits are distributed.

(*b*) Use your answer to explain the merits and the dangers of high gearing.

(University of London GCE 'A' level)

38.3A Martha is the accountant of a trading business. During the past year she produced interim accounts for the six months ended 30 November 19-5, and draft final accounts for the year ended 31 May 19-6, as follows:

	Interim Accounts	Draft Final Accounts
	£	£
Sales (all on credit terms)	140,000	336,000
Cost of sales (note 1)	42,000	112,000
Gross profit	98,000	224,000
less expenses	56,000	168,000
Net profit	42,000	56,000
Fixed assets	70,000	63,000
Current assets (note 2)	42,000	71,000
Current liabilities (note 3)	(22,000)	(30,000)
	90,000	104,000
Share capital	30,000	30,000
Retained earnings	60,000	74,000
	90,000	104,000

Notes:

1 Average stock was £14,000 during the first six months.

2 Current assets were:

	30 Nov 19-5	31 May 19-6
	£	£
Stock	16,000	25,000
Debtors	24,000	28,000
Bank	2,000	18,000
	42,000	71,000

3 Current liabilities consisted entirely of trade creditors.

Martha informs you that the business leased additional premises from 1 December 19-5, and that sales arising therefrom totalled £70,000 for the six months to 31 May 19-6, with an average mark-up on cost prices of 150% being made on those goods.

Expenses relating to these additional premises totalled £21,000 for the period. Two-fifths of the closing stock of the business was located at these premises.

Prepare a report, using appropriate accounting ratios, to explain the changes in the financial situation of the business during the year ended 31 May 19-6.

(University of London GCE 'A' level)

38.4 John Jones is considering purchasing shares in one of two companies and has extracted the following information from the balance sheet of each company.

	Company A Plc £000s	Company B Plc £000s
Authorised Share Capital		
£1 Ordinary shares	600	1,000
8% £1 Preference shares	400	
Issued Share Capital		
£1 Ordinary shares	300	800
8% £1 Preference shares	200	
Reserves		
Share premium	300	400
Retained earnings	400	200
Loan Capital		
10% Debentures (1990)		200
12% Debentures (1996)	400	

Required

(*a*)　Define the term 'gearing' stating clearly what is meant by a low gearing ratio.

(*b*)　Calculate the gearing factor for each company.

(*c*)　Explain to John Jones the significance of gearing to an ordinary shareholder in each of the companies above.

(*d*)　Assuming for each company a trading profit of £200,000 before interest and an ordinary dividend of 15% complete the profit and loss appropriation account for a year for each company. You should ignore taxation.

(*Associated Examining Board GCE 'A' level*)

38.5A The following are extracts from the balance sheets as at 31 March 19-4 and 31 March 19-5 of Glebe Ltd:

	31 March 19-4 £	£	31 March 19-5 £	£
Current Assets				
Stocks	20,000		25,000	
Trade debtors	10,000		17,000	
Cash	5,000		3,000	
		35,000		45,000
Less				
Current Liabilities				
Trade creditors	12,000		16,000	
Proposed dividends	6,000		5,000	
Bank overdraft	7,000		29,000	
		25,000		50,000
		10,000		(5,000)

Required

(*a*)　Calculate for each of the two years two ratios that indicate the liquidity position of the company.

(b) (i) From the information given, give reasons for the changes which have occurred in the working capital.

(ii) What other information regarding the current assets and current liabilities would you consider necessary to assess the ability of the business to continue in operation?

(c) Discuss any other information available from a balance sheet that may affect an assessment of the liquidity of a business.

(*Associated Examining Board GCE 'A' level*)

38.6 Colin Black is considering investing a substantial sum in the ordinary shares of Jacks Ltd. Having some accounting knowledge he has extracted the following information from the accounts for the last two financial years.

	as at 31 March 19-4 £	as at 31 March 19-5 £
Issued Share Capital		
£1 ordinary shares, fully paid	100,000	150,000
Reserves		
Share premium	10,000	60,000
Retained earnings	140,000	160,000
Loan Capital		
10% debentures 1987-89	40,000	40,000
	for year ended 31 March 19-4 £	for year ended 31 March 19-5 £
Net profit after tax	60,000	70,000

Because he was disappointed with the result he obtained when he calculated the return on the equity capital employed, Colin Black has asked for your advice.

Required

(a) Calculate the figures which prompted Colin Black's reaction.

(b) Prepare a memorandum to Colin Black pointing out other information to be considered when comparing the return on equity capital employed over two years as a basis for his investment decision.

(c) Explain why a company builds up and maintains reserves.

(*Associated Examining Board*)

38.7A The following information has been extracted from the accounts of Witton Way Ltd:

Profit and loss account for the year to 30 April 19-6

	19-5 £'000	19-6 £'000
Turnover (all credit sales)	7,650	11,500
less Cost of sales	(5,800)	(9,430)
Gross Profit	1,850	2,070
Other expenses	(150)	(170)
Loan interest	(50)	(350)
Profit Before Taxation	1,650	1,550
Taxation	(600)	(550)
Profit After Taxation	1,050	1,000
Dividends (all ordinary shares)	(300)	(300)
Retained Profits	£ 750	£ 700

Balance sheet at 30 April 19-6

	19-5 £'000	19-6 £'000
Fixed Assets		
Tangible assets	10,050	11,350
Current Assets		
Stocks	1,500	2,450
Trade debtors	1,200	3,800
Cash	900	50
	3,600	6,300
Creditors: Amounts falling due within one year	2,400	2,700
Net Current Assets	1,200	3,600
Total Assets Less Current Liabilities	11,250	14,950
Creditors:		
Amounts falling due after more than one year		
Loans and other borrowings	350	3,350
	£10,900	£11,600
Capital and Reserves		
Called up share capital	5,900	5,900
Profit and loss account	5,000	5,700
	£10,900	£11,600

Additional information:

During the year to 30 April 19-6, the company tried to stimulate sales by reducing the selling price of its products and by offering more generous credit terms to its customers.

Required

(*a*) Calculate six accounting ratios specifying the basis of your calculations for each of the two years to 30 April 19-5 and 19-6 respectively which will enable you to examine the company's progress during 19-6.

(*b*) From the information available to you, including the ratios calculated in part (*a*) of the question, comment upon the company's results for the year to 30 April 19-6 under the heads of 'profitability', 'liquidity', 'efficiency' and 'shareholders' interests'.

(*c*) State what additional information you would require in order to assess the company's attempts to stimulate sales during the year to 30 April 19-6.

(*Association of Accounting Technicians*)

38.8 You are presented with the following information for three quite separate and independent companies:

Summarised balance sheets at 31 March 19-7

	Chan plc £'000	Ling plc £'000	Wong plc £'000
Total assets *less* current liabilities	600	600	700
Creditors: amounts falling due after more than on year			
10% Debenture stock	–	–	(100)
	£600	£600	£600
Capital and reserves:			
Called up share capital			
Ordinary shares of £1 each	500	300	200
10% Cumulative preference shares of £1 each	–	200	300
Profit and loss account	100	100	100
	£600	£600	£600

Additional information:

1 The operating profit before interest and tax for the year to 31 March 19-8 earned by each of the three companies was £300,000.

2 The effective rate of corporation tax for all three companies for the year to 31 March 19-8 is 30%. This rate is to be used in calculating each company's tax payable on ordinary profit.

3 An ordinary dividend of 20p for the year to 31 March 19-8 is proposed by all three companies, and any preference dividends are to be provided for.

4 The market prices per ordinary share at 31 March 19-8 were as follows:

	£
Chan plc	8.40
Ling plc	9.50
Wong plc	10.38

5 There were no changes in the share capital structure or in long-term loans of any of the companies during the year to 31 March 19-8.

Required

(*a*) Insofar as the information permits, prepare the profit and loss account for each of the three companies (in columnar format) for the year to 31 March 19-8 (formal notes to the accounts are not required):

(b) calculate the following accounting ratios for each company:

(i) earnings per share;

(ii) price earnings;

(iii) gearing [taken as total borrowings (preference share capital and long-term loans) to ordinary shareholders' funds];

and

(c) using the gearing ratios calculated in answering part (b) of the question, briefly examine the importance of gearing if you were thinking of investing in some ordinary shares in one of the three companies assuming that the profits of the three companies were fluctuating.

(*Association of Accounting Technicians*)

38.9A The Chairman of a family business has been examining the following summary of the accounts of the company since it began three years ago.

Balance Sheet (at 30 June) £'000s

	19-4 Actual		19-5 Actual		19-6 Actual	
Freehold land and buildings		150		150		150
Plant	150		150		450	
less Depreciation	15	135	30	120	75	375
		285		270		525
Stock and work in progress	20		45		85	
Debtors	33		101		124	
Bank and cash	10		15		–	
	63		161		209	
less Creditors	20		80		35	
Taxation	4		17		6	
Overdraft	–	39	–	64	25	143
		324		334		668
less Loan		–		–		200
		324		334		468
Ordinary share capital						
(£1 shares)		300		300		300
General reserve		17		25		45
Deferred tax account		7		9		23
		324		334		468

Profit and Loss Account (for year to 30 June) £'000s

	19-4 Actual		19-5 Actual		19-6 Draft	
Sales		260		265		510
Trading profit		53		50		137
Depreciation	15		15		45	
Loan interest	–	15	–	15	30	75
Net profit		38		35		62
Taxation (including transfer to or from deferred tax account)		11		15		15
Net profit after tax		27		20		47
Dividend (proposed*)		10		12		14*
Extraordinary expense (public liability claim)		–		–		13
Retained		17		8		20

The Company's products are popular in the locality and in the first two years sales could have been higher if there had been extra machine capacity available.

On 1 January 19-6, additional share and loan capital was obtained which enabled extra machinery to be purchased. This gave an immediate increase in sales and profits.

Although 19-5/-6 showed the best yet results, the Chairman is not very happy; the accountant has suggested that a dividend should not be paid this year because of the overdraft. The account has, however, shown a proposed dividend of £14,000 (£2,000 up on last year) for purposes of comparison pending a decision by the directors.

Naturally, the Chairman is displeased and wants some explanations from the accountant regarding the figures in the accounts.

He specifically asks:

(i) Why, if profits are the best ever and considering the company has obtained extra capital during the year, has the company gone into overdraft? Can there really be a profit if there is no cash left in the bank to pay a dividend?

(ii) Why is the freehold still valued at the same price as in 19-4? The real value seems to be about £225,000. Why is this real value not in the balance sheet?

Required:

Write a report to the Chairman:

(a)   commenting on the state and progress of the business as disclosed by the accounts and the above information, supporting your analysis by appropriate key accounting ratios, and

(b)   giving reasoned answers, in the context of recognised accounting law, rules and practices, to each of the questions raised by the Chairman.

(*Institute of Chartered Secretaries and Administrators*)

38.10 The following information is provided for Bessemer Ltd which operates in an industry subject to marked variations in consumer demand.

(i) Shareholders' equity at 30 September 19-5.

	£'000s
Issued ordinary shares of £1 each fully paid	5,000
Retained profits	1,650
	6,650

There were no loans outstanding at the balance sheet date.

(ii) Profit and loss account extracts: year to 30 September 19-5.

	£'000s
Net profit before tax	900
less Corporation tax	270
	630
less Dividends	600
Retained profit for the year	30
Retained profit at 1 October 19-4	1,620
Retained profit at 30 September 19-5	1,650

(iii) The directors are planning to expand output. This will require an additional investment of £2,000,000 which may be financed either by issuing 1,000,000 ordinary shares each with a nominal value of £1, or by raising a 12% debenture.

(iv) Forecast profits before interest charges, if any, for the year to 30 September:

	£'000s
19-6	1,800
19-7	500
19-8	2,200

A corporation tax rate of 30% on reported profit before tax may be assumed; the directors plan to pay out the entire post-tax profit as dividends.

Required:

(*a*) The forecast profit and loss appropriation accounts for each of the next three years and year-end Balance Sheet extracts, so far as the information permits, assuming that the expansion is financed by:

(*i*) issuing additional shares, or

(*ii*) raising a debenture.

(*b*) Calculate the forecast return on shareholders' equity, for each of the next three years, under the alternative methods for financing the planned expansion.

(*c*) An assessment of the merits and demerits of the alternative methods of finance based on the calculations made under (*a*) and (*b*) and any other relevant methods of comparison.

(*Institute of Chartered Secretaries and Administrators*)

38.11A An investor is considering the purchase of shares in either AA plc or BB plc whose latest accounts are summarised below. Both companies carry on similar manufacturing activities with similar selling prices and costs of materials, labour and services.

Balance Sheets at 30 September 19-7

	AA plc £'000s	£'000s	BB plc £'000s	£'000s
Freehold Property at revaluation 19-5		2,400		–
Plant, Machinery and Equipment:				
at cost	1,800		1,800	
depreciation	1,200		400	
		600		1,400
Goodwill		–		800
Stocks: finished goods		400		200
work in progress		300		100
Debtors		800		500
Bank deposit		–		400
		4,500		3,400
less Liabilities due within one year				
Creditors	600		900	
Overdraft	200		–	
	800		900	
Liabilities due after one year	1,400		1,000	
		2,200		1,900
		2,300		1,500
Ordinary £1 shares		1,000		500
Reserves		1,300		1,000
		2,300		1,500

Profit and Loss Accounts – Year to 30 September 19-7

	AA plc		BB plc	
	£'000s	£'000s	£'000s	£'000s
Sales		2,500		2,500
Operating profit		400		600
Depreciation – plant, machinery and equipment	180		180	
Loan interest	150		160	
		330		340
		70		260
Bank interest		–		100
		70		360
Taxation		20		90
Available to ordinary shareholders		50		270
Dividend		40		130
Retained		£ 10		£ 140
Price/earnings ratio	30		5	
Market value of share	£1.50		£2.70	

Required:

(*a*)   Write a report to the investor, giving an appraisal of the results and state of each business, and

(*b*)   advise the investor whether, in your opinion, the price earnings ratios and market price of the shares can be justified in the light of the figures in the accounts, giving your reasons.

(*Institute of Chartered Secretaries and Administrators*)

38.12 The following are the summarised accounts for B Limited, a company with an accounting year ending on 30 September.

Summarised balance sheets for	19-5/6		19-6/7	
	£000	£000	£000	£000
Tangible fixed assets – at cost				
less depreciation		4,995		12,700
Current assets:				
Stocks	40,145		50,455	
Debtors	40,210		43,370	
Cash at bank	12,092		5,790	
	92,447		99,615	
Creditors: amounts falling due				
within one year:				
Trade creditors	32,604		37,230	
Taxation	2,473		3,260	
Proposed dividend	1,785		1,985	
	36,862		42,475	
Net current assets		55,585		57,140
Total assets *less* current liabilities		60,580		69,840
Creditors: amounts falling due				
after more than one year:				
10% Debentures 2006/2010		19,840		19,840
		40,740		50,000
Capital and reserves:				
Called-up share capital of £0.25 per share		9,920		9,920
Profit and loss account		30,820		40,080
Shareholders' funds		40,740		50,000

Summarised Profit and Loss accounts for	19-5/6	19-6/7
	£000	£000
Turnover	486,300	583,900
Operating profit	17,238	20,670
Interest payable	1,984	1,984
Profit on ordinary activities		
before taxation	15,254	18,686
Tax on profit on ordinary activities	5,734	7,026
Profit for the financial year	9,520	11,660
Dividends	2,240	2,400
	7,280	9,260
Retained profit brought forward	23,540	30,820
Retained profit carried forward	30,820	40,080

You are required to

  (*a*) calculate, for each year, two ratios for each of the following user groups, which are of particular significance to them:

    (i)   shareholders,

    (ii) trade creditors,

    (iii) internal management:

  (*b*) make brief comments upon the changes, between the two years, in the ratios calculated in (*a*) above.

(*Chartered Institute of Management Accountants*)

38.13A The following are the financial statements of D Limited, a wholesaling company, for the year ended 31 December:

Profit and loss accounts	19-4	19-4	19-5	19-5
	£000	£000	£000	£000
Turnover – credit sales	2,200		2,640	
cash sales	200		160	
		2,400		2,800
Cost of sales		(1,872)		(2,212)
Gross profit		528		588
Distribution costs		(278)		(300)
Administration expenses		(112)		(114)
Operating profit		138		174
Interest payable		–		(32)
Profit on ordinary activities before tax		138		142

Balance sheets as at 31 December	19-4	19-4	19-5	19-5
	£000	£000	£000	£000
Tangible fixed assets		220		286
Current assets: Stocks	544		660	
Debtors	384		644	
Cash at bank	8		110	
	936		1,414	
Creditors: amounts falling due within one year:				
Trade creditors	(256)		(338)	
Net current assets		680		1,076
Total assets *less* current liabilities		900		1,362
Creditors: amounts falling due after more than one year:				
Debenture loans				(320)
Shareholders' funds		900		1,042

The following information should be taken into consideration.

1 You may assume that:

(i) The range of products sold by D Limited remained unchanged over the two years;

(ii) the company managed to acquire its products in 19-5 at the same prices as it acquired them for in 19-4;

(iii) the effects of any inflationary aspects have been taken into account in the figures.

2 Ignore taxation.

3 All calculations must be shown to one decimal place.

You are required, using the information above, to assess and comment briefly on the company, from the point-of-view of:

(*a*) profitability;

(*b*) liquidity.

(*Chartered Institute of Management Accountants*)

38.14 G plc is a holding company with subsidiaries that have diversified interests. G plc's board of directors is interested in the group acquiring a subsidiary in the machine tool manufacturing sector. Two companies have been identified as potential acquisitions, A Ltd and B Ltd. Summaries of both these companies' accounts are shown below:

Profit and loss accounts for the year ended 30 April 19-8

	A Ltd £000	B Ltd £000
Turnover	985	560
Cost of goods sold		
Opening stock	150	145
Materials	255	136
Labour	160	125
Factory overheads	205	111
Depreciation	35	20
Closing stock	(155)	(140)
	650	397
Gross profit	335	163
Selling and administration expenses	(124)	(75)
Interest	(35)	(10)
Profit before taxation	176	78
Taxation	65	25
Profit after taxation	111	53

Balance Sheets at 30 April 19-8

	A Ltd £000	A Ltd £000	B Ltd £000	B Ltd £000
Fixed assets		765		410
Current assets				
Stock	155		140	
Debtors	170		395	
Bank	50		45	
	375		580	
Current liabilities				
Trade creditors	235		300	
Other	130		125	
	365		425	
Net current assets		10		155
Debentures		(220)		(70)
		555		495
Share capital		450		440
Profit and loss account		105		55
		555		495

You are required to prepare a report for the board of G plc assessing the financial performance and position of A Ltd and B Ltd. Your report should be prepared in the context of G plc's interests in these two companies and should be illustrated with financial ratios where appropriate. You should state any assumptions you make as well as any limitations of your analysis.

(*Chartered Institute of Management Accountants*)

39
Alternatives to historic cost accounting

The attempts of the accounting profession through the Accounting Standards Committee (ASC) to produce an acceptable alternative to historic cost accounting were outlined in Chapter 45 of the first volume. A student may be forgiven for being confused if not dismayed by the often tortuous efforts over more than twenty years to produce an acceptable standard to apply to the published accounts of companies. Yet all that remains of numerous reports, books, exposure drafts and standards is the ASC Handbook *Accounting for the Effects of Changing Prices* published in 1986. No Standard is in place nor looks likely to be at the time of publishing this book. This is particularly remarkable since the overwhelming mass of evidence indicates the inadequacy of historic cost accounting.

A Treasury report *Accounting for Economic Costs and Changing Prices* published in August 1986 and known as the *Byatt Report* reached the following conclusion 'that the measurement errors involved in estimating the cost of using resources in current prices pales into insignificance compared with those involved in ignoring the effect of changing prices, in spite of the extra degree of judgement involved.'

Despite the continuing weight of informed opinion supporting the adjustment of historic cost accounts, so far it is the implacable opposition of management and to some extent auditors of the organisations affected which has been dominant. This situation reflects a very unsatisfactory hiatus. It is impossible to see how accounts can suitably be considered to show a 'true and fair' view when they are quite clearly neither true nor fair. It appears that only the Government will have sufficient authority to overcome the interest of management in favour of the investing public, or public interest at large.

In the rest of this chapter some of the detailed issues and adjustments required to convert historic cost accounts to current costs will be examined. Only the most important adjustments will be considered.

Accounting values

The cost of an asset purchased in the open market is an objective measure of its value at the point of time when it was acquired. What is meant by this is that there exists in properly kept records, quite easily verifiable evidence of the purchase value, from items such as invoices and cheques paid out. Objectivity is important because it means that there will be a high degree of uniformity in the way that different accountants in separate organisations will record similar transactions. Most users would prefer accounts to be based on objective evidence rather than on the subjective guesses of the managers.

However the problem with historic costs is that if they are not adjusted they very quickly cease to reflect values that have much meaning. One of the most significant features of the twentieth century has been the ever increasing rate at which values have changed. This is due to a wide variety of causes including technological advances, population growth, energy and food shortages as well as the pervading influence of monetary inflation. Thus whilst historic cost accounting has the considerable advantage of being based on objective evidence it fails entirely to cope with the problem of reflecting current values of the assets, capital and liabilities or revenues and expenses in a business.

Once the historic cost basis is departed from the problem of deciding on an alternative basis of valuation has to be tackled. It is important to remember that accounting is concerned to record economic values and not moral, social or other values. Economics values in our kind of society are based on market prices, that is the price at which goods are bought and sold by producers and consumers.

The basis of a market value depends on a complex array of factors. Fundamentally, value depends on the expectations the people in the market have about the future worth of something. If an asset promises to yield economic benefits in the future it will have a current value. The current value however will take account of the inherent uncertainty of the future and also will charge interest for delay in obtaining a benefit. Cash in hand now is worth more than cash in the future because it can earn interest. In our economy markets for most goods are 'efficient' in that they incorporate all the significant knowledge that is available to fix the current price. Thus market prices incorporate the knowledge and experience of a wide range of expert dealers and thus form a reasonable basis of value for accounting purposes.

Market prices are readily available for a wide range of commodities and goods, but some things are unique so there is nothing exactly the same being bought or sold. For instance there is a market price for butter which is quoted daily for example in the *Financial Times*, but if you own a plot of land there can be nothing which is exactly the same. However in this situation there is often something sufficiently similar being bought and sold to enable a qualified valuer to arrive at a reasonable estimate of the value.

Using index numbers

Because a business may own thousands of different assets the process of revaluing every individual item each year could assume vast proportions. Thus it is often much more convenient to revalue groups of assets in line with the change in market value for the whole group. Index numbers are prepared by the UK Government Statistical Service which indicate the change in value in the market of particular asset groups. For example if a firm equipped a new factory on 1 January 19-1 with one hundred machine tools costing £5,000,000 what is their market value at the accounting date 31 December 19-1? Instead of trying to estimate for each individual machine the firm could obtain the market price index for machine tools as at 1 January and 31 December 19-1. Let us assume that at 1 January the index was 150 and at 31 December 180. To convert the value from the date of purchase to the accounting date we multiply the purchase price by:

$$\frac{\text{The Index at the Accounting Date}}{\text{The Index at the Date of Purchase}} \quad \text{i.e.} \quad \frac{180}{150} \times 5{,}000{,}000 = 6{,}000{,}000$$

The value of £6,000,000 is the estimated present market price of similar new machinery. For accounting purposes depreciation to cover one year's usage would then have to be charged.

A firm which has assets that are different from most other firms may feel that it is worth preparing its own index numbers to convert the figures on the accounts, perhaps also because there are no suitable published index numbers available. In the case of specialised items like land and buildings it will normally be appropriate to employ a qualified valuer to estimate changes in the market price.

Value to the business

In a market there are two levels of value – the buying price and the selling price. For some things the difference may be small but often there is quite a significant gap. For many products there is a middleman or dealer who operates between the buyer and the seller and who takes some remuneration for his services. The more specialised and complex the product the larger the gap is likely to be between buying and selling prices.

For example a firm in the textile industry may have ordered dyestuffs to their own colour specifications which cost £5,000 from the producer. If the firm finds that the order for which the dyestuffs were purchased has been cancelled it may wish to dispose of them. If the colours are non-standard nobody else may wish to buy them, their market price may be nothing and they will be scrapped.

The buying price on the market is generally called the Replacement Value of an asset. The price at which it can be sold in the market is its Realisable Value. For accounting purposes it has been proposed that the appropriate basis of value should be 'Value to the Business.' In order to determine this you need to decide what a business would do if it were deprived of the asset. If the business owns a machine which cost £5,000, what is its value? If in the event of the machine being irreparably damaged the firm would buy another machine then its value is its replacement cost. If however the machine would not be replaced then its value would be based on Realisable Value, which is what it could be sold off for.

In a normal business where continuity of production and development exists you would expect most values to be based on Replacement Value. However with technological product change being very rapid it is sometimes the case that replacement does not imply buying an identical item. When you replace something you buy the best thing available to satisfy your requirements. In other words you are concerned with the replacement of the services obtained from the asset not the asset in its own right. The judgement about replacement or realisation can only be made by the management. However it is a judgement and therefore basically subjective in nature.

Adjusting accounts to their current values

In order to illustrate how adjustments to current value accounting take place a simple example will be worked through the Balance Sheet for Copperfield Ltd which in abbreviated form and at historic cost is shown in Exhibit 39.1.

Exhibit 39.1

Copperfield Ltd
Balance Sheet at 31 December 19-1

Fixed Assets	Cost	Aggregate Depreciation	£
Land and Buildings	50,000	5,000	45,000
Plant & Machinery	100,000	20,000	80,000
	150,000	25,000	125,000

Current Assets		
Stock in Trade		20,000	
Trade Debtors		14,000	
Cash at Bank		9,000	
		43,000	
Current Liabilities			
Trade Creditors		13,000	30,000
			155,000
less 10% Loan Stock			65,000
			90,000

	£
Share Capital	
Authorised and Issued	50,000
Ordinary Shares	
of £1	
Reserves	
Profit retained	40,000
	90,000

The Directors state that all the assets would be replaced if the business were deprived of them. A revaluation of the Land and Buildings by a qualified valuer has revealed that the replacement cost of the Land and Buildings in their current state would be £90,000. In terms of their condition when bought ten years ago this would be equivalent to £100,000 replacement cost and the depreciation on buildings therefore would be £10,000.

The Plant and Machinery was bought two years ago when the index for the relevant type of plant was 160. The index at 31 December 19-1 is 240. Converting the Balance Sheet figures to current value at 31 December 19-1 gives:

$$\text{Plant and Machinery at cost} \times \frac{\text{Index at Balance Sheet date}}{\text{Index when Asset purchased}} = 100,000 \times \frac{240}{160} = £150,000$$

The Aggregate Depreciation will be converted at the same rate as the Asset to which it relates. Thus the current value of depreciation is $£20,000 \times \dfrac{240}{160} = 30,000$

Stock in Trade represents raw materials purchased evenly over the last two months of the year when the average price index for replacement was 250. At 31 December 19-1 the index had risen to 255. The current value of stock in trade is therefore

$$£20,000 \times \frac{255}{250} = £20,400$$

The current value for trade debtors (after allowance has been made for bad debts) ought to take account of the fact that there is a time delay in obtaining payment. Normally however because the delay is not long the debtors are treated at their cash face value. Thus debtors and cash are treated the same way and for this purpose are different from the other assets we have been dealing with. Because money is the medium of exchange its face value must be its market value. If you have a five pound note which you have held for five years it is still only worth its face value. Assets such as cash or debtors which have a fixed monetary value are called Monetary Assets. Monetary Assets of course lose value in an inflationary period because you can buy less with each unit of money as time passes. This type of loss will be dealt with when we examine the Profit and Loss Account.

All the assets in the Balance Sheet have now been reviewed in current terms. In summary the position is as shown in Exhibit 39.2.

Exhibit 39.2

Historic cost £	Fixed Assets	Current Value £	Aggregate Depreciation £	£	Change £
45,000	Land and Building	100,000	10,000	90,000	+45,000
80,000	Plant and Machinery	150,000	30,000	120,000	+40,000
125,000		250,000	40,000	210,000	
	Current Assets				
20,000	Stock in Trade	20,400			+400
14,000	Trade Debtors	14,000			–
9,000	Cash at Bank	9,000		43,400	–
168,000				253,400	85,400

The increase in the value of assets of £85,400 over historic costs represents a profit to the business. However it is not a profit that has been realised through a sale, nor is it a profit that the business can afford to distribute as dividends if it wishes to retain the real value of resources in the business. Thus the increase on revaluation of assets should be credited to a Capital Maintenance Reserve. The Balance Sheet after this adjustment will be as shown on Exhibit 39.3.

Exhibit 39.3

Copperfield Ltd
Balance Sheet at 31 December 19-1

Fixed Asset		Current Value	Aggregate Depreciation
	£	£	£
Land and Building	100,000	10,000	90,000
Plant and Machinery	150,000	30,000	120,000
	250,000	40,000	210,000
Current Assets			
Stock in Trade		20,400	
Trade Debtors		14,000	
Cash at Bank		9,000	
		43,400	
Current Liabilities			
Trade Creditors		13,000	30,400
			402,400
less 10% Loan Stock			65,000
			175,400
Share Capital Authorised & Issued			
Ordinary Shares of £1			50,000
Reserves			
Capital maintenance			85,400
Retained Profit			40,000
			175,400

So far attention has been directed only to the Balance Sheet, however the impact of changing values is also important in calculating Profit or Loss. Adjustments in calculating the current cost of expenses will arise from items already mentioned.

Depreciation adjustment

Firstly depreciation on Fixed Assets will need to be changed to current cost. This is done by using the index numbers which are appropriate for the Fixed Assets concerned. If we have for example an asset bought on 1 January 19-1 for 2,000 and to be fully depreciated over 10 years straight line, i.e. 10% per annum, the historic cost depreciation at 31 December 19-1 will be £200. Assuming the price index for this asset at 1 January 19-1 were 200 and at 31 December 250 the depreciation for the year would be $£2,000 \times \dfrac{250}{200} \times 10\% = £250$ in current cost terms. The Balance Sheet would show:

Asset at Current Value	£2,500
less Aggregate Depreciation	250
	£2,250

If we continue with this asset to 31 December 19-2 when the index is 300 the situation would show that current cost depreciation for the year is $£2,000 \times \dfrac{300}{200} \times 10\% = £300$

i.e. current cost depreciation requires £100 more than historic cost. If we adjust the asset value for the Balance Sheet this would now be $£2,000 \times \dfrac{300}{200} = £3,000$. Depreciation for its two years of life should have grown to 20% or £600. However we have so far only changed £550, i.e. £250 in 19-1 and £300 in 19-2. The problem is that £50 too little was charged in 19-1 in current value terms. Thus as the original cost value of an asset is adjusted so also must be aggregate depreciation. The depreciation for earlier years is known as backlog depreciation. In preparing a profit and loss account only the adjustment for the current year would be included.

The backlog adjustment would be set against the Capital Maintenance Reserve. In the example we have just used the fixed asset figures in the Balance Sheet would be:

Balance Sheet at 31 December 19-2

19-1	*Fixed Assets*	
2,500	Plant and Machinery at current value	£3,000
250	*less* Aggregate Depreciation	600
2,250		2,400

The Capital Maintenance Reserve would include the following adjustments in 19-2:

Credit (i.e. increase the Reserve) for the rise in value of plant	£500
Debit (i.e. reduce the Reserve) for backlog depreciation	£50

The Profit and Loss Account will be debited with the depreciation for 19-2, i.e.

Historic cost depreciation	£200
Plus in the Current Cost Adjustment Statement Current value adjustment	£100
Total Current Value Depreciation	£300

Applying this approach to Copperfield Ltd would mean that the historical cost depreciation for the year to 31 December 19-1 would have to be adjusted by the index relating to the asset concerned. Thus assuming the historic cost depreciation figures for year to 31.12.19-1 were:

	£	
Land and Buildings	1,000	
Plant and Machinery	10,000	11,000

Then the conversion to current costs would be

£

Land and Buildings $1,000 \times \dfrac{100}{50} =$ 2,000

Plant and Machinery $10,000 \times \dfrac{240}{160} =$ 15,000   17,000

The Current Cost of depreciation for the year is £6,000 more than historic cost. Note that the index for Land and Buildings is developed from the Revaluation figures. Backlog depreciation would have to be allowed for when current cost accounting had been in operation for more than one year.

Cost of sales adjustment

In the calculation of the Profit and Loss account for most firms one of the most important elements in the calculation of profit or loss is the Cost of Sales (often called Cost of Goods Sold). The Sales during an accounting period will be recorded at their actual invoiced prices over the period. The Purchases made during the period will also be at the cost prices over the period. Assuming that activity is reasonably constant the total Purchases and Sales will reflect the average price for the period. However under Historic Cost accounting methods with rising prices the opening and closing stock in trade figures will reflect values which differ from the average cost for the period. In order to ensure that the Cost of Sales reflects the same (i.e. average) prices as Purchases and Sales it is necessary to adjust the Stock in Trade figures to average cost levels. Example:

Index Numbers Reflecting Stock in Trade Values are:

Opening Stock was valued when the index averaged	150
The index average for the year to 31 December 19-1	200
Closing Stock was valued when the index averaged	250
The Index at 31 December 19-2	255

The Cost of Sales in Historic Cost Values for years to 31.12.19-1 is:

Opening Stock in Trade	£15,000
Purchases	200,000
	215,000
less Closing Stock in Trade	20,000
Cost of Sales	195,000

The Current Cost of Sales adjusted to average values for the year would be:

Opening Stock in Trade $15,000 \times \dfrac{200}{150} =$	20,000	
Purchases at actual cost	200,000	
	220,000	
Closing Stock in Trade $20,000 \times \dfrac{200}{250} =$	16,000	
Current Cost of Sales	204,000	

The Current Cost of Sales is thus £9,000 (204,000 − 195,000) greater than the Historic Cost of Sales, and in the Current Cost Accounts a deduction (debit) of this amount from Historic Profit would be made and described as Cost of Sales Adjustment. The corresponding credit will go to Capital Maintenance Reserve.

If the business for example is very seasonal in nature it may not be correct to assume that Purchases and Sales are at 'average' values. Where this exists the management will have to make adjustments to the Sales and Purchase figures to convert them to a current value base.

Monetary working capital adjustment

The next adjustment in the Profit and Loss Account is an attempt to allow for the loss which arises when holding 'monetary assets' in an inflationary period. This adjustment known as the Monetary Working Capital Adjustment is based on the additional or reduced finance needed, in a period of changing prices due to the price change rather than a change in volume of working capital. Monetary Working Capital does not include Stock in Trade for which adjustment has already been made, but for most businesses consists of trade debtors and trade creditors. Strictly cash balances ought to be included, but because a business often has cash which is surplus to operating needs – because for example it is about to buy other assets in the near future, the calculation of Monetary Working Capital for convenience can be restricted to Debtors and Creditors. They are felt to be assets which are limited to operating requirements of the existing business. The adjustments to be made for Monetary Working Capital gains or losses is similar in method to that used for Stock in Trade. The opening and closing figures of working capital are adjusted to average values for the year. Working through an example:

	1 January 19-1	21 December 19-1
	£	£
Trade Debtors	11,000	14,000
Trade Creditors	10,200	13,000

The index numbers should reflect the current values of the goods or services which comprise the sales or purchases included in debtors and creditors, those appropriate for the business are:

1 January 19-1	150.0
31 December 19-1	250.0
Average for the year	200.0

The monetary working capital at 1 January 19-1 is £800 (11,000−10,200) in historic terms. In average values for the year it would be:

$$£800 \times \frac{200.0}{150.0} = 1066.7$$

The monetary working capital at 31 December 19-1 is £1,000 (14,000−13,000) in historic terms. In average values for the year it would be:

$$£1000 \times \frac{200}{250} = £800$$

In historic terms the change in working capital is:

31 December 19-1	£1000
1 January 19-1	£800
Increase in working capital	200

The adjusted Figures show:

31 December 19-1	£800.0
1 January 19-1	1066.7
Reduction in working capital	−266.7

The adjusted figures show that if valued at the same point in terms of prices the working capital reduced by £266.7. That is there is a real fall in working capital amount or volume of £266.7. If this is deducted from the change in working capital shown in historic terms the figure given will represent the impact of price changes on working capital £200 − (−266.7) = £466.7 (Note the double negative).

In summary:

	£
Price increase in working capital	466.7
Volume reduction in working capital	−266.7
Net change in working capital at historic values	200.0

The Price increase in working capital is the figure shown in the Profit and Loss Account as Monetary Working Capital Adjustment.

The way to calculate Monetary Working Capital Adjustment can be summarised as:

1 Calculate the opening and closing working capital figures in historic terms, and calculate the change in the year: – Closing Working Capital – Opening Working Capital. If the opening Working Capital is larger than closing then the answer will be negative.

2 Obtain index numbers at the start and end of the year and an average for the year.

3 Convert the opening and closing working capital figures to average values. Using these averages calculate the volume increase in working capital: closing working capital at average value – opening working capital at average value. Again if the opening value exceeds the closing value the result will be negative.

4 Deduct from your answer in (1), the answer in (3), i.e. from the historic cost change in monetary working capital deduct the average value change in monetary working capital. The answer will be the Monetary Working Capital Adjustment for Price.

5 If prices are rising and debtors exceed creditors the result will be as in our illustration – a debit to Profit and Loss Account with the corresponding credit to Capital Maintenance Reserve.

If prices are rising and creditors exceed debtors there will be a credit to Profit and Loss reflecting benefit of owing amounts fixed in money units in an inflationary period.

The current cost operating profit

The adjustments made so far can now be summarised to show the adjustments which are made to convert the traditional historic cost net profit before interest and tax into the Current Cost Operating Profit.

For illustration purposes information which has been worked out in the text will be combined with assumed figures to show the layout in Exhibit 39.4.

Exhibit 39.4

Profit and Loss Account for the year ended 31 December 19-1

		Current Cost £	Historic Cost £
Sales		150,000.0	150,000.0
Trading Profit (Historic Cost)		16,000.0	16,000.0
Current Cost Adjustments:			
Depreciation	6000.0		
Cost of Sales	9000.0		
Monetary Working Capital	466.7	15,466.7	
Current Cost Operating Profit		533.3	

Gearing adjustment

Having arrived at the Current Cost Operating Profit the final adjustment required is designed to allow for the fact that most businesses do not run exclusively on funds provided by the shareholders. If all the funds are provided by shareholders no further adjustment is required but if some funds are provided by lenders or creditors then part of the loss incurred due to inflation is offset.

If during an inflationary period you hold £100 in cash for a year when the retail price index moves from 200 to 300, you make a loss of £50 because your buying power has been reduced. In order to be as well off at the end of the year in buying power you would need cash of £150 ($£100 \times \frac{300}{200}$). If the £100 had been borrowed however there would be no loss because you could repay the £100 loan in full at the end of the year with your cash without having to compensate the lender for his loss in buying power terms of £50. This does not take into account interest payments to the lender, which are assumed to be simply for the use of the money, although in inflationary periods they are higher to compensate lenders for inflationary losses.

To take account of the fact that a business can offset some of its losses from inflation by borrowing – a gearing adjustment is calculated by working out the funds which are borrowed as a proportion of total funds. If a business for example obtains 20% of its funds from creditors and lenders then 20% of the Current Cost Adjustments are shown as an addition back to profits, i.e. this amount is a gain to the shareholders of the business.

The calculation required is as follows:

(*a*) Ascertain the average net borrowing for the period. The average can be a simple average from the opening and closing Balance Sheets unless there have been material charges, i.e. new borrowing or repayment during the year, in which case a weighted average would be necessary. Net borrowing is defined as the sum of all Liabilities and Provisions apart from those included in Monetary Working Capital (Trade Creditors) and Proposed Dividends, less the sum of all current assets apart from those included in the Cost of Sales adjustment (stock in trade) and Monetary Working Capital (trade debtors). Let average net borrowing be L.

(*b*) Ascertain the average shareholders' interest as the average of share capital, reserves and proposed dividends, as shown in the opening and closing current cost balance sheets. Let the average shareholders' interest be S.

(*c*) The gearing proportion is the ratio of average net borrowing to the sum of this and the shareholders interest, i.e. $\dfrac{L}{L + S}$.

Using the information from Copperfield Ltd the details can be worked as in Exhibit 39.5.

Exhibit 39.5

Copperfield Ltd
Current Cost Balance Sheet at 31 December 19-1

19-0	*Fixed Assets*	*Current Value*	*Aggregate Depreciation*	*£*
80,000	Land and Building	100,000	10,000	90,000
10,000	Plant and Machinery	150,000	30,000	120,000
180,000		250,000	40,000	210,000
	Current Assets			
16,000	Stock in Trade	20,400		
11,000	Trade Debtors	14,000		
8,200	Cash in Bank	9,000		
215,200		43,400		
	Current Liabilities			
10,200	Trade Creditors	13,000		30,400
205,000				240,400
65,000	*less* 10% Loan Stock			65,000
140,000				175,400
19-0	*Share Capital*			
	Authorised and Issued			
50,000	Ordinary Shares of £1			50,000
	Reserves			
70,000	Capital Maintenance			85,400
20,000	Retained Profit			40,000
140,000				175,400

Net borrowings:

	19-0	19-1
	£	£
10% Loan Stock	65,000	65,000
less Cash at Bank	(8,200)	(9,000)
	56,800	56,000

Average for year L = £56,400.

Shareholder interest:

	19-0	19-1
	£	£
Share Capital plus Reserves	140,000	175,400

Average for year S = £157,700.

The gearing proportion is therefore $\dfrac{L}{L+S} = \dfrac{56,400}{56,400 + 157,700} = 26.3\%$.

Applying the gearing percentage of 26.3 to the total value of the Current Cost Adjustments in the Profit and Loss Account of £15,466.7 gives a value for the gearing adjustment of £4,067.7.

The final form of the Profit and Loss Account adjusted to Current Costs will be in the form shown in Exhibit 39.6.

Exhibit 39.6

Profit and Loss Account for the year ended 31 December 19-1

		Current Cost £		Historic Cost £
Sales		150,000		150,000
Trading Profit		16,000		16,000
Current Cost Adjustments:				
Depreciation	6,000			
Cost of Sales	9,000			
Monetary Working Capital	467	15,467		
Current Cost Operating Profit		533		
Gearing Adjustment		4,068		
		4,601		
less Net Interest Payable		6,500		6,500
Before tax	Loss	(1,899)	Profit	9,500
Corporation Tax		2,000		2,000
Attributable to Shareholders				
after tax	Loss	(3,899)	Profit	7,500
Ordinary Dividend		500		500
Balance to Retained Earnings	Loss	(4,399)	Profit	7,000

The above examples have been based on the operating capital maintenance concept. The ASC handbook also recommends calculating profit under the financial capital maintenance concept. The way in which this is done is explained in the first volume, Chapter 45 and is not repeated here.

Review questions

39.1 Write down whether you consider the following statements are true or false.

(*a*) Objectivity exists in historic cost accounting when there is an independently verifiable cost price.

(*b*) Historic cost accounting in general reflects the current value of assets in a business.

(*c*) Economic values in our society tend to be based on market prices.

(*d*) Value depends on the current position and does not take account of future expectations.

(*e*) Index numbers can be useful in converting historic costs to current values.

39.2A Write down whether you consider the following statements are true or false.

(*a*) The buying price of assets in the market is known as realisable value.

(*b*) The 'value to the business' of an asset is the lower of replacement or realisable value.

(*c*) Monetary Assets include items like trade debtors which lose value in an inflationary period.

(*d*) Backlog depreciation is charged to the Current Cost Profit and Loss Account as soon as it arises.

(*e*) The gearing adjustment is based on the proportion of borrowed funds to those provided by shareholders.

39.3A Using Motor Cars as the basis prepare index numbers showing how the 'new' car prices of two popular models of your own choice have changed in the last five years. Prepare a similar index for the one year old second-hand value of the same cars. Try to think of reasons for any differences which emerge from the comparison. What difficulties arise in preparing the index numbers?

39.4 A firm owns machinery which was bought on 1 January 19-4 for £20,000. It is preparing current cost accounts at 31 December 19-6 and wishes to calculate the equipment replacement cost value at that date. The index of machinery prices at 1 January 19-4 was 150 and at 31 December 19-6 had risen to 180. What is the current cost value at 31 December 19-6?

39.5A The machinery whose details are given in question 39.4 is depreciated at 10% per annum on a straight line basis. At the 31 December 19-7 the index was 200. What would the depreciation in current costs be for the year ended 31 December 19-7.

39.6 Using the information in 39.5A what would the amount of backlog depreciation be on the machinery requiring adjustment at 31 December 19-7.

39.7A Plant and Machinery was bought on 1 July 19-3 for £50,000 when the relevant price index was 200. The index at 30 June 19-4 was 250 and at 30 June 19-5, 300. Depreciation is to be provided at 20% per annum straight line. Show the entries that would appear in the Current Cost Balance Sheets at 30 June 19-4 and 30 June 19-5 in respect of the fixed asset Plant and Machinery, and calculate the adjustments necessary to the Capital Maintenance Reserve.

39.8 The historic Cost of Sales for Beanco Ltd was calculated as follows for the year ended 31 December 19-1:

	£
Opening Stock in Trade	30,000
Purchases	500,000
	530,000
Closing Stock in Trade	60,000
Cost of Sales	470,000

The following price index numbers have been obtained:

Index when opening stock on trade was bought	140
Average index for the year	160
Index when closing stock in trade was bought	180
Index at 31 December 19-1	200

Assuming that purchases were made evenly during the year, what is the Current Cost of Sales for 19-1?

39.9A The following balances are taken from the records of Hi-Fli Ltd. Calculate from this information what the Monetary Working Capital adjustment should be at 31 December 19-1:

	1 January 19-1	31 December 19-1
	£	£
Trade Debtors	25,000	30,000
Trade Creditors	19,000	20,000

The index numbers which relate to purchases and sales for Hi-Fli Ltd are:

1 January	200
Average for year	220
31 December	240

39.10 Using the information in question 38.9A but assuming the index numbers were as follows calculate the Monetary Working Capital adjustment

1 January	250
Average for year	275
31 December	300

39.11A The following information has been calculated for the Wrede Organisation Ltd for the year ended 31 December 19-5. Prepare a statement showing the Current Cost Operating Profit.

	£
Sales	1,400,000
Operating Profit (using historic costs)	700,000
Current Cost Adjustments:	
Additional depreciation	300,000
Additional cost of sales	400,000
Monetary Working Capital	15,000

39.12 From the following abridged balance sheet for Apex Corporation Ltd calculate the Gearing Adjustment percentage $\dfrac{L}{L+S}$

Apex Corporation Ltd
Balance Sheet at 31 December

19-1		19-2	19-1		19-2
£		£	£		£
	180,000 Fixed Assets at net current value	200,000	90,000	Ordinary Share Capital	90,000
	Current Assets			*Reserves*	
30,000	Stock in Trade	50,000	30,000	Capital Maintenance	40,000
20,000	Trade Debtors	30,000	35,000	Retained Profit	65,000
15,000 65,000	Cash at Bank	10,000 90,000		*Loans*	
			75,000	Debenture Stock	75,000
				Current Liabilities	
			15,000	Trade Creditors	20,000
	245,000	290,000	245,000		290,000

39.13A From the accounts of Brayco Ltd you have obtained the following information for the year ending 31 December 19-8.

		£
Sales		8,000,000
Trading Profit using historic cost		3,500,000
Current Cost Adjustments (increases in cost)		
Depreciation	180,000	
Cost of Sales	750,000	
Monetary Working Capital	400,000	1,330,000
Interest payable		430,000
Corporation Tax for the year		1,700,000
Proposed Ordinary Dividend		500,000
Gearing Adjustment $\dfrac{L}{L+S}$		20%

Set out a Current Cost Profit and Loss Account for the year to 31 December 19-8.

39.14 During a period of inflation, many accountants believe that financial reports prepared under the historical cost convention are subject to the following major limitations:

1 stocks are undervalued;

2 depreciation is understated;

3 gains and losses on net monetary assets are undisclosed;

4 balance sheet values are unrealistic;
  and

5 meaningful periodic comparisons are difficult to make.

Required:

Explain briefly the limitations of historical cost accounting in periods of inflation with reference to each of the items listed above.

(*Association of Accounting Technicians*)

Appendix I
Examination techniques

If you were completely devoid of examination technique you would probably not have advanced to this stage of the examinations. All of the advice given to you in *Business Accounting 1* is still applicable. If you have not already read that advice you should try to borrow a copy of the book from a friend, or read it in a library.

A lot of what follows was written in *Business Accounting 1*. Don't avoid reading it just because you used it. In your first examination you were competing with people who had probably never sat an accounting examination before. A lot of them will not get past stage 1. In stage 2 you are competing against people who have already proved they have a certain degree of competence in the subject. You might have got away with a certain amount of poor examination technique at stage 1, but that will not be as easy at stage 2.

Here I want to concentrate on the main deficiencies noted by examiners. These have never changed for the past 40 years. Students really should read examiners' reports, they will learn a lot from them.

Students do not read the questions properly

A large number of students do not answer the questions as set by the examiner, because they have not read the question properly. They answer what they think the examiner wants, not what he is asking for.

Let me take a simple example. Suppose the examiner sets the following question: 'Describe the use of accounting ratios in assessing the performance of businesses.'

A lot of students will immediately start to describe how to calculate various accounting ratios. Marks which will be obtained – nil. The question asked for the *use* of accounting ratios, not *how to calculate* them.

Many other students will have concentrated on the word *use*. They will then write their answer based on comparing this year's accounting ratios in a business with those of last year. They may well even mention trend ratios which will earn them some extra marks. If they keep their discussion to comparing ratios in a business in the year with other years however, they cannot get top marks, no matter how well they have written their answers.

Why not? Well, they picked up the word use, but from then on they stopped reading properly. The question does not in any way limit itself to the ratios of one business only. First of all you can compare the performance of a business with its own performance in the past. Secondly, you may be able to compare one business with another business of a similar kind. In addition, if you miss out mentioning inter-firm comparisons you will lose marks.

Therefore, (a) *read* the question carefully, (b) *underline* the *key* words to get to the meaning of the questions, (c) *think carefully* about how widespread your answer should be.

On the other hand there is no point in widening the question more than is needed. It is for the *use* of *accounting* ratios, *not* the use of *all types* of ratios. Besides accounting ratios there are marketing ratios – e.g. size of share of market, how long it takes to supply orders, ratios of defective goods etc. The question does not ask for all of these. If you give them, you will not get any extra marks.

Poor time management

Using time well to gain the highest possible marks is essential. Examiners constantly report that examinees are very poor in this aspect of tackling an examination. How then can you avoid the usual pitfalls

First of all read the *rubric* carefully. These are the instructions at the top of the paper, e.g. 'Attempt four questions only: the three questions in Section A and one from Section B. Begin each answer on a separate page.'

You would be surprised to know that a lot of students would try to answer more than one question from Section B. If you tackle two questions from Section B you will get marks for only one of your answers. No examiner will mark both and then give you marks for your highest marked answer. They will mark the first of the optional questions answered and ignore the next unnecessary answer.

Secondly, don't annoy the examiner by not starting your answer on a separate page. It is your job to make the examiner's work as easy as possible. Examiners are only human, and it would not be surprising if their annoyance did not result in it influencing the marking of your paper.

You really must attempt each and every question to fulfil the examination requirements. If you have to answer five questions then you must not tackle only four questions.

Students often feel that they would be better off by handing in the complete answers to only four questions, instead of five incomplete answers. In accounting examinations this is not true. Why is this so?

1 Examiners use positive marking in accounting examinations. If you have done 80 per cent of an answer worth 20 marks in total, and you have got it absolutely correct, then you get 80% × 20 = 16 marks.

2 The first marks in a question are the easiest to obtain. Thus it is easier to get the first 10 marks out of 20 than it is to get the second lot of marks to get full marks. By ensuring that you get the easiest marks on every question it therefore makes your task easier.

To ensure that you tackle (not necessarily finish) each question you should mark the number of minutes to be allowed by *yourself* for each question. Thus a 20-mark question, in a 100-mark examination, should be given 20 per cent of the time, i.e. 3 hours × 20% = 36 minutes. When 36 minutes have gone by, *stop answering the question* unless it is the last question to be attempted, and go on to the next question.

If you don't know the answer, or part of an answer, you should guess. You don't lose marks for guessing, and if you guess correctly you get the marks. Intuition will often give the correct answer. Very often if you don't guess on part of a computational question you will be unable to go on to the remainder of the question which you can answer.

Workings

You may wonder why I have put this under a separate heading. I cannot emphasise enough how important it is that you should:

(a) submit all your workings, and

(b) ensure that the workings are set out so that the examiner can follow them.

A very high percentage of candidates in an examination are near the pass mark, within either a few percentage points above it or below it. You should know that from your study of natural curves in statistics. If you are one of these candidates, and, as we have said, there are a lot of them, handing in workings which can be understood by the examiner will often ensure you a pass mark. Conversely, no workings, or completely unintelligible workings may well ensure your failing the examination.

Tackle the easiest questions first

Never start off your examination by tackling a difficult question. You have got to be able to settle down properly, and not let your nerves get out of control. Starting off on the easiest question is the best way to enable you to get off to a good start. Much more about this was written in *Business Accounting 1*.

State your assumptions

It does happen that sometimes a question can contain ambiguities. Examination bodies try to prevent it happening, but it does occur occasionally. The questions do (unfortunately) sometimes contain errors.

In both of these cases you must point out the ambiguity/error. You should then make an assumption, based on what you thought the examiner meant, and carry on with your answer. You must, however, state what your assumption is. Try to make your assumption as sensible as possible. The examiner will then mark your answer accordingly. If you make a ridiculous assumption it is unlikely that he will give you any marks for that part of your answer. Don't be sarcastic in your comments or complain about inefficiency, there are other times and places for that.

Answering written questions

The problem

Unlike computational-type answers you will not know whether your written answers are up to the mark until you receive your examination result. Likewise written questions lack the certainty and precision of accounting problems and it is often difficult to fathom out exactly what the examiners require of you. For this reason sound examination technique is absolutely essential together with precise knowledge of relevant law and regulations.

There are several major aspects to success in written papers. These are to *plan* your answer, to answer the question *as set*, to pay attention to good *layout* and to explain in clear and simple terms what you are doing. Remember you can only be marked on what you write down. You have no opportunity to explain some ambiguity or other and if what you write is unclear you will *not* get the benefit of the doubt.

Plan

First read the question and jot down the key *verb*, i.e. your instructions; this may be to discuss, explain, advise, set out, list, draft an audit programme, write a letter etc.

If the question requires a discussion or an explanation it should be written in proper paragraph form. Each paragraph should be self-contained and explain the point it makes. Sentences should be short and to the point. The ideal length for a paragraph is 3 sentences with 4 as a maximum. Over 4 and you are probably making more than one point and should have gone into 2 paragraphs.

Plan how many points you are going to make and what the answer is. This is essential as otherwise your answer will 'drift' as you struggle to come to some conclusion. The plan should consist of arrows connecting points to each other so that the answer will flow and be logical. The plan need not be too extensive; it is silly to waste time on a 'mini-answer'. It should consist of the *headings* you are going to use.

Layout

Whenever examiners meet to discuss results, or write down their commentary on students' performance they all agree on the importance of good layout; yet students generally tend to take no notice. The range of marks between good papers and poor papers tends to be quite small. Anything you can do to put the examiner on your side will pay off in those few extra marks.

The main areas for good layout are:

1   *Tabulate* in numbered points, unless you are writing an essay-type question (as explained above).

2   Leave at least a clear line between each point or paragraph.

3   Use headings whenever possible to indicate what major point or series of points you are about to make. Make it easy for the examiner to read your work and follow what you are doing.

A solid mass of material is difficult to read, provides no respite for the eye and shows a lack of discipline. Remember that you are taking a *professional* examination and there is no room for academic licence.

4   Take care with your *language*. Be objective and avoid the use of the words 'I' or 'we' at too frequent intervals. Be direct and concise, say what you mean, do not use pompous terminology and use technical words in their correct meaning.

Short sentences are far more effective and punchy than long ones. An accounting programme or evaluation of an internal control system could well start with a series of *verbs*. Good ones are: test, examine, inspect, calculate, reconcile, compare, summarise, inquire, investigate. These key words will help you to make answers to these types of questions much more direct and to the point. If you start with them you are bound to avoid falling into the trap of being long-winded, or of padding-out your answer. You only have a limited time and everything you write down must earn you marks.

5   *Think* while you are writing out your answer to make sure you are answering the question *as set*. Keep on reading the instructions and make sure you are following them. Use the question to help you to get the answer and, while this should be tackled at the planning stage, it is always possible that inspiration will strike while you are writing out your answer. In which case jot the point down on your plan, otherwise you might forget it and that can cause frustration.

What you say should be relevant but if you are in doubt about the relevance but sure about the accuracy – give it to him! You can not lose and it may be one of the key points he was looking for.

Key points

Do try to find a couple of key points to each question. These are points which you feel are vital to answer the question. You may well be right, and anyway jotting them down after you have read the question carefully can help to give your answer much needed direction.

Practice

You will need to practise the above routine. Written answers in fact need more practice than computational ones. Have a go at the question. Write out the answer as you would in the examination. Compare with the suggested answers.

Write out at the foot of your answer *what you left out* and *what you got wrong*.

Learn from the answers and from the work you do, so that when you see a similar question you will produce a better answer.

Time pressure

You will experience a lot of time pressure as you progress with written questions. Do not worry; this is a good sign.

In the examination spread your time sensibly. Start with the questions you like the look of most and if you have to go slightly over time do so. End with the question you think you cannot answer, but do give yourself time to have a reasonable go at it.

If a written question is included in a computational paper do not go over the time on it but do spend the allocated time. Examiners pay great attention to the written parts of computational papers, so do not skimp this part.

All this sounds formidable and, of course, it is. It requires skill and application and above all confidence. Practice makes perfect and once the skill is acquired then, like riding a bicycle, it will not be forgotten. Take pride in your work and be critical of your own efforts, but do not imagine your answers will have to be perfect to pass the examination. Suggested answers tend to be too long because tutors are afraid to reveal any signs of weakness or ignorance.

Go for the main points and make them well. That is the secret of success.

Appendix II
Interest tables

Table 1

Compound Sum of £1

Year	1%	2%	3%	4%	5%	6%	7%	8%	9%	10%
1	1.010	1.020	1.030	1.040	1.050	1.060	1.070	1.080	1.090	1.100
2	1.020	1.040	1.061	1.082	1.102	1.124	1.145	1.166	1.188	1.210
3	1.030	1.061	1.093	1.125	1.158	1.191	1.225	1.260	1.295	1.331
4	1.041	1.082	1.126	1.170	1.216	1.262	1.311	1.360	1.412	1.464
5	1.051	1.104	1.159	1.217	1.276	1.338	1.403	1.469	1.539	1.611
6	1.062	1.126	1.194	1.265	1.340	1.419	1.501	1.587	1.677	1.772
7	1.072	1.149	1.230	1.316	1.407	1.504	1.606	1.714	1.828	1.949
8	1.083	1.172	1.267	1.369	1.477	1.594	1.718	1.851	1.993	2.144
9	1.094	1.195	1.305	1.423	1.551	1.689	1.838	1.999	2.172	2.358
10	1.105	1.219	1.344	1.480	1.629	1.791	1.967	2.159	2.367	2.594
11	1.116	1.243	1.384	1.539	1.710	1.898	2.105	2.332	2.580	2.853
12	1.127	1.268	1.426	1.601	1.796	2.012	2.252	2.518	2.813	3.138
13	1.138	1.294	1.469	1.665	1.886	2.133	2.410	2.720	3.066	3.452
14	1.149	1.319	1.513	1.732	1.980	2.261	2.579	2.937	3.342	3.797
15	1.161	1.346	1.558	1.801	2.079	2.397	2.759	3.172	3.642	4.177

Year	12%	14%	15%	16%	18%	20%	24%	28%	32%
1	1.120	1.140	1.150	1.160	1.180	1.200	1.240	1.280	1.320
2	1.254	1.300	1.322	1.346	1.392	1.440	1.538	1.638	1.742
3	1.405	1.482	1.521	1.561	1.643	1.728	1.907	2.097	2.300
4	1.574	1.689	1.749	1.811	1.939	2.074	2.364	2.684	3.036
5	1.762	1.925	2.011	2.100	2.288	2.488	2.932	3.436	4.007
6	1.974	2.195	2.313	2.436	2.700	2.986	3.635	4.398	5.290
7	2.211	2.502	2.660	2.826	3.185	3.583	4.508	5.629	6.983
8	2.476	2.853	3.059	3.278	3.759	4.300	5.590	7.206	9.217
9	2.773	3.252	3.518	3.803	4.435	5.160	6.931	9.223	12.166
10	3.106	3.707	4.046	4.411	5.234	6.192	8.594	11.806	16.060
11	3.479	4.226	4.652	5.117	6.176	7.430	10.657	15.112	21.199
12	3.896	4.818	5.350	5.936	7.288	8.916	13.215	19.343	27.983
13	4.363	5.492	6.153	6.886	8.599	10.699	16.386	24.759	36.937
14	4.887	6.261	7.076	7.988	10.147	12.839	20.319	31.691	48.757
15	5.474	7.138	8.137	9.266	11.974	15.407	25.196	40.565	64.359

Year	36%	40%	50%	60%	70%	80%	90%
1	1.360	1.400	1.500	1.600	1.700	1.800	1.900
2	1.850	1.960	2.250	2.560	2.890	3.240	3.610
3	2.515	2.744	3.375	4.096	4.913	5.832	6.859
4	3.421	3.842	5.062	6.544	8.352	10.498	13.032
5	4.653	5.378	7.594	10.486	14.199	18.896	24.761
6	6.328	7.530	11.391	16.777	24.138	34.012	47.046
7	8.605	10.541	17.086	26.844	41.034	61.222	89.387
8	11.703	14.758	25.629	42.950	69.758	110.200	169.836
9	15.917	20.661	38.443	68.720	118.588	198.359	322.688
10	21.647	28.925	57.665	109.951	201.599	357.047	613.107
11	29.439	40.496	86.498	175.922	342.719	642.684	1164.902
12	40.037	56.694	129.746	281.475	582.622	1156.831	2213.314
13	54.451	79.372	194.619	450.360	990.457	2082.295	4205.297
14	74.053	111.120	291.929	720.576	1683.777	3748.131	7990.065
15	100.712	155.568	437.894	1152.921	2862.421	6746.636	15181.122

Table 2

Present Value of £1

Year	1%	2%	3%	4%	5%	6%	7%	8%	9%	10%	12%	14%	15%
1	0.990	0.980	0.971	0.961	0.952	0.943	0.935	0.926	0.917	0.909	0.893	0.877	0.870
2	0.980	0.961	0.943	0.925	0.907	0.890	0.873	0.857	0.842	0.826	0.797	0.769	0.756
3	0.971	0.942	0.915	0.889	0.864	0.840	0.816	0.794	0.772	0.751	0.712	0.675	0.658
4	0.961	0.924	0.889	0.855	0.823	0.792	0.763	0.735	0.708	0.683	0.636	0.592	0.572
5	0.951	0.906	0.863	0.822	0.784	0.747	0.713	0.681	0.650	0.621	0.567	0.519	0.497
6	0.942	0.888	0.838	0.790	0.746	0.705	0.666	0.630	0.596	0.564	0.507	0.456	0.432
7	0.933	0.871	0.813	0.760	0.711	0.665	0.623	0.583	0.547	0.513	0.452	0.400	0.376
8	0.923	0.853	0.789	0.731	0.677	0.627	0.582	0.540	0.502	0.467	0.404	0.351	0.327
9	0.914	0.837	0.766	0.703	0.645	0.592	0.544	0.500	0.460	0.424	0.361	0.308	0.284
10	0.905	0.820	0.744	0.676	0.614	0.558	0.508	0.463	0.422	0.386	0.322	0.270	0.247
11	0.896	0.804	0.722	0.650	0.585	0.527	0.475	0.429	0.388	0.350	0.287	0.237	0.215
12	0.887	0.788	0.701	0.625	0.557	0.497	0.444	0.397	0.356	0.319	0.257	0.208	0.187
13	0.879	0.773	0.681	0.601	0.530	0.469	0.415	0.368	0.326	0.290	0.229	0.182	0.163
14	0.870	0.758	0.661	0.577	0.505	0.442	0.388	0.340	0.299	0.263	0.205	0.160	0.141
15	0.861	0.743	0.642	0.555	0.481	0.417	0.362	0.315	0.275	0.239	0.183	0.140	0.123
16	0.853	0.728	0.623	0.534	0.458	0.394	0.339	0.292	0.252	0.218	0.163	0.123	0.107
17	0.844	0.714	0.605	0.513	0.436	0.371	0.317	0.270	0.231	0.198	0.146	0.108	0.093
18	0.836	0.700	0.587	0.494	0.416	0.350	0.296	0.250	0.212	0.180	0.130	0.095	0.081
19	0.828	0.686	0.570	0.475	0.396	0.331	0.276	0.232	0.194	0.164	0.116	0.083	0.070
20	0.820	0.673	0.554	0.456	0.377	0.319	0.258	0.215	0.178	0.149	0.104	0.073	0.061
25	0.780	0.610	0.478	0.375	0.295	0.233	0.184	0.146	0.116	0.092	0.059	0.038	0.030
30	0.742	0.552	0.412	0.308	0.231	0.174	0.131	0.099	0.075	0.057	0.033	0.020	0.015

Year	16%	18%	20%	24%	28%	32%	36%	40%	50%	60%	70%	80%	90%
1	0.862	0.847	0.833	0.806	0.781	0.758	0.735	0.714	0.667	0.625	0.588	0.556	0.526
2	0.743	0.718	0.694	0.650	0.610	0.574	0.541	0.510	0.444	0.391	0.346	0.309	0.277
3	0.641	0.609	0.579	0.524	0.477	0.435	0.398	0.364	0.296	0.244	0.204	0.171	0.146
4	0.552	0.516	0.482	0.423	0.373	0.329	0.292	0.260	0.198	0.153	0.120	0.095	0.077
5	0.476	0.437	0.402	0.341	0.291	0.250	0.215	0.186	0.132	0.095	0.070	0.053	0.040
6	0.410	0.370	0.335	0.275	0.227	0.189	0.158	0.133	0.088	0.060	0.041	0.029	0.021
7	0.354	0.314	0.279	0.222	0.178	0.143	0.116	0.095	0.059	0.037	0.024	0.016	0.011
8	0.305	0.266	0.233	0.179	0.139	0.108	0.085	0.068	0.039	0.023	0.014	0.009	0.006
9	0.263	0.226	0.194	0.144	0.108	0.082	0.063	0.048	0.026	0.015	0.008	0.005	0.003
10	0.227	0.191	0.162	0.116	0.085	0.062	0.046	0.035	0.017	0.009	0.005	0.003	0.002
11	0.195	0.162	0.135	0.094	0.066	0.047	0.034	0.025	0.012	0.006	0.003	0.002	0.001
12	0.168	0.137	0.112	0.076	0.052	0.036	0.025	0.018	0.008	0.004	0.002	0.001	0.001
13	0.145	0.116	0.093	0.061	0.040	0.027	0.018	0.013	0.005	0.002	0.001	0.001	0.000
14	0.125	0.099	0.078	0.049	0.032	0.021	0.014	0.009	0.003	0.001	0.001	0.000	0.000
15	0.108	0.084	0.065	0.040	0.025	0.016	0.010	0.006	0.002	0.001	0.000	0.000	0.000
16	0.093	0.071	0.054	0.032	0.019	0.012	0.007	0.005	0.002	0.001	0.000	0.000	
17	0.080	0.060	0.045	0.026	0.015	0.009	0.005	0.003	0.001	0.000	0.000		
18	0.069	0.051	0.038	0.021	0.012	0.007	0.004	0.002	0.001	0.000	0.000		
19	0.060	0.043	0.031	0.017	0.009	0.005	0.003	0.002	0.000	0.000			
20	0.051	0.037	0.026	0.014	0.007	0.004	0.002	0.001	0.000	0.000			
25	0.024	0.016	0.010	0.005	0.002	0.001	0.000	0.000					
30	0.012	0.007	0.004	0.002	0.001	0.000	0.000						

Table 3

Sum of an Annuity of £1 for N Years

Year	1%	2%	3%	4%	5%	6%	7%	8%
1	1.000	1.000	1.000	1.000	1.000	1.000	1.000	1.000
2	2.010	2.020	2.030	2.040	2.050	2.060	2.070	2.080
3	3.030	3.060	3.091	3.122	3.152	3.184	3.215	3.246
4	4.060	4.122	4.184	4.246	4.310	4.375	4.440	4.506
5	5.101	5.204	5.309	5.416	5.526	5.637	5.751	5.867
6	6.152	6.308	6.468	6.633	6.802	6.975	7.153	7.336
7	7.214	7.434	7.662	7.898	8.142	8.394	8.654	8.923
8	8.286	8.583	8.892	9.214	9.549	9.897	10.260	10.637
9	9.369	9.755	10.159	10.583	11.027	11.491	11.978	12.488
10	10.462	10.950	11.464	12.006	12.578	13.181	13.816	41.487
11	11.567	12.169	12.808	13.486	14.207	14.972	15.784	16.645
12	12.683	13.412	14.192	15.026	15.917	16.870	17.888	18.977
13	13.809	14.680	15.618	16.627	17.713	18.882	20.141	21.495
14	14.947	15.974	17.086	18.292	19.599	21.051	22.550	24.215
15	16.097	17.293	18.599	20.024	21.579	23.276	25.129	27.152
16	17.258	18.639	20.157	21.825	23.657	25.673	27.888	30.324
17	18.430	20.012	21.762	23.698	25.840	28.213	30.840	33.750
18	19.615	21.412	23.414	25.645	28.132	30.906	33.999	37.450
19	20.811	22.841	25.117	27.671	30.539	33.760	37.379	41.446
20	22.019	24.297	26.870	29.778	33.066	36.786	40.995	45.762
25	28.243	32.030	36.459	41.646	47.727	54.865	63.249	73.106
30	34.785	40.568	47.575	56.085	66.439	79.058	94.461	113.283

Year	9%	10%	12%	14%	16%	18%	20%	24%
1	1.000	1.000	1.000	1.000	1.000	1.000	1.000	1.000
2	2.090	2.100	2.120	2.140	2.160	2.180	2.200	2.240
3	3.278	3.310	3.374	3.440	3.506	3.572	3.640	3.778
4	4.573	4.641	4.779	4.921	5.066	5.215	5.368	5.684
5	5.985	6.105	6.353	6.610	6.877	7.154	7.442	8.048
6	7.523	7.716	8.115	8.536	8.977	9.442	9.930	10.980
7	9.200	9.487	10.089	10.730	11.414	12.142	12.916	14.615
8	11.028	11.436	12.300	13.233	14.240	15.327	16.499	19.123
9	13.021	13.579	14.776	16.085	17.518	19.086	20.799	24.712
10	15.193	15.937	17.549	19.337	21.321	23.521	25.959	31.643
11	17.560	18.531	20.655	23.044	25.738	28.755	32.150	40.238
12	20.141	21.384	24.133	27.271	30.350	34.931	39.580	50.895
13	22.953	24.523	28.029	32.089	36.766	42.219	48.497	64.110
14	26.019	27.975	32.393	37.581	43.672	50.818	59.196	80.496
15	29.361	31.722	37.280	43.842	51.659	60.965	72.035	100.815

Year	28%	32%	36%	40%	50%	60%	70%	80%
1	1.000	1.000	1.000	1.000	1.000	1.000	1.000	1.000
2	2.280	2.320	2.360	2.400	2.500	2.600	2.700	2.800
3	3.918	4.062	4.210	4.360	4.750	5.160	5.590	6.040
4	6.016	6.326	6.725	7.104	8.125	9.256	10.503	11.872
5	8.700	9.398	10.146	10.846	13.188	15.810	18.855	22.370
6	12.136	13.406	14.799	16.324	20.781	26.295	33.054	41.265
7	16.534	18.696	21.126	23.853	32.172	43.073	57.191	75.278
8	22.163	25.678	29.732	34.395	49.258	69.916	98.225	136.500
9	29.369	34.895	41.435	49.153	74.887	112.866	167.983	246.699
10	38.592	47.062	57.352	69.814	113.330	181.585	286.570	445.058
11	50.399	63.122	78.998	98.739	170.995	291.536	488.170	802.105
12	65.510	84.320	108.437	139.235	257.493	467.458	830.888	1444.788
13	84.853	112.303	148.475	195.929	387.239	748.933	1413.510	2601.619
14	109.612	149.240	202.926	275.300	581.859	1199.293	2403.968	4683.914
15	141.303	197.997	276.979	386.420	873.788	1919.869	4087.745	8432.045

Table 4

Present Value of Annuity of £1 per period

Year	1%	2%	3%	4%	5%	6%	7%	8%	9%	10%
1	0.990	0.980	0.971	0.962	0.952	0.943	0.935	0.926	0.917	0.909
2	1.970	1.942	1.913	1.886	1.859	1.833	1.808	1.783	1.759	1.736
3	2.941	2.884	2.829	2.775	2.723	2.673	2.624	2.577	2.531	2.487
4	3.902	3.808	3.717	3.630	3.546	3.465	3.387	3.312	3.240	3.170
5	4.853	4.713	4.580	4.452	4.329	4.212	4.100	3.993	3.890	3.791
6	5.795	5.601	5.417	5.424	5.076	4.917	4.766	4.623	4.486	4.355
7	6.728	6.472	6.230	6.002	5.786	5.582	5.389	5.206	5.033	4.868
8	7.652	7.325	7.020	6.733	6.463	6.210	6.971	5.747	5.535	5.335
9	8.566	8.162	7.786	7.435	7.108	6.802	6.515	6.247	5.985	5.759
10	9.471	8.983	8.530	8.111	7.722	7.360	7.024	6.710	6.418	6.145
11	10.368	9.787	9.253	8.760	8.306	7.887	7.499	7.139	6.805	6.495
12	11.255	10.575	9.954	9.385	8.863	8.384	7.943	7.536	7.161	6.814
13	12.134	11.348	10.635	9.986	9.394	8.853	8.358	7.904	7.487	7.103
14	13.004	12.106	11.296	10.563	8.899	9.295	8.745	8.244	7.786	7.367
15	13.865	12.849	11.938	11.118	10.380	9.712	9.108	8.559	8.060	7.606
16	14.718	13.578	12.561	11.652	10.838	10.106	9.447	8.851	8.312	7.824
17	15.562	14.292	13.166	12.166	11.274	10.477	9.763	9.122	8.544	8.022
18	16.398	14.992	13.754	12.659	11.690	10.828	10.059	9.372	8.756	8.201
19	17.226	15.678	14.324	13.134	12.085	11.158	10.336	9.604	8.950	8.365
20	18.046	16.351	14.877	13.590	12.462	11.470	10.594	9.818	9.128	8.514
25	22.023	19.523	17.413	15.622	14.094	12.783	11.654	10.675	9.823	9.077
30	25.808	22.397	19.600	17.292	15.373	13.765	12.409	11.258	10.274	9.427

Year	12%	14%	16%	18%	20%	24%	28%	32%	36%
1	0.893	0.877	0.862	0.847	0.833	0.806	0.781	0.758	0.735
2	1.690	1.647	1.605	1.566	1.528	1.457	1.392	1.332	1.276
3	2.402	2.322	2.246	2.174	2.106	1.981	1.868	1.766	1.674
4	3.037	2.914	2.798	2.690	2.589	2.404	2.241	2.096	1.966
5	3.605	3.433	3.274	3.127	2.991	2.745	2.532	2.345	2.181
6	4.111	3.889	3.685	3.498	3.326	3.020	2.759	2.534	2.339
7	4.564	4.288	4.089	3.812	3.605	3.242	2.937	2.678	2.455
8	4.968	4.639	4.344	4.078	3.837	3.421	3.076	2.786	2.540
9	5.328	4.946	4.607	4.303	4.031	3.566	3.184	2.868	2.603
10	5.650	5.216	4.833	4.494	4.193	3.682	3.269	2.930	2.650
11	5.988	5.453	5.029	4.656	4.327	3.776	3.335	2.978	2.683
12	6.194	5.660	5.197	4.793	4.439	3.851	3.387	3.013	2.708
13	6.424	5.842	5.342	4.910	4.533	3.912	3.427	3.040	2.727
14	6.628	6.002	5.468	5.008	4.611	3.962	3.459	3.061	2.740
15	6.811	6.142	5.575	5.092	4.675	4.001	3.483	3.076	2.750
16	6.974	6.265	5.669	5.162	4.730	4.033	3.503	3.088	2.758
17	7.120	5.373	5.749	4.222	4.775	4.059	3.518	3.097	2.763
18	7.250	6.467	5.818	5.273	4.812	4.080	3.529	3.104	2.767
19	7.366	6.550	5.877	5.316	4.844	4.097	3.539	3.109	2.770
20	7.469	6.623	5.929	5.353	4.870	4.110	3.546	3.113	2.772
25	7.843	6.873	6.907	5.467	4.948	4.147	3.564	3.122	2.776
30	8.055	7.003	6.177	5.517	4.979	4.160	3.569	3.124	2.778

Appendix III
Answers to review questions

1.1 (a) Gudgeon's books (years omitted)

R Johnson Ltd

Jul 1 Sales	2,460	Jul 1 Bills Receivable	2,460

B Scarlet & Co Ltd

Jul 1 Sales	1,500	Jul 1 Bills Receivable	1,500
Sep 4 Bills Receivable (dishonour)	1,500		
" 4 Bank: Noting charge	6		

Bills Receivable

Jul 1 R Johnson Ltd	2,460	Jul 4 Bank	2,460
" 1 B Scarlet & Co Ltd	1,500	" 4 Bank	1,500

Bank

Jul 4 Bills Receivable	2,460	Jul 4 Discounting Charges	80
" 4 Bills Receivable	1,500	" 4 Discounting Charges	65
		Sep 4 B Scarlet (discounted bill)	1,500
		" 4 Noting charge (Scarlet)	6

Discounting Charges

Jul 4 Bank	80
" 4 "	65

Bills Payable

Sep 1 N Gudgeon (discounted bill)	1,500	Jul 1 N Gudgeon	1,500

(b) Scarlet's books

N Gudgeon

Jul 1 Bills Payable	2,460	Jul 1 Purchases	2,460

Bills Payable

Sep 1 Bank	2,460	Jul 1 N Gudgeon	2,460

Bank

		Sep 1 Bills Payable	2,460

Johnson's books

N Gudgeon

Jul 1 Bills Payable	1,500	Jul 1 Purchases	1,500

Bills Payable

Sep 1 Bank	1,500	Jul 1 N Gudgeon	1,500
" 4 Noting Charge	6		

Noting Charges

Sep 4 N Gudgeon	6

1.3 Sales Ledger Control (years omitted)

Aug 1 Balances b/d	12,370	Aug 1 Balances b/d	105
" 31 Sales	16,904	" 31 Returns In	407
" 31 Bills Receivable Dishonoured	177	" 31 Bank	15,970
" 31 Balances c/d	88	" 31 Bills Receivable	1,230
		" 31 Cash	306
		" 31 Bad Debts	129
		" 31 Discounts Allowed	604
		" Balances c/d*	10,788
	29,539		29,539

*difference

1.4

(a) Noone: Accounts

		Dr	Cr
Jan 1 Purchases	Iddon	420	
	Iddon		420
	Bills Payable	420	
Feb 29 Goods Destroyed	Cost of Goods Sold	3,600	
Apl 1 Insurance Company	Goods Destroyed	3,000	
Apl 4 Bills Payable	Iddon	420	
Apl 4 Iddon	Interest Charges	10	
	Bills Payable		430
Apl 9 Bank	Insurance Co.	3,000	
May 7 Bills Payable	Bank	430	

(b) Iddon: Accounts

		Dr	Cr
Jan 1 Noone	Sales	420	
Jan 1 Bills Receivable	Noone	420	
Jan 1 Bank	Discounting Charges	412	
	Bills Receivable	8	
	Bills Receivable		420
Apl 4 Noone	Bank	420	
Apl 4 Bills Receivable	Noone	430	
	Interest Receivable	420	
May 7 Bank	Bills Receivable		430

2.1 Ollier's Books (dates ignored)

Joint Venture with Avon

Cars	900	Sales	1,600
Repairs & Respraying	60		
Profit on Venture	237		
Balance c/d	403		
	1,600		1,600
Cash to Avon	403	Balance b/d	403

Avon's Books

Joint Venture with Ollier

Garage Rental	20	Balance c/d	403
Advertising	10		
Licence and Insurance	36		
Car	100		
Profit on Venture	237		
	403		403
Balance b/d	403	Cash from Ollier	403

Memorandum Joint Venture Account

Cars	1,000	Sales	1,600
Repairs & Respraying	60		
Garage Rental	20		
Advertising	10		
Licence and Insurance	36		
Profit on Venture			
Ollier ½	237		
Avon ½	237	474	
	1,600		1,600

2.2

Plant's Books

Joint Venture with Hoe and Reap

Rent	156	Balance c/d	620
Labour: Planting	105		
Labour: Fertilising	36		
Sundries	10		
Labour	18		
Fertiliser	29		
Share of Profit	266		
	620		620
Balance c/d	620	Cash from Reap	620

Hoe's Books

Joint Venture with Plant and Reap

Seeds	48	Balance c/d	179
Motor Expenses	17		
Share of Profit	114		
	179		179
Balance b/d	179	Cash from Reap	179

Reap's Books

Joint Venture with Plant and Hoe

Lifting	73	Sales	987
Sale Expenses	39		
Share of Profit	76		
Balances c/d	799		
	987		987
Cash to Plant	620	Balance b/d	799
Cash to Hoe	179		
	799		799

Plant, Hoe and Reap, Memorandum Joint Venture Account

Rent	156	Sales	987
Labour: Planting	105		
Labour: Fertilising	36		
Sundry Expenses	18		
Lifting	73		
Fertiliser	29		
Motor Expenses	17		
Seeds	48		
Sale Expenses	39		
Sundries	10		
Profit shared: Plant	266		
Hoe	114		
Reap	76	456	
	987		987

3.1

Consignment to MB

	£		£
Goods	3,000	Sales	3,500
Carriage	147	Stock c/d 20/120 × 3,666	611
Insurance	93		
Freight	240		
Port charges	186		
	3,666		
Commission	175		
Profit	270		
	4,111		4,111

MB

	£		£
Freight	240	Sales	3,500
Port Charges	186		
Commission	175		
Bank	2,899		
	3,500		3,500

3.2

Account Sales for Hughes of London From Galvez of Madrid

	£	£
Bicycle Sales 250 × £20 =		5,000
50 × £18 =		900
		5,900
less: Port & Duty Charges	720	
Storage & Carriage	410	
Commission 6% of £5,900	354	
		1,484
		4,416

Consignment Inwards

	£		£
Port and Duty Charges	720	Sales 250 × £20	5,000
Storage & Carriage Charges	410	50 × £18	900
Commission	354		
Cash	4,416		
	5,900		5,900

4.1

Realisation

	£		£
Buildings	2,700	Cash: Debtors	800
Tools & Fixtures	400	Buildings	850
Debtors	950	Tools etc.	2,800
Cash: Expenses	200	Discounts	100
Loss on Realisation:			
Moore	150		
Stephens	150		
	4,550		4,550

Capital Accounts

	Moore	Stephens		Moore	Stephens
Loss on Realisation	150	150	Balance b/fwd	2,000	1,500
Cash	1,850	1,350			
	2,000	1,500		2,000	1,500

Cash

	£		£
Balance b/fwd	1,800	Expenses Realisation	100
Debtors	2,700	Creditors	2,550
Buildings	400	Capitals: Moore	1,850
Tools	950	Stephens	1,350
	5,850		5,850

4.2

(a) Realisation

	£		£	£
Fixed Assets	14,000	Bank: Fixed Assets		8,000
Stock	5,000	X: Fixed Assets		7,000
Debtors	21,000	Bank: Stock		4,000
Bank: Dissolution Costs	800	Bank: Debtors		3,000
		Discounts on Creditors		500
		Loss: X ³⁄₆	9,150	
		Y ²⁄₆	6,100	
		Z ¹⁄₆	3,050	18,300
	40,800			40,800

(b) Capitals

	X	Y	Z		X	Y	Z
Fixed Assets taken over	7,000			Balances b/f	4,000	4,000	2,000
Loss Shared	9,150	6,100	3,050	Deficiency Shared X			525
Deficiency	525	525		Y			525
Bank to settle				Bank to settle	12,675	2,625	
	16,675	6,625	3,050		16,675	6,625	3,050

Bank (as proof only)

	£		£
Realisation: Fixed Assets	8,000	Balance b/f	13,000
Stock	4,000	Creditors	16,500
Debtors	3,000	Realisation: Costs	800
Capital X	12,675		
Y	2,625		
	30,300		30,300

553

4.5 (a) (i)

Amis, Lodge & Pym

Trading and Profit & Loss Account for the year ended 31 March 19-8

Sales			404,500
less Cost of Goods Sold:			
Opening Stock		30,000	
Add Purchases		225,000	
Add Carriage Inwards		4,000	
		259,000	
less Closing Stock		35,000	224,000
Gross Profit			180,500
add Bank Interest		750	
Discounts Received		4,530	5,280
			185,780
less Office Expenses (30,400 + 405)		30,805	
Rent, Rates, Light & Heat (8,800 – 1,500)		7,300	
Carriage Outwards		12,000	
Discounts Allowed		10,000	
Provision for bad debts		295	
Depreciation: Motor		15,000	
Plant		20,000	95,400
Net Profit			90,380
add Interest on Current Accounts & Drawings:			
Amis		1,000	
Lodge		900	
Pym		720	2,620
			93,000
less Salary – Pym		13,000	
Interest on Capitals: Amis	8,000		
Lodge	1,500		
Pym	500	10,000	23,000
			70,000
Balance on Profit shared:			
Amis 50%		35,000	
Lodge 30%		21,000	
Pym 20%		14,000	70,000

(a) (ii)

Current Accounts

	Amis	Lodge	Pym		Amis	Lodge	Pym
Balances b/f	1,000	500		Salary			13,000
Drawings	25,000	22,000	15,000	Interest on Capital	8,000	1,500	500
Interest on Drawings	1,000	900	720	Balance on Profits	35,000	21,000	14,000
Transfer to Capital	16,000	–	11,380	Transfer to Capital			900
	43,000	23,400	27,500		43,000	23,400	27,500

(b) (i)

Realisation

Motors (80,000 – 35,000)			45,000
Plant (100,000 – 56,600)			43,400
Debtors (14,300 – 715)			13,585
Stock			35,000
Profit on realisation			
Amis 50%		10,000	
Lodge 30%		6,000	
Pym 20%		4,000	20,000
			156,985

Discount on Creditors		500
Amis: Motor		5,000
Bank: debtors		12,985
Fowles Ltd (75,000 + 63,500)		138,500
		156,985

(ii)

Bank

Balance b/f			4,900
Realisation: Debtors			12,985
Rent Rebate			1,500
Fowles Ltd			63,500
Capitals: Lodge			4,900
Pym			4,620
			92,405

Office Expenses		405
Creditors		16,000
Capital: Amis		76,000
		92,405

(iii)

Capitals

	Amis	Lodge	Pym		Amis	Lodge	Pym
Current A/c		900		Balances b/f	80,000	15,000	5,000
Fowles Ltd Shares	25,000	25,000	25,000	Current A/c	16,000		11,380
Realisation: Motor	5,000			Profit on Real.	10,000	6,000	4,000
Bank	76,000			Bank		4,900	4,620
	106,000	25,900	25,000		106,000	25,900	25,000

4.7

(a)

Lock, Stock and Barrel
Profit & Loss Account for the six months ended 1 February 19-7

Sales of completed Houses		280,000
less Costs of completing houses		
Houses in course of construction at start	115,000	
Materials used	35,750	
Land used (75,000 × ⅓)	25,000	
Wages & Subcontractors	78,000	253,750
Gross Profit		26,250
less Administration Salaries	17,250	
General Expenses	12,500	
Depreciation: Freehold land	300	
Plant & Equipment (6/12 × 10%)	7,500	
Vehicles (25% × 6/12)	4,500	42,050
Net Loss		15,800

Shared:		
Lock	40%	6,320
Stock	30%	4,740
Barrel	30%	4,740
		15,800

Capitals

	Lock	Stock	Barrel		Lock	Stock	Barrel
Drawings	6,000	5,000	4,000	Balances b/f	52,000	26,000	4,000
Loss Shared	6,320	4,740	4,740	Balance c/d			4,740
Balances c/d	39,680	16,260					
	52,000	26,000	8,740		52,000	26,000	8,740

Lock, Stock and Barrel
Balance Sheet as at 1 February 19-7

	Cost	Depreciation	
Fixed Tangible Assets			
Freehold Land & Buildings	20,000	3,300	16,700
Plant & Equipment	150,000	89,500	60,500
Motor Vehicles	36,000	27,500	8,500
	206,000	120,300	85,700
Current Assets			
Stock of Land for Building		50,000	
Stocks of Materials		7,500	
Debtors for completed houses		35,000	
		92,500	
less Current Liabilities			
Trade Creditors	52,250		
Bank Overdraft	75,250	127,500	
Working Capital			(35,000)
Net Assets			50,700

Financed by:		
Capitals:	Lock	39,680
	Stock	16,260
	Barrel	(5,240)
		50,700

(b)

Amounts distributable to partners
On 28 February there was only (6,200 + 7,000 + 72,500 − 75,250) 10,450 there was nowhere near enough to pay off the creditors, and so payment to partners could not be made.
On 30 April we treat it as though no more cash will be received.

First Distribution

	Lock	Stock	Barrel
Capital Balances before Dissolution	39,680	16,260	(5,240)
Loss if no further assets realised (85,700 + 92,500 − 6,000 − 6,200 − 7,000 − 72,500 − 35,000 − 50,000) = 1,500			
Loss shared in profit/Loss ratios	(600)	(450)	(450)
Cars taken over	(2,000)	(2,000)	(2,000)
	37,080	13,810	(7,690)
Barrel's deficience shared profit/loss ratio	4,394	3,296	7,690
Paid to Partners	32,686	10,514	–

Second and Final Distribution

	Lock	Stock	Barrel
Capital balances before dissolution	39,680	16,260	(5,240)
Profit finally ascertained 100,000 − 1,500 = 98,500			
Shared	39,400	29,550	29,550
	79,080	45,810	24,310
less Distribution & Cars	34,686	12,514	2,000
Final Distribution (100,000)	44,394	33,296	22,310

(c) (dates omitted)

Realisation

Assets at balance sheet values		
Fixed Assets	85,700	
Current Assets	92,500	
Profit on Realisation		
Lock 40%	39,400	
Stock 30%	29,550	
Barrel 30%	29,550	98,500
		276,700

Partners: Vehicles taken over	6,000
Bank: Stocks	7,000
Vehicles	6,200
Land	72,500
Debtors	35,000
Plant	50,000
Land	100,000
	276,700

Capitals

	Lock	Stock	Barrel
Balance b/f			
Cars	2,000		
Bank 1st	32,686	10,514	22,310
Bank: final	44,394	33,296	
	79,080	45,810	29,550

Balances	Barrel	Lock	Stock	Barrel
b/f	5,240	39,680	16,260	
Profit	2,000			
shared	22,310	39,400	29,550	29,550
	29,550	79,080	45,810	29,550

5.1

Branch Stock (dates omitted)

	Memo				Memo	
Balance b/f	4,400	3,300	Branch Debtors		21,000	21,000
Goods from Head Office	24,800	18,600	Cash Sales		2,400	2,400
Gross Profit		5,850	Returns to H.O.		1,000	750
			Goods Stolen		600	450
			Profit & Loss:			
			Normal Wastage		100	75
			Profit & Loss:			
			Excess Wastage		152	114
			Balance c/f		3,948	2,961
	29,200	27,750			29,200	27,750

Branch Debtors

Balances b/fwd	3,946	Bad Debts		148
Branch Stock: Sales	21,000	Discounts Allowed		428
		Bank		22,400
		Balance c/fwd		1,970
	24,946			24,946

5.2 **(a)**

Branch Stock (Selling Prices)

Goods from Head Office		Cash Sales	89,940
(82,400 + 10% 8,240 =		Sales: Branch Debtors	1,870
90,640 + 25%)	113,300	Goods to other branches	3,300
		Branch Stock Adjustment:	
		Reductions	2,250
		Balance c/d	15,940
	113,300		113,300

Branch Stock Adjustment *(Profit Margin)*

Goods to other branches	660	Branch Stock	22,660
Branch Stock: Reductions	2,250	(113,300 − 90,640)	
Profit and Loss	16,562		
Balance c/d	3,188		
	22,660		22,660

*As cost to branch (Original cost + 10%) is subject to further mark-up of 25%, therefore margin is 20%, and this is profit margin used in this account.

(b)

Book stock per branch stock account	15,940
Physical Stock	14,850
	1,090

Four possible reasons for deficiency:
(i) Thefts by customers
(ii) Thefts by staff
(iii) Wastages due to breakages, mis-counting etc.
(iv) Cash misappropriated

(c) Figure to be taken for RST balance sheet:

Actual stock at selling price	14,850
less 20% Margin	2,970
	11,880
Cost to Branch	
less Head Office Loading	1,080
(+ 10% = 1/11th of adjusted figure) 1/11th	
Actual cost to company	10,800

Therefore (iii) 10,800 is correct answer.

5.4

Stone & Millington

Trading & Profit & Loss Account for the year ended 31 December 19-1

	Head Office		Branch		Combined	
Sales		60,000		40,000		100,000
less Cost of Goods Sold						
Opening Stock	4,000		4,800		8,800	
Add Purchases	50,000				50,000	
	54,000					
Goods sent to branch	14,400		14,400			
	39,600		19,200		58,800	
less Closing Stock	6,600	33,000	5,600	13,600	12,200	46,600
Gross Profit		27,000		26,400		53,400
less Expenses:						
Salaries	3,500		2,500		6,000	
Rent	7,500		4,500		12,000	
Administration	6,000				6,000	
Depreciation: Fixtures	2,000	19,000	2,400	9,400	4,400	28,400
Net Profit		8,000		17,000		25,000
less Partners' Commission: Stone			1,200			
Millington			2,550	3,750		
Interest on Capitals: Stone			1,100			
Millington			1,100	2,200		
				5,950		
Balance of Profits Stone ½			9,525			
Millington ½			9,525	19,050		25,000

Balance Sheet as at 31 December 19-1

Fixed Assets	22,000	
less Depreciation	4,400	17,600
Current Assets		
Stock	12,200	
Bank	3,000	
	15,200	
less Current Liabilities		
Creditors	1,800	
Working Capital		13,400
		31,000

	Stone	Millington
Capitals		
Balances 1.1.19-1	11,000	11,000
add Partners Commission	1,200	2,550
,, Interest on Capitals	1,100	1,100
,, Balance of Profits	9,525	9,525
	22,825	24,175
less Drawings	8,000	8,000
	14,825	16,175
		31,000
		31,000

Packer & Stringer

Trading & Profit & Loss Account for the year ended 31 December 19-4

	HO		Branch	
Sales		39,000		26,000
less: Cost of Goods Sold				
Opening Stock	13,000		4,400	
add Purchases	37,000			
	50,000			
Goods to Branch	17,200		17,200	
	32,800		21,600	
less Closing Stock	15,240	17,560	6,570	15,030
		21,440		10,970
Bad Debt provision not required				20
				10,990
Salaries	4,500		3,200	
Administrative Expenses	1,440		960	
Carriage	2,200		960	
General Expenses	3,200		1,800	
Provision for Bad Debts	50		110	
Depreciation	150		360	
Manager's Commission		11,540		7,390
Net Profit		9,900		3,600
				13,500
Packer: Commission		900		
Interest on Capital: Packer	840			
Stringer	240	1,080		
		1,980		
Balance of Profits: Packer ¾	8,640			
Stringer ¼	2,880	11,520		
		13,500		

Balance Sheet as at 31 December 19-4

			£
Fixed Assets			
Furniture		2,600	
less Depreciation		1,110	1,490
Current Assets			
Stock		10,000	21,810
Debtors		10,000	
less Provision for Bad Debts		830	9,170
Cash & Bank			3,000
			33,980
less Current Liabilities			
Creditors		6,200	
Bank Overdraft		1,350	
Manager's Commission		120	7,670
Working Capital			26,310
			27,800

5.7 *Conversion of Branch Trial Balance to Pounds Sterling*

	Fl	Fl	Rate	£	£
Freehold Buildings	63,000		7	9,000	
Debtors and Creditors	36,000	1,560	8 9	4,460	195
Sales		432,000	9		48,000
Head Office		504,260	Actual		60,100
Branch cost of sales	360,000		*below	40,400	
Depreciation: Machinery		56,700	below	8,100	
Administration costs	18,000		9	2,000	
Stock 30.6.19-8	11,520		8	1,440	
Machinery at cost	126,000		7	18,000	
Remittances	272,000		Actual	29,990	
Balances at bank	79,200		8	9,900	
Selling & Distribution	28,800		9	3,200	
Profit on Exchange			–		1,995
	994,520	994,520		118,390	118,390

*Cost of Sales: Branch   Fl 360,000

Less Depreciation   Fl 12,600 ÷ 7 = £1,800

Fl 347,400 ÷ 9 = £38,600

£40,400

E G Company Ltd

Trading & Profit & Loss Accounts for the year ended 30 June 19-8

	Head Office		Branch	
Sales		104,000		48,000
less Cost of Sales	58,400		38,600	
Depreciation	600		1,800	
		59,000		40,400
Gross Profit		45,000		7,600
Goods to Branch		35,000		
		80,000		
Administration Costs	15,200		2,000	
Selling & Distribution	23,300		3,200	
Provision for unrealised profit on branch stock	300			
Manager's Commission			114	
		38,800		5,314
Net Profit		41,200		2,286

		43,486
add Balance from last year		2,000
Balance carried forward to next year		45,486

Balance Sheet as at 30 June 19-8

Fixed Assets			
Freehold Buildings at cost			23,000
Machinery at cost		24,000	
less Depreciation		9,600	14,400
			37,400
Current Assets			
Stock		30,040	
Debtors		13,360	
Bank		14,500	
Cash in Transit		1,990	
		59,890	
less Current Liabilities			
Creditors*		9,809	
Working Capital			50,081
			87,481
Financed by:			
Share Capital: Authorised and Issued			40,000
Reserves			
Difference on Exchange		1,995	
Profit & Loss		45,486	47,481
			87,481

*Creditors HO 9,500 + Branch 195 + Manager 114 = 9,809.

(HO Books) Branch Account

	£	Fl		£	Fl
Balance b/d	25,136	189,260	Cash from debtors	36	320
Components	35,000	315,000	Remittances	28,000	256,000
Net Profit	2,286	*24,000	Cash in transit	1,990	16,000
Difference on Exchange	1,995	–	Balance c/d	34,391	255,940
	64,417	528,260		64,417	528,260

*This represents the profit per branch profit and loss account if it had been drawn up using florins.

5.8

(a)

Trial Balance as at 31 December 19-9

	Crowns	Crowns	Rate	£	£
Bank	66,000		4	16,500	
Creditors		92,400	4		23,100
Debtors	158,400		4	39,600	
Fixed Assets	145,200		5	29,040	
Head Office		316,800	Actual		65,280
Profit & Loss		79,200	4.4		18,000
Stocks	118,800		4.4	29,700	
Difference on Exchange			4		8,460
	488,400	488,400		114,840	114,840

(b) (Books of Head Office) Highland Branch

	£			£
Balance b/d	65,280		Balance c/d	91,740
Difference on Exchange	8,460			
Net Profit	18,000			
	91,740			91,740

(c)

Balance Sheet as at 31 December 19-0

	£	£
Fixed Assets		68,640
Current Assets		
Stocks	56,100	
Debtors	58,080	
Bank	27,060	
	141,240	
less Current Liabilities		
Creditors	44,220	
Working Capital		97,020
		165,660
Financed by:		
Issued Share Capital		86,400
Reserves	70,800	
Profit & Loss	8,460	
Difference on Exchange		79,260
		165,660

6.1 (a) (dates omitted)

Containers Stock

	Rate	Qty	£		Rate	Qty	£
Stocks b/d:				Scrapped	–	120	–
Warehouse	10	2,000	20,000	Container Suspense:			
At Customers	10	5,500	55,000	Kept by Customers (W1)	20	250	5,000
Bank: purchases	10	1,250	12,500	Containers Missing (W2)	–	40	–
Profit and Loss				Stocks c/d			
Profit on Containers			900	Warehouse	10	3,390	33,900
				At Customers	10	4,950	49,500
		8,750	88,400			8,750	88,400

Containers Suspense

	Rate	Qty	£		Rate	Qty	£
Debtors	20	9,050	181,000	Deposits on Crates returnable b/d	20	5,500	110,000
Container Stock				Debtors: charged out	20	8,750	175,000
Kept by Customers (W1)	20	250	5,000				
Deposits on crate returnable c/d	20	4,950	99,000				
		14,250	285,000			14,250	285,000

Workings: (W1) Balancing item needed for container suspense, caused by customers keeping containers beyond the permitted time limit.

(W2) Balancing item – quantities only. 40 containers are missing. An investigation should be made into how this could have happened.

6.2 (balances not carried down)

Note: It would have been possible to have these records kept in only two accounts, a Containers Suspense Account and a Containers Stock Account. However the examiner has asked for another method, using four accounts, now illustrated. The same eventual answer is the same as per the shorter textbook method.

(a) Cases Stock (at valuation £5 per case)

	No	£		No	£
Balances b/fwd:			Cases Profit & Loss	–	2,000
In warehouse	1,000	5,000	(Purchases written down to £5 each)		
At customers	3,000	15,000	Retained by Customers	1,500	7,500
Purchases	2,000	12,000	Cases damaged to p/l	100	500
			Cases sold	50	250
			Balances c/d		
			In Warehouse	850	4,250
			At Customers	3,500	17,500
	6,000	32,000		6,000	32,000

(b)

Cases Suspense (at £8 returnable price each)

	No	£		No	£
Returned by Customers	23,000	184,000	Balances b/f with Customers	3,000	24,000
Cases Stock (Purchases)	1,500	12,000	Charged to Customers	25,000	200,000
Balances c/d	3,500	28,000			
	28,000	224,000		28,000	224,000

(c)

Cases sent to Customers (at chargeable price £10)

	No	£		No	£
Balances b/d	3,000	30,000	Cases returned	23,000	184,000
Cases charged out	25,000	200,000	Bank: cases kept	1,500	15,000
Cases Profit & Loss		50,000	Bank: Cash from		
			Customers (23,000 × £2)		46,000
			Balances c/d	3,500	35,000
	28,000	280,000		28,000	280,000

(d)

Cases Profit & Loss Account

Cases Stock: Purchases		Cases to customers		
written down	2,000	(25,000 × £2)		50,000
Cases sold	250	Profit on cases retained		4,500
Cases damaged	500	Cash Sales		100
Cash: repairs	1,400			
Profit to main profit & loss	50,450			
	54,600			54,600

7.1

Royalties

19-1 Dec 31	Smoker	600	19-1 Dec 31	Manufacturing	600	
19-2 Dec 31	Smoker	800	19-2 Dec 31	Manufacturing	800	
19-3 Dec 31	Smoker	1,200	19-3 Dec 31	Manufacturing	1,200	
19-4 Dec 31	Smoker	1,400	19-4 Dec 31	Manufacturing	1,400	

Smoker

19-1 Dec 31	Balance c/d	1,000	19-1 Dec 31	Royalties	600	
			" 31	Short Workings	400	
		1,000			1,000	
19-2 Jan 31	Bank	1,000	19-2 Jan 1	Balance b/d	1,000	
Dec 31	Balance c/d	1,000	Dec 31	Royalties	800	
			" 31	Short Workings	200	
		2,000			2,000	
19-3 Jan 31	Bank	1,000	19-3 Jan 1	Balance b/d	1,000	
Dec 31	Short workings	200	Dec 31	Royalties	1,200	
" 31	Balance c/d	1,000				
		2,200			2,200	
19-4 Jan 31	Bank	1,000	19-4 Jan 1	Balance b/d	1,000	
Dec 31	Short Workings	200	Dec 31	Royalties	1,400	
" 31	Balance c/d	1,200				
		2,400			2,400	
19-5 Jan 31	Bank	1,200	19-5 Jan 1	Balance b/d	1,200	

Short Workings

19-1 Dec 31	Smoker	400	19-3 Dec 31	Smoker	200	
19-2 Dec 31	Smoker	200	" 31	Written off to Profit & Loss	200	
			" 31	Balance c/d	200	
		600			600	
19-4 Jan 1	Balance b/d	200	19-4 Dec 31	Smoker	200	

7.3

(a) Royalties

19-6 Dec 31	Landlord	200	19-6 Dec 31	Trading	200	
19-7 Dec 31	Landlord	400	19-7 Dec 31	Trading	400	
19-8 Dec 31	Landlord	600	19-8 Dec 31	Trading	600	
19-9 Dec 31	Landlord	500	19-9 Dec 31	Trading	500	

(b)

Shortworkings

19-6	Dec 31	Landlord	c/d	300	19-6 Dec 31 Balance	300
19-7	Jan 1	Balance	b/d	400	19-7 Dec 31 Landlord	400
	Dec 31	Landlord	c/d	400		100
				__400__		__400__
19-8	Jan 1	Balance	b/d	400	19-8 Dec 31 Landlord: Recouped	200
					Profit & Loss: Irrecoupable	100
					Balance c/d	100
				__400__		__400__
19-9	Jan 1	Balance	b/d	100	19-9 Dec 31 Landlord: Recouped	100

(c)

Landlord

19-6	Dec 31	Balance	c/d	500	19-6 Dec 31 Royalties	200
					Shortworkings	300
				__500__		__500__
19-7	Jan 31	Cash		500	19-7 Jan 1 Balance b/d	500
	Dec 31	Balance	c/d	500	Dec 31 Royalties	400
					Shortworkings	100
				__1,000__		__1,000__
19-8	Jan 31	Cash		500	19-8 Jan 1 Balance b/d	500
	Dec 31	Shortworkings Recouped		200	Dec 31 Royalties	600
		Balance	c/d	400		
				__1,100__		__1,100__
19-9	Jan 31	Cash		400	19-9 Jan 1 Balance b/d	400
	Dec 31	Shortworkings Recouped		100	Dec 31 Royalties	500
		Balance	c/d	400		
				__900__		__900__

8.1

Machinery

19-3	Jan 1	Vendor	6,000		6,000

Vendor's Account

19-3	Jan 1	Bank	846	19-3 Jan 1 Machinery		6,000
	Dec 31	Bank	2,000	Dec 31 HP Interest		412
	" 31	Balance	c/d 3,566			
			__6,412__			__6,412__
19-4	Dec 31	Bank	2,000	19-4 Jan 1 Balance		3,566
	" 31	Balance	c/d 1,851	Dec 31 HP Interest		285
			__3,851__			__3,851__
19-5	Dec 31	Bank	2,000	19-5 Jan 1 Balance	b/d	1,851
				Dec 31 HP Interest		149
			__2,000__			__2,000__

Provision for Depreciation: Machinery

				19-3 Dec 31 Profit & Loss		600
				19-4 Dec 31 Profit & Loss		540
19-4	Dec 31	Balance	c/d 1,140			1,140
			1,140			
				19-5 Jan 1 Balance	b/d	1,140
				Dec 31 Profit & Loss		486
19-5	Dec 31	Balance	c/d 1,626			1,626
			1,626			

Balance Sheet as at 31 December 19-5

Machinery at cost	6,000
less Depreciation	600
	5,400
(Included in Liabilities) Owing on HP	3,566

562

8.3

Bulwell's books

Motor Lorries

19-1	Granby Garages	54,000				

Hire Purchase Interest

19-1	Granby	11,250	19-1	Profit & Loss	11,250
19-2	Granby	8,063	19-2	Profit & Loss	8,063
19-3	Granby	4,078	19-3	Profit & Loss	4,078

Bank

19-1	Granby (Jan 1)	9,000
19-1	Granby (Dec 31)	24,000
19-2	Granby	24,000
19-3	Granby	20,391

Granby Garages

19-1	Bank	9,000	19-1	Motor Lorries	54,000
19-1	Bank	24,000		HP Interest	11,250
	Balance c/d	32,250			
		65,250			65,250
19-2	Bank	24,000	19-2	Balance b/d	32,250
	Balance c/d	16,313		HP Interest	8,063
		40,313			40,313
19-3	Bank	20,391	19-3	Balance b/d	16,313
				Interest	4,078
		20,391			20,391

Depreciation

19-1	Balance c/d	12,500	19-1	Profit & Loss	12,500
19-2	Balance c/d	25,000	19-2	Balance b/d	12,500
				Profit & Loss	12,500
		25,000			25,000
19-3	Balance c/d	37,500	19-3	Balance b/d	25,000
				Profit & Loss	12,500
		37,500			37,500
19-4	Balance c/d	50,000	19-4	Balance b/d	37,500
				Profit & Loss	12,500
		50,000			50,000

Balance Sheet as at 31 December

	19-1		19-2		19-3		19-4	
Motor Lorries cost	54,000	12,500	54,000	25,000	54,000	37,500	54,000	50,000
less Depreciation to date		41,500		29,000		16,500		4,000
Liabilities:								
HP Debt outstanding		32,250		16,313				–
Charge against profit:								
HP Interest	11,250	11,250	8,063	8,063	4,078			
Depreciation	12,500	12,500	12,500	12,500	12,500	12,500	12,500	12,500

NB Calculation of Interest

19-1 25% × £45,000 = £11,250
19-2 25% × £32,250 = £ 8,063
19-3 25% × £16,313 = £ 4,078

(b) Granby's books

Bulwell Aggregates

19-1	Bank – deposit	9,000	19-1	HP Sales	54,000
	Bank – instalment	24,000		HP Interest	11,250
	Balance c/f	32,250			
		65,250			65,250
19-2	Bank – instalment	24,000	19-2	Balance b/d	32,250
	Balance c/f	16,313		HP Interest	8,063
		40,313			40,313
19-3	Bank – instalment	20,391	19-3	Balance b/d	16,313
				HP Interest	4,078
		20,391			20,391

Bank

19-1	Bulwell	9,000
19-1	Bulwell	24,000
19-2	Bulwell	24,000
19-3	Bulwell	20,391

HP Interest

19-1	HP Trading	11,250	19-1	Bulwell	11,250
19-2	HP Trading	8,063	19-2	Bulwell	8,063
19-3	HP Trading	4,078	19-3	Bulwell	4,078

Hire Purchase Trading

(19-1)

HP Sales		54,000	
HP Interest		11,250	65,250
Cost of Lorries		43,200	
Provision for Unrealised Profit c/f		6,450	49,650
Gross Profit			15,600

(19-2)

HP Interest		8,063
Provision for Unrealised Profit b/f	6,450	
less Provision for Unrealised Profit c/f	3,263	3,187
Gross Profit		11,250

(19-3)

HP Interest		4,078
Provision for Unrealised Profit b/f		3,263
Gross Profit		7,341

Working: Unrealised Profit

$$\text{Profit margin} \quad \frac{10,800}{54,000} \times \frac{100}{1} = 20\%$$

$$20\% \times £32,250 = £6,450$$
$$20\% \times £16,313 = £3,263$$

8.5 *RJ*

Hire Purchase Trading & Profit & Loss Account for the year ended 31 December 19-8

Sales at Hire Purchase Price (850 × 300)			255,000
Purchases		180,000	
less Stock (50 × 200)		10,000	
		170,000	
Cost of Goods Sold		170,000	
Provision for Unrealised Profit		59,500	229,500
Gross Profit			25,500
less Wages & Salaries		12,800	
General Expenses		5,500	
Bank Interest		400	18,700
Net Profit			6,800

Balance Sheet as at 31 December 19-8

Fixed Assets			10,000
Current Assets			
Stock in Warehouse		10,000	
Hire Purchase Debtors	178,500		
less Provision for Unrealised Profit	59,500	119,000	
		129,000	
less Current Liabilities			
Creditors	16,600		
Bank Overdraft	19,600	36,200	92,800
			102,800
Financed by:			
Capital			100,000
Cash Introduced			
add Net Profit			6,800
			106,800
less Drawings			4,000
			102,800

8.8

Motor Coaches

Date	Particulars	£	Date	Particulars	£
1.1.-4	Bank (Polly)	20,000	31.12.-4	Balance c/d	134,000
	Moneconomic	43,200			
30.9.-4	Bank (Dolly)	20,400			
	Moneconomic	50,400			
		134,000			134,000
1.1.-5	Balance b/d	134,000	31.12.-5	Balance c/d	216,600
31.7.-5	Bank (Molly)	17,800			
	Moneconomic	64,800			
		216,600			216,600
1.1.-6	Balance b/d	216,600	31.3.-6	Motors Disposal (Polly)	63,200
31.3.-6	Bank (Ena)	24,600	30.6.-6	″ ″ (Dolly)	70,800
	Moneconomic	75,600	1.12.-6	″ ″ (Tina)	116,400
30.6.-6	Motors Disposal	33,600	31.12.-6	Balance c/d	182,800
	Moneconomic	82,800			
		433,200			433,200

Accumulated Depreciation

31.12.-5	Balance c/d	106,295		Profit & Loss (W1)	46,900
			31.12.-4	" (W2)	59,395
		106,295	31.12.-5		106,295
31.3.-6	Motors Disposal (W4)	36,498	1.1.-6	Balance b/d	106,295
30.6.-6	" (W5)	40,887	31.12.-6	Profit & Loss (W3)	53,862
31.12.-6	Balance c/d	82,772			
		160,157			160,157

Motors Disposal

31.3.-6	Motor Coaches	63,200		Bank	22,000
30.6.-6	"	70,800		Depreciation (W4)	36,498
		116,400		Motor Coaches	33,600
				Depreciation (W5)	40,887
				Moneconomic	60,000
				Profit & Loss	57,415
		250,400			250,400

Hire Purchase Interest

31.12.-4	Profit & Loss	8,337		Bank (W6) 6,019 + 2,318	8,337
31.12.-5	"	13,594		Bank (W6) (2,592 + 6,250 + 4,752)	13,594
31.12.-6	"	29,751		Bank (W6) (29 + 1,402 + 6,998 + 9,072 + 12,250)	29,751

Hire Purchase Creditors (Moneconomic)

1.1.-4		22,983	31.12.-4	Bank (W9)	43,200
30.9.-4		70,617		Balance c/d	50,400
		93,600			93,600
1.1.-5		58,766	31.12.-5	Bank (W9)	70,617
		76,651		Balance c/d	64,800
		135,417			135,417
1.1.-6		88,740	31.12.-6	Bank (W9)	76,651
31.3.-6		60,000		Motor Coaches	75,600
30.6.-6		94,752		Balance c/d	82,800
31.12.-6	Interest owing on Tina	8,441			
		243,492			243,492

Workings

(W1, W2 & W3)

	Polly	Dolly	Molly	Ena	Total Depn
19-4 Cost	63,200	70,800			
Depn 35%	22,120	24,780			46,900 (W1)
	41,080	46,020			
19-5 Cost			82,600		59,395 (W2)
Depn 35%	14,378	16,107	28,910		
	26,702	29,913	53,690		
19-6 Cost			53,690	100,200	53,862 (W3)
Depn 35%			18,792	35,070	
Sold for	22,000	33,600			
Profit (Loss)	(4,702)	3,687			

(W4) Polly 22,120 + 14,378 = 36,498
(W5) Dolly 24,780 + 16,107 = 40,887

(W6) Interest charged

	Cost-Deposit	Interest	Instalments	Year	Fraction*	Charge
Polly	43,200	8,640	11	19-4	209/300	6,019
			12	19-5	90/300	2,592
			1	19-6	1/300	29
		8,640				8,640
Dolly	50,400	10,080	3	19-4	69/300	2,318
			12	19-5	186/300	6,250
			6	19-6	(see W7)	1,402
		(see W7)				9,970
Molly	64,800	12,960	5	19-5	110/300	4,752
			12	19-6	162/300	6,998
Ena	75,600	15,120	9	19-6	180/300	9,072
Tina	82,800	16,560	3	19-6	(see W8)	12,250

*Using Rule of 78 method See Chapter 36.

(W7) interest in 19-6 for Dolly
Total payable 50,400 + 10,080
Paid 21 × 2,520 (i.e. 60,480 ÷ 24)

	60,480
	52,920
Still owing	7,560
But settled for	7,450
Therefore interest rebate	110

Therefore total interest amended to 10,080 − 110 = 9,970 (as above)
Therefore balance = interest for 19-6 i.e. 1,402

(W8) Tina Repossession

	HP Principal	2 Years Interest	Fraction
Bought 30.6.-6			69/300
less Paid 3 × 4,410	82,000	16,560	
	8,611	3,809	
Proceeds	60,000		39,000
Owing 30.9.-6	14,189	12,751	
Settled for	14,189	8,441	
Therefore interest reduced by		4,310	1,975

(W9) Repayments

	Paid	Interest (W6)	Principal Repaid
19-4 Polly 11 × 2,160	23,760	6,019	
Dolly 33 × 2,520	7,560	2,318	
	31,320	8,337	22,983
19-5 Polly 12 × 2,160	25,920	2,592	
Dolly 12 × 2,520	30,240	6,250	
Molly 5 × 3,240	16,200	4,752	
	72,360	13,594	58,766
19-6 Polly 1 × 2,160	2,160	29	
Dolly 6 × 2,520	15,120	1,402	
Settlement on Dolly	7,450		
Molly 12 × 3,240	38,880	6,998	
Ena 9 × 3,780	34,020	9,072	
Tina 3 × 4,140	12,420	3,809 (W8)	
	110,050	21,310	88,740

Cosy Fires Ltd

10.1

Application & Allotment

Dr		Cr	
Cash: return of unsuccessful applications 5,000 × 0.60	3,000	Cash: application for 65,000 × 0.60	39,000
Share Capital: Due on application & allotment: 40,000 × 0.70	28,000	Cash: Balance due on allotment (see workings)*	1,975
Share Premium: 40,000 × 0.25	10,000	Balance c/d: Due from allottee in respect of 500 shares:	
		500 × 0.35 = 175	
		less o/paid on application	
		250 × 0.60 = 150	25
	41,000		41,000
Balance b/d	25	Forfeited Shares	25

Share Capital

Dr		Cr	
Forfeited Shares: amount called on shares forfeited: 500 × 0.70	350	Balance b/f	75,000
Balance c/fwd	115,000	Application & Allotment	28,000
		Call	11,850
		Forfeited Shares	500
	115,350		115,350

Share Premium

Dr		Cr	
Balance c/fwd	10,375	Application & Allotment	10,000
		Forfeited Shares	375
	10,375		10,375

Forfeited Shares

Dr		Cr	
Share Capital	350	Application & Allotment	25
Cash: 500 × 1.10 per share	550	Share Capital	500
		Share Premium	375
	900		900

Call

Dr		Cr	
Share Capital 39,500 × 0.30	11,850	Cash	11,850

Balance Sheet as at 31 May 19-7

Share Capital		
Authorised: 160,000 Ordinary Shares of 1 each		160,000
Issued and fully paid: 115,000 Ordinary Shares of 1 each		115,000
Capital Reserve:		
Share Premium		10,375

*Workings:

Due on application 0.60 × 40,000	24,000	
Due on allotment 0.35 × 40,000	14,000	38,000
Received on application: 0.60 × 65,000	39,000	
less refunded 5,000 × 0.60	3,000	36,000
Balance due on allotment		2,000
less Amount due on application & allotment 500 × 0.95	475	
Received on application 750 × 0.60	450	25
		1,975

Share Capital

Forfeited Shares	5,000	Balance b/d	500,000
Balance c/d	1,000,000	Application & Allotment	250,000
		First & Final Call	250,000
		Forfeited Shares	5,000
	1,005,000		1,005,000

First & Final Call

Share Capital	250,000	Cash	247,500
		Forfeited Shares	2,500
	250,000		250,000

Forfeited Shares

First & Final Call	2,500	Share Capital	5,000
Share Capital	5,000	Cash	4,500
Share Premium	2,000		
	9,500		9,500

Given format 1 of the Companies Act 1985, there are two places where uncalled capital can be shown. These are either place A or C II (5).

If C II (5) is chosen it becomes:

Current Assets		
II Debtors		
(5) Called up share capital not paid		2,500
Issued Share Capital		
1,000,000 ordinary shares of £1 each		1,000,000
Reserves		
Share Premium		302,000

The authorised share capital should be shown also as a note only.

The increase in share premium would also be shown as a note in the statement showing changes in reserves.

10.3 M Ltd
Ledger Accounts (dates omitted)

Application & Allotment

Cash (750,000 × 85p)	637,500	Cash (Refund 125,000 × 85p)	106,250
Application & Allotment (500,000 × 25p – overpaid 125,000 × 85p)	18,750		
First & Final Call (495,000 × 50p)	247,500		
Forfeited Shares (5,000 × 90p)	4,500		

Share Capital

Application & Allotment	250,000	Cash	637,500
Share Premium	300,000	Cash	18,750
Cash	106,250		
	656,250		656,250

Share Premium

Balance c/d	302,000	Application & Allotment	300,000
		Forfeited Shares	2,000
	302,000		302,000

11.1 (i)

	Dr	Cr
(A1) Bank	5,000	
(A2) Ordinary Share Applicants		5,000
Cash received from applicants		
(B1) Ordinary Share Applicants	5,000	
(B2) Ordinary Share Capital		5,000
Ordinary shares allotted		
(C1) Preference Share Capital	5,000	
(C2) Preference Share Redemption		5,000
Shares to be redeemed		
(D1) Preference Share Redemption	5,000	
(D2) Bank		5,000
Payment made to redeem shares		

	Balances Before	Effect Dr	Effect Cr	Balances After
Net Assets (except bank)	20,000			20,000
Bank	13,000	(A1) 5,000	(D2) 5,000	13,000
	33,000			33,000
Preference Share Capital	5,000	(C1) 5,000		–
Preference Share Redemption	–	(D1) 5,000	(C2) 5,000	–
Ordinary Share Capital	15,000		(B2) 5,000	20,000
Ordinary Share Applicants	–	(B1) 5,000	(A2) 5,000	–
Share Premium	2,000			2,000
	22,000			22,000
Profit & Loss	11,000			11,000
	33,000			33,000

11.1 (ii)

	Dr	Cr
(A1) Preference Share Capital	5,000	
(A2) Preference Share Redemption		5,000
Shares to be redeemed		
(B1) Preference Share Redemption	5,000	
(B2) Bank		5,000
Cash paid on redemption		
(C1) Profit & Loss Appropriation	5,000	
(C2) Capital Redemption Reserve		5,000
Transfer per Companies Act		

	Balances Before	Effect Dr	Effect Cr	Balances After
Net Assets (except Bank)	20,000			20,000
Bank	13,000		(B2) 5,000	8,000
	33,000			28,000
Preference Share Capital	5,000	(A1) 5,000		–
Preference Share Redemption	–	(B1) 5,000	(A2) 5,000	–
Ordinary Share Capital	15,000			15,000
Capital Redemption Reserve	–		(C2) 5,000	5,000
Share Premium	2,000			2,000
	22,000			22,000
Profit & Loss	11,000	(C1) 5,000		6,000
	33,000			28,000

11.1 (iii)

	Dr	Cr
(A1) Bank		
(A2) Ordinary Share Applicants		
Cash received from applicants		
(B1) Ordinary Share Applicants	1,500	
(B2) Ordinary Share Capital		1,500
Ordinary shares allotted		
(C1) Profit & Loss Appropriation	3,500	
(C2) Capital Redemption Reserve		3,500
Part of redemption not covered by new issue, to comply with Companies Act.		
(D1) Preference Share Capital	5,000	
(D2) Preference Share Redemption		5,000
Shares to be redeemed		
(E1) Preference Share Redemption	5,000	
(E2) Bank		5,000
Payment made for redemption		

11.1 (iv)

	Balances before	Effect Dr	Effect Cr	Balances after
Net Assets (except bank)	20,000			20,000
Bank	13,000	(A1) 1,500	(E2) 5,000	9,500
	33,000			29,500
Preference Share Capital	5,000	(D1) 5,000		–
Preference Share Redemption	–	(E1) 5,000	(D2) 5,000	–
Ordinary Share Capital	15,000		(B2) 1,500	16,500
Ordinary Share Applicants	–	(B1) 1,500	(A2) 1,500	–
Capital Redemption Reserve	–		(C2) 3,500	3,500
Share Premium	2,000			2,000
	22,000			22,000
Profit & Loss	11,000	(C1) 3,500		7,500
	33,000			29,500

	Dr	Cr
(A1) Preference Share Capital	5,000	
(A2) Preference Share Redemption		5,000
Shares to be redeemed		
(B1) Profit & Loss Appropriation	1,250	
(B2) Preference Share Redemption		1,250
Premium on redemption of shares *not* previously issued at premium		
(C1) Profit & Loss Appropriation	5,000	
(C2) Capital Redemption Reserve		5,000
Transfer because shares redeemed out of distributable profits		
(D1) Preference Share Redemption	6,250	
(D2) Bank		6,250
Payment on redemption		

11.1 (v)

	Balances before	Effect Dr	Effect Cr	Balances after
Net Assets (except bank)	20,000			20,000
Bank	13,000		(D2) 6,250	6,750
	33,000			26,750
Preference Share Capital	5,000	(A1) 5,000		–
Preference Share Redemption	–	(D1) 6,250	(A2) 5,000 (B2) 1,250	–
Ordinary Share Capital	15,000			15,000
Capital Redemption Reserve	–		(C2) 5,000	5,000
Share Premium	2,000			2,000
	22,000			22,000
Profit & Loss	11,000	(C1) 5,000 (B1) 1,250		4,750
	33,000			26,750

	Dr	Cr
(A1) Bank	7,000	
(A2) Ordinary Share Applicants		7,000
Cash received from applicants		
(B1) Ordinary Share Applicants	7,000	
(B2) Ordinary Share Capital		7,000
Ordinary shares allotted		
(C1) Preference Share Capital	5,000	
(C2) Preference Share Redemption		5,000
Shares being redeemed		
(D1) Share Premium Account	1,500	
(D2) Preference Share Redemption		1,500
Amount of Share Premium account used for redemption		
(E1) Profit & Loss Appropriation	500	
(E2) Preference Share Redemption		500
Excess of premium payable over amount of share premium account usable for the purpose		
(F1) Preference Share Redemption	7,000	
(F2) Bank		7,000
Amount payable on redemption		

11.3 (i)

	Balances before	Effect Dr	Effect Cr	Balances after
Net Assets (except bank)	20,000			20,000
Bank	13,000	(A1) 7,000	(F2) 7,000	13,000
	33,000			33,000
Preference Share Capital	5,000	(C1) 5,000	(C2) 5,000	–
Preference Share Redemption	–	(F1) 7,000	(D2) 1,500	–
			(E2) 500	
Ordinary Share Capital	15,000		(B2) 7,000	22,000
Ordinary Share Applicants	–	(B1) 7,000	(A2) 7,000	–
Share Premium Account	2,000	(D1) 1,500		500
	22,000			22,500
Profit & Loss	11,000	(E1) 500		10,500
	33,000			33,000

Dr   Cr

(A1) Ordinary Share Capital   6,000
(A2) Ordinary Share Purchase   6,000
Shares to be purchased

(B1) Ordinary Share Purchase   6,000
(B2) Bank   6,000
Payment for shares purchased

(C1) Profit and Loss   4,500
(C2) Capital Redemption Reserve   4,500
Transfer of deficiency of permissible capital payment to comply with Companies Act

11.3 (ii)

	Balances before	Effect Dr	Effect Cr	Balances after
Net Assets (except bank)	12,500			12,500
Bank	13,000		(B2) 6,000	7,000
	25,500			19,500
Preference Share Capital	5,000			5,000
Ordinary Share Capital	10,000	(A1) 6,000		4,000
Ordinary Share Purchase		(B1) 6,000	(A2) 6,000	6,000
Non-Distributable Reserves	6,000			6,000
Capital Redemption Reserve	–		(B2) 4,500	4,500
	21,000			19,500
Profit & Loss	4,500	(C1) 4,500		–
	25,500			19,500

Dr   Cr

(A1) Ordinary Share Capital   6,000
(A2) Ordinary Share Purchase   6,000
Shares to be purchased

(B1a) Profit and Loss   4,500
(B2b) Non-Distributable Reserves   1,500
(B2) Ordinary Share Capital   6,000
Transfers of profit and loss and Non-Distributable Reserves per Companies Act

(C1) Ordinary Share Purchase   12,000
(C2) Bank   12,000
Payment to shareholders

	Balances before	Effect Dr	Effect Cr	Balances after
Net Assets (except bank)	12,500			12,500
Bank	13,000		(C2) 12,000	1,000
	25,500			13,500
Preference Share Capital	5,000			5,000
Ordinary Share Capital	10,000	(A1) 6,000		4,000
Ordinary Share Purchase	–	(C1) 12,000	(A2) 6,000	–
			(B2) 6,000	
Non-Distributable Reserves	6,000	(B1b) 1,500		4,500
	21,000			13,500
Profit & Loss	4,500	(B1a) 4,500		–
	25,500			13,500

11.5 Workings: Opening Balance 10% Debentures (A/c below)

Originally issued	375,000	
less redeemed previously	150,000	225,000

10% Debentures

30/9 Debenture Redemption	225,000	1/7 Balance b/f	225,000

Workings: Sinking Fund Investments (A/c below)

Appropriations to date	334,485
Interest invested (39,480 – 2,475)	37,005
	371,490
less sold – at cost	144,915
	226,575

Sinking Fund Investments

1/7 Balance b/f	226,575	2/8	Bank No 2 Sale	73,215
2/8 Sinking Fund: Profit	3,893	25/9	Bank No 2 Sale	160,238
(73,215 – 69,322)				
25/9 Sinking Fund: Profit	2,985			
(Cost 226,575 – 69,322 =				
157,253. Sold for 160,238)				
	233,453			233,453

Workings: Sinking Fund (A/c below)

Previous contributions	334,485
Interest on investments	39,480
Profit: previous sales of investments (147,234 – 144,915)	2,328
Profit: previous purchase debentures (150,000 – 147,243)	2,757
	379,050
less Transfer to general reserve sum equal to debentures redeemed.	150,000
	229,050

Sinking Fund A/c

30/9 Debenture Redemption (Premium 1%)	2,250	1/7	Balance b/f	229,050
30/9 General Reserve	236,889	7/7	No 2 Bank: Interest	1,756
		2/8	S.F. Investments: Profit	3,893
		13/9	No 2 Bank: Interest	1,455
		25/9	S F Investments: Profit	2,985
	239,139			239,139

No 2 Bank A/c

1/7	Balance b/f	2,475	30/9 W Bank plc (Deposit)	15,150
7/7	Sinking Fund: Interest	1,756	30/9 Debenture Redemption	212,100
2/8	SF Investments: Sale	73,215	30/9 No 1 Bank Transfer	11,889
13/9	Sinking Fund: Interest	1,455	of balance	
25/9	SF Investments: Sale	160,238		
		239,139		239,139

Debenture Redemption A/c

30/9 No 2 Bank	212,100	30/9 10% Debentures	225,000
(225,000 Debentures		30/9 Sinking Fund (Premium)	2,250
– 15,000 B Ltd = 210,000			
at 1% premium			
30/9 Balance c/d	15,150		
(15,000 outstanding at			
premium 1%)			
	227,250		227,250

W Bank A/c

30/9 No 2 Bank	15,150	

12.1 (a)

Checkers Ltd
Profit & Loss Account for the year ended 31 December 19-5

	Total	Basis of Allocation	Pre-Incorporation 8,000	Post-Incorporation 20,000
Gross Profit	28,000	Turnover	8,000	20,000
less				
Salaries of Vendors	1,695	Actual	1,695	
Wages	8,640	Time	2,160	6,480
Rent	860	Time	215	645
Distribution	1,680	Turnover	480	1,200
Commission	700	Turnover	200	500
Bad Debts	314	Actual	104	210
Interest	1,650	Time	990	660
Directors Remuneration	4,000	Actual		4,000
Directors Expenses	515	Actual		515
Depreciation*				
Motors	1,900	Actual	400	1,500
Machinery	575	Actual	125	450
Bank Interest	168	Actual		168
	22,697		6,369	16,328
Net Profit	5,303		1,631	3,672
	28,000		8,000	20,000

*Depreciation:
Motors to 31 March 19-5 20% × 3 months × 7,000 + 20% × 1 month × 3,000 = 400
After 20% × 9 months × 7,000 + 20% × 9 months × 3,000 = 1,500
(b) Transfer to a Capital Reserve
(c) Charge to a Goodwill Account.

12.2 *Adjusted Profits*

	16,400	23,920	19,650
Profit per accounts	16,400	23,920	19,650
add Motor Expenses saved	620	660	700
,, Depreciation overcharged	1,500	700	60
,, Wrapping Expenses saved	420	480	510
,, Bank Interest	180	590	740
,, Preliminary Expenses		690	
	2,720	3,120	2,010
	19,120	27,040	21,660
less Extra Management Remuneration	1,500	1,500	1,500
,, Investment Income	290	340	480
,, Rents Received	940	420	
,, Opening Stock		1,900	
,, Profit on Property			
	2,730	4,800	1,980
Profits as adjusted	16,390	18,080	19,680

Average profit

$$16,390$$
$$18,080$$
$$19,680$$
$$54,150 \div 3 = 18,050$$

If 18,050 is a return of 25% on investment, then
$$\frac{18,050}{25} \times 100 = 72,200 \text{ purchase price}$$

12.3 (a)

CK
Realisation

Freehold Premises	8,000	CK Ltd: Value at which assets taken over	27,200
Plant	4,000	Discount on Creditors	150
Stock	2,000		
Debtors	5,000		
Profit on Realisation	8,350		
	27,350		27,350

Capital

CK Ltd: Shares	24,150	Balance b/d	16,000
Cash	200	Profit on Realisation	8,350
	24,350		24,350

CK Ltd (not asked for in question)

Realisation	27,200	Creditors	3,050
		Shares	24,150
	27,200		27,200

RP Ltd – Realisation

Freehold Premises	4,500	CK Ltd Value at which assets taken over	13,000
Plant	2,000		
Stock	1,600		
Debtors	3,400		
Profit on Realisation	1,500		
	13,000		13,000

Sundry Shareholders

CK Ltd	5,000	Share Capital	4,000
Cash	3,000	Profit on Realisation	1,500
Shares		Revenue Surplus	2,500
	8,000		8,000

CK Ltd (not asked for in question)

Realisation	13,000	Bank Overdraft	3,500
		Creditors	1,500
		Sundry Shareholders: Cash	5,000
		Shares	3,000
	13,000		13,000

Journal of CJK Ltd

(b) Have omitted narratives

Cash	5,000	
Share Premium		3,000
Ordinary Shares		2,000
Cash	7,840	
Discount on issue	160	
7 per cent Debentures		8,000
Goodwill	7,000	
Freehold Premises	10,000	
Plant	3,500	
Stock	2,000	
Debtors	5,000	
Provision for Discounts Receivable		150
Creditors		3,200
Provision for Bad Debts		300
Ordinary Shares		24,150
Goodwill	500	
Freehold Premises	5,500	
Plant	2,000	
Stock	1,600	
Debtors	3,400	
Creditors		1,500
Bank Overdraft		3,500
Cash		5,000
Ordinary Share Capital		3,000
Formation Expenses	1,200	
Cash		1,200

(c)
CJK Ltd
Balance Sheet as at 1st January 19-0

	£	£
Fixed Assets: at cost		
Freehold Premises		15,500
Plant		5,500
Goodwill		7,500
		28,500
Current Assets		
Stock	8,400	
Debtors	300	
less Provision for Bad Debts		8,100
Cash at Bank		3,140
		14,840
less Current Liabilities		
Creditors	4,700	
Less Provision	150	
		4,550
Working Capital		10,290
		38,790

13.1

Debenture Interest

		£				£
19-3				19-3		
Dec 31	Bank	9,600		Dec 31	Profit & Loss	12,800
,, 31	Income Tax	3,200				
		12,800				12,800

Income Tax

		£				£
19-3				19-3		
Dec 31	Balance c/d	3,200		Dec 31	Debenture Interest	3,200

Ordinary Dividends

		£				£
19-3				19-3		
Jul 1	Bank	20,000		Dec 31	Profit & Loss	50,000
Dec 31	Accrued c/d	30,000				
		50,000				50,000

Deferred Taxation

		£				£
19-3				19-3		
Dec 31	Balance c/d	14,000		Dec 31	Profit & Loss*	14,000

*35% of (£90,000 − £50,000) = £14,000

Corporation Tax

		£				£
19-3				19-3		
Dec 31	Balance c/d	90,000		Dec 31	Profit & Loss	90,000

Advance Corporation Tax

		£				£
19-3				19-3		
Sept 30	Bank (⅓ × £20,000)	6,667		Dec 31	Balance c/d	6,667

Profit & Loss Account (extracts) year to 31 December 19-3

	£	£
Net trading profit		220,000
less debenture interest		12,800
Profit on ordinary activities before taxation		207,200
Corporation Tax	90,000	
Deferred Tax	14,000	
		104,000
Profit on ordinary activities after taxation		103,200
less Ordinary Dividends: Interim	20,000	
Final proposed	30,000	
		50,000

Balance Sheet (extracts) as at 31 December 19-3

	£
Creditors: Amounts Falling Due Within One Year	
Proposed ordinary dividend	30,000
Corporation Tax	90,000
Deferred Tax (14,000 − ACT recoverable 6,667)	7,333
Income Tax	3,200

13.3
Workings
(W1) Tax deducted from franked investment income is

$$\frac{25}{100-25} \times £900 = \frac{1}{3} \times £900 = £300$$

Tax deducted from fixed interest income is ⅓ × £24,000 = £8,000

(W2) Changes in Deferred Taxation account.
Timing difference:
Capital allowances allowable for tax (E)
Depreciation actually charged (E)

Transferred to Deferred Tax Account £40,000 × 35% = £14,000

Deferred Tax

Dr		£		Cr		£
19-2				19-2		
Dec 31	Balance c/d	81,000		Jan 1	Balance b/f (J)	67,000
				Dec 31	Tax on Profit on Ordinary Activities (W1)	14,000
		81,000				81,000

Income Tax

Dr		£		Cr		£
19-2				19-2		
Oct 31	Interest Receivable (CI)	8,000		Nov 30	Debenture Interest (B)	20,000
Dec 15	Bank	12,000				
		20,000				20,000

Interest Receivable

Dr		£		Cr		£
19-2				19-2		
Dec 31	Profit & Loss	32,000		Oct 31	Bank (CI)	24,000
				„ 31	Income Tax (CI)	8,000
		32,000				32,000

Debenture Interest

Dr		£		Cr		£
19-2				19-2		
Nov 30	Bank (B)	60,000		Dec 31	Profit & Loss	80,000
„ 30	Income Tax (B)	20,000				
		80,000				80,000

Franked Investment Income

Dr		£		Cr		£
19-2				19-2		
Dec 31	Profit & Loss	1,200		Sept 1	Bank (C2)	900
				Sept 1	Tax on Profit on Ordinary Activities* (W1)	300
		1,200				1,200

* See note following balance sheet

Advance Corporation Tax

Dr			£		Cr			£
19-2					19-2			
Jan 31	Balance b/f (N)		49,000		Sept 30	Corporation Tax set-off of (N)		49,000
May 31	Bank (ACT on I) *1		30,000					
Aug 31	Bank (ACT on F)		6,000					
Sept 15	Bank (ACT on G) *2		24,700		Dec 31	Balance c/d *3		60,700
			109,700					109,700

Notes *1 The ACT on the final dividend for 19-1 cannot be set off against the Corporation Tax for 19-1. This is because it was paid in 19-2 and should therefore be set off against the 19-2 Corporation Tax payment.
*2 The ACT on (G) is calculated 1/3 × £75,000 less tax credit on investment income (C2) £300 = £24,700.
*3 Deductible against 19-2 tax payable in 19-3.

Corporation Tax

Dr			£		Cr			£
19-2					19-2			
Sept 30	ACT set-off (N)		49,000		Jan 1	Balance b/f (K)		115,000
„ 30	Bank *1		63,000		Dec 31	Tax on Profit on Ordinary Activities (L)		154,000
„ 30	Tax on Profit on Ordinary Activities *2 (K)		3,000					
Dec 31	Balance c/d (L)		154,000					
			269,000					269,000

Notes *1 £115,000 owing – £3,000 reduction (K) – ACT set offs deducted in 19-1, £49,000 = £63,000.
*2 Adjustment for amendment in tax bill.

Tax on Profit on Ordinary Activities

Dr			£		Cr			£
19-2					19-2			
Sept 1	Investment Income (W1)		300		Sept 30	Corporation Tax (K)		3,000
Dec 31	Corporation Tax		154,000		Dec 31	Profit & Loss		165,300
„ 31	Deferred Tax (W1)		14,000					
			168,300					168,300

Preference Dividends

		£				£
19-2				19-2		
Jun 30	Bank	18,000	(F)	Dec 31	Profit & Loss	18,000

Ordinary Dividends

		£					£
19-2				19-2			
Mar 31	Bank	90,000	(I)	Jan 1	Accrued b/d	(I)	90,000
Jul 15	Bank	75,000	(G)	Dec 31	Profit & Loss		195,000
Dec 31	Accrued c/d	120,000					
		285,000					285,000

Barnet Ltd

Profit & Loss (extracts) for the year ended 31 December 19-2

		£	£
Net trading profit			560,000
add fixed rate interest (C1) (gross)	(A)	32,000	
franked investment income (C2) (gross)		1,200	33,200
			593,200
less debenture interest (B) (gross)			80,000
Profit on ordinary activities before taxation			513,200
Tax on profit on ordinary activities *1			151,300
			361,900
less Dividends:			
Preference Dividend		18,000	
Ordinary: interim		75,000	
final		120,000	120,000
			213,000

*1 Notes attached to accounts giving make-up of this figure.

Balance Sheet (extracts) as at 31 December 19-2

	£	£
Creditors amounts falling due within one year		
Proposed ordinary dividend	120,000	
Corporation tax	154,000	
Deferred tax (81,000 – ACT recoverable 60,700)	20,300	

A final point concerns the difference in treatment of tax on franked investment income as compared with tax on other income, such as interest. It is only the tax on franked investment income which is treated as part of the final tax costs, while the tax on interest is simply deducted from charges paid by the company. You would have to study taxation in detail to understand why this happens.

BG Ltd

Profit & Loss Account for the year ended 31 December 19-7

	£	£
Trading Profit		50,000
Income from shares in related companies	3,000	
Other interest receivable and similar income	1,100	4,100
		54,100
Interest payable and similar charges		3,600
Profit on ordinary activities before taxation		50,500
Tax on profit on ordinary activities		24,000
Profit on ordinary activities after taxation		26,500
Undistributed Profits from last year		9,870
		36,370
Transfers to Reserves	5,000	
Dividends Proposed	21,000	26,000
Undistributed Profits carried to next year		10,370

14.1 Either Ltd

Profit per draft accounts

			£000
			157
(i)	Stock: reduce to net realisable value	+	–
(ii)	Directors' remuneration		35
(iii)	Bad Debt		43
(iv)	Corporation Tax saved on (i) + (ii) + (iii) × 50%	54	30
(v)	Depreciation adjustment (W1)		30
(vi)	Revaluation Reserve (realised on sale)	125	
(vii)	General Reserve	80	
(viii)	Loss brought forward (W2)	259	144
			282
		net –23	

Maximum possible dividend	net –23	134

Preference dividend 6%	£9,000
Ordinary dividend	£125,000

Research and development expenditure: assumed to have been carried forward in accordance with SSAP 13 and can be justified. Failing this it would have to be a realised loss.

For a plc no changes required, except that the payment should not reduce net assets below called up share capital and undistributable reserves = 400 + 150 + 100 = 650. A further bad debt might change this position.

15.1 (a)

Merton Manufacturing Co Ltd

Balance Sheet as at . . .

Fixed Tangible Assets				
Freehold Land & Buildings at cost	(W1)			95,000
Plant & Equipment at written down value				104,350
				199,350
Current Assets				
Stocks			25,000	
Debtors			50,000	
Bank	(W2)		14,150	
			89,150	
Creditors: Amounts falling due within one year				
Creditors			63,500	
				25,650
Net Current Assets				
Total Assets less Current Liabilities				225,000
Long Term Loans: 8 per cent Debentures	(W3)			150,000
				75,000
Capital & Reserves				
Called-up Share Capital	(W4)			75,000
150,000 50p Ordinary Shares				

Workings:

			Capital Reduction	
(W1)				
Ordinary Shares 50p (new)	7,500		Ordinary Shares £1 (old)	90,000
(1 for 6 = 15,000 × 50p)			6% Preference Shares (old)	150,000
Ordinary Shares 50p (new)	25,000		11½% Debenture (old)	100,000
(1 for 3 – preference –			Share Premium written off	25,000
50,000 × 50p)				
8% Debentures	50,000			
(1 for 3 preference)				
8% Debenture	100,000			
(exchange for 11½%)				
Ordinary Shares 50p	12,500			
(1 for every £4 old debenture)				
Goodwill written off	50,000			
Profit & Loss written off	38,850			
Plant & Equipment *	81,150			
	365,000			365,000

* per (vii) of question – amount needed to balance.
(W2) Shares issued 60,000 shares × 50p = 30,000
Cash 30,000 – Overdraft 15,850 = balance 14,150

(W1)

Reducing balance	
Cost 1.12 19-1	100,000
Depreciation 19-2	25,000
Cost 1.6 19=3	75,000
	25,000
	100,000
Depreciation 19-3	25,000
Cost 29.2.84	75,000
„ 31.5.84	28,000
	45,000
	148,000
Depreciation 19-4	37,000
	111,000
Cost 1.12 19-4	50,000
	161,000
Depreciation 19-5	40,250
	120,750

Total 25,000 + 25,000 + 37,000 + 40,250 = 127,250

Straight-line

		19-2	19-3	19-4	19-5
Cost 1.12.19-2	100,000	25,000	25,000	25,000	25,000
1.6.19-3			3,125	6,250	6,250
29.2.19-4	28,000				7,000
31.5.19-4	45,000			5,250	11,250
1.12.19-4	50,000			5,625	12,500
			28,125	42,125	62,000
		25,000			
		Total 157,250			

Extra depreciation 157,250 – 127,250 = 30,000

(W2) As profits after tax were 157,000 but yet shown in balance sheet as £13,000.
means that a deficit of £144,000 had been brought forward from last year.

(W3) See Capital Reduction – debit side (W1) new debentures 50,000 + 100,000 = 150,000

(W4) See (W1) 7,500 + 25,000 + 12,500 + new shares issued for cash 30,000 = 75,000

(b) (Main points)

	Old Shareholdings	New Shareholders
Expected profit	22,500	12,000
less Interest 11½%	11,500	
" 8%		
Taxable profits	11,000	10,500
less Corporation Tax 33⅓%	3,667	3,500
Profits before dividends	7,333	7,000
Preference dividends – if profits sufficient	9,000	–

Before construction
(Old) Preference Shareholders

Before reconstruction it would have taken over 5 years at this rate before preference dividends payable, as probably deficit of 38,850 on the profit & loss account would have to be cleared off first.

(Old) Ordinary Shares

Even forgetting the profit & loss account deficit, the preference dividends were bigger than available profits. This would leave nothing for the ordinary shareholder.

After reconstruction

The EPS (Earnings per Share) is £7,000 ÷ 150,000 = 4.67p
If all profits are distributed the following benefits would be gained:

By Old Preference Shareholders		
50,000 shares × 4.67p	2,335	
£50,000 8% Debentures	4,000	
	6,335	

Plus any benefits from tax credits.

By Old Ordinary Shareholders	
15,000 shares × 4.67p	700

Plus any benefits from tax credits.

(c)
(i) Preference Shareholders – points to be considered:
What were prospects for income?
Based on projected earnings would have been no income for over 5 years, then earnings of 7.333 per annum if all profits distributed.
(ii) What are new prospects for income?
Total income of 6.333 per annum immediately.
(iii) Is it worth exchanging (i) for (ii)?

Obviously depends on whether forecasts are accurate or not. If above are accurate would seem worthwhile.

(iv) What have preference shareholders given up?
Some of exchange consists of ordinary shares which are more risky than preference shares, both in terms of dividends and of payments on liquidation.
(v) What have they gained?
Debenture interest payable whether profits made or not.

15.2 (a) (Narratives omitted)

	Dr	Cr
Preference Share Capital	37,500	
Ordinary Share Capital	175,000	
Capital Reduction		212,500

Preference Shares reduced 25p each (0.25 × 15,000) &
Ordinary Shares reduced by 0.875 (200,000 × 0.875)

	Dr	Cr
Capital Reduction	3,375	
Ordinary Share Capital		3,375

Ordinary Shares issued re Preference dividend arrears,
27,000 × 0.125

	Dr	Cr
Share Premium	40,000	
Capital Reduction		40,000

Share Premium balance utilised

	Dr	Cr
Provision for Depreciation	62,500	
Capital Redemption	72,500	
Plant & Machinery		135,000

Plant & Machinery written down to 75,000

	Dr	Cr
Capital Reduction	176,625	
Profit & Loss		114,375
Preliminary Expenses		7,250
Goodwill		55,000

Profit & Loss Account and intangible assets written off

	Dr	Cr
Cash	62,500	
Ordinary Share Applicants		62,500

Applications for shares 500,000 × 0.125

	Dr	Cr
Ordinary Share Applicants	62,500	
Ordinary Share Capital		62,500

500,000 Ordinary Shares issued

(b)   Balance Sheet as at 31 December 19-5

Finer Textiles Ltd
Balance Sheet as at 31 March 19-6

Fixed Assets			
Intangible:	Goodwill		15,000
Tangible:	Plant		169,800
	Furniture		6,000
			190,800
Current Assets			
Stock		170,850	
Debtors		65,100	
Bank		107,400	
Cash		150	
		343,500	
Creditors: Amounts Falling due within 1 year			
Creditors		31,800	
Net Current Assets			311,700
Total Assets less Current Liabilities			502,500
Creditors: Amounts falling due after more than 1 year			
Debentures			150,000
			352,500
Capital and Reserves			
Called-up Share Capital			352,500

Fixed Assets			
Leasehold Property at cost		80,000	
Less Provision for Depreciation		30,000	50,000
Plant and Machinery at valuation			75,000
			125,000
Current Assets			
Stock		79,175	
Debtors		31,200	
		110,375	
less Current Liabilities			
Bank Overdraft	51,000		
Creditors	43,500	94,500	
Working Capital			15,875
			140,875
Financed by:			
Share Capital: Preference Shares 150,000 shares £0.75			112,500
Ordinary Shares 227,000 ordinary shares £0.125			28,375
			140,875

15.3   The Journal (narratives omitted)

	Dr	Cr
(i) Preference Share Capital	37,500	
Capital Reduction		37,500
(ii) Ordinary Share Capital	360,000	
Capital Reduction		360,000
(iii) Capital Reserve	48,000	
Capital Reduction		48,000
(iv) Preference Share Capital	112,500	
Ordinary Share Capital	240,000	
New Ordinary Share Capital		352,500
(v) (a) Debenture Holders	150,000	
Debentures		150,000
(b) Cash	150,000	
Debenture Holders		150,000
(vi) Capital Reduction	445,500	
Goodwill etc		210,000
Plant		45,000
Furniture		6,600
Profit & Loss		183,900

16.1 (a) Following is a brief answer:

(i) Such closure costs should be treated as an extraordinary item. because
  • It is (probably) a material item.
  • These are costs not likely to recur regularly or frequently.
  • The cessation is outside normal activities of the business.

(ii) This should be adjusted for tax change for 19-7. Because it is not material (probably) it does not need to be disclosed separately.

(iii) The excess should be credited to a reserve account, and a note attached to the balance sheet. Depreciation to be based on revalued amount and on new estimate of remaining life of the asset, this to be disclosed in a note to the accounts.

(iv) Treat as bad debt and write off to profit and loss. Because it is a material item it should be disclosed as an exceptional item in the profit and loss account.

(v) This is a prior year adjustment. The retained profit brought forward should be amended to allow for the change in accounting policy in the current year. The reasons: (a) it is material, (b) relates to a previous year, (c) as a result of change in accounting policy. The adjustment should be disclosed in a note to the accounts.

(b) See textbook.

16.2

(i) The replacement cost is irrelevant. The stock should be shown at the cost of £26,500. This assumes historic cost accounts.

(ii) Paramite: Stock to be valued at direct costs £72,600 plus fixed factory overhead £15,300 = £87,900. Under no circumstances should selling expenses be included.

Paraton: As net realisable value is lower than the costs involved, this figure of £9,520 should be used (SSAP 9).

(iii) In this case there is a change of accounting policy. Accordingly a prior year adjustment will be made. On a straight line basis net book value would have been:

Cost 160,000 less 12½% × 2 years = 120,000

Value show   90,000

Therefore prior year adjustment of   30,000 to be added to retained profit at 1 November 19-4.

For 19-5 and each of the following 5 years depreciation will be charged at the rate of £20,000 per annum. (SSAP 6)

(iv) The cost subject to depreciation is £250,000 less land £50,000 = £200,000. With a life of 40 years this is £5,000 per annum.

This also will result in a prior year adjustment, in this case 10 × £5,000 = £50,000. This will be debited to retained profits at 1 November 19-4. For 19-5 and each of the following 29 years the yearly charge of depreciation will be £5,000. (SSAP 6)

(v) Write off £17,500 to Profit & Loss. (SSAP 13)

(vi) As this development expenditure is almost definitely going to be recovered over next 4 years it can be written off over that period. (SSAP 13)

(vii) As this is unlikely to happen often it is an extraordinary item. Charge to Profit & Loss – to be shown after, 'Profit on Ordinary Activities after Taxation'.

(viii) As this is over 20% it is material and appears to be long-term. This means that Litteshall Ltd is an associated company and accounts should be prepared accordingly. The post-acquisition profits to be brought in is 30% × £40,000 = £12,000.

(c) The concepts which are applicable here are (i) going concern. (ii) consistency. (iii) accruals, (iv) prudence.

Following on the revelations in (b) and the effect on sales so far of the advertising campaign, is the partnership still able to see itself as a going concern? This would obviously affect the treatment of valuations of all assets.

Given that it can be treated as a going concern, the next point to be considered is that of consistency. The treatment of the expense item should be treated consistently.

The accruals concept is concerned with matching up revenues and costs, and will affect the decision as to how much of the costs should be carried forward. Some revenue in future periods needs to be expected with a high degree of certainty before any of this expenditure should be carried forward. It does not seem highly likely that large revenues can be expected in future in this case. In any case 75 per cent is a very large proportion of such expenditure to be carried forward. There is no easy test of the validity of the partners' estimates. Granted that under SSAP 13 for development expenditure some of it, under very stringent conditions, can be carried forward. If the partners' estimates can be accepted under this, then profits would be increased by 75% × (50,000 + 60,000 + 25,000) = £82,500.

(d) The expected profits/loss are as follows:

	Project A	Project B	Project C
Direct Costs to date	30,000	25,000	6,000
Overheads to date	4,000	2,000	500
Future expected direct costs	10,000	25,000	40,000
" " overheads	2,000	2,000	3,000
Total of expected costs	46,000	54,000	49,500
Sale price of project	55,000	50,000	57,500
Expected total profit/loss	9,000	(4,000)	8,000
% Complete	75%	50%	15%

When a project is sufficiently near completion then a proportion of the profits can be taken as being realised.

Project A is 75% complete and this indicates profit being taken. Whether or not 75% can be taken, i.e. £6,750, will depend on the facts of the case. If completion at the above figures can be taken for granted then it might be reasonable to do so. Prudence dictates that a lesser figure be taken.

With project B there is an expected loss. Following the prudence concept losses should be always accounted for in full as soon as they become known.

In project C it is too early in the project, 15% completed, to be certain about the outcome. No profit should therefore be brought into account.

Profit, dependent on comments about project A, will therefore be increased by £6.750 – £4,000 = £2,750.

(e) This is a case where the examiner has dipped into topics from other subjects. What is needed here is a tree diagram to show the probabilities.

16.5

The fact that this is a partnership does not mean that SSAPs are not applicable, they are just as applicable to a partnership as they are to a limited company.

(a) (i) These should be included as Sales £60,000 in the accounts for the year to 31 May 19-7. This is because the matching concept requires that revenue, and the costs used up in achieving it, should be matched up. Profits: increase of £60,000.

(ii) Stock values are normally based on the lower of cost or net realisable value.
In this case it depends how certain it is that the stock can be sold for £40,000. If a firm order can definitely be anticipated, then the figure of £40,000 can be used as this then represents the lower figure of net realisable value. Profit: an increase of £15,000.
However, should the sale not be expected, then the concept of prudence dictates that the scrap value of £1,000 be used. Profit: a reduction of £24,000.

(b) It is important to establish the probability of the payment of the debt of £80,000. If it is as certain as possible as it can be that payment will be made, even though it may be delayed, then no provision is needed. Profit change: nil.

However effect on future profits can be substantial. A note to the accounts detailing the possibilities of such changes should be given.

Dear Sir/Mr . . . .

Report on Draft Profit & Loss Account for the year ended 30 September 19-6

Further to your letter/our meeting of . . . I would like to offer my suggestions for the appropriate accounting treatment of items (i) to (v).

(i) Redundancy payments: £100,000

In an age of changing technology such payments might be looked at as part of the normal expenses of operating a company. If it is not material in terms of its effect on profit then it would not have to be disclosed. If on the other hand it is judged material then a note should be appended to the accounts as to the size of payments and the effect on profits. In this case, as it equals approximately 13% of profits before taxation it would appear to be a material item, needing a note to the accounts.

(ii) Closure costs of a factory

As this refers to the closure of a significant part of the business the closure costs should be treated as 'extraordinary' playing no part in normal trading. According to SSAP 6, the correct treatment would be to show it as a extraordinary item, (net after Corporation Tax deducted), immediately after the figure for profit and taxation in the profit and loss account, i.e. before dividends.

(iii) Change of basis of Depreciation: £258,000.

There should only be a change in the basis of depreciation if it brings about a fairer presentation of the accounting results and financial position of the company, see SSAP 12. This SSAP also requires that the depreciation should be shown as normal expenses, rather than as a prior year adjustment.

Because the item is a material one, and make comparison difficult, a note as to the details should be appended to the accounts.

(vi) Additional expenses covered by fire: £350,000.

These expenses are covered by SSAP 17 as post-balance sheet non-adjusting events. The fire happened after the balance sheet date, and therefore did not affect conditions as at that date. The figures in this year's accounts should not therefore be altered.

If the event was such as to call into question the continuation of the business, then there should be a note to the accounts on the going-concern basis. In this particular instance this does not seem to be the case, but good practice, although not necessary, would be to give details of the event in notes to the accounts.

(v) Bad debt £125,000.

The accounts have not yet been approved by the directors, and it does affect the valuation of assets at the year end. SSAP 17 would be to treat it as a post-balance sheet adjusting event. It should therefore be written off as a bad debt.

Where it is considered to be a material and unusual event, there should also be a note attached to the accounts.

Should you like to have further discussions concerning any of the points raised, will you please contact me. I hope that you will find my comments to be of use.

Yours faithfully.

CACA

Address
Date

There is a probability of 0.75 of achieving £50,000 sales. As this is greater than the specified figure of 0.70 then the stocks should not be written down. Effect on profits: nil.

(f) The opening stock should be shown as the revised figure. If error had not been found this year's profit would have been £7,000 greater.

The adjustment should be shown as a prior year adjustment in the current accounts.

16.6 (a)
The Chief Accountant
Uncertain Ltd

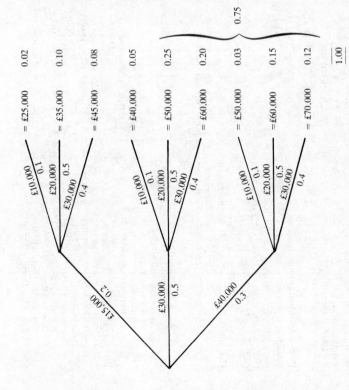

£10,000 0.1	= £25,000 0.02
£20,000 0.5	= £35,000 0.10
£30,000 0.4	= £45,000 0.08
£10,000 0.1	= £40,000 0.05
£20,000 0.5	= £50,000 0.25
£30,000 0.4	= £60,000 0.20
£10,000 0.1	= £50,000 0.03
£20,000 0.5	= £60,000 0.15
£30,000 0.4	= £70,000 0.12

0.75
1.00

16.6

(b) Uncertain Ltd

Draft profit & loss account for the year ended 30 September 19-6

Sales			5,450,490
Manufacturing cost of sales (W1)			2,934,500
			2,515,990
Administration expenses		785,420	
Selling expenses (W2)		1,013,600	1,799,020
Profit before tax			716,970
Corporation Tax (50%) (W3)			358,485
Profit after tax			358,485
Extraordinary item			
Factory closure costs		575,000	
less Corporation tax		287,500	287,500
			70,985
Proposed dividend on ordinary shares			125,000
Reduction in retained profits			(54,015)

(W1) 3,284,500 − 350,000 (iv) = 2,934,500
(W2) 629,800 + (iii) 258,800 + (v) 125,000 = 1,013,600
(W3) 50% of profits before tax

Depreciation: Motors	6,500		22,210
Equipment	700		
Administrative Expenses:			
Salaries and Wages	5,600		
Rent and Rates	2,500		
General Administrative Expenses	3,320		
Motor Expenses	3,600		
Auditors' Remuneration	500		
Discounts Allowed	3,940		
Bad Debts	570		
Depreciation: Motors	3,500		
Equipment	1,100	24,630	46,840
Other Operating Income: Royalties Receivable			72,860
			1,800
			74,660
Income from shares in related companies	660		
Interest on bank deposit	770		1,430
			76,090
Interest Payable: Debenture Interest			2,400
Profit on ordinary activities before taxation			73,690
Tax on Profit on ordinary activities			30,700
Profit on ordinary activities after taxation			42,990
Retained Profits from last year			15,300
			58,290
Transfer to General Reserve		8,000	
Proposed Ordinary Dividend		30,000	38,000
Retained profits carried forward to next year			20,290

17.1 (a) (for internal use)

Rogers plc

Trading & Profit & Loss Account for the year ended 31 December 19-2

	£	£	£
Sales		288,000	
less Returns Inwards		11,500	276,500
less Cost of Sales:			
Stock 1 January 19-2		57,500	
add Purchases	164,000		
less Returns Outwards	2,000	162,000	
Carriage Inwards		1,300	
		220,800	
less Stock 31 December 19-2		64,000	156,800
Gross Profit			119,700
Distribution Costs:			
Salaries and Wages	2,800		
Rent and Rates	3,750		
General Distribution Expenses	4,860		
Motor Expenses	3,600		

17.1 (b) (published accounts)

Rogers plc
Profit and Loss Account for the year ended 31 December 19-2

	£	£
Turnover		276,500
Cost of Sales		156,800
Gross Profit		119,700
Distribution Costs	22,210	
Administrative Expenses	24,630	46,840
		72,860
Other Operating Income		1,800
		74,660
Income from Shares in Related Companies	660	
Other Interest Receivable	770	1,430
		76,090
Interest Payable		2,400
Profit on Ordinary Activities before Taxation		73,690
Tax on Profit on Ordinary Activities		30,700
Profit on the year on Ordinary Activities after Taxation		42,990
Retained Profits from last year		15,300
		58,290
Transfer to General Reserve	8,000	
Proposed Ordinary Dividend	30,000	38,000
Retained Profits carried forward to next year		20,290

(for internal use)

	£	£	£
Turnover			506,750
Cost of Sales:			
Wages	11,350		
Depreciation of Plant and Machinery	1,500		
			336,450
Gross Profit			
Distribution Costs:			
Salaries and Wages	29,110		
Rent and Rates	20,000		
Motor Expenses	10,400		
General Distribution Expenses	8,220		
Haulage Costs	2,070		
Depreciation: Motors	15,000		
Plant and Machinery	8,000	92,800	
Administrative Expenses:			
Salaries and Wages	20,920		
Rent and Rates	5,000		
Motor Expenses	5,200		
General Administrative Expenses	2,190		
Bad Debts	840		
Discounts Allowed	5,780		
Auditors' Remuneration	2,000		
Directors' Remuneration	5,000		
Depreciation: Motors	7,000		
Plant and Machinery	5,000	58,930	
less Discounts Received		6,800	52,130
			144,930
			191,520
Income from shares in related companies		3,500	
Interest from Government Securities		1,600	5,100
			196,620
Amount written off investment in related companies		14,000	
Debenture Interest		3,800	17,800
Profit on Ordinary Activities before Taxation			178,820
Tax on Profit on Ordinary Activities			74,000
Profit on Ordinary Activities after Taxation			104,820
Retained Profits from last year			37,470
			142,290
Transfer to Debenture Redemption Reserve		20,000	
Proposed Ordinary Dividend		50,000	70,000
Retained Profits carried forward to next year			72,290

Notes to accounts on debenture interest and auditors' remuneration.

17.2 (a)

Federal plc
Trading & Profit & Loss Account for the year ended 31 December 19-4

	£	£	£
Sales			849,000
less Returns Inwards			5,800
			843,200
less Cost of Sales:			
Stock 1 January 19-4			64,500
add Purchases	510,600		
less Returns Outwards	3,300	507,300	
Carriage Inwards		4,900	
		576,700	
less Stock 31 December 19-4		82,800	
Cost of Goods Sold		493,900	

583

17.2 (b) (published accounts) **Federal plc**
Profit and Loss Account for the year ended 31 December 19-4

	£	£
Turnover		843,200
Cost of Sales		506,750
Gross Profit		336,450
Distribution Costs	92,800	
Administrative Expenses	52,130	144,930
		191,520
Income from Shares in Related Companies	3,500	
Other Interest Receivable	1,600	5,100
		196,620
Amounts written off Investments	14,000	
Interest Payable	3,800	17,800
Profit on Ordinary Activities before Taxation		178,820
Tax on Profit on Ordinary Activities		74,000
Profit on Ordinary Activities after Taxation		104,820
Retained Profits from last year		37,470
		142,290
Transfer to Reserves	20,000	
Proposed Ordinary Dividend	50,000	70,000
Retained Profits carried forward to next year		72,290

17.3 (a) **Rufford plc**
Profit and Loss Account for the year ended 31 March 19-6

	Notes	£000	£000
Turnover	(1)		642
Cost of Sales (60 + 401 – 71)			390
Gross Profit			252
Distribution Costs (33 + 19)		52	
Administrative Expenses (97 + 8)		105	157
Operating Profit			95
Income from other fixed asset investments (14 × 100/70)	(2)	20	
Other interest receivable	(3)	25	45
			140
Interest Payable	(4)		6
Profit on Ordinary Activities before Taxation			134
Tax on Profit on Ordinary Activities	(5)		50
Profit for the year on Ordinary Activities after Taxation			84

		£000	£000
Extraordinary Items, less taxation	(6)		12
			72
Retained profits brought forward from last year	(7)	160	
Prior year adjustment		15	145
			217
Dividends (21 + 42)			63
Retained profits carried forward to next year			154

Notes to the Accounts:

1 Turnover is net of VAT.

2 Operating profit is shown after charging the following:

	£000	£000
Depreciation: distribution costs	19	
administrative expenses	8	27
Authors' remuneration		20
Directors' emoluments		45
Hire of plant		12

3 Income from fixed asset investment is in respect of a listed company.

4 Interest payable is on a bank overdraft, repayable within 5 years.

5 Tax on Profit on Ordinary Activities:

	£000
Corporation Tax at 50% on profits	38
Tax credits on dividends received	6
Transferred to deferred taxation	9
Overprovision in 19-5	(3)
	50

6 Factory closure expenses, and tax thereon, to be shown here – only net figure given in question.

7 Dividends:

	£000
Interim 5p per share	21
Final: proposed 10p per share	42
	63

8 Earnings per share.
EPS of 20p per share based on earnings of £84,000 and on average 420,000 shares on issue throughout the year.

(b)

Balance Sheet extracts as at 31 March 19-6

	£000	£000
Creditors: amounts falling due within one year		
Other creditors including taxation and social security (W1)		95
Provisions for liabilities and charges		
Taxation, including deferred taxation (W2)		15

Workings:

(W1)	£000	£000
Corporation tax for year to 31 March 19-6	38	
ACT paid on 14.10.19-5	3	35
Proposed dividend		42
ACT on proposed dividend		18
		95

(W2)		
Deferred tax as given		24
From profit and loss		9
		33
less ACT on proposed dividend		18
		15

		£000	£000
Retained profits brought forward from last year		160	
Prior year adjustment		15	145
	(7)		217
Dividends (21 + 42)			63
Retained profits carried forward to next year			154

Notes to the Accounts:

1 Turnover is net of VAT.

2 Operating profit is shown after charging the following:

	£000	£000
Depreciation: distribution costs	19	27
administrative expenses	8	20
Authors' remuneration		45
Directors' emoluments		
Hire of plant		12

3 Income from fixed asset investment is in respect of a listed company.

4 Interest payable is on a bank overdraft, repayable within 5 years.

5 Tax on Profit on Ordinary Activities:

	£000
Corporation Tax at 50% on profits	38
Tax credits on dividends received	6
Transferred to deferred taxation	9
Overprovision in 19-5	(3)
	50

6 Factory closure expenses, and tax thereon, to be shown here – only net figure given in question.

7 Dividends:

	£000
Interim 5p per share	21
Final: proposed 10p per share	42
	63

8 Earnings per share.

EPS of 20p per share based on earnings of £84,000 and on average 420,000 shares on issue throughout the year.

17.3 **Rufford plc**

(a) *Profit and Loss Account for the year ended 31 March 19-6*

	Notes	£000	£000
	(1)		
Turnover			642
Cost of Sales (60 + 401 – 71)			390
Gross Profit			252
Distribution Costs (33 + 19)		52	
Administrative Expenses (97 + 8)		105	157
Operating Profit	(2)		95
Income from other fixed asset investments	(3)	20	
Other interest receivable (14 × 100/70)		25	45
			140
Interest Payable	(4)		6
Profit on Ordinary Activities before Taxation			134
Tax on Profit on Ordinary Activities	(5)		50
Profit for the year on Ordinary Activities after Taxation			84
Extraordinary Items, less taxation	(6)		12
			72

(b)

Balance Sheet extracts as at 31 March 19-6

	£000	£000
Creditors: amounts falling due within one year		
Other creditors including taxation and social security (W1)		95
Provisions for liabilities and charges		
Taxation, including deferred taxation (W2)		15

Workings:

	£000	£000
(W1) Corporation tax for year to 31 March 19-6	38	
ACT paid on 14.10.19-5	3	35
Proposed dividend		42
ACT on proposed dividend		18
		95
(W2) Deferred tax as given	24	
From profit and loss	9	33
less ACT on proposed dividend		18
		15

Creditors: amounts falling due within one year

Debentures	6,000	
Bank Overdrafts	4,370	
Trade Creditors	12,410	
Bills of Exchange Payable	1,600	24,380
Net current assets		19,330
Total assets less current liabilities		118,400
Creditors: amounts falling due after one year		
Debentures	4,000	
Bills of Exchange Payable	2,000	6,000
		112,400
Capital and reserves		
Called-up Share Capital		75,000
Share Premium Account		20,000
Other Reserves:		
Capital Redemption Reserve	5,000	
General Reserve	4,000	9,000
Profit and loss account		8,400
		112,400

18.1 Owen Ltd

Balance Sheet as at 31 December 19-1

	£	£	£
Called-up Share Capital Net Paid			150
Fixed assets			
Intangible assets			
Development Costs		3,070	
Goodwill		21,000	24,070
Tangible assets			
Land and Buildings		32,000	
Plant and Machinery		7,100	39,100
Investments			
Shares in Related Companies		35,750	
			98,920
Current assets			
Stock			
Raw Materials and Consumables		3,470	
Finished Goods and Goods for Resale		18,590	22,060
Debtors			
Trade Debtors		17,400	
Amounts Owed by Related Companies		3,000	
Prepayments		1,250	21,650
			43,710

Notes:

(i) Called-up Share Capital consists of:

	£
50,000 £1 Ordinary Shares	50,000
50,000 Preference Shares of 50p each	25,000
	75,000

(ii) Land and Buildings:

	£	£
Cost		48,000
Depreciation to 31 December 19-0	12,000	
Depreciation for year to 31 December 19-1	4,000	16,000
		32,000

(iii) Plant and Machinery

	£	£
Cost		12,500
Depreciation to 31 December 19-0	3,600	
Depreciation for year to 31 December 19-1	1,800	5,400
		7,100

18.2

Belle Works plc
Balance Sheet as at 30 September 19-4

	£	£	£
Fixed assets			
Intangible assets			
Concessions, patents, licences, trade marks and similar rights and assets	1,500		
Goodwill	17,500	19,000	
Tangible Assets			
Land and Buildings	72,500		
Plant and Machinery	19,400	91,900	110,900
Current assets			
Stock			
Raw Materials and Consumables	14,320		
Work in Progress	5,640		
Finished Goods and Goods for Resale	13,290	33,250	
Debtors			
Trade Debtors	11,260		
Other Debtors	1,050		
Prepayments and Accrued Income	505	12,815	
		46,065	
Creditors: amounts falling due within one year			
Debenture Loans	6,000		
Bank Loans and Overdrafts	3,893		
Trade Creditors	11,340		
Bills of Exchange Payable	4,000		
Other creditors including taxation and Social Security	14,675	39,908	
Net current assets			6,157
Total assets less current liabilities			117,057
Creditors: amounts falling due after more than one year			
Debenture Loans	12,000		
Trade Creditors	1,260	13,260	
Provisions for liabilities and charges			
Pensions and Similar Obligations	1,860		
Taxation, including Deferred Taxation	640	2,500	
			15,760
			101,297

	£	£
Capital and reserves		
Called-up Share Capital		70,000
Share Premium Account		5,000
Revaluation reserve		10,500
Other reserves		
General reserve	6,000	
Foreign Exchange Reserve	3,500	9,500
Profit and loss account		6,297
		101,297

Notes appended to the accounts on the details of Tangible Assets and Depreciation, also exact details of items lumped under group descriptions.

18.3

Baganza plc
Profit and Loss Account for the year ended 30 September 19-7

	£000	£000
Turnover		19,500
Cost of Sales (W1)		14,700
Gross Profit		4,800
Distribution Costs	600	
Administrative Expenses (W2)	1,390	1,990
		2,810
Other Operating Income (W3)		341
Profit on Ordinary Activities before Taxation		3,151
Tax on Profit on Ordinary Activities (W4)		962
Profit on Ordinary Activities after Taxation		2,189
Extraordinary Item		1,500
Profit for the Financial Year		3,689
Retained Profits from last year		2,109
		5,798
Dividends (W5)		756
Retained Profits carried to next year		5,042
Earnings per share (W6)		182.4p

Workings: (in £000's)
(W1) Opening stock 2,300 + Purchases 16,000 – Closing stock 3600 = £14,700
(W2) Per trial balance 400 + Research 75 + Depreciation: Property (5% × 2,700)
135 + Plant (15% × 5,200) 780 = £1,390
(W3) Dividends received 249 + 27/73 of 249 = 341
(W4) Corporation tax 850 + tax credit 92 + deferred tax 40 – overpayment last
year 20 = 962

(W5) Dividends: Interim 36 + Final 720 = 756
(W6) EPS = Profit 2,189,00 ÷ shares 1,200,000 = 182.4p

Baganza plc
Balance Sheet as at 30 September 19-7

	£000	£000	£000
Fixed Assets			
Tangible Assets			
Land & Buildings	2,305		
Plant & Machinery	820		
		3,125	
Investments		2,000	
			5,125
Current Assets			
Stocks	3,600		
Debtors	2,700		
Cash at Bank	60		
		6,360	
Creditors: amounts falling due within one year			
Trade Creditors	2,900		
Corporation Tax (850 + 360 – 87)	1,123		
Order taxation and social security	266		
(ACT 27/73 × 720)			
Proposed dividend	720		
		5,009	
Net Current Assets			1,351
			6,476
Total Assets less Current Liabilities			
Taxation, including deferred taxation			234
(460 + 40 – 266)			6,242
Capital and Reserves			
Called up Share Capital			1,200
Profit and Loss Account			5,042
			6,242

19.1

X Limited
Balance sheet at 31 March 19-7

	£000	£000	£000
Fixed Assets			
Intangible assets			
Development costs	35		
Tangible assets			
Freehold properties	1,040		
Plant and machinery	850		
Vehicles	285		
	2,175		
			2,410
Investments			
Investments in listed shares	200		
Current Assets			
Stocks	500		
Debtors and prepayments (see workings)	654		
Cash at bank	439		
		1,593	
Creditors: amounts falling due within 1 year			
Trade creditors and accrual	878		
Other creditors (see workings)	640		
		1,518	
Net Current Assets			75
Total Assets less Current Liabilities			2,485
Creditors: amounts falling due after more than 1 year			
12% Debentures 1996			500
Provisions for liabilities and charges			
Deferred taxation			8
			1,977
Capital and Reserves			
Called-up share capital			1,000
Share premium			150
Revaluation reserve			612
Profit and loss account (see workings)			215
			1,977

Workings:

	£000	£000
Profit and Loss	386	
less Bad Debt (225,000 × 76%)	171	215
Debtors	825	
less Bad Debt (225,000 × 76%)	171	654
Other creditors: Proposed dividend	280	
Corporation Tax	360	640

Notes to the balance sheet

1 Research and Development

Research costs are written off immediately. Development costs are carried forward when there is a reasonable certainty of profitable outcome of the project and amortised over the useful life of the project.

2 Tangible Assets

	Freehold Property £000	Plant & Machinery £000	Vehicles £000
Cost on 1 April 19-6*	800	1,500	220
Disposal at cost	(320)		
Addition			200
Revaluation adjustment	612		
On 31 March 19-7	1,092	1,500	420
Depreciation at 1 April 19-6*	80	500	55
Depreciation on Disposals	(40)		
Provision in year	12	150	80
	52	650	135
Net Book Values	1,040	850	285

*Exam note only. Found by working backwards, leaving these figures as difference.

Note: Freehold Property was valued by Messrs V & Co. Chartered Surveyors at a market value of £1,040,000 as compared with net book value of £428,000. The valuation figure has been included in balance sheet, and £612,000 has been credited to a revaluation reserve. Depreciation for 19-7 has been based on the revalued figure.

3 Investments

These had a market value of £180,000 on 31 March 19-7, but as this is not considered by the directors to be a permanent fall in value, the cost figure has been retained.

4 Stock

	£000
Finished Goods	250
Raw Materials	200
Work-in-Progress	50
	500

The current replacement cost of goods is £342,000.

5 Deferred Taxation

Provision as at 1 April 19-6	78	
add Provision during year	50	128
less ACT recoverable		120
		8

6 Share Capital

1,000,000 ordinary shares of £1 each is the authorised capital, which has been fully issued and called up.

7 Reserves

	Profit & Loss Account	Share Premium	Revaluation Reserve
Balance at 1 April 19-6	?	150	—
Change during the year			612
	215	150	612

19.2

Billinge plc
Profit and Loss Account for the year to 30 June 19-6

	Notes	£000	£000	£000
Turnover				1,500
Cost of Sales (W1)				825
Gross Profit				675
Distribution Costs	(2)		55	
Administrative Expenses (W2)	(3)		320	375
Profit on Ordinary Activities before Taxation				300
Tax on Profit on Ordinary Activities	(3)			115
Profit on Ordinary Activities after Taxation				185
Extraordinary Charges (W4)	(4)			15
Profit for the Financial Year				170
Retained Profits from last year				40
				210
Dividends paid and proposed	(5)			90
Retained Profits carried to next year				120
Earnings per share	(6)			41p

Billinge plc
Balance Sheet as at 30 June 19-6

	Notes	£000	£000	£000
Fixed Assets				
Tangible Assets	(7)			
Fixtures & Fittings				187
Current Assets				
Stocks: Finished Goods & Goods for resale			100	
Debtors			500	
Cash at Bank			107	
			707	
Creditors: amounts falling due within one year				
Trade Creditors		64		
Other Creditors, Taxation and Social Security (W4)		70		
Advance Corporation Tax		39		
Proposed Dividend		90		
			263	

			£000
Net Current Assets			444
			631
Total Assets less Current Liabilities			
Provisions for liabilities and charges			
Taxation including deferred taxation	(8)		61
			570
Capital and Reserves			
Called-up Share Capital	(9)		450
Profit and Loss Account			120
			570

Workings:

(W1)			
Opening Stock	70		
Purchases	855	925	
less Closing Stock	100		
	825		

(W2)			
Depreciation		340	
less disposals		20	320
Additions			60
			380
$20\% \times 380$			76
Loss on disposals			20

(W3)			
C/T for year	85		
Deferred Taxation	40		
	125		
less previous overprovision	10	(15)	
	115	,, cash (3)	2
			78

(4)			
C/T for year	85	Administrative expenses	242
			340
less tax relief extraordinary	15		
	70		

Notes to the accounts:

1 Accounting policies
  (a) The financial statements have been drawn up using the historical cost convention.
  (b) Turnover consists of sales to external customers less VAT.
  (c) Stocks are valued at lower of cost or net realisable value.
  (d) Depreciation of fixed assets is based on cost, using the straight-line method over 5 years, salvage values being ignored.
  (e) Deferred taxation is at the anticipated rate, taking into account the differing periods and the probability that a liability will occur.
2 Administrative expenses include depreciation £78,000.

3 Taxation

	£000
Corporation Tax at 35% on profit for the period	85
Deferred taxation	40
	125
less adjustment re last year's corporation tax	10
	115

4 Extraordinary changes have arisen from the closure of a factory, costs being £30,000 less taxation relief of £15,000 = £15,000.

5 Proposed ordinary dividend of 20p per share — 90

6 EPS calculated by dividing profit after taxation (but before extraordinary charges) by number of ordinary shares on issue during the period.

7 Tangible fixed assets:

	£000	£000	£000
Fixtures etc at 1.7. 19-5		340	
Additions		60	
		400	
less Disposals		20	
		380	
Depreciation at 1.7. 19-5	132		
For the period	76		
	208		
less Disposals	15		
		193	
		187	

8

	£000	£000
Deferred taxation at 1.7. 19-5	60	
Profit and Loss charge	40	
	100	
ACT (3/7 × 90,000)	39	
		61
		450

9 Authorised, issued × fully paid ordinary £1 shares

19.6

Scampion plc
Profit and Loss Account for the year ended 31 May 19-7

	£000	£000
Turnover		3,232
(3,489 − VAT 259)		
Cost of Sales (1,929 + 330 + 51)		2,310
Gross Profit		922
Administrative Expenses (595 + 25 + 45)		665
Operating Profit		257
Income from shares in related companies	5	
Other interest receivable (note 2)	10	15
		272

	£000	£000
Interest payable (note 3)	18	
Written off investments/note	4	22
Profit on ordinary activities before taxation		250
Tax on profit on ordinary activities (note 4)		100
Profit on ordinary activities after taxation		150
Proposed ordinary dividend		66
Retained profits carried forward to next year		84

Scampion plc
Balance Sheet as at 31 May 19-7

	£000	£000
Fixed Assets		
Tangible Assets (note 5)		1,372
Investments (note 6)		60
		1,432
Current Assets		
Stock	230	
Debtors (67−45)	22	
Investments (market value £115,000)	103	
Cash at bank and in hand	84	
	439	
	553	
Creditors: amounts falling due within one year (note 7)		(114)
Net Current Liabilities		
Total Assets less Current Liabilities		1,318
Creditors: amounts falling due after more than one year (note 8)		50
		1,268
Capital and Reserves		
Called-up Share Capital		660
Share Premium Account		225
Profit and Loss Account (note 9)		383
		1,268

Notes:

1 Accounting policies

The historical cost convention has been used.

Provisions for depreciation are to write off the cost or valuation over the expected useful lives of the assets, by equal instalments, as follows:

Freehold buildings	40 years
Fixtures, fittings or equipment	10 years
Motor vehicles	5 years

Depreciation provisions have not been made on freehold land. The basis of the valuation of stock is the lower of cost or net realisable value.

2 Other interest receivable.
This is income from government securities £10,000.

3 Interest payable.

Interest on loans repayable within 1 year	12,000
Interest on loans repayable in more than 5 years' time	6,000
	£18,000

4 Taxation
(It has been assumed, that 'tax charge based on the accounts for the year' means that the profit shown of £250 is same as the taxable profits.)
Corporation Tax at the rate of 40 per cent on profits have been provided for.

5 Tangible Assets £000

	Valuation or Cost at 31/5/86	Additions at cost	less Disposals	Depreciation to 31/5/-6	31/5/-7	Net
Freehold Land and Buildings	1,562	50	400	29	5	1,178
Fittings, Fittings and Equipment	141	40		38	18	125
Motor Vehicles	117	20		40	28	69
	1,820	110	400	107	51	1,372

6 Investments

Valuation by directors of shares in related companies	64,000
less written off during the year	4,000
	60,000

7 Creditors

Trade creditors (487,000 – Tax 120,000)	367,000
Corporation Tax	100,000
Proposed dividend	66,000
Bank loan	20,000
	553,000

8 Creditors – amounts falling due after more than one year £50,000 12% Debentures repayable in X years' time.

9 Reserves

	Revaluation	Profit & Loss
Balance 31.5.19-6	150	149
Transfer to Profit and Loss	(150)	150
Retained profits for year to 31.5.-7		84
	–	383

20.1

J J Ltd
Statement of Source and Application of Funds
Year ended 31 December 19-5

Source of Funds		
Profit before tax		2,408
Add Depreciation		1,015
		3,423
Total generated from operations		
Application of Funds		
Purchase of fixed assets	2,520	
Dividend paid	500	
Taxation paid	856	
		3,876
		453
Decrease in working capital		
Decrease in stock	(116)	
Increase in debtors	105	
Decrease in creditors	218	
		207
Decrease in bank balances		(660)
		453

20.3

Albert Dejonge
Source and Application of Funds Statement
Year to 31 December 19-5

		£
Sources		
Net Profit (after uninsured fire loss)		22,000
add Depreciation		4,000
		26,000
Contribution from trading		
Long-term loan		5,000
		31,000
less Applications		
New Motor Vehicle	6,000	
Drawings	12,000	
		18,000
Net Increase in funds		13,000
Working Capital Change		
Increase in Stock (reduced by fire loss 6,000)		12,300
Increase in Debtors	3,000	
Owing from insurance	3,000	
		6,000
Reduction in Expenses owing		500
		18,800
Increase in Creditors	(1,500)	
Reduction in Expenses in Advance	(400)	
Reduction in Balance at Bank	(4,500)	
Increase in Cash	600	
Reduction in Net Liquid Funds		(3,900)
Increase in Net Liquid Funds		5,800
Increase in Working Capital Funds		13,000

20.5

Whitehead Ltd
Sources and Application of Funds Statement
Year ended 31 May 19-7

Sources of Funds

	£
Trading Profit for the Year (20,000 + Proposed Dividend 30,000 + Interim Dividend 10,000)	60,000
add Depreciation (15,000 + 5,000)	20,000
	80,000
Contribution from Trading	
Sale of Fixtures at net book value	2,000
	82,000

Application of Funds

	£	£
Purchase of Plant and Machinery		30,000
Purchase of Investments		8,000
Dividends Paid 19-6	20,000	
Interest 19-7	10,000	30,000
		68,000
Net Increase in Working Capital Funds		14,000

		£
Increase in Working Capital		
Increase in Stock		4,000
Increase in Bank Balance		20,000
Reduction in Creditors		4,000
		28,000
Reduction in Working Capital		
Reduction in Debtors		14,000
Net Increase in Working Capital		14,000

20.8

Forest plc
Statements of source and application of funds
for the three years to 31 October 19-5—7

	19-5 £000	19-6 £000	19-7 £000
Source of Funds			
Profit/(loss) before tax	(85)	(95)	(20)
Extraordinary items	150	(30)	(40)
	65	(125)	(60)
Adjustments for items not involving the movement of funds:			
Depreciation:	185	200	200
Total generated from operations	250	75	140
Funds from other sources			
Issue of debentures	–	250	–
	250	325	140
Application of Funds			
Dividends paid	(50)	(50)	–
Tax paid	(5)	–	–
Purchase of fixed assets	(95)	(90)	–
	(150)	(140)	–
	£100	£185	£140
Increase/Decrease in Working Capital			
Stocks	190	(210)	50
Debtors	(20)	315	225
Creditors	(20)	10	(165)
Movement in net liquid funds:			
Cash balances	(50)	70	30
	£100	£185	£140

20.10 (a)

Blackley Limited
Forecasted net cash position for the three months to 31 March 19-7

	31 Jan 19-7 £000	Month to 28 Feb 19-7 £000	31 Mar 19-7 £000
Receipts			
Trade debtors (Wkg 1)	235	290	345
Tangible fixed assets	12	–	–
Investments	10	–	–
Debentures	–	–	50
	257	290	395
Payments			
Trade creditors (Wkg 2)	150	230	285
Administration, selling and distribution expenses	37	40	42
Tangible fixed assets	–	240	–
Investments	–	–	5
Taxation	8	–	–
Dividend	15	–	–
	210	510	332
Forecasted net cash flow	47	(220)	63
add Opening cash	80	127	(93)
Forecasted closing cash	£127	£(93)	£(30)

Blackley Limited
(b) Forecasted source and application of funds statement for the three months to 31 March 19-7

	£'000	£'000
Source of funds		
Profit before tax (£10 + 24)		34
Adjustments for items not involving the movement of funds		
Depreciation (£3 + 20 +4)		27
Total generated from operations		61
Funds from other sources		
Issue of debentures for cash	50	
Sale of investments	10	
Sale of fixed assets	12	72
		133
Application of funds		
Dividends paid	(15)	
Tax paid	(8)	
Purchase of fixed assets	(240)	
Purchase of investments	(5)	(268)
		(135)
Increase/decrease in working capital		
Increase in stock (£55 – 40)	15	
Increase in trade debtors (£80 – 50)	30	
(Increase) in trade creditors (£150 – 80)	(70)	
Movement in net liquid funds:		
(Decrease) in cash balances (£80 + 30)	(110)	
		(135)

Workings

Trade debtors: forecasted cash receivable

	31 Jan 19-7 £000	28 Feb 19-7 £000	31 March 19-7 £000
Sales	250	300	350
less Closing trade debtors	65	75	80
	185	225	270
add Opening trade debtors	50	65	75
Forecasted cash receipts from trade debtors	£235	£290	£345

Trade creditors: forecasted cash payable

	31 Jan 19-7 £000	28 Feb 19-7 £000	31 March 19-7 £000
Opening stock	40	30	40
Purchases (by deduction)	190	250	295
	230	280	335
less Closing stock	30	40	55
Cost of sales	£200	£240	£280
Purchases (as above)	190	250	295
less Closing trade creditors	120	140	150
	70	110	145
add Opening trade creditors	80	120	140
Forecasted cash payments to trade creditors	£150	£230	£285

21.1

Consolidated Loan 4%

	Nominal	Income	Capital			Nominal	Income	Capital
19-6					19-6			
Jul 1 Bank	12,000	200	7,060	Aug 1 Bank		240	
19-7					19-7			
Jan 2 Adjustment for 1 month's interest on sale		10		Jan 2 Bank: Sale at 61 ex div	3,000		1,830
					" 2 Adjustment contra			10
Jun 30 Investment Income Account		420		Feb 1 Bank		240	
" 30 Profit & Loss: Profit on Sale			75	Jun 30 Balances c/f	9,000	150	5,295
	12,000	**630**	**7,135**		**12,000**	**630**	**7,135**

Abee Ltd: Ordinary Shares

	Nominal	Income	Capital			Nominal	Income	Capital
19-6								
Jul 12 Bank	2,000		4,000	Aug 15 Bank: Sale	2,500	225	2,500
Aug 15 Bonus Issue	3,000	–		Mar 1 Bank: Dividend		225	
Jun 30 Investment Income		225		Jun 30 Balances c/f	2,500		2,000
Jun 30 Profit on Sale to Profit & Loss			500				
	5,000	**225**	**4,500**		**5,000**	**225**	**4,500**

Ceedee Ltd: Ordinary Shares

	Nominal	Income	Capital			Nominal	Income	Capital
19-7								
Apl 1 Bank	5,000		3,875	Apl 1 Bank: Sale of Rights	2,500		625
Apl 1 Rights Issue	2,500	–	625	Jun 1 Bank: Dividend		625	
Jun 30 Investment income		625		Jun 30 Balance c/f	5,000		3,250
	7,500	**625**	**3,875**		**7,500**	**625**	**3,875**

21.2

Shares in Composite Interest Ltd

	Nominal	Income	Capital			Nominal	Income	Capital
19-5								
Apl 1 Balance b/f	6,000		7,200	Bank: Sale of Shares	1,000		1,965
Bonus Issue	3,000	–		Bank: Sale of Rights	1,890		210
Bank	1,800		1,890	Bank: Dividend		1,000	
Profit & Loss			765	Bank: Dividend 5%		490	
Investment Income		1,490		Balance at cost c/f	9,800		7,680
	10,800	**1,490**	**9,855**		**10,800**	**1,490**	**9,855**

22.1

Contract

Year 1			Year 1	
Plant	16,250		Work Certified	58,000
Materials	25,490		Plant c/d	10,250
Wages	28,384		Stock & Work in Progress c/d	12,200
Direct Expenses	2,126			
Gross Profit to Profit & Loss	8,200			
	80,450			**80,450**
Year 2			**Year 2**	
Plant b/d	10,250		Work Certified	116,000
Stock & Work in Progress b/d	12,200		Sale of Plant	4,100
Materials	45,432			
Wages	33,226			
Direct Expenses	2,902			
Penalty	700			
Gross Profit to Profit & Loss	15,390			
	120,100			**120,100**

Workings:

Computation Profit of Year 1

Contract Price		174,000
Less Actual Expenditure 25,490 + 28,384 + 2,126	56,000	
Estimated Cost of Plant (16,250 − 4,250)	12,000	
Estimated Expenses Year 2	81,400	149,400
Estimated total contract profit-estimate made at end of year 1		24,600

Using Formula given by question.

$$\frac{\text{WORK CERTIFIED}}{\text{TOTAL CONTRACT PRICE}} \times \text{TOTAL ESTIMATED PROFIT} = \text{PROFIT FOR YEAR 1}$$

$$= \frac{52,200 + 5,800}{174,000} \times 24,600 = 8,200$$

22.2

Stannard and Sykes Ltd
Pier Contract Account
Contract for Seafront Development Corporation
valued at £300,000

	£	£		£
Materials – direct	58,966		Materials on site carried	
– from store	10,180	69,146	down	11,660
Wages		41,260	Work in progress carried	
			down	151,167
Hire of Plant		21,030		
Direct Expenditure		3,065		
Overheads		8,330		
Wages accrued carried down		2,826		
		145,657		
Profit & Loss Account				
(proportion of profit to				
date).		17,170		
		£162,827		£162,827
Materials on site brought down		11,660	Wages accrued brought down	2,826
Work in progress brought down		151,167		

A suggested method for prudently estimating the amount of profit to be taken to November 30th is:

$$\frac{2}{3} \times \frac{\text{Cash received}}{\text{Value of work certified}} \times \text{Estimated profit (Value of work certified less cost of work certified).}$$

	£	£
Total expenditure to date		145,657
less Materials on site at November 30th,		
19-8	11,660	
	12,613	24,273
Cost of work not yet certified		
Cost of work certified (a)		121,384
Value of work certified (b)		150,000
Total Profit to date (b) − (a)		£28,616

23.1

(a) Board of Directors
Manvers Ltd
Report on Advantages of Value Added Statement
Such statements were recommended for use in the Corporate Report as published by the professional accountancy bodies in 1975.
The advantages can be listed as:

(1) It avoids using profit as the important factor. This is useful, as 'profit' is something misunderstood by many people.
(2) Clarity. As it is concerned with linking revenue to the inputs and services paid for, it gives a clear picture of the operation of the business.
(3) It illustrates interdependence between the various factors in a business.
(4) Value added can also be related to capital employed.

The Profit & Loss Account is legally necessary. The Value Added Statement may use the same information, but it is used to demonstrate different factors and sheds light on matters which might have escaped attention otherwise.
The Source & Application Funds Statement is quite different. It is concerned with all items of a capital nature, whereas value added deals with performance on a revenue basis.

(b)

Manvers Ltd

Profit & Loss Account for the year ended 31 May 19-6

Turnover (204,052 − 30,608)		173,444
less Expenses		
Materials & Services	146,928	
Depreciation	1,835	
Pension Scheme	2,810	
Salaries	16,468	
Profit Sharing Schemes	525	
Welfare & Staff Amenities	806	
Rates	325	
Bank Interest	250	
Loan Interest	1,600	171,547
Profits before Taxation		1,897
Corporation Tax		985
Profits after Taxation		912
Dividends		500
Retained Profits		412
(c) Profits before tax		1,897
add back non-cash item – depreciation		1,835
Operating Profits		3,732

25.1 *H & S Consolidated Balance Sheet*

Goodwill	10
Stock	140
Bank	50
	200
Share Capital	200
	200

25.2 *H & S Consolidated Balance Sheet*

Fixed Assets	3,800
Stock	1,500
Debtors	700
Bank	300
	6,300
Share Capital	6,000
Capital Reserve	300
	6,300

25.3 *H & S Consolidated Balance Sheet*

Fixed Assets	62,000
Stock	27,000
Debtors	8,000
Bank	3,000
	100,000
Share Capital	100,000
	100,000

25.6 *H & S Consolidated Balance Sheet*

Goodwill	300
Fixed Assets	2,000
Stock	1,300
Debtors	900
Bank	300
	4,800
Share Capital	4,000
Minority Interest	800
	4,800

25.7 *H & S Consolidated Balance Sheet*

Fixed Assets	3,325
Stock	3,000
Debtors	2,000
Bank	200
	8,525
Share Capital	8,000
Capital Reserve	375
Minority Interest	150
	8,525

25.10 *H & S Consolidated Balance Sheet*

Fixed Assets	12,600
Current Assets	5,900
	18,500
Share Capital	10,000
Profit & Loss	6,500
Capital Reserve*	600
Minority Interest	1,400
	18,500

*Goodwill S1 300, Capital Reserve 900 = Net Capital Reserve 600

25.11 *H & S Consolidated Balance Sheet*

Goodwill*	350
Fixed Assets	9,450
Current Assets	6,000
	15,800
Share Capital	10,000
Profit & Loss	2,000
General Reserve	1,400
Minority Interest	2,400
	15,800

*Goodwill (S1) 600, Capital Reserve (S2) 250 = Net Goodwill 350.

26.1   *H & S Consolidated Balance Sheet as at 31 December 19-6*

Goodwill		950
Fixed Assets		10,950
Current Assets		3,900
		15,800
Share Capital		10,000
Profit & Loss (H 4,000 + S 1,800)		5,800
		15,800

26.2   *H & S Consolidated Balance Sheet as at 31 December 19-9*

Fixed Assets	47,400
Current Assets	27,100
	74,500
Share Capital	50,000
Profit & Loss (H 14,000 – S 400)	13,600
General Reserve	5,000
Capital Reserve	1,790
Minority Interest	4,110
	74,500

26.4   *H & S Consolidated Balance Sheet as at 31 December 19-5*

Goodwill	1,390
Fixed Assets	36,900
Current Assets	20,900
	59,190
Share Capital	40,000
Profit & Loss	8,270
General Reserve	5,000
Minority Interest	5,920
	59,190

Minority Interest 60% of 10,000 + 2,800 + 2,000 = 5,920
Goodwill S1 Cost 8,150–60% of 10,000 + 1,100 + 2,000 = 290, S2 Cost 11,400 –
(8,000 + 500 + 1,800) = 1,100
Profit & Loss H 7,550 + S11,020 – S2 300 = 8,270.

27.1   *H & S Consolidated Balance Sheet as at 31 December 19-9*

Goodwill		850
Fixed Assets		2,300
Current Assets		
Stock (1,200 + 900 – 90)	2,010	
Debtors (2,100 + 1,400 – 220)	3,280	
Bank	500	
	5,790	
less Current Liabilities		
Creditors (900 + 700 – 220)	1,380	
Net Current Assets		4,410
		7,560
Financed by		
Share Capital		2,000
Profit & Loss		4,760
(H 3,700 – 90 + S 1,150)		
General Reserve		800
		7,560

27.2   *H & S Consolidated Balance Sheet as at 31 December 19-4*

Goodwill		1,600
Fixed Assets		14,200
Current Assets		
Stock (3,100 + 7,200 – 50)	10,250	
Debtors (4,900 – 600 + 3,800)	8,100	
Bank	2,500	
	20,850	
less Current Liabilities		
Creditors (3,800 + 2,100 – 600)	5,300	
Net Current Assets		15,550
		31,350
Financed by:		
Share Capital		20,000
Profit & Loss (H 4,000 – 50 + S 60% of 2,000)		5,150
Minority Interest (40% of 10,000 + 5,500)		6,200
		31,350

27.3 *H, S1 and S2 Consolidated Balance Sheet as at 31 December 19-8*

Fixed Assets		65,000
Current Assets		
Stock (£46,000 – £640)	45,360	
Debtors (£28,000 – £1,400)	26,600	
Bank	9,000	
	80,960	
less Current Liabilities		
Creditors (21,000 – 1,400)	19,600	
Net Current Assets		61,360
		126,360
Financed by:		
Share Capital		100,000
Profit and Loss Account:		
(£23,000 – £400 – £240 – S1 £5,000 + S2 5/6ths of £1,800)		18,860
General Reserve		2,000
Minority Interest (1/6th of £30,000 + £3,000)		5,500
		126,360

S1 Capital Reserve: Cost £39,000 – £30,000 – £8,000 – £4,000 = £3,000.
S2 Goodwill: Cost £29,000 – 5/6ths of £30,000 + £1,200 = £2,800.
Net Goodwill = £3,000 – £3,000 = NIL.

28.1

Shares bought 31.12.19-4	10,000	
Proportion Profit & Loss at 31.12.19-4 (25% of 24,000)	6,000	
		16,000
Shares bought 31.12.19-6	14,000	
Proportion Profit & Loss at 31.12.19-6 (35% of 30,000)	10,500	
		24,500
		40,500
Paid 31.12.19-4	23,500	
Paid 31.12.19-6	31,000	
		54,500

Goodwill therefore 54,500 – 40,500 = 14,000

28.3

Shares bought	36,000	
Profit & Loss balance 31.12.19-7	28,000	
	64,000	
add proportion 19-8 profits before acquisition 8/12 × 42,000		50,000

Proportion of pre-acquisition profit

$$\frac{50,000}{80,000} \times 64,000 = 40,000$$

	90,000

Paid for shares 158,000
Therefore goodwill is 158,000 – 90,000 = 68,000.

29.1 *H & S Consolidated Balance Sheet as at 31 December 19-7*

Goodwill		1,000
Fixed Assets		57,000
Current Assets		15,000
		73,000
Share Capital		50,000
Profit & Loss Account (H 19,000 + S 4,000)		23,000
		73,000

Workings: Goodwill: Cost 29,000 – 20,000 – 3,000 – Dividend 5,000 = 1,000.

29.3 *H & S Consolidated Balance Sheet as at 31 December 19-9*

Goodwill		14,000
Fixed Assets		80,000
Current Assets	33,000	
Less Current Liabilities		
Proposed Dividend	1,500	
Net Current Assets		31,500
		125,500
Share Capital		80,000
Profit & Loss Account: (H 23,000 + S ¾ of 6,000 + ¾ of 7,000)		32,750
Minority Interest (¼ of 40,000 + 11,000)		12,750
		125,500

Workings: Goodwill: (Cost 47,000 – ¾ of 40,000 + 4,000) 14,000.

29.5 *Consolidated Balance Sheet of H Ltd & S Ltd as at 31 December 19-6*

Fixed Assets		
Intangible Assets		
Goodwill (see Workings)		55,000
Tangible Assets (note 1)		680,000
Current Assets		
Stocks	160,000	
Debtors	140,000	
Bank	40,000	
	340,000	
Creditors: amounts falling due within one year		
Trade Creditors	212,000	
Preference Dividend proposed	8,000	
	220,000	
Net Current Assets		120,000
Total assets less current liabilities		855,000

Capital and Reserves
Called-up Share Capital: Ordinary Shares

	Cost	Depreciation to date	Net
£1 fully paid			500,000
Reserves			185,000
Minority Interest			170,000
			855,000

Note 1 Tangible Fixed Assets

	Cost	Depreciation to date	Net
Buildings	420,000	110,000	310,000
Plant & Machinery	320,000	70,000	250,000
Motor Vehicles	210,000	90,000	120,000
	950,000	270,000	680,000

Workings
(i) Goodwill

Cost of investment		250,000
less ordinary shares (75%)	150,000	
reserves (75%)	37,500	187,500
		62,500
less dividend from pre-acquisition profits		7,500
		55,000

(ii) Minority Interest

Preference Shares	100,000
Reserves 25% × 80,000	20,000
Ordinary Shares 25%	50,000
	170,000

The proposed preference dividend could be shown as part of the minority interest.

(iii) Reserves

H Limited		170,000
S Ltd 75% of extra reserves since acquisition 80,000 − 50,000 = 30,000		22,500
		192,500
less dividends received by H Ltd which were from pre-acquisition profits		7,500
		185,000

29.6 Workings:
Cost of Control (Remember to calculate it as on 1/1/-6) £000

Cost of investment		300
less Nominal Value shares bought 80%	120	
Reserves 80% × 90	72	192
		108

Minority Interest

20% of Reserves at 1.1.-6 × 90	18	
20% of 19-6 retained profit × 18	3.6	
20% of shares × 150	30	51.6

Stock

X	80		
Y	70		153
In transit	3		
less Profit element in Y's stock	2		
goods in transit	0.4	24	24
			150.6

Bank

X 10 + Y 12 + in transit 2	24

Reconciliation of current accounts

	X		Y
Bal b/d			19
Bal c/d		19	
In transit		2	
Bank (1)		3	
Stock (2)		19	
		19	19
Bal b/d		14	

Reserves

X		
19-6 Retained profits	220	
Proposed dividend Y 80%	20	
80% Y profits for 19-6 × 18	8	
	14.4	
	262.4	
− Cost of Control (above) written off	108	
− Profit in goods in transit	0.4	
− Profit in Y's stock	2	110.4
		152

600

Consolidated Balance Sheet for X plc & subsidiary Y plc as at 31 December 19-6

	£000 Cost	£000 Depreciation to date	£000 Net
Tangible Fixed Assets			
Freehold Property	280	18	262
Plant and Machinery	245	52	193
	525	70	455
Current Assets			
Stock (see workings)		150.6	
Debtors		250	
Bank		24	
		424.6	
less Current Liabilities			
Trade Creditors (130 + 80 + 2)		212	
Taxation		44	
Proposed Dividends		20	
		276	148.6
			603.6
Called-up Share Capital			
400,000 ordinary shares £1			400
Reserves (see workings)			152
			552
Minority Interest (see workings)			51.6
			603.6

30.1 *H & S Consolidated Balance Sheet as at 31 December 19-8*

Goodwill		100,000
Fixed Assets	500,000	
– Depreciation	138,000	362,000
Current Assets		205,000
		667,000
Share Capital		500,000
Profit and Loss Account:		
(H 143,000 – 10,000 + S 32,000 + 2,000)		167,000
		667,000

30.3 *H & S Consolidated Balance Sheet as at 31 December 19-7*

Goodwill		19,000
Fixed Assets	185,000	
Less Depreciation	33,500	151,500
Current Assets		68,000
		238,500
Share Capital		150,000
Profit & Loss (H 77,000 + S 14,000 – 2,500)		88,500
		238,500

31.1 *H & S1, & S2 Consolidated Balance Sheet as at 31 December 19-7*

Goodwill		9,320
Fixed Assets		127,000
Current Assets		33,000
		169,320
Share Capital		100,000
Profit & Loss Account:		
(H 37,000 + S1 90% of 16,000 + S2 63% of 3,000)		53,290
General Reserve		10,000
Minority Interest		6,030
		169,320

Minority interest:			
Shares in S1	1,000		
Shares in S2 37% of 5,000	1,850	2,850	
Profit & Loss S1 10% of 23,000	2,300		
S2 37% of 4,000	1,480	3,780	
		6,630	
Less Cost of Shares in S2 for minority interest of S1 10% of 6,000		600	
		6,030	
Goodwill: Cost of shares to group in S1		23,000	
in S2 90% of 6,000		5,400	
		28,400	
Less Shares: In S1		9,000	
In S2 63% of 5,000		3,150	
Profit & Loss S1 90% of 7,000		6,300	
S2 63% of 1,000		630	19,080
			9,320

601

31.6

Sales Ltd & subsidiaries
Balance sheet as at 31 October 19-5

Fixed assets	Cost	Depreciation	Net
Buildings	184,000	–	184,000
Plant (W1)	260,000	92,400	167,600
	362,900	203,700	159,200
	806,900	296,100	510,800

Current Assets
Stock (W2)	247,400
Debtors (W3)	275,200
Bank	50,600
	573,200

Less Current Liabilities
Creditors (W4)	297,400	
Bank Overdraft (W5)	26,100	
Corporation Tax	129,100	
Proposed Dividends	80,000	
Proposed Dividends Relating to Minority Interests (W6)	16,000	548,600
Net Current Assets		24,600
		535,400

Ordinary Share Capital	200,000
Revenue Reserves (W7)	189,390
Capital Reserve (W8)	9,000
	398,390
Minority Interest (W9)	137,010
	535,400

Workings: *Note* S Lt owns 75% of M Lt & 75% × 80% = 60% of C Ltd

(W1) *less* (note g) intercompany profit

Plant 102,900 + 170,000 + 92,000 =	364,900
	2,000
	362,900
Depreciation 69,900 + 86,000 + 48,200 =	204,100
less 2 years on intercompany profit element 10 % × 2,000 × 2 =	400
	203,700

(W2)
Stock 108,500 + 75,500 + 68,400	252,400
– Unrealised profit (note f) 20% × 25,000	5,000
	247,400

(W3) Debtors 196,700 + 124,800 – 83,500 405,000

– Interindebtedness (note h)		56,900	
– Dividends: 80% of (note h)	10,000	28,900	
,, 75% of	48,000	36,000	
			129,800
			275,200

(W4)
Creditors 160,000 + 152,700 + 59,200		371,900
– Interindebtedness (note h)	28,900	
	45,600	74,500
		297,400

(W5)
Overdraft	37,400
– cheque in transit (note i)	11,300
	26,100

(W6) Minority Interests: Shares of Proposed Dividends
Components Ltd: Ordinary 20% × 10,000	2,000
Preference	2,000
Machinery Ltd: Ordinary 25% × 48,000	12,000
	16,000

(W7)
Reserves S Ltd	154,000	
M Ltd	85,000	
C Ltd	74,000	
		313,000
add Reduction in Depreciation of Components 2,000 × 10% × 2 yrs = 400 × 60% ownership of Components		240
		313,240

less Profit of Machinery		2,000
Unrealised profit on stock		5,000
Cost of Control of C Ltd on 1/4/83 60% × 60,000		36,000
Minority Interest in C Ltd 40% × 74,000		29,600
Cost of Control of M Ltd on 1/4/83 75% × 40,000		30,000
Minority Interest in M Ltd 25% × 85,000		21,250
		123,850
		189,390

Brodick plc & subsidiaries

32.1

Consolidated Profit & Loss Account for the year ended 30 April 19-7

	£000	£000
Turnover (1,100 + 500 + 130)		1,730
Cost of Sales (630 + 300 + 70)		1,000
Gross Profit		730
Administrative Expenses (105 + 150 + 20)		275
Profit on Ordinary Activities before Taxation		455
Tax on Profit and Ordinary Activities (65 + 10 + 20)		95
Profit on Ordinary Activities after Taxation		360
Minority Interests (20% × 40 + 40% × 20)		16
Profit for the Financial Year		344
Retained Profits from last year (W1)		506
		850
Dividends Paid & Proposed		200
Retained Profits carried to next year (note 1)		650

Note (1)

Retained Profits carried to next year comprise		
Brodick plc (see W1)		590
Subsidiaries (see W1)		60
		650

Workings

(W1)	Retained profits b/f			
	Brodick			460
	Lamlash	106		
	less Minority (20%)	(21.2)		
	less Pre-acquisition (80% × 56)	(44.8)	40	
			30	
	Corrie	24		
	less Minority (40%)	12		
	less Pre-acquisition (60% × 20)	12	6	
				506
	Retained profits for year (344 − 200)			144
				650

(W8) Cost of Control

C Ltd at date of purchase. Capital:	Ordinary Shares	100,000	
	Reserves	60,000	160,000

M Ltd had owned 80% =	128,000	
Then had paid	96,000	32,000

Bringing about a Capital Reserve of this 25% is owned by Minority Interest of M Ltd 8,000

M Ltd at date of purchase. Capital	120,000	
Reserve	40,000	160,000

S Ltd owns 75%	120,000	
S Ltd paid	135,000	15,000
Cost of Control		
Net figure for Capital Reserve		9,000

(W9) Minority Interest

Ordinary Shares: 25% M Ltd	30,000
40% C Ltd	40,000
	40,000

Preference Shares		
Increase in Profit because of		
Depreciation change 40% × 400	160	
25% Revenue Reserves M Ltd × 85,000	21,250	
40% " " C " × 74,000	29,600	
		161,010

less 25% payment made by M Ltd for investment in C Ltd × 96,000	24,000
	137,010

603

32.2

Norbreck plc & its subsidiary Bispham Ltd
Consolidated Profit & Loss Account for the year ended 30 September 19-7

	£000	£000
Turnover		2,150
Cost of Sales		995
Gross Profit		1,155
Administrative Expenses		475
Profit on Ordinary Activities before Taxation		680
Tax on Profit on Ordinary Activities		50
Profit on Ordinary Activities after Taxation		630
Minority Interest (20% × 180)		36
Profit for the Financial Year		594
Retained Profits from last year		196
		790
Dividends		360
Retained Profits carried to next year		430
Earnings per share (594/900)		66p

Norbreck plc & its subsidiary Bispham Ltd
Consolidated Balance Sheet as at 30 September 19-7

	£000	£000	£000
Fixed Assets			
Tangible Assets			1,720
Current Assets			
Stocks	550		
Debtors (280 + 150 – 80 dividend)	350		
Cash and Bank	50		
		950	
Creditors: Amounts Falling Due Within One Year			
Trade Creditors	240		
Other Creditors, Taxation & Social Security	230		
Proposed Dividends (270 + 20% × 100)	290		
		760	
Net Current Assets			190
Total Assets less Current Liabilities			1,910
Provisions for Liabilities and Charges			
Taxation, including deferred taxation			480
			1,430

	£000	£000
Capital and Reserves		
Called-up Share Capital		900
Profit & Loss Account		430
		1,330
Minority Interest (20% × £500)		100
		1,430

Workings	£000	£000	£000
Goodwill			
Investment			400
Nominal Value of Shares (80% x 400)		320	
Profit & Loss (80% x 40)		32	
			352
Goodwill on acquisition			48
Retained profits			
b/fwd Norbreck			220
Bispham	70		
– Pre-acquisition	40		
		30	
– Minority Interest (20%)		6	
		24	
		244	
– Goodwill on Acquisition (see above)		48	
		196	
Retained Profits of Group b/fwd		196	
For the year (per Consolidated P/L 594 – 360)		234	
C/fwd		430	

33.1 *(a)* **Large Ltd & its subsidiary Small Ltd**
Consolidated Profit & Loss Account for the year ended 30 September 19-6

	£000
Turnover (10,830 + 2,000 × 108)	12,722
Cost of Sales & Production (3,570 + 1,100 – (108 × ⅔))	4,598
	8,124
Administrative & Marketing Expenses	2,772
Unpurchased Goodwill written off (per Companies Act 1985)	50
Research Costs written off (see SSAP 13)	50
	2,872
Profit on Ordinary Activities before Taxation	5,252
Tax on Profit on Ordinary Activities	2,504
Profit on Ordinary Activities after Taxation	2,748
Minority Interests	121
	2,627

Retained Profits from last year 1,290

                                               3,917

Dividend 2,400

Retained Profits carried to next year 1,517

(c) In this case merger accounting is not permitted. It can only be used when 90% of the consideration is given as equity share capital, and here Large obtained 75% for cash.

If merger treatment had been used the profits made before the merger could be distributed as dividends.

(b) Large Ltd & its subsidiary Small Ltd

Consolidated Balance Sheet as at 30 September 19-6

	£000	£000	£000
Fixed Assets			
Intangible Assets			
Development Costs	180		
Goodwill	48		228
Tangible Assets			
At cost less depreciation			4,648
			4,876
Current Assets			
Stock (594 + 231 − 27)		798	
Debtors		2,620	
Bank		123	3,541
Creditors: Amounts falling due within one year			
Trade Creditors		453	
Net Current Assets			3,088
			7,964
Capital and Reserves			
Called-up Share Capital			6,000
Capital Reserve (W1)			129
Profit & Loss Account			1,517
Minority Interest (W2)			7,964
			7,964

Note: Minority Interest = 318

Workings

(W1) Investment in small cost 525

    less Share Capital 600

        75% Retained Earnings × 72 ... 54 654

    Capital Reserve on Acquisition 129

(W2) Share Capital 200

    25% Retained Earnings × 472 118

                                    318

35.1

	Jan	Feb	Mar	Apl	May	Jun
Opening Stock	740	690	780	1,100	1,400	1,160
add Production	750	1,010	1,410	1,620	1,240	800
	1,490	1,700	2,190	2,720	2,640	1,960
less Sales	800	920	1,090	1,320	1,480	1,020
Closing stock	690	780	1,100	1,400	1,160	940

140

35.2 (a)

Opening stock	?	
add Production	(C)	
	(B)	
less Sales total – see question		1,550
Closing Stock		150

Missing figure (B) must be 1,700

Missing figure (C) must then be 1,560

Equal production per month 1,560 ÷ 12 = 130 units.

Given figures per (*a*)

(b)

	(J)	(F)	(M)	(A)	(M)	(J)	(J)	(A)	(S)	(O)	(N)	(D)
Opening Stock	140	160	110	70	50	60	90	150	250	210	230	210
add production	130	130	130	130	130	130	130	130	130	130	130	130
	270	290	240	200	180	190	220	280	380	340	360	340
less Sales	110	180	170	150	120	100	70	30	170	110	150	190
Closing Stock	160	110	70	50	60	90	150	250	210	230	210	150

Lowest closing figure is April 50 units.

If stock is not to fall below 80 units an extra 80 − 50 = 30 units will have to be produced in January making production for that month of 160 units.

35.4 (i) *B Ukridge: Cash Budget*

	May	June	July	Aug	Sept	Oct
Balance b/fwd		5,305	4,305	1,305		
Overdraft b/fwd					6,695	9,695
Receipts from debtors	400	4,000	8,000	12,000	9,000	5,000
Capital	5,005					
	5,405	9,305	12,305	13,305	2,305	(4,695)
Payments	100	5,000	11,000	20,000	12,000	7,000
Balance c/fwd	5,305	4,305	1,305			
Overdraft c/fwd				6,695	9,695	11,695

(ii) There are the possibilities of delaying payments to creditors, delaying purchases or somehow of getting debtors to pay up more quickly. Apart from these it is possible that a credit factoring firm could help in 'buying' the amounts of debtors from Ukridge..

If none of these are possible only a really fantastic product could warrant interest at 100 per cent per annum. This could be the case, although there are many people whose optimism about their products exceeds the true profitability.

35.5

N Morris: Cash Budget

	Jul	Aug	Sept	Oct	Nov	Dec
Balance b/fwd	1,200		250			
Overdraft b/fwd		260		160	540	420
Receipts	4,000	6,400	5,800	8,000	6,000	9,500*
	5,200	6,140	6,050	7,840	5,460	9,080
Payments (see schedule)	5,460	5,890	6,210	8,380	5,880	5,410
Balance c/fwd		250				3,670
Overdraft c/fwd	260		160	540	420	

*Includes £2,500 legacy

Payments Schedule

Jul
Raw Materials 320 (Jul) × £4	1,280
300 (Jun) × £1	300
Direct Labour 320 × £8	2,560
Variable 300 × £1 + 320 × £1	620
Fixed Expenses	400
Drawings	300
	5,460

Aug
Raw Materials 350 (Aug) × £4	1,400
320 (Jul) × £1	320
Direct Labour 350 × £8	2,800
Variable 350 × £1 + 320 × £1	670
Fixed Expenses	400
Drawings	300
	5,890

Sept
Raw Materials 370 (Sep) × £4	1,480
350 (Aug) × £1	350
Direct Labour 370 × £8	2,960
Variable 370 × £1 + 350 × £1	720
Fixed Expenses	400
Drawings	300
	6,210

Oct
Raw Materials 380 (Oct) × £4	1,520
370 (Sep) × £1	370
Direct Labour 380 × £8	3,040
Variable 380 × £1 + 370 × £1	750
Fixed Expenses	400
Drawings	300
Machinery	2,000
	8,380

Nov
Raw Materials 340 (Nov) × £4	1,360
380 (Oct) × £1	380
Direct Labour 340 × £8	2,720
Variable 340 × £1 + 380 × £1	720
Fixed Expenses	400
Drawings	300
	5,880

Dec
Raw Materials 310 (Dec) × £4	1,240
340 (Nov) × £1	340
Direct Labour 310 × £8	2,480
Variable 310 × £1 + 340 × £1	650
Fixed Expenses	400
Drawings	300
	5,410

35.6 (a) **Stock Budget 19-7**

	Aug	Sept	Oct	Nov	
Opening Stock	5,000*	7,000	8,000	7,000	(A)
add Purchases	20,000	23,500	21,500	31,000	(B)
	25,000	30,500	29,500	38,000	(C)
less Cost of Sales	18,000	22,500	22,500	27,000	(D)
Closing Stock	7,000	8,000	7,000	11,000	(E)

*After special sale of £8,000 goods at cost.

To work out missing figures:

August (A) is known. (C) is 24,000 − 25% = 3

(D) 18,000

As stockturn is 3 therefore $\left(\dfrac{(A)\ 5,000 + (E)\ ?}{} \right) \div 2 = 3$

Therefore bottom line is 6,000 so (E) must be 7,000.

Repeat following months.

(b) **Cash Budget 19-7**

	Aug	Sept	Oct	Nov
Receipts:				
Capital	10,000			
Soul's Debtors	20,250			
Debtors	–		24,000	30,000
Special Sale	8,000	–	–	
	38,250		24,000	30,000
Payments:				
Creditors	10,000	20,000	23,500	21,500
General Expenses	700	700	700	700
	10,700	20,700	24,200	22,200
Bank: Opening	(20,000)	7,550	(13,150)	(13,350)
Closing	7,550	(13,150)	(13,350)	(5,550)

35.9

Cash Budget

	Jan	Feb	Mar	Apl	May	June
Opening Balance	25,000	+890				
Opening Overdraft			–370	–600	–740	–600
Received (see schedule)	400	600	1,750	2,200	2,900	3,550
	25,400	1,490	1,380	1,600	2,160	2,950
Payments (see schedule)	24,510	1,860	1,980	2,340	2,760	3,460
Closing Balance	+890					
Closing Overdraft		–370	–600	–740	–600	–510

Cash Receipts Schedule

	Jan	Feb	Mar	Apl	May	June
Cash Sales	400	600	800	1,000	1,300	1,400
Credit Sales	-	-	800	1,200	1,600	2,000
Rent received			150			150
	400	600	1,750	2,200	2,900	3,550

Cash Payments Schedule

	Jan	Feb	Mar	Apl	May	June
Drawings	250	250	250	250	250	250
Premises	20,000					
Shop Fixtures	3,000					
Motor Van	1,000					
Salaries of Assistants	260	260	260	260	260	260
Payments to Creditors		1,200	1,320	1,680	2,100	2,800
Other Expenses		150	150	150	150	150
	24,510	1,860	1,980	2,340	2,760	3,460

Current Assets		
Stock-in-Trade		910
Debtors		5,400
		6,310
less Current Liabilities		
Creditors	2,310	
Other Expenses Owing	150	
Bank Overdraft	510	
		2,970
Working Capital		3,340
		27,090

Financed by:		
Capital		25,000
Cash Introduced		3,590
Add Net Profit		28,590
		1,500
less Drawings		27,090

D Smith

Forecast Trading and Profit and Loss Accounts for the 6 months ended 30 June 19-4

Sales		16,500
less Cost of Goods Sold:		
Purchases	11,410	
Less Closing Stock (130 × £7)	910	
		10,500
Gross Profit		6,000
Add Rent Received		300
		6,300
less Expenses:		
Assistants Salaries	1,560	
Other Expenses	900	
Depreciation: Shop Fixtures	150	
Motor Van	100	
		2,710
Net Profit		3,590

Balance Sheet as at 30 June 19-4

	Cost	Depn	Net
Fixed Assets			
Premises	20,000	-	20,000
Shop Fixtures	3,000	150	2,850
Motor Van	1,000	100	900
	24,000	250	23,750

35.11 Cash Payments Schedule

	Jul	Aug	Sept	Oct	Nov	Dec
Direct Materials	240	140	160	220	200	160
Direct Labour	450	450	450	450	450	450
Variable Overhead	210	270	270	270	270	270
Fixed Overhead	90	90	90	90	90	90
Machine	500					
Motor Vehicle			2,000			
	1,490	950	2,970	1,030	1,010	970

Cash Receipts Schedule

	Jul	Aug	Sept	Oct	Nov	Dec
Debenture					5,000	
Receipts from Debtors	990	900	1,080	1,440	1,800	1,850
	990	900	1,080	1,440	6,800	1,850

(a) Cash Budget (in £'s)

	Jul	Aug	Sept	Oct	Nov	Dec
Opening Balance	7,100	6,600	6,550	4,660	5,070	10,860
add Receipts	990	900	1,080	1,440	6,800	1,850
	8,090	7,500	7,630	6,100	11,870	12,710
less Payments	1,490	950	2,970	1,030	1,010	970
	6,600	6,550	4,660	5,070	10,860	11,740

(b) Debtors Budget (in £'s)

	Jul	Aug	Sept	Oct	Nov	Dec
Opening Balance	1,890	1,980	2,520	3,240	3,650	3,515
add Sales	1,080	1,440	1,800	1,850	1,665	1,295
	2,970	3,420	4,320	5,090	5,315	4,810
less Receipts	990	900	1,080	1,440	1,800	1,850
Closing Balance	1,980	2,520	3,240	3,650	3,515	2,960

(c) Creditors Budget (in £'s)

	Jul	Aug	Sept	Oct	Nov	Dec
Opening Balance	540	520	580	580	500	440
add Purchases	220	200	160	140	140	180
	760	720	740	720	640	620
less Payments	240	140	160	220	200	160
Closing Balance	520	580	580	500	440	460

(d) Raw Materials Budget (in £'s)

	Jul	Aug	Sept	Oct	Nov	Dec
Opening Stock	300	340	360	340	300	260
add Purchases	220	200	160	140	140	180
	520	540	520	480	440	440
less used in production	180	180	180	180	180	180
Closing Stock	340	360	340	300	260	260

(e) Gregg Ltd: Forecast Operating Statement for the six months ended 31 December 19-6

Sales		9,130
less Cost of Goods Sold		
Operating Stock Finished Goods	1,800	
add Cost of Goods Completed (£10 × 540)	5,400	
	7,200	
less Closing Stock Finished Goods (220 × £10)	2,200	
		5,000
Gross Profit		4,130
less Expenses:		
Fixed Overhead		540
Depreciation: Machinery	700	
Motor Vehicles	600	
Office Fixtures	30	1,330
		1,870
Net Profit		2,260

(f) Forecast Balance Sheet as at 31 December 19-6

	Cost	Depreciation to date	Net
Fixed Assets:			
Tangible Assets			
Land and Buildings	40,000	–	40,000
Plant and Machinery	10,500	6,700	3,800
Motor Vehicles	8,000	3,400	4,600
Office Fixtures	500	250	250
	59,000	10,350	48,650
Current Assets:			
Stocks Finished Goods		2,200	
Raw Materials		260	
Debtors		2,960	
Cash and Bank		11,740	
		17,160	
Creditors: amounts falling due within 1 year			
Creditors for Raw Materials	460		
Creditors for Variable Overhead	270	730	
Net Current Assets			16,430
Total Assets less Current Liabilities			65,080
Creditors: amounts falling due after more than 1 year			
Debentures			5,000
			60,080
Capital and Reserves			
Called-up Share Capital			50,000
Profit & Loss Account (7,820 + 2,260)			10,080
			60,080

36.1 (a) $5,300 \times 0.17 \times \dfrac{62}{365}$ = £153.05

(b) $9,000 \times 0.19 \times \dfrac{70}{365}$ = £327.95

The Bank will pay £9,000 − 327.95 = £8,672.05.

36.3 The amount borrowed is:

£1,000 × ¼ =	250.0
750 × ¼ =	187.5
500 × ¼ =	125.0
250 × ¼ =	62.5
Equivalent loan for 1 year	625.0

$$r = \frac{200}{625 \times 1} = 0.32 \text{ or } 32\%$$

36.4 £4,000 will accumulate to $4,000 (1 + .1)^{10} = £10,375$.
Interest is therefore £10,375 − 4,000 = £6,375.
(Using the tables 4,000 × 2.594 = £10,376 – note slight rounding errors.)

36.7 The present value of an annuity of £5,000 p.a. for seven years at 12% = 5,000 × 4.564 = **£ 22,820**

$$R = \frac{Ar}{(1+r)^n - 1}$$

or

$$\left[\frac{1 - \dfrac{1}{(1 + 0.12)^7}}{0.12} \right] \times 5,000 \;=\; £\,22,820$$

The offer of £20,000 would therefore appear less attractive than retaining the rental income.

36.9

$$R = \frac{Ar}{(1 + r)^n - 1} = \frac{100,000 (0.10)}{(1 + 0.10)^5 - 1}$$

= £16,380 per annum.

36.11

	Year 19-1	Year 19-2
Purchase of machine	50,000	—
Sale of old machine	—	(8,000)
Installation Cost	10,000	
Commissioning Cost	15,000	8,000
Rent of premises to date of completion	5,000 (9 months)	3,750
Training Labour		
Working Capital	10,000	2,000
Net Cash Outlay	90,000	5,750

36.12

		£	
	Capital Cost 19-1	90,000	
19-1	25% writing down	22,500	@ 50% tax 11,250 Rc'd 19-2
	Balance c/d	67,500	
	New expenditure excluding scrap value	13,750	
		81,750	
19-2	25% writing down	20,312	@ 50% tax 10,156 rec'd 19-3
		60,938	
19-3	25% writing down	15,234	@ 50% tax 7,617 rec'd 19-4
		45,704	

This calculation will proceed over the life of the account. In 19-3 the scrap value received for old plant will be taxed @ 50%, i.e., cash outflow of £4,000.

	19-1	19-2	19-3	19-4	
Capital cash flow	90,000	5,750			
Tax relief		(11,250)	(10,156)	(7,617)	etc
Tax on scrap			4,000		
Net Cash Flow	90,000	(5,500)	(6,156)	(7,617)	etc

36.13

	Net Cash Flow	15% Present Value Factor	£
19-1	90,000	0.870	78,300
19-2	5,500	0.756	4,158
19-3	6,156	0.658	4,051
19-4	7,617	0.572	4,357
			90,866

NPV at start of period 90,866

36.17 Exactly 3 years when the cumulative cash flow will be – nil –.

36.18

Year	Net Cash Flow	Present Value Factor for 10%	NPV £
1	9,000	0.909	8,181
2	(6,000)	0.826	(4,956)
3	(3,000)	0.751	(2,253)
4	(2,000)	0.683	(1,366)
Net Present Value of Cash (inflow)			(394)

36.19

Year	Net Cash Flow	Present Value Factor for 12%	NPV 12%	Present Value Factor for 14%	NPV 14%
1	9,000	0.893	8.037	0.877	7.893
2	(6,000)	0.797	(4.782)	0.769	(4.614)
3	(3,000)	0.712	(2.136)	0.675	(2.025)
4	(2,000)	0.636	(1.272)	0.592	(1.184)
			(153)		70

12% Discount Rate gives NPV (153)
14% Discount Rate gives NPV 70
223

The IRR is $\frac{70}{223} \times 2\%$ below 14% = 14 − 0.63 = 13.37%

36.23

	Internal Rate of Return	NPV using 12%
Project A	16%	(£2.433)
Project B	14%	(£3.270)

Using IRR the choice would be Project A but using NPV with 12% interest would suggest Project B. The crucial factor is therefore the rate of interest that funds would be invested at when generated by the project, if approximating to 12% then the NPV is more realistic but if closer to the IRR rates then they would give better solution.

36.25

Year	Net Cash Flow £	Factor for 12%	Present Value £
0	8,000	1.000	8.000
1	(4,000)	0.893	(3.572)
2	(2,000)	0.797	(1.594)
3	(6,000)	0.712	(4.272)
			(1.438)

1 The NPV at 12% interest is £1,438.
2 The Present Value of an annuity of £1 for three years at 12% interest = £2.402. therefore Present Value £1,438 = 2.402 × The annual sum

therefore the annual sum = $\frac{1438}{2.402}$ = £598.7

36.26 The Present Value of an annuity of £1 for six years at 12% interest = £4.111
Present Value £2.624 = 4.111 × the annual sum

therefore annual sum = $\frac{2,624}{4.111}$ = £638.3 which is a better annual return than for

machine in 30.3.

36.28 £13,190 × PV factor an annuity of £1 = £50,000

PV factor for an annuity of £1 = $\frac{50,000}{13,190}$ = 3.79

Referring to the tables along the 5 period row gives 10% interest for 3.79.

36.29

£

Cost of Asset 80,000 (1−0.4) = 48,000
Cost of Leasing 26.338 (1−0.4) = 15.803

PV factor for four years = $\frac{48,000}{15.803}$ = 3.04

From PV of annuity tables 3.04 represents 12% interest over 4 years.

36.30 Factor for PV of an annuity of £1 for 10 years at 14% = 5.216
5,000 × 5.216 = £26,080 Capital Value of Lease.

36.31 (a)
BN
Roadhog

	0	1	2	3	4	5
Cash inflow		(12,500)	(15,000)	(20,000)	(20,000)	(20,000)
Cash outflow						
fixed		2,000	2,000	2,200	2,400	2,400
variable		3,000	3,000	4,800	4,800	4,800
Operating cashflow		(7,500)	(9,400)	(13,000)	(13,000)	(13,000)
Capital	40,000					(8,000)
	40,000	(7,500)	(9,400)	(13,000)	(13,000)	(21,000)
	1.00	0.909	0.826	0.751	0.683	0.621
	40,000	(68,17)	(7,764)	(9,763)	(8,879)	(13,041)

NPV = (6,264)

FX Sprinter

FX Sprinter	0	1	2	3	4	5
Cash inflow		(12,500)	(15,000)	(20,000)	(20,000)	(20,000)
Cash outflow						
fixed		1,800	1,800	1,800	2,000	2,200
variable		4,000	4,800	6,400	6,400	6,400
Operating Cash Flow		(6,700)	(8,400)	(11,800)	(11,600)	(11,400)
Capital	45,000					
	45,000	(6,700)	(8,400)	(11,800)	(11,600)	(20,400)
	1.00	0.909	0.826	0.751	0.683	0.621
	45,000	(6,090)	(6,938)	(8,862)	(7,923)	(12,668)

NPV = 2,519

VR Rocket

VR Rocket	0	1	2	3	4	5
Cash inflow		(12,500)	(15,000)	(20,000)	(20,000)	(20,000)
Cash outflow						
fixed		1,500	1,500	1,400	1,400	1,400
variable		3,500	4,200	5,600	5,600	5,600
		(7,500)	(9,300)	(13,000)	(13,000)	(14,000)
	50,000					
	50,000	(7,500)	(9,300)	(13,000)	(13,000)	(27,000)
	1.00	0.909	0.826	0.751	0.683	0.621
	50,000	(6,817)	(7,682)	(9,763)	(8,879)	(16,767)

NPV = 92

To the Directors of Road Wheelers Ltd
The NPV anticipated for the three vehicles are as follows:

BN Roadhog £6,264 Positive
FX Sprinter £2,519 Negative
VR Rocket £ 92 Positive

On the basis on NPV assessment using a discount rate of 10% the BN Roadhog appears to be the best option although the VR Rocket is also positive and may also be considered if there are significant 'non-financial' features in its favour.

The payback position on the three vehicles is as follows:

BN Roadhog 3 years 9.3 months
FX Sprinter 4 years 3.8 months
VR Rocket 4 years 3.2 months

This indicates that the BX Roadhog recovers the cash outlay faster than the other two options which is in its favour.

Since the capital outlay on the BX Roadhog is also significantly lower than the other options this indicates a lower risk and will enhance the ROC on the Balance Sheet figures.

The BN Roadhog appears to be the best choice.

(b) The problems in evaluating capital projects are essentially related to the estimates involved in forecasting the revenues and cuts associated with the project. In this evaluation the relative performance of the three alternatives may be more reliable than overall estimates of the environment. In some situations important factors in the decision may not be readily quantified especially in areas of new technology where many factors are unknown.

The techniques of evaluating the cash flow data are well understood but care must be taken that an appropriate 'cost of capital' is chosen and that risk is taken into account.

36.33 (a) Revised Operating Budget

Ship A	19-6	19-7	19-8	19-9	19-0
Estimated Revenue Receipts	5	7	9	11	13
Extra Revenue 10%	0.5	0.7	0.9	1.1	1.3
Operating Payments	5.5	7.7	9.9	12.1	14.3
	4.0	5.0	6.5	7.5	9.0
Net Cash Flow Ship A	1.5	2.7	3.4	4.6	5.3

Ship B	19-6	19-7	19-8	19-9	19-0
Estimated Revenue Receipts Private	2.5	3.5	5.0	6.5	7.5
Commercial	3.45	4.6	5.85	6.5	7.8
Operating Payments	5.95	8.1	10.85	13.0	15.3
	4.80	6.0	7.9	9.0	10.8
Net Cash Flow Ship B	1.15	2.1	2.95	4.0	4.5

$$\frac{20 + \text{Debenture Interest } 3}{200} = 11.5\%$$

Net Profit/Owners Equity $\frac{20}{140}$ = 14.3% Stock Turnover $\frac{100}{30}$ = 3.3 times.

Sales/Fixed Assets $\frac{150}{120}$ = 1.3 times. Days Sales in Debtors = 122.

Net Worth/Total Assets $\frac{140}{290}$ = 48.3% Fixed Assets/Net Worth $\frac{120}{140}$ = 85.7%.

Coverage of Fixed Charges $\frac{20+3}{3}$ = 7.7 times.

37.10 Current Ratios (1) 2.4:1 (2) 2.4:1, Acid Test Ratio (1) 1.2:1 (2) 1.2:1 Gross Profit/Sales (1) 21.3 (2) 20.3 Net Profit/Sales (1) 5% (2) 4.5% Operating Profit/Capital Employed:

(1) $\frac{30,000}{200,000}$ = 15% (2) $\frac{38,000}{294,000}$ = 12.9% Net Profit/Owners Equity:

(1) $\frac{30,000}{200,000}$ = 15% (2) $\frac{34,000}{234,000}$ = 14.5% Stock Turn (using year end figures)

(1) $\frac{472}{120}$ = 3.9 times (2) $\frac{596}{188}$ = 3.2 times. Sales/Fixed Assets (1) $\frac{600}{60}$ = 10 times

(2) $\frac{748}{80}$ = 93 times. Collection Period for Debtors (1) = 60.8 days (2) = 80 days

Net Worth/Total Assets (1) $\frac{200}{300}$ = 0.67 (2) $\frac{234}{446}$ = 0.52 Coverage of fixed charges.

(1) n/a (2) $\frac{38,000}{4,000}$ = 9.5

38.2 19-4

	A £'000		B £'000		C £'000
(a) Return on Capital of 20% = Profit*	120.0		120.0		120.0
Interest less tax	–	24.0	10.5	66.0	29.7
		13.2		36.3	
Profit for Ordinary Shares	£120.0		109.2		90.3
Ordinary Share Capital	£600		400		50
Profit Return	%20		27.3		180.6

(b) Cash Flows

	Ship A	Factor 15%	Ship B		Factor 15%	
0	(10.0)	1.0	(10.0)	(14.0)	1.0	(14.0)
19-6	1.5	0.870	1.3	1.15	0.87	1.0
19-7	2.7	0.756	2.0	2.1	0.756	1.6
19-8	3.4	0.658	2.2	2.95	0.658	1.9
19-9	4.6	0.572	2.6	4.0	0.572	2.3
19-0	5.3	0.497	2.6	4.5	0.497	2.2
NPV	7.5	0.497 × cost	0.7	3.7	0.497	5.0 5.2
			4.4	10.5		0.2

Assumed Value of Ship on market $^{15}/_{20}$ × cost

Note The calculation has been done with a zero assumption about cash value of ships at the end of year 5 and then with an assumed value equal to the unexplained cost value based on a 20-year life.

(c) The evaluation assumes an interest rate of 15% and evaluates cash flows over the first five years life of the ships. If the assumption is that at the end of five years the ships will have no value then Ship A has a positive NPV of £0.7m whilst B has a negative NPV of £5.0m. However, it is likely that the ships would be valueless at the end of year 5 and if an assumption is made to take 15/20 of the cost as the realisable value then both NPVs become positive at £4.4m and £0.2m respectively.

From this evaluation Ship A looks to give a better return. It is worth noting however, that Ship B does have much higher capacity. If operating revenues were to expand more than forecast over the five years and thereafter, this ship might provide much higher returns. This operating forecast and the likely market values of the two vessels should therefore be closely examined.

37.4
1 A, C, E.
2 A, C, E.
3 E.
4 D, F (assuming current assets exceed current liabilities)
5 No Effect.

37.6
(a) = $\frac{.1}{1.5}$ = 6.7%

= $\frac{15,000}{100,000}$ = £0.15 per share

(b) = $\frac{1.5}{0.15}$ = 10.0

(c) = 10.0

37.8 Selection of five from:
Current Ratio 1.89:1; Acid Test Ratio 0.78:1 (Note Only Bank and Debtor Balances included) Gross Profit/Sales 33⅓% Net Profit/Sales (no tax assumed) 13.3%. Net Operating Profit/Capital Employed

Return on Capital of 10% = Profit
Interest *less* tax

	60.0	60.0	60.0
– 24.0		66.0	
13.2	10.8 36.3	29.7	
		30.3	
Ordinary Share Capital	60.0 37.2	50	
	600 400		
Profit Return	% 10 12.3	60.6	

*Profit is assumed to be after tax but before interest.

(b) High gearing accentuates the rate of return to the ordinary shareholder. In the zero-geared position of A the return to the shareholder supply reflects the change in profits earned on trading. In the high-geared position of Company C the return to the shareholder decreases from 108.6% to 60.6%, i.e. to a reduction of 66.5% as profits reduce by only 50%. Company B reflects an intermediate position with a relatively moderate level of gearing.

High gearing increases risk to shareholders for two reasons. First if the profits earned are not sufficiently high to meet interest charges then the company may find itself failing since the lenders may seek a winding up order. Second the risk is increased simply because of exaggerated fluctuations in the returns which are accentuated in the high-geared situation.

However, it can be seen that if profits earned are higher than the interest rate, this will produce a significantly higher return to the shareholder in a high-geared company. The fact that interest is allowed as a deduction for tax purposes indicates that gearing may give an overall advantage. The market's assessment of the risk position will counter this, and will be based on the nature of the business and management.

38.4 (a) refer to the text.
(b)

	Company A			B	
	£000	%		£000	%
Ordinary Shares	300			800	
Revenue Share Premium	300			400	
Retained Profit	400			200	
	1,000	62.5		1,400	87.5
8% Preference Shares	200			–	
1% Loan – Debentures				200	
12% Loan – Debentures	400				
	600	37.5		200	12.5
Total Share Capital and Loan	1,600	100.0		4,600	100.0

Company A Debt/Equity = $\frac{37.5}{62.5}$ = 60%

B   "   = $\frac{12.5}{87.5}$ = 14.3%

(c) Company A is more highly geared than B since it is committed to paying a higher proportion of fixed dividend and interest payments for its profits. A higher level of gearing increases risk. (Note the answer in 38.2(b) is appropriate.)

(d)

		A	B
Trading Profit before intent		200,000	20,000
less interest charges		48,000	180,000
Net Profit after interest charge		152,000	–
Preference Dividend	16,000		120,000
Ordinary Dividend	45,000	61,000	
Retained Profit		91,000	60,000

38.6

(a)

	19-4	19-5
Equity Shares	100,000	150,000
Reserves	150,000	220,000
Total Equity Capital	250,000	370,000
Loans	40,000	40,000
Total Capital Employed	290,000	410,000
Profits (net after tax)	60,000	70,000
Return on Total Equity	24%	18.9%

To Mr C Black

(b) The reduction in profits from 24% to 18.9% of Total Equity needs to be analysed into its causal factors. During the year the net profits have increased but act as fast as the equity capital which has gone up by £120,000 over the year. If the increase reflected an investment late in 19-5 it would reduce returns because a full year's profit could not be earned.

It is therefore essential to examine the nature of the investment and the future. Before shares are bought it is essential to examine future prospects. If these are good the historic analysis may not be important. However, if the new funds were used – clearly prospects may not be good and shares should not be bought.

(c) Reserves are profits retained within the business. The profits may be from revenue, i.e. from profits which could be distributed as dividends to shareholders or capital – for example where fixed amounts are revalued upwards to reflect current market value.

The creation of reserves reflects an increase in capital in the organisation which would normally be to reflect increasing sales of operation. In this sense reserves reflect an alternative to issuing new shares. In the case of capital reserves from revaluation – there are simply 'paper adjustments' to value which do not in themselves indicate more resources in the organisation.

Revenue reserves may in fact be distributed as dividends whereas Capital reserves would not normally be available for this purpose and are more akin to share capital.

shareholders' funds. It should be noted that other definitions of gearing are possible and are sometimes used.

Any company with a gearing ratio of, say, 70% would be considered to be high geared, whilst a company with a gearing ratio of, say, 20% would be low geared.

Gearing is an important matter to consider when investing in ordinary shares in a particular company. A *high-geared* company means that a high proportion of the company's earnings are committed to paying either interest on any debenture stock and/ or dividends on any preference share capital *before* an ordinary dividend can be declared. If a company is low geared, then a high proportion of the company's earnings can be paid out as ordinary dividends.

Chan plc has not issued any long-term loans or any preference share capital. Gearing does not, therefore, apply to this company, and all of the earnings may be paid out to the ordinary shareholders.

Ling plc is a relatively low-geared company. It has no debenture stock, and only a small proportion of its earnings are committed to paying its preference shareholders. The balance may then all be declared as an ordinary dividend.

Wong plc is an extremely high-geared company. A high proprotion of borrowings (in this case consisting of both debenture stock and preference share capital), means that a high proportion of its earnings has to be set aside for both its debenture holders and its preference shareholders before any ordinary dividend can be declared. As a result, if the profits of the company are low, no ordinary dividend may be payable.

If profits are rising a high geared company may not be a particularly risky company in which to purchase some ordinary shares, but the reverse may apply if profits are falling.

For the year to 31 March 19-8, Chan, Ling and Wong's operating profit is identical. Wong is committed to paying interest on its debenture stock (which is allowable against tax), and both Ling and Wong have to pay a preference dividend (which is *not* allowable against tax).

In deciding whether to invest in any of the three companies, there are a great many other factors to be considered, including future prospects of all three companies. However, *ceteris paribus*, when profits are fluctuating an ordinary shareholder is more likely to receive a higher return by investing in Chan rather than by investing in either Ling or Wong. Similarly, an ordinary shareholder can expect a higher return by investing in Wong.

Based on the limited amount of information given in the question, therefore, an investor considering purchasing ordinary shares in only one of these three companies would be recommended to buy shares in Chan plc.

It should be noted that if profits were *increasing*, an investor would be recommended to buy shares firstly in Wong, then in Ling and finally in Chan. The earnings per share in both Ling and Wong are far higher than in Chan, so there is a much greater chance of an increase in the ordinary dividend, but this is not necessarily the case if profits are falling or fluctuating.

38.8 (a) Profit and loss accounts for the year to 31 March 19-8

	Chan plc £'000	Ling plc £'000	Wong plc £'000
Operating profit	300	300	300
Interest payable	–	–	(10)
	300	300	290
Profit on ordinary activities before tax			
Taxation (30%)	(90)	(90)	(87)
Profit on ordinary activities after tax	210	210	203
Dividends: Preference	–	(20)	(30)
Ordinary	(100)	(60)	(40)
	(100)	(80)	(70)
Retained profit for the year	£ 110	£ 130	£ 133

(b) (i) Earnings per share	Chan plc	Ling plc	Wong plc
Net profit after tax and preference dividend	210	210 – 20	203 – 30
Number of ordinary shares in issue	500	300	200
=	42p	63.3p	86.5p

(ii) Price/earnings ratio			
Market price of ordinary shares	840	950	1038
Earnings per share	42	63.3	86.5
=	20	15	12

(iii) Gearing ratio

$$\frac{\text{Loan capital} + \text{preference shares}}{\text{Shareholders' funds}} \times 100 :$$

Chan plc = Nil

Ling plc $= \dfrac{200}{300+100+130} \times 100 = 37.7\%$

Wong plc $= \dfrac{300+100}{200+100+133} \times 100 = 92.4\%$

(c) A gearing ratio expresses the relationship that exists between total borrowings (that is, preference share capital and long-term loans), and the total amount of ordinary

614

38.10 (a) (i) *Forecast profit and loss appropriation accounts*

	19-6 £'000	19-7 £'000	19-8 £'000
Forecast profits	1,800	500	2,200
less corporation tax (30%)	540	150	660
	1,260	350	1,540
less Dividends proposed	1,260	350	1,540

Balance sheet extracts

	19-6 £'000	19-7 £'000	19-8 £'000
Shareholders' equity			
Issued ordinary shares of £1 each fully paid	6,000	6,000	6,000
Share premium account	1,000	1,000	1,000
Retained profits	1,650	1,650	1,650
	8,650	8,650	8,650
Current liabilities			
Dividends proposed	1,260	350	1,540

(a) (ii) *Forecast profit and loss appropriation accounts*

	19-6 £'000	19-7 £'000	19-8 £'000
Forecast profits	1,800	500	2,200
less interest (12% × £2m)	240	240	240
	1,560	260	1,960
less corporation tax (30%)	468	78	588
	1,092	182	1,372
less Dividends proposed	1,092	182	1,372

Balance sheet extracts

	19-6 £'000	19-7 £'000	19-8 £'000
Shareholders' equity			
Issued ordinary shares of £1 each full paid	5,000	5,000	5,000
Retained profits	1,650	1,650	1,650
	6,650	6,650	6,650
Deferred liabilities			
12% Debentures	2,000	2,000	2,000
Current liabilities			
Dividend proposed	1,092	182	1,372

(b) (i) If planned expansion is financed by share issue, the forecast return on shareholders' equity for the next three years will be:

$$19\text{-}6 \quad 1,260/8,650 \times 100 = 14.6\%$$
$$19\text{-}7 \quad 350/8,650 \times 100 = 4.0\%$$
$$19\text{-}8 \quad 1,540/8,650 \times 100 = 17.8\%$$

(ii) If planned expansion is financed by debenture issue, the forecast return on shareholders' equity for the next three years will be:

$$19\text{-}6 \quad 1,092/6,650 \times 100 = 16.4\%$$
$$19\text{-}7 \quad 182/6,650 \times 100 = 2.7\%$$
$$19\text{-}8 \quad 1,372/6,650 \times 100 = 20.6\%$$

Note: All the above figures are, of course, net of tax and should be grossed by a factor of 100/70 if comparison with gross interest rates is to be made.

(c) The return on shareholders' equity for the year ended 30 September 19-5 was 600/6,620 × 100 = 9.1% and it could have been 9.5% if full distribution of the year's profit had been made. To have the return fluctuate between 2.7% and 20.6%, as it will do if the planned expansion is financed by the debenture issue, will surely unnerve all but the most sturdy shareholders. Such a violent swing from year to year will confuse, confound and alarm anyone looking at the shares as an investment.

To finance the planned expansion by a share issue does not improve matters greatly, as it will be seen that the return will still fluctuate between 4.0% and 17.8%. But since we are told that the industry is 'subject to marked variations in consumer demand' it does seem more appropriate to use share capital (by definition risk-bearing) rather than a debenture. The poor profits forecast for 1987 suggest that it would not take much of a variation from the expected results to show no profit at all, and were this to occur, is there not a possibility that the debenture holders could not be paid their due interest? Failure to pay debenture interest on time would bring in a receiver (assuming the debentures were secured): his function would then be to collect not only the unpaid interest but the capital as well, as failure to pay interest would be a breach in the conditions under which the debenture was issued.

If shareholders are to miss a year's dividends as a result of there being no profits for distribution, the directors can expect a stormy annual general meeting, but that is far less dangerous than the entry of a receiver.

In practice, of course, it is unusual for a company to pay out all profits as dividends, and since shareholders will pay more attention usually to the level of dividends paid than to profits earned, it would make better financial sense if the 1986 dividend were maintained at or slightly above the 1985 level, enabling an addition to be made to retained profits. This in turn would enable a fund to be built up to supplement current profits for dividends and/or to redeem the debentures.

The all-shares or all-debentures choice is also an unrealistic one. Although there is much to be said for a broad share base to support what is obviously a risky business, it could make better sense to raise part of the required £2,000,000 by shares and part by debentures. A restrained dividend policy coupled with the use of the (probably enlarged) depreciation charge arising after the expansion had taken place could enable a debenture redemption programme to be established over the course of the next few years.

38.12 (a) (i) *Shareholders*

Earnings per share (EPS)

$$\frac{19\text{-}6}{} \quad \frac{9,520}{39,680} = 24\text{p} \qquad \frac{19\text{-}7}{} \quad \frac{11,660}{39,680} = 29.4\text{p}$$

Dividend cover
(EPS ÷ dividend per share)

$$\frac{24\text{p}}{5.6\text{p}} \quad (2,240 \div 39,680) = 4.3 \text{ times} \qquad \frac{24\text{p}}{6\text{p}} \quad (2,400 \div 39,680) = 4.9 \text{ times}$$

Note: In this case, as only ordinary shares, could divide profit after tax by hotel dividends, to obtain some answers.

(ii) *Trade Creditors*

Current Ratio $\quad \dfrac{92,447}{36,862} = 2.5 \qquad \dfrac{99,615}{42,475} = 2.3$

Acid Test $\quad \dfrac{40,210 + 12,092}{39,862} = 1.4{:}1 \qquad \dfrac{43,370 + 5,790}{42,475} = 1.2$

(iii) *Internal Management*

Debtor Ratio/Sales* $\quad \dfrac{40,210}{486,300} \times 52 = 4.3 \text{ weeks} \qquad \dfrac{43,370}{583,900} \times 52 = 3.9$
*assumed credit sales

Return on Capital Employed (before tax) $\quad \dfrac{15,254}{40,740} = 37.4\% \qquad \dfrac{18,686}{50,000} = 37.4\%$

(b) *Shareholders*

EPS. An increase of 5.4p per share has occurred. This was due to an increase in profit without any increase in share capital.

Dividend cover. Increased by 0.6 times because increase in profit not fully reflected in dividends.

Trade Creditors

Current ratio. This has fallen but only marginally and it still appears to be quite sound.

Acid test. This has also fallen, but still seems to be quite reasonable.

Internal Management

Debtor ratio. There appears to have been an increase in the efficiency of our credit control. Return on capital employed. This has stayed the same for each of the two years. The increase in capital employed has seen a proportional increase in profits.

38.14

To the Board of G plc

From AN Other, Accountant

Subject: *Potential acquisition of either of companies A Ltd and B Ltd as subsidiaries in the machine tool manufacturing sector. Financial performances assessed.*

As instructed by you I have investigated the financial performances of these two companies to assist in the evaluation of them as potential acquisitions.

It should be borne in mind that financial ratio analysis is only partial information. There are many other factors which will need to be borne in mind before a decision can be taken.

The calculations of the various ratios are given as an appendix.

Profitability

While the main interest to the board is what G plc could obtain in profitability from A Ltd and B Ltd, all I can comment on at present is the current profitability enjoyed by these two companies.

Here the most important ratio is that of ROCE (Return on Capital Employed) A's ROCE is 27.2% as compared with B 15.6%.

The great difference in ROCE can be explained by reference to the secondary ratios of profit and asset utilisation. Both ratios are in A's favour. The profit ratios are A 34% : B20%. The asset utilisation ratios are A 0.9 : B 0.6, showing that A is utilising its assets 50% better than B. It is the effect of these two ratios that give the ROCE for each company.

The very low working capital employed by A Ltd very much affects the asset utilisation ratio. How far such a low working capital is representation of that throughout the whole year is impossible to say.

Liquidity

It would not be sensible to draw final conclusion as to the liquidity positions of the two companies based on the balance sheet figures. As a balance sheet is based at one point in time it can sometimes be misleading, as a reading of figures over a period would be more appropriate.

A Ltd does appear to have a short-term liquidity problem, as the current assets only just cover current liabilities. The 'quick' or 'acid test ratio' on the face of it appears to be very inadequate at 0.6.

By contrast, B Ltd with a current ratio of 1.4 and a 'quick ratio' of 1.0 would appear to be reasonably liquid.

However, much more light is shed on the position of the companies when the debtors' collection period is examined. A collects its debts with a credit period of 9 weeks. In the case of B Ltd this rises to an astonishing 36.7 weeks. Why is this so? It could be due simply to very poor credit control by B Ltd. Such a long credit period casts considerable doubt on the real worth of the debtors. There is a high probability that many of them may prove difficult to collect. It might be that B Ltd, in order to maintain sales has lowered its requirements as to the credit-worthiness of its customers. If the credit period was reduced to a normal one for the industry it might be found that many of the customers might go elsewhere.

The problem with debtors in the case of B Ltd is also carried on to stock. In the case of A Ltd the stock turnover is 4.3 falling to 2.8 in B Ltd. There could be a danger that B Ltd has stock increasing simply because it is finding it difficult to sell its products.

Capital Gearing

A Ltd is far more highly geared than B Ltd. 93.6% as compared with 14.1%. A comparison with this particular industry by means of inter-firm comparison should be undertaken.

Limitations of Ratio Analysis

You should bear in mind the following limitations of the analysis undertaken:

(i) One year's accounts are insufficient for proper analysis to be undertaken. The analysis of trends, taken from say 5 years' accounts would give a better insight.

(ii) Differences in accounting policies between A Ltd and B Ltd will affect comparisons.

(iii) The use of historical costs brings about many distortions.

(iv) The use of industry inter-firm comparisons would make the ratios more capable of being interpreted.

(v) The plans of the companies for the future expressed in their budgets would be of more interest than past figures.

Conclusions

Depending on the price which would have to be paid for acquisition, I would suggest that A Ltd is the company most suitable for takeover.

A N Other
Accountant

Appendix

(i) *Return on Capital Employed*

	A Ltd	B Ltd
$\dfrac{\text{Profits before interest and tax}}{\text{Capital employed}}$	$\dfrac{211}{775} \times 100 = 27.2\%$	$\dfrac{88}{565} \times 100 = 15.6\%$

(ii) *Asset Utilisation Ratios*

		A Ltd	B Ltd
Total Assets Turnover:	$\dfrac{\text{Turnover}}{\text{Total assets}}$	$\dfrac{985}{1,140} = 0.9$	$\dfrac{560}{990} = 0.6$
Fixed Assets Turnover:	$\dfrac{\text{Turnover}}{\text{Fixed assets}}$	$\dfrac{985}{765} = 1.3$	$\dfrac{560}{410} = 1.4$
Working Capital Turnover:	$\dfrac{\text{Turnover}}{\text{Working Capital}}$	$\dfrac{985}{10} = 98.5$	$\dfrac{560}{155} = 3.6$

(iii) *Profitability Ratios*

		A Ltd	B Ltd
Gross Profit %:	$\dfrac{\text{Gross profit}}{\text{Turnover}} \times 100$	$\dfrac{335}{985} \times 100 = 34\%$	$\dfrac{163}{560} \times 100 = 29\%$
Profit before taxation and interest as % Turnover		$\dfrac{211}{985} \times 100 = 21\%$	$\dfrac{88}{560} \times 100 = 16\%$

(iv) *Liquidity Ratios*

		A Ltd	B Ltd
Current ratio:	$\dfrac{\text{Current assets}}{\text{Current liabilities}}$	$\dfrac{375}{365} = 1.0$	$\dfrac{580}{425} = 1.4$
Acid test or 'quick ratio':	$\dfrac{\text{Current assets} - \text{stock}}{\text{Current liabilities}}$	$\dfrac{220}{365} = 0.6$	$\dfrac{440}{425} = 1.0$
Debtor ratio:	$\dfrac{\text{Trade Debtors} \times 52}{\text{Credit sales}}$	$\dfrac{170}{985} \times 52 = 9.0$ wks	$\dfrac{395}{560} \times 52 = 36.7$ wks

(v) *Capital Structure*

		A Ltd	B Ltd
Gearing ratio:	$\dfrac{\text{Long term borrowing}}{\text{Shareholders' funds}} \times 100$	$\dfrac{220}{555} \times 100 = 93.6\%$	$\dfrac{70}{495} \times 100 = 14$
Proprietary ratio:	$\dfrac{\text{Shareholders' funds}}{\text{Tangible assets}}$	$\dfrac{555}{1,140} = 0.5$	$\dfrac{495}{990} = 0.5$

39.1 (a) T (b) F (c) T (d) F (e) T.

39.4 £24,000

39.6 Total Depreciation at 31.12.19-7 required £10,667 (40% of £26,667). Provision at 31.12.19-6 = £7,200 (30% of £24,000) + Provision for y/e 31.12.19-7 £2,667 gives a provision of £9,867. The backlog is therefore 10,667 – 9,867 = £800.

39.8 Opening Stock $30,000 \times \dfrac{160}{140} = 34,286$ + Purchases $500,000$ − Closing Stock $60,000 \times \dfrac{160}{180} = 53,000$ = Current Cost of Sales £480,953.

Adjustment therefore $480,953 - 470,000 = £10,953$.

39.10 Working Capital 1 January £6,000. 31 December £10,000, therefore change in the year = £4,000.

At average index values working Capital is 1 January $6,000 \times \dfrac{220}{200} = £6,600$ and 31 December $10,000 \times \dfrac{220}{240} = £9,167$. Change in the year $9,167 - 6,600 = £2,567$. The Monetary Working Capital Adjustment for Price is $£4,000 - 2,567 = £1,433$.

39.12 Average Net Borrowings 19-0 Debenture Stock $75,000$ − Cash at Bank $15,000 = £60,000$ 19-1 Debenture Stock $75,000$ − Cash $10,000 = £65,000$.

Average = $\dfrac{60,000 + 65,000}{2} = £62,500 = $ L

Average Shareholders' Interest 19-0 $90,000 + 30,000 + 35,000 = £155,000$ 19-1 $90,000 + 40,000 + 65,000 = £195,000$. Average = $\dfrac{155,000 + 195,000}{2}$

$= £175,000 = $ S

Gearing Proportion $= \dfrac{L}{L + S} = \dfrac{62,500}{62,500 + 175,000} = 26.3\%$

39.14 Many accountants believe that during a period of inflation financial reports prepared under the historical cost convention are subject to a number of severe limitations. The question lists five such limitations, and a brief explanation of each one is as follows:

1 Stocks are undervalued.

Stock values are normally based on historical costs. This means that the historic closing stock will usually have cost less than its current economic value. Hence the costs of sales will tend to be higher than it would be if the closing stock was revalued at its current cost. As a result, the gross profit will be higher, and the entity may then pay out a higher level of net profit.

If the entity pays out a high level of profit and at the same time it has to pay more for its stocks (because prices are rising), it may be left with insufficient funds for it to be able to replace its stocks with the same quantity of goods that it had sold during the previous period. Hence it will not be able to operate at the same level of activity as it had previously experienced.

2 Depreciation is understated.

Depreciation is usually based on the historic cost of fixed assets. Such assets will normally increase in price during a period of inflation. The annual depreciation charge, therefore, may not reflect the amount needed to be able to replace the assets at their increased cost. Consequently, the accounting profit tends to be over-stated, and this may mean that too much profit is withdrawn from the business. The cash resources may then prove insufficient to replace the assets at the end of their useful life. Like the stock valuation problem, therefore, the business may not be able to operate at the same level of activity that it has previously experienced.

3 Gains or losses on net monetary assets are undisclosed.

Net monetary assets include both long and short-term loans made to and by the entity, for example, debentures, and trade debtors and trade creditors. During a period of inflation, an entity gains on both long and short-term borrowings. The gain arises because although the amount originally borrowed will eventually be repaid at its face value, its purchasing power will have been reduced; for example, £5,000 borrowed in 19-1 will not purchase the same quantity of goods in 19-5 as it did in 19-1. In 19-5 the borrower may have to pay (say) £8,000 to purchase the same quantity of goods as he might have done in 19-1. Hence the entity will have, in effect, gained £3,000 by borrowing during an inflationary period, because it is effectively having to pay back less in purchasing power (or in real terms, as it is known) than it borrowed.

By contrast, if the entity has *loaned* money during a similar period (perhaps by allowing its customers to buy goods on credit), it loses money because the purchasing power of the respective debts (which are fixed in monetary terms) will purchase fewer goods when they are eventually settled than they would have done when they were first incurred.

In financial reports prepared under the historical cost system, neither the gross nor the net effect of these types of transactions is disclosed.

4 Balance sheet values are unrealistic.

Fixed assets are normally recorded in the balance sheet at their original cost, that is, at their historic cost. During a period of inflation, the historic cost of the assets may be far less than their *current* cost, that is, at the value the entity places on them at the time that the financial reports are prepared. Hence the financial reports give a misleading impression of the entity's net worth as at the time that they are prepared.

5 Meaningful periodic comparisons are difficult to make.

A meaningful comparison of financial reports prepared under the historic cost convention over several accounting periods may be misleading since such accounts will normally have been prepared using, say, pounds sterling in one period and pounds sterling in all subsequent periods.

Financial reports prepared in such a way are not, however, strictly comparable. For example, £100 in 19-1 is not the same as £100 in 19-5, because £100 would not purchase the same amount of goods in 19-5 as it did in 19-1. In fact the comparison is just as meaningless as comparing financial reports prepared, say, in dollars with, say, reports prepared in marks. It is obvious to most users of such reports that 100 dollars are not the same as 100 marks, but it is less obvious that £19-1 are not the same as £19-5.

In order to be able to make a meaningful comparison between financial reports prepared in different time periods, therefore, it is desirable to translate them into the same currency, that is, to use the same price base. The argument behind this point is similar in principle to that used in translating dollars into marks or marks into dollars.

Index

Teachers' Manuals are available free of charge to lecturers using Business Accounting Volumes 1 and 2. The manuals include:

● Fully displayed answers to all questions not answered in the textbook.
● Guidelines on how to prepare students for examinations.
● Background to SSAPs.

These manuals are available from the local agents listed below. Apply for your copy on official letterheaded paper.

Longman Group (Far East) Ltd
PO Box 223
Cornwall House
18th Floor
Taikoo Trading Estate
Tong Chong Street
Quarry Bay
HONG KONG

Longman Jamaica Ltd
43 Second Street
Newport West
PO Box 489
Kingston 10
JAMAICA

Longman Kenya Ltd
PO Box 18033
Kjabe Street
PO Box 47540
Nairobi
KENYA

Longman Singapore Publishers (Pty) Ltd
25 First Lok Yang Road
Off International Road
Jurong Town
SINGAPORE 2262

RIK Services Ltd
104 High Street
San Fernando
TRINIDAD

Longman Zimbabwe (Pvt) Ltd
PO Box ST 125
Southerton
Harare
ZIMBABWE